Lecture Notes in Computer Science   11434

Commenced Publication in 1973
Founding and Former Series Editors:
Gerhard Goos, Juris Hartmanis, and Jan van Leeuwen

Editorial Board Members

Services Science

Subline of Lectures Notes in Computer Science

Subline Editors-in-Chief

Subline Editorial Board

More information about this series at http://www.springer.com/series/7408

Xiao Liu · Michael Mrissa ·
Liang Zhang · Djamal Benslimane ·
Aditya Ghose · Zhongjie Wang ·
Antonio Bucchiarone · Wei Zhang ·
Ying Zou · Qi Yu (Eds.)

Service-Oriented Computing – ICSOC 2018 Workshops

ADMS, ASOCA, ISYyCC, CIoTS, DDBS, and NLS4IoT
Hangzhou, China, November 12–15, 2018
Revised Selected Papers

 Springer

Editors
Xiao Liu
Deakin University
Melbourne, VIC, Australia

Liang Zhang
Fudan University
Shanghai Shi, China

Aditya Ghose
School of IT and Computer Science
University of Wollongong
Wollongong, NSW, Australia

Antonio Bucchiarone
Scientific and Technological Hub
Fondazione Bruno Kessler (FBK)
Trento, Italy

Ying Zou
Queen's University
Kingston, ON, Canada

Michael Mrissa
University of Pau and Pays
Pau Cedex, France

Djamal Benslimane
LIRIS Lab
University Lyon 1, IUT
Villeurbanne Cedex, France

Zhongjie Wang
Harbin Institute of Technology
Harbin, China

Wei Zhang
Macquarie University
Sydney, NSW, Australia

Qi Yu
Rochester Institute of Technology
Rochester, NY, USA

ISSN 0302-9743   ISSN 1611-3349 (electronic)
Lecture Notes in Computer Science
ISBN 978-3-030-17641-9   ISBN 978-3-030-17642-6 (eBook)
https://doi.org/10.1007/978-3-030-17642-6

LNCS Sublibrary: SL2 – Programming and Software Engineering

This Springer imprint is published by the registered company Springer Nature Switzerland AG
The registered company address is: Gewerbestrasse 11, 6330 Cham, Switzerland

Preface

This volume presents the proceedings of the scientific satellite events that were held in conjunction with the 2018 International Conference on Service-Oriented Computing, which took place in Hangzhou, China, November 12–15, 2018. Since the first edition in Trento in 2003, ICSOC has become one of leading conferences in the rapidly evolving areas of service research.

The satellite events provide venues for specialist groups to meet, to generate focused discussions on specific sub-areas within service-oriented computing, and to engage in community-building activities. These events helped significantly enrich the main conference by both expanding the scope of research topics and attracting participants from a wider community. The selected scientific satellite events were organized around three main tracks, i.e., a workshop track, a PhD symposium track, and a demonstration track.

We received a good number of proposals for the ICSOC 2018 workshop track and six of them were finally selected. The workshop track included a wide range of topics that fall into the general area of service computing. A special focus this year was on the Internet of Things, data analytics, and smart services. These technology trends in combination with novel application domains led to inspiring research results.

- The First International Workshop on Data-Driven Business Services (DDBS)
- The First International Workshop on Networked Learning Systems for Secured IoT Services and Its Applications (NLS4IoT)
- The 8th International Workshop on Context-Aware and IoT Services (CIoTS)
- The Third International Workshop on Adaptive Service-Oriented and Cloud Applications (ASOCA2018)
- The Third International Workshop on IoT Systems for Context-Aware Computing (ISyCC)
- The First International Workshop on AI and Data Mining for Services (ADMS)

The workshops were held on November 12, 2018. Each workshop had its own chairs and Program Committee, who were responsible for the selection of papers. The overall organization for the workshop program, including the selection of the workshop proposals, was carried out by Xiao Liu, Michael Mrissa, and Liang Zhang. The ICSOC PhD Symposium is an international forum for PhD students to present, share, and discuss their research in a constructive and critical atmosphere. It also provides students with fruitful feedback and advice on their research approach and thesis. The PhD Symposium Track was chaired by Djamal Benslimane, Aditya Ghose, and Zhongjie Wang.

The ICSOC Demonstration Track offers an exciting and highly interactive way to show research prototypes/work in service-oriented computing (SOC) and related areas. The Demonstration Track was chaired by Antonio Bucchiarone, Wei Zhang, and Ying Zou.

We would like to thank the workshop, PhD symposium, and demonstration authors, as well as keynote speakers and workshop Organizing Committees, who together contributed to this important aspect of the conference.

We hope that these proceedings will serve as a valuable reference for researchers and practitioners working in the SOC domain and its emerging applications.

January 2019

Xiao Liu
Michael Mrissa
Liang Zhang
Djamal Benslimane
Aditya Ghose
Zhongjie Wang
Antonio Bucchiarone
Wei Zhang
Ying Zou
Qi Yu

Organization

General Chairs

Michael Sheng   Macquarie University, Australia
Zhaohui Wu   Zhejiang University, China
Xiaofei Xu   Harbin Institute of Technology, China

Program Chairs

Claus Pahl   Free University of Bozen-Bolzano, Italy
Maja Vukovic   IBM Research, USA
Jianwei Yin   Zhejiang University, China

Workshop Chairs

Xiao Liu   Deakin University, Australia
Michael Mrissa   University of Pau and Pays Adour, France
Liang Zhang   Fudan University, China

PHD Symposium Chairs

Djamal Benslimane   Lyon University, France
Aditya Ghose   University of Wollongong, Australia
Zhongjie Wang   Harbin Institute of Technology, China

Demonstration Chairs

Antonio Bucchiarone   FBK, Italy
Wei Zhang   Macquarie University, Australia
Ying Zou   Queen's University, Canada

Panel Chairs

Athman Bouguettaya   University of Sydney, Australia
Jian Yang   Macquarie University, Australia

Local Organization Chair

Shuiguang Deng   Zhejiang University, China

Publicity Chairs

Bin Cao   Zhejiang University of Technology, China
Qiang He   Swinburne University of Technology, Australia
Yanjun Shu   Harbin Institute of Technology, China
Paul de Vrieze   Bournemouth University, UK

Publication Chair

Qi Yu   Rochester Institute of Technology, USA

Financial Chair

Bernd J. Krämer   FernUniversität, Germany

Web Chairs

Hai Dong   RMIT University, Australia
Adnan Mahmood   Macquarie University, Australia

Industry Chairs

Min Fu   Alibaba, China
Lijie Wen   Tsinghua University, China

Sponsorship Chairs

Dongjin Yu   Hangzhou Dianzi University, China
Jun Shen   University of Wollongong, Australia

Steering Committee Liaison

Jian Yang   Macquarie University, Australia

Steering Committee

Boualem Benatallah   UNSW, Australia
Fabio Casati   University of Trento, Italy
Bernd J. Krämer   FernUniversität, Germany
Winfried Lamersdorf   University of Hamburg, Germany
Heiko Ludwig   IBM, USA
Mike Papazoglou   Tilburg University, The Netherlands
Jian Yang   Macquarie University, Australia
Liang Zhang   Fudan University, China

Workshop on Data-Driven Business Services

Yezheng Liu   Ministry of Education, Hefei, Anhui, China,
Yuanchun Jiang   Hefei University of Technology, Anhui, China
Jennifer Shang   The Joseph M. Katz Graduate School of Business,
                       University of Pittsburgh, USA

Workshop on Networked Learning Systems for Secured IoT Services and Its Applications

Frank Jiang   Deakin University, Australia
Haiying Xia   Guangxi Normal University, China

Workshop on Context-Aware and IoT Services

Yanbo Han   North China University of Technology, Beijing, China,
Liang Zhang   Fudan University, Shanghai, China
Jian Yu   Auckland University of Technology, New Zealand,
Guiling Wang   North China University of Technology, Beijing, China
Sira Yongchareon   Auckland University of Technology, New Zealand

Workshop on Adaptive Service-Oriented and Cloud Applications

Khalil Drira   LAAS-CNRS and Université de Toulouse, France
Ismael Bouassida Rodriguez ReDCAD, University of Sfax, Tunisia

Workshop on IoT Systems for Context-Aware Computing

Sami Yangui   CNRS LAAS, Toulouse, France
Mohamed Mohamed   IBM Research, Almaden, San Jose, USA
Zhangbing Zhou   China University of Geosciences, Beijing, China

Workshop on AI and Data Mining for Services

Anup Kalia   IBM T.J. Watson Research Center, USA
Jin Xiao   IBM T.J. Watson Research Center, USA
Fanjing Meng   IBM Research Lab, Beijing, China
Larisa Shwartz   IBM T.J. Watson Research Center, USA
Ying Li   Peking University, Beijing, China

Contents

ASOCA: Adaptive Service-Oriented and Cloud Applications and ISyCC: IoT Systems for Context-Aware Computing

ADMS: AI and Data Mining for Services

PhD Symposium

Demonstrations

DDBS: Data-Driven Business Services

Introduction of the First International Workshop on Data-Driven Business Services

We are entering the era of Big Data which brings new opportunities and challenges to design and optimize business services. The aim of data-driven business services is to employ big data to uncover the hidden service patterns, the unknown correlations, personalized customer preferences and other useful business information in various service fields. The analytical findings can lead to more effective marketing, new revenue opportunities, better customer service, improved operational efficiency, competitive advantages over rival organizations and other business benefits.

Our workshop encourages submission of innovative technologies, methodologies, and theories in data-driven business services, which can facilitate and/or provide insights on the practices, challenges, and solutions of data-based service computing and optimization. We welcome studies taking various quantitative methods, such as algorithm, econometrics, analytical modeling, simulation, etc.

We totally received 10 papers in the scope of the workshop topics. After the double-blind peer review of the paper, we accept 5 high-quality papers. The title and author information are listed as follows:

(1) Ming Liu, Xifen Xu, A data-driven optimization method for reallocating the free-floating bikes
(2) Qing Guo, Bing Li, Xuan Luo, Study on Airport De-icing Schedule Problem Balancing Fairness and Efficiency
(3) Pirelli, Natalia Nessler, Gorica Tapandjieva, Alain Wegmann, Co-Design of Business and IT services - a Tool-Supported Approach Blagovesta
(4) Cong Xin, Zi Lingling, Shuang Kai, Energy-aware and Location-constrained Virtual Network Embedding in Enterprise Network
(5) Zerun Chen, Rui Gu, WeChat Red Envelops: Literature Review and Future Directions

Five authors of the accepted papers gave presentations of their works during the workshop day. The authors also discussed the issues about data-driven business services with other scholars.

A Data-Driven Optimization Method for Reallocating the Free-Floating Bikes

Ming Liu[(✉)] and Xifen Xu

School of Economics and Management, Nanjing 210094,
People's Republic of China
liuming@njust.edu.cn

Abstract. Free-floating bike sharing (FFBS) is a new bike sharing mode when compared to the traditional station-based bike sharing (SBBS). It brings convenience for users since bikes can be picked up and returned anywhere but not the fixed stations. However, it also brings difficulty for managers because reallocation of free-floating bikes is totally different from any traditional ones. Using data-driven method, we define two types of nodes in this paper (i.e., easily and hardly accessed nodes), to represent different convenience levels of getting bikes from the FFBS. We collect bikes at hardly accessed nodes and reallocate them to the easily accessed nodes. Our objective is to move the needed bikes in the shortest distance and meanwhile to maximize the operation revenue. The problem is formulated as a multi-objective mixed integer programming model and an effective algorithm is designed to solve it. The test results can provide several constructive suggestions for reallocating the free-floating bikes.

Keywords: Free-floating bike sharing · Static reallocation ·
Multi-objective optimization

1 Introduction

Bike sharing, especially free-floating bike sharing, is flourishing all over the world. These shared systems have the advantages of zero pollution, zero emission, flexibility and convenience, and are especially suited for short-distance trips. In 2015, Mobike, the pioneer who opened a new era of bike-sharing services, developed a bike that can be located and rented through their Mobike App, and returned anywhere but not the fixed stations. It perfectly solves the last mile problem and revolutionizes the traditional bike-sharing market. And now the free-floating bike sharing has been implemented in many large cities (countries) in China, the United Kingdom, Netherlands, and other countries [1].

In FFBS, a specific App provides the user interface for locating, unlocking, locking, and payment. By tracking bicycles in real-time with GPS, a user can easily locate and find bikes. Then the user can unlock the bike by scanning its QR code and the ride starts. After the ride, the user can pay via mobile phone [2]. Different from the SBSS, where bikes can only be accessed at fixed stations and returned to unoccupied lockers in the stations after use, users can hire and lock the free-floating bikes anywhere.

© Springer Nature Switzerland AG 2019
X. Liu et al. (Eds.): ICSOC 2018 Workshops, LNCS 11434, pp. 3–13, 2019.
https://doi.org/10.1007/978-3-030-17642-6_1

Thus, FFBS saves the cost of construction by eliminating the need for docking stations. And users of FFBS don't worry about finding an empty station when renting a bike, or a station where is a shortage of vacant piles when returning a bike.

Admitting that FFBS is more user-friendly and flexible, the emergency of such transport systems implies various problems. Especially, the distribution of the free-floating bikes is more dispersed, compared to the SBSS. Some bicycles are parked in places that are hard for the public to search. This increases the difficulty for users to find available bikes by GPS [3]. Reallocating the free-floating bikes is important for the sustainable development of FFBS. Bike reposition can either be static or dynamic. At present, there are more literature on the reallocation of the SBBS. For instance, Chemla et al. (2013) combined the branch-and-cut algorithm and the tabu search to rebalance bikes aiming to minimize the operation cost [4]. Mauro et al. (2014) presented four mixed integer linear programming formulations and tailored a branch and cut algorithms to solve them [5]. Christian et al. (2014) adapted greedy and PILOT construction heuristic, variable neighborhood search and GRASP to improve users' satisfaction rate in the dynamic case [6]. Zhang et al. (2016) proposed a dynamic bicycle repositioning methodology, using a novel heuristic algorithm to solve the multi-commodity time-space network flow model [7]. However, very few papers focused free-floating bikes reallocation. Pal and Zhang (2017) considered a multiple-vehicle static repositioning for the FFBSS [8]. Liu et al. (2018) studied a bike repositioning problem with multiple depots, multiple visits, and multiple heterogeneous vehicles for FFBSS [9].

Nowadays, Big Data attracts more and more attention. The subversion and innovation of Big Data is reflected in almost every industry, especially FFBSS. In FFBSS, a lot of data is generated every day, such as bike status, traffic flow, etc. And it offers significant opportunities for smart management. Based on Big data analysis, we find that some bikes are almost never used as they are parked in uncommon locations. The utilization of those bikes remains at a low level, such services may cause financial losses to the company or have negative impact on user satisfaction. Hence, we consider to increase revenue by reallocating bikes that are put in inconvenience positions. Using data-driven method, we define two types of nodes in this paper (i.e., easily and hardly accessed nodes), to represent different convenience levels of getting bikes from the FFBS (Liu et al. 2018). Easily accessed nodes stand for the sites popular to the public, where the utilization rate of bicycles is high (e.g., supermarket, school), while hardly accessed nodes are defined as the locations sparsely populated, hard to be found, where bikes are generally less and rarely used (e.g., alley). In this paper, our objective is to transport bikes at hardly accessed nodes to easily accessed nodes to maximize operation revenue in the shortest possible distance. We formulate a multi-objective mixed integer programming model and use a genetic algorithm to solve it.

The rest of this paper is organized as follows: In Sect. 2, we elaborate the model. In Sect. 3, the solution procedure is proposed. Section 4 presents a numerical example. Finally, Sect. 5 concludes the paper with directions for future research.

2 Model Formulation

As stated in the "Introduction", our objective of the optimization model includes two aspects, the maximum revenue which represents the sum income of all the easily accessed nodes, and the operating costs that are the total distance travelled by the vehicle. The weighted difference of the two components is the total operation profit of the problem. In this paper, we assume that the vehicle departs from the warehouse and ends in the warehouse. And we note that there is no bike in the depot. We also assume that the demand at hardly accessed nodes is 0, so bikes at hardly accessed nodes can't bring revenue, only bikes at easily accessed nodes can bring income. The FFBRP in our paper is to determine the route of the vehicle, load all bikes at hardly accessed nodes and unload reasonably at easily accessed nodes in the shortest distance, such that the total profit is maximized.

2.1 Notation

To facilitate model formulation, we first give the notations used as follows:

Sets:

V_E: A set of nodes which are easily accessed by users

V_H: A set of nodes which are hardly accessed by users

V_0:   A set of nodes, including the depot (denoted by $i = 0$), easily and hardly accessed nodes

Parameters:

θ_i: Number of bicycles on the vehicle after the point i

q_i: Number of bicycles loading or unloading, $q_i > 0, i \in V_H$, q_i. bikes should be removed at hardly accessed nodes; $q_i < 0, i \in V_E$, q_i. bikes should be supplied at easily accessed nodes;

s_i^0:   The initial inventory level at node $i \in V_0$.

s_i: Inventory level at node i at the end of the reallocation operation

$f_i(s_i)$:   A convex income function for station $i \in V_E$, the function is defined over the integers $s_i = 0, \ldots, n$.

Q: Vehicle capacity

β: Difficulty coefficient

M: Big M

d_{ij}:   Distance between the point i and the point j

a_i: The increased revenue for each additional bike at easily accessed nodes, $i \in V_E$

b_i: The increased fee for each additional bike at easily accessed nodes, $i \in V_E$

D_i: The maximum demand of easily accessed nodes, $i \in V_E$

Decision variables:

$$x_{ij} = \begin{cases} 1 & \textit{the vehicle from the point i to j} \\ 0 & \text{else} \end{cases}$$

2.2 Optimization Model

Since it's hard to find those bikes at hardly accessed nodes and it will increase operating costs, we introduce a new parameter, the difficulty coefficient β, to depict the difficulty to find bikes at hardly accessed nodes. Based on the above notations, we can formulate the model as follows:

$$\text{Max} \sum_{i \in V_E} f_i(s_i) - \alpha \left(\sum_{i \in V_0} \sum_{j \in V_H, i \neq j} (1 + \beta) d_{ij} x_{ij} + \sum_{i \in V_0} \sum_{j \in V_0 \setminus \{V_H\}, j \neq i} d_{ij} x_{ij} \right) \tag{1}$$

$$\sum_{i \in V_0} x_{ij} = 1 \quad j \in V_0, j \neq i \tag{2}$$

$$\sum_{i \in V_0} x_{ji} = 1 \quad j \in V_0, j \neq i \tag{3}$$

$$s_i = s_i^0 + q_i \quad i \in V_0 \tag{4}$$

$$s_0 = 0 \tag{5}$$

$$s_0^0 = 0 \tag{6}$$

$$q_i = s_i^0 \quad i \in V_H \tag{7}$$

$$\theta_j \geq \theta_i + q_j - M(1 - x_{ij}) \quad i \in V_0, j \in V_0, j \neq i \tag{8}$$

$$\theta_i \geq \theta_j - q_j - M(1 - x_{ij}) \quad i \in V_0, j \in V_0, j \neq i \tag{9}$$

$$\max\{0, q_j\} \leq \theta_i \leq \min\{Q, Q + q_j\} \quad i \in V_0, j \in V_0, j \neq i \tag{10}$$

$$\sum_{i \in S} \sum_{j \in S} x_{ij} \leq |S| - 1 \quad S \in V_0 \setminus \{0\}, S \neq \emptyset \tag{11}$$

$$x_{ij} \in \{0, 1\} \quad i \in V_0, j \in V_0, j \neq i \tag{12}$$

The objective (1) aims to maximize the total profit of the system, consisting of maximizing the income of all easily accessed nodes and minimizing the total operation costs, that is, minimizing the total distance, appropriately weighted by a factor of α. Constraints (2) and (3) impose that every node and the depot is visited exactly once. Constraints (4) represents the final inventory of all nodes. Constraints (5) and (6) ensure that the depot does not have bikes at the beginning and ending of vehicle's operation. Constraints (7) stipulates that the vehicle must collect all bikes when the vehicle travel to the hardly accessed nodes. Constraints (8) and (9) demonstrate that, if $x_{ij} = 1$, then $\theta_j = \theta_i + q_j$, modeling the flow conservation. Constraints (10) simply gives lower and upper bounds on the loads. Constraints (11) is the subtour elimination constraints. Constraints (12) represents that x_{ij} is a 0–1 variable.

Our next step is to define the income function of easily accessed nodes. For easily accessed nodes, there is a certain amount of bicycle riding demand. The income will increase first and then decrease with the increase in the number of bicycles. When the number of bicycles exceeds the demand, the unused bikes may occupy a lot of public space or increase the maintenance cost, resulting in a decline in revenue. Hence, we formulate the income function as follows.

$$f_i(s_i) = \begin{cases} a_i \times x_i - b_i \times x_i \, x_i \le D_i \\ a_i \times D_i - b_i \times x_i \, x_i > D_i \end{cases} x_i \in N \tag{13}$$

The function image is shown in Fig. 1.

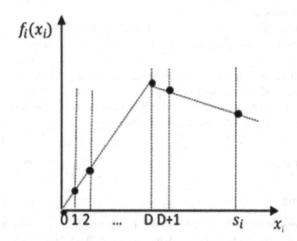

Fig. 1. The income function

3   Solution Procedure

In this paper, the genetic algorithm is used to solve the problem. The genetic algorithm (GA) is a global search algorithm by simulating biological evolutionary mechanisms. The GA obtains the optimal solution or satisfactory solution to the problem by a cyclical process with selection, crossover, mutation, and improvement. The procedure is described as follows:

Step 1: Initialization. Set the population size, the maximum number of iterations, the selection rate, the crossover rate and the mutation rate of the genetic algorithm.

Step 2: Chromosome coding. According to the nature of the problem, real number encoding method is adopted. More specifically, we layer the chromosomes: the first layer is the route of vehicle, and the second layer is the number of bikes increased per easily accessed node. For example, let's assume that 5 and 6 are easily accessed nodes.

The chromosome, 32541683, is divided into two parts. 325416, means the six nodes are visited with the order. 83, means that easily accessed nodes 5 and 6 obtain 8 bikes and 3 bikes respectively. According to the coding rules and problem constraints, randomly generate the original generation.

Step 3: Fitness evaluation. Fitness is a criterion for measuring the quality of individuals and an important basis for genetic operations. The greater the fitness value of an individual, the greater the probability of being selected to the next generation. Therefore, the fitness function is defined as Eq. (1).

Step 4: Selection. The classic proportionate selection, the roulette wheel selection, is used to choose the new population.

Step 5: Crossover. Pairs of parents are selected for crossover in the population according to the crossover rate. We cross each of the two layers of any two chromosomes to obtain two new chromosomes. To prevent the node from repeating twice in a chromosome, we use the elimination function to remove the repeat nodes in the first layer of the chromosome.

Step 6: Mutation. We also mutate the two layers of the chromosome separately. We select a chromosome at the desired probability and exchange any two points of this chromosome.

Step7: Termination. The process will be terminated after a fixed number of generations. The route and the number of bicycles added at easily accessed nodes corresponding to the individual with the best fitness values in the last generation of populations is the optimal solutions to the problem.

4 Case Study

4.1 Data Setting

In order to assess the performance of the proposed model, we perform several numerical tests. We assume that Area A has one depot. And there are 5 easily accessed nodes, where the utilization ratio of bicycle is much higher than other 20 hardly accessed nodes in which bicycles are barely used. We must collect all bikes at hardly accessed nodes and reallocate them to the easily accessed nodes with a 50-capacity vehicle. The related parameters are set as follows: $\alpha = 0.6$, $\beta = 0.1$. The other data setting are illustrated in Tables 1 and 2.

4.2 Test Result

As mentioned above, our model pursues the maximum profit with the shortest possible distance. The test results are demonstrated in the following Fig. 1. Figure 1 is the convergence process of the proposed GA. We find that the reallocation profit is stable around ¥335. The total income is around ¥530, and the total cost is around ¥195 (Fig. 2).

Table 1. The number of bikes in hardly accessed nodes

Node	Quantity	Node	Quantity
1	6	11	3
2	7	12	6
3	6	15	5
4	3	14	4
5	5	15	6
6	8	16	4
7	3	17	10
8	6	18	6
9	1	19	9
10	8	20	5

Table 2. Parameters of easily accessed nodes

Node	a_i	b_i	D_i
21	5.5	1.5	20
22	6.3	1.5	22
23	6.8	1.5	22
24	6.9	1.5	28
25	5.8	1.5	24

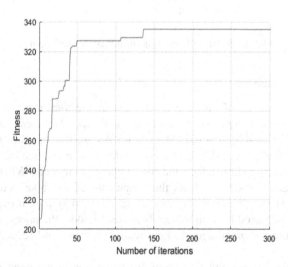

Fig. 2. Convergence procedure of the GA

It is important to note that there is a trade-off between the revenue and the distance that can be increased when the vehicle travels to the next easily accessed node. For example, the easily accessed node 24 is far from other nodes, but its unit income is higher than other easily access node. The route shows that more bikes will be transported to 24. Because long-distance transportation makes sense only when there is enough revenue. Due to the limitation of the total number of bicycles, the easily accessed nodes with smaller unit income are often supplied with fewer bicycles. Therefore, we need to consider transporting more bicycles to higher-income easily accessed nodes as much as possible while meeting vehicle constraints, even if the transport distance is long.

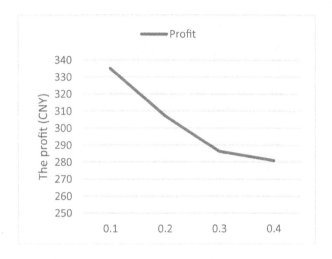

Fig. 3. Sensitivity analysis on difficulty coefficient

4.3 Sensitivity Analysis

To understand the impact of difficulty coefficient of the total profit of the proposed model, we conducted sensitivity analysis with β. We test five situations β = 0.1, β = 0.2, β = 0.3, β = 0.4. The test results are illustrated in Figs. 3 and 4.

Obviously, as the level of difficulty increase, the total profit declines. The increase in the level of difficulty mainly affects the costs rather than income. When the user rides the bike to a remote place, it affects the usage rate of the bike and increases the reallocation cost. Hence, the operation can set up a reward system, if the user rides the bike at the hardly accessed node to the easily accessed node, the user can get a reward. In this way, the user is encouraged to help reallocate bikes and reduce the operation cost of the company.

More interestingly, we find that there are some hardly accessed nodes that are relatively far away from other nodes and have fewer bikes. Therefore, collecting bicycles at these hardly accessed nodes may result in income less than cost. We simply sort by the ratio of the bicycle stock level at that hardly accessed nodes to the total distance from that hardly accessed node to other nodes. Then we delete one, two, three nodes with the smallest ratio. The test results are illustrated in Figs. 4 and 5.

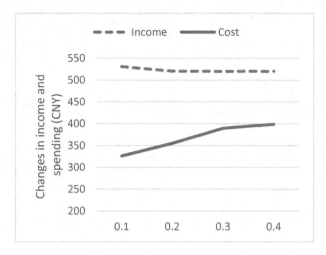

Fig. 4. Sensitivity analysis on difficulty coefficient

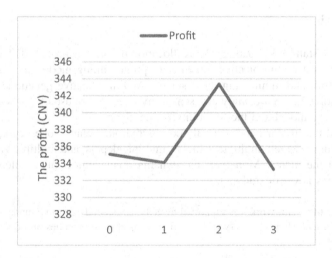

Fig. 5. The profit with the decline of hardly access nodes

It is particularly noteworthy that when the two nodes are deleted, the profit after reallocation is increased. As shown in Fig. 6, although the revenue is reduced, the cost is relatively lower, so the total profit increases instead. When there are only a few bikes at some hardly accessed nodes but it costs a lot of money to collect, the company can give up these bikes appropriately and wait for the users to ride the bicycles.

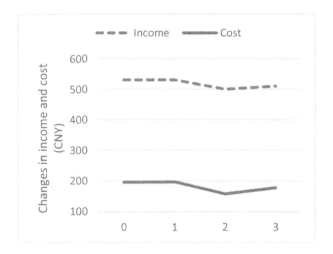

Fig. 6. The income and cost with the decline of hardly access nodes

5 Conclusion

In this paper, a static free-floating bike reallocation problem is proposed. The problem is formulated as a multi-objective mixed inter programming model, including maximizing the profit and minimizing the distance. And an effective genetic algorithm is designed to solve it. A case study and sensitivity analysis are used to demonstrate the rationality of the model and the feasibility of the algorithm.

It is noted that in our paper we only considered one vehicle, one depot, and once visited. In future research, multiple vehicles, multiple depots, and multiple visits can be considered in the model. Moreover, the dynamic management of free-floating bike-sharing systems is worth studying.

Acknowledgments. This work was supported by National Natural Science Foundation of China (No. 71771120) and MOE (Ministry of Education) Project of Humanities and Social Sciences (No. 17YJA630058).

References

1. Caggiani, L., Camporeale, R., Ottomanelli, M.: Wai Yuen Szeto.: A modeling framework for the dynamic management of free-floating bike-sharing systems. Transp. Res. Part C **87**, 159–182 (2018)
2. Yi, A., Zongping, L., Mi, G.: A solution to measure travel's transfer tolerance for walking mode and dockless bike-sharing mode. J. Supercomput. **1**, 1–18 (2018)
3. Bike-sharing: Users share perks, gripes. https://www.straitstimes.com/singapore/bike-sharing-users-share-perks-gripes. Accessed 26 Sept. 2018
4. Chemal, D., Meunier, F., Calvo, R.W.: Bike sharing systems: Solving the static rebalancing problem. Discrete Optim. **10**, 120–146 (2013)

5. Dell' Amico, M., Hadjicostantinou, E., Iori, M., Novellani, S.: The bike sharing rebalancing problem: mathematical formulations and benchmark instances. Omega **87**, 7–19 (2014)
6. Kloimüllner, C., Papazek, P., Hu, B., Raidl, Günther R.: A cluster-first route-second approach for balancing bicycle sharing systems. In: Moreno-Díaz, R., Pichler, F., Quesada-Arencibia, A. (eds.) EUROCAST 2015. LNCS, vol. 9520, pp. 439–446. Springer, Cham (2015). https://doi.org/10.1007/978-3-319-27340-2_55
7. Zhang, D., Yu, C., Desai, J., Lau, H.Y.K., Srivathsan, S.: A time-space network flow approach to dynamic repositioning in bicycle sharing systems. Transp. Res. Part B **103**, 188–207 (2017)
8. Pal, A., Zhang, Y.: Free-floating bike sharing: solving real-life large-scale static rebalancing problems. Transp. Res. Part C **80**, 92–116 (2017)
9. Liu, Y., Szeto, W.Y., Ho, S.G.: A static free-floating bike repositioning problem with multiple heterogeneous vehicles, multiple depots, and multiple visits. Transp. Res. Part C **92**, 208–242 (2018)

Study on Airport De-icing Schedule Problem Balancing Fairness and Efficiency

Qing Guo[1], Bing Li[1(✉)], and Xuan Luo[2]

[1] School of Information Technology and Management,
University of International Business and Economics, Beijing, China
a378602672@163.com, lb0501@126.com
[2] Lancaster University, Lancaster, UK
silence9476@163.com

Abstract. Taking the airport de-icing resources optimization arrangements as the research object. When the airport de-icing resources are tense and large-scale delays occur at the airport, airport decision-makers need to consider both fairness and efficiency. At present, the FCFS method is widely used at home and abroad for de-icing scheduling, which has certain defects in fairness and efficiency. To improve the efficiency of airport de-icing and the fairness of resource allocation, through research and analysis of the theory and method of airport de-icing process scheduling problem, a multi-objective mathematical optimization model with the minimum number of strands as the efficiency goal and the minimum weighted dissatisfaction value as the fairness goal is established. An algorithm based on fully combination thinking is designed, and a multi-objective decision-making strategy is proposed for decision makers to choose a satisfactory solution as the airport de-icing resource allocation scheme. Based on the algorithm simulation of the model and comparative analysis, the results show that this algorithm is able to solve the problem of aircraft de-icing scheduling problem, which can improve the resource utilization efficiency better compared with the existing manual scheduling method and ensure the fairness of resource allocation to a certain extent.

Keywords: Aircraft de-icing · Parallel machine scheduling ·
Fairness and efficiency · Resource constraint · Multi-objective optimization

1 Introduction

With the rapid development of China's civil aviation industry, the number of passengers that need to be carried has increased year by year. It is the most important thing to consider how to ensure the flight operating efficiency and flight safety. During the snow and ice weather, the surface of the civil aircraft becomes rough due to condensation cream and ice, which cause and the flight resistance increases. The safety in the air is difficult to be guaranteed. And so far, many air crashes have been caused, such as the "2004.11.21" air crash in China Baotou and the United Kingdom "2002.1.4" Birmingham air crash, causing the death of more than a thousand passengers. On the other hand, aircraft de-icing in cold weather may cause delays in airport area, which is likely to seriously affect operational efficiency of the airport, and cause substantial

© Springer Nature Switzerland AG 2019
X. Liu et al. (Eds.): ICSOC 2018 Workshops, LNCS 11434, pp. 14–26, 2019.
https://doi.org/10.1007/978-3-030-17642-6_2

economic losses. Comprehensive and effective de-icing of aircraft has become the key to the normal operation of winter airports. Under such circumstances, there is important practical significance to study the problem of aircraft de-icing (mainly the aircraft de-icing sequence) for improving the operational support capability and operational efficiency of civil aviation airports.

The strategy of "first come first served" is mostly used by large domestic airports to do de-icing operations. That is so say, allocate resources according to application time for de-icing. Under the snow and ice weather, all flights belonging to various airlines are waiting in line for the de-icing platform. This method is simple to operate. However, due to the limited resources of the de-icing equipment provided by the airport, the de-icing efficiency is extremely low, and the fairness problem is not being considered. The situation that an airline may not be able to obtain de-icing resources for a long time is likely to happen. As a result, the airport is possible to show a disorderly state, resulting in a large loss of manpower and material resources. Optimizing the existing de-icing scheduling strategy and using a more efficient and fairer way to arrange aircraft de-icing sequences is conducive to increasing the economic efficiency of the airport and maintaining airport stability. Therefore, the research in this paper is very necessary and valuable.

2 Literature Review

The operation scheduling problem of airport equipment is always a research hotspot in the field of civil aviation. Voulgarellis et al. [1] used computer tools such as Matlab to systematically model all important aspects of airport operations and conduct simulation experiments on different modules. Thereby, they explored the links between the in every department, providing a certain basis for the systematic optimization of airport dispatch services. In order to improve the efficiency of de-icing, for the design and construction of scheduling algorithms for de-icing resources, experts in related fields have done a lot of research: Lin et al. [2] improved the pheromone and state change rules in ant colony algorithm. This improvement makes the convergence speed of the ant colony algorithm increase and enhances the quality of understanding. Shi et al. designed a scheduling model for de-icing equipment using genetic algorithms, which improves the efficiency of de-icing vehicles in large-scale airports. However, they did not consider environmental and resource constraints. Juran et al. [3] discussed the problem of parallel service resource allocation from the perspective of bottleneck resources. But there are few studies on the allocation of de-icing resources. In the actual process of airport operations, especially in the case of emergencies, this problem is very prominent. Mao and Mors [4] introduced the competition and coordination mechanism into the aircraft de-icing plan, and proposed the aircraft-based de-icing scheduling framework and various optimization algorithms. However, the dynamic response during the actual operation is not effective. Based on the relevant knowledge of game theory, Xing made a systematic study on the allocation of multiple de-icing resources, and achieved good results. But that method still needs further improvement.

Although the above literature improves the operational efficiency of airport de-icing resource scheduling and reduces the probability of large-scale delay events, it does not delve into the issue of fairness in the process of resource allocation. When de-icing resources are scarce, airport decision makers need to consider the fairness of resource allocation while considering the maximization of resource allocation efficiency. Otherwise, it is easy to cause instability, disorder, and even lead to conflicts.

At present, there is no exact principle of fair distribution at home and abroad. The research on the fairness of emergency resource allocation mainly includes maximum and minimum fairness, and proportional fairness. Maximum and minimum fairness is the maximization of the worst individual performance within the system to achieve fairness. Proportional fairness refers to the allocation of emergency supplies in the same proportion of the demand of each company. For example, Vitoriano et al. [5] expresses fairness by setting the minimum ratio of resources and demand to the demand point; Huang et al. [6] achieves fairness through the convex function with unsatisfied demand as the objective function.

Although the above literature considers the fairness of resource allocation, it does not explore the relationship between fairness and efficiency. Bertsimas [7] has studied the relationship between resource fairness allocation strategy and system efficiency loss, and proved the inverse relationship between these two. Medernach et al. pointed out the problem of equitable distribution of resources under different demand scenarios, proposing the solution of efficiency and fairness pareto solution based on lexico-graphical order. Li et al. established a multi-objective hybrid programming model with minimum and maximum dissatisfaction as the fair goal and system utility maximization as the efficiency goal.

In summary, scholars have begun to study the issue of resource allocation that balances fairness and efficiency, but with fewer results. And many of them believe that fairness should focus on the equality of "physical distribution", while a few scholars believe that they should focus more on "psychological utility". The former refers to realizing the distribution of materials according to a certain proportion of demand points. While the latter focuses on subjectivity, which is emphasizing whether people's inner feelings are unfair. For example, the definition of fairness in the New Palgrave Economics Dictionary is that "if in one distribution, no one is married to another, then this distribution is called fair distribution". Therefore, this paper argues that in the process of emergency material distribution, it is necessary to consider the equalization of "physical distribution" and "psychological utility" of each demand point. Therefore, this paper establishes a multi-objective mathematical optimization model with the minimum dissatisfaction value of satisfying the equal utility of each airline, the efficiency goal of minimizing the number of stranded passengers, and the proportional fairness as the constraint condition of satisfying the equality of physical distribution.

Therefore, compared with the existing literature above, here are the main contributions of this paper. ① Consider the de-icing efficiency of the airport while taking into account the fairness of de-icing resource allocation. ② In terms of fairness, consider the equalization of "physical distribution" and "psychological utility" at the same time. ③ Construct multi-objective mathematical optimization model, design solving algorithm, and propose multi-objective decision-making strategy for airport decision makers to weigh.

3   Aircraft De-icing Scheduling Model

3.1   Problem Setting

The problem of airport de-icing scheduling involved in this paper can be described as below. In ice and snow weather, there are n aircrafts waiting for de-icing operations at the airport. And these aircrafts are affiliated to different airlines. The airport has m de-icing rigs (where small aircrafts can be de-iced on large de-icing rigs but large aircrafts cannot be de-iced on small de-icing rigs). In the case of known time-consuming de-icing of various types of aircraft, the designed scheduling scheme minimizes the number of passengers stranded in a period of time, while at the same time the company has the lowest total weighted dissatisfaction. For this study, the most important issue is to determine which aircraft to choose and the de-icing sequence for each de-icing aircraft.

Taking the actual de-icing process of an airport as an example, the airport centralized de-icing scheduling process mainly includes airport command centres, airlines, and ground service centres. The relationship between these three is shown in Fig. 1.

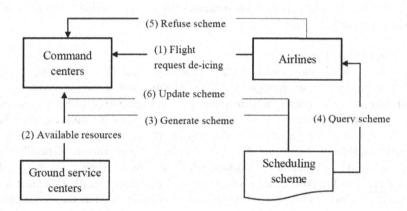

Fig. 1. Flow chart of de-icing scheduling

The goal of the airport command centre is to minimize the number of passengers stranded during a certain period of time and maintain the stability of the airport; the airlines hope that their subordinate flights can be de-iced in time. The design of the de-icing scheduling scheme proposed in this study optimizes the existing first-come-first service mode, and obtains a scheduling scheme that can minimize the number of stranded passengers and balance the fairness of each airline.

3.2   Quantification of Fairness Indicator

In ice and snow weather, de-icing resources are scarce and cannot meet the needs of all airlines at the same time. When one airline believes that other airlines are being "privileged" to get more de-icing resources, it is subjectively considered to be unfair.

This subjective sense of injustice is the main cause of dissatisfaction. Based on this, this study builds a function that describes the dissatisfaction of each airline based on the principle of mutual dissatisfaction.

3.2.1   Minimum Dissatisfaction

In the early days of ice and snow, de-icing resources are in short supply. Therefore, when the unsatisfied demand of the i company is higher than the unsatisfied demand of the j company, the i company generates a dissatisfaction value, and otherwise, i does not have dissatisfaction. Therefore, the dissatisfaction function is recorded as $e_{ij} = \max\{0, r_i - r_j\}$, and e_{ij} is recorded as the dissatisfaction value of i company to j company. And $r_i = d_i - s_i$ indicates that the unsatisfied demand of i company is equal to the actual demand of i company minus the demand satisfaction amount. On the other hand, considering that the more passengers, the more likely generating group events, and the weight of their dissatisfaction function should be greater. According to the principle of normalization, the weight is $h_i = d_i/D$, that is, the weight of i company is the ratio of the demand of i company to the total demand of all companies. In summary, the total weighted dissatisfaction value of all airlines is $f = \sum_{i \in I} \sum_{j \in I} h_i e_{ij}$. The lower value of this function, the smaller the dissatisfaction of each airline, which confirms that the "psychological utility" is more equal.

3.2.2   Proportional Fairness

Fair or unfair resource allocation is a relative concept. If the study only pays attention to the equalization of "psychological utility", it will result in airlines with smaller demand being allocated only a small amount of de-icing resources, or even completely undistributed. It makes another kind of unfairness while pursuing fairness. Therefore, in order to solve this contradiction, the equality of "physical distribution" needs to be moderately considered. This study draws on the idea of "proportional fairness", which is to set a minimum demand satisfaction rate λ for each airline $(\lambda = \sigma \sum s_i/D)$. $\sum s_i/D$ represents the ratio of total supply to total demand; $\sigma \in [0, 1]$ indicates the degree of proportional fairness; $\sigma \to 0$ indicates that the proportional fairness is getting lower and lower, and $\sigma = 0$ means the equal allocation of emergency supplies in full accordance with the "psychological utility"; $\sigma \to 1$ indicates that the proportional fairness is getting higher and higher, and $\sigma = 1$ means that emergency materials are equally distributed according to "physical distribution".

3.3   Model Building

The establishment of the de-icing resource allocation model in this paper is based on the following assumptions:

① Each de-ice land can only de-ice one aircraft at a time, and all de-icing lands can start de-icing sat the same time.

② De-icing and aircraft are classified according to their size. And large aircraft can only be de-iced on large de-icing platforms while small aircraft can be de-iced on both larger and small de-icing platforms.

③ The secondary de-icing is not considered, that is, each aircraft can be ready to take off after once de-icing.

④ The de-icing treatment time is taken as the time when the aircraft is operated on the de-icing platform, which means the starting time, the inspection time are excluded.

⑤ The de-icing time of all aircraft is counted from zero and cannot be stopped once de-icing is started.

3.3.1 Symbol Description

(1) Aircraft Collection A: To simplify the complexity of the problem, this article assumes that there are three types of aircraft waiting for de-icing:

$$A_1 = \{a_1, a_2, \ldots, a_{m1}\}$$
$$A_2 = \{a_{m1+1}, a_{m1+2}, \ldots, a_{m1+m2}\}$$
$$A_3 = \{a_{m1+m2+1}, a_{m1+m2+2}, \ldots, a_{m1+m2+m3}\}$$
$$A = A_1 \cup A_2 \cup A_3$$

A represents all aircraft collections; A_1 represents a collection of large aircraft; A_2 represents a combination of medium aircraft; and A_3 represents a collection of small aircraft. m_1, m_2 and m_3 represent the number of large, medium, and small types of aircraft to be de-iced, respectively.

(2) De-icing Platform B: This paper assumes that there are two types of de-icing platforms:

$$B_1 = \{b_1, b_2, \ldots, b_{l1}\}$$
$$B_2 = \{b_{l1+1}, a_{l1+2}, \ldots, a_{l1+l2}\}$$
$$B = B_1 \cup B_2$$

l_1 and l_2 respectively represent the number of de-icing positions included in each of the two de-icing platforms B_1 and B_2. And the aircraft in A_1 cannot be de-icing by the de-icing position (small de-icing position) included in the de-icing platform B_2. In addition to the de-icing position (large de-icing position) in the ice floor B_1, de-icing operations can be performed on any type of aircraft.

(3) De-icing time t(k): indicates the de-icing time of aircraft k. Therefore, when $k = 1, 2, 3, \ldots, m_1$, $t(k) = t_1$; when $k = m_1 + 1$, $m_1 + 2, \ldots, m_1 + m_2$, $t(k) = t_2$; when $k = m_1 + m_2 + 1, \ldots, m_1 + m_2 + m_3$, $t(k) = t_3$.

(4) Scheduling time window length w: one scheduling period.

(5) 0–1 variable y_{ku}: If $y_{ku} = 1$, it means that the aircraft k is de-icing on the u de-icing platform; $y_{ku} = 0$, the result is the opposite.

(6) Number of passengers in the aircraft p_k: the number of passengers in the aircraft k, and the demand for the airline i is $d_i = \sum_{k \in A} p_k$.

3.3.2 Mathematical Model

According to the above variable definition, the de-icing resource scheduling model is established as follows:

$$\min \quad Z_1 = \sum_{i \in I} \sum_{j \in I} h_i e_{ij} \tag{1}$$

$$\min \quad Z_2 = d - \sum_{k \in A} \sum_{u \in B} y_{ku} p_k \tag{2}$$

s.t.

$$y_{ku} = 0, \text{ when } k \in \{1, 2, \ldots, m_1\} \text{ and } u \in \{l_1 + 1, l_1 + 2, \ldots, l_1 + l_2\} \tag{3}$$

$$\sum_{k \in A} t_k y_{ku} \leq T \tag{4}$$

$$s_i \geq \lambda d_i \tag{5}$$

The objective function (1) is a fairness indicator, which means that the total weighted dissatisfaction value of each airline is minimized. The objective function (2) is an efficiency indicator, which means that the number of stranded passengers is minimized. The constraint function (3) indicates that a large aircraft cannot de-ice at a small de-icing location. The constraint function (4) is a time window constraint. The formula (5) indicates that the acquisition amount of de-icing resources of an airline is not less than the minimum demand, that is, the proportional fairness constraint.

4   Aircraft de-Icing Scheduling Algorithm

In the multi-objective optimization problem, each target is often a reciprocal relationship. So there is generally no optimal solution, and only non-inferior solutions exist. The methods for solving multi-objective problems can be roughly divided into two categories: ① a priori method, that is, the decision-maker has a certain preference in advance, and then transforms the multi-objective into a single-objective solution through linear weighting, ideal points, hierarchical sequences; ② The posterior method is to first obtain a set of non-inferior solutions of the problem by multi-objective evolutionary algorithm or other multi-objective solving method, and then the decision-makers choose the satisfactory scheme according to their own preferences. This study is based on the principle of weighting in the prior method to design an algorithm based on the idea of fully combination.

Step 1. De-icing aircraft plan selection. Assume the time window of 60 min, for B1 de-icing platform,

$$60 - t_3 < n_1 t_1 + n_2 t_2 + n_3 t_3 < 61 \tag{6}$$

It is possible to find all the de-icing schemes in a certain B_1 de-icing platform, that is, select n_1 large aircraft, n_2 medium-sized aircraft, and n_3 small aircraft. For B_2 de-icing platforms (large aircraft cannot be de-iced on B_2 de-icing platforms), and according to

$$60 - t_3 < n_4 t_2 + n_5 t_3 < 61 \tag{7}$$

That is to choose n_4 medium-sized aircraft, n_5 small aircraft. Applying this method to all de-icing ridges, n different schemes can be obtained, each of which corresponds to the number of different large, medium and small aircrafts. And the constraints on time window conditions are completed.

Step 2. Standardize the process. Since the dimensions of the two objective functions are inconsistent, standardization processing is required. It is assumed that Z_1^* is the single-objective model optimal value considering only the objective function (1). And the corresponding objective function value (2) is Z_2'; Z_2^* is a single-objective model optimal value considering only the objective function (2), and its corresponding objective function (1) has a value of Z_1'. Then the objective function of the weighting method can be expressed as

$$\min \left(w_1 \frac{Z_1' - Z_1}{Z_1' - Z_1^*} + w_2 \frac{Z_2' - Z_2}{Z_2' - Z_2^*} \right) \tag{8}$$

In the formula, $w_1 + w_2 = 1$ and $w_1 \geq 0 w_2 \geq 0$.

Step 3. Single objective optimal value calculation. ① Select one of the n schemes mentioned in step 1 and assume that the scheme needs to select x large aircraft, y medium aircraft, and small z aircraft. From the aircraft waiting for de-icing, select x, y, z large, medium and small aircraft for full combination. ② Since each aircraft has its own ownership, each combination can determine the total number of passengers that each airline can take off, that is, the demand satisfaction of each airline, and thus the total weighted dissatisfaction value and the passengers who can not take off. ③ Repeating the first two steps n times can solve all the schemes: the minimum number of stranded persons and the corresponding total weighted dissatisfaction values, namely Z_2^* and Z_1'; the total weighted dissatisfied value minimum and the corresponding number of stranded persons, and Z_1^* and Z_2'.

Step 4. Find the Pareto optimal solution. On the basis of steps 2 and 3, a set of Pareto optimal solutions can be obtained by adjusting the weights of the value of w1 and w2. With 0.02 as the step change weight, 51 solutions are able to obtained theoretically. But due to repeated solutions, the actual number of solutions is less than the theoretical value.

Step 5. Solve the aircraft scheduling sequence. According to the solution obtained in step 4, each solution represents which aircraft is selected. The concept of de-icing efficiency is introduced, which means that the number of passengers in the aircraft/the de-icing time of the aircraft to sort the selected aircraft. The higher the efficiency value, the higher the de-icing queue is, ensuring that more passengers will take off in the short term.

The time complexity of the core algorithm in the above algorithm is $O(2^n)$ and this algorithm can solve a set of Pareto optimal solutions of the problem. The smaller the w_1 value, the more important the number of stranded passengers, that is, the efficiency target; the smaller the w_2 value, the more important the total weighted dissatisfaction value, that is, the fair goal. Decision makers can choose the satisfactory solution as the de-icing resource allocation scheme according to their own preferences.

5   Analytical Properties

5.1   Test Cases

Firstly, this study conducted a single-example experiment. Suppose that there are now 34 aircrafts that are stranded at the airport to be taken off, and there are There are each 2 aircrafts in the B_1 and B_2 de-icing platforms. The number of passengers carried by the aircraft was randomly generated by MATLAB (see Table 1 for data). The first six large aircraft required de-icing for 20 min, the medium-sized aircraft numbered 7–18 required de-icing for 18 min, and the last 16 small aircraft required de-icing for 15 min. In a fixed time-window of 60 min, it is necessary to dispatch the aircraft to each de-icing platform in order to achieve the minimum number of stranded passengers and the lowest total weighted dissatisfaction of each airline. In addition, the proportional fairness coefficient $\sigma = 0.5$.

Table 1. Date of aircrafts

No	1	2	3	4	5	6	7	8	9	10	11	12	13	14	15
p_k	215	110	286	246	248	113	120	165	173	65	77	104	59	128	100
i	2	3	1	4	3	4	4	2	1	2	2	1	4	2	2
	16	17	18	19	20	21	22	23	24	25	26	27	28	29	30
	76	180	110	140	95	70	82	184	61	86	58	116	102	109	106
	1	4	3	1	3	2	2	3	1	1	3	3	3	2	3
	31	32	33	34											
	117	93	104	84											
	2	3	2	1											

According to the algorithm design, using Matlab language programming and according to the weight adjustment every 0.02 step, the solution combination of 51 solutions (11 non-repetitive solutions) is calculated, as shown in Fig. 2. The specific scheme can be seen in Table 2. The x-axis refers to dissatisfaction value and the y-axis is the number of stranded passengers. It can be seen from the figure that the total weighted dissatisfaction value Z_1 and the number of stranded passengers Z_2 have an inverse relationship. The efficiency of the allocation scheme corresponding to the solution closer to the x-axis is higher, and the fairness of the allocation scheme corresponding to the solution closer to the y-axis is better. Airport decision makers can choose their options based on their own preferences.

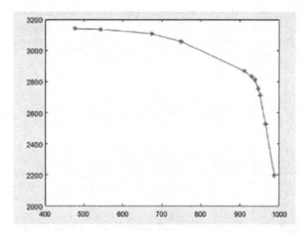

Fig. 2. Experimental results

Table 2. Scheme

No	Dissatisfaction value	Stranded persons	b1	b2	b3	b4
1	477.8	3141	6 10 11	13 15 16	18 21 22	24 25 26 34
2	543.4	3137	6 10 11	12 13 16	18 21 22	24 25 26 34
3	674.2	3107	6 7 10	11 12 13	16 21 24	25 26 28 34
4	748.7	3059	6 7 10	11 12 13	15 16 17	18 24 26
5	910.2	2869	4 6 7	10 11 12	13 16 17	18 21 32
6	929.0	2834	4 6 7	10 11 13	16 17 20	21 24 28 34
7	937.4	2815	4 6 7	11 12 13	14 16 17	18 24 32
8	945.4	2756	4 6 7	10 11 13	17 19 21	24 25 27 32
9	950.3	2711	4 6 7	9 10 13	17 18 21	22 24 25 30
10	964.2	2527	3 4 6	7 10 12	13 17 21	23 24 26 29
11	987.1	2198	3 4 6	7 8 9	13 14 17	19 23 30 34

5.2 Sensitivity Analysis

5.2.1 Impact of Proportional Fairness

If the other parameters are unchanged and the proportional fairness indicator is changed, from Fig. 3, it shows that the fair value of the fold line from right to left is 0.1, 0.5, 0.9. The endpoint solution can be seen in Table 3. According to the experimental results, the lower the proportional fairness, the more the number of solutions obtained, which may be due to the increase of the feasible domain of the model; as the proportional fairness increases, the range of values of the dissatisfaction Z_1 and the number of stranded persons Z_2 is gradually decreasing. At the same time, it can be seen that when the proportional fair value is large, the value of the total weighted dissatisfaction value is small, indicating that the equality of "physical distribution" and the equality of "psychological utility" are also inversely related. The higher the proportional fairness, the companies with smaller demand are more favourable, and vice versa, for companies with large demand.

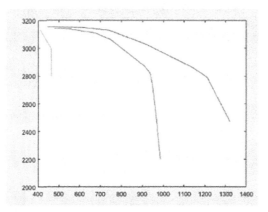

Fig. 3. Experimental results of different proportional fairness

Table 3. Endpoint solution

	Scheme	Dissatisfaction value	Stranded persons
0.1	Z1 min	444.9	3150
	Z2 min	1321.4	2468
0.5	Z1 min	477.8	3141
	Z2 min	987.0	2198
0.9	Z1 min	411	3131
	Z2 min	464	2795

5.3   Algorithm Comparison

So far, the FCFS algorithm is still the most commonly used in large domestic airports, that is, the order of aircraft de-icing is arranged on a first-come, first-served basis. Therefore, here we compare the algorithm of this paper with the FCFS algorithm, the company of each aircraft and the application for de-icing time can be seen in Table 4. The results are shown in Table 5, which can be compared with Table 2. It can be seen from the simulation results that the algorithm of this paper is superior to the FCFS algorithm in terms of fairness, time utilization, and passenger carrying capacity.

Table 4. The flight conversion information

No	Company no	Apply for de-icing time	No	Company no	Apply for de-icing time
1	2	10:25	18	3	10:05
2	3	10:10	19	1	10:15
3	1	10:30	20	3	10:00
4	4	10:25	21	2	10:18

(*continued*)

Table 4. (*continued*)

No	Company no	Apply for de-icing time	No	Company no	Apply for de-icing time
5	3	10:28	22	2	10:12
6	4	10:15	23	3	10:40
7	2	10:40	24	1	10:18
8	2	10:35	25	1	10:21
9	1	10:20	26	3	10:25
10	2	10:05	27	3	10:30
11	2	10:15	28	3	10:08
12	1	10:00	29	2	10:05
13	4	10:10	30	3	10:10
14	2	10:05	31	2	10:20
15	2	10:22	32	3	10:30
16	1	10:00	33	2	10:40
17	4	10:25	34	1	10:02

Table 5. Results obtained using the FCFS algorithm

Dissatisfaction value	Stranded persons	b1	b2	b3	b4
1520	3136	20 18 28 21	34 29 2	12 10 13	16 14 30

6 Concluding Remarks

This study establishes a de-icing scheduling model that considers both fairness and efficiency, and designs a multi-objective solving algorithm based on full combination. Using the model and algorithm of this paper can effectively improve the de-icing efficiency of the airport and the fairness of resource allocation, and improve the airport economic efficiency and better maintain the stability of the airport. Through the case analysis, the validity and practicability of the model and algorithm are proved. In addition, the following conclusions are drawn.

1. By constructing a multi-objective model and algorithm that combines fairness and efficiency, the de-icing resource allocation scheme with different preferences can be obtained. Compared with the single-objective model, the multi-objective model can better balance the fairness and efficiency of de-icing resource allocation, and is conducive to maintaining the stability of the airport.
2. Characterize the equal dissatisfaction of the "psychological utility" of each airline and the equalization of "physical distribution". And there is a contradiction between proportional fairness. Also airport decision makers need to weigh the considerations based on actual conditions.

The limitations of this study are showed as follows. ① The performance of the machine used in this study is poor, so the amount of data is small. But this algorithm has good scalability. If the machine performance is good enough, the algorithm of this study can carry more calculations of data. ② This research model is still a little idealized, and more complex factors need to be considered in the actual decision-making. There are some research directions which still need to be further expanded: research on the best aircraft de-icing scheme after joining the interest of the ground service company; research new aircraft airports inside during time window; the impact of time nodes on the dissatisfaction of airlines.

Acknowledgments. The research was partially supported by the National Social Science Fund Project, China (No. 16BTQ065) "Multi-source intelligence fusion research on emergencies in big data environment".

References

1. Voulgarellis, P.G., Christodoulou, M.A., Boutalis, Y.S.: A MATLAB based simulation language for aircraft ground handling operations at hub airports (SLAGOM). In: Proceedings of the 2005 IEEE International Symposium on, Mediterrean Conference on Control and Automation, pp. 334–339. IEEE (2005)
2. Lin, B.M.T., Lu, C.Y., Shyu, S.J., Tsai, C.Y.: Development of new features of ant colony optimization for flow shop scheduling. Int. J. Prod. Econ. **112**(2), 742–755 (2007)
3. Juran, I., Prashker, J.N., Bekhor, S.: A dynamic traffic assignment model for the assessment of moving bottlenecks. Transp. Res. Part C Emerg. Technol. **17**(3), 240–258 (2009)
4. Mao, X.Y., Mors, A.T., Roos, N., et al.: Agent-based scheduling for aircraft deicing. In: Proceedings of the 18th Belgium-Netherlands Conference on Artificial Intelligence, Brussels, pp. 229–236 (2007)
5. Vitoriano, B., Ortuño, M.T., Tirado, G., et al.: A multi-criteria optimization model for humanitarian aid distribution. J. Global Optim. **51**(2), 189–208 (2011)
6. Huang, M., KarenSmilowitz, B.: Models for relief routing: Equity, efficiency and efficacy. Transp. Res. Part E **48**(1), 2–18 (2011)
7. Bertsimas, D., Farias, V.F., Nikolaos, T.: On the efficiency-fairness trade-off. Manage. Sci. **58**(12), 2234–2250 (2012)

Co-design of Business and IT Services - A Tool-Supported Approach

Blagovesta Pirelli[✉], Natalia Nessler, and Alain Wegmann

School of Computer and Communication Sciences, Ecole Polytechnique Fédérale de Lausanne (EPFL), 1015 Lausanne, Switzerland
{blagovesta.pirelli,natalia.nessler,alain.wegmann}@epfl.ch

Abstract. Service modeling is an important step in designing service-oriented systems. There are multiple levels of design because service science includes both the business rationale and the IT implementation of the services. As business and IT perspectives differ, the modeling techniques are different, and often the respective modeling languages are disconnected or ad-hoc. We propose a new service-modeling approach for connecting the business modeling and the web service modeling by presenting these two perspectives in a single model. We present a multi-stage modeling process for capturing different perspectives and creating models iteratively by working with levels of abstraction from higher to lower. The model is then used as an input in order to generate a REST API specification in the OpenAPI format to feed the next stages of the service life-cycle.

Keywords: Service description · Service modeling · Service specification · OpenAPI · REST

1 Introduction

In today's API economy, many business-information systems make use of web services or develop interfaces for other systems to interact with them [14]. During the development of these systems, a major part of the work is the definition and configuration of the web services. The business requirements for these services are often captured with user stories, or other informal or semi-formal descriptions. However, the development of the actual services requires a fine level of detail.

We use SEAM [15], a modeling technique based on service science, to bring together abstract business models and precise specifications. SEAM enables us to understand the business environment and to define the actors' responsibilities for the information managed by them. We observe that service-modeling techniques fall into two categories: business-service modeling and IT-service modeling. On the one hand, the business-service models are not precise enough to fully describe web services (e.g., which identifiers to use, which status to return to the user). On the other hand, IT-service models do not preserve the business semantics.

© Springer Nature Switzerland AG 2019
X. Liu et al. (Eds.): ICSOC 2018 Workshops, LNCS 11434, pp. 27–40, 2019.
https://doi.org/10.1007/978-3-030-17642-6_3

Therefore, our research question is: *How do we extend existing service modeling to simultaneously design business and IT services?*

We present a service-modeling approach for generating web-service specifications by using an ontological extension of service models that captures the minimum amount of annotations necessary to define the web services. With these annotations, a single model captures all business and technical requirements, and enables hiding or showing information as necessary. For web services, we chose the Representational State Transfer (REST) [6], the widely adopted architectural style for web services. There are many languages that describe REST services, e.g., WADL [7]. We chose to work with the OpenAPI[1] specification (previously Swagger), as it is the *de facto* industry standard. We developed a supporting tool that generates the OpenAPI specification corresponding to the service models. Our tool removes the necessity of transferring the business models to technical specifications and is a part of the toolbox for service designing with SEAM.

Using our proposed modeling approach, a service designer (i.e., a business analyst, a requirements engineering practitioner, or a project manager) goes through the following process. First, the service designer captures the business environment in a service-system model. Then, they describe the information entities that the business actors use in the service process. Next, they annotate the models with additional information necessary for describing IT services that each actor requires. Finally, our tool generates the web specification from the models.

This paper's structure is the following: In Sect. 2, we present a brief literature review and background work. In Sect. 3, we describe our approach for the generation of REST API specifications from service models. In Sect. 4, we conclude and outline future work.

2 Literature

2.1 Services in Business and IT

A service system is a set of elements that collaborate in a service delivery process [8]. A service system is most often a socio-technical system that presents the interaction between both human and technical elements. Modeling complex systems, with the help of conceptualization and formalization of the target service system, is a necessary step for understanding their behavior. Service models show only an abstraction, i.e., abstract away any underlying implementations. With simplifications such as modularization, abstraction, and interfaces, services are defined in a minimalistic way, and understandable by the people to whom service designers communicate the models.

One of the earliest works on service modeling, service blueprinting [13], lays the four fundamental steps to modeling and designing services: (1) identify processes, (2) isolate fail points, (3) timebox the execution, and (4) analyze profitability. The service blueprint is generic and does not take into account the

---

[1] http://archive.today/ZSNFJ.

recent developments of the IT infrastructure involved in the service process because it was developed in the 80's. Recently, Estañol et al. [5] used service blueprinting to extend service modeling and designing to a set of executable logic rules to check the validity of the service blueprint.

For specialized modeling of business processes within an organization, Business Process Modeling and Notation (BPMN) is widely used. BPMN's logic is similar to an activity diagram, which makes the notation easy to understand. The models can be executed (if complete). However, BPMN does not tolerate ambiguity that is present at the beginning of service design.

IT-service modeling techniques include mostly formal description languages in order to specify the behavior of web services. For example, WADL [7] and the OpenAPI are such specifications. The resulting specifications are highly technical and detailed, and they do not accommodate a more abstract view of who uses the services for which purpose. Nevertheless, these formal specifications are necessary for developing the service according to its life-cycle steps [12].

Recently, web-service verification has been a subject of interest to researchers as it is a means to prove that services implementation complies with the rules and policies that service designers define at a business level. It is still a non-trivial task to verify distributed systems without a coordination module (a gateway in traditional SOA terms), but the advancements of formal methods are promising even if still incomplete and costly, as shown by Camilli et al. [2] and Panda et al. [11]. For such verification, a formal specification is a necessary but insufficient condition. The verification models need to include the information from the context, as well as the local conditions of the service state. Complex scenarios that require business logic and rules co-exist with the web service descriptions.

In this paper, we use SEAM, a service science modeling method, for the basis of our work. SEAM models show different levels of abstraction by instantiating a service model with only one single perspective. The type of information and the level of detail of a service model depend on whether the model is meant for business people or for engineers. A SEAM diagram shows these perspectives (levels) in a hierarchy of systems [15]. The typical levels of an enterprise are a business segment, an organization, a department/team, and an IT system (infrastructure). These levels are refined in the same way as an interface (black box) is a refinement of the module that implements the interface (white box). In the same way, service system models form a hierarchy of refined service system models.

The SEAM method includes service behavioral models that capture the service system's actors and the relationships between them. A behavioral model (illustrated in Fig. 1) contains working objects (either business- or human-working objects) and relationships between them. The models are hierarchical: a working object as a whole (noted with "[w]") hides its implementation details from other working objects. With the refinement relationship between working objects, we relate and refine working objects as a whole to the working object as a composite (noted with "[c]"), and we "see" how the service system is organized. Service-system refinement means that a working object as a whole is an

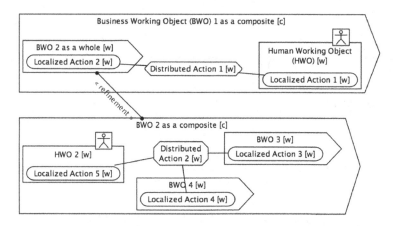

Fig. 1. Service system's graphical notation

abstraction of a working object as a composite; and vice-versa, a working object as a composite is a refinement for a working object as a whole.

2.2   Web Services Generation

The generation of REST APIs from different sources is an active research domain. Recent work in the area includes projects that show how to generate an OpenAPI specification from HTML documentation [3] or how to extract automatically REST specifications from deployed web sites or from code analysis [4]. These generative tools rely on already existing web resources and do not connect the business services to the web services.

The semantic annotation of web services has yielded many results, most notably OWL-S [9,10]. However, OWL-S is a bottom-up approach. It is based on WSDL and requires a level of technical detail unfeasible to achieve at the business-service level.

There are other methods in the domain of service-oriented software development, for example, the SOMA method [1] for building service-oriented solutions. SOMA uses different models to represent business and IT requirements for the specification of services. Furthermore, there is no automation of the specification process, which makes it costly to develop, update, and coordinate the models corresponding to business and the models corresponding to IT services.

2.3   Summary

None of the existing service-design and modeling methods binds together the rigor of formal methods and the vigor of the service-design process. The business environment poses constraints (e.g., policies, business rules, semantics) to the implementation; these constraints are hard to maintain or to express formally because of the different ways of modeling human cognition (natural language, informal formulation) and of IT services (formal syntax and semantics of web service definition languages and specifications). Generative tools are useful for avoiding mistakes by carrying out repetitive, mechanical actions. These tools also ease the subsequent design steps but do not substitute human input in the design process. As design is iterative, at each step, system designers need to provide constraints (input, outputs, and invariants) and implementation details.

Instead of abstracting all details of the IT implementation from the business perspective, we add to the business service models a few annotations for web services descriptions and provide a tool in order to automate model translations. All details of the requirements of the web-service specification are captured where the benefits and the use of the web service are captured. Not all web services are specified from the business-service model. Infrastructural services and other utilities are not visible at the business level of abstraction. However, the generated service specification would suffice as an input for initiating the web-service contract design and the web-service implementation.

3   Proposed Modeling Method

Recall that our proposed modeling method is based on SEAM, a service design method [15]. Our proposed method includes the following four modeling steps (Fig. 2):

1. Business-service modeling – the service designer creates the high-level business-service system models
2. Information-properties definition – the service designer includes the information that each actor operates on; this information represents the data entities on which a web service operates as well
3. REST annotations – the designer includes the annotations necessary for the specification of RESTful web services
4. IT-services specification – our tool generates a concrete REST API specification in the form of an OpenAPI specification

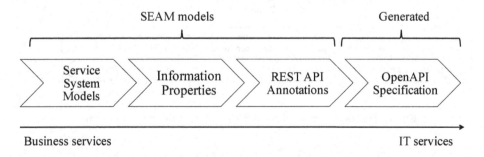

Fig. 2. Co-design modeling approach for business and IT services

The first three steps require the service designer to model the services: observe the environment, conceptualize their observations in the form of models, and/or design new service systems for prototyping. During these steps, the service designer uses a CAD tool to create formal service models. The last step is where our tool generates the web service specification. The modeling method is iterative in its nature and helps service designers quickly develop minimal service-specifications for both business and IT.

We use a running example to explain the modeling steps in detail. The example we model is the maintenance service for airplanes with a particular type of engine. The example models show how an airplane club receives the service provided by the value network for maintaining airplanes with an engine manufacturer's (EM) engine.

3.1   Step 1: Service System Model

To model both the business service and the corresponding REST API, service designers analyze the environment and prepare the service system models of the business case. The business-service system includes the actors involved in the service process, the services they provide, and the process in which they interact. The service designer models the service system with the help of a CAD tool that generates both an XML meta model and a graphical representation of a service behavioral model.

Business-Service Model of the Interaction with the Client. The service designer models the service model of the service provider and their clients (or service adopters). Figure 3 depicts the service system called *airplane maintenance*. There are two actors: a business working-object named *engine manufacturer's (EM) value network* and a human working-object named *airplane club*. The process in which they interact is the *airplane maintenance* process. The *engine workshop* provides the service *fix an airplane with an EM's engine*.

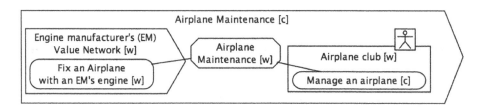

Fig. 3. Business service model of the interaction with the client

Business Service Model of the Interaction with the Client and the Refined Value Network of the Provider. Next, the service model includes the details about who is a part of the value network that delivers the service *fix*

an airplane with an EM's engine. The details are depicted in Fig. 4. The model is refined with the service system as a composite of the *EM's value network.* The composite service system includes *EM*, a *certified technician*, and an *engine repair shop.* The value network disregards organizational boundaries and includes all actors who collaborate in a service process based on the service they provide.

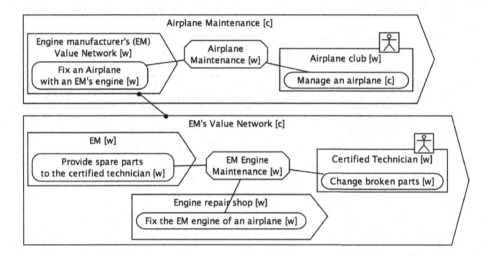

Fig. 4. Business service model of the interaction with the client and the refined value network of the provider

3.2   Step 2: Information Properties

An important step in understanding the context of the service is to define the concepts related to the service process. Different actors have different vocabularies. A classic way of looking at these concepts is with the help of entity-relationship diagrams and domain-specific languages (DSL). Our models capture the information necessary for providing a service with its localized properties.

In the case of the plane maintenance service-system, we define the information properties of the services of each working object (Fig. 5). On the level the services related to airplane maintenance, the vocabulary of the actors includes information properties for *Airplane, Repair,* and *Repair of Airplanes.* In the model, the airplane club has both *airplanes* and *repairs,* as they manage airplanes that sometimes break and need repairs. The EM's information includes only *repair of airplanes* because they are not concerned with the airplanes, only with their repair. The refined model includes actors that manage the information related to airplanes and airplane parts (e.g., *airplane, engine, part*), and that have a vocabulary related to handling broken parts (e.g., *certification*).

The *part* and *Certification* information properties are connected with dashed lines to show the relationship between the concepts for different actors. The *engine repair shop* has the information on the broken part (which belongs to

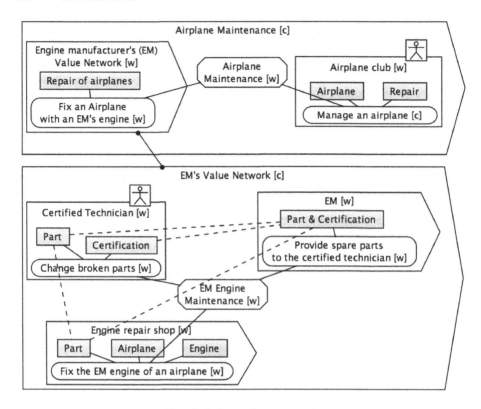

Fig. 5. Information properties

an engine, hence, to an airplane). This information initiates other information flows; *EM* now knows which part has to be shipped to the technician who has the appropriate level of *certification* to change the broken part. In this service interaction, the status attributes of the *part* are transformed, but the *part* remains the same information property.

3.3   Web Services Annotation

After the information properties are defined, the service model includes a minimal annotation for describing the web services necessary to operate with this information. We create our annotations by using the fact that there are only four required properties to create a valid OpenAPI specification. These properties are a base URL, the path templates, the HTTP verbs, and the formal parameters.

Inside a localized action, the SEAM meta model includes localized actions that correspond to web-service operations. Thus, we include the HTTP verb, e.g., POST, GET, PUT, DELETE, in the localized action as the additional XML property *stereotype*. In Fig. 6, the *manage an airplane* localized action includes three sub-localized actions that correspond to managing the information known to the *airplane club*. These three sub-localized actions are (1) <<POST>>

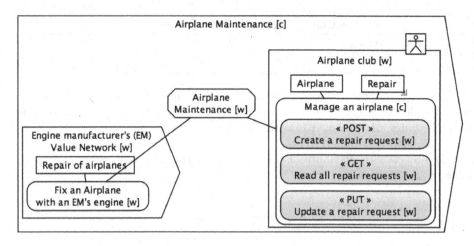

Fig. 6. Web services operations annotations

Create a repair request, (2) <<GET>> Read all repair requests, and (3) <<PUT>> Update a repair request. They can be automatically generated to include a sub-localized action for each pair <*HTTP verb, Information Property*>.

Furthermore, the sub-localized actions include the rest of the required web-service description parts: the parameters and the path. In Fig. 7, the parameters are included as localized properties, annotated semantically with a *stereotype* property <<*in*>> for input parameters and <<*out*>> for output parameters. The path template is described by a sequence edge which points from the input to the output parameter and is labeled with the path template. The parameters have a predefined syntax for describing what type of object the parameter assumes (a built-in type in the OpenAPI, e.g., `string`, `integer`, etc., or a complex type, e.g., `enum`, `array`, `schema`). We give examples for possible input and output parameters in Listing 1.1 for `built-in` parameters, in Listing 1.2 for `schema` parameters, in Listing 1.3 for `enum` parameters, and in Listing 1.4 for `array` parameters.

Listing 1.1. Built-in type parameters example

```
name: string ,
age: integer
```

Listing 1.2. Schema parameter example

```
person {
    name: string ,
    age: integer
}
```

Listing 1.3. Enumeration parameter example

```
count: enum(one , two , three )
```

Listing 1.4. Array parameters example

```
people: array(string),
students: array(person),
profs: array(person {name: string, age: integer})
```

Figure 7 shows the syntax for the three services defined for the airplane club. For example, <<*POST*>> *Create a repair request* expects a `NewRepair` object with attributes `clientId`, `planeId`, `date`, `description` as an input parameter. The output parameter, which the web service sends after execution, is a `Repair` object with attributes `repairId` and a `status` of an *enum* type and values `new`, `wip`, `done`.

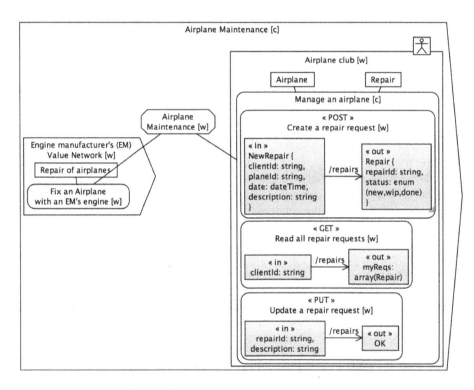

Fig. 7. Web service's parameters annotation

3.4   OpenAPI Specification

We developed a tool[2] that takes as an input the XML file of the service model and generates the OpenAPI specification from it. During our research, we created new annotations for our models. Figure 8 shows the relationship between the graphical model and the meta model for these annotations. In our tool, we use the standard SEAM meta model without changing it.

---

[2] https://github.com/lams-epfl/gen-rest/.

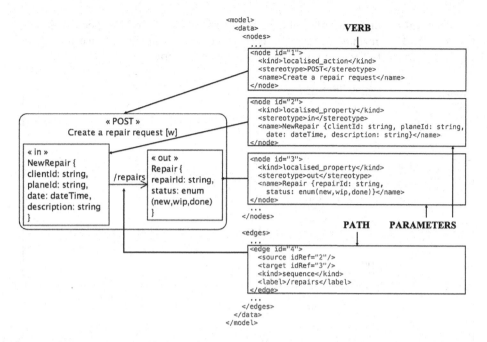

Fig. 8. Meta model annotations for web services

There are only two types of elements in the SEAM meta model: `nodes` and `edges`. Nodes represent elements and edges represent relationships between elements. Nodes have a name, an ID, a stereotype, a kind, and other attributes. Edges have an ID, a source, a target, a label, a kind, and other attributes. We use only existing attributes to store the information from the web-service annotations. Existing tools can still parse the models but do not give semantic meaning to the new annotations stored in the attributes. Our tool, when it parses the model, assumes a semantic meaning for creating the web-service specifications for these attributes.

Within every `node` of type `localized_action` that requires a web service, we add one or many sub-`localized_actions`. The `node` then has a property `stereotype` that defines the `verb` of the web service. Within the `localized_action` node, there are two other `nodes`. The `edge` defining which `node` includes which other `nodes` is not in the figure. The two nodes of the same type of `localized_property` also include a `stereotype` property. The `stereotype` of these two `nodes` is either `in` or `out` in order to show which parameter the `node` describes. Our tool interprets the property `stereotype` of a `node`, based on the property `kind` of the type of the `node`, either a `localized_property` or a `localized_action`). The last piece of information is the `path` of the web service. The path is described by the `edge` that connects the input and the output parameters. The property `label` of the `edge` contains the path template.

The final result from our tool is a correct runnable OpenAPI specification in the YAML data format and can be used to continue the web-service life-cycle. Listing 1.5 depicts the generated output for our example.

Listing 1.5. Generated OpenAPI 3.0.0 YAML

```yaml
openapi: 3.0.0
servers: []
info:
  version: 1.0.0
  title: Airplane maintenance
tags:
  - name: EM VN
  - name: Airplane club
  - name: Technician
  - name: Engine repair shop
  - name: EM
paths:
  /repairs:
    post:
      tags:
        - Airplane club
      description: Create a repair request
      responses:
        '200':
          description: request successful
          content:
            application/json:
              schema:
                $ref: '#/components/schemas/Repair'
      requestBody:
        content:
          application/json:
            schema:
              $ref: '#/components/schemas/NewRepair'
        required: true
    get:
      tags:
        - Airplane club
      description: Read all repair requests
      parameters:
        - name: clientId
          in: query
          required: true
          schema:
            type: string
      responses:
        '200':
          description: request successful
          content:
            application/json:
              schema:
                type: array
                items:
                  $ref: '#/components/schemas/Repair'
    put:
      tags:
        - Airplane club
      description: Update a repair request
      responses:
        '200':
          description: OK
      requestBody:
        content:
          application/json:
            schema:
              type: object
```

```
                    properties:
                      clientId:
                        type: string
                      description:
                        type: string
              required: true
components:
  schemas:
    NewRepair:
      type: object
      properties:
        clientId:
          type: string
        planeId:
          type: string
        date:
          type: string
          format: date—time
        description:
          type: string
    Repair:
      type: object
      properties:
        repairId:
          type: string
        status:
          type: string
          enum:
            - new
            - wip
            - done
```

4   Conclusion and Future Work

In this paper, we have proposed a method how to co-design business-service systems and their corresponding REST API specifications. Our method consists of four modeling steps: (1) modeling of the business service system, (2) conceptualization of domain information; (3) annotation of the service system model with attributes describing RESTful services, and (4) generation of the REST specification in the form of an OpenAPI specification.

The next steps of the project are to develop a bidirectional connection between models and to automate the generation of SEAM models from an OpenAPI specification. Despite the fact that bringing semantics to web-service annotations is an already established research area, our approach differs because it brings these annotations to the business-model level.

Moreover, we will work on model checkers and parsers that ensure correctness of the models. The first step would be to parse the OpenAPI definition in order to propose to the CAD users what they could use when developing the services. Our long-term goal is to integrate support for REST APIs that have been already developed and published in order to help designers with the modeling process when there is no need for a web-service implementation but a web-service configuration.

References

1. Arsanjani, A., Ghosh, S., Allam, A., Abdollah, T., Ganapathy, S., Holley, K.: Soma: a method for developing service-oriented solutions. IBM Syst. J. **47**(3), 377–396 (2008)
2. Camilli, M., Bellettini, C., Capra, L., Monga, M.: A formal framework for specifying and verifying microservices based process flows. In: Cerone, A., Roveri, M. (eds.) SEFM 2017. LNCS, vol. 10729, pp. 187–202. Springer, Cham (2018). https://doi.org/10.1007/978-3-319-74781-1_14
3. Cao, H., Falleri, J.-R., Blanc, X.: Automated generation of REST API specification from plain HTML documentation. In: Maximilien, M., Vallecillo, A., Wang, J., Oriol, M. (eds.) ICSOC 2017. LNCS, vol. 10601, pp. 453–461. Springer, Cham (2017). https://doi.org/10.1007/978-3-319-69035-3_32
4. Choudhary, S., Kimura, K., Sekiguchi, A.: Spec2rest: an approach for eliciting web API resources from existing applications. In: 2017 IEEE International Conference on Web Services (ICWS), pp. 910–913. IEEE (2017)
5. Estañol, M., Marcos, E., Oriol, X., Pérez, F.J., Teniente, E., Vara, J.M.: Validation of service blueprint models by means of formal simulation techniques. In: Maximilien, M., Vallecillo, A., Wang, J., Oriol, M. (eds.) ICSOC 2017. LNCS, vol. 10601, pp. 80–95. Springer, Cham (2017). https://doi.org/10.1007/978-3-319-69035-3_6
6. Fielding, R.T., Taylor, R.N.: Principled design of the modern web architecture. ACM Trans. Internet Technol. (TOIT) **2**(2), 115–150 (2002)
7. Hadley, M.J.: Web application description language (WADL). Technical report, Mountain View, CA, USA (2006)
8. Maglio, P.P., Vargo, S.L., Caswell, N., Spohrer, J.: The service system is the basic abstraction of service science. Inf. Syst. e-bus. Manag. **7**(4), 395–406 (2009)
9. Martin, D., et al.: OWL-S: semantic markup for web services. W3C Memb. Submiss. **22**(4) (2004)
10. Martin, D., et al.: Bringing semantics to web services: the OWL-S approach. In: Cardoso, J., Sheth, A. (eds.) SWSWPC 2004. LNCS, vol. 3387, pp. 26–42. Springer, Heidelberg (2005). https://doi.org/10.1007/978-3-540-30581-1_4
11. Panda, A., Sagiv, M., Shenker, S.: Verification in the age of microservices. In: Proceedings of the 16th Workshop on Hot Topics in Operating Systems, pp. 30–36. ACM (2017)
12. Papazoglou, M.P., Van Den Heuvel, W.J.: Service-oriented design and development methodology. Int. J. Web Eng. Technol. **2**(4), 412–442 (2006)
13. Shostack, G.L.: Designing services that deliver. Harv. Bus. Rev. **62**(1), 133–139 (1984)
14. Tan, W., Fan, Y., Ghoneim, A., Hossain, M.A., Dustdar, S.: From the service-oriented architecture to the web API economy. IEEE Internet Comput. **20**(4), 64–68 (2016)
15. Wegmann, A.: On the systemic enterprise architecture methodology (SEAM). In: ICEIS 2003, Proceedings of the 5th International Conference on Enterprise Information Systems, Angers, France, 22–26 April 2003, pp. 483–490 (2003)

Energy-Aware and Location-Constrained Virtual Network Embedding in Enterprise Network

Xin Cong[1], Lingling Zi[1(✉)], and Kai Shuang[2]

[1] School of Electronic and Information Engineering,
Liaoning Technical University, Huludao 125105, China
`chongzi610@163.com`, `lingling19812004@126.com`
[2] State Key Laboratory of Networking and Switching Technology,
Beijing University of Posts and Telecommunications, Beijing 100876, China
`shuangk@bupt.edu.cn`

Abstract. Network virtualization can integrate the servers and computers from different locations in the large enterprises. Most of prior studies on the network virtualization execute on the cloud platform and they are not suit for the enterprise network. Therefore, the problem of the energy-aware and location-constrained virtual network embedding (EL-VNE) in the enterprise network is proposed and solved in this paper. Firstly, both the computing capability and bandwidth capability are unified by adopting the complex number theory and their corresponding capabilities of nodes, including physical and virtual nodes are determined. Then EL-VNE model is presented and proved to be a NP-complete problem, so as to make the virtual network embedding process only need node mapping without link mapping. Finally, a heuristic algorithm is presented to minimize the energy consumption on the condition of location constraint of nodes. The experiments show that the proposed EL-VNE can get less energy consumption compared with EAD, and simultaneously have better performance compared with GLC.

Keywords: Energy aware · Location constraint · VNE · Enterprise network

1 Introduction

With the rapid development of large enterprises, more and more data is need to be analyzed and dealt every day, while simultaneously, some sensitive data must be protected and transmitted only in local network of the enterprises. So, it is better to construct the private data center (DC) instead of renting the cloud platforms. To decrease the construction costs of DC, utilizing existed servers and computers to compose the substrate network is a good scheme, which serves as a feasible platform for analyzing and dealing enterprise data. However,

X. Liu et al. (Eds.): ICSOC 2018 Workshops, LNCS 11434, pp. 41–52, 2019.
https://doi.org/10.1007/978-3-030-17642-6_4

how to efficiently share the resources is an inevitable problem. To settle this problem, the technique of network virtualization is well adopted. This technique permits heterogeneous virtual networks to coexist in the same substrate network [1,2] and allows different types of task to share the resources, in which a key issue, resource allocation mechanism (namely virtual network embedding VNE) is widely researched in cloud platforms [3,4].

Compared with the existed mechanism in cloud platform, the researches of VNE in the enterprise network are less. The designs of VNE meet some unique features, mainly containing the following four points. (1) In view of the fact that the distributed computers in the different offices could provide limited resources, two virtual machines cannot be embedded on the same physical machine in one VNE process. (2) The arrival of virtual requests (VRs) is dynamic rather than static. (3) The capabilities of computers are various and the quantities of resources provided from them are different. So the VRs should be embedded with the location constraint. (4) For the personal purpose, a DC is built and it will not obtain benefits. So, the costs of energy should be minimized. According to the above features, three challenges are faced, including modeling the dynamic requests of VRs, designing the VNE algorithm with the condition of location-constraint, and minimizing the energy costs.

In this paper, an energy-aware and location-constrained virtual network embedding model (EL-VNE) is designed for the enterprise network. Firstly, the nodes in both the substrate network and virtual network are defined by adopting the complex number theory. Secondly, a virtual request with the dynamic feature is fitted to associate with the virtual nodes. Finally, an energy and location constrained model is built to minimize the energy costs in the EL-VNE. This model is proved to be a NP-complete problem, which is solved by the proposed heuristic algorithm. In summary, our contributions are described as follows.

(1) As far as we know, the complex number theory is first introduced to VNE and it is adopted to describe the computing and bandwidth capabilities of nodes in both substrate and virtual network. (2) A virtual request is fitted by Gaussian distribution reflecting the computing capability of VRs, which is a good way to embody the dynamic feature. (3) EL-VNE is designed and proved to be a NP-complete problem and its solution is to use an elite heuristic algorithm to minimize the energy costs.

The rest of this paper is organized as follows. Section 2 summarizes the related work. Section 3 demonstrates the proposed EL-VNE. Section 4 evaluates the performance of EL-VNE. Section 5 concludes the paper.

2   Related Work

As an important issue in network virtualization, VNE has received intensive attention. Recently, the resource allocation and the VM placement algorithms mainly focus on the goals of cloud providers, such as available computing and bandwidth capabilities, energy consumption [5–7] etc. The objective of VNE is to decrease the energy costs and it is studied by many researches. The authors in [8] proposed an energy optimization method by minimizing the number of the active physical servers. The authors presented a VM assignment problem to minimize the power consumption [9], but they ignored the power consumption of the physical links. To settle this problem, some solutions that concentrate on putting the servers into the sleepy mode are presented, such as integrated coverage and connectivity configuration method [10]. Recently, considering the dynamic feature of VNE, the requirement of VN is modeled as the combination of basic sub-requirements and variable sub-requirements. In [11], the bandwidth demands were described as a Gaussian distribution and a sliding window approach was built to maximize the revenue, but the dynamic feature of CPU demands were not considered.

Meanwhile, the problem of location-constrained VNE has also attracted many researchers. In [12], an augmented graph was used to model LC-VNE as a multi-commodity flow problem. In [5], considering resource requirements with different dimensional on both virtual nodes and virtual links, the MILP model was extended and a quality-of-service issue was presented. Then the future work formulated a path MILP model and a column generation to solve LC-VNE. In [13] the compatibility graph and heuristic algorithms were proposed to map nodes and links efficiently, but their virtual demands were static.

3   The Proposed EL-VNE

3.1   The Definition of Nodes and Network in EL-VNE

Generally, the resource provision of physical nodes in the substrate network has two types of attributes, computing capability and bandwidth capability, respectively. Similarly, the resource requirement of virtual nodes is also divided into the above types. Based on these observations, the complex number theory is utilized to define nodes in EL-VNE, shown as follows.

Definition 1 (Physical Node): A physical node is represented as a complex number, where its real part is the provision of computing capability and its imaginary part is the provision of bandwidth capability.

Definition 2 (Virtual Node): A virtual node is represented as a complex number, in which its real part is the requirement of computing capability and its imaginary part is the requirement of the bandwidth capability.

We model a substrate network as an undirected and weighted graph $G_s(V_s, E_s)$, where V_s denotes the set of physical nodes and E_s denotes the set of links. Each physical node $\forall v_s^i \in V_s$ has a computing capability with the complex number (Definition 1) and each physical link $\forall b_s^i \in E_s$ has a bandwidth capability, which is computed by the starting node and the ending node and various at different time. Similar to the studies [14], the node attributes contain computing capability and location, and the link attributes contain bandwidth in this paper.

Similar to G_s, we model a virtual network as an undirected and weight graph $G_v(V_v, E_v, LC_v)$. Differently, the introduction of LC_v is to denote location constraint, and each location constraint $\forall lc_v^{v_v^i} \in LC_v$ has its preferred location corresponding to virtual node v_v^i. Based on the location constraint, v_v^i can only be mapped onto a set of candidate physical nodes $\Psi_{v_v^i}^{\rho} \in V_s$. Here, ρ is a radius and $\Psi_{v_v^i}^{\rho} = \{v_s^k \in V_s \,|\, \|v_s^k - v_v^i\| \leq \rho\}$, where $\|v_s^k - v_v^i\|$ is the distance between two locations.

Both CPU and bandwidth always vary a lot over time in the cloud. However, for the reason of lacking the application types of bandwidth in the enterprise network, the variations of the bandwidth requirements are more steady than the ones in the cloud. Hence, the dynamic feature of bandwidth requirement is ignored here. The various data is shown in [15], the CPU requirement obeys the Gaussian distributions, i.e. $CPU_v \sim N(\mu_v, \sigma_v)$, where μ_v denotes the mean value and σ_v denotes the standard deviation.

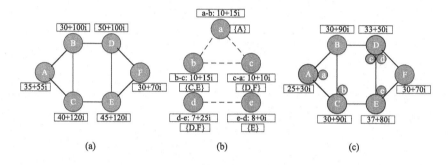

Fig. 1. An example of EL-VNE.

In Fig. 1(a) and (b) show the substrate network and the virtual requirements respectively, and (c) demonstrates the solution of EL-VNE. In (a), the computing capability of node A is 35 and its bandwidth capability is 55, in which the bandwidth capability can be allocated to nodes B and C. In (b), virtual requirement a demands 10 computing capabilities and transmits data to b with 15 bandwidth capabilities. $\{A\}$ is the candidate set of a. In (c), a is embedded to A, b is embedded to C, and c is embedded to D. Hence, for node A, its computing capability is 25, which is computed as 35 minus 10. And its bandwidth capability is 30, which is computed as 55 minus 15 and the result minus 10 again.

3.2   Problem Description of EL-VNE

Generally, VNE provides substrate resources to support virtual network requirements, and the process of embedding is either node mapping first or link mapping first. Since EL-VNE is a special scenario, the attributes of physical nodes contain both computing capability and bandwidth capability. Only node mapping is considered here, and each virtual node chooses a unique physical node to satisfy its computing, bandwidth and location requirements, while minimizing the energy costs.

Node energy model. Similar to [14], the linear model of node energy is reported as follows.

$$P = \begin{cases} P_b + (P_{max} - P_{min}) \cdot CPU & if\ the\ node\ is\ active \\ 0 & otherwise \end{cases} \quad (1)$$

where P_b is the baseline power, P_{max} is the full workload power, P_{min} is the empty workload power and CPU is the current workload.

According to the dynamical requirements in the enterprise network, the whole energy cost in time T can be calculated as follows.

$$E_1(T) = \int_0^T \left[P_b(H(t) + F(t)) + (P_{max} - P_{min}) \sum_{i=1}^{V_v(t)} CPU_i(t) \right] dt \quad (2)$$

where $H(t)$ and $F(t)$ denote the total number of the hosting and forwarding nodes at the time t, $V_v(t)$ is the number of the virtual nodes at the time t, and $CPU_i(t)$ is the CPU requirement of the virtual node i at the time t.

Link energy model. In EL-VNE, the bandwidth is changed with the bandwidth attribute (the imaginary part) of physical nodes. As shown in [14], the energy of unit bandwidth is a fixed value, and denoted as P_{fix}. The link energy can be described as follows.

$$E_2(T) = P_{fix} \cdot \int_0^T \sum_{i=1}^{V_v(t)} \sum_{v_v^j \in \phi(v_v^i)} \sum_{v_s \in f(v_v^i \to v_v^j)} |v_s| \cdot b(t) \, dt \quad (3)$$

v_v^i is the starting virtual node which sends data, and v_v^j is the ending virtual node which receives data. $\phi(\cdot)$ is defined as a set of forwarding nodes which relays data when v_v^i transfers data to $v_v^j (v_v^i \to v_v^j)$. $|v_s|$ denotes the hop-count corresponding to $v_v^i \to v_v^j$, i.e. the number of the forwarding nodes. $b(t)$ is the bandwidth requirement which can satisfy when $v_v^i \to v_v^j$ at the time t. v_v^{ij} denotes the link connection relation between two virtual nodes, i.e. $v_v^{ij} = \{v_v^j | v_v^j = \phi(v_v^i)\}$.

Then we formulate the EL-VNE problem as that whether there is an EL-VNE solution scheme, the overall energy consumption of which is no more than EQ, shown as Eq. 4.

$$E = E_1 + E_2 \leq EQ \quad (4)$$

where EQ is a positive number.

The core of solution scheme is to establish the related mapping $V_r \to V_s$, so as to complete the node mapping and link mapping simultaneously. The following three constraints need to be satisfied.

(1) Node mapping constraint. Each physical node in the same virtual network can accommodate only one virtual node in one VNE process. Assuming $g(\cdot)$ to be a mapping function, the condition is established:

$$v_s = g(v_v) \tag{5}$$

$$g(v_v^1) = g(v_v^2) \quad iff \ v_v^1 = v_v^2 \tag{6}$$

(2) Location constraint. The virtual nodes can choose many physical nodes as mapping nodes to form the set of candidate physical nodes in the enterprise network.

$$v_s = \left\{ v_s^k \ \middle| \ v_s^k \in \Psi_{v_v^i}^\rho \ \&\& \ v_s^k = g(v_v^i) \right\} \tag{7}$$

(3) Node capability constraint. For the computing capability, the requirement of the virtual node must be less than the surplus of the physical node. For the bandwidth capability, two virtual nodes v_v^i and v_v^j communicate from one side to the other, and their requirement must be less than the minimized bandwidth of the physical nodes, which lie in the communication path $v_v^i \rightarrow v_v^j$.

$$c_v^{v_v^i} < c_s^{v_s^k}, \ if \ v_s^k = g(v_v^i) \tag{8}$$

$$b_v^{v_v^{ij}} < min(b_s^{v_s}), \ if \ v_s^k \in \phi(v_v^i) \tag{9}$$

3.3   Complexity and Solution Algorithms of EL-VNE

As shown in [16], a popular problem named graph bisection problem is widely studied and proved to be the NP-complete problem. The bisection problem is described as: given a graph $G(V, E)$ and a positive integer K, whether there exit two subsets V_1 and V_2, satisfying $V = V_1 \cup V_2$, $V_1 \cap V_2 = \phi$, $|V_1| = \lceil |V|/2 \rceil$, $|V_2| = \lfloor |V|/2 \rfloor$ and the number of links between V_1 and V_2 is less than or equal to K. On this basis, we have the following theorem.

Theorem 1. *The EL-VNE problem is NP-complete.*

Proof. First, we prove that the EL-VNE problem belongs to a NP problem. If the solution of Eq. 4 can be found, it is easy to check that whether Eqs. 5, 4, 7, 8 and 9 can be satisfied in polynomial time.

Then we prove that EL-VNE has a desired solution if and only if there is a desired bisection graph. Suppose that two networks are G_s and G_v, and a positive integer is EQ. As shown in the bisection graph $G(V, E)$, EL-VNE also has $G_v(V_v, E_v)$ satisfying $V_v = V$ and $E_v = E$. The node directly comes from the virtual network, denoting by $V_v^1 = \{\alpha_v^i\}(i \in [1, |V_v|])$. And the corresponding node α_i comes from G_v. The situation of links E_v^1 is similar to nodes. Assuming the sub-graph with V_v^1 and E_v^1 is $\alpha - island$. Suppose that the other set is $V_v^2 = \{\beta_v^k\}$, where $k \in [1, |V_v|]$. This set is used to construct the bisection graph of EL-VNE, and the contained nodes are extra nodes. Also, the links satisfy $E_v^2 = \phi$. Assuming the sub-graph with V_v^2 and E_v^2 is $\beta - island$. Noting that β_v^i is corresponding to α_v^i.

For the substrate network, there are also two complete sub-graphs, $\alpha' - island$ and $\beta' - island$. $\alpha' - island$ satisfies the condition:

$$V_s^1 = \bigcup \{\alpha_s^i\}, E_s^1 = \{(\alpha_s^i, \alpha_s^j) \in V_s^1 \times V_s^1, i \neq j, i, j \in [1, |V_s^1|]\} \tag{10}$$

$\beta' - island$ satisfies the condition:

$$V_s^2 = \bigcup \{\beta_s^k\}, E_s^2 = \{(\beta_s^k, \beta_s^h) \in V_s^2 \times V_s^2, k \neq h, k, h \in [1, |V_s^2|]\} \tag{11}$$

Supposing that the nodes that are in-bridge and out-bridge are denoted as o_s^{in} and o_s^{out}. For the physical nodes in the $\alpha' - island$ and o_s^{out}, they are connected to o_s^{in} and o_s^{out} respectively. In addition, two types of paths exist in the bridge. The first one is to directly connect form o_s^{in} to o_s^{out}, and the second one is to connect by through a Δ-hops line topology. Therefore, for all the physical nodes, links with the bridge described in detail are as follows.

$V_s' = \bigcup \{v_s^i\} \bigcup \{o_s^{in}, o_s^{out}\}$ $i \in [1, \Delta + 1]$, where is the node in the Δ-hops line topology.

$E_s^{1'} = \{(\alpha_s^i, o_s^{in}) | \alpha_s^i \in V_s^1\} \bigcup \{(\beta_s^i, o_s^{out}) | \beta_s^i \in V_s^2\}$, which is the set of links in the Δ-hops line topology.

$E_s^{2'} = \{(o_s^{in}, o_s^{out})\}$, which is the first type of path.

$E_s^{3'} = \{(o_s^{in}, v_s^i)\} \bigcup \{(v_s^k, o_s^{out})\} \bigcup (\bigcup \{(v_s^i, v_s^k) | |v_s^i \rightarrow v_s^k| = \Delta\})$, which is the second type of path. $|v_s^i \rightarrow v_s^k|$ is the number of forwarding nodes which are locating in the communication path.

On this basis, the location constraints are described as $\Psi_{\alpha_v^i}^\rho = \{\alpha_s^i, \beta_s^i\}$, $\Psi_{\beta_v^i}^\rho = V_s^1$ if $i \leq \lceil |V|/2 \rceil$ and $\Psi_{\beta_v^i}^\rho = V_s^2$ if $i > \lfloor |V|/2 \rfloor$. Assuming all the physical nodes have a unit energy of computing capability and bandwidth capability. Hence, positive K is defined as: $EQ = 2\left(|V| + EQ + \lfloor |V|/2 \rfloor^2 + \lceil |V|/2 \rceil^2\right) + |E| + |V|^2$. In summary, the above processes can be completed in polynomial time.

Then we obtain the mapping function from G_v to G_s in EL-VNE, including node mapping and link mapping. Node mapping function is shown as follows:

$$\Theta(\alpha_v^i) = \begin{cases} \alpha_s^i & \alpha_v^i \in V_1 \\ \beta_s^i & \alpha_v^i \in V_2 \end{cases} \tag{12}$$

$$\Theta(\beta_v^i) = \begin{cases} \alpha_s^{\bar{i}} & \alpha_v^{\bar{i}} \in V_1, i \leq \lceil |V|/2 \rceil, \alpha_v^i \bigcap \alpha_v^{\bar{i}} = \phi, \alpha_v^i \bigcup \alpha_v^{\bar{i}} = V_1 \\ \beta_s^{\bar{i}} & \alpha_v^{\bar{i}} \in V_2, i > \lfloor |V|/2 \rfloor, \beta_v^i \bigcap \beta_v^{\bar{i}} = \phi, \beta_v^i \bigcup \beta_v^{\bar{i}} = V_2 \end{cases} \tag{13}$$

The link mapping function is obvious when the node mapping function is determined. According to the above mapping functions, EL-VNE can be converted to the bisection graph and the expected solution of EL-VNE is to find a desired bisection graph. Therefore, EL-VNE is a NP-complete problem. ∎

In order to solve EL-VNE problem, the algorithm named minimum energy maximum set (MEMS) is designed to solve the EL-VNE problem. A virtual node usually has a set of candidate nodes, which makes $V_1 \bigcap V_2 \neq \phi$. Hence, a pre-dealing process needs to be designed to make the candidate node lonely. In MEMS, a matching graph (MG) that suited for both the attributes of nodes (complex number) and bisection graph is constructed. The construction rules of MG are described as follows. (1) A node in MG represents a candidate substrate path. (2) A link in MG is drawn if two substrate paths are connected to a common physical node. In other words, two substrate paths should satisfy that either they are the candidate paths for two adjacent virtual links with one common node or they can accommodate two candidate paths which are not adjacent. Table 1 is presented to preform pre-dealing process and MG construction. In order to minimize the energy in EL-VNE, a maximum set in MG needs to be found. This set should cover all the links of the virtual requirements and meet the constraints in Eqs. 5, 6, 7, 8 and 9. Therefore, a heuristic algorithm is designed to find the near-optimal MEMS in MG, which is shown in Table 2.

4 Experiments and Evaluation

In this section, the performance of EL-VNE is evaluated using GT-ITM tools [17]. The experiments ran on the substrate network with 50 computers and 4 servers. Similar to the work [13,14], we set the 100*100 grid. The computers are randomly mapped into this grid, but the servers are in the same office. The number of virtual network requirements is randomly selected from 1 to 10. The probability that any two virtual nodes are connected is set as 0.5. The virtual node v_v^i chooses some physical nodes located in a circle and finally these physical nodes form a candidate set. In this circle, the center is v_v^i and its radium ρ is 10. The number of nodes in the candidate set is randomly chosen from 1 to 10. The virtual requirements arrive following a Poisson process with the

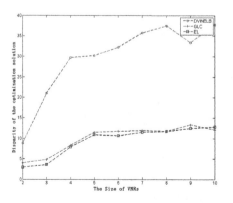

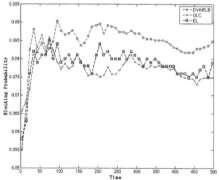

Fig. 2. The disparity of optimization solution.

Fig. 3. The blocking probability.

Table 1. The description of algorithm 1.

Algorithm 1. The pre-dealing process and MG construction.

Input: Complex number of physical nodes and virtual nodes, original candidate set of
each virtual node.

Output: MG.

For(each $v_v \in V_v$){//utilize the complex number to remove the dissatisfied elements
from the candidate set;

  For(each $v_s \in \Psi_{v_v}^\rho$){

    If($c_s^{v_s} < c_v^{v_v} \| b_s^{v_s} < b_v^{v_v}$) {

      Remove v_s from $\Psi_{v_v}^\rho$;

    }

  }

}

Utilize pre-dealing process methods to form a new candidate set $v_s \in \Psi_{v_v}^\rho$ corresponding
to each v_v;

For(each connection between v_v^i and v_v^j){ //construct the nodes in MG

  For(each v_s^i in the candidate set of v_v^i){

    For(each v_s^j in the candidate set of v_v^j){

      If(v_s^i is a neighbor of v_s^j){

        Construct a node in MG and mark with "v_s^i-v_s^j";

      }else{

        Find a shortest path between v_s^i and v_s^j, and mark with "v_s^i -...- v_s^j";

      }

    }

  }

}

Mark the nodes to represent the same candidate path of v_s^i and v_s^j in one group;

For (each node v_{MG}^m in MG){ //constructing the links in MG

  For(each node v_{MG}^n in MG && $m \neq n$ && (v_{MG}^m and v_{MG}^n) are not in the same group){

    If(two adjacent candidate paths accommodate the same common node "v_s^i" || two
adjacent candidate paths accommodate two virtual links){

      Build a link between v_{MG}^m and v_{MG}^n;

    }

  }

}

Output MG.

---

average arrival rate λ per time-unit and the average holding time $1/\mu$. The
CPU requirements of virtual nodes obey Gaussian distribution with $N(\mu, \sigma)$,
$\mu \in [0, 20]$ and $\sigma \in [0, 10]$. Liking [14], the value of parameter p_b is set as 165 W
and $P_{max} - P_{min}$ is set as 15 W/CPU unit.

To evaluate the performance of the EL-VNE solution, MILP is introduced.
The pre-process of MILP is computed to be suit for EL-VNE. Then the optimal
solution is obtained and marked as E^*. At the same time, our obtained solution
of EL-VNE is marked as E. Parameter ω denoting the disparity of optimization
solution is introduced to identify the distance between the optimal solution of
MILP and EL-VNE, which is computed as $\omega = (E^* - E)/E$. The other parameter is the blocking probability, denoting as the ratio of the blocked to the total

Table 2. The description of algorithm 2.

Algorithm 2. The near-optimal MEMS algorithm.
Input: G_s, G_v, MG.
Output: The maximum set M.
$M = \phi$;
If(each v_v^i is connected to v_v^j && $v_s^i = g\left(v_v^i\right)$ && $v_s^j = g\left(v_v^j\right)$ && (" v_s^i-...-v_s^{j}" || " v_s^i - v_s^{j} ")   is the mark of a node in MG) {
Compute the bandwidth requirement $b_v^{v^{ij}}$;
}
Order $b_v^{v^{ij}}$ to form a decreasing sequence DS;
For (each $b_v^{v^{ij}} \in DS$){
If($min\left(b_s^{v_s^k}\right) \geq b_v^{v^{ij}}, v_s^k \in \{v_s^i, \cdots, v_s^j\}$ && $c_s^{v_i} < c_v^{v_i}$ && $c_s^{v_j} < c_v^{v_j}$){
$M' \leftarrow \Lambda$;
} else {
Return "Finding the maximum set is failed!";
}
Select the node with minimum tops in M' and add it to M;
Update the computing and bandwidth resources (the complex value of the physical node);
}
Return M.

VNRs and it is computed as $\varpi = \lim\limits_{t \to T} \frac{|\Gamma_{blocked}(t)|}{|\Gamma_{blocked}(t)| + |\Gamma_{accepted}(t)|}$, where t is the current time, T is the deadline of running time. If the servers are always powered on, then $T \to +\infty$. $\Gamma_{blocked}(t)$ is the set of the blocked VNRs and $\Gamma_{accepted}(t)$ is the accepted VNRs. The goals of our paper are to accommodate VNRs as many as possible and to save the energy.

Figure 2 shows the comparison results of ω using DVINELB [12], GLC [13] and the proposed EL(EL-VNE). The curves between GLC and EL are close to each other, but EL takes less time to compute the solution. The reasons include (1) each physical node in EL can get only one virtual node at one VNE process, so the residual resources become more balanced; (2)the introduction of complex number theory makes EL only pay attention on node mapping, so less time could be spent to compute the solution compared with GLC and DVINELB.

Figure 3 shows the comparison results of ϖ and from this figure, we observe that the blocking probability of EL is between GLC and DVINELB, in which that of GLC is the lowest. Since GLC is used in cloud platform, its adequate resources guarantee that the optimal solution can be obtained in a long time. However, as the resource allocation in the enterprise network, the residual resources are not enough to accommodate EL-VNE to select the best optimal solution. Hence, the blocking probability of EL is higher than GLC. However, EL-VNE can get better performance than DVINELB.

Figures 4 and 5 evaluate energy consumption using EL and EAD. In Fig. 4, a small size of VNRs arrival and the energy consumption of EL is less than EAD. The reason is that only node mapping in EL are used, so as to save the energy consumption for link mapping in VNE. In addition, when the size of VNRs is

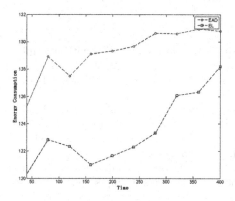
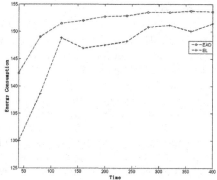

Fig. 4. The average energy consumption with small size VNRs.

Fig. 5. The average energy consumption with middle size VNRs.

small, the number of residual resources in enterprise network is large. Hence, the physical nodes are gathered relatively and the number of forwarding nodes is reduced. However, in Fig. 5, a middle size of VNRs arrival, the distance between the EAD curve and the EL one becomes closer. The reason is that with the increasing of the number of VNRs, the residual resources of current physical nodes become less, and it is more difficult to compute the best solution of EL, so more and more physical nodes participate in the VNE, which will cause more energy consumption. A possibility may occur that the energy consumption of EL can be larger than EAD when the number of VNRs is very large.

5   Conclusion

In this paper, an optimal solution of EL-VNE is proposed to solve the problem of energy-aware and location-constrained virtual network embedding in the enterprise network. Firstly, a complex number theory is introduced to identify the computing capability and bandwidth capability of nodes. Then the EL-VNE problem is modeled with the location constraint. Thirdly, a method is presented to transform EL-VNE to a bisection graph, and the complexity of EL-VNE is proved to be NP-complete. Fourthly, a heuristic algorithm is demonstrated to find an optimal solution of EL-VNE. Finally, the performance of EL-VNE has shown that our algorithm gets lower value of energy consumption than that of EAD and simultaneously, it is closer to the best optimal solution than GLC in terms of algorithm performance.

Acknowledgment. This work is partially supported by The National Natural Science Foundation of China (No. 61602227, 61702241); The Foundation of the Education Department of Liaoning Province (No. LJYL019); The Doctoral Starting up Foundation of Science Project of Liaoning Province (No. 201601365); National Key Research and Development Program of China(No. 2016QY01W0200); The Foundation of Liaoning Educational Committee (No. LJYL019).

References

1. Ogino, N., Kitahara, T., Arakawa, S.: Virtual network embedding with multiple priority classes sharing substrate resources. Comput. Netw. **112**, 52–66 (2017)
2. Chochlidakis, G., Friderikos, V.: Mobility aware virtual network embedding. IEEE Trans. Mob. Comput. **16**(5), 1343–1356 (2017)
3. Cao, Z., Lin, J.: Optimal cloud computing resource allocation for demand side management in smart grid. IEEE Trans. Smart Grid **8**(4), 1943–1955 (2017)
4. Yousafzai, A., Gani, A., Noor, R.M.: Cloud resource allocation schemes: review, taxonomy, and opportunities. Knowl. Inf. Syst. **50**(2), 347–381 (2017)
5. Papagianni, C., Leivadeas, A., Papavassiliou, S.: On the optimal allocation of virtual resources in cloud computing networks. IEEE Trans. Comput. **62**(6), 1060–1071 (2013)
6. Hong, H.J., Chen, D.Y., Huang, C.Y.: Placing virtual machines to optimize cloud gaming experience. IEEE Trans. Cloud Comput. **3**(1), 42–53 (2015)
7. Fard, S.Y.Z., Ahmadi, M.R., Adabi, S.: A dynamic VM consolidation technique for QoS and energy consumption in cloud environment. J. Supercomput. **73**(10), 4347–4368 (2017)
8. Esfandiarpoor, S., Pahlavan, A., Goudarzi, M.: Structure-aware online virtual machine consolidation for datacenter energy improvement in cloud computing. Comput. Electr. Eng. **42**, 74–89 (2015)
9. Elijorde, F., Lee, J.: Attaining reliability and energy efficiency in cloud data centers through workload profiling and SLA-aware VM assignment. Int. J. Soft Comput. Appl. **7**(1), 41–58 (2015)
10. Wu, J., Zhang, Y., Zukerman, M.: Energy-efficient base-stations sleep-mode techniques in green cellular networks: a survey. IEEE Commun. Surv. Tutor. **17**(2), 803–826 (2015)
11. Sun, G., Yu, H., Li, L.: Exploring online virtual networks mapping with stochastic bandwidth demand in multi-datacenter. Photonic Netw. Commun. **23**(2), 109–122 (2012)
12. Chowdhury, M., Rahman, M.R., Boutaba, R.: Vineyard: virtual network embedding algorithms with coordinated node and link mapping. IEEE/ACM Trans. Netw. (TON) **20**(1), 206–219 (2012)
13. Gong, L., Jiang, H., Wang, Y.: Novel location-constrained virtual network embedding LC-VNE algorithms towards integrated node and link mapping. IEEE/ACM Trans. Netw. **24**(6), 3648–3661 (2016)
14. Zhang, Z., Su, S., Zhang, J.: Energy aware virtual network embedding with dynamic demands: online and offline. Comput. Netw. **93**, 448–459 (2015)
15. Wang, M., Meng, X., Zhang, L.: Consolidating virtual machines with dynamic bandwidth demand in data centers. In: INFOCOM, 2011 Proceedings IEEE, pp. 71–75 (2011)
16. Garey, M.R., Johnson, D.S.: Computers and Intractablity: A Guide to the Theory of NP-Completeness. Freeman, San Francisco (1990). 210, problem ND17
17. Zegura, E.W., Calvert, K.L., Bhattacharjee, S.: How to model an internetwork. In: INFOCOM, Proceedings IEEE, vol. 2, pp. 594–602. IEEE (1996)

WeChat Red Envelops: Literature Review and Future Research Directions

Zerun Chen and Rui Gu[✉]

School of Information Technology and Management,
University of International Business and Economics, Beijing 100029, China
doudouelisa@126.com, gurui@uibe.edu.cn

Abstract. As an innovative Internet product grounded in Chinese particular-
istic culture, WeChat Red Envelops has received increasing attention from both
academics and practitioners. A considerable number of studies have been conducted to investigate the WeChat Red Envelops phenomenon. However, the
extant literature has been very scattered and little effort has been devoted to
integrating the existing findings. Consequently, our understanding of the
WeChat Red Envelops phenomenon is fragmented and limited. Against this
background, this study conducted a systematic review of extant studies, summarized the current research status, identified the research gaps and accordingly
provide future research directions. We believe that this study offers an important
foundation for future research to conduct in-depth investigation and advance our
understanding regarding WeChat Red Envelops.

Keywords: WeChat Red Envelops · Mobile social media · Mobile internet ·
Product innovation · Gamification

1 Introduction

According to the mUserTracker report of iResearch (2017), China has more than 600
million mobile social netizens, accounting for nearly 90% of the total mobile netizens.
The annual growth rate of China's mobile social netizens is higher than the global
level, and more than 50% of the netizens are above 30 years old (iResearch 2017). The
development of the Internet is accompanied by the growth of netizens. Internet users
are more familiar with the use of mobile Internet, and they are more willing to try new
social games and new features. Among the various social media platforms, WeChat is
one of the most influential (Kantar 2017).

WeChat Red Envelops[1] is an Internet product launched by Tencent on January 27,
2014. The product has quickly occupied the market with its convenience, entertainment, and practicality. It was reported that 768 million people have used the WeChat
Red Envelops to send and receive a total of 60 billion red envelops as greetings to their
family, friends, and colleagues during the 2018 Spring Festival (WeChat 2018). On
Chinese New Year's Eve, 688 million people have participated in the red envelops

---

[1] WeChat Red Envelops is used as a term which refers particularly to the red envelops function of
WeChat. It is an Internet product from a consumer perspective.

© Springer Nature Switzerland AG 2019
X. Liu et al. (Eds.): ICSOC 2018 Workshops, LNCS 11434, pp. 53–66, 2019.
https://doi.org/10.1007/978-3-030-17642-6_5

activities, accounting for more than half of the Chinese population (WeChat 2018). Distinct from traditional red envelops, WeChat red envelops eliminate the limitations of time and space. The high level of ease of use and interestingness has made WeChat Red Envelops quite a phenomenal product in China.

As the WeChat red envelops prevail, we have witnessed an increasing number of studies on this intriguing phenomenon. However, the extant literature has been very scattered and thus has rendered our understanding of the WeChat Red Envelops phenomenon fragmented and limited. Furthermore, various theories and perspectives have been employed to investigate such phenomenon and little effort has been devoted to integrating the existing findings. Against this background, this paper presents a systematic review of extant studies on WeChat Red Envelops to identify the research gaps and accordingly provide future research directions.

The remainder of this paper proceeds as follows. In the next section, we outline the development of WeChat Red Envelops and summarize the characteristics of the product. We then describe the method used in the literature search and identification, and delineate the current state of research on WeChat Red Envelops. Subsequently, we present the major research themes and identify the research gaps. Finally, a discussion of future research directions and limitations is offered.

2   WeChat Red Envelops

WeChat Red Envelops is the product of the integration of Internet technology and traditional Chinese red envelops culture (Holmes et al. 2015; Park 2016; Xie et al. 2017). In the early studies, researchers have regarded WeChat Red Envelops as a product and have categorized its functions into two types: giving red envelops and receiving red envelops (Sun 2016). Giving red envelops means that users can select a WeChat group or a certain person in advance, set the monetary value and the number of red envelops, and then send them. Receiving red envelops means that users can receive the red envelops from a WeChat group or another person who is in the users' friend list on WeChat (Liang 2014; Wu 2014). Some researchers have emphasized that WeChat red envelops not only have the blessing significance but also break through the time and space restrictions of the traditional red envelops, which makes WeChat Red Envelops convenient and innovative (Feng 2015; Holmes et al. 2015; Tian 2016; Xu 2016).

As the needs of users change, WeChat Red Envelops offers the "grab red envelops" function and the researchers' attention has accordingly shifted. Researchers believed that the emergence of "grab red envelops" has enabled WeChat Red Envelops to be upgraded and differentiated, thereby making it more intriguing for users (Yan 2015). In view of this, some researchers have regarded WeChat Red Envelops as a game (Feng 2014; Liang 2014; Tian 2016). When users participate in grabbing red envelops, they feel happy and excited. Adding the element of "grab red envelops" leads WeChat Red Envelops to be a representative of the similar products such as Red Envelops by Alipay and Sina Weibo. The key factors of the success of WeChat Red Envelops include its high level of ease of use, interestingness, and social entertainment as well as the positive online word of mouth and the wide media propaganda (Xu and Song 2014).

With the prevailing of mobile payment, WeChat Red Envelops has increasingly become an indispensable application in people's daily life, and has gradually developed into a phenomenal Internet product.

Based on a review of the existing literature, the key characteristics of WeChat Red Envelops are identified and summarized in Table 1.

Table 1. Characteristics of WeChat Red Envelops

Characteristic	Definition	Studies
Simplicity	WeChat Red Envelops is quite easy to operate. The threshold for participating in the WeChat Red Envelops is low, which facilitates the participation of a wide variety of users (e.g., different ages and occupations)	Wu (2014), Zeng (2014), Feng (2015), Liu et al. (2015), Wang (2015), Sun (2016), Wang and Wang (2016), Xu (2016), Yang and Chen (2016)
Interactivity	WeChat Red Envelops is embedded in the mobile social networking platform WeChat. User participation in WeChat Red Envelops is accompanied by interactions, greetings, and blessings of friends and relatives	Feng (2014), Zeng (2014), Li and Zhang (2015), Wang (2015), Ye (2015), Sun (2016), Wang and Wang (2016)
Interestingness	WeChat Red Envelops highlights the "grab" feature and shifts user attention from the monetary value of Red Envelops to the interestingness of the game	Feng (2014), Zeng (2014), Wang (2015), Sun (2016), Wang and Wang (2016)
Innovativeness	WeChat Red Envelops combines the Chinese tradition of giving Red Envelops with the electronic wallets, and brings users a personalized experience by designing the Red Envelops as a social game	Feng (2015), Yang and Chen (2016)
Economic benefits	The money users obtain from participating in WeChat Red Envelops can be used for real-life consumption and brings economic benefits to both businesses and users	Liu et al. (2015), Chen and Rau (2016), Sun (2016), Yang and Chen (2016), Vodanovich et al. (2017), Wu and Ma (2017)

WeChat Red Envelops is an innovation of commercial services in the mobile Internet era. Researchers have employed the innovation diffusion theory as a lens to understand its development process (Feng 2014, 2015). As an IT innovation product, WeChat Red Envelops was initially learned about and accepted by innovators and early adopters on the mobile social networking platform WeChat, and then was disseminated and known by more users through the sharing of these early users. With the continuous improvement of WeChat Red Envelops and the participation of more users, WeChat Red Envelops attracts more and more attention and ultimately penetrates among a huge number of users (Feng 2014, 2015).

3 Literature Search and Analysis

3.1 Literature Search and Identification

In order to systematically analyze the research development and the current status of WeChat Red Envelops, we employed a two-stage approach to search and identify the relevant literature (Webster and Watson 2002). In the first stage, considering that WeChat Red Envelops is a typical phenomenon in the Chinese context, we first conducted electronic search using the Chinese words "微信红包" as the search term for articles' keyword or title in the three major Chinese academic databases: China National Knowledge Infrastructure (CNKI, cnki.net), Wanfang Data (wanfangdata.com.cn), and VIP (vipinfo.com.cn). Unlike VIP which includes only journal articles, CNKI and Wanfang Data are comprehensive databases which also include newspaper articles, reports, and patents. Therefore, we limited our search to the academic type of literature, including journal articles, dissertations, and conference proceedings in CNKI and Wanfang Data. Consequently, we obtained 239 articles in CNKI, 322 in Wanfang Data, and 113 in VIP. Given that some articles are simultaneously indexed in more than one database, we conducted a screening of those duplicate articles. As a result, we identified 416 Chinese articles with the keyword or title including the Chinese words "微信红包" in the three Chinese academic databases. To identify English articles, we conducted a search on Google Scholar using the keywords "WeChat red envelop", "WeChat red packet", and "WeChat red bag", respectively. A total of 65 articles were obtained.

In the second stage, we applied the exclusion criteria to the initial set of articles. Specifically, we excluded the articles that did not focus on WeChat Red Envelops by reading the abstract of the articles. As for the Chinese articles, we also excluded articles that are cited less than three times (median of the citation counts of all articles collected) to ensure the quality of the studies included in our literature analysis. Consequently, we identified a total of 73 articles by September 2018.

3.2 Literature Analysis and Review

We conducted a quantitative analysis of the literature, including the evolution of the number of articles, research trends and priorities. Among the 73 articles, 11 were published in 2014, 29 in 2015, 26 in 2016, and 7 in 2017 (Fig. 1). With regard to the research trends and priorities, we found that the research on WeChat Red Envelops can be divided into two major themes: (1) the reasons of the popularity of WeChat Red Envelops and (2) the dark side of WeChat Red Envelops. For the theme on the reasons of the popularity, two perspectives were analyzed: (1) the user perspective: WeChat

Red Envelops meets users' diverse needs and motivations, and (2) the company perspective: Tencent adopted various marketing tactics to promote WeChat Red Envelops. For the theme on the dark side of WeChat Red Envelops, there are two categories of issues: (1) the negative impact of WeChat Red Envelops on interpersonal relationships, and (2) the legal issues caused by WeChat Red Envelops. Each research theme is discussed in detail below.

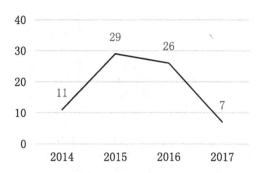

Fig. 1. Annual distribution of the number of WeChat Red Envelops articles

3.2.1   Theme 1: Reasons of the Popularity of WeChat Red Envelops

With the continuous development of WeChat Red Envelops, many researchers were interested in studying why WeChat Red Envelops has been so popular and widely adopted. Our review revealed that the reasons can be classified as two categories: the user perspective and the company perspective.

The User Perspective: Needs and Motivations The widespread popularity of WeChat Red Envelops stems from the fact that they meet the diverse needs of users. Among the employed theories, the uses and gratifications theory is the most popular (Hu 2016; Li and Zhang 2015; Shen and Chen 2015; Wang 2016; Wei 2015; Yang and Chen 2016). According to this theory, individuals are motivated by their self-defined psychological and social needs to access and use a medium (Katz et al. 1973b). There are five categories of needs which motivate individuals' choice and use of media: (1) cognitive needs – access to information, knowledge, and understanding, (2) affective needs – emotional, pleasant or aesthetic experiences, (3) personal integrative needs – strengthening confidence and stability, (4) social integrative needs – strengthening contact with family and friends, and (5) tension-release needs – escape or divert attention (Katz et al. 1973a). Our literature review showed that the various needs identified in extant literature can be mapped into the five categories of Katz et al. (1973a) (see Table 2).

Table 2. User needs through the lens of uses and gratifications theory

Article	Cognitive needs	Affective needs	Personal integrative needs	Social integrative needs	Tension-release needs
Yang and Chen (2016)	Feeling fresh New ways of communication Gain new experience	Happy Pleasant Content	Approval Honor Prestige	Communication Interaction Keep up with others Sense of belonging Identity	Passing time Relax Relieve stress
Wang (2016)	Curiosity	Happy Interesting	Equal opportunity to participate	Enrich chat topics	Release emotions Escape from burden and pressure
Shen and Chen (2015)		Joy	Self-image construction Respect Self-realization	Maintain relationships Meet new friends	
Wei (2015)	Interested in new things	Entertainment Fun Excitement	Possess equal status as participants	Learn about social topics Appear to be social and integrated with the people around Avoid outdated	Passing time Release emotions Escape from burden and stress
Cai et al. (2017)		Joyful Pleasure		Enhance social communication Expand relationship network	Leisure

Some researchers have examined users' participation motivations with other theoretical approaches, such as Maslow's hierarchy of needs theory (Liao 2014; Zhang 2016), mental accounting theory (Zhou 2015), psychological reactance theory (Li et al. 2016), self-determination theory (Li et al. 2016), and interaction ritual chains theory (Zhang 2016). Notably, Zhou (2015) emphasized that users create a separate mental account for the WeChat red envelops and thus they perceive greater value from the money obtained from the red envelops than from other channels. Moreover, Zhang (2016) suggested that grabbing red envelops creates a social ritual and invokes users' emotional energy, which make users feel full of impulses to participate in the red envelops activities. In sum, the aforementioned various theoretical perspectives have provided us with rich understanding of the user-side reasons of the popularity of WeChat Red Envelops.

The Company Perspective: Marketing Tactics Tencent company's various marketing tactics have been considered as another driving force of the WeChat Red Envelops' success. As of 2017, Tencent has stayed ahead in the competition against Alipay, Sina Weibo, Baidu, and other businesses which have launched Red Envelops in the same period (Tecent 2017). Our literature review suggested that Tencent has used event marketing, public relations marketing, viral marketing, and multi-channel marketing tactics to promote the WeChat Red Envelops (Table 3). Lessons learned from the WeChat Red Envelops suggested that to attain effective marketing outcomes, companies not only need to understand consumers' psychological needs, but also and more important, they need to delicately leverage the appropriate opportunities, engage consumers, and lower the engaging threshold as well (Liu 2014; Zhao 2015). Furthermore, companies should leverage consumer sharing to be more cost-efficient in the marketing activities (Ye 2015; Zhu 2015).

Table 3. Tencent's marketing tactics

Marketing Tactic	Illustration	Studies
Event marketing	Tencent has implemented intensive marketing activities before and during the Chinese Spring Festival, a special time period in which people have the tradition of sending Red Envelops, to promote the use of WeChat Red Envelops	Liu et al. (2015), Wu et al. (2016), Yan (2016)
Public relations marketing	Tencent has propagandized itself via third-party authorities and publicly recognized media outlets. For example, a renowned website *huxiu.com* published an eye-catching article "WeChat Red Envelops detonates the society! What does Tencent do right and what will it get?" The newspaper *First Financial Daily* posted the article "WeChat Red Envelops are suddenly popular: fighting against Alibaba."	Yang and Li (2015), Yan (2016)
Viral marketing	Tencent has leveraged the relationship chain to encourage users to disseminate and spread the WeChat Red Envelops to facilitate public awareness and acceptance	Ye (2015), Yan (2016)
Multi-channel marketing	Tencent has simultaneously released their ads in offline channels, TV programs, Internet, and the mobile Internet platforms	Zeng (2014), Ye (2015), Zhao (2015)

3.2.2   Theme 2: Dark Side of WeChat Red Envelops

As a new mobile Internet product, WeChat Red Envelops has also incurred negative consequences which are to be addressed appropriately. For instance, the increased online interaction through "screen" has exerted a negative impact on interpersonal relationships such that it weakens the interpersonal trust and closeness compared to face-to-face communication (Sun 2016). Moreover, WeChat Red Envelops has been used for such illegal purposes as commercial bribery and gambling (Cheng 2016; Li 2016c; Shang and Feng 2016; Shi 2016).

The Negative Impact on Interpersonal Relationships WeChat Red Envelops has occupied users' time of face-to-face communication with friends and family, thereby squeezing the interpersonal communication space in reality (Hu 2016; Liu et al. 2015; Wang and Wang 2016; Wang 2015). Besides, the emotions formed on the basis of entertainment tend to be unstable, posing a threat to the establishment of a firm interpersonal relationship (Wang and Wang 2016; Wang 2015). Furthermore, in some cases, individuals deliberately request red envelops, resulting in a friendship crisis (Sun 2016).

The Legal Issues The first issue is the personal information security (Li 2016a, 2016b, 2016c; Shen and Chen 2015; Shi 2016). As WeChat Red Envelops is bound to the users' bank card, sensitive information such as users' ID number, mobile phone number, personal bank card number and password is at the risk of being stolen, increasing the possibility of users' financial loss. Furthermore, as giving and receiving WeChat red envelops are conducted anonymously, users cannot turn to legal authorities to protect their interests if a transaction dispute or fraud occurs.

The second issue is with the deposit funds and their interest (Cheng 2016; Huang and Gao 2015; Li 2016b, 2016c; Mo 2014; Tian 2015). In most cases, users do not immediately take out the money or use it after obtaining WeChat red envelops, which leads to a large amount of deposit funds in WeChat accounts. Moreover, if the red envelops sent by a user are not opened by other users within 24 h, the money in the red envelops will be returned to the sender, before which the money is deposited in Tenpay's pool of funds. According to the regulations of the People's Bank of China, the interest derived from the deposits should be paid to the users, so there is still much controversy on the issue of interest. Besides, although the WeChat platform only provides payment services, it has accumulated a large amount of funds. In this sense, the WeChat platform is performing a function of commercial bank savings, however, it does not have a license for such business (Huang and Gao 2015). Therefore, WeChat Red Envelops has caused the suspicion of illegally raising funds for the Tencent company.

The third issue is the gambling behavior using WeChat Red Envelops (Huang et al. 2016; Qi 2017; Shang and Feng 2016). WeChat Red Envelops has provided a random-amount-distribution function to enhance user experience, however, this function has been used by speculators for gambling (Dong 2017; Du 2016; Luo and Zhao 2018; Xiong 2016). Since gambling is addictive per se, WeChat Red Envelops gambling behavior must not be ignored.

3.3 Summary of Extant Literature

Based on the review of extant literature, we identified the following gaps. First, although multiple theories have been used to investigate the user-side reasons of the popularity of WeChat Red Envelops, most of the studies (except for Huang 2016;

Li et al. 2016) are conceptual in nature and have not been empirically validated. Second, extant studies have suggested the user-side and the company-side reasons of the popularity of WeChat Red Envelops, however, few studies have attended to the artifact design elements that give rise to the success of WeChat Red Envelops.

Third, although researchers have noted the negative impact on interpersonal relationships, few has collected data to empirically investigate this issue. Fourth, multiple papers have discussed the legal issues caused by WeChat Red Envelops, however, feasible and specific solutions have yet to be proposed. Finally, little attention is given to the business value of WeChat Red Envelops.

4 Discussion

4.1 Future Research Directions

Based on the aforementioned research gaps, we suggest the following future research directions regarding WeChat Red Envelops. First, more empirical research is required to quantitatively examine the user-side reasons for the wide adoption of WeChat Red Envelops, such as user needs and motivations, given that merely applying theories to qualitatively explicate a phenomenon is undoubtedly insufficient for a high-quality academic research with both rigor and relevance (Lee and Hubona 2009). Furthermore, the empirical research is encouraged to employ more theories from other disciplines such as cognitive science and behavioral economics to enrich our understanding of the user-side factors of the WeChat Red Envelops popularity.

Second, since WeChat Red Envelops is a successful Internet product innovation, ascertaining its design elements which contribute to its success warrants future research efforts. Toward this end, researchers are suggested to refer to the design science paradigm (Gregor and Hevner 2013) and the case study methodology (Yin 2013). Specifically, researchers can apply the design science research guidelines and take the WeChat Red Envelops as a real-world case. Data can be collected through interviews, reports, and corporate documents to identify those unique and contributing design elements. A mixed methods approach combining qualitative and quantitative methods will be helpful to enhance the research findings and offer rich and significant insights (Venkatesh et al. 2013). Furthermore, as WeChat Red Envelops has the component of gaming, the emerging research stream of gamification can also be taken as a frame of reference. Researchers are encouraged to delve into the gamification literature (e.g., Liu et al. 2017) to identify and attest the design principles of gamification. We believe that these future research efforts have significant implications for both theory and practice. In particular, they will benefit the practitioners with specific and actionable guidelines on product innovations in the mobile Internet and social media contexts.

Third, theory-grounded empirical studies and case studies are needed to rigorously investigate the dark side of WeChat Red Envelops. The extant literature is mostly descriptive and lacks a theoretical foundation. Consequently, our understanding of the dark side associated with the use of WeChat Red Envelops is incomplete and fragmented. Indeed, the negative impact of IT use is an important research area for IS scholars, "given the results from [prior related] studies and considering that the ubiquitous and functionally pervasive nature of IT use is expected to expose users to ever greater levels of conditions that are potent for experiencing negative outcomes" (Tarafdar et al. 2013, p. 270). Hence, more research following a scientific research methodology is encouraged to examine various aspects of the dark side of the WeChat Red Envelops use as well as the antecedents and consequences at the levels of individuals, groups, organizations, culture, and society. Such research will contribute to our knowledge base regarding the negative impact of WeChat Red Envelops. Practically, it can offer actionable intervention measures for platform operators, government agencies, and organizations to mitigate or eliminate the negative impact.

Finally, as WeChat Red Envelops has been widely used, the potential business value it affords is enormous and awaits exploration and exploitation. WeChat Red Envelops is not only used for social entertainment among friends and family members but also is adopted in corporate marketing and promotion activities (Ye 2015). In the era of data technology, big data plays a critical role in improving business operations and management (Guha and Kumar 2018). The data generated by the WeChat Red Envelops has great potential for corporate use. For instance, companies can give customers WeChat red envelops as coupons and encourage them to repatronize their stores. By so doing, companies can monitor and measure the effectiveness of their promotion activities by time, day, and season. They can accordingly adjust the business operations and marketing plans. In this case, the question of how to quantify the effectiveness of promotion activities implemented via WeChat Red Envelops needs to be addressed. Furthermore, future research can integrate the data generated in users' WeChat Red Envelops activities (e.g., offline payment using WeChat Red Envelops) with other sources of data on users (e.g., online shopping data) to construct a complete and more accurate user profile. Toward this end, such work as the design of methods and algorithms needs to be done. Undoubtedly, WeChat Red Envelops has the potential to generate tremendous commercial value and warrants more in-depth future research from multiple disciplines.

4.2 Limitations

This study has a few limitations. First, although we have conducted a relatively comprehensive and structured search of the literature, it is likely that we did not identify all relevant papers. While the citation frequency is a recognized indicator of article quality, our selection of having less than three citation counts as an exclusion criterion for Chinese articles is somewhat arbitrary. Future research could build on our study and expand the literature body for further analysis. Second, as the research on WeChat Red Envelops is at a nascent stage, most articles are conceptual and empirical research is still emerging. Our study takes a first step in synthesizing extant literature and providing an overview of the research status and trends. Nonetheless, future research is recommended to conduct a follow-up review to gain an up-to-date understanding of the literature.

5   Conclusion

This paper takes a lead in presenting a systematic review of extant literature on WeChat Red Envelops. The analysis reveals two major themes, namely, reasons of the popularity of WeChat Red Envelops and the dark side associated with the use of WeChat Red Envelops. Based on the research gaps identified in the literature, we recommend that future studies conduct more theory-based and empirical research and employ theories from other disciplines as well as multiple methods to enhance our knowledge base of the WeChat Red Envelops phenomenon. We also recommend that future studies explore the business value of WeChat Red Envelops and conduct research on the approaches, methods, and algorithms associated with the exploration and exploitation of the business value. We hope that our study helps researchers and practitioners to gain an initial overview of the literature and inspires more future research to gain a better understanding of the WeChat Red Envelops related phenomena.

Acknowledgements. This research was supported in part by the National Natural Science Foundation of China (71501042), the Social Science Foundation of Beijing City (17XCC008), the Program for Young Excellent Talents of UIBE (17YQ16), the China Scholarship Council (201806645005), and the Foundation for Disciplinary Development of SITM in UIBE.

References

Cai, C., Shang, H., Lertsiriworapong, T.: A study of motivation factors of grab red envelopes phenomenon: a case study of WeChat, In: Proceedings of the Fourth International Conference on Management Science, Innovation, and Technology, Bangkok, Thailand, pp. 120–132 (2017)

Chen, N., Rau, P.-L.P.: Group participation influence on members' gifting behaviors in a social game. In: Rau, P.-L.P. (ed.) CCD 2016. LNCS, vol. 9741, pp. 34–42. Springer, Cham (2016). https://doi.org/10.1007/978-3-319-40093-8_4

Cheng, B.: Criminal law issues and regulatory path of WeChat red envelops. J. Tianshui Adm. Coll. **17**(5), 27–30 (2016). (in Chinese)

Dong, T.: An empirical analysis of the WeChat cases of WeChat red envelops. Leg. Syst. Soc. **4**, 59–63 (2017). (in Chinese)

Du, L.: The status quo and prevention of WeChat gambling. Net Moon Acad. J. **4**, 80–85 (2016). (in Chinese)

Feng, J.: Research on communication strategy based on network social relation structure—from WeChat red envelops. Southeast. Commun. **4**, 80–82 (2014). (in Chinese)

Feng, L.: Research on the popular situation of WeChat red envelops. Journal. Commun. **18**, 74–76 (2015). (in Chinese)

Gregor, S., Hevner, A.R.: Positioning and presenting design science research for maximum impact. MIS Q. **37**(2), 337–355 (2013)

Guha, S., Kumar, S.: Emergence of big data research in operations management, information systems, and healthcare: past and future roadmap. Prod. Oper. Manag. **27**(9), 1724–1735 (2018)

Holmes, K., Balnaves, M., Wang, Y.: Red bags and WeChat (wēixìn): online collectivism during massive chinese cultural events. Global Media J. Aust. Ed. **9**(1), 1–12 (2015)

Hu, B.: An exploratory study of the influence of interpersonal communication on WeChat red envelops. West. Acad. J. (News Commun.) **4**, 43–45 (2016). (in Chinese)

Huang, C., Gao, X.: The legal risk of WeChat red envelops under the background of internet finance and its prevention. J. Beijing Polit. Law Vocat. Coll. **4**, 77–82 (2015). (in Chinese)

Huang, D., He, J., Cai, H., Lin, J.: Analysis on the characteristics of WeChat red envelops gambling and countermeasures. J. Zhejiang Police Coll. **4**, 76–80 (2016). (in Chinese)

Huang, X.: An Empirical Study on the Use Behavior of WeChat Red Envelops and Its Influencing Factors. Hua Zhong University of Science and Technology, Wuhan (2016). (in Chinese)

iResearch.: 2017 China Social Application Demand Value White Paper (2017). (in Chinese). http://report.iresearch.cn/report/201709/3072.shtml

Kantar.: 2017 China Social Media Impact Report (2017). (in Chinese). http://b2b.toocle.com/detail–6408264.html

Katz, E., Blumler, J.G., Gurevitch, M.: On the use of the mass media. Am. Sociol. Rev. **38**(2), 164–181 (1973a)

Katz, E., Blumler, J.G., Gurevitch, M.: Uses and gratifications research. Pub. Opin. Q. **37**(4), 509–523 (1973b)

Lee, A.S., Hubona, G.S.: A scientific basis for rigor in information systems research. MIS Q. **33**(2), 237–262 (2009)

Li, D.: Research on space-time utility of WeChat payment, In: Proceedings of the Second International Conference on Humanities and Social Science Research, pp. 228–232. Atlantis Press (2016a)

Li, D., Liu, J., Ma, M., Zhang, C.: WeChat red envelops, consumers grab or not grab: interpretation based on mediation model of participation motivation and psychological resistance. J. Acad. Mark. Sci. **12**(1), 18–37 (2016). (in Chinese)

Li, S.: Perspective on the legal risk of WeChat red envelops. Jinan J. (Philos. Soc. Sci. Ed.) **38**(10), 74–81 (2016b). (in Chinese)

Li, W.: On the duality of WeChat red envelops related crimes and criminal regulations. J. Guangxi Polit. Leg. Manag. Cadre Coll. **25**(4), 66–71 (2016c). (in Chinese)

Li, X., Zhang, J.: Discussion on the rise of WeChat red envelops from the perspective of communication. Today Media **23**(6), 105–107 (2015). (in Chinese)

Liang, F.: WeChat red envelops. News Outpost **4**, 92 (2014). (in Chinese)

Liao, L.: Grab WeChat red envelops, can't stop it! China Telecom Ind. **3**, 50–51 (2014). (in Chinese)

Liu, D., Santhanam, R., Webster, J.: Toward meaningful engagement: a framework for design and research of gamified information systems. MIS Q. **41**(4), 1011–1034 (2017)

Liu, J.: Looking at the WeChat red envelops from the internet thinking marketing. Mark. Res. **3**, 37–38 (2014). (in Chinese)

Liu, W., He, X., Zhang, P.: Application of red envelopes–new weapon of WeChat payment, In: Proceedings of the Fifth International Conference on Education, Management, Information and Medicine, pp. 704–708. Atlantis Press, Shenyang (2015)

Luo, K., Zhao, Y.: Organizing others to grab wechat red envelops and tapping the profit should open a casino crime. China Prosec. **18**, 11–13 (2018). (in Chinese)

Mo, D.: WeChat red envelops triggers mobile payment battle. Comput. Netw. **5**, 13 (2014). (in Chinese)

Park, L.J.: WeChat Red Bags: How International Students from China Use Social Media While Attending a Public University in California. University of California, Los Angeles (2016)

Qi, T.: An exploratory study of the investigation of online gambling crime cases—taking WeChat red envelops gambling as an example. J. Beijing Police Coll. **3**, 76–82 (2017). (in Chinese)

Shang, X., Feng, Y.: How to rectify WeChat red envelops gambling. Mod. World Police **2**, 91–92 (2016). (in Chinese)

Shen, S., Chen, Y.: An exploratory study of the influence of WeChat red envelops propagation on interpersonal relationship. Sci. Technol. Commun. **8**, 110–111 (2015). (in Chinese)

Shi, X.: Fraudulent behavior and legal supervision in wechat red envelops mobile payment. People's Forum **11**, 111–113 (2016). (in Chinese)

Sun, R.: Analysis on the characteristics of WeChat red envelops and its propagation effect. Journal. Commun. **3**, 22–23 (2016). (in Chinese)

Tarafdar, M., Gupta, A., Turel, O.: The dark side of information technology use. Inf. Syst. J. **23** (3), 269–275 (2013)

Tecent, T.: New Trend Report of 2017 Mobile Red Envelops (2017). (in Chinese). http://tech.qq.com/a/20170204/004129.htm#p=23

Tian, H.: Legal problems and countermeasures in WeChat red envelops. J. Chongqing Ind. Trade Vocat. Tech. Coll. **1**, 81–86 (2015). (in Chinese)

Tian, J.: Analysis of the Chinese new year red envelops customs in WeChat red envelops. News Res. Guide 7(19), 88–89 (2016). (in Chinese)

Venkatesh, V., Brown, S.A., Bala, H.: Bridging the qualitative-quantitative divide: guidelines for conducting mixed methods research in information systems. MIS Q. **37**(1), 21–54 (2013)

Vodanovich, S., McKenna, B., Cai, W.: Cultural values inherent in the design of social media platforms: a case study of WeChat, In: Pucihar, A., Borštnar, M.K., Kittl, C., Ravesteijn, P., Clarke, R., Bons, R. (eds.) Proceedings of the Thirtieth BLED eConference, Bled, Slovenia, pp. 617–627 (2017)

Wang, H., Wang, S.: Analysis of the influence of WeChat red envelops on the construction of interpersonal relationship. Southeast. Commun. **4**, 64–67 (2016). (in Chinese)

Wang, N.: Study on the Phenomenon of WeChat Red Envelops Propagation. Liaoning University, Shenyang (2016). (in Chinese)

Wang, R.: Analysis of the positive and negative effects of WeChat red envelops on interpersonal communication. Southeast. Commun. **7**, 77–80 (2015). (in Chinese)

Webster, J., Watson, R.T.: Analyzing the past to prepare for the future: writing a literature review. MIS Q. **26**(2), 13–23 (2002)

WeChat.: WeChat Data Report During the Spring Festival of 2018 (2018). (in Chinese). https://mp.weixin.qq.com/s/ALLqMzV2Tubg2-6kQjVWwg

Wei, Y.: Communication analysis of the prevalence of WeChat red envelops. Mod. Audiov. **5**, 271–273 (2015). (in Chinese)

Wu, J., Liu, L., Huang, L.: Exploring user acceptance of innovative mobile payment service in emerging market: the moderating effect of diffusion stages of WeChat Payment in China, In: Proceedings of the Twentieth Pacific Asia Conference on Information Systems, pp. 1–16. AIS Electronic Library (2016)

Wu, L.: Thinking behind WeChat red envelops fanaticism. Mod. Women (late) **6**, 321 (2014). (in Chinese)

Wu, Z., Ma, X.: Money as a social currency to manage group dynamics: red packet gifting in chinese online communities. In: Proceedings of the 2017 ACM SIGCHI Conference on Human Factors in Computing Systems, Denver, CO, USA, pp. 2240–2247. ACM (2017)

Xie, C., Putrevu, J.S.H., Linder, C.: Family, friends, and cultural connectedness: a comparison between wechat and facebook user motivation, experience and NPS among Chinese people living overseas. In: Rau, P.-L.P. (ed.) CCD 2017. LNCS, vol. 10281, pp. 369–382. Springer, Cham (2017). https://doi.org/10.1007/978-3-319-57931-3_30

Xiong, W.: WeChat red envelops: characteristics of new gambling activities and countermeasures. Public Secur. Educ. **2**, 29–34 (2016). (in Chinese)

Xu, Q., Song, Q.: New thoughts on WeChat red envelops: using WeChat as an example to analyze the success factors of new media products. China Media Technol. **3**, 27–30 (2014). (in Chinese)

Xu, X.: The influence of WeChat red envelops on chinese new year culture from the perspective of new media. Today Media **24**(10), 45–48 (2016). (in Chinese)

Yan, M.: Talking about the functional tendency of social media communication—taking WeChat red envelops as an example. News Res. Guide **6**(10), 5–6 (2015). (in Chinese)

Yan, W.: Looking at the network marketing method from WeChat red envelops. Time Finan. **3**, 222–223 (2016). (in Chinese)

Yang, K., Li, S.: An exploratory study of tencent's marketing thinking behind WeChat red envelops. Mark. Wkly. Theor. Res. **2**, 54–55 (2015). (in Chinese)

Yang, S., Chen, J.: Research on Audience demand based on use and satisfaction theory—from WeChat red envelops. Publ. Wide Angle **10**, 67–69 (2016). (in Chinese)

Ye, Q.: Research on marketing strategy of WeChat red envelops based on social relationship. News World **4**, 133–134 (2015). (in Chinese)

Yin, R.K.: Case Study Research: Design and Methods. Sage Publications, Thousand Oaks (2013)

Zeng, T.: Analysis on the product marketing thinking of WeChat red envelops. Mark. Wkly (Theory Res. **6**, 76–77 (2014). (in Chinese)

Zhang, X.: Interactive research on WeChat red envelops in the perspective of interactive ceremony chain. Journal. Res. Guide **3**, 8–9 (2016). (in Chinese)

Zhao, W.: Behind the WeChat red envelops: the key points of new media brand marketing. Audiovisual **6**, 150–151 (2015). (in Chinese)

Zhou, S.: On the basis of communication audience psychology to explore the madness of online red envelops. Journal. Res. Guide **8**, 224 (2015). (in Chinese)

Zhu, W.: From the marketing strategies in didi WeChat red envelops to see the user sharing behavior in the mobile internet. News World **4**, 97–98 (2015). (in Chinese)

NLS4IoT: Networked Learning Systems for Secured IoT Services and Its Applications

Introduction to the 1st International Workshop on Networked Learning Systems for Secured IoT 2018

The NLS4IoT 2018 workshop was held in conjunction with the 16th International Conference on Service Oriented Computing (ICSOC 2018) on November 12–15, 2018 in Hangzhou, China. This workshop provides an exciting and highly interactive forum for researchers and practitioners to exchange new ideas, developments, and experiences in Networked learning systems, secured sensing and Its Applications for Big Data Analytics in Internet and Web of things, Cloud Computing, Ubiquitous Computing, Big Data Analytics, and Complex Networks.

This workshop clearly showed interesting research efforts in the field and offered the ability to fruitful discussions:

- IoT Security/Privacy preservation
- Cyber Security, Intrusion Detection Systems, Malware and Botnets
- Security of storage systems, operating systems
- Intrusion detection, prediction, classification, and their response models for survivable, resilient, and self-healing systems
- Actuate-sensory network security, web security, wireless security, digital forensics, security information analytics
- Neural network-based learning, including the intelligent structures, algorithms and applications
- Heterogeneous learning on multi-modality data, including Multi-view learning, Multitask learning, Transfer learning, Semi-supervised learning, Active learning; Reinforcement learning
- Data-driven learning and control and goal-oriented learning, prediction, and control
- Complexity analysis of distribution algorithms
- Non-iidness learning; Coupled learning and coupled relationship discovery
- Anomaly detection in social networks

We would like to thank the authors for their submissions, the program committee for their reviewing work, and the organizers of the ICSOC 2018 conference for their support which made this workshop possible.

Frank Jiang
Haiying Xia
NLS4IoT 2018 Programme Chairs

Research and Design of CMOS Fully Differential Telescopic Operational Amplifier with Common Mode Feedback

Zhongqiu Pang, Pinqun Jiang[✉], Shuxiang Song, and Mingcan Cen

College of Electronic Engineering, Guangxi Normal University,
Guilin 541004, Guangxi, China
pangzq_ic@163.com, pqjiang@163.com

Abstract. In the medium or low frequency cases, the performance such as the gain or bandwidth of the fully differential operational amplifier is not good. In this paper, a fully differential telescopic two-stage operational amplifier with two-stage common-mode feedback is designed by using TSMC 250 nm technology. The first stage operational amplifier is telescopic structure, while the second stage operational amplifier is common source structure. The inner structure of common-mode feedback is continuous-time common-mode feedback circuit, and the outer structure is switched capacitor CMFB structure. It has the advantages of high gain and good linearity. It overcomes the shortcomings of common mode feedback circuit in limiting the output swing. It can stabilize the DC operating point and improve the output swing effectively. Cadence Spectre simulation results show that the common mode feedback structure keeps the common mode level at 1.25 V, the open loop gain is 67.7 dB, the phase margin is 45°, and the unit gain bandwidth is 150.7 MHz under the 2.5 V supply voltage.

Keywords: Common mode feedback · Telescopic type structure ·
Operational amplifier

1 Introduction

With the development of integrated circuits, the operational amplifier, one of the core circuits of analog integrated circuits, has attracted people's attention. Operational amplifier is widely used in analog integrated circuits, such as ADC circuit (Analog to Digital Converter), comparator circuit and so on [1–3]. Therefore, high performance operational amplifiers have always been one of the hot topics in current integrated circuit research [4, 5].

This paper endeavors to study the CMOS operational amplifier is studied. A fully differential operational amplifier with two-stage operational amplifier and two-stage common-mode feedback is designed. The circuit has high gain and bandwidth, and the common-mode output voltage can be stabilized near half of the power supply voltage to ensure the maximum voltage swing [6–10].

There are three main structures of operational amplifiers: (1) two-stage operational amplifier; (2) folded-cascode; (3) telescopic cascode amplifier. The gain of the two-stage

© Springer Nature Switzerland AG 2019
X. Liu et al. (Eds.): ICSOC 2018 Workshops, LNCS 11434, pp. 69–79, 2019.
https://doi.org/10.1007/978-3-030-17642-6_6

operational amplifier is very high, and the differential output swing is also very large, but the high-order poles cause a limited stable bandwidth, requiring Miller compensation and other compensation methods, increasing the complexity of the circuit; foldable cascode operational amplifier has good frequency characteristics, but more branches, power consumption. By contrast, the output swing of the telescopic operational amplifier is similar to the folded cascade amplifier, with good frequency characteristics and relatively low power consumption. Therefore, the main circuit operational amplifier uses the telescopic operational amplifier [11–14].

2   Circuit Structure and Design

2.1   Subsection Sample

The fully differential telescopic operational amplifier designed in this paper consists of five parts: bias circuit, first-order operational amplifier, second-order operational amplifier, first-order common-mode feedback circuit and second-order common-mode feedback circuit, as shown in Fig. 1.

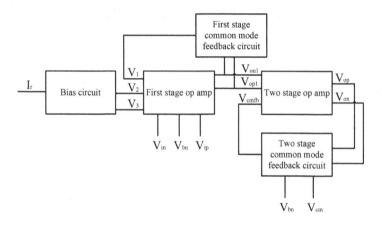

Fig. 1. Block diagram of fully differential telescopic operational amplifier

Figure 2, the overall circuit of the operational amplifier is shown. The left M_0–M_8 transistor is a bias circuit, the right M_9–M_{21} transistor is a fully differential telescopic operational amplifier, the continuous-time CMFB is an inner common mode feedback circuit or the first common mode feedback circuit, and the SC-CMFB is an outer common mode feedback structure or the second common mode feedback circuit.

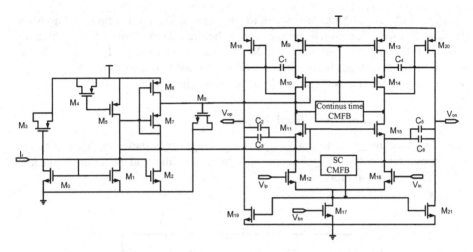

Fig. 2. Fully differential telescopic amplifier circuit diagram

3   Analysis of Each Module Circuit

3.1   Bias Circuit Analysis

As shown in Fig. 3, the bias circuit mainly consists two current mirrors, M_0 and M_1 constitute a current mirror, M_0 and M_2 constitute the other current mirror, and the output signals of the gate and drain of M_0 are input as reference current because

$$\frac{W_0}{L_0} = \frac{W_1}{L_1} = \frac{W_2}{L_2} \tag{1}$$

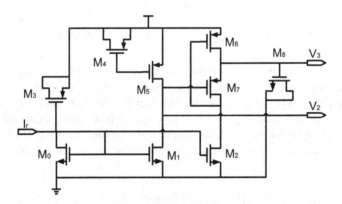

Fig. 3. The bias circuit

Type (1) W_n/L_n is MOS tube width to length ratio. The current flowing into M_0 is duplicated through the current mirror so that the drain current through M_0, the drain current of M_1 and the drain current of M_2 are equal. That is $I_{D1} = I_{D2} = I_{D3}$. M_5, M_6 and M_7 are used as loads in the circuit to adjust the drain voltage V_2 and V_3 generated by the M_1 and M_2 drains. M_3 and M_8 serve as matching tubes.

3.2   Main Circuit of Operational Amplifier

The main structure of the two-stage operational amplifier is shown in Fig. 4. The first stage uses a fully differential telescopic operational amplifier and the second stage uses a common source amplifier.

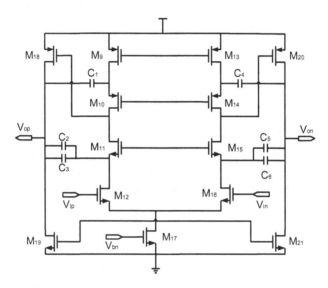

Fig. 4. Main structure of two stage operational amplifier

Cascaded structure has high output impedance, and MOS transistor is used to construct cascode constant current source structure, but this is at the cost of consuming voltage redundancy. The fully differential amplifier is symmetric, and only the left half side circuit can be analyzed. M_{17}, is a bias tube for the first stage operational amplifier, providing bias current for the first level operational amplifier in Fig. 4. The PMOS tube M_9 and M_{10} are cascaded to form a cascade amplifier of the current source. Its cascaded resistance is

$$R_1 = [1 + (g_{m10} + g_{mb10})r_{o10}]r_{o9} + r_{o10} \tag{2}$$

For M_{11} and M_{12} cascaded cascade cascades, the output impedance is the same as the above formula, and the impedance is

$$R_2 = [1 + (g_{m11} + g_{mb11})r_{o11}]r_{o12} + r_{o11} \tag{3}$$

Therefore, the total output impedance is two impedance parallel.

$$R_o = R_1//R_2 \tag{4}$$

M_1 as amplifier tube, transconductance is $G_{m1} = g_{m1}$, and its first gain is

$$|A_{v1}| \approx g_{m1}R_o = g_{m1}(R_1//R_2) \tag{5}$$

The voltage swing of the first stage operational amplifier is

$$2[V_{DD} - (V_{GSn} - V_{thn})_{PMOS} - |V_{GSn} - V_{thn}|_{NMOS} - V_{CSS}] \tag{6}$$

V_{GSn}–V_{thn} is the overdrive voltage, $(V_{GSn}$–$V_{thn})_{PMOS}$ is PMOS overdrive voltage, $|V_{GSn}$–$V_{thn}|_{NMOS}$ is PMOS overdrive voltage, V_{CSS} is the voltage at both ends of the current source M_{17}. In order for the input tube M_1 to work in the saturation region, the input voltage V_{ip} must satisfy the following conditions

$$V_A \geq V_{in} \geq V_{CSS} + V_{th12} \tag{7}$$

$$V_A = V_{DD} - [(V_{GS11} - V_{th11}) + |V_{GS10} - V_{th10}| + |V_{GS9} - V_{th9}|] + V_{th12} \tag{8}$$

When the tail current source is large, it can be found that the input voltage range is very small.

Due to the limitation of the structure of the telescopic operational amplifier, the output swing is relatively low, so the second stage uses a common source amplifier, so that the second stage operational amplifier can improve the overall circuit output swing. M_{19} is a two-stage operational amplifier offset tube and M_{18} is an amplifier of the two-stage operational amplifier. The gain of second level is

$$|A_{v2}| \approx g_{m18}(r_{o18}//r_{o19}) \tag{9}$$

So the two level gain is

$$A_v = A_{v1} \cdot A_{v2} = g_{m1}(R_0//R_1) \cdot g_{m18}(r_{o18}//r_{o19}) \tag{10}$$

In order to increase the bandwidth or phrase margin of the circuit, the capacitors C_1, C_2, C_3, C_4, C_5, C_6 are used to compensate for the cascade structure of the four cascades. The compensating capacitor is divided into two channels, which are connected to the cascode structure composed of PMOS transistor and the cascode structure composed of NMOS transistor respectively, so that the conjugate pole can be pushed away, and the gain and phase margin can be improved.

3.3 Inner Layer Common Mode Feedback Circuit

Figure 5 is the inner common-mode feedback circuit of a telescopic full-differential operational amplifier, which is constructed as a continuous-time common-mode feedback circuit. The CT CMFB circuit is also symmetrical. M_{28} provides bias current for CT CMFB with current leakage structure. M_{22} and M_{23}, M_{23} and M_{24} constitute two current mirror structures, namely

$$\frac{W_{22}}{L_{22}} = \frac{W_{23}}{L_{23}} = \frac{W_{23}}{L_{23}} \tag{11}$$

Type (11) W_n/L_n is MOS tube width to length ratio. The current flowing into M_{22} and M_{24} is duplicated through the current mirror so that the drain current passing through M_{22}, the drain current of M_{23} and the drain current of M_{24} are equal, i.e.

$$I_{D_{22}} = I_{D_{23}} = I_{D_{24}} \tag{12}$$

The output V_{op1} and V_{on1} of the first stage operational amplifier are used as the differential inputs of the common mode feedback circuit M_{25} and M_{27}, so that the M_{25} and M_{27} operate in the saturation region. The principle is as follows: when the output voltage V_{op1} increases, that is, when the gate voltage of M_{25} increases, the gate voltage V_{bn} of M_{28} remains unchanged, the voltage at both ends of M_{28} increases, the bias current provided by M_{28} for the continuous-time common-mode feedback circuit (CT CMFB) increases, and the feedback output voltage V_1 decreases through the current mirror M_{22} image current; That is, when the gate voltage of M_{25} transistor is reduced, the gate voltage V_{bn} of M_{28} is unchanged, the voltage at both ends of M_{28} is decreased, the bias current provided by M_{28} for continuous time common mode feedback circuit (CT CMFB) is reduced, and the feedback output voltage V_1 is increased by the mirror current of M_{22}. V_{on1} is equally rational.

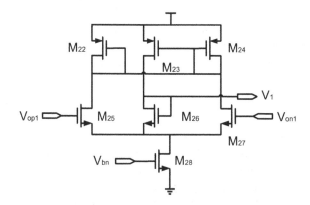

Fig. 5. Continuous time common mode feedback circuit

Because the first stage cascode structure makes the output voltage swing small, the use of Continuous time CMFB can appropriately increase the output swing. The load of the first stage operational amplifier is small. Although the use of short channel devices will produce a lot of noise, this signal is mainly a common mode signal.

3.4   Outer Common Mode Feedback Circuit

Figure 6 below is the outer common-mode feedback circuit of a fully telescopic differential operational amplifier, which is constructed as a switched capacitor common-mode feedback circuit, called SC CMFB for short. The stability and linearity of the outer common-mode feedback circuit are required to be high, so the circuit is used. The two sets of switched capacitors operate alternately under the control of the clock, with high linearity. Due to the high output swing, linearity is necessary, the output stage can drive large capacitors, common-mode feedback circuit will not have a significant impact on the amplifier.

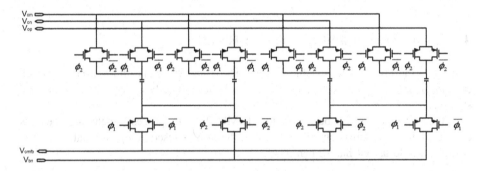

Fig. 6. Switched capacitor common mode feedback circuit

V_{cm} is a common-mode voltage, generally half of the supply voltage, that is, 1.25 V. V_{op} and V_{on} is the differential output of the secondary operational amplifier, V_{bn} is the bias voltage, V_{cmfb} is the output common-mode voltage of SC-CMFB, that is, the gate voltage of the secondary operational amplifier bias tube. ϕ_1, ϕ_2, $\overline{\phi_1}$ and $\overline{\phi_2}$ are the signals generated by the clock circuit, ϕ_1 and $\overline{\phi_1}$ are the clock signals which are not overlapping. The situation of ϕ_2 and $\overline{\phi_2}$ is the same as that of and. Each PMOS tube and NMOS tube is composed of 12 transmission gates respectively, and the clock signal controls the turn-on and turn-off of the transmission gate circuit to achieve common mode feedback.

Figure 7 is equivalent circuit diagram of switched capacitor common mode feedback circuit.

V_{op} and V_{on} are the differential outputs of two-stage operational amplifiers, C_7 and C_8 are the equivalent capacitors of SC-CMFB, C_9 is the equivalent power supply generated by capacitors. When the capacitance of C_9 is large, the stored charge capacity is large, which can be regarded as power supply. M_{19} and M_{21} are two op offset tubes. When $[(V_{op}+V_{on})/2] < V_{cm}$, V_{cm} remains unchanged, and equals to 1.25 V, C_9 as the

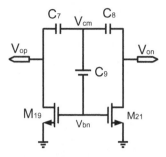

Fig. 7. Equivalent circuit diagram of switched capacitor common mode feedback circuit

equivalent constant voltage source also remains unchanged, then V_{bn} decreases and V_{op} increases. When $[(V_{op}+V_{on})/2] > V_{cm}$, V_{cm} remain unchanged and V_{bn} increase, V_{op} decreases and the feedback regulation is achieved, so that the gate voltage V_{cmfb} of the original secondary operational amplifier bias tube can always remain near V_{bn}.

4   Layout Design and Simulation Results

Therefore, the layout is reasonable with unified connections and through-holes, which contributes to the consistent parasitic effect of the two fully differential symmetrical structures.

The overall circuit is based on the TSMC 250 nm process, including the bias circuit, timing generation circuit and fully differential telescopic operational amplifier. And the whole layout has shown in Fig. 8.

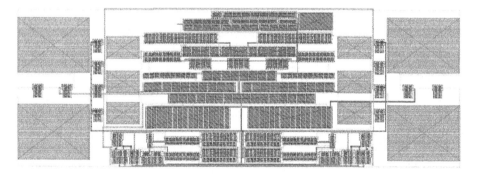

Fig. 8. Overall circuit layout

Figure 9 shows the value of gain, bandwidth and phase margin for the pre imitation case. When the supply voltage is 2.5 V, the gain is 67.7 dB, the bandwidth is 150.7 MHz, and the phase margin is 45°.

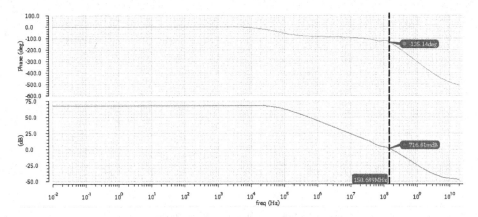

Fig. 9. Forward simulation results

Due to the limitations of the analog circuit design's octagon rule and integrated circuit design process, the gain, bandwidth and phase margin restrict each other. For example, increasing gain can lead to phase margin and bandwidth reduction. The simulation result shows that parameters have good results.

By calculating the circuit and verifying the simulation model, the W/L of MOS tube is determined. The following Table 1 is the list of MOS tube parameters. Since each transmission gate in SC-CMFB is of the same size, the PMOS and NMOS tubes that constitute the transmission gate are not listed in the Table 1. The W/L of the PMOS is 1.6/0.28 (μm) and the W/L of the NMOS is 0.72/0.26 (μm).

Table 1. Device parameters of the circuit.

	W/L (μm)		W/L (μm)		W/L (μm)
M_0	2/1	M_{10}	3/0.3	M_{20}	15/0.33
M_1	2/1	M_{11}	5/0.5	M_{21}	40/1
M_2	2/1	M_{12}	10/1	M_{22}	4/1
M_3	10/10	M_{13}	3/0.3	M_{23}	4/1
M_4	10/10	M_{14}	3/0.3	M_{24}	4/1
M_5	0.5/1	M_{15}	5/0.5	M_{25}	2/1
M_6	4/1	M_{16}	10/1	M_{26}	2/1
M_7	2/0.3	M_{17}	20/1	M_{27}	2/1
M_8	2/13	M_{18}	15/0.33	M_{28}	5.36/1
M_9	3/0.3	M_{19}	40/1		

Figure 10 shows the post imitated graph. From the graph, we can see that the gain is 62 dB, the bandwidth is 109.7 MHz, and the phase margin is 41°.

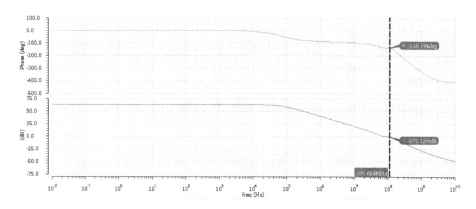

Fig. 10. Post imitated simulation results

Table 2 lists the parameters compared with literatures.

Table 2. The operational performance of this paper is compared with other literatures

Op amp	Process/nm	Gain/dB	Phase/(°)	Bandwidth/MHz
Literature [6]	40	51.3	57.8	201
Literature [7]	130	75	37	171.9
Literature [11]	350	51.94	44	26.1
This work	250	67.7	45	150.7

Acknowledgements. This work was supported by the Natural Science Foundation of China (No.61361011), the Natural Science Foundation of Guangxi (No. 2017GXNSFAA198363), the Basic Ability Enhancement Program for Young and Middle-aged Teachers of Guangxi.

References

1. Yong, L.: A 1 mW 71.5 dB SNDR 50 MS/s 13 bit fully differential ring amplifier based SAR-assisted pipeline ADC. IEEE J. Solid-State Circuits **50**(12), 2901–2911 (2015)
2. Wang, W.C.: A 118 dB PSRR 0.00067% (−103.5 dB) THD+N and 3.1 W fully differential class-D audio amplifier with PWM common mode control. IEEE J. Solid-State Circuits **51** (12), 2808–2818 (2016)
3. Khateb, F.: Low-voltage fully differential difference transconductance amplifier. IET Circuits Devices Syst. **12**(1), 73–81 (2018)
4. Saso, J.M.: Power-efficient class AB fully differential amplifier. Electron. Lett. **53**(19), 1298–1300 (2017)
5. Tian, Y.: Silicon carbide fully differential amplifier characterized up to 500 °C. IEEE Trans. Electron Devices **63**(6), 2242–2247 (2016)
6. Centurelli, F., Monsurrò, P.: A fully-differential class-AB OTA with CMRR improved by local feedback. In: European Conference on Circuit Theory and Design, pp. 1–4. IEEE (2017)

7. Wang, J., Bu, S.: An efficient frequency compensation scheme for CMFB loop in fully differential amplifiers. In: IEEE International Conference on Electron Devices and Solid-State Circuits, pp. 415–418. IEEE (2015)
8. Rahim, S.A.E.A., Azmi, I.M.: A CMOS single stage fully differential folded cascode amplifier employing gain boosting technique. In: International Symposium on Integrated Circuits, pp. 234–237. IEEE (2011)
9. Uhrmann, H., Zimmermann, H.: A fully differential operational amplifier for a low-pass filter in a DVB-H receiver. In: Mixed Design of Integrated Circuits & Systems, pp. 197–200. IEEE (2009)
10. Meysam, A.: High gain and high CMRR two-stage folded cascode OTA with nested miller compensation. J. Circ. Syst. Comput. **24**(04) (2015)
11. Arbet, D., Kovac, M.: High dynamic range and low distortion fully differential difference amplifier in CMOS. In: Radioelektronika, pp. 114–117. IEEE (2015)
12. Harb, A.: A rail-to-rail full clock fully differential rectifier and sample-and-hold amplifier. In: IEEE International Symposium on Circuits and Systems, pp. 1571–1574. IEEE (2010)
13. Mahmoud, S.A.: Low voltage fully differential CMOS current feedback operational amplifier. In: Circuits and Systems 2004, vol. 1, pp. 49–52. IEEE (2004)
14. Nerurkar, S.B., Abed, K.H.: CMOS fully differential operational transconductance amplifier design for delta-sigma modulators. In: Southeastcon, pp. 52–57. IEEE (2008)

Parallel Concatenated Network with Cross-layer Connections for Image Recognition

Peng Li, Pinqun Jiang$^{(\boxtimes)}$, Shangyou Zeng, and Rui Fan

College of Electronic Engineering,
Guangxi Normal University, Guilin 541004, China
gxsd_roc@163.com, pqjiang@163.com

Abstract. The traditional convolutional neural networks are heavy with millions of parameters and the classification accuracy is not high. To address this issue, we propose a novel model called parallel concatenated convolutional neural network with cross-layer connections. The model mainly includes parallel processing and concatenate operation. In parallel processing, the diversity of features is increased by using different sizes of convolution kernels. The parallel outputs are integrated together by concatenate operation. Meanwhile, an improved cross-layer connection structure is also added to the model. At the experimental stage, the model was tested on the Caltech-256 and Food-101 datasets, the experiment results indicate that the constructed PCNet (without cross-layer connections) increases the recognition accuracy by 2.54% and 7.31% compared to AlexNet, and the proposed RPCNet (with cross-layer connections) is improved by 6.12% and 12.28% compared to AlexNet.

Keywords: Convolution neural network · Parallel processing ·
Cross-layer connections · Image classification

1 Introduction

With the rapid development of computer hardware (such as GPU), feature extraction based on deep learning [1] has attracted wide attention of researchers, and has made a great breakthrough in the field of image recognition [2]. Convolutional neural network (CNN) extracts feature vectors from input images by alternating transformation of multiple convolution layers and pooling layers, and has translation and scale invariance to a certain extent. The depth of network often determines the classification accuracy of the model. If the layers of convolution neural network are shallow, it may not be able to extract characteristic vectors, which lead to poor performance. However, with the deepening of network layers, the network parameters and overall complexity will increase, which may lead to over-fitting problem or difficult to converge.

The earliest CNN was LeNet5 [3] model proposed by LeCun et al. in 1998. Because of the shallow layers of network, the number of target classes is small and the background is single, the classification accuracy of network is not high when recognizing the images with many other classes and complex background. Krizhevsky et al. designed an AlexNet [4] network to win the 2012LSVRC championship with more than 10% accuracy ahead

© Springer Nature Switzerland AG 2019
X. Liu et al. (Eds.): ICSOC 2018 Workshops, LNCS 11434, pp. 80–88, 2019.
https://doi.org/10.1007/978-3-030-17642-6_7

of the second place. It was a great success of deep learning in image classification. In [5], the Network in Network proposed by Lin Min first used a 1×1 convolution kernel, and the fully connection layer is replaced by global pooling. In [6], Szegedy et al. used GoogleNet to classify images, proposed the Inception module of parallel convolution, and achieved the first result of ILSVRC classification accuracy. However, the network size is huge, not only requires high hardware equipment, but also converges slowly. Inspired by the Network in Network, the Google team proposed computational bottle-necks and applied the 1×1 convolution kernel to the Inception module, resulting in several improved Inception models. In [7], He et al. proposed deep residual networks (ResNet), which can greatly improve performance by learning residual, and won the championship in the ILSVRC competition in 2015. More complex networks, such as VGGNet [8], DenseNet [9], and MobileNet [10], the huge amount of parameters increase the complexity of the network and require higher memory computing power of the hardware. For the general hardware researchers, this can only be tradeoff between sac-rificing accuracy and adapting to the hardware environment. Therefore, we try to improve the AlexNet network structure, improve the training efficiency and achieve better clas-sification accuracy under the current hardware equipment.

In this paper, when training the original AlexNet network, the memory usage is very high, the training is slow, and the accuracy of the experiment is difficult to guarantee. We first constructed a parallel concatenate structure to replace the convo-lution kernel of AlexNet, called PCNet. Then, we try to add an improved cross-layer connection structure, called RPCNet. Experiments are presented on publicly datasets: Caltech-256 and Food-101. In comparison, RPCNet perform better than some of the existing methods. We present the details of approaches in Sect. 2 and the experimental process in Sect. 3. Finally, we make a conclusion in Sect. 4.

2 Method

2.1 Analysis of AlexNet Network and Basic Improvement

Similar convolution kernels of 5×5 and 3×3 are used in VGGNet and GoogLeNet, and the recognition accuracy is better. Multiple small-scale convolution kernels are more nonlinear than large-scale convolution kernels. We can replace the 11×11 convolution kernels in AlexNet with small-scale convolution kernels (7×7 and 5×5 kernels).

Although there are only three layers in the full-connection layer, the parameters account for about 80% of the total parameters. The parameters of the full-connection layer directly affect the overall efficiency. Some excellent network models, such as ResNet and GoogLeNet, are pooled by global average pool layer. Reducing the full-connection layer can reduce the network parameters without greatly weakening the network performance.

For the first time, LRN layer was used in AlexNet, but in Wu Enda's [11] view, LRN can't play a big role. Therefore, we use BN [12] layer instead of the original LRN layer, the advantage of adding BN layer is to reduce the dependence on initialization, make gradient transfer more smoothly, and to a certain extent prevent the network from over fitting. But adding BN layer will increase the amount of computation and make the network training relatively slow. The calculation method of the BN layer can be obtained by formula 1:

$$
\begin{cases}
\mu_B \longleftarrow \frac{1}{m} \sum_{k=1}^{m} x_k \\
\sigma_B^2 \longleftarrow \frac{1}{m} \sum_{k=1}^{m} (x_k - \mu_B)^2 \\
\hat{x}_k \longleftarrow \frac{x_k - \mu_B}{\sqrt{\sigma_B^2 + \varepsilon}} \\
y_k \longleftarrow \gamma \hat{x}_k + \beta \equiv BN_{\gamma,\beta}(x_k)
\end{cases}
\tag{1}
$$

2.2 Parallel Concatenated Structure

Figure 1(a) gives a schematic diagram of traditional parallel concatenated convolution, and an improved convolution structure is shown in Fig. 1(b).

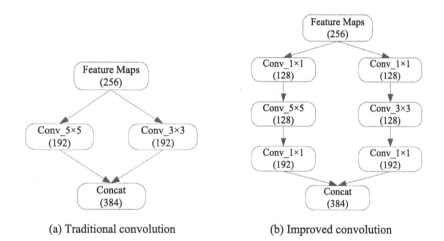

(a) Traditional convolution   (b) Improved convolution

Fig. 1. Parallel concatenated convolution.

It can be seen that the improved method is to reduce the dimension with 1×1 convolution kernel, and then to convolute in parallel with 5×5 and 3×3 convolution kernel. In order to ensure the number of original output feature maps, the 1×1 convolution kernel is used to increase the dimension, and finally the parallel outputs are concatenated. Parameters in Fig. 1(a) P = $256 \times 5 \times 5 \times 192 + 256 \times 3 \times 3 \times 192$ = 1671168. In Fig. 1(b) P = $256 \times 1 \times 1 \times 128 + 128 \times 5 \times 5 \times 128 + 128 \times 1 \times 1 \times 192 + 256 \times 1 \times 1 \times 128 + 128 \times 3 \times 3 \times 128 + 128 \times 1 \times 1 \times 192 = 671744$. In Fig. 1(b), the improved method reduces parameters and facilitates feature extraction.

2.3   Parallel Concatenated Structure with Cross-layer Connections

CNN with different architectures can be constructed through residual learning modules. For example, in literature [13], the Inception-ResNet convolutional neural network is built by combining residual learning module with Inception model. The network has achieved excellent performance in the classification of ImageNet dataset.

Based on traditional residual learning [7] structure, a new $h(x)$ function is constructed by using linear transformation to make full use of the information learned from the lower-level layers, as shown in Fig. 2(a). The output y of module is defined as Eq. (2):

$$y = F(x, W_i) + h(x) \qquad (2)$$

As described, we continue to improve the Fig. 1(b) by using the structure of Fig. 2 (a), the improved parallel concatenated structure with cross-layer connections can be obtained as shown in Fig. 2(b).

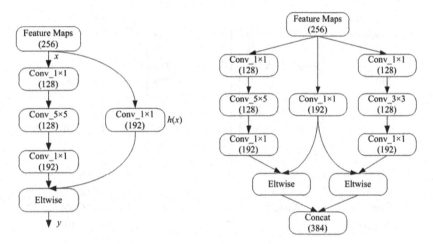

(a) Cross-layer connection   (b) Improved structure with cross-layer connections

Fig. 2. Parallel concatenated structure with cross-layer connections.

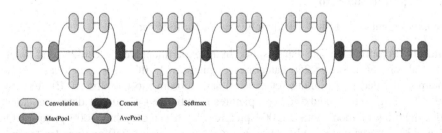

Fig. 3. Proposed parallel concatenated network with cross-layer connections (RPCNet).

Simulating the structure of AlexNet, we replace the original 11×11 convolution kernel with two small size convolution kernels, 7×7 and 5×5, stacking multiple Fig. 2(b) structures, and replace the original full-connected layer with an average pool layer. Finally, proposed the parallel concatenated convolutional neural network with cross-layer connections structure as shown in Fig. 3, and the basic network structure settings as shown in Table 1.

Table 1. Basic network structure parameters.

Layer name	Filter size/stride/pad/number		Output size
Input			$227 \times 227 \times 3$
Conv1	$7 \times 7/2/0/96$		$111 \times 111 \times 96$
Conv2	$5 \times 5/2/1/96$		$55 \times 55 \times 96$
Maxpool2	$3 \times 3/2$		$27 \times 27 \times 96$
Module3	$\begin{bmatrix} 1 \times 1/1/0/96 \\ 5 \times 5/1/2/96 \\ 1 \times 1/1/0/128 \end{bmatrix}$	$\begin{bmatrix} 1 \times 1/1/0/96 \\ 3 \times 3/1/1/96 \\ 1 \times 1/1/0/128 \end{bmatrix}$	$27 \times 27 \times 256$
Maxpool3	$3 \times 3/2$		$13 \times 13 \times 256$
Module4	$\begin{bmatrix} 1 \times 1/1/0/128 \\ 5 \times 5/1/2/128 \\ 1 \times 1/1/0/192 \end{bmatrix}$	$\begin{bmatrix} 1 \times 1/1/0/128 \\ 3 \times 3/1/1/128 \\ 1 \times 1/1/0/192 \end{bmatrix}$	$13 \times 13 \times 384$
Module5	$\begin{bmatrix} 1 \times 1/1/0/128 \\ 5 \times 5/1/2/128 \\ 1 \times 1/1/0/192 \end{bmatrix}$	$\begin{bmatrix} 1 \times 1/1/0/128 \\ 3 \times 3/1/1/128 \\ 1 \times 1/1/0/192 \end{bmatrix}$	$13 \times 13 \times 384$
Module6	$\begin{bmatrix} 1 \times 1/1/0/96 \\ 5 \times 5/1/2/96 \\ 1 \times 1/1/0/128 \end{bmatrix}$	$\begin{bmatrix} 1 \times 1/1/0/96 \\ 3 \times 3/1/1/96 \\ 1 \times 1/1/0/128 \end{bmatrix}$	$13 \times 13 \times 256$
Maxpool6	$3 \times 3/2$		$6 \times 6 \times 256$
Conv7	$3 \times 3/1/1/512$		$6 \times 6 \times 512$
Conv8	$1 \times 1/1/0/256/101$		$6 \times 6 \times 256/101$
Avgpool8	$6 \times 6/1$		$1 \times 1 \times 256/101$

3 Experiment

3.1 Experimental Setup

The experiment is as follows. It mainly consists of four parts.

Datasets Introduction: The datasets used in the experiment are Caltech-256 and Food-101. Caltech-256 contains 256 categories of pictures. In this paper, each category is randomly divided into training set and test set according to the ratio of 4:1. Finally, 23919 training pictures and 5862 test pictures are obtained. Food-101 dataset contains 101 categories of food, with 101000 pictures. Each category has 1000 pictures. Of these, 750 pictures were used for training and the remaining 250 pictures for testing. A total of 75750 training pictures and 25250 test pictures were obtained.

Image Preprocessing: This process mainly includes scale normalization, de mean and data-augmentation. Firstly, the image sizes of the two datasets are scaled to 256×256, and the mean values are removed before training. Finally, the image is scaled to 227×227 from the upper left corner, the upper right corner, the lower left corner, the lower right corner and the middle of the two datasets by using the image augmentation technique. The advantage of this approach is that the data set is 10 times as large as the original one, to a certain extent preventing over-fitting and increasing generalization capabilities.

Experimental Environment: All the network structures are deployed with Caffe [14] framework. The experimental results of each model are accomplished on i7-6700 K quad-core CPU, Ubuntu 14.04 operating system, 32 GB memory and NVIDIA-GTX 1070 GPU.

Neural Network Training: The basic settings of learning parameters are shown in Table 2.

Table 2. Caffe learning parameters setting.

Parameters	Caltech-256	Food-101
Test batch_size	50	50
base_lr	0.005	0.005
gamma	0.1	0.1
momentum	0.9	0.9
weight_decay	0.004	0.004
lr_policy	multistep	multistep
max_iteration	60000	150000

3.2 Experimental Results

It mainly compares the performances of classical AlexNet, PCNet (without cross-layer connections) and RPCNet (with cross-layer connections). Tables 3 and 4 show the performance of the models on Caltech-256 and Food-101 datasets respectively.

As shown in Table 3, the performances of PCNet and RPCNet are superior to traditional ALexNet in classification accuracy of Caltech-256. It is worth noting that if the cross-layer connections are added to PCNet, the recognition accuracy will be increased by 3.58%. In other words, RPCNet achieved the best performance 60.41%.

Table 3. Performance comparison on Caltech-256.

Model	Parameters(M)	Accuracy(%)
AlexNet + BN	59.33	54.29
PCNet	3.71	56.83
RPCNet	3.90	60.41

Table 4 summarized the experimental results obtained on the Food-101. The results are similar to Table 3. RPCNet got the best result 72.25% compared with other network in this paper. Figures 4 and 5 show the accuracy curves of each model on Caltech-256 and Food-101 datasets respectively.

Table 4. Performance comparison on Food-101.

Model	Parameters(M)	Accuracy(%)
AlexNet + BN	58.70	59.97
PCNet	3.63	67.28
RPCNet	3.82	72.25

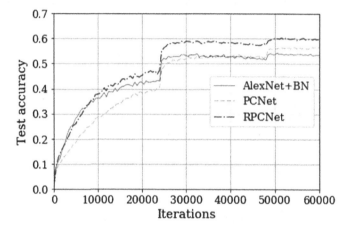

Fig. 4. Accuracy of different network classifications on Caltech-256.

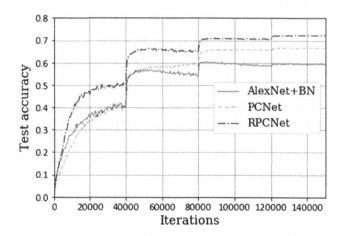

Fig. 5. Accuracy of different network classifications on Food-101.

To sum up the above, the RPCNet network proposed in this paper, not only improves the recognition rate by 6.12% and 12.28% compared with AlexNet, but also reduces the network parameters ten times as much as AlexNet, and realizing the lightweight of the network. RPCNet has the following characteristics:

(1) Using parallel concatenate module, more image features can be extracted than a single channel. By using 1×1 convolution kernel reasonably, the number of output feature maps of convolution layer can be controlled and the network parameters can be reduced.

(2) Adding cross-layer connections structure in parallel concatenate module can improve the classification accuracy to a certain extent. In addition, due to the increase of the depth and width of the RPCnet network, the training time will also lengthen.

At last, the RPCNet network proposed in this paper is compared with other methods on the Food-101 dataset as shown in Table 5. Our method is superior to some existing methods.

Table 5. Classification rates on Food-101.

Method	Classification accuracy (%)
RFDC [2]	50.76
Neural Networks [15]	56.40
PCNet	**67.28**
Resnet18 [15]	67.59
DCNNFOOD [16]	70.41
EnsembleNet [17]	72.12
RPCNet	**72.25**

4 Conclusion

In this paper, a parallel concatenated convolutional neural network with cross-layer connections (RPCNet) is proposed, which uses two kinds of convolution kernels to extract features from feature maps to increase the diversity of feature extraction. At the same time, the convolution kernel of 1×1 is used to optimize the parameters, which increases the depth and width of the network. At the experimental stage, the network was tested on the Caltech-256 and Food-101 datasets, the experiment results indicate that the constructed PCNet increases the recognition accuracy by 2.54% and 7.31% compared to AlexNet, and the proposed RPCNet is improved by 6.12% and 12.28% compared to AlexNet. It is proved that the method proposed in this paper can effectively improve the network performance and improve the accuracy of image classification. Meanwhile, this method is superior to some existing methods. The next work is to continue to improve the network, and to test and optimize on a larger scale of data sets to analyze the performance of the network, to further improve network performance.

Acknowledgments. Authors acknowledge support of the National Natural Science Foundation of China (Grant Nos. 11465004). Authors are also thankful to the anonymous reviewers whose constructive suggestions helped improve and clarify this manuscript.

References

1. Deng, L., Yu, D.: Deep learning: methods and applications. Found. Trends Signal Process. **7**(3), 197–387 (2014)
2. Bossard, L., Guillaumin, M., Van Gool, L.: Food-101 – Mining Discriminative Components with Random Forests. In: Fleet, D., Pajdla, T., Schiele, B., Tuytelaars, T. (eds.) ECCV 2014. LNCS, vol. 8694, pp. 446–461. Springer, Cham (2014). https://doi.org/10.1007/978-3-319-10599-4_29
3. LeCun, Y., Bottou, L., Bengio, Y., Haffner, P.: Gradient-based learning applied to document recognition. Proce. IEEE **86**(11), 2278–2324 (1998)
4. Krizhevsky, A., Sutskever, I., Hinton, G.: Imagenet classification with deep convolutional neural networks. In: NIPS, pp. 1097–1105 (2012)
5. Lin, M., Chen, Q., Yan, S.: Network in network. arXiv preprint (2013) arXiv:1312.4400
6. Szegedy, C., Liu, W., Jia, Y., et al.: Going deeper with convolutions. In: Proceedings of the IEEE Conference on Computer Vision and Pattern Recognition, pp. 1–9 (2015)
7. He, K., Zhang, X., Ren, S., et al.: Deep residual learning for image recognition. In: Proceedings of the IEEE Conference on Computer Vision and Pattern Recognition, pp. 770–778 (2016)
8. Simonyan, K., Zisserman, A.: Very deep convolutional networks for large-scale image recognition. arXiv preprint (2014). arXiv:1409.1556
9. Huang, G., Liu, Z., Maaten, L.V.D., et al.: Densely connected convolutional networks. In: 2017 IEEE Conference on Computer Vision and Pattern Recognition (CVPR), pp. 2261–2269. IEEE (2017)
10. Howard, A.G., Zhu, M., Chen, B., et al.: Mobilenets: efficient convolutional neural networks for mobile vision applications. arXiv preprint (2014). arXiv:1704.04861
11. Coates, A., Ng, A., Lee, H.: An analysis of single-layer networks in unsupervised feature learning. In: Proceedings of the Fourteenth International Conference on Artificial Intelligence and Statistics, pp. 215–223 (2011)
12. Ioffe, S., Szegedy, C.: Batch normalization: accelerating deep network training by reducing internal covariate shift. arXiv preprint (2015). arXiv:1502.03167
13. Szegedy, C., Ioffe, S., Vanhoucke, V., et al.: Inception-v4, inception-resnet and the impact of residual connections on learning. In: 31st AAAI Conference on Artificial Intelligence, pp. 4278–4284. AAAI Press, San Francisco (2017)
14. Jia, Y., Shelhamer, E., Donahue, J., et al.: Caffe: convolutional architecture for fast feature embedding. In: Proceedings of the 22nd ACM international conference on Multimedia, pp. 675–678. ACM (2014)
15. Attokaren, D.J., Fernandes, I.G., Sriram, A., et al.: Food classification from images using convolutional neural networks. In: TENCON 2017 IEEE Region 10 Conference, pp. 2801–2806. IEEE (2017)
16. Yanai, K., Kawano, Y.: Food image recognition using deep convolutional network with pre-training and fine-tuning. In: 2015 IEEE International Conference on Multimedia & Expo Workshops (ICMEW), pp. 1–6. IEEE (2015)
17. Pandey, P., Deepthi, A., Mandal, B., et al.: FoodNet: recognizing foods using ensemble of deep networks. IEEE Signal Process. Lett. **24**(12), 1758–1762 (2017)

Application of System Calls in Abnormal User Behavioral Detection in Social Networks

Shizhen Zhang, Frank Jiang[(✉)], and Min Qin

Guangxi Normal University, Guilin 541004, China
fjiang@gxnu.edu.cn

Abstract. Abnormal user detection is one of the key issues in online social network security research. Attackers spread advertising and other malicious messages through stolen accounts, and malicious actions seriously threaten the information security of normal users with the credit system of social networks. For this reason, in the literature, there are a considerable amount of research work which detect abnormal accounts in social networks, however, these efforts ignore the problem of the seamless integration of machine learning with human behaviour-based analysis. This paper reviews the main achievements of abnormal account detection in online social networks in recent years from three aspects: behavioral characteristics, content-based, graph-based, and proposes a new social network abnormal user detection method based on system calls in computer's kernel. Using enumeration sequence and hidden semi-Markov method, a hierarchical model of anomaly user detection in social networks is established.

Keywords: Coupled Behavior Analysis ·
Coupled hidden Semi-Markov model · Abnormal behavior detection ·
System call

1 Introduction

While online social networks bring people various conveniences and meet people's needs, the massive number of users also attracts attackers [1–3] to gain huge profits by illegal means. Attackers publish advertisements, pornography, and other malicious information on social networking sites by creating many fake accounts and embezzling normal user accounts [4, 5]. For example, Twitter adds 3 million pieces of spam every day [6]. About 8.7% of Facebook's accounts are fake accounts created by attackers. These fake accounts and stolen normal accounts are collectively referred to as abnormal accounts. Because of the trust relationship between social network users, malicious information is more dangerous than malicious information contained in traditional spam. The study found that the click-through rate of spam links in Twitter was two orders higher than the link click rate [7] in spam. These malicious behaviors pose a serious threat to the normal user's private information, account security, and user experience. At the same time, attackers obtain benefits by performing malicious actions, adding friends through abnormal accounts. Aiming at the threats posed by abnormal accounts in online social networks, a large number of detection schemes have been proposed by academics and industry. According to the different core algorithms used in these schemes, these programs are mainly divided into three categories.

© Springer Nature Switzerland AG 2019
X. Liu et al. (Eds.): ICSOC 2018 Workshops, LNCS 11434, pp. 89–101, 2019.
https://doi.org/10.1007/978-3-030-17642-6_8

1.1   Detection Scheme Based on Behavior Characteristics

Abnormal accounts can increase the frequency of the release of news or send a large number of friend requests in a short time to maximize the benefits. Therefore, there are differences in some behavioral characteristics between abnormal account and normal account. Some works have detected anomalies according to the different behaviors between abnormal and normal accounts. Amleshwaram et al. [8] proposed 15 features of message content to detect abnormal accounts in Twitter, and then used the k-means algorithm to cluster these abnormal accounts to detect Spam Campaigns. Stringhini et al. [9] detected the Spam accounts on Facebook and Twitter using the friend relationship feature and the message content feature, and then detected the Spam Campaign by aggregating the Spam accounts based on the final address of the URL published by the account. Yang et al. [10] used the features of the friend relationship such as the number of friend requests and the number of friend requests accepted to detect the Sybil account in RenRen networks. The detection method based on behavior characteristics is fast, but the sample data need to be pre-trained. At the same time, it requires a sample of normal account and abnormal account number. When the number of features is relatively large, the training time under the line is longer.

The detection scheme based on behavior characteristics can detect abnormal behavior only after the occurrence of abnormal behaviors. Therefore, it is impossible to detect malicious behavior in real time.

1.2   Content-Based Detection Scheme

The content-based detection scheme uses the difference between the content posted by the abnormal account and the content published by the normal account. Therefore, the focus of the detection is to determine whether the message published by the user is a malicious message. Gao et al. [11] clustered the messages published by the Facebook users, namely found a group that published a large number of identical or similar messages, and then judged whether the messages published by the users in these groups were malicious through a blacklist. If the message is malicious, then these accounts are considered as the Spam Campaign account. The content-based detection scheme can determine whether a message is malicious when a user publishes a message, and is more timely than the detection method based on behavior characteristics. However, when the data set is large, the recognition efficiency of the content-based detection scheme will decrease.

1.3   Graph-Based Detection Scheme

The essence of the graph-based detection scheme is to use a different structures or connections between the abnormal accounts and the normal ones in the graph formed by social relationships, and then use the graph mining related algorithm to find the specific abnormal structures or abnormal nodes in the graph. SybilGuard [12] calculates the transfer path of each node through the modified random walk algorithm, and determines whether it is a normal node according to whether the path of the node intersects the path of a given normal node. Hung et al. [5] believe that the Sybil detection scheme based on the random walk algorithm assumptions for the network structure and the attack model does not hold in the real network. Based on Andersen, Chung, and Lang's community discovery algorithm [6] proposed an ACL detection scheme to transform the Sybil detection scheme from normal nodes and Sybil nodes to determine the normal probability of other nodes in the community where the normal node is located, and to provide mathematical proofs [6], and experimental results show that ACL detection is better than Sybil-Limit.

Compared with behavior-based or content-based detection schemes, graph-based detection schemes do not require training of samples in advance, but the simple use of graph structure to detect abnormal accounts has a large false positive rate and can only detect abnormalities that can make up the graph structure. At the same time, some graph-based detection schemes need to be based on certain assumptions. However, due to the complexity of social networks in real life, abnormal account numbers in different social networks have different characteristics. Therefore, it is necessary to strictly verify the hypothesis of the detection scheme when applying a graph-based detection scheme.

The existing abnormal user analysis methods of social networks are based on the difference in characteristics between normal users and abnormal users. Therefore, feature selection is particularly important in the detection of abnormal users in social networks. However, for different social platforms, the valuable features for analyzing social networks may vary, which requires a specific analysis of each social software. This paper draws lessons from the method of anomaly intrusion detection based on system calls, and uses computer system calls to detect anomalous users on Sina Weibo. In a social network, mobile phones, computers, and other electronic devices are carriers for attackers to perform abnormal operations. Each operation request of a social network user can find a mapping about it in the system call of the machine. Therefore, the system call serves as a medium for connecting the user operation request and the user command executed by the computer. We mode and analyze the system call sequence of the machine and use the abnormal mode of the system call as an indicator for judging whether the user has an abnormal operation request. The advantage of this method is that it has good mobility and is suitable for various social platforms.

2 Methodology

2.1 Coupled Behavior Analysis Problem

We classify Coupled Behavior as intra-coupling and inter-coupling [13]. Suppose there are I social network user, a user i performed mi actions, that is to say, issued MI system call requests to the computer, namely $\{b_{i1}, b_{i2}, \ldots, b_{im_i}\}$. Therefore, we get the behavioral characteristics matrix as follows:

$$FM(b) = \begin{bmatrix} b_{11} & b_{12} & \cdots & b_{1m_{max}} \\ b_{21} & b_{22} & \cdots & b_{2m_{max}} \\ \vdots & \vdots & \ddots & \vdots \\ b_{n1} & b_{n2} & \cdots & b_{nm_{max}} \end{bmatrix} \tag{1}$$

Where $m_{max} = \max\{m_1, m_2, \ldots, m_i\}$, $\{b_{ij}|m_i < m_{max}\}$ for each set of behaviors, the corresponding element $b_{i,j}$ is recognized as $(/)$ when $m_i < m < m_{max}$. Further, each (i, j) element of this matrix FM(b) is actually a row vector, expressed as $\overrightarrow{b}_{ij} = ([q_{ij}]_1, [q_{ij}]_2, \ldots, [q_{ij}]_K)$, where $[p_{ij}]_k (1 < k < K)$ is the kth property of the behavior b_{ij}.

Definition: Relationship $\Re = <\varepsilon(\cdot), \eta(\cdot)>$ is a tuple which reveals complex interactions within an user's behaviors (named intra-coupled behaviors, represented by function $\varepsilon(\cdot)$ and that between multiple behaviors of different users (inter-coupled behaviors by relationship function $\eta(\cdot)$.

The intra-coupling is the relationship within one row of the above matrix, while how the behaviors interact is embodied among the columns of FM(b), indicated as inter-coupling.

Specifically, user i's behavior bij are intra-coupled with other behaviors of the same user in terms of the corresponding function $\varepsilon_p^i(\cdot)(1 < j \le m_i, p \ne j)$ and inter-coupled with other actors' behaviors in terms of the corresponding function $\eta_p^i(\cdot)(1 < p \le I, p \ne i)$, with non-determinism.

Coupled behaviors b refer to behaviors $b_{i_1 j_1}$ and $b_{i_2 j_2}$ that are coupled in terms of the relationship $f(\varepsilon_{j_1 j_2}^{i_1 i_2}(\cdot))((i_1 = i_2) \wedge (j_1 \ne j_2))$ or $f(\eta_{j_1 j_2}^{i_1 i_2}(\cdot))((i_1 \ne i_2) \wedge (j_1 \ne j_2))$, where $(1 \le i_1, i_2 \le I) \wedge (1 \le j_1, j_2 \le m_{max})$.

Theorem 1 (Coupled Behavior Analysis (CBA)): The analysis of coupled behavior is to build the objective function g(·) under the condition that behaviors are coupled with each other by coupling function $f(\cdot)$, and satisfy the following conditions:

$$f(\cdot) := f(\varepsilon(\cdot), \eta(\cdot)).$$
$$g(\cdot) \,|\, (f(\cdot) \ge f_0) \ge g_0. \tag{2}$$

2.2 Hidden Semi-Markov Model (HSMM)

The hidden Semi-Markov model (HSMM) is an extension of Hidden Markov Model. The underlying process is a semi-Markov chain, which has a variable sojourn time at each state. During the period, there are a sequence of observations while in the same state. The HSMM has been successfully applied in many areas.

We consider a classical HSMM model with state space $N = \{1, 2, \ldots, S\}$ and sojourn time set $\delta = \{1, 2, \ldots, L\}$, which can be described as follows:

$$\lambda = \{a_{(i,l')(j,l)}, b_{j,l}(u_{r_1:r_l}), \pi_{i,l}\} \tag{3}$$

where $a_{(i,l')(j,l)}, i, j \in N, l, l' \in \delta$ denotes the state transition probability that the process transits to next state j and the sojourn time at this state is t, when the state is i and the sojourn time at state i is t', that is,

$$a_{(i,l')(j,t)} := P\{N_{[t+1:t+l]} = j | N_{[t-l'+1:t]} = i\} \tag{4}$$

which is independent to time t. $b_{j,d}(u_{r_1:r_l})$ is the observation probability that d observations $u_{r_1:r_l}$ occur during the sojourn time l of state j, which can be denoted by

$$b_{j,d}(u_{r_1:r_l}) := P\{O_{[t+1:t+l]} = u_{r_1:r_l} | N_{[t+1:t+l]} = j\}; \tag{5}$$

$\pi_{i,l}$ denotes the initial distribution that the process starts from state i with sojourn time l, that is,

$$\pi_{i,l} = P\{N_{[t-l+1:t]} = i\}, t \leq 0, l \in \delta. \tag{6}$$

Define the forward variable and the backward variable:

$$\alpha_t(j, l) = P\{N_{[t-l+1:t]} = j, O_{1:t} | \lambda\} \tag{7}$$

$$\beta_t(j, l) = P\{O_{t+1:T} | N_{[t-l+1:t]} = j, \lambda\} \tag{8}$$

Similar to deriving the formulas for the HMM, it is easy to obtain the forward-backward algorithm for a general HSMM:

$$\partial_t(j, l) = \sum_{i \in N/\{j\}} \sum_{l' \in \delta} \partial_{t-l}(i, l') a_{(i,l')(j,l)} b_{j,l}(O_{t-l+1:t}) \tag{9}$$

for $t > 0, l \in \delta, j \in N$ with an initial condition $\partial_0(j, l) = \pi_{j,l}, \partial_\tau(j, l) = 0, \tau < 0$ and

$$\beta_t(j, l) = \sum_{i \in N/\{j\}} \sum_{l' \in \delta} a_{(j,l)(i,l')} b_{i,l'}(O_{t+1:t+l'}) \beta_{t+l'}(i, l') \tag{10}$$

for t < T with an initial condition $\beta_T(j, l) = 1, \beta_\tau(j, l) = 0, \tau > T$.

The probability that state j started at t − l + 1 and ends at t, with sojourn time d and partial observed sequence is $O_{1:T}$ can be computed by

$$\gamma_t(j, l) := P\{S_{[t-l+1:t]} = j, O_{1:T} | \lambda\} = \partial_t(j, l) \beta_t(j, l) \tag{11}$$

2.3   Social Network Abnormal User Detection Based on System Call Analysis

Abnormal intrusion detection based on system call analysis can be divided into two phases. The first phase is the training phase which scanning the normal behavior trace and building a normal behavior pattern database based on the system call sequence; the second phase is the detection phase which scanning the new trace that may contain abnormal behavior, and looking for patterns that not appear in the normal behavior pattern database to detect if there are abnormal behaviors.

This paper proposes a new method which applies computer system calls to detect abnormal users and analysis their coupling relationships in social networks. Compared with traditional methods based on network structure, content, and user behavior characteristics, the method proposed in this paper first uses the mapping of social network user operation requests on the machine behavior for sequence modeling. The system call is used as a medium to analyze whether a social network user has an abnormal operation and the coupling relationship of the user behaviors are considered. This is a new attempt in the field of social network user behavior analysis. The abnormal user detection process based on system calls analysis is shown in Fig. 1.

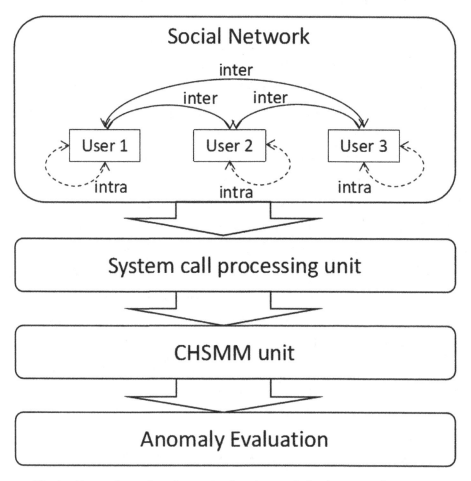

Fig. 1. Abnormal user detection process based on analysis of system call sequences

3   CHSMM-Based Abnormal Coupled User Behavior Analysis in Social Networks

3.1   Data Preprocessing

Once we collected the sequence of system calls from the running privilege process the next step to be data preprocessing. Collected system call information are raw data type, applying some preprocessing techniques on raw information and change the data set into processing dataset. On the original data, we only extract the time and symbols of the system call. The parameters and return values are not considered. A partial system calls of a normal user at a certain moment are shown in Fig. 2. And the system call symbols at each time of user i(i = 1, 2, ···,K) are extracted to form the sequence S_i^t. This sequence is a mapping of a social network user's operation request at a certain moment on the computer. In the test process, we rely on the analysis of sequence S_i^t to determine whether the user has abnormal behavior at a certain moment. Because each sequence of St is very long, in order to facilitate the study, whether in the training phase or in the testing phase, we use the window of length r to divide each St into N short equidistantly sequences: $S(t) = \{s_t^1, s_t^2, s_t^3, \ldots s_t^N\}$. All these system call names are replaced by unique number which reduced the complexity of data. For example, 6 is open, 7 is close, 72 is mmap and so on. So we can access them easily and format them to sequence of numbers. Once we build the preprocessed data base from raw data we can easily extract the normal behavior rule from these data set. After finishing this step, missing system call numbers are replaced with −1 and stored in the data base.

18:19:53 execve	18:19:53 open
18:19:53 open	18:19:53 old_mmap
18:19:53 open	18:19:53 close
18:19:53 old_mmap	18:19:53 open
18:19:53 close	18:19:53 fstat
18:19:53 open	18:19:53 read
18:19:53 fstat	18:19:53 old_mmap
18:19:53 read	18:19:53 mprotect
18:19:53 old_mmap	18:19:53 old_mmap
18:19:53 mprotect	18:19:53 old_mmap
18:19:53 old_mmap	18:19:53 execve
18:19:53 execve	18:19:53 open
18:19:53 open	18:19:53 old_mmap
18:19:53 open	18:19:53 close

Fig. 2. Partial system call at a certain time for a normal user

3.2 The System Framework

A CHSMM based system has been built for detecting abnormal group-based behaviors of social network users. The CHSMM captures and models a group of users' system call sequences and their relationships following Data Structure:

$$\frac{User - Operation}{Attributes} \tag{12}$$

Sequences at 'Time' moment are constructed as per

$$\left\{ \frac{User - Operation}{Time_i - SCS_i} \longrightarrow \rho \frac{User - Operation}{Time_j - SCS_j} \right\}_{i,j=1}^{I,J} \tag{13}$$

where SCS represents System call sequence at 'Time' moment, Following this structure, the coupled trading behaviors in Table 1 are converted into the sequences presented in Fig. 3.

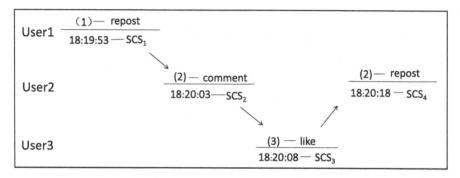

Fig. 3. Behavior sequences - Data Structure

The system of CHSMM based abnormal coupled behavior detection is illustrated in Fig. 4. It consists of two key components: Sequence Extractor, CHSMM Detector. Its working process is as follows. During the training period, only 'normal' system call sequences are fed into the Sequence Extractor and converted into K sequences by following Data Structure. Such sequences are fed into the CHSMM, which learns the relationship and dynamics of the sequential data. Since the CHSMM is trained on 'normal' data, it can fit the 'normal' data very well but not the abnormal sequences.

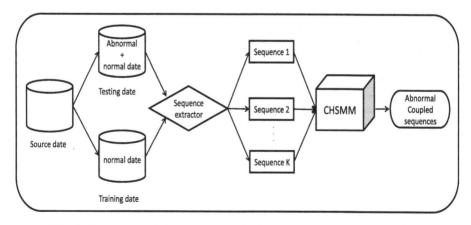

Fig. 4. Framework of abnormal coupled behavior detection in social network

The new system call sequences of a group are judged to be abnormal or not according to the probability of fitting in the learned CHSMM models. If the fit probability is low, it means that the group's behaviors do not fit the model well, and they are treated as anomalies.

3.3 CHSMM-Based Coupled Behavior Modeling

We propose a coupled HSMM on the basis of HSMM [14]. The standard fully-coupled HSMMs generally refer to a group of HSMM models, here we consider K models, in which the state of one model after time t+1 depends on the states of all models (including itself) before time t. Here, we consider a special coupled HSMM. For K HSMM coupled together, the coupled transition probability has the following structure:

$$P\{N_{[t+1:t+l]}^c = j | N_{[t-l^1+1:t]}^1 = i^1, \ldots, N_{[t-l^c+1:t]}^c = i, \ldots, N_{[t-l^K+1:t]}^K = i^K\}$$

$$= \sum_{c'=1}^K \theta_{c'c} P(N_{[t+1:t+l]}^c = j | N_{[t-l^{c'}+1:t]}^{c'} = i^{c'})$$ (14)

Under this special structure, the coupled HSMM can be described by a quadruplet

$$\lambda = \{\pi, A, B, \Theta\}, \ A = \left\{a_{(i,l)(j,l')}^{(c',c)}\right\}, \ B = \left\{b_{j,l}^c(u_{r_1:r_l})\right\}, \ \pi = \{\pi^c(i, l)\}$$ (15)

Coupling coefficient $\Theta = \{\theta_{c'c}\}$ such that $\sum_{c'=1}^K \theta_{c'c} = 1$

For the coupled HSMM, we can also obtain the forward-backward procedure. We define the extended forward variable as:

$$\alpha_t(j_1, l^1, j_2, l^2, \ldots, j_K, l^K) = P(S_{[t-l^1+1,t]}^1 = j_1, \ldots, S_{[t-l^K+1,t]}^K = j_K, O_{1:t}|\lambda)$$ (16)

and the extended backward variable

$$\beta_t(j_1, l^1, j_2, l^2, \ldots, j_K, l^K) = P(O_{t+1:T}|S_{[t-l^1+1,t]}^1 = j_1, \ldots, S_{[t-l^K+1,t]}^K = j_K, \lambda)$$ (17)

The coupling matrix between two coupled system call sequence is represented by $\Theta = \{\theta_{c'c}\}$, where $\theta_{c'c}$ represents the effect of model c' on c.

$$\theta_{c'c} = \Pr(N_{t+1}' = N_c | N_t = N_{c'})$$ (18)

where N_c and $N_{c'}$ denote the hidden states of two interacting sequences Ψ_c and $\Psi_{c'}$ respectively. Correspondingly, a CHSMM modeling K system call sequences can be expressed as

$$\lambda^{CHSMM} = \{\pi, A, B, \Theta\}$$ (19)

3.4   The Algorithms

The main algorithm for abnormal user detection based on the CHSMM is to find the abnormal system call sequence through the trained CHSMM model. Because the model is trained on a normal sequence set, it cannot fit the abnormal data very well. The output of the model will inform us whether the input data is normal.

The algorithm is to calculate the distance from the test sequence to the centroid of the trained model. If the distance exceeds the threshold, the sequence is considered anomalous.

Algorithm. CHSMM for detecting abnormal coupled system call sequences

---

Step1:   Construct   system   call   sequences   including   training   sequences $Seq_1, Seq_2, ..., Seq_Z$ and   test   sequences $Seq_1', Seq_2', ..., Seq_{Z'}'$

Step2: Train the CHSMM models on the training sequences;

Step3: Compute the mean (μ) and standard deviation (σ) of probability of training sequences according to the following formulas:

$$\mu = \frac{\sum_{i=1}^{Z} Pr(Seq_i \mid CHSMM)}{Z}$$

$$\sigma = \sqrt{\frac{1}{Z} \sum_{i=1}^{Z} [Pr(Seq_i \mid CHSMM) - \mu]^2}$$

where Z is the total number of training sequences, mean μ represents the centroid of model CHSMM, and the standard deviation σ represents the radius of models CHSMM

Step 4: For each test sequence Seq Seq_i', calculate its distance Di to the centroid of

model by $$D_i = \frac{\mu - Pr(Seq_i' \mid M)}{\sigma}$$

Consequently, Seq_i' is an abnormal pattern, if it satisfies: $D_i > \rho_0$, where ρ_0 is a given threshold.

---

4   Experiments and Evaluation

4.1   Experimental Data

We collect system calls when multiple Weibo accounts send operation request on multiple linux system computers. However, the data processing is very time consuming because of the large number of system calls and the redundant parameters. We only collect ten normal Weibo users' system call data as our training dataset in terms of operating Weibo in an hour. It contains 10300 system call symbols. System call data collected additionally which contain abnormal user operations are used as test data, making the test data a mixture of both normal and abnormal behaviors. We manually mark the system call sequence as normal or not based on the message content. If the following exception occurs in the message content, the system call sequence at this time is marked as an exception.

1. Pornography contents and viruses in the message content;
2. Phishing URL in the message content;
3. Advertisement contents including texts and images take over more than 50% in the message content

The ratio of training data to test data is set to 7:3. Following Data Structure and Data Preprocessing rules, we convert the data sets as Table 1 shown, which are associated with corresponding user, time, operation type and system call sequence.

Table 1. Samples of experimental data

User	Time	Operation	System call sequence
1	18:19:53	Repost	5, 12, 9, 6, 32, 8, 24, 24, 18, ..., 55, 43
2	18:20:03	Comment	7, 8, 8, 23, 56, 32, 2, 18, 44, ..., 13, 71
3	18:20:08	Like	12, 25, 34, 11, 8, 4, 32, 21, ..., 55, 26
2	18:20:18	Repost	5, 12, 7, 7, 6, 32, 8, 24, 22, 18, ..., 21, 56

CHSMM-based models are trained on such labeled normal data to capture the characteristics and dynamics in so-called 'normal' user operation. The trained models are deployed on the mixed test data to detect abnormal behaviors. Alerts fired on those possibly problematic system call sequence are treated as a rough benchmark for us to evaluate the CHSMM. The detected abnormal sequence indicates the anomalous user behavior operation at that moment.

4.2   Performance Evaluation

We evaluate the performance of our proposed model based on the technical perspective, where $Accuracy = \frac{TP+TN}{TP+TN+FP+FN}$, $Precision = \frac{TP}{TP+FP}$ $Recall = \frac{TP}{TP+FN}$, $Specificity = \frac{TN}{FP+TN}$. TP is true positive, TN is true negative, FP is false positive, and FN is false negative. TP, TN, FP and FN are counted in terms of the abnormal cases identified in the data.

We compare the performance of the proposed CHSMM model with the HMM and HSMM models. As shown in Fig. 5, the proposed CHSMM model performs best among three models whatever in accuracy, precision, recall or specificity. For instance, the precision of CHSMM is 70.2%, HSMM is 68.5%, while HMM is only 64.2%. This shows that performance of the HMM only modeling one sequence is much lower than the CHSMM modeling several coupled sequences. Further, CHSMM is generally significantly better than HSMM. One state in HSMM corresponds to one segment of observation which is different from the conventional HMM. HSMM overcomes the limitation of HMM modeling caused by the assumption of Markov chain, and provides better modeling and analysis ability in solving practical problems, improves the ability and accuracy of pattern classification. As we can see, HMM and HSMM only capture one sequence. However, CHSMM is proposed to model multiple processes with coupling relationships based on HSMM and reflects the real situation of social network users' behavior.

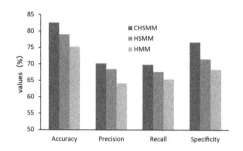

Fig. 5. Performance comparision of three models

Acknowledgements. We applied system calls and investigated their relations to the detection of abnormal behaviors of social network users for the first time. It is a completely new approach. The article has only described the fundamental work in this direction, more work will be reported in the next stage on the new progress on this basis. The authors would like to thank the support of National Natural Science Foundation of China (61762018), the Guangxi 100 Youth Talent Program (F-KA16016) and the Colleges and Universities Key Laboratory of Intelligent Integrated Automation, Guilin University of Electronic Technology, China (GXZDSY2016-03), the research fund of Guangxi Key Lab of Multi-source Information Mining & Security (18-A-02-02), Natural Science Foundation of Guangxi (2018JJA170109).

References

1. Gao, H., Hu, J., Huang, T.: Security issues in online social networks. IEEE Internet Comput. **5**(4), 56–63 (2011)
2. Caviglione, L., Fire, M., Goldschmidt, R., Elovici, Y.: Online social networks: threats and solutions survey. IEEE Commun. Surv. Tutor. **16**(4), 2019–2036 (2013)
3. Merlo, M.A.: A taxonomy-based model of security and privacy in online social networks. Int. J. Comput. Sci. Eng. **9**(4), 325–338 (2014)
4. Thomas, K., McCoy, D., Grier, C., Kolcz, A., Paxson, V.: Trafficking fraudulent accounts: The role of the underground market in Twitter spam and abuse. In: Usenix Security Symposium, pp. 195–210 (2013)
5. Huang, T.K., Rahman, M.S., Madhyastha, H.V., Faloutsos, M., Ribeiro, B.: An analysis of socware cascades in online social networks. In: International Conference on World Wide Web, Riode Janeiro, Brazil, pp. 619–630 (2013)
6. Chu, Z., Gianvecchio, S., Wang, H.: Who is tweeting on Twitter: Human, bot, or cyborg? In: Proceedings of the 26th Annual Computer Security Applications Conference, Austin, USA, pp. 21–30 (2010)

7. Kanich, C., Kreibich, C., Levchenko, K.: Spamalytics: an empirical analysis of spam marketing conversion. In: Proceedings of the 15th ACM Conference on Computer and Communications Security, Alexandria, USA, pp. 3–14 (2008)
8. Amleshwaram, A.A., Reddy, N., Yadav, S.: CATS: characterizing automation of Twitter spammer. In: Proceedings of the 5th International Conference on Communication Systems and Networks, Bangalore, India, pp. 1–10 (2013)
9. Stringhini, G., Kruegel, C., Vigna, G.: Detecting spammers on social networks. In: Proceedings of the 26th Annual Computer Security Applications Conference, Austin, USA, pp. 1–9 (2010)
10. Yang, Z., Wilson, C., Wang, X.: Uncovering social network Sybils in the wild. ACM Trans. Knowl. Discov. 8(1), 2 (2014)
11. Gao, H., Hu, J., Wilson, C.: Detecting and characterizing social spam campaigns. In: Proceedings of the 10th ACM SIGCOMM Conference on Internet Measurement, Melbourne, Australia, pp. 35–47 (2010)
12. Yu, H., Kaminsky, M., Gibbons, P.B.: Sybilguard: defending against Sybil attacks via social networks. IEEE Trans. Netw. 16(3), 576–589 (2008)
13. Cao, L., Ou, Y., Yu, P.: Coupled behavior analysis with applications. IEEE Trans. Knowl. Data Eng. 24, 1378–1392 (2011)
14. Brand, M., Oliver, N., Pentland, A.: Coupled hidden markov models for complex action recognition. In: Proceedings of the 1997 IEEE Computer Society Conference on Computer Vision and Pattern Recognition, pp. 994–999 (1997)

Multi-branch Aggregate Convolutional Neural Network for Image Classification

Rui Fan, Pinqun Jiang$^{(\boxtimes)}$, Shangyou Zeng, and Peng Li

College of Electronic Engineering, Guangxi Normal University,
Guilin 541004, China
18677356119@163.com, pqjiang@163.com

Abstract. In terms of image classification, in order to obtain higher classification accuracy, different levels of feature information need to be extracted from the image. Convolutional neural networks are increasingly applied to image classification. However, the traditional convolutional neural network has insufficient feature information extraction, poor classification accuracy, and easy over-fitting. This paper proposes Multi-branch aggregation network framework based on deep convolutional neural network that can be applied to image classification. Based on the traditional convolutional nerve, the network width and depth network are increased without increasing the parameters to optimize and improve the network to further enhance the feature expression ability of the network, Enriched the diversity of feature sampling, increased image classification accuracy and prevented overfitting. The framework and traditional frameworks and other frameworks were compared and analyzed through a series of comparative experiments in two standard databases, CIFAR-10 and CIFAR-100, and the validity of the framework was demonstrated.

Keywords: Image classification · Convolutional neural network · Classification accuracy · Convergence

1 Introduction

Image classification is one of the key research contents of computer vision and artificial intelligence [1]. The main task is to classify the same type of pictures in image data, which has a wide range of applications in scientific research, medical applications and industrial applications. At present, the research of image classification is mainly divided into two parts: image feature extraction and classification algorithm research. Although there are many excellent classification algorithms, such as traditional classification methods: based on support vector machine (SVM) classifier [2] and the bag of visual word (BoVW) [3] has achieved good results on many datasets, but with the breakthrough of deep network in image processing and the convenience of convolution neural network in image processing, both academic and industrial circles tend to use convolution neural network for image classification.

The most influential application of convolutional neural networks in image classification is the AlexNet [4] proposed by Krizhevsky et al. Since this model won the ILSVRC 2012 ImageNet image classification competition, the upsurge of convolution

© Springer Nature Switzerland AG 2019
X. Liu et al. (Eds.): ICSOC 2018 Workshops, LNCS 11434, pp. 102–112, 2019.
https://doi.org/10.1007/978-3-030-17642-6_9

neural network (CNN) has swept the whole field of computer vision. The convolutional neural network replaces the classifier and traditional hand-crafted features, which refreshes the accuracy of each image race task and exceeds the accuracy of the human eye. For example, VGGNet [5] developed by the Computer Vision Group at Oxford University, explored the relationship between the depth of a convolutional neural network and its performance by repeatedly stacking 3×3 small convolution kernels and 2×2 maximum pooling layers. It successfully constructed a 16–19-layer deep convolutional neural network and won the second place in the ILSVRC 2014 competition classification project. ResNet [6], proposed by He et al., successfully trained 152-layer deep neural networks using residual block, and The structure can accelerate the training of the ultra-deep neural network very quickly, and the accuracy of the model has been greatly improved. It won the championship in ILSVRC 2015, and achieved a top-5 error rate of 3.57%. At the same time, the parameter is lower than VGGNet, and the effect is very outstanding. SENet [7], designed by Momenta's Hu et al., studied channel coding, modeled channel relations through feature re-calibration, and further enhanced the expression ability of convolution network, and the winner of ILSVRC2017 image classification achieved a Top-5 error rate of 2.251%.

Convolutional neural network models are exponentially increasing in depth as they continue to approach the precision limits of computer vision tasks. As the network size increases, the computational complexity of the network increases, which consumes more computing resources. The deeper the network depth, the more likely the gradient dispersion phenomenon will occur, which will make it difficult to optimize the network model parameters and increase the difficulty of network training, and too many network parameters, in the case of a limited amount of training data, the network is prone to over-fitting. This paper improves the traditional network structure and designs a suitable structure with fewer layers, to reduce the parameters while widening and deepening the network, improve the accuracy of network classification, and reduce the harsh hardware requirements of the network. We explore a generalized and efficient infrastructure that can satisfy the limited conditions.

2   Convolution Neural Network

2.1   Convolutional Neural Network Basic Operations

Convolutional neural networks are a branch of research and application in deep learning. They are specialized in processing neural networks with similar network data structures. Its basic idea is to build multiple convolution operations, pool operations, and so on. Trained by large-scale data, a large number of representative feature information to classify and predict samples.

The function of convolution is to train less parameters to extract the feature information of the input data. It is conducive to construct a deeper and larger network structure to solve more complex problems.

Pooling is an effective dimensionality reduction method that prevents over-fitting, pooling includes the maximum pool and the average pool.

The formula for ReLu [8] is defined as follows:

$$ReLu = \begin{cases} x, x > 0 \\ 0, x \leq 0 \end{cases} \tag{1}$$

As a function of the activation function of the convolutional network, this function effectively overcomes the problem of gradient dispersion in back-propagation that compared with the traditional sigmoid and tanh activation functions, so that the network can be trained deeper and faster.

During the model training process, dropout [9] randomly discards some of the intermediate calculation results, which makes the network more anti-interference and prevents over-fitting, as show in Fig. 1.

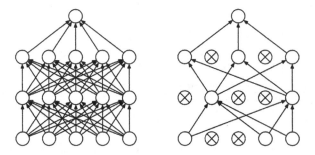

Fig. 1. Dropout diagram.

2.2   Convolutional Neural Network Training Process

CNN is actually a mapping function that has input to output (with many hidden layers between them). Through the training process of the network, it has the ability to map between input and output pairs. The training process of network is shown in Fig. 2.

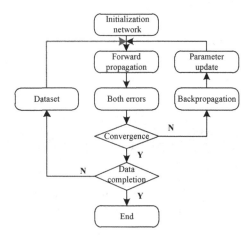

Fig. 2. Flow chat of training.

The training of convolutional neural networks can be divided into two parts: forward computing and error back propagation. Forward computing is to get the eigenvectors through a series of transformations of convolution layer, pool layer and full connection layer, and then classify them by Softmax classifier. Back propagation is used to correct errors. Gradient descent method is used to update the weights and other parameters of the network layer by layer.

The output of the convolutional layer can be obtained by Eq. (2), where x_i^{l-1} is the output feature map of the upper layer, M_j is the subset of the upper layer feature map, $k_{i,j}^l$ is the weight of the convolution kernel, and b_j^l is the corresponding bias, $f(\cdot)$ is the activation function.

$$x_j^l = f\left(\sum_{i \in M_j} x_i^{l-1} \times k_{i,j}^l + b_j^l\right) \tag{2}$$

The parameters of the pooling layer can be obtained by Eq. (3), where β_j^l and b_j^l are weight and offset parameters, $down(\cdot)$ is down sampling functions and $f(\cdot)$ is activation functions.

$$x_j^l = f(\beta_j^l down(x_j^{l-1}) + b_j^l) \tag{3}$$

The output of the fully connected layer can be obtained by Eq. (4), where ω_l and b_l are weight and offset parameters, $f(\cdot)$ is the activation function.

$$x_j^l = f(\omega_l x_{l-1} + b_l) \tag{4}$$

The average error cost function of the network can be obtained by Eq. (5), and the weight update can be obtained by Eq. (6), where N is the number of samples, C is the input category, and ∂ is the learning rate. In practice, to prevent over-fitting, L_2 regularization term is added to the cost function.

$$E = \frac{1}{2}\sum_{n=1}^{N}\sum_{k=1}^{C}(u_k^n - x_k^n)^2 \tag{5}$$

$$\omega_i = \omega_{i-1} + \partial\frac{\partial E}{\partial \omega_{i-1}} \tag{6}$$

The network adjusts the weights, offsets and other parameters by alternating the forward operation and the error back propagation, so as to minimize the error until the network reaches the convergence requirement.

3 Improved Model

3.1 Model Principle

The traditional convolutional neural network is a convolution operation of the upper layer output by convolution kernel to obtain the output feature map of the convolutional layer, but the convolution operation has only one channel, and the extracted image features may be insufficient. Multi-branch aggregation module proposed in this paper convolves the upper feature map through three channels, and then fuses the output feature maps of the two channels. Finally, the merged output feature map is cascaded with the third channel to obtain the final output. Make the collected feature information more adequate. The principle is as shown in Eq. (7):

$$
\begin{cases}
x_{j,1.1}^l = f_1\left(\sum_{i \in M} x_i^{l-1} \times k_{i,j}^{l,1.1} + b_j^l\right) \\[2mm]
x_{j,1.2}^l = f_1\left(\sum_{i \in M} x_i^{l-1} \times k_{i,j}^{l,1.2} + b_j^l\right) \\[2mm]
x_{j,2}^l = f_1\left(\sum_{i \in M} x_i^{l-1} \times k_{i,j}^{l,2} + b_j^l\right) \\[2mm]
x_{j,1}^l = f_2\left(x_{j,1.1}^l, x_{j,1.2}^l\right) \\[2mm]
x_j^l = f_3\left(x_{j,1}^l, x_{j,2}^l\right)
\end{cases}
\tag{7}
$$

Where M is a subset of the upper feature map, $f_1(\cdot)$ is the activation function, $x_{j,1.1}^l$ is the convolution output of the first channel, $f_2(\cdot)$ is the feature map fusion mode of the two channels, and $x_{j,1}^l$ is the output of the fusion. $f_3(\cdot)$ is the feature graph cascading

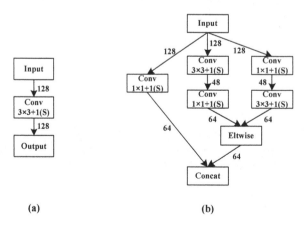

(a)　　　　　　　　(b)

Fig. 3. Flow chat of training two convolution modules (a) Traditional convolution module (b) Multi-branch aggregation convolution module.

mode of two channels, and x_j^l is the cascade output. The specific model settings are shown in Fig. 3.

Replace the traditional model (a) with the improved (b) as shown in Fig. 3. The 1×1 convolution is placed before and after the 3×3 convolution as a module that changes the dimension (height), increasing the depth and width of the convolutional neural network without increasing computational complexity, To prevent over fitting. At the same time, the change of the convolution position of the two sizes allows the network to extract the information in each detail of the input, reducing the error value. The network is then integrated through convergence, and finally concatenated with convolutions of different scales to improve accuracy again. Accelerate convergence speed by using the principle of sparse matrix decomposition into dense matrix calculation The feature is extracted on multiple scales of the module, and the output features are no longer uniformly distributed, but the related features are gathered together, and the unrelated non-key features are weakened, and the natural convergence speed is faster.

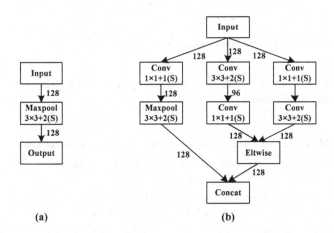

Fig. 4. Two pooling modules (a) Traditional pooling module (b) Multi-branch aggregation pooling module.

In the traditional model, the pooling layer is usually used, and the extracted features have translation invariance, but some key information is still lost. This paper links the pooling and the Multi-branch aggregation convolution layer together. The specific model settings are shown in Fig. 4.

Replace the traditional model (a) with the improved (b) as shown in Fig. 4. This model can extract the missing information from the traditional pooling operation and increase the accuracy.

3.2 Model Setting

The specific model settings are shown in Fig. 5. The optimization of the entire network is mainly divided into three parts, and Module A and Module B are alternately stacked. Reduce the size of the output by Module A and double the number of channels. Module B improves the accuracy by repeatedly extracting feature values without changing the feature size and number of channel. (The first Module A does not change the size of the feature map to ensure that the feature information at the beginning of the input is not lost.) The feature map after the three-layer stack is reduced and the number of channels is expanded.

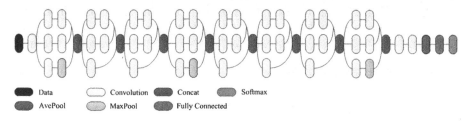

Fig. 5. Multi-branch aggregation network.

The overall structure and specific parameter settings of Multi-branch aggregation network are shown in Table 1.

Table 1. Multi-branch aggregation network overall parameter setting.

Type	Filter size/ Stride/Pad	Output size	Depth
Input image		$31 \times 31 \times 3$	1
Conv1	$5 \times 5/1/0$	$27 \times 27 \times 64$	1
Module A2		$27 \times 27 \times 128$	1
Module B3	As in Fig. 3	$27 \times 27 \times 128$	2
Module A4	As in Fig. 4	$13 \times 13 \times 256$	1
Module B5		$13 \times 13 \times 256$	3
Module A6		$7 \times 7 \times 512$	1
Conv7	$3 \times 3/1/1$	$7 \times 7 \times 512$	1
Conv8	$1 \times 1/1/0$	$7 \times 7 \times 512$	1
Avgpool9		$1 \times 1 \times 512$	1
FC10		10/100	1

4   Experiment

4.1   Experiment Setup

All the network structures in this experiment are deployed using the Caffe [10] framework based on C++ programming language. The experimental platform is configured on i7-6700K quad-core CPU, Ubuntu 14.4 operating system, 32 GB memory and NVIDIA-GTX 1070 GPU.

The datasets used in the experiment are open datasets CIFAR-10 and CIFAR-100. CIFAR-10 contains 10 kinds of natural images. Each kind of natural image has 5 000 training images and 1 000 test images. There are 60 000 RGB three-channel images with a size of 32 × 32. CIFAR-100 is similar to the data set CIFAR-10. However, the CIFAR-100 dataset contains 100 classes of natural images. Each class of images has 500 training images and 100 test images. There are 60,000 RGB three-channel images with a size of 32 × 32. The number of data sets is obviously more than CIFAR-10, and the number of each category is less, which makes the difficulty of classification increase.

A major challenge for convolutional neural networks is the need for very large data sets to train and learn all the basic parameters of the model. But even if the current large-scale data sets, such as ImageNet, have more than one million image data sets, still cannot meet the needs of deep convolution structure training. In order to improve the accuracy of the training model, the input image is normalized and de-averaged before training. The network uses data enhancement technology to cut each image from the upper left corner, the lower left corner, the upper right corner, the lower right corner and the middle to 31 × 31 pixels smaller than the original image size, then horizontal inversion, this can expand the training set to 10 times the original, it can very good increase the diversity of data, can effectively alleviate the over-fitting model, while improving the performance of the model and generalization ability of the effect to improve robustness.

The various hyper-parameters of the solver file for the two data sets of the experiment were set to be trained on CIFAR-10, the initial learning rate is set to 0.001, the gamma is set to 0.9, the type of learning rate is set to poly, the power is set to 1.5, the dropout_ratio is set to 0.5, and the test_batch _size is set to 100, and the network performance is tested once every 500 times. When training on the CIFAR-100, the initial learning rate is set to 0.005, The type of learning rate is set to multistep, the step value is set to 24000 and 48000, the maximum number of iterations is set to 70000, the dropout_ratio is set to 0.5, the test_batch_size is set to 100, and the network performance is tested once every 500 times. In this paper, the experimental results of the frame model are the average of the 5 results.

4.2   Experimental Results and Analysis

In order to validate the method in this paper, the framework model was tested on two public datasets. In order to compare with the traditional network, Fig. 6 shows the accuracy curve of the two networks tested on CIFAR-10. When the highest number of iterations is reached, it is significantly higher than the traditional network, 3.1% more

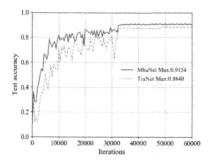

Fig. 6. Accuracy of different network classifications on the CIFAR-10.

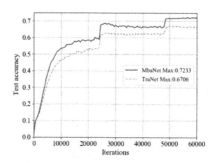

Fig. 7. Accuracy of different network classifications on the CIFAR-100.

than the traditional network. It can be seen from Fig. 7 that due to the increased difficulty of the CIFAR-100 classification task, the classification accuracy obtained on this data is low. However, it still achieved an accuracy rate of 72.33%, which is superior to the traditional method.

Tables 2 and 3 show the comparison between the proposed network framework and traditional and recently popular network frameworks. It can be seen that the framework has certain advantages. The learning rate on CIFAR-100 is multistep, and the learning rate varies every 24,000 times. On CIFAR-10, the learning rate is poly, and the learning rate varies every iteration.

Table 2. Compare the accuracy of different methods in CIFAR-10.

Method	Accuracy (%)
CNN + Spearmint [11]	85.02
Conv.maxout + Dropout [12]	88.32
NIN + Dropout [13]	89.59
DSN + Dropout [14]	90.31
NIN + Dropout + Data Augmentation [13]	91.31
AlexNet + Fine-tuning [15]	89.40
TraNet	88.40
Multi-branch aggregation Net	91.53

The experimental results show that the improved MbaNet has better performance than the traditional network, and the test results are good on both data sets, with generalization. It improves the diversity of feature extraction and increases robustness. It shows that multi-scale extraction features are cascaded together, and aggregation operations and convolution operations are cascaded together to improve the classification accuracy of the network.

Table 3. Compare the accuracy of different methods in CIFAR-100.

Method	Accuracy (%)
NIN + Dropout [13]	64.32
DSN + Dropout [14]	65.43
RCNN-96 + Dropout [16]	65.82
RCNN-128 + Dropout [16]	67.41
RCNN-160 + Dropout [16]	68.25
AlexNet + Fine-tuning [15]	67.38
Highway Network [17]	67.61
TraNet	67.06
Multi-branch aggregation Net	72.33

5   Conclusions

This paper proposes Multi-branch aggregation image classification framework based on traditional convolutional neural networks. The framework uses a variety of convolution kernels to feature extraction, which increases the diversity of feature extraction, and combines the features of multiple convolution extractions in a cascade and fusion manner. At the same time, Pooling and convolution parallel connection instead of traditional pool layer to reduce information loss in pool layer. The comparison experiments and theoretical analysis are carried out on the two databases of CIFAR-10 and CIFAR-100 with the traditional network framework and the recent popular network framework. The results show that the proposed framework has good performance and the classification accuracy is obviously improved. Future work will further adjust the network framework based on the current image classification, learn more accurate feature representation, and try to apply it to other tasks such as image retrieval and target recognition.

Acknowledgments. Authors acknowledge support of the National Natural Science Foundation of China (Grant Nos. 11465004). Authors are also thankful to the anonymous reviewers whose constructive suggestions helped improve and clarify this manuscript.

References

1. Bossard, L., Guillaumin, M., Van Gool, L.: Food-101 – mining discriminative components with random forests. In: Fleet, D., Pajdla, T., Schiele, B., Tuytelaars, T. (eds.) ECCV 2014. LNCS, vol. 8694, pp. 446–461. Springer, Cham (2014). https://doi.org/10.1007/978-3-319-10599-4_29
2. Burges, C.J.C.: A tutorial on support vector machines for pattern recognition. Data Min. Knowl. Disc. **2**(2), 121–167 (1998)
3. Penatti, O.A.B., Silva, F.B., Valle, E., et al.: Visual word spatial arrangement for image retrieval and classification. Pattern Recogn. **47**(2), 705–720 (2014)
4. Krizhevsky, A., Sutskever, I., Hinton, G.: Imagenet classification with deep convolutional neural networks. In: NIPS (2012)

5. Redmon, J., Divvala, S., Girshick, R., et al.: You only look once: unified, real-time object detection. In: Proceedings of the IEEE Conference on Computer Vision and Pattern Recognition, pp. 779–788 (2016)
6. He, K., Zhang, X., Ren, S., et al.: Deep residual learning for image recognition. In: Proceedings of the IEEE Conference on Computer Vision and Pattern Recognition, pp. 770–778 (2016)
7. Hu, J., Shen, L., Sun, G.: Squeeze-and-excitation networks. arXiv preprint arXiv:1709.01507 (2017)
8. Zhang, Z., Fu, S.: Profiling and analysis of power consumption for virtualized systems and applications. In: 2010 IEEE 29th International Performance Computing and Communications Conference (IPCCC), pp. 329–330. IEEE (2010)
9. Srivastava, N., Hinton, G., Krizhevsky, A., et al.: Dropout: a simple way to prevent neural networks from overfitting. J. Mach. Learn. Res. **15**(1), 1929–1958 (2014)
10. Jia, Y., Shelhamer, E., Donahue, J., et al.: Caffe: convolutional architecture for fast feature embedding. In: Proceedings of the 22nd ACM International Conference on Multimedia, pp. 675–678. ACM (2014)
11. Snoek, J., Larochelle, H., Adams, R.P.: Practical Bayesian optimization of machine learning algorithms. In: Advances in Neural Information Processing Systems, pp. 2951–2959 (2012)
12. Goodfellow, I.J., Warde-Farley, D., Mirza, M., et al.: Maxout networks. arXiv preprint arXiv:1302.4389 (2013)
13. Chen, Y., Yang, X., Zhong, B., et al.: Network in network based weakly supervised learning for visual tracking. J. Vis. Commun. Image Represent. **37**, 3–13 (2016)
14. Lee, C.Y., Xie, S., Gallagher, P., et al.: Deeply-supervised nets. In: Artificial Intelligence and Statistics, pp. 562–572 (2015)
15. Yang, H.F., Lin, K., Chen, C.S.: Supervised learning of semantics-preserving hash via deep convolutional neural networks. IEEE Trans. Pattern Anal. Mach. Intell. **40**(2), 437–451 (2018)
16. Liang, M., Hu, X.: Recurrent convolutional neural network for object recognition. In: Proceedings of the IEEE Conference on Computer Vision and Pattern Recognition, pp. 3367–3375 (2015)
17. Srivastava, R.K., Greff, K., Schmidhuber, J.: Highway networks. arXiv preprint arXiv:1505.00387 (2015)

Remote Sensing Image Deblurring Algorithm Based on WGAN

Haiying Xia[(✉)] and Chenxu Liu

College of Electronic Engineering, Guangxi Normal University, Guilin 541004, China
xhyhust@gmail.com

Abstract. Remote sensing images are blurred due to large and wide imaging, long shooting distance, fast scanning speed, interference from external light, etc. At the same time, because of that remote sensing images have the characteristics of diverse and dense shooting objects, deblurring remote sensing images is a major problem in remote sensing research. Therefore, we propose a remote sensing image deblurring algorithm, which based on WGAN. The algorithm is different from the traditional method in estimating the blur kernel of image. What's more our method does not require an explicit estimation of the blur kernel, and it implements an end-to-end image deblurring process. We use a WGAN-based deblurring model. First, the training images are processed in pairs. Then, in order to increase the generalization ability, a image of 256 * 256 that is a sub-region cropped at the random position in the original image is chosen as the input image. Finally, to achieve a better deblurring effect, a content loss function and a perceptual loss function are added to the loss function to achieve the specific implementation. The remote sensing image deblurring model trained by the proposed method has achieved better results on the remote sensing image dataset. The experimental results show that the proposed algorithm have better performance than the traditional method in filtering out the blur of remote sensing images, which could optimize the overall visual effect subjectively and improve the peak signal-to-noise ratio of the image objectively.

Keywords: Remote sensing image · Motion blur · Deblurring · Generative Adversarial Networks · Deep learning

1 Introduction

In the actual working environment, remote sensing images are often face the problem of the noise interference during the optical information acquisition, conversion and transmission, causing the image quality to decrease and become blurred. Therefore, the deblurring analysis, the evaluation and the filtering of remote sensing images have been the focus of remote sensing applications, as well as a hotspot of remote sensing image. The main purpose of deblurring remote sensing images is to preserve the edges of the remote sensing image and the important feature information while removing the blur. At present, the deblurring methods of remote sensing images mainly focus on estimating blur kernel based on regularization [1–3]. In [1], bilateral and shock filters are

© Springer Nature Switzerland AG 2019
X. Liu et al. (Eds.): ICSOC 2018 Workshops, LNCS 11434, pp. 113–125, 2019.
https://doi.org/10.1007/978-3-030-17642-6_10

used to handle blurred images, and a variational Bayesian iterative model is applied to determine the optimal solution by considering prior knowledge of the sparsity feature of the blur kernel, and then the deblurring result can be obtained by non-blind deconvolution based on gradient sparsity. In [2], Cheng firstly used the improved edge method to quickly estimate the size and shape of the blur kernel, and used the direct edge detection method to predict the blur kernel, and then used the non-blind deconvolutional method to recover the images. The original image was compensated by the regular deconvolutional and high frequency compensation with the weighted deblurring method, which would suppress the ringing effect caused by the error of blur kernel estimation. However, these traditional remote sensing image deblurring methods need to estimate the blur kernel accurately and effectively. The biased kernel estimation will directly affect the quality of the potential sharp image, resulting in undesired ringing artifacts. Therefore, the estimations of the blur kernels not only could affect the efficiency but also the effect of deblurring. At present, with the development of deep learning, the research on image deblurring based on deep learning has became more and more popular [4–6]. It does not need to predict the blur kernel, but outputs the corresponding sharp image directly through the training network, which is an end-to-end deblurring process. Nah et al. [5] proposed a dynamic scene deblurring method based on multi-scale convolutional neural networks, which can restore the blurred images in an end-to-end manner from the blur caused by various sources. Kupyn et al. [6] proposed a multi-component loss function to optimize the conditional adversarial networks for blind motion deblur. These methods have achieved good results on conventional blurred image data. However, due to the particularity of remote sensing images, these methods are not effective in deblurring remote sensing images.

Aiming at the characteristics of remote sensing image such as the scale diversity, perspective specificity and imaging complexity, this paper proposes a remote sensing image deblurring method based on WGAN. In order to achieve better deblurring effect, the loss function is redesigned in this paper. The content loss function and the perceptual loss function are added to the original loss function to realize the end-to-end remote image deblurring model. The effectiveness of the method is proved by theory and experiment. The rest of the article is structured as follows: Sect. 2 circumstantiates the network structure and loss functions used in this article. Section 3 describes the datasets used in this article, as well as experimental analysis and evaluation. Section 4 summarizes the work.

2   Remote Sensing Image Deblurring Model Based on WGAN

2.1   Theoretical Basis

Generative Adversarial Networks (GANs) were proposed by Goodfellow et al. [7], whose idea stems from the two-person zero-sum game in game theory. GANs has powerful data generation capabilities, which has achieved good results in image/text generation, image restoration, and super-resolution analysis. The basic framework of GANs consists of a Generative Model (G) and a Discriminative Model (D), as shown in Fig. 1.

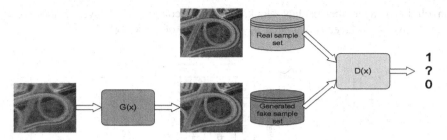

Fig. 1. The basic framework of GANs

The Generative Model is generally represented by the function G(x), and the Discriminative Model is represented by the function D(x). The process of GANs training is divided into two steps. The first step is to train the Discriminative Model D (x). The Discriminative Model is a two-class model, the positive sample is the real sample x, and the negative sample is the generated data G(z) of the Generative Model. The second step is to train the Generative Model G(x), which the input is random noise z (in this case, the blurred image), and the output is the fake sample G(z) of the same dimension as the real sample. The purpose of Generative Model is to make D(G(z)) as same as possible to D(x), and the aim of the Discriminative Model is to make D(G(z)) and D(x) as different as possible. In the end, the network models become balanced in the mutual game between the two.

It can be seen from the principle of GANs that the difficulty lies in designing a reasonable loss function. The loss function of the original GANs uses the JS distance, which makes the original GANs network very difficult to train. Arjovsky et al. [8] proposed Wasserstein GAN (WGAN) for the problem of the original GAN. WGAN introduces the Wasserstein distance in the loss function, which solves the shortcomings of the original GANs. This paper uses the WGAN model.

The generative adversarial network only proposes a network framework, and does not specify the specific form of the generator and the discriminator. It only needs to fit the generator function and the discriminator function well. Since the convolutional neural network has achieved unprecedented effects in image processing, the design of the generator and discriminator are convolutional neural network structures in this paper. Design a good generative adversarial network includes three aspects mainly: the Generative Network, the Discriminative Network and loss function. The design of these three aspects often needs to be combined with specific application scenarios. A detailed description can be seen as follows.

2.2 Network Architecture

Residual Networks (ResNets) proposed by He et al. [9] can solve the problems of difficult training and gradient disappearance of deep convolutional neural networks effectively. Therefore, the Generative Network of this paper is designed as a convolutional neural network based on residual block. The Generative Network structure is shown in Fig. 2. The conv, Residual Block, and Upconv in the figure represent the convolutional layer, the residual block, and the deconvolutional layer, respectively. Every convolution layer is activated by the function of LeakyReLU.

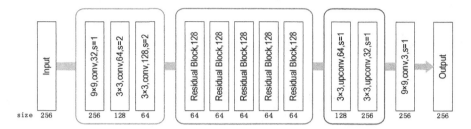

Fig. 2. Generative network structure

It can be seen that the structure of the Generative Network is mainly divided into four parts: an encoder network, a residual block network, a decoder network, and a convolution unit. The encoder network is composed of three downsampling units, the residual block network is composed of five residual units, and the decoder network is composed of two upsampling units. The structure of the downsampling unit, the residual unit and the upsampling unit are shown in Figs. 3, 4 and 5.

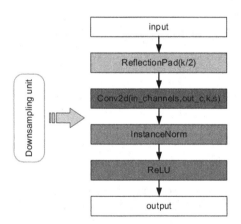

Fig. 3. Downsampling unit structure

Firstly, in order to increase the generalization ability, the original image is randomly clipped at the time of training. Specifically, a 256×256 sub-region is randomly selected from the original image as the input image, and 128 feature maps are obtained through the encoder network. Then there are 5 residual blocks arranged, and finally the decoder network is arranged, and 128 feature maps are converted into the dimensions of the input image. By setting the padding boundary of each convolutional layer to 0, the resolution of the input and output images could remain unchanged. The 3×3 convolutional kernel used in the convolution process not only could have the same

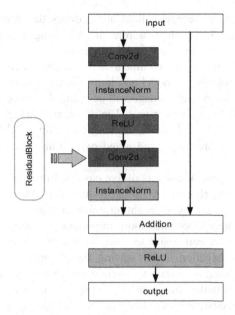

Fig. 4. Residual unit structure

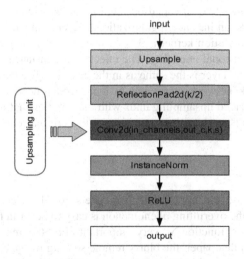

Fig. 5. Upsampling unit structure

Receptive Field as the 5×5 and the 7×7, but also can reduce many training parameters. Batch normalization is set in each module to prevent over-fitting in training.

The input of the encoder will pass through three cascaded downsampling units. The downsampling unit is composed of a convolutional layer in series, an instance regularizational layer, and a nonlinear active layer. The size of the convolution kernel is

3×3, which increases the receptive field and reduces the size of the image. The instance regularizational layer plays a role in stabilizing and accelerating model training by normalizing the mean and standard deviation of the input samples of the same batch. The addition of the nonlinear active layer prevents the model from degenerating into a simple linear model and improves the model's descriptive ability. In the encoder, the size of the input image will be reduced to the original one-half (i.e., from 256 to 128 to 64) for each such unit. The downsampling units, while extracting the input image feature map, scale down the image size, improve the accuracy, reduce the dimension of the feature maps, and avoid over-fitting phenomenon to a certain extent.

The residual block network consists of five cascaded residual blocks. The residual block does not change the shape of the input feature map. The idea of residuals is to remove the same main part, thus highlighting minor changes. Adding residual blocks makes the change of output becomes more important for weight adjustment, which makes the network deeper and easier to train, so that the effect is better. From the perspective of back-propagation, it is "solving the phenomenon of gradient disappearance". Gradient is used to update the weight parameters to make the network fit better, and the error term that is the sensitivity to the network loss value is used to find. Therefore, from the perspective of back-propagation, adding the residual unit can directly propagate and add the error term to the previous network layer. By one's way, it can solve the problem of gradient disappearance and make the network deeper.

The decoder includes two cascaded upsampling units, which consist of a series of deconvolutional layers, an instance regularizational layer, and a nonlinear active layer. The size of the deconvolution kernel is 3×3, which serves to enlarge the size of the image from low-dimensional encoding. The effect of the instance regularization layer and the nonlinear active layer is the same as in the encoder. The feature map processed by the residual block network was input to the decoder network, and then it was amplified by two cascaded upsampling units with the function that make the size of the input feature image restored to the same size as the original one (the image size is 256×256).

2.3 Loss Functions

It is difficult to choose the appropriate parameters for the Generative Adversarial Network model, and the overfitting phenomenon is easy to occur in training. Therefore, the design of the loss function is very important. For the remote sensing image deblurring problem in this paper, the blurry remote sensing image and the clear remote sensing image share a lot of information, such as color, brightness and other information, which is more difficult to reconcile during training. This requires choosing a suitable loss function to assist the training better.

Traditionally, the L_1 or L_2 loss of the restored image and the real image is used as the target equation for image restoration tasks. However, only using L_1 or L_2 loss in a deep convolutional neural network results in a smoother restored image because of that the pixel-level error equation tends to converge at the average of all possible solutions. This will cause the image losing sharp edges, and the blur at the edges will still be present mostly. Therefore, in order to optimize this neural network model, the loss function we use consists of content loss, perceptual loss, and WGAN-GP loss [10], as in expression (1). Where $L_{content}^2$ represents the corresponding pixel subtraction, that is, content loss, $L_{content}^1$ represents the perceptual loss, and L_{GAN-GP} represents the WGAN-GP loss.

$$L_G = L_{content}^2 + L_{content}^1 + L_{GAN-GP} \tag{1}$$

(1) Content Loss:

In order to ensure the similarity between the generated image and the sharp image, we added the L_1 loss to the loss function. What $L_{content}^2$ denotes is the corresponding pixel subtraction, that is, content loss, as shown in the expression (2). X_g and X_{sharp} represent the image generated by the generator and the true clear image, respectively.

$$L_{content}^2 = \left\| X_{sharp} - X_g \right\| \tag{2}$$

(2) Perceptual Loss:

During the training of the network, we found that the chromatic aberration at the boundary position of the generated image could not be eliminated, resulting in distortion of some objects in the remote sensing image. In response to this problem, we introduced a new kind of perceptual loss in model training. Perceptual loss was first proposed by Johnson et al. [11], introducing a pre-trained convolutional network model to optimize the boundary information of the image. The pre-trained $VGG - 16$ model is first used to extract features by removing the last Softmax layer and then calculates the perceptual loss, as in expression (3). X_g and X_{sharp} represent the image generated by the generator and the real sharp image respectively. The $VGG - 16$ network [12] has 5 convolution blocks from top to bottom, and the two convolution blocks are distinguished by the MaxPooling layer, and each convolution block has 2–3 convolutional layers, each convolution layer is followed by a ReLU active layer, and VGG_{5-3} represents the active layer (ReLU) output of the 3rd convolutional layer of the 5th convolutional block.

$$L_{content}^1 = \left\| VGG_{5-3}(X_{sharp}) - VGG_{5-3}(X_g) \right\| \tag{3}$$

(3) L_{GAN-GP} Loss:

WGAN's training is relatively stable, but sometimes it still produces bad samples or can't converge. So, with the method of cutting weights, it can stabilize the various GAN architectures without adjusting the hyperparameters. As shown in the expression

(4), X_{blur} denotes a blurry image (note: $G(X_{blur}) = X_g$), P_{blur} denotes a distribution from which the blurry image comes, E denotes an expectation, and $D(\cdot)$ denotes a corresponding probability.

$$L_{GAN-GP} = \min\left\{ \underset{X_{blur} \sim p_{blur}}{-E} [D(G(X_{blur}))] \right\} \qquad (4)$$

2.4 Model Training

The hardware configuration of the model training platform is I5-7300HQ CPU, 16G memory, NVIDIA GTX 1060 6G GPU, and the remote sensing image datasets in training are derived from DOTA, NWPU VHR-10, INRIA aerial image dataset and RSOD-Dataset. Before training, the data in the datasets is processed in advance, and the blurred image is spliced together with the sharp image. In order to increase the generalization ability, the original image is randomly clipped during training. Specifically, in the original image, a randomly generated position crops a 256×256 sub-region as an input image. The model epoch is set to 200. With the advantage of GPU parallel computing, the time required to complete 200 epoch is 9 h. Considering that the sample data is not large, we set the batchsize to 5. When there are too much training data, you could increase the corresponding bachsize value to improve the training speed. The learning rate algorithm uses Adam and the learning rate is 0.0001. In the actual test, it is found that the Adam method used in the remote sensing image deblurring model is better than other adaptive methods, and its convergence speed is faster and the learning efficiency is higher.

3 Experimental Results and Analysis

3.1 Datasets

The effect of deblurring changes due to different training datasets. This paper collects and organizes training datasets from multiple sources and compares the results. Remote sensing images are different from general scene images. Remote sensing images have the characteristics of long shooting distance and wide viewing angle. Therefore, the types of objects covered are relatively complex. This paper collects and organizes remote sensing images in different situations and combines them into high-quality remote sensing image dataset.

A total of four datasets were collected in this paper, as follows:

(1) DOTA: A Large-scale Dataset for Object Detection in Aerial Images, which is a dataset jointly developed by Xia Guisong, the State Key Laboratory of Remote Sensing of Wuhan University, and Baixiang, Huake Telecom College. 2806 remote sensing images are divided into 15 categories.

(2) NWPU VHR-10: The aerospace remote sensing target detection dataset marked by Northwestern Polytechnical University, with 800 images, including 650 targets, 150 background images, and 10 categories: aircraft, ships, tanks Baseball field, tennis court, basketball court, track and field, port, bridge, vehicle.

(3) INRIA aerial image dataset: Inria is the abbreviation of the French National Institute of Information and Automation. The institution has a large number of databases, which is one of the database of urban building inspections. There are only two types: building and not building. There are 5,500 sheets in total.

(4) RSOD-Dataset: Wuhan University team marked, including four types of targets: aircraft, playgrounds, overpasses, oil drums. There are 4993 aircrafts in 446 images, 191 playgrounds in 189 images, 180 overpass in 176 overpass, and 1586 oiltanks in 165 images.

In this paper, the above four training sets are used to train individually or in combination, and 1000 pictures are selected for testing. Table 1 lists the average quality of several training pictures. By comparison, the selected training sets will make the deblurring effect different. It can be clearly seen that we use a mixed dataset, and the deblurred quality of the remote sensing image is improved when more and more useful information is included. The size of the training set also could affect the results of the reconstruction. We use a specific number of training sets during training and then test the quality of the resulting image. As shown in Fig. 7, it can be seen from the figure that when the number of pictures in the training set is gradually increased, the quality evaluation index of the tested image – peak signal to noise ratio (PSNR) and structural similarity index (SSIM) are continuously improved. When it is increased to a certain extent, the improvement of quality tends to be stable, and the size of the dataset is no longer the main influencing factor.

Table 1. Deblurred results after training different datasets

Evaluation index	Training set									
	(1)	(2)	(3)	(4)	(1) + (2)	(2) + (3)	(3) + (4)	(1) + (4)	(1) + (3) + (4)	(1) + (2) + (3) + (4)
PSNR	22.57	26.07	26.95	25.42	27.67	28.61	29.14	28.53	29.21	29.22
SSIM	0.81	0.82	0.83	0.78	0.85	0.87	0.89	0.87	0.91	0.93

The size of the training set also affects the results of the reconstruction. We use a specific number of training sets during training and then test the quality of the resulting image. As shown in Fig. 6, it can be seen from the figure that the quality evaluation index of the tested image–peak signal to noise ratio (PSNR) and structural similarity index (SSIM) are continuously improved when the number of pictures in the training set is gradually increased. When it is increased to a certain extent, the quality improvement tends to be stable, and the size of the dataset is no longer the main influencing factor.

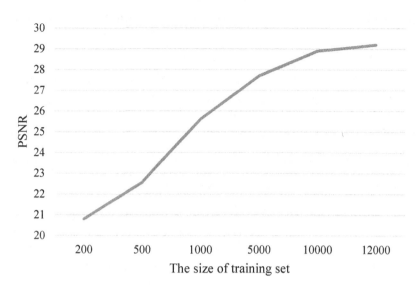

Fig. 6. Relationship between the size of dataset and PSNR

3.2   Subjective Evaluation of the Algorithm

We select some test pictures to show the deblurring effect, and Fig. 7 shows the effect of deblurring the remote sensing images in different scenes. The first scene is the residential area and the school. In the deblurred picture, the letters on the lawn and in the middle of the playground and the layout of the surrounding houses can be clearly seen. The second scene is the interlaced road area. The picture shows the location of each car on the road and the size of the car in the parking lot clearly after deblurring; the third scene is the airport, which the clear outline of each aircraft and the location of the surrounding objects can be seen in the deblurred picture. It can be seen from the comparison of the three groups that the deblurred model tested can effectively highlight the details and avoid the ringing effect, and achieve good results. The left side of each line is the deblurred image restored by our algorithm, and the right side is the blurry remote sensing image.

We select the deblurring results of some images and compare them with other remote sensing image deblurring methods [1]. Some deblurring effects are shown in Fig. 8. We noticed from the results of Tan et al. [1] that the whole picture has pixel stitching and ringing effect. Our results did not have the above problems, and the restored images were clear and achieved good results. (from top to bottom, blurry images, Tan et al. [1] 's deblurred images, ours and real sharp images)

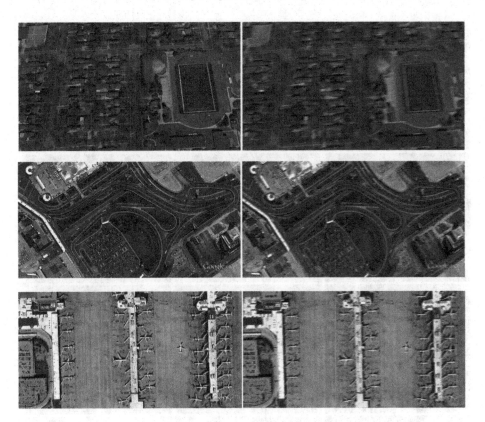

Fig. 7. Partial test image deblurring effect

3.3 Objective Evaluation of the Algorithm

To objective evaluation of image quality, peak signal to noise ratio (PSNR) and structural similarity (SSIM) are generally used. Table 2 gives the comparison results on the test set. As can be seen from Table 2, compared with other neural network algorithms, the average PSNR and SSIM on the test set exceed the other methods. It can be seen that the deblurring algorithm proposed in this paper is more suitable for the multi-dimensional and dense features of remote sensing image imaging. This way not only could improve the subjective visual effect of remote sensing image deblurring, but also improve the image quality evaluation index and improve the objective quality of the image.

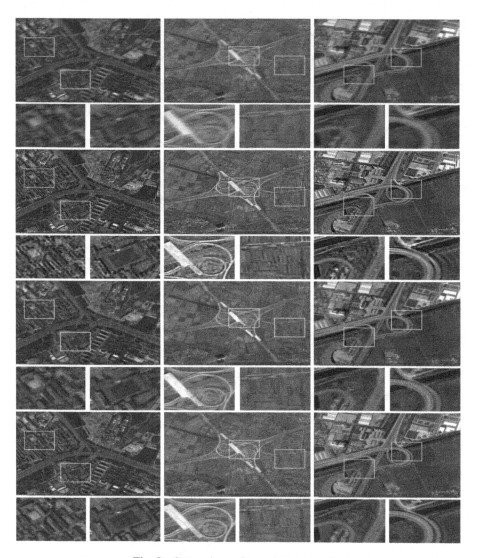

Fig. 8. Comparison of experimental results

Table 2. Comparison of the quality of the blurred image on the test set

Algorithm	Ours	Nah's method [5]	Kupyn's method [6]
PSNR	29.20	25.60	27.93
SSIM	0.9185	0.8177	0.8765

4 Conclusion

In this paper, the remote sensing image is deblurred by WGAN-based remote sensing image deblurring algorithm. The algorithm does not need to estimate the blur kernel explicitly, and realizes the end-to-end image deblurring process. We use the WGAN loss function, the content loss function, and the perceptual loss function to implement it. We improved the existing Generative Adversarial Networks and introduced a perceptual loss function through the VGG network to make the generated deblurred image closer to the real image. This method effectively avoids the ringing phenomenon caused by the inaccuracy of blur kernel estimation by traditional methods. The superiority and reliability of the algorithm are proved by experiments. Although the deblurring effect is better, there is still room for improvement in processing speed.

Acknowledgement. This work is supported by the National Natural Science Foundation of China (No. 61762014). The project was funded by a major project of Guangxi Science and Technology (Guike AA18118009).

References

1. Tan, H.P., et al.: Multi-scale deblurring of remote sensing images based on regularization constraints. J. Image Graph. **20**(3), 386–394 (2015)
2. Cheng, F.: Deblurring of optical remote sensing image based on estimated point spread function. Shanghai Aerosp. **33**(3), 105–112 (2016)
3. Zhang, G.M., et al.: Remote image restoration method based on blurry image and noise image. Electron. Des. Eng. **25**(18), 82–86 (2017)
4. Ren, J.J., et al.: Image deblurring based on fast convolutional neural networks. J. Comput. Aided Des. Comput. Graph. **29**(8), 1444–1456 (2017)
5. Nah, S., Kim, T.H., et al.: Deep multi-scale convolutional neural network for dynamic scene deblurring. In: IEEE Conference on Computer Vision and Pattern Recognition 2017, pp. 257–265 (2017)
6. Kupyn, O., Budzan, V., et al.: DeblurGAN: blind motion deblurring using conditional adversarial networks. arXiv preprint arXiv:1711.07064, pp. 1–7 (2018)
7. Goodfellow, I.J., Pouget-Abadie, J., et al.: Generative adversarial nets. In: Advances in Neural Information Processing System, pp. 2672–2680 (2014)
8. Arjovsky, M., Chintala, S., et al: Wasserstein GAN. arXiv preprint arXiv:1701.07875 (2017)
9. He, K., Zhang, X., Ren, S., Sun, J.: Identity mappings in deep residual networks. In: Leibe, B., Matas, J., Sebe, N., Welling, M. (eds.) ECCV 2016. LNCS, vol. 9908, pp. 630–645. Springer, Cham (2016). https://doi.org/10.1007/978-3-319-46493-0_38
10. Gulrajani, I., Ahmed, F., et al.: Improved Training of Wasserstein GANs. arXiv preprint arXiv:1704.00028 (2017)
11. Johnson, J., Alahi, A., Fei-Fei, L.: Perceptual losses for real-time style transfer and super-resolution. In: Leibe, B., Matas, J., Sebe, N., Welling, M. (eds.) ECCV 2016. LNCS, vol. 9906, pp. 694–711. Springer, Cham (2016). https://doi.org/10.1007/978-3-319-46475-6_43
12. Simonyan, K., Zisserman, A., et al.: Very deep convolutional networks for large-scale image recognition. In: Proceedings of International Conference on Learning Representations, abs/1409.1555 (2014)

Text Classification Research Based on Improved Word2vec and CNN

Mengyuan Gao, Tinghui Li[✉], and Peifang Huang

Guangxi Normal University, Guilin 541000, China
tinghuili@gxnu.edu.cn

Abstract. In view of the traditional classification algorithm, the problem of high feature dimension and data sparseness often occurs when text classification of short texts. This paper proposes a text feature combining neural network language model word2vec and document topic model Latent Dirichlet Allocation (LDA). Represents a matrix model. The matrix model can not only effectively represent the semantic features of the words but also convey the context features and enhance the feature expression ability of the model. The feature matrix was input into the convolutional neural network (CNN) for convolution pooling, and text classification experiments were performed. The experimental results show that the proposed matrix model has better classification effect than the traditional text classification methods based on word2vec and CNN. In the text classification accuracy rate, recall rate and F1 three evaluation indicators increased by 8.4%, 8.9% and 8.6%.

Keywords: Text classification · Word2vec · LDA · CNN

1 Introduction

In recent years, with the rapid development of Internet technology, mainstream social platforms have generated massive amounts of text information all the time. Among them, short texts account for a large proportion. These texts are short in length and strong in context, and have high research value in the fields of information retrieval, text recommendation and relationship extraction [1]. Short text classification, as a basic task in the field of natural language processing, has been closely watched by researchers. Therefore, efficient and accurate text classification methods are of great significance for data mining, information processing and network maintenance.

The feature representation and classification algorithm of text is an important part of text classification work, which has a direct impact on text classification effect. The traditional text feature representation is based on the word bag model (BOW) [2]. Using the word bag principle, the words are disorderly represented to a high-dimensional vector space model, ignoring the context structure information of the words, making the text classification work face. Great challenge. In 2013, Mikolov et al. proposed a word2vec word vector model based on previous studies, mapping words to a real vector [3]. The word2vec model has been widely used in Chinese word segmentation [3], POS Tagging [4], and emotional classification [5]. However, how to use the word vector to better represent the text has always been a difficult point in the

© Springer Nature Switzerland AG 2019
X. Liu et al. (Eds.): ICSOC 2018 Workshops, LNCS 11434, pp. 126–135, 2019.
https://doi.org/10.1007/978-3-030-17642-6_11

current work. The current common methods are: averaging all the word vectors contained in a document [6], doc2vec model [7], clustering word vectors [8]. However, these methods ignore the influence of a single word on the entire document, so the effect is not satisfactory.

Traditional machine learning classification algorithms include Naive Bayes (NB), Support Vector Machine (SVM), Logistic Regression, etc. (LR). Most of these classification algorithms are based on vector space models, and these classification algorithms generally use artificially designed feature selection algorithms such as TF-IDF, information gain (IG), chi-square statistics (CHI), and weighted likelihood logarithm (WLLR). Wait. These feature selection algorithms have problems such as insufficient feature representation and easy to ignore the relationship between categories. AGARWAL proposes to extract feature information by detecting simple grammar patterns [9]. In response to the problem of TF-IDF feature selection, data loss is easy to occur. Narayanan et al. proposed a class descriptor (CTD) to reduce the impact of data skew. In addition, compared with the traditional machine learning classification algorithm, SVM has the characteristics of high efficiency and stability. The final decision function is determined by only a few support vectors, which avoids dimensional disaster [10, 11]. However, SVM also has certain limitations when it comes to training large-scale data sets.

Deep learning is a hot topic in the field of machine learning research. Convolutional neural networks (CNN) were originally applied in the field of computer vision [12]. At present, CNN has also achieved very good results in the field of natural language processing. Kim combines word vectors with CNN and applies them to topic classification and semantic analysis to achieve good results [13]. Meng J.E. et al. proposed a pooling technique based on attention mechanism, which can acquire more semantic information to better model sentences [14].

The CNN input matrix only extracts the word vector matrix of the word granularity level and ignores the overall semantic feature expression of the text granularity level, which leads to the incompleteness of the text feature representation, which affects the accuracy of text classification. This paper attempts to combine the word2vec model with the LDA model to form a new text feature representation matrix, which is then passed to CNN for text classification, and has achieved good classification results.

2 Related Work

2.1 Text Preprocessing

The process of text preprocessing generally includes the following steps:

(1) Standard encoding format, generally the web page information storage format crawled from the Internet is rather confusing, which will directly affect the experimental effect, so the unified encoding format such as GBK or utf-8.

(2) Text segmentation, the words of the text will be used as features to characterize the text in the following experiments. English can divide words by space characters, and Chinese needs to re-segment the continuous man into words according to the rules. At present, the Chinese word segmentation system ICTCLAS developed by

the Institute of Computer Technology of the Chinese Academy of Sciences and the Python Chinese word segmentation component Jieba can be used to implement word segmentation, add custom dictionary, keyword extraction, and part-of-speech tagging.

(3) To stop words, including a large number of auxiliary words, function words, prepositions in the text, such words appear at high frequency, may form noise, affect the classification effect, usually we will directly filter out the stop words in the text.

2.2   Text Representation

In the Natural Language Processing (NLP) task, we let the machine learning algorithm to deal with the natural language, but the machine can't directly understand the human language, so the language is mathematicalized, that is, a word is represented as a vector. One-hot encoding is the simplest way to characterize a text, using a long vector to represent a word. The length of the vector is the size N of the dictionary D, the component of the vector has only one "1", the others are all "0", and the position of "1" corresponds to the index of the word in the dictionary. This representation is very simple but usually faces problems with too high dimensions, and the default words and words are isolated, ignoring the semantic information of the context. Therefore, it is not often used. In addition, Mathew J. et al. use the LDA model to represent the semantic features of text and construct a word vector model based on topic distribution [15]. Tang Ming considers the influence of a single word on the whole document, uses TF-IDF to calculate the weight of words in each document, and combines the word2vec word vector model to generate a document vector for Chinese document classification [16]. The Word2vec model can train word vectors quickly and efficiently. After training, the Word2vec model can be used to map each word to a vector to represent the relationship between words and words. The LDA theme model was proposed by Blei et al. in 2003 and is also known as the three-layer Bayesian probability model. The LDA contains words, topics, and document structures. By briefly describing the documents and retaining the essential feature information, the LDA helps to efficiently process large-scale data sets [17].

2.3   Text Classification

Text classification models are generally divided into two categories: machine learning and deep learning. Taiyong Guo's characteristics of traditional TF-IDF extraction are not well reflected in the importance of the internal and category categories. It is proposed to introduce a position factor to correct the features and perform classification verification on the support vector machine [18]. Yuting S. proposed a text classification method based on LDA and SVM. The topic feature model describes the document, which is more accurate than the traditional feature extraction method [19]. Because the CNN convolutional neural network model has good adaptability to text classification tasks, Nguyen, TH, etc. assume that the positions of all text elements are known, and each input sample contains only one relationship, exploring CNN in relation mining and relationships. The application in the classification task [20]. In summary, the application of the text surface feature extraction method is relatively mature, but it is easy to lead to high-dimensional data and incomplete feature expression. The LDA model extracts the semantic features and ignores the semantic features. The word2vec model trains the word vector model and ignores the semantic features. If these two representation features are used as the input matrix of the CNN, the classification effect will be unsatisfactory.

3   Word2vec and LDA Combination Model

3.1   Construct CNN Input Matrix

Training Word Vector.
Word2vec mainly contains two important models, Continuous Bag-of Words (CBOW) model and Skip-gram model. Both models include an input layer, a projection layer, and an output layer. The CBOW model uses the $C(C = 2)$ words before and after $M(t)$ to predict the current word; the Skip-gram model is just the opposite. It uses the word $M(t)$ to predict the C words before and after it. In this paper, the Skip-gram model is used to train the no-learning term rule by random combination. Let $M(t)$ be any word in the data set, then the formula is as follows:

$$P(M_{t-k}M_{t-k+1}M_{t+k-1}|M_t) \tag{1}$$

Among them: $M_{t-k}M_{t-k+1}M_{t+k-1}$ is the probability of $M(t)$ appearing by jumping combination. When the word vector trains text, it outputs the N-dimensional vector representation of any word:

$$M = \begin{bmatrix} M_{11} & M_{12} & M_{13} & \cdots & M_{1N} \\ M_{21} & M_{22} & M_{23} & \cdots & M_{2N} \\ \vdots & \vdots & \vdots & \vdots & \vdots \\ M_{k1} & M_{k2} & M_{k3} & \cdots & M_{kN} \end{bmatrix} \tag{2}$$

Where: M is any text of the data set and M_{kN} is the weight of the term.

Training Theme Vector
The LDA model treats a document as a collection of word vectors. The process is as follows: For a document, the document and the topic satisfy a polynomial distribution, and the words in the topic and vocabulary also satisfy a polynomial distribution. Both polynomials are Dirichlet prior distributions with hyperparameters α and β, respectively. Therefore, the composition process of the document d can be regarded as: extracting a topic from the document topic distribution θ, and then extracting a word from the word distribution $\varnothing$ corresponding to the extracted topic, repeating the above process times, forming an article containing N words. The probability model formula is as follows:

$$p(\theta, z, w | \alpha, \beta) = p(\theta|\alpha) \prod_{n=1}^{N} (z_n|\theta) p(w_n | z_n, \beta) \tag{3}$$

Through the LDA model, the probability distribution of the word on the subject (4) and the probability distribution of the article on the subject (5) can be obtained, where K is the subject number and C_{wk} is the number of times the word w is given the subject k, C_{dk} Indicates the number of times document d is given to topic k.

$$p(k|w) = \frac{C_{wk} + \beta}{\sum_{k=1}^{K} C_{wk} + K\beta} \tag{4}$$

$$p(k|d) = \frac{C_{dk} + \alpha}{\sum_{k=1}^{K} C_{dk} + K\alpha} \tag{5}$$

After the LDA model is finished, the topic distribution matrix of the arbitrary data of the output data set is as follows:

$$Z = \begin{bmatrix} Z_{11} & Z_{12} & Z_{13} & \cdots & Z_{1N} \\ Z_{21} & Z_{22} & Z_{23} & \cdots & Z_{2N} \\ \vdots & \vdots & \vdots & \vdots & \vdots \\ Z_{k1} & Z_{k2} & Z_{k3} & \cdots & Z_{kN} \end{bmatrix} \tag{6}$$

Where: Z_{MN} is the subject probability vector corresponding to the text M, N is the corpus size, N is the vector dimension, and the number is the same as the word vector dimension.

Vector Stitching

The improved text representation method is to superimpose the matrices obtained by training the above two models to form a new feature matrix, which includes both semantic features and semantic features.

$$M_{new} = M \oplus Z \tag{7}$$

Where: $\oplus$ is a vector stitching operation. The splicing is completed to obtain a new matrix M_{new}, which serves as the input matrix of the CNN.

$$M_{new} = \begin{bmatrix} M_{11} & M_{12} & M_{13} & \cdots & M_{1N} \\ M_{21} & M_{22} & M_{23} & \cdots & M_{2N} \\ \vdots & \vdots & \vdots & \vdots & \vdots \\ M_{k1} & M_{k2} & M_{k3} & \cdots & M_{kN} \\ Z_{l1} & Z_{l2} & Z_{l3} & \cdots & Z_{lN} \end{bmatrix} \tag{8}$$

3.2   Convolutional Neural Network Model

CNN is an optimized convolutional neural network. The core lies in the convolution operation between the input matrix and different convolution kernels. The pooled convolution result is used as the data feature of the classification operation. Therefore, the convolutional neural network is mainly composed of convolutional layer, pooling layer and classification layer. The structure is shown in Fig. 1:

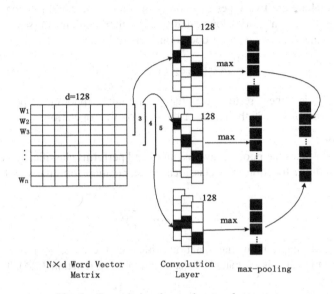

Fig. 1. Convolutional neural network structure

Input Layer

The input layer is a word vector matrix of words in a sentence. Assuming that there are n words and the word vector dimension is d, the size of the input matrix is $n \times d$. The value of the word vector can be fixed or optimized as a parameter during the training of the model.

Hidden Layer

The hidden layer includes a convolution layer and a pooling layer. The convolution essence is a weighted superposition of the input signal, which is a volume of the text by a different size of the convolution kernel (Filter) $h \times d$ (h is the number of words contained in the convolution kernel window, d represents the vector dimension of each word). The product operation extracts local features of different granularities. The experimental convolution kernels are designed in three sizes, namely $3 \times d$, $4 \times d$, $5 \times d$, and CNN convolution operations as follows:

$$c_i = f\left(\sum W_1 \cdot X_{i:i+h-1} + b_1\right) \tag{9}$$

Where c_i represents the result of the convolution operation, that is, the point multiplication of the output matrix and the convolution kernel plus the activation output after the offset. h is the window size, $X_{i:i+h-1}$ is the word vector matrix in the i to $i+h-1$ window of the input, W_1 is the convolution kernel or the weight matrix, b_1 is the offset, and f is the *relu* activation function.

After the features are obtained by convolution, the features are extracted to simplify the computational complexity of the network, and the features are compressed at the pooling layer. There are two types of pooling operations: average pooling and maximum pooling. Text categorization usually uses max-pooling to select the most important information. The pooling operation is as follows:

$$\hat{c} = max\{c_1, c_2, c_3 \cdots c_{n-h+1}\} \tag{10}$$

Where: $\hat{c}$ is the result of the maximum pooling operation, and $c_i (i = 1, 2, \ldots, n-h+1)$ is the result of the convolution operation.

Output Layer

The output layer takes the pooling layer as input and performs classification calculation through the *Softmax* function. The classification calculation formula is as follows:

$$f(x)_\varnothing = \frac{1}{1 + exp(-\varnothing^T x)} \tag{11}$$

exp represents the exponential function with e as the base, $\varnothing$ is the evaluation parameter, and the value is estimated by the minimum cost function $J(\varnothing)$. The formula is as follows:

$$J(\varnothing) = \sum_{i=1}^{M} y(i) log f_\varnothing \left(x^{(i)} \right) \tag{12}$$

The return value of the function is the probability value of C components, and each component corresponds to the probability of an output category, thereby dividing the type information of the text and completing the classification.

4   Experiment Studies

4.1   Experimental Environment and Data

The experiment in this paper is carried out under the Win7 system. The CPU is Inter Core i5-3230M 2.6 GHz, the memory size is 8G, the experimental programming language is Python3.5, the development tool is Pycharm, and the deep learning framework used is Tensorflow1.0.0. The experimental data in this paper is from Sogou Lab's text classification corpus. It selects 8,000 documents from sports, military, tourism, finance, IT, real estate, education, entertainment, and eight categories of 1000 experiments. The data is verified by ten-fold cross-validation. The set is divided into 80% training set and 20% test set.

4.2 Experimental Setup

The data in this paper is unified in UTF-8 encoding format, calling the Jieba participle component in Python for word segmentation, and using the stop word list of Harbin Institute of Technology to stop words. Create a text feature representation matrix and enter CNN for text classification. The specific settings of the CNN model parameters are shown in Table 1:

Table 1. CNN parameter configuration.

Parameter name	Parameter value
Num_filters	128
Kernel_size	3, 4, 5
Embedding_dim	128
Pooling	Max-pooling
Batch_size	64
Droupout_prob	0.5
Num_epochs	10
Learning_rate	1e–3

4.3 Evaluation Indicators

For the classification results, the internationally accepted evaluation indicators are adopted: the precision rate P, the recall rate R, and the F1 value. The calculation formulas of the three evaluation indicators are as follows:

$$P = \frac{A}{A+B} \tag{13}$$

$$R = \frac{A}{A+C} \tag{14}$$

$$F_1 = \frac{2PR}{P+R} \tag{15}$$

Where A indicates that a certain type of text is correctly identified as the number of samples of the class, B indicates that a certain type of text is recognized as the number of samples of other categories, and C indicates that the text of other categories is recognized as the number of samples of the class.

In order to verify the effectiveness of the improved input feature matrix, the word2vec-based CNN text classification method is compared with the experiment in this paper. Compare the precision of the precision P and the recall rate of R and F1. The experimental data is shown in Table 2:

As can be seen from the above table, the average accuracy, recall rate and F1 of the traditional CNN-based word2vec text classification method are: 0.836, 0834, and 0.835, respectively. The average precision, recall and F1 values of the classification

Table 2. Comparison of classification results.

Date_set	P		R		F1	
	Word2vec	Word2vec-LDA	Word2vec	Word2vec-LDA	Word2vec	Word2vec-LDA
Military	0.836	0.917	0.850	0.932	0.843	0.924
PE	0.840	0.932	0.833	0.927	0.836	0.929
Travel	0.827	0.906	0.841	0.914	0.834	0.910
Finance	0.817	0.928	0.840	0.913	0.834	0.920
IT	0.846	0.935	0.825	0.923	0.835	0.929
Property	0.825	0.901	0.867	0.942	0.845	0.921
Education	0.850	0.943	0.808	0.915	0.828	0.929
Entertainment	0.844	0.905	0.817	0.921	0.830	0.913
Average	0.836	0.920	0.834	0.923	0.835	0.921

methods in this paper are: 0.920, 0.923, and 0.921. In comparison, the improved method has a better classification effect, and the average accuracy rate, recall rate, and F1 value are increased by about 8%. The reason is that the improved text representation matrix has strong feature representation ability and is more representative, which can provide more category information for text classification.

5 Conclusion

The improved text classification method in this paper solves the problem that the traditional CNN input matrix features are not fully represented and affects the text classification effect. A word-vector based on word granularity and a specific improvement method based on semantic granularity are proposed. The word vector matrix and the topic vector matrix are superimposed to form a new matrix that can reflect both part-of-speech features and semantic features. The input matrix features of the product neural network make it better for text representation and improve classification performance. It provides a new idea for text classification research based on convolutional neural networks.

References

1. Severyn, A., Moschitti, A.: Learning to rank short text pairs with convolutional deep neural networks. In: Proceedings of the 38th International ACM SIGIR Conference on Research and Development in Information Retrieval - SIGIR 2015, pp. 373–382 (2015)
2. Zhang, Y., Jin, R., Zhou, Z.H.: Understanding bag-of-words model: a statistical framework. Int. J. Mach. Learn. Cybern. 1, 43–52 (2010)
3. Mikolov, T., Sutskever, I., Chen, K., Corrado, G., Dean, J.: Distributed representations of words and phrases and their compositionality. In: Advances in Neural Information Processing Systems, vol. 26, pp. 3111–3119 (2013)

4. Zheng, X., Chen, H., Xu, T.: Deep learning for Chinese word segmentation and POS tagging. In: EMNLP, pp. 647–657 (2013)
5. Xue, B., Fu, C., Shaobin, Z.: A study on sentiment computing and classification of Sina Weibo with Word2vec. In: 2014 IEEE International Congress on Big Data, pp. 358–363 (2014)
6. Xing, C., Wang, D., Zhang, X., Liu, C.: Document classification with distributions of word vectors. In: Asia-Pacific Signal and Information Processing Association Annual Summit and Conference, APSIPA 2014 (2014)
7. Le, Q.V., Mikolov, T.: Distributed representations of sentences and documents. In: International Conference on International Conference on Machine Learning, pp. 1–9 (2014)
8. Kim, H.K., Kim, H., Cho, S.: Bag-of-concepts: comprehending document representation through clustering words in distributed representation. Neurocomputing **266**, 336–352 (2017)
9. Agarwal, A., Xie, B., Vovsha, I.: Sentiment analysis of Twitter data. In: The Workshop on Languages in Social Media, pp. 30–38. Association for Computational Linguistics (2011)
10. Yang, F., Li, Z., Zeng, S., Hao, B., Qi, P., Pang, Z.: A novel method for wireless communication signal modulation recognition in smart grid. J. Commun. **11**, 813–818 (2016)
11. Jie, C., Zhiyi, F., Dan, Z., Guannan, Q.: Network traffic classification using feature selection and parameter optimization. Int. J. Appl. Eng. Res. **10**, 5663–5679 (2015)
12. Luong, M., Pham, H., Manning, C.D.: Effective approaches to attention-based neural machine translation. In: Proceedings of the 2015 Conference on Empirical Methods in Natural Language Processing, pp. 1412–1421 (2015)
13. Kim, Y.: Convolutional neural networks for sentence classification. In: The 2014 Conference on Empirical Methods in Natural Language Processing (EMNLP), pp. 1746–1751 (2014)
14. Zhang, Y., Wallace, B.: A sensitivity analysis of (and practitioners' guide to) convolutional neural networks for sentence classification. In: The 8th International Joint Conference on Natural Language Processing, pp. 253–263 (2015)
15. Mathew, J., Radhakrishnan, D.: An FIR digital filter using one-hot coded residue representation. In: IEEE, pp. 1–4 (2015)
16. Ming, T., Lei, Z., Xianchun, Z.: Document vector representation based on Word2Vec. Comput. Sci. **43**, 214–219 (2016)
17. Carrera-trejo, V., Sidorov, G., Miranda-jiménez, S., Ibarra, M.M., Martínez, R.C.: Latent Dirichlet allocation complement in the vector space model for multi-label text classification. Int. J. Comb. Optim. Probl. Inform. **6**, 7–19 (2015)
18. Taiyong, G.: A method based on TF-IDF and improved support vector machine research on Chinese text categorization. Comput. Eng. **37**, 141–145 (2016)
19. Yuting, S., Dehua, X.: Research on Chinese text classification based on LDA and SVM. Res. Dev. **2**, 18–23 (2016)
20. Nguyen, T.H., Grishman, R.: Relation extraction: perspective from convolutional neural networks. In: Workshop on Vector Modeling for NLP, pp. 39–48 (2015)

Retinal Image Registration Based on Bifurcation Point and SURF

Haiying Xia[(⊠)] and Danhua Chen

College of Electronic Engineering,
Guangxi Normal University, Guilin 541004, China
xhyhust@gmail.com

Abstract. Retinal image registration is the process of matching and superimposing two retinal images of the same patient. The traditional feature-based retinal image registration algorithm is computationally expensive during the matching process. This paper proposes a fast and efficient registration method based on the combination of bifurcation point and SURF algorithm. First, the eight-neighbor search algorithm is used to detect the bifurcation points of the reference image and the target image, and then the SURF feature is extracted in the rectangular template region centered on the bifurcation point. The Euclidean distance is used to perform rough matching on the extracted features, then RANSAC is used for fine matching, and finally the transformation model is estimated. Experiments show that this method can quickly and effectively achieve the registration of retinal images while reducing a large number of unnecessary searches and achieving a great registration result.

Keywords: Retinal image registration · Bifurcation point · SURF ·
Feature extraction · RANSAC

1 Introduction

With the rapid development of computer vision technology, image registration technology has gradually received widespread attention. At present, it has been widely studied and applied in the fields of computer vision, medical diagnosis, automatic tracking and positioning, face recognition, and image 3D reconstruction. Image registration is the process of matching and superimposing the same content of two or more images of the same scene. This article focuses on the techniques of retinal fundus image registration that are important in practical medical clinical practice. Retinal fundus images are an important basis for the diagnosis of diabetes, glaucoma, hypertension, coronary heart disease and other diseases. The doctor can obtain a variety of complementary information of the diseased tissue or organ while two retinal fundus images of the same patient at different times or different modalities are registered, thereby providing a more comprehensive basis for the diagnosis of the disease.

Currently, related retinal image registration methods can be roughly divided into three categories: region-based methods, feature-based methods, and hybrid methods [1]. Region-based methods, such as mutual information [2, 3], cross-correlation [4], etc.,

© Springer Nature Switzerland AG 2019
X. Liu et al. (Eds.): ICSOC 2018 Workshops, LNCS 11434, pp. 136–146, 2019.
https://doi.org/10.1007/978-3-030-17642-6_12

require a large search space, resulting in a large amount of computational cost and not suitable for fast registration. Feature-based methods, representative features of the retina are bifurcations, optic discs, and dimples. Among them, bifurcation [5–7] has a wide range of applications in image registration. [8] proposed the idea of bifurcation structure, which effectively reduced the many-to-one mismatch caused by the single bifurcation point matching, but the registration effect is not accurate enough. In addition, there are other point features that are widely used for retinal image registration, such as the iterative closest point algorithm ICP [9], dual bootstrap ICP [10], and generalized dual bootstrap ICP [11]. The hybrid approach combines region-based and feature-based methods to improve registration effects. For example, [12] proposed the Harris-PIIFD registration framework, but it is very sensitive to large mismatches; [13] using the SURF-PIIFD registration framework to improve Harris-PIIFD framework. The outliers are effectively eliminated, but the algorithm is time consuming.

In order to improve the registration accuracy, reduce the computational cost, and improve the speed of the algorithm, this article proposes a fast and efficient registration algorithm based on the advantages of two different features of the bifurcation point and the SURF key point. First, an eight-neighbor search algorithm is used to detect the bifurcation points of the reference image and the target image. Then, the SURF key points are searched within a given rectangular template area centered on the bifurcation point, and the extracted features are coarsely matched by Euclidean distance. Finally, the RANSAC algorithm is used to finely match for eliminating the mismatch and enhancing the robustness of the algorithm so that the accurate point pairs are obtained for the final transform model estimation. Further experiments show that the method can quickly and effectively achieve the registration of retinal images while reducing a large number of unnecessary searches and achieving a good registration effect.

2 Proposed Method

Our improved retinal image registration framework, as shown in the Fig. 1, mainly includes the following four parts: detecting the position bifurcation point and SURF candidate point position; searching the feature points in the rectangular template; Euclidean distance coarse matching and RANSAC Fine matching; transform estimation.

The image is pre-processed prior to extracting local feature points with the SURF detector. The color image consists of three channels, and the image contrast is most noticeable in the green co-channel, so we select the green component in the input RGB image format.

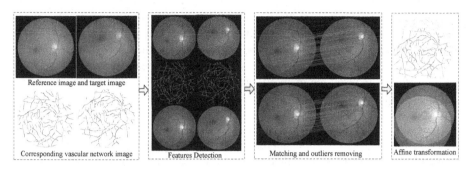

Fig. 1. Improved retinal image registration framework. Input a pair of retinal images and their corresponding blood vessel images, one as a reference image and the other as a target image. Extract the SURF feature points around the bifurcation points by locating the bifurcation points. Then use the Euclidean distance preliminary point match and then use RANSAC to remove the mismatch. Finally, the retinal images are aligned on the same spatial axis by affine transformation.

2.1   Bifurcation Point Extraction

The vascular vasculature can represent the entire retinal fundus image. The bifurcation point is the most prominent visual feature in the vascular network. Therefore, the bifurcation point is usually extracted to register the retinal image. This paper uses the eight neighborhood search algorithm to extract the bifurcation point. Assuming the centerline of the vessel is given, we can detect the bifurcation point through a $3 * 3$ window. Whether the seed point is a candidate bifurcation point is determined by detecting the gray value of the eight neighborhood pixels. If the gray value of three or more pixels in a neighborhood of a seed point has a gray value of 1, it is determined that the seed point is a candidate bifurcation point.

If only the eight neighborhood search algorithm is used to detect the bifurcation point, there will be some error points, as shown in the Fig. 2(a). In order to eliminate the error point, we further detect the connectivity of the surrounding blood vessels and the candidate bifurcation points in the surrounding $7 * 7$ region centered on the candidate bifurcation point, and use the vector of one circle around the rectangular region as the angle vector of the candidate bifurcation point. If three branch angles are detected around a candidate point, it is determined to be a bifurcation point. The filtered bifurcation point is as shown in the Fig. 2(b), which can effectively eliminate the trifurcation point and the false bifurcation point.

The bifurcation point is a typical feature in the retinal image. If the bifurcation points are precisely aligned, the entire retinal image is aligned. However, it easily causes mismatch due to the high similarity of the bifurcation points because the feature vector of each bifurcation point is mainly composed of its three bifurcation angles.

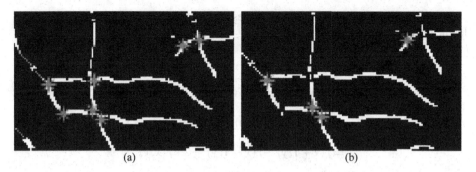

Fig. 2. Extract the bifurcation point. (a) is the bifurcation point extracted by the eight-neighbor algorithm; (b) is the bifurcation point after filtering.

2.2   SURF Algorithm

The Speeded Up Robust Feature (SURF) [14] is a robust local feature point detection and description algorithm proposed by H. Bay et al. SURF has two major advantages in terms of execution efficiency. One is to use the integral graph on the Hessian matrix, and the other is to use the dimensionality reduction feature descriptor.

The Hessian matrix is a square matrix of the second-order partial derivatives of the multivariate function describing the local curvature of the function. For image F, its Hessian matrix is as follows:

$$H(f(x,y)) = \begin{bmatrix} \dfrac{\partial^2 f}{\partial x^2} & \dfrac{\partial^2 f}{\partial x \partial y} \\ \dfrac{\partial^2 f}{\partial x \partial y} & \dfrac{\partial^2 f}{\partial y^2} \end{bmatrix} \tag{1}$$

Gaussian filtering of the image is required before constructing the Hessian matrix. The filtered Hessian matrix is expressed as:

$$H(x, \sigma) = \begin{bmatrix} L_{xx}(x,\sigma) & L_{xy}(x,\sigma) \\ L_{xy}(x,\sigma) & L_{yy}(x,\sigma) \end{bmatrix} \tag{2}$$

When the discriminant of the Hessian matrix obtains a local maximum, it determines that the current point is brighter or darker than other points in the surrounding neighborhood, thereby locating the position of the key point.

We know that in discrete digital images, the first derivative is the grayscale difference of adjacent pixels:

$$Dx = f(x+1, y) - f(x, y) \tag{3}$$

The second derivative is the re-derivation of the first derivative:

$$Dxx = [f(x+1, y) - f(x, y)] - [f(x, y) - f(x-1, y)] \tag{4}$$

$$= f(x+1, y) + f(x-1, y) - 2 * f(x, y)$$

The discriminant of the Hessian matrix is actually the second-order partial derivative of the current point to the horizontal direction multiplied by the second-order partial derivative in the vertical direction and then subtracted the quadratic square of the horizontal and vertical second-order partial derivatives of the current point:

$$\det(H) = Dxx * Dyy - Dxy * Dxy \tag{5}$$

The $f(x, y)$ in the Hessian matrix discriminant is the Gaussian convolution of the original image. Since the Gaussian kernel obeys the normal distribution and the coefficient is getting lower from the center point. SURF uses a box filter to approximate Gaussian filter in order to improve the operation speed, therefore multiplying Dxy by a weighting factor of 0.9 to balance the error caused by the approximation using the box filter:

$$\det(H) = Dxx * Dyy - (0.9 * Dxy)^2 \tag{6}$$

Box filters can increase the speed of the operation which involves the use of integral graph. Filtering the image by a box filter is converted to the problem of calculating the addition and subtraction of pixels between different regions of an image. This is the strength of the integral graph which can be completed by simply finding the integral graph several times.

In the SURF algorithm, a 4 * 4 rectangular block of the direction along the main direction of the feature point is taken around the feature point. Each sub-area counts the Haar wavelet features of the horizontal and vertical directions of 25 pixels. The Haar wavelet feature is the four directions as after the horizontal direction value, after the vertical direction value, after the horizontal absolute value, and after the vertical absolute value. These four values are used as feature vectors for each sub-block region such that a total of 4 * 4 * 4 = 64-dimensional vectors is used as descriptors for SURF features. The results of the SURF algorithm in extracting feature points in the retina fundus image are shown in the Fig. 3:

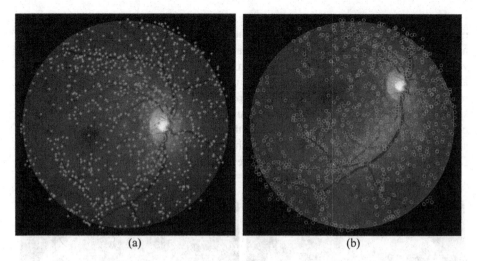

(a)   (b)

Fig. 3. Extract feature points in retinal images by SURF. (a) is the SURF point detected in the reference image; (b) is the SURF point detected in the target image.

Figure 3(a) detects 912 points, and Fig. 3(b) detects 891 points. The number of points of interest detected by the SURF algorithm is too dense and contains a large number of unnecessary redundant points which leads to high computational cost and increases the duration of the algorithm in the process of searching for point matching. The key to image registration is to find high-quality, high-reliability representative points, so that even if the number of detected points is small, it can be accurately registered.

2.3 Algorithm Design

Combining the advantages of the two different features of the bifurcation point and the SURF key point, we first find the bifurcation point and SURF point position information, and then extract the SURF feature descriptor in a rectangular template area Ω centered on the bifurcation point. Then, perform coarse matching by Euclidean distance and fine matching by RANSAC algorithm, and the transformation model is estimated subsequently. The entire algorithm flow is as follows:

Algorithm 1: Proposed registration algorithm

    Input: Retinal, Retinal vascular image pair, parameters r, η, κ, t

    Output: Correspondence set χ, transformation T

1   Color image preprocessing, select green channel

2   Locating the bifurcation point position: pt

3   Extracting candidate points using SURF: p

4   **For** creating a region Ω centered on each pt

    Judge whether p belongs to Ω or not

        Yes: put p into pm and go to step 4

    Until judge each point p, and pm is the selected feature points

5   Inner point set χ is determined by Eq. (7) and RANSAC algorithm

6   Estimate affine transformation T from all inner points

The rectangular template constrains the range of feature point search. This algorithm for filtering feature points can make the selected feature points along the vascular network distribution and the number of feature points greatly reduced. The vascular venation can represent the transformation of the entire retinal image. Therefore, although the number of feature points is limited, the selected feature points are more representative, the reliability of the registration result is improved, and the registration speed is also faster. The size of the rectangular template must ensure the quality of the points in the template area, as well as the number of feature points. Therefore, according to the experimental experience, the size of the rectangular template is set to $\Omega = 21 * 21$. The filtered feature points are distributed as shown in the Fig. 4:

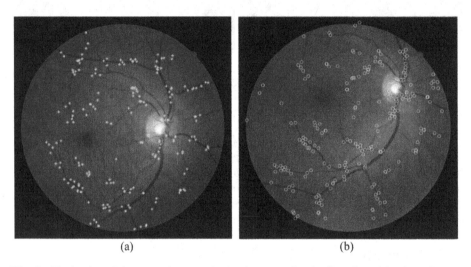

(a)   (b)

Fig. 4. Final selected feature points. (a) is the feature point finally selected in the reference image; (b) is the feature point finally selected in the target image.

Figure 4(a) extracts 206 points, and Fig. 4(b) extracts 212 points. These points are distributed along the vascular network and the number of feature points is significantly less than that in Fig. 3, but more typical. The feature matching process will search for matching pairs with good similarities between the feature points that are ultimately selected. In this paper, the Euclidean distance is used to measure the similarity of any feature point pairs. The expression is as follows:

$$s = d(x, y) = \sqrt{\sum_{i=1}^{n} (x_i - y_i)^2} \tag{7}$$

Where x and y represent feature vectors in the two images, respectively, and symbol $d(\cdot)$ represents the distance measure between the feature vectors. The matching points of the two images obtained by the rough matching of the Euclidean distance are as shown in the Fig. 5 (a):

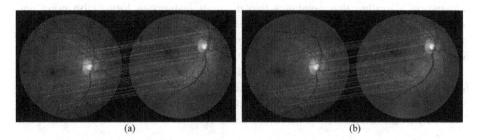

(a)   (b)

Fig. 5. Point matching. (a) is the result of the initial point matching of the Euclidean distance; (b) is the result of removing the mismatch point by RANSAC.

Obviously, there are still some mismatched points in the image. In order to obtain a finer matching point, RANSAC is used to further obtain a new interior point. As shown in the Fig. 5 (b), it is clear that there is almost no error in the matching points. Finally, all fine interior points can be used together to estimate the transformation model, such as an affine transformation. The registration results are as shown in the Fig. 6:

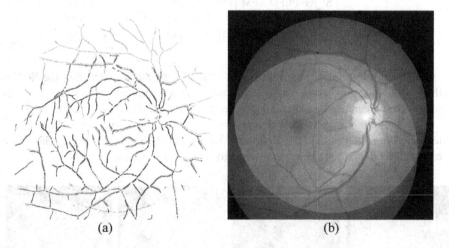

(a)   (b)

Fig. 6. Result of registration of the retinal images. (a) is the result of vascular fusion; (b) is the result of image fusion.

3 Experiments and Results

We implemented the algorithm in MATLAB R2016a. The experimental computer system is configured as: CPU is Intel(R) core(TM) i3-6100. We use the public fundus database FIRE to verify the performance of the proposed algorithm. This paper is a registration algorithm that combines two different features of bifurcation point and SURF key point. Therefore, the proposed method is compared with the bifurcation structure algorithm [8] based on bifurcation point and the registration algorithm of SURF combined with PIIFD [13].

Five pairs of retinal fundus images of the FIRE database were randomly selected for comparison. N1 is the number of detected matching points, N2 is the number of points finally used in the registration step, and t is the running time of the algorithm. The comparison results are shown in the Table 1:

Table 1. Comparison of proposed methods and SURF-PIIFD-RPM [13]

Image pairs	Methods	N1	N2	Percentage	t/(s)
A14	The proposed	80	64	80%	4.195
	SURF-PIIFD-RPM [13]	201	132	66%	12.019
P03	The proposed	80	65	81%	4.661
	SURF-PIIFD-RPM [13]	199	154	77%	18.380
P18	The proposed	80	37	46%	4.542
	SURF-PIIFD-RPM [13]	124	51	41%	11.463
P21	The proposed	80	56	70%	4.537
	SURF-PIIFD-RPM [13]	208	130	63%	12.971
S34	The proposed	80	75	94%	4.309
	SURF-PIIFD-RPM [13]	234	189	81%	11.225

Compared with the [13] algorithm, our method runs much faster than the SURF-PIIFD-RPM algorithm because it greatly reduces the search range of matching pairs. In addition, the percentage can also indicate that the number of feature points extracted is small, but the reliability is high. The matching points occupy a higher proportion in the detection points than in the [13] algorithm. Taking the P18 and P21 image pairs as an example, the effect diagrams of the two algorithms are illustrated in the Fig. 7:

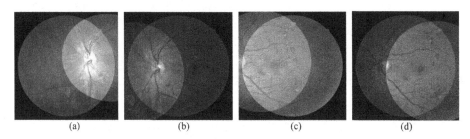

(a)   (b)   (c)   (d)

Fig. 7. Image registration results. (a) is the result of the proposed method in P18; (b) is the result of [13] in P18; (c) is the result of the proposed method in P21; (d) is the result of [13] in P21.

As can be seen from the registration results, our algorithm is clearer in details of the image registration than [13]. In addition, our method is also compared with the bifurcation structure algorithm in [8] by testing the experimental image of [8], and the result is as shown in the Fig. 8:

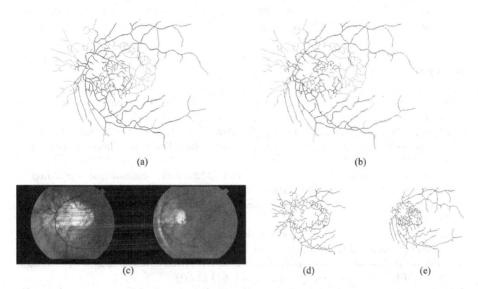

Fig. 8. Image registration results. (a) is the result of the proposed method; (b) is the result of the registration of the bifurcation structure [8]; (c) is the point matching result of the proposed method; (d) and (e) are the matching pair of the bifurcation structure [8].

Experimental results show that the algorithm is more accurate than the algorithm proposed in [8]. There are few matching bifurcation structures in [8] which containing only three pairs of matching bifurcation structures in the (d) and (e). By removing the repeated bifurcation points, only 10 pairs of matching bifurcation points are obtained, and the bifurcation points are unevenly distributed which resulting in local blood vessels to be out of alignment obviously. Meanwhile, as shown in the (c), our method extracts 51 pairs of matching points. And the feature points are distributed along the vascular network so that the transformation parameters can be accurately estimated.

4 Conclusion

This paper mainly studies the extraction problem of feature point sets. We propose a fast and efficient registration algorithm by using the advantages of bifurcation point and SURF two different features. This method not only can extract representative and reliable feature points from images, but also effectively remove incorrect matching point pairs. It can be seen from the experimental results that the method has higher registration accuracy, lower computational cost, faster algorithm speed and great registration effect on the international public database FIRE. However, the optimal solution is not always obtained every time because RANSAC removes outliers with an uncertain probability to obtain a reliable model. In the following work, we will focus on designing a better way to remove outliers.

Acknowledgement. This work is supported by the National Natural Science Foundation of China (No. 61762014). The project was funded by a major project of Guangxi Science and Technology (Guike AA18118009).

References

1. Brown, L.G.: A survey of image registration techniques. ACM Comput. Surv. **24**(4), 325–376 (1992)
2. Maes, F., Collignon, A., Vandermeulen, D., Marchal, G., Suetens, P.: Multimodality image registration by maximization of mutual information. IEEE Trans. Med. Imaging **16**(2), 187–198 (1997)
3. Pluim, J.P.W., Maintz, J.B.A., Viergever, M.A.: Mutual-information-based registration of medical images: a survey. IEEE Trans. Med. Imaging **22**(8), 986–1004 (2003)
4. Cideciyan, A.V.: Registration of ocular fundus images. IEEE Eng. Med. Biol. Mag. **14**, 52–58 (1995)
5. Zana, F., Klein, J.C.: A multimodal registration algorithm of eye fundus images using vessels detection and hough transform. IEEE Trans. Med. Imaging **18**(5), 419–428 (1999)
6. Laliberte, F., Gagnon, L., Sheng, Y.: Registration and fusion of retinal images-an evaluation study. IEEE Trans. Med. Imaging **22**(5), 661–673 (2003)
7. Fang, B., Tang, Y.Y.: Elastic registration for retinal images based on reconstructed vascular trees. IEEE Trans. Biomed. Eng. **53**(6), 1183–1187 (2006)
8. Chen, L., Huang, X., Tian, J.: Retinal image registration using topological vascular tree segmentation and bifurcation structures. Biomed. Signal Process. Control **16**, 22–31 (2015)
9. Besl, P.J., Mckay, N.D.: A method for registration of 3-D shapes. IEEE Trans. Pattern Anal. Mach. Intell. **14**(2), 239–256 (1992)
10. Stewart, C.V., Tsai, C.L., Roysam, B.: The dual-bootstrap iterative closest point algorithm with application to retinal image registration. IEEE Trans. Med. Imaging **22**(11), 1379–1394 (2003)
11. Yang, G., Stewart, C.V., Sofka, M., Tsai, C.L.: Registration of challenging image pairs: initialization, estimation, and decision. IEEE Trans. Pattern Anal. Mach. Intell. **29**(11), 1973–1989 (2007)
12. Chen, J., Tian, J., Lee, N., Zheng, J., Smith, R.T., Laine, A.F.: A partial intensity invariant feature descriptor for multimodal retinal image registration. IEEE Trans. Biomed. Eng. **57**(7), 1707–1718 (2010)
13. Wang, G., Wang, Z., Chen, Y., Zhao, W.: Robust point matching method for multimodal retinal image registration. Biomed. Signal Process. Control **19**, 68–76 (2015)
14. Bay, H., Tuytelaars, T., Van Gool, L.: SURF: speeded up robust features. In: Leonardis, A., Bischof, H., Pinz, A. (eds.) European Conference on Computer Vision, vol. 3951, pp. 404–417. Springer, Heidelberg (2006)

CIoTS: Context-Aware and IoT Services

Introduction to the 8th International Workshop on Context-Aware and IoT Services CIoTS 2018

The CIoTS 2018 workshop was held in conjunction with the 16th International Conference on Service Oriented Computing (ICSOC 2018) on November 12–15, 2018 in Hangzhou, China. This workshop provides an exciting and highly interactive forum for researchers and practitioners to exchange new ideas, developments, and experiences in Internet and Web of things, Context-Aware Services, Cloud Computing, Ubiquitous Computing, Big Data Analytics, and Complex Networks.

This workshop clearly showed interesting research efforts in the field and offered the ability to fruitful discussions:

- Augmented Reality in IoT
- Hydrologic IoT Data Processing
- Sensor Data Correlation Aware Service Composition
- Dynamic Service Adaptation for Cloud Infrastructure and Edge Devices
- Multi-Workflow Scheduling Strategy in Fog Computing
- IoT Privacy
- Real-time Road Traffic Speed Estimation
- Data Cleaning Service for Massive Spatio-temporal Data
- Smart Home behaviour Tracking
- R-tree Construction Scheme for Spatio-Temporal Data Stream

We would like to thank the authors for their submissions, the program committee for their reviewing work, and the organizers of the ICSOC 2018 conference for their support which made this workshop possible.

Jian Yu
Guiling Wang
Sira Yongchareon
CIoTS 2018 Programme Chairs

Augmented Reality in IoT

Gary White[(⊠)], Christian Cabrera, Andrei Palade, and Siobhán Clarke

School of Computer Science and Statistics, Trinity College Dublin, Dublin, Ireland
{whiteg5,cabrerac,paladea,siobhan.clarke}@scss.tcd.ie

Abstract. IoT is a combination of physical objects with virtual representations and services. Augmented reality provides an ideal interface to IoT applications by superimposing virtual information about smart objects and services on a user's view of the real world. This allows a user to interact with the physical object as well as receiving additional context-aware information about the object e.g., size, speed and temperature, as well as information about nearby objects. However, users do not have to directly interact with the physical objects or sensors as augmented reality can be an effective method of providing additional information about IoT services in the environment, such as the QoS attributes of a service or the ratings that other users have provided during previous invocations. In this paper, we describe the use of augmented reality in IoT to provide contextual information to service users and providers and give a demonstration of an augmented reality application that we have developed and three projections of how users may interact with future context-aware applications. We also discuss some of the current research challenges and the future work that needs to be carried out to address these challenges.

1 Introduction

The development of Internet of Things (IoT) technology has made it possible to connect various smart devices together through a range of communication protocols. The number of devices connected to the IoT is predicted to grow at an exponential rate, with forecasts predicting that there will be around 26 billion connected devices by 2020 [1]. These devices will lead to a wide variety of services from multiple sources such as monitoring sensors, surveillance cameras and actuators. The management of the services provided by these devices is recognised as one of the most important areas of future technology and has gained wide attention from research institutes and industry in a number of different domains including transportation, healthcare and emergency response [2,3].

Both service providers and consumers need to be able to engage with IoT applications in a context-aware manner where they sense and react based on the environment and user context. Augmented reality (AR) provides an intuitive interface to IoT as it allows for context as well as superimposing virtual information in the real world such as in cognitive buildings [4]. Service consumers can interact naturally, in a visual manner with suggested nearby services, which

X. Liu et al. (Eds.): ICSOC 2018 Workshops, LNCS 11434, pp. 149–160, 2019.
https://doi.org/10.1007/978-3-030-17642-6_13

are handled by a context-oriented middleware. Service providers can use AR to debug and repair failing IoT devices, by showing key QoS metrics of the services provided by the device such as the response time and throughput. Device-related metrics such as the temperature, CPU and memory usage of the device can also be shown. The internal components of the device can be connected objects, which will allow the field operator to see a specific visualisation to repair the faulty internal component of the IoT device that is not operating correctly [5]. This allows for easy repair and a return to a suitable operating performance.

IoT applications can be used in a range of domains that have different QoS requirements based on the sensitivity and criticality of the application. IoT application QoS can typically be categorised as best effort (no QoS), differentiated services (soft QoS) and guaranteed services (hard QoS) [6]. In the hard QoS case, there are strict hard real-time QoS guarantees. This is appropriate for safety critical applications such as monitoring patients in a hospital or collision avoidance in a self-driving car system. Soft QoS does not require hard real-time guarantees but needs to be able to reconfigure and replace services that fail. This could be a routing application, which uses air quality, flooding and pedestrian traffic predictions, to provide the best route through the city. If one of the services is about to fail, the application should be recomposed using suitable replacement services. The final case is best effort, where there are no guarantees when a service fails, such as a simple atomic service that measures the temperature in a house. For hard and soft QoS AR could provide an intuitive way to alert users that a service may be about to fail and that they may need to retake control especially in the self-driving car scenario. Forecasting the failure of IoT service can be accomplished through the use of LSTM networks [7].

The remainder of the paper is organised as follows: Sect. 2 outlines some of the recent developments in AR that will reduce the barrier to entry and make these applications much more common in an IoT environment. Section 3 demonstrates a service-oriented middleware that can be used to provide context in an IoT environment and a deep edge architecture that provides a scalable solution for AR applications in IoT. Section 4 demonstrates some of the augmented reality applications that we have developed and discusses how they can be used for both service providers and consumers in IoT. We also create some projections of how users may interact with future context-aware applications. Finally in Sect. 5 we outline the conclusions from this paper and some of the open research questions that need to be explored.

2   Augmented Reality in IoT

AR has quickly evolved in recent years and there is a range of commercial software and hardware that can allow for the creation of AR experiences. Today, there are a variety of APIs at the consumer level that makes it possible to create AR experiences with most of them making use of mobile technologies such as smartphones or tablets. Apple has recently launched ARKit [8] that allows building AR environments with little knowledge of the technology behind it.

Another example that we use in our demonstration is the Vuforia developer library for Unity, which includes Google's ARCore allowing AR applications on all modern android devices [9]. This will allow for much more devices to interact with IoT services through an AR interface and will encourage developers to create AR based IoT applications.

With the wide penetration of smart phones and the new APIs released by Apple and Google we project there will be an increase in mobile augmented reality in the next few years. The use of mobile phones as augmented reality visors will be a necessary step to allow the development of applications and to evaluate the effectiveness of AR in IoT. The transition after this can be to a number of alternative head-mounted displays such as Google Glass, Microsoft Hololens or Magic Leap Lightwear. These head-mounted displays allow for hands free interaction with IoT services and objects, which will be useful for field technicians to interact with devices and view visualisations showing which connected components to replace in order to repair a smart device.

Considering the enormous potential of AR and IoT and the large amount of research that has been invested in each technology, the integration of both components is still at an early stage. Most current approaches show characteristics of objects without taking into account additional context such as the user preference, nearby object/locations, time, weather, etc. Some proposals such as a Sentient Visor infer a high level context of the user using a context interface server to alter the manner in which information is displayed to the user [10]. However, the application of a smart watering plant is simplistic and only needs the local sensor information, also a central server for reasoning don't take into account the vision of IoT as intelligent objects. In our demonstration we show more advanced examples combining dynamic and heterogeneous services from traditional web services and IoT services and using additional context information to provide intuitive applications. More recent work such as ARIoT provides a scalable AR framework for interacting with IoT devices but focuses on targeting objects rather than derived context through connected objects [11]. Other approaches such as Second Surface, where users are able to create, tag and share data around everyday objects are implemented through a remote server in the cloud [12]. The deep edge architecture that we describe in Sect. 3 allows all the analysis to take place at the edge of the network reducing response time and jitter and creating a more immersive AR experience.

3   Context-Aware Middleware

Figure 1a shows a context-aware service oriented-middleware that can be deployed on the deep edge architecture in Fig. 1b to manage the registration, execution and context of IoT services in the city. The middleware manages the context of users in the environment in a distributed way across each of the gateways. When a user requests an application the middleware first receives the user request at the request handler, which establishes a request/response communication channel with the user and forwards the request to the context manager. The context manager is responsible for acquiring and maintaining metadata about the services and the environment to support smart service management. The meta-data includes service attributes (e.g., location, type, domain, etc.), QoS properties (e.g., response time, energy consumption, etc.), urban-context (e.g., places and their meaning in the city, points of interest, etc.), and user preferences (e.g., user feedback, QoS experience, user behaviour, etc.). Service attributes and QoS prop-erties are acquired from providers and the monitoring process. This data is stored as part of the service descriptions. Urban-context is acquired from Open Street Maps (OSM) and formalised using ontologies in OWL format. User preferences are acquired from the discovery and composition process. This data is stored as independent JSON documents in the service registry.

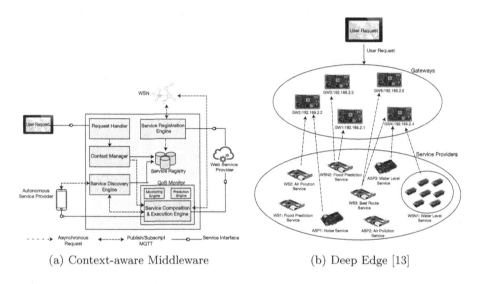

(a) Context-aware Middleware   (b) Deep Edge [13]

Fig. 1. Context-aware middleware and architecture for deep edges

For example, if a user is in a car dealership and searches for Jaguar we can search nearby IoT services to see if there are any Jaguar cars available at this dealership with additional context-aware information such as the price, year, fuel efficiency. If a user is at the zoo and searches for Jaguar, then we look for any nearby IoT beacons that are advertising a Jaguar exhibition. Additional context-aware information can then also be supplied such as the amount of jaguars, where they are from and what food they eat. This component can process traditional user information from a request such as the location and time but the component can also be extended to run a deep convolutional neural network to process the image sent by the AR device in real time at the edge [14]. This can add additional specific information about the contents of the image that the user is currently looking at. This would allow for additional context-aware information not available in previous IoT applications, providing more immersive and user-specific applications with an AR interface.

The other main components of the middleware as shown in Fig. 1a are the Service Registration Engine (SRE), the Service Discovery Engine (SDE), the QoS Monitor and the Service Composition & Execution Engine (SCEE). The SRE registers the available services in the environment according to domain. The SDE uses a backward-planning algorithm to identify concrete services, which can be used to satisfy the non-functional requirements of the request and sends this list of services to the SCEE. The QoS monitor is used to monitor these services and identify possible candidate services to switch to if one of the services begins to degrade, using a matrix factorisation based collaborative filtering algorithm in the prediction engine [15,16]. The prediction engine also contains an algorithm to forecast future QoS values of currently executing services, to identify that a service may be about to fail using an LSTM based neural network and service recomposition is needed [7]. The SCEE uses an optimisation algorithm to maximise the available QoS in the response.

The "deep edge" architecture, which we define in a previous work, allows for much more processing to take place at the edge of the network, without access to the cloud [13]. These devices can be arranged as a network of gateways as shown in Fig. 1b. Here the embedded GPUs (Jetson Tx2) have a number of services registered on them that would be distributed throughout the city such as traffic and weather data that can be used for a range of IoT applications. The additional processing power in deep edges compared to other traditional IoT gateways (e.g. raspberry pi) allows them to run the prediction engine in the middleware locally to make predictions for IoT services in the environment instead of offloading this to the cloud. This makes the IoT applications in the environment much more reliable. As these devices are one hop away from users they can provide much lower end-to-end latency and jitter. This makes them suitable to handle augmented reality applications that require reduced latency and jitter with the additional benefit of being able to take advantage of the GPU on each device for increased graphical processing for higher resolution augmented reality applications. Application can offload the graphical processing from a users phone to a GPU to make the applications higher resolution, while also keeping the short response time available using edge networks to provide a fully immersive experience.

4   Demonstrations

In this section we give a demonstration of some of the use cases of AR in IoT. We consider both service providers and consumers to show how AR provides an easy interface to the virtual information of connected objects and services.

4.1   Provider

Service providers want to be able to interact with devices that they are using to provide services in the environment. Figure 2 shows the augmented information for the sensor on a stones marker. In this case this device provides a simple

temperature service that is used by other smart applications. By interacting
with the device the field technician can identify that the response time of the
service is quite high as shown by the orange background on the text. The other
key QoS factors are normal as shown by the green background. A time-stamp is
also provided for logging when services have failed or are acting abnormally.

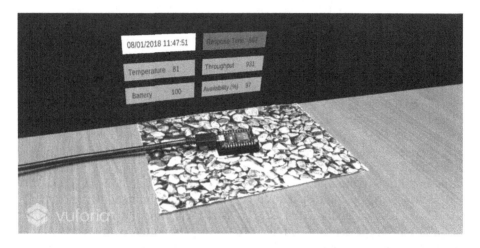

Fig. 2. AR showing QoS of service on device (Color figure online)

Fig. 3. Phone used for AR experience

The device can further be interacted with to identify the problem and choose a suitable replacement part. Figure 3 shows how a field technician may currently activate the AR experience by using a mobile phone. In the future with the reduction in cost of headware accessories such as Magic Leap Lightwear this will allow for hands-free operation. Hands-free operation allow for more complicated repair operations on larger devices [17].

4.2   Consumer

For consumers, AR provides a low entry barrier for interacting with IoT services. The management of the services will be handled by a context-aware middleware that can make suggestions to the user of relevant applications that may be available in the area. It will manage the registration, QoS, composition and execution of the services. The user just needs to interact with the augmented suggestions on their headset to add additional virtual information to their environment. In this section, we provide some scenarios of consumers interacting with IoT services in the future and show how AR could be used to augment our experience by adding context-aware information from IoT services. These projections provide a top-down view of the possibility of combination of IoT and AR.

The first scenario is a tourist walking into a smart campus in Trinity College Dublin. Location based AR is used to provide additional context aware information of the buildings that the tourist is looking at, as they walk through the campus in Fig. 4. The contextual information is taken from a web service, which provides some details on the design and superstition of the Campanile on the campus. As the person has never been to the campus before and has visited other tourist locations in the city, the middleware can provide suggested locations to visit next such as the Book of Kells. Additional information such as the waiting time in the queue can accurately be measured by IoT devices located at the attraction and reviews retrieved from a web service.

We can also see some advertised services in the environment that the user has not interacted with yet. These IoT beacons provide further information about two statues in the front square of George Salmon and William E.H. Lecky. These advertised services have predicted response time using the IoTPredict algorithm [16] as that is the QoS metric that the user most interested in. The metrics are coloured green to show the services have acceptable response times. This first example shows the importance of context in the scenario as if a student is walking to class and looks at the same building they may not want additional information about the history and design of the building and nearby tourist attractions but may be interested in their calender application to find the location of their first class and the length of the queue at the coffee shop.

The second scenario that we envisage is a smart agricultural scenario. In this case, a farmer is making hay to use as animal feed during the winter months in Fig. 5. The grass has been cut and the farmer needs information about the weather and moisture content of the grass in order to make hay. The farmer can retrieve a seven day weather forecast from a service provider but can also use additional contextual information provided by dynamic and heterogeneous

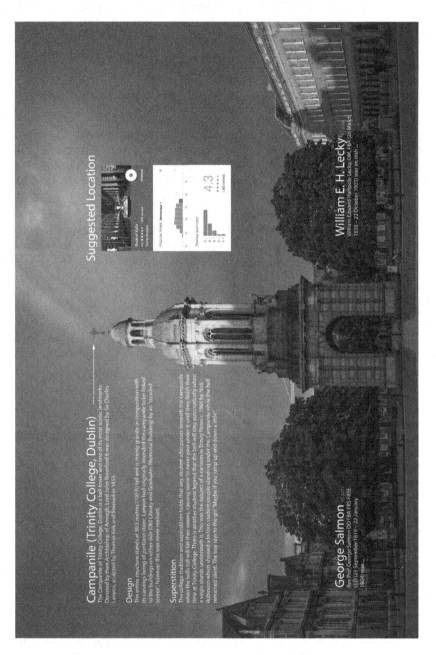

Fig. 4. Tourist interacting with services in AR

Fig. 5. Farmer interacting with services in AR

Fig. 6. Commuter interacting with services in AR

sensors deployed across the field. These sensors provide additional information about the current moisture content of the grass and the soil temperature. Based on the additional context information provided by the services the farmer has an estimated time when the grass will reach the 18% moisture content needed for large round bales from the current 85% of 6 days. The bailing equipment, which is also a smart device can provide a status update showing that it is ready for use or that some replacement parts must be ordered (Fig. 6).

The final scenario that we consider is a smart city scenario of a commuter planning a trip home. In this case IoT sensors in the surrounding location have detected an extreme weather event and the presence of snow and ice on the roads. The commuter is looking at some city bikes available at a bike stand. Based on the additional information from IoT services in the environment the user is given a weather warning that it is unsafe to travel on the bikes due to the snow and ice on the roads. Initially the application shows the bus timetable but when the buses are cancelled due to the weather the application dynamically adapts and gives the user the option to book a taxi or uber. This example shows the importance of context and managing heterogeneous and dynamic services.

5 Conclusion and Future Work

In this paper we have shown how both users and providers can use AR to interact with IoT devices and services. AR can be used to quickly debug devices as well as providing an easy way to interact with services in a local environment. In our demonstration of some possible future AR experiences we have shown the importance of context and having accurate information about the surrounding environment from nearby IoT devices. Additional information about the user is also beneficial, for example whether they are a student or a tourist to further personalise the experience. These figures demonstrated the possibilities when combing AR and IoT and we hope will encourage further research.

There are a number of open research questions in the combination of IoT and AR such as the architecture to run these applications due to the low latency and jitter requirements. We have described a deep edge architecture in our previous work [13] and plan to conduct experimentation on a campus wide level to show the suitability of this architecture for AR applications in IoT. This will provide an experimental platform that we can use to conduct additional experiments with students and tourists that investigates additional factors, that may effect the quality of experience such as the resolution, suitability of augmented information and response time of the application.

Acknowledgment. This work was funded by Science Foundation Ireland (SFI) under grant 13/IA/1885.

References

1. Bauer, H., Patel, M., Veira, J.: The Internet of Things: Sizing Up the Opportunity. McKinsey, New York (2014)
2. Lee, I., Lee, K.: The Internet of Things (IoT): applications, investments, and challenges for enterprises. Bus. Horiz. **58**(4), 431–440 (2015)
3. Al-Fuqaha, A., Guizani, M., Mohammadi, M., Aledhari, M., Ayyash, M.: Internet of Things: a survey on enabling technologies, protocols, and applications. IEEE Comm. Surv. Tutor. **17**(4), 2347–2376 (2015)
4. Ploennigs, J., Ba, A., Barry, M.: Materializing the promises of cognitive IoT: how cognitive buildings are shaping the way. IEEE Internet Things J. **5**(4), 2367–2374 (2018)
5. Abate, A.F., Narducci, F., Ricciardi, S.: Mixed reality environment for mission critical systems servicing and repair. In: Shumaker, R. (ed.) VAMR 2013. LNCS, vol. 8022, pp. 201–210. Springer, Heidelberg (2013). https://doi.org/10.1007/978-3-642-39420-1_22
6. White, G., Nallur, V., Clarke, S.: Quality of service approaches in IoT: a systematic mapping. J. Syst. Softw. **132**, 186–203 (2017). http://www.sciencedirect.com/science/article/pii/S016412121730105X
7. White, G., Palade, A., Clarke, S.: Forecasting QoS attributes using LSTM networks. In: International Joint Conference on Neural Networks (IJCNN) (2018)
8. Apple Inc.: ARKit. https://developer.apple.com/arkit/
9. Vuforia Engine. https://developer.vuforia.com/
10. García-Macías, J.A., Alvarez-Lozano, J., Estrada-Martinez, P., Avilés-López, E.: Browsing the Internet of Things with sentient visors. Computer **5**, 46–52 (2011)
11. Jo, D., Kim, G.J.: ARIoT: scalable augmented reality framework for interacting with Internet of Things appliances everywhere. IEEE Trans. Consum. Electron. **62**(3), 334–340 (2016)
12. Kasahara, S., Heun, V., Lee, A.S., Ishii, H.: Second surface: multi-user spatial collaboration system based on augmented reality. In: SIGGRAPHAsia 2012 Emerging Technologies, p. 20. ACM (2012)
13. White, G., Clarke, S.: Smart cities with deep edges. In: ECML International Workshop on Urban Reasoning (2018)
14. Redmon, J., Divvala, S.K., Girshick, R.B., Farhadi, A.: You only look once: unified, real-time object detection (2015). http://arxiv.org/abs/1506.02640
15. Braubach, L., Murillo, J.M., Kaviani, N., Lama, M., Burgueño, L., Moha, N., Oriol, M. (eds.): ICSOC 2017. LNCS, vol. 10797. Springer, Cham (2018). https://doi.org/10.1007/978-3-319-91764-1
16. White, G., Palade, A., Cabrera, C., Clarke, S.: IoTPredict: collaborative QoS prediction in IoT. In: IEEE International Conference on Pervasive Computing and Communications (PerCom) (PerCom 2018), Greece, March 2018
17. Henderson, S., Feiner, S.: Exploring the benefits of augmented reality documentation for maintenance and repair. IEEE Trans. Visual Comput. Graphics **17**(10), 1355–1368 (2011)

The Tentative Research of Hydrological IoT Data Processing System Based on Apache Flink

Feng Ye[1,2(✉)], Peng Zhang[3], Cheng Hu[1], Songjie Zhu[1], and Ling Li[1]

[1] College of Computer and Information, Hohai University, Nanjing, China
yefeng1022@hhu.edu.cn
[2] Postdoctoral Centre, Nanjing Longyuan Micro-Electronic Company,
Nanjing, China
[3] Jiangsu Province Water Resources Department, Nanjing, China

Abstract. With the widespread application of sensor and IoT technology in the field of water conservancy informatization, the traditional application systems based on Java EE or pure NoSQL databases for hydrological data processing and analysis have been difficult to meet the new requirements for processing and analyzing large-scale hydrological IoT stream data. How to select a suitable big data processing platform and how to implement application systems for hydrological IoT stream data requires in-depth theoretical foundations, more experimental comparisons, effective design paradigm and practical implementations. This paper summarizes the research status of big data in water conservancy domain, and then proposes a hydrological IoT data processing system based on Apache Flink. We use the sensor data obtained in Chuhe river as the experimental dataset, and take the common and daily operations for hydrological data as example. The experimental results show that the processing capability of the hydrological IoT data processing system is far superior to the traditional multi-tier architecture system based on Java EE or pure NoSQL databases, and it obviously becomes an appreciable solution for water conservancy informatization.

Keywords: Apache Flink · Stream data · Water conservancy informatization · IoT

1 Introduction

With the widespread use of Internet of things (IoT) [1] and the rapid development of the mobile Internet, diverse data has been growing explosively. How to deal with large-scale IoT data has become a research hotspot [2]. Meanwhile, in the field of water conservancy informatization, the hydrological IoT data acquisition capability has also continuously improved. Because of the diversity, dynamics and large-scale of the hydrological IoT stream data, the traditional multi-tier architecture system based on Java EE or pure NoSQL databases for hydrological data processing and analysis have been difficult to meet the new requirements for processing and analyzing these hydrological IoT stream data. In this context, how to select a suitable big data processing platform and how to implement an appreciable solution for hydrological IoT

X. Liu et al. (Eds.): ICSOC 2018 Workshops, LNCS 11434, pp. 161–168, 2019.
https://doi.org/10.1007/978-3-030-17642-6_14

stream data become a key challenge. According to existing research and the present situation of the information development in water conservancy informatization, we think it requires in-depth theoretical foundations, more experimental comparisons, effective design paradigm and practical implementations.

By comparing the mainstream big data processing platforms, we propose a novel hydrological IoT data processing system based on Apache Flink [3, 4], which is an open source framework and distributed processing engine for stateful computations over unbounded and bounded data streams. To our knowledge, though Apache Flink powers business-critical applications in many companies and enterprises around the globe, such as Alibaba.com and Ericsson, there are no cases in the field of water conservancy informatization. Using the sensor data obtained from Chuhe river as the experimental data, the proposed system is proved to be advanced in water conservancy informatization domain.

The rest of the paper is organized as follows. Section 2 describes some works related to this topic of interest. In Sect. 3, after introducing the Apache Flink, the architecture and components of the proposed hydrological IoT data processing system is described. In Sect. 4, comparing with the traditional multi-tier architecture system based on Java EE or pure NoSQL databases, we analyzes the performance of the proposed the hydrological IoT data processing system using the sensor data obtained in Chuhe river. At last, conclusion along with the direction for future research is provided in Sect. 5.

2 Relate Works

According to Feng [5], after long-term application practice, a large number of heterogeneous business data have been accumulated in water conservancy domain. By 2012, the hydrological data alone had exceeded 100 TB nationwide. With the development and widespread application of IoT related technologies such as remote sensing, sensor and so on, the hydrological IoT data acquisition capability has been continuously improved, and more and more hydrological data have been collected and utilized in water conservancy informatization. These hydrological IoT data often have the following characteristics [6]: (1) Multi-source: data is captured by sensors at different locations; (2) Heterogeneous stream data; (3) Thematic diversity: there are many topics such as water quality, hydrology and irrigation, and different topics require different computing patterns. (4) Presence of outliers: observations considerably higher or lower than most of the data, which infrequently but regularly occur. (5) Autocorrelation: consecutive observations tend to be strongly correlated with each other. (6) Dependence on other uncontrolled variables: values strongly co-vary with water discharge, hydraulic conductivity, sediment grain size, or some other variable. From the perspective of data type, these massive data includes both batch and stream data. From the perspective of timeliness, certain hydrological data such as flood warnings require timely and efficient processing and feedback. Moreover, because the data lineage for location, environment, weather and other related factors is often missing in the process of data acquisition, there is a wealth of spatial-temporal correlation information between data lost. Therefore, when the traditional hydrological data processing systems based on Java EE or pure NoSQL databases cannot effectively face the large-scale hydrological IoT data, it is necessary to adopt a suitable big data processing engine to improve the processing capabilities of such data [7].

Currently, there are already many typical big data processing platforms. The Map-Reduce [8] framework has become a de facto standard for big data technology and is widely used to manage large clusters. Hadoop [9] is an open source implementation of the MapReduce framework and plays an active role in the big data technology system. However, in practice, industry and academia also gradually find that the MapReduce framework and Hadoop implementation are not one-size-fits-all big data processing solutions [10]. For example, the Hadoop platform is not suitable for second - or micro-second interactive queries [11]. Therefore, Map-Reduce and Hadoop are difficult to apply to hydrological IoT data processing effectively. Apache Spark [12, 13], is an another large data parallel computing framework based on in-memory computing that can be used to build large, low-latency data analysis applications. On the speed side, Apache Spark extends the popular Map-Reduce model to efficiently support ore types of computations, including interactive queries and stream processing. On the generality side, Apache Spark is designed to cover a wide range of workloads that previously required separate distributed systems, including batch applications, iterative algorithms, interactive queries and streaming. Although the throughput has improved, the biggest problem is that Apache Spark lacks low end-to-end latency with exactly-once guar-antees [14–16]. Obviously, they are unable to satisfy some high throughput and low latency processing scenarios, such as flood warning and forecasting.

Compared with mainstream big data platforms like Apache Spark and Hadoop, Apache Flink is considered to be the fourth generation and the latest generation big data processing engine. Specifically speaking, Apache Flink is a framework and dis-tributed processing engine for stateful computations over bounded and unbounded data streams. It has been designed to run in all common cluster environments, perform computations at in-memory speed and at any scale. The core computational fabric of Apache Flink, labeled "Flink runtime" in Fig. 1, is a distributed system that accepts streaming dataflow programs and executes them in a fault-tolerant manner in one or more machines. Apache Flink also offers developer-friendly APIs that layer on top of the runtime and generate these streaming dataflow programs.

As far as I know, though Apache Flink powers business-critical applications in many companies and enterprises around the globe, such as Alibaba.com and Ericsson, there are no cases in the field of water conservancy informatization. Therefore, from the above, we can see that Apache Flink is a versatile processing framework that can handle any kind of stream, and it is necessary to study how to design and implement IoT data processing system in combination with Apache Flink in water conservancy domain.

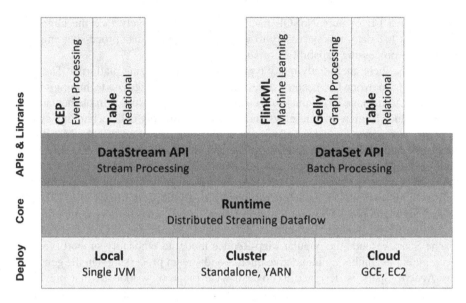

Fig. 1. The key components of the Apache Flink stack

3 The Proposed Hydrological IoT Data Processing System

The system architecture proposed is shown in Fig. 2, and there are four tiers: infrastructure layer, virtualization layer, dataset processing layer and visualization layer. The infrastructure layer provides the hardware foundation for big data processing, such as PCs, various servers and network equipment. Various resources are abstracted into different resource pools, such as data resource pool, network resource pool.

In virtualization layer, Apache CloudStack is installed, configured and deployed to construct virtual machines cluster and then used to manage the infrastructure resource. Hadoop, NoSQL, relational databases and other tools can be installed in virtual machines cluster. In this layer, according to a variety of business requirements, multiple data management solutions can be coexist, such as MySQL cluster, HBase or Hadoop Distributed File System (HDFS). Different data management solutions and diverse storage tools are applicable for different scale or types of data. For example, if local resource of single virtual machine is sufficient for data processing, it is not necessary to use YARN [17].

Above the virtualization layer, it is dataset processing layer, and Apache Flink is the most direct support for building this layer. It provides three layered APIs, and each API offers a different trade-off between conciseness and expressiveness and targets different use cases. ProcessFunctions is used to process individual events from one or two input streams or events that were grouped in a window and has fine-grained control over time and state. The DataStream API provides primitives for many common stream processing operations, such as windowing, record-at-a-time transformations, and enriching events by querying an external data store. Table API and SQL are used for unified stream and batch processing. Apache Flink features several libraries for

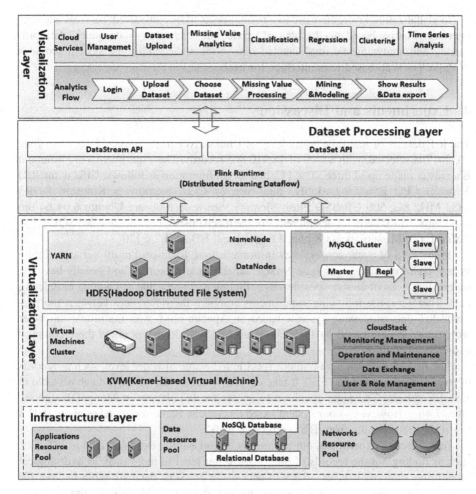

Fig. 2. The architecture of hydrological IoT data processing system

common data processing use cases. The libraries are typically embedded in an API and not fully self-contained. Based on such a rich API, we can implement many business functions and perform computations for hydrological IoT stream data at in-memory speed and at any scale. In addition, in order to implement an effective stream-first architecture and to gain the advantages of using Apache Flink, a common pattern is to implement a streaming architecture by using a message transport such as Apache Kafka [18], which can collect and deliver data from continuous events from a variety of sources (producers) and make this data available to applications and services that subscribe to it (consumers). Thus, having a message-transport system that decouples producers from consumers is better because it can support a micro-services approach and allows processing steps to hide their implementations, and provides them with the freedom to change those implementations.

In visualization layer, there are two main aspects to be considered: services and user interface. Firstly, based on the idea of service-oriented, many data query, data processing and analyzing are implemented into services. Secondly, the system provides WYSIWYG Web-based user interface for users.

4 Experiments and Discussion

The IoT dataset of real-time water level of Chuhe river from January 1, 2015 to June 30, 2017 is selected, with a total of 18,910,865 records. The experimental environment is a cluster made up of three same PC, and its configuration as follows: CPU is Intel(R) Xeon(R) CPU E5645@2.40 GHz dual-core 24 CPU; memory is Kingston DDR3 1333 MHz 8G, 500 GB SSD Flash Memory. Software tools are Ubuntu 6.04 64-bit, and Linux 3.11.0 kernel. For different storage mechanisms, our choice is MySQL 5.7.x, Kafka 1.1.0, MongoDB 2008 plus 3.6.3[19] and HBase 1.2.6 [20].

In the field of water conservancy informatization, traditional multi-tier architecture system based on Java EE or pure NoSQL databases are common and usually have the normal functions of finding specific value, finding extreme value and adding or deleting data. Therefore, the following experiments compare the differences between the proposed IoT data processing systems based on Apache Flink with traditional multi-tier architecture system based on Java EE or pure NoSQL databases under these common and daily operations.

The first experiment is to find out specific IoT value of water level, such as records of river water level above "5.5". It takes 8.41 s to access the MySQL database table in Java EE system. The same operation to access the IoT dataset in MongoDB directly takes 7.46 s. However, in our system based on Apache Flink, it only takes about 0.03 s to get the same results from HBase through Kafka.

In the second experiment, our purpose is to find out the extreme value in IoT data, such as finding out the records of the lowest water level in more than 70 hydrological monitoring stations. It takes 16.2 s to access the MySQL database table in Java EE system. The same operation to access the IoT dataset in MongoDB directly takes 10.3 s. In our system based on Apache Flink, it only takes about 0.07 s to finish the task from HBase through Kafka.

In the third experiment, the deletion operation for IoT data is tested. For large-scale IoT stream data, it does not need to be maintained for a long time, and it is often cleaned up after a period of time. For this reason, taking 5 million records as an example, we verify the effect. It only takes 3.22 s using the IoT data processing systems based on Apache Flink and HBase, far less than the 122 s needed to use MySQL logic in Java EE system and the 55 s needed to use logic for accessing MongoDB.

The experimental results are shown in Fig. 3. below, and it is not hard to see that the system based on Apache Flink platform makes full use of the parallelization mechanism, and significantly improves the execution efficiency of common operations.

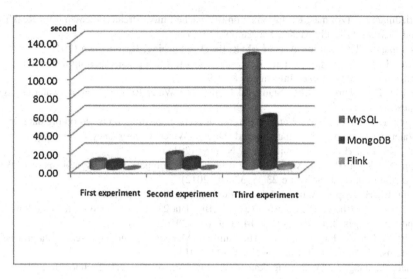

Fig. 3. Comparison of execution time in different experiments

5 Summary and Prospect

In this paper, we summarize the characters of big data of water conservancy domain, and then propose a hydrological IoT data processing system based on Apache Flink. Then, we analyze the performance of the proposed the hydrological IoT data processing system using the IoT data obtained in Chuhe river. By comparing the efficiency of common operations, our proposed system is significantly superior to the traditional application based on Java EE or pure NoSQL databases system.

In follow-up studies, we will focus on study the machine learning algorithms combined with the analysis of the hydrological IoT data on Apache Flink platform, especially for real-time analysis of stream data, and provide more support for flood control and drought control.

Acknowledgement. This work is partly supported by the 2018 Jiangsu Province Key Research and Development Program (Modern Agriculture) Project under Grant No.BE2018301, the 2017 Jiangsu Province Postdoctoral Research Funding Project under Grant No. 1701020C, the 2017 Six Talent Peaks Endorsement Project of Jiangsu under Grant No. XYDXX-078, and the Fundamental Research Funds for the Central Universities under Grant No. 2013B01814.

References

1. Yu, R., Yang, X., Huang, J., et al.: QoS-aware service selection in virtualization-based cloud computing. In: Proceedings of 14th Asia-Pacific Network Operations and Management Symposium: Management in the Big Data and IoT Era, pp. 1–8. IEEE Computer Society (2012)
2. Walker, S.J.: Big data: a revolution that will transform how we live, work, and think. Math. Comput. Educ. **47**(17), 181–183 (2013)

3. Friedman, E., Tzoumas, K.: Introduction to Apache Flink: Stream Processing for Real Time and Beyond. O'Reilly Media, Sebastopol (2016)
4. Deshpande, T.: Learning Apache Flink. Packt Publishing, Birmingham (2017)
5. Feng, J., Xu, X., Tang, Z., et al.: Research on key technology of water big data and resource utilization. Water Resour. Informatiz. **8**, 6–9 (2013)
6. Helsel, D.R., Hirsch, R.M.: Statistical Methods in Water Resources. http://water.usgs.gov/pubs/twri/twri4a3/
7. Gong, H., Liu, W., et al.: Water resources data center construction based on big data. In: 3rd Water Conservancy Information and Digital Water Conservancy Technology Forum, pp. 243–248. Hohai University Press, Nanjing (2015)
8. Qin, X., Wang, H., Du, X., et al.: Big data analysis-competition and symbiosis of RDBMS and MapReduce. J. Software **23**(1), 32–45 (2012)
9. Lam, C.: Hadoop in Action. Manning Publications, Stamford (2011)
10. Bajaber, F., Elshawi, R., Batarfi, O., et al.: Big data 2.0 processing systems: taxonomy and open challenges. J. Grid Comput. **14**, 379–405 (2016)
11. Sakr, S., Liu, A., Fayoumi, A.G.: The family of MapReduce and large-scale data processing systems. ACM Comput. Surv. **46**(1), 10–11 (2013)
12. Zhao, S., Jiang, J.: Typical big data computing frameworks. ZTE Technol. J. **22**(2), 14–18 (2016)
13. Estrada, R., Ruiz, I.: Big Data SMACK: A Guide to Apache Spark, Mesos, Akka, Cassandra, and Kafka. Apress, New York (2016)
14. Zhang, P., Li, P., Ren, Y., et al.: Distributed stream processing and technologies for big data: a review. J. Comput. Res. Develop. **51**(Suppl), 1–9 (2014)
15. Sakr, S.: Big Data 2.0 Processing Systems: A Survey, pp. 74–89. Springer, Cham (2016). https://doi.org/10.1007/978-3-319-38776-5
16. Liu, X., Iftikhar, N., Xie, X.: Survey of real-time processing systems for big data. In: Proceedings of the 18th International Database Engineering and Applications Symposium. Association for Computing Machinery, pp. 356–361 (2014)
17. Chintapalli, S., Dagit, D., Evans, B., et al.: Benchmarking streaming computation engines: storm, Flink and spark streaming. In: Proceedings of IEEE 28th International Parallel and Distributed Processing Symposium Workshops, pp. 1789–1792. IEEE Computer Society (2016)
18. Narkhede, N., Shapira, G., Palino, T.: Kafka: The Definitive Guide. O'Reilly Media, Sebastopol (2017)
19. Tiwari, S.: Professional NoSQL. Wiley, Indianapolis (2011)
20. George, L.: HBase: The Definitive Guide. O'Reilly Media, Sebastopol (2011)

Runtime Service Composition Modification Supporting Situational Sensor Data Correlation

Chen Liu[1,2(⊠)], Zhongmei Zhang[1,2], Shouli Zhang[1,2], and Yanbo Han[1,2]

[1] Beijing Key Laboratory on Integration and Analysis of Large-Scale Stream Data, North China University of Technology, Beijing, China
{liuchen,hanyanbo}@ncut.edu.cn, gloria_z@126.com, zhangshoulia@163.com
[2] Cloud Computing Research Center, North China University of Technology, Beijing, China

Abstract. Although IoT service and service composition provide effective means to develop IoT applications, the dynamic and time-varying correlation among massive sensors rises up new challenges to the traditional model-based approaches, and the extra uncertainty and complexity of service composition become apparent. This paper proposes a data-driven service composition method based on our previous *proactive data service* model. We utilize real-time correlation analysis of sensor data to refine model-based service composition at runtime. The correlation among sensor data is usually asynchronous. In this paper, we adopt and improve a Dynamic Time Warping (DTW) algorithm to obtain one-way lag-correlation, and realize dynamic sensor data correlation through refining existing service composition. Based on the real sensor data set in a coal-fired power plant, a series of experiments demonstrate the effectiveness of our service composition method.

Keywords: Service composition · IoT applications · Data-driven · Lag-correlation

1 Introduction

Today, more and more sensors are deployed in our physical world. The collaboration of large-scale autonomous and heterogeneous sensors rises up new challenges for developing IoT application. IoT service becomes a hot topic as it can provide consistent method to access and utilize sensor data from different stakeholders [1–4], and composition of IoT service can apparently achieve more valuable capacity. In our previous work [1], we proposed a novel type of service abstraction, called as proactive data service following the thought of software-defined sensors. And we preliminarily applied our service in an anomaly detection application. Based on anomaly detection rule, we can define service composition plan at design time and composite certain services for detecting specific equipment anomalies based on multiple indicator anomalies. Our previous service composition method was model based, which considered indicator

© Springer Nature Switzerland AG 2019
X. Liu et al. (Eds.): ICSOC 2018 Workshops, LNCS 11434, pp. 169–181, 2019.
https://doi.org/10.1007/978-3-030-17642-6_15

(or sensor) in isolation without accounting correlation of sensors, and can only detect anomalies when they have happened already.

In practice, sensors are not independent with each other. One sensor data may be normal individually, but when collectively accounting for other sensor data, it may be anomalous [5]. In this paper, we assume that if we modify the model-based service composition for considering more related sensors, we can detect anomalies much earlier and avoid serious damage. However, the situational and time-varying correlation among massive sensors rises up new challenges. It is apparent that correlations among sensors are difficult to accurately enumerate because of the plenty number of sensors. What's more, the correlation among sensors is situational and time-varying, fixed correlations cannot ensure the accuracy and sufficiency of service composition. Hence, it is crucial to dynamically modify service composition plan at runtime.

Recently, many studies proposed their dynamic service composition methods to help construct the service composition plan at runtime. Automatic re-planning schemes [6–8] allow composition plans to be adapted when matching services are unavailable, but existing approaches depend on central knowledge bases. Some works [9, 10] presented data-driven approaches to realize service composition at runtime relying on semantic matching or history composition plan mining. However, for proactive data services, it is hard to correlate them based on semantic matching because their underling sensor data are generally described with weak semantic.

In this paper, we present a data-driven service composition method based on our proactive data service model, which can dynamically refine the model-based service composition based on real-time sensor data analysis at runtime. In practice, the correlation among sensor data is usually asynchronous and time-varying. Based on the time difference and situational correlation among sensors, we can correlate more sensors and improve the effectiveness of service composition. Specifically, we classify the correlation among sensor data into one-way lag-correlation and two-way lag-correlation in respect of correlation difference's direction. And then we utilize one way lag-correlation among sensor data and mapping among service and sensor data to realize the modification of model-based service composition. At present, we only obtain the one-way lag-correlation among sensor data, and we adopt and improve a Dynamic Time Warping (DTW) based algorithm to analyze underlying sensor data of services. We apply our method in the real anomaly detection for a coal-fired power plant, and verify the effectiveness of our service composition method through a series of experiments.

2   Scenario

The motivation example in this paper is a real-time anomaly detection application for coal-fired power plant. The deployed sensors can reflect running indicators through collecting sensor data. And equipment anomaly can be inferred based on multiple indicator anomalies relying on expert experience. Figure 1 shows an anomaly detection example in Primary Air Fan (PAF). For simplicity, we only mark 5 sensors in Fig. 1, which are *import air volume* as *A*, *bearing temperature* as *B*, *bearing vibration* as *C*, and *motor electricity* as *D*.

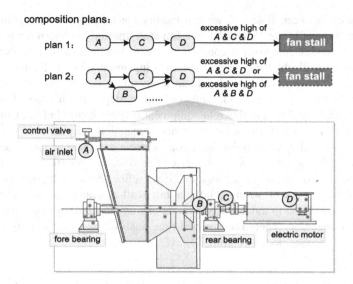

Fig. 1. An anomaly detection example in primary air fan

With our proactive data service model, we can coordinate certain sensors and realize equipment anomaly detection based on service composition [1]. Based on an anomaly detection rule "excessive high of $A \rightarrow$ excessive high of $C \rightarrow$ excessive high of $D \rightarrow$ **fan stall anomaly**", we can compose service *import_air_volume*, *bearing_vibration*, and *valve_degee* as the first composition plan showed in Fig. 1, and detect **fan stall anomaly** when excessive high of A, C and D happens. However, it can only detect anomalies when they have already happened. It is crucial to detect anomalies as earlier as possible to avoid irreparable damage. We assume that we can detect equipment anomaly much earlier if we consider more related sensors as well as their situations. As showed in Fig. 2(a), sensor B and sensor C have a correlation, and when an anomaly happens in B, there is an anomaly happens in C latter. Considering the time difference

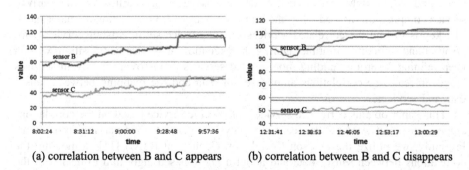

(a) correlation between B and C appears   (b) correlation between B and C disappears

Fig. 2. The Varied correlation between sensor B and C

and correlation between *B* and *C*, we can modify the first composition plan into the second plan showed in Fig. 1, and detect a **fan stall anomaly** before it really happens.

Although service composition considered sensor data correlation can obtain better effect, there are still challenges when coordinating more sensors. Firstly, given the plenty number of sensors involved, human intervention is rendered insufficient and inaccurate. There are over ten thousands of sensors deployed in a coal-fired power plant, and sensors deployed in different equipment may have correlations. Correlations defined based on expert experiences or sensors' semantic descriptions are not accurate enough. And secondly, the correlations among sensors are dynamic and time-varying, which will affect the effectiveness of service composition. As showed in Fig. 2(b), sensor *B* and *C*'s correlation disappears, and if we refine service composition based on fixed correlation, we will wrongly infer a **fan stall anomaly**. In summarize, it is insufficient and difficult to modify service composition plan at design time for realizing sensor data correlation. Therefore, the real-time analysis of sensor data is needed to advise service composition at runtime.

3 Data-Driven Service Composition Method

3.1 Method Overview

In our previous work [1], we introduced event mechanism in service model and gave some basic definitions preliminarily. Each proactive data service is mapped by certain set of sensors though receiving sensor data stream as its input sensor event streams. Input sensor event streams can be transformed into multiple service event streams with richer semantics through operations. With the proactive data service, we can composite certain services based on predefined rules.

Definition 1: service composition plan. A service composition plan is defined as a tuple <*S*, ***Links***, *condition*>, in which *S* is a set of service, ***Links*** is a set of *link* = <s_{source}, s_{target}> which indicate the connection of services, and *condition* indicates when to output the result of composition.

Through considering more sensor data, we can refine the existing service composition and obtain higher effect such as detect anomaly much earlier. Our data-driven service composition method takes the real-time sensor data correlation as major basis. The key is to find the correlated services for the service set in existing service composition and refine it at runtime. During the execution of service composition, we can keep refining it through adding more related services or removing irrelevant services based on real-time correlations among sensor data and the mapping between sensor data and services.

This paper obtains correlated services for specific service based on the correlations among sensor data, and utilizes real-time analysis to generate time-varying correlations. Presently, we utilize the Pearson Correlation Coefficient (PCC) [11] to measure the correlations between sensor data and adopt a DTW-based algorithm to deal with the problem of asynchronous correlation. There are two steps in our method: we firstly generate real-time sensor data correlation based on the analysis of sensor data, and then we find the service correlation based on the mapping between sensor data and service and refine the existing service composition at runtime.

3.2   Sensor Data Correlation Analysis

The correlation among sensor data usually shifts in time, which can be regard as Lag-correlation [12]. When analyzing correlation among sensor data, misjudgment of correlation also occurs if correlation lags are not considered. After observing large amounts of sensor data, there are generally the one-way lag-correlation shifts between sensors, which is shown in Fig. 3.

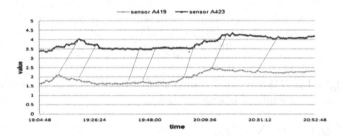

Fig. 3. Two types of correlation among sensor data

The lag-correlation analysis problem can be considered to find the time lag vector to maximize the PCC, which can be formalized as follows:

Definition 2: One-way Lag-correlation Analysis Problem. Given two sensor data sets E_i and E_j, suppose $E_i = \{e_{i(t1)}, e_{i(t2)}, \ldots, e_{i(tm)}\}$ and $E_j = \{e_{j(t1)}, e_{j(t2)}, \ldots, e_{j(tm)}\}$ in a slide window, if there exists a time lag vector $\Delta = \{t'_1, t'_2, \ldots, t'_n \mid t'_k \geq 0\}$ makes

$$cor_{(E_i, E_j, \Delta)} = \frac{\sum_1^n \left(e_{i(t)} - \overline{e_i}\right)\left(e_{j(t + tk')} - \overline{e_j}\right)}{\sqrt{\sum_1^n \left(e_{i(t)} - \overline{e_i}\right)^2} \times \sqrt{\sum_1^n \left(e_{j(t + tk')} - \overline{e_j}\right)^2}} \geq \delta_{cor},$$

in which δ_{cor} is a given threshold, we regard there is a one–way lag-correlation between E_i and E_j. Each time lag is positive, which can insure that E_{fj} always changes after E_{fi}'s changes.

To analyze the correlation between two sensor data, we can firstly obtain a time lag vector that makes $MAX(cor_{(E_i,E_j,\Delta)})$, and then justify if there is a lag-correlation through comparing with given threshold. Expectation Maximization (EM) algorithm [13] can be used to calculate the lag vector. However, the time complexity relies on the number of data records and iterations. Hence, we transform the function model for calculating time lag vector based on follow theorem.

Theorem 1: The Pearson Correlation Coefficient rises when the Euclidian Distance of the normalized series falls.

Proof:

$$\rho_{E_i,E_j} = \frac{\sum_{t=0}^{n} \left(e_{i(t)} - \overline{e}_i\right) \times \left(e_{j(t)} - \overline{e}_j\right)}{\sqrt{\sum \left(e_{i(t)} - \overline{e}_i\right)^2} \times \sqrt{\sum \left(e_{j(t)} - \overline{e}_j\right)^2}} \tag{1}$$

$$\cos \theta = \frac{E_i \cdot E_j}{\|E_i\|\|E_j\|} = \frac{\sum_{t=0}^{n} e_{i(t)} \times e_{j(t)}}{\sqrt{\sum e_{i(t)}^2} \times \sqrt{\sum e_{j(t)}^2}} \tag{2}$$

According to Eqs. (1) and (2), it is obvious that the Pearson correlation coefficient is equivalent to the centralized cosine similarity.

$$\begin{aligned} d\left(E_i, E_j\right) &= \sum_{t=1}^{n} \left(e_{i(t)} - e_{j(t)}\right)^2 \\ &= \sum_{t=1}^{n} e_{i(t)}^2 + \sum_{t=1}^{n} e_{j(t)}^2 - 2\sum_{t=1}^{n} e_{i(t)} \cdot e_{j(t)} \\ &= 2 - 2\cos \theta \end{aligned} \tag{3}$$

Based on Theorem 1, we can calculate the time lag vector makes the minimum Euclidian distance of the normalized series, and then calculate the PCC of the original series based on the time lag vector.

3.3   Sensor Data Correlation Generation

DTW algorithm [14] is a robust method used to measure similarity of time series, which can shift and distort the time-series to ignore the problem of time axis scaling and shifting. In this paper we adopt a DTW-based algorithm to find the time lag vector of two sensor data series. For analysis the lag-correlation more accurately, we improve the traditional DTW algorithm when calculating the cost matrix in two respects: (1) for confirming that one sensor data series always changes after the other, we only calculating the upper triangular or lower triangular matrix; and (2) to avoid excessive time warping, we set a maximum value for the time lag vector. The pseudo-code of our DTW-based algorithm is showed as follows:

```
Algorithm 1: sensor event correlation generation
Input:
    E_i={e_{i(t1)}, e_{i(t2)},...,e_{i(tn)}} and E_j={e_{j(t1)}, e_{j(t2)},...,e_{j(tn)}};
    δ_cor : the threshold of PCC;
    Limit: the maximum value for the time lag vector;
Output:
    true or false
1.  get E_i', E_j' through normalizing E_i and E_j;
2.  generate matrix distance[n][n] for each event in E_i'
    and E_j';
3.  for j =0, i=0→n & i=0,j=0→n;
4.     output[i][i]=distance[i][j]
5.  estimate whether calculating the upper triangular or
    lower triangular matrix
6.  if flag == upper
7.     for(j:1→n; i:1→j)
8.        if (j-i>=limit)
9.           output[i][j] = Min(output[i][j-1],output[i-
    1][j-1])+distance[i][j];
10.       else
11.          output[i][j] = Min(output[i-1][j-1], out-
    put[i][j-1], output[i-1][j])+distance[i][j];
12. if flag ==downer
13.    ...
14. get path for E_i and E_j based on output[n][n] and cal-
    culate correlation coefficient cor
15. if cor >= δ_cor
16.    return true;
17. else
18.    return false;
```

Through calculating the correlation coefficient of sensor data sets in slide window, we can obtain the real-time specific sensor data pair's correlation.

3.4 Correlation-Based Service Composition

After generating the one-way lag-correlation among sensor data, we can obtain the service correlation based on the mapping between sensor data and service, and refine the existing service composition at runtime by considering more correlated service. When the latest sensor data correlations are generated, we will find the correlated service for each primitive service in the existing service composition plan, and add new related services with corresponding links, and remove irrelevant services and corresponding links. In this way, the service composition can keep refining based on dynamic correlations for obtaining better effect. The pseudo-code of service composition refining is showed as follow:

```
Algorithm 2: Service composition refining
Input:
    sp, an existing service composition plan;
    cor_f, all the latest sensor data correlations;
Output:
    sp, new service composition plan;
1.  s is the primitive service set in sp;
2.  links is the primitive link set in sp;
3.  for each s in s
4.      s_new is new service set added in sp and related s;
5.      links_new is new link set added in sp and involved
    s_new;
6.      for each cor_f = <E_i, E_j> in cor_f'
7.          if E_j is underlying sensor data of s
8.              s_new'.add(s');
9.              for each link in links
10.                 if link.s_source = s
11.                     link' = <s, link.s_target>;
12.                     link_new'.add(link');
13.                 else if link.s_target = s;
14.                     link' = <link.s_source, s>;
15.                     link_new'.add(link');
16.                 end if
17.             end for
18.         end if
19.     end for
20.     sp.remove(s_new - s_new');
21.     sp.remove(links_new - link_new');
22.     sp.add(s_new' - s_new);
23.     sp.add(link_new' - links_new);
24. end for
25. return sp;
```

The algorithm will keep executing once the latest correlation is generated, so that the service composition plan keeps refining for realizing dynamic correction of sensor data.

4 Experiments

In this section, we firstly verify that if our method can detect anomaly much earlier, and then verify the accuracy of our method.

4.1 Experiment Setup

Datasets: The datasets used in our experiments is the real sensor data and artificial maintenance records from a fire power plant. Each sensor generated one value per 30 s from 2015-01-31 00:00:00 to 2016-01-31 23:59:59. The detail information is shown in Table 1. We choose sensor data of 5 main systems to verify the effectiveness of our data-driven service composition method.

Table 1. Detail information of dataset in our experiments

System name	Equipment number	Sensor number	Anomaly number
Coal Mill System (GMS)	36	334	141
Turbonator System (TS)	50	299	101
Air and Gas System (AGS)	32	344	44
Water Supply System (WSS)	69	725	61
Environmental Protection System (EPS)	10	49	119
Total	197	1751	466

Environment: We implemented our method in a cluster consisting of 5 nodes, and the nodes are running in virtual machines with CentOS 6.4, four Intel Core i5-2400 CPUs 3.10G Hz and 4.00 GB RAM. All the algorithms are implemented in Java with JDK 1.8.0.

Evaluation Criterion: To verify the effectiveness of our method, we design following criterion:

(1) **Time Ahead:** let *LTime* be the time when our method predicted an indicator anomaly, *CTime* be the time when the anomaly is actually happened, the time ahead can be calculated as follow:

$$Time_{ahead} = CTime - LTime$$

(2) **Precision:** the precision can be calculated as follow:

$$precision = \frac{|L \cap T|}{|L|} \times 100\%$$

(3) **Recall:** the recall can be calculated as follow:

$$recall = \frac{|L \cap T|}{|T|} \times 100\%$$

In which $L = \{l_1, l_2, ..., l_m\}$ is the list of indicator anomalies predicted by service composition method, and $T = \{t_1, t_2, ..., t_n\}$ is the actually indicator anomalies happened in practice.

4.2   Effectiveness Evaluation

For evaluating the effectiveness of our data-driven service composition method, we respectively and randomly select 10 periods of data from 5 systems, and simulate stream data for each sensor strictly according to the real sensor data's timestamp. We realize the model-based service composition based on 102 equipment detection rules, and compared with our method. Table 2 shows the average time ahead for all anomalies of our method. Our method can warn anomalies at least 10 min and at most 45 min in advance. The result shoes that our method can detect anomalies much earlier.

Table 2. The average time ahead of our method

System name	GMS	TS	AGS	WSS	EPS
Time ahead	12 m 30 s	10 m	21 m 30 s	45 m	17 m 30 s

Then we artificially set some correlated sensors for sensors involved in the anomaly detection rules based on sematic matching and expert experiences, and refine the existing service composition as set of fixed service composition. Then we utilize our method and fixed service composition to predict anomalies respectively, and compare each system's average precision and recall.

As shown in Fig. 4, our method has a precision over 79% and a recall over 70%. Comparing to service composition based on fixed plans, our method has both higher precision and recall. This is because our method can refine service compositions at runtime based on real-time sensor event correlation. It can detect new correlations and composite related services, and increase the precision of anomaly prediction consequently. What's more, our method doesn't have to follow invalid sensor correlation, and can relatively avoid predict wrong anomalies. Thereby, our method can miss much fewer anomalies and obtain higher recall.

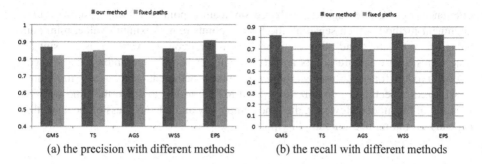

Fig. 4. The effectiveness of anomaly detection with different methods

5 Related Work

5.1 Dynamic Service Composition

A dynamic services composition allows determining and replacing service components during runtime [15].

Hossain et al. [10] presented a big data-driven approach to handle service composition in mobile environment, which utilized parallel processing to select the optimum required services in a minimal time. Wu et al. [16] presented an AI planning approach for the automatic composition of web services. Canfora et al. [17] proposed a re-planning approach based on general algorithm. When the actual QoS deviates from the estimation during the execution of workflow, the re-planning approach determines the re-planning slice and re-binds the concrete services. Kalasapur et al. [18] proposed a graph-theory based service composition mechanism, and defined a composition result as a directed acyclic graph. Zhang et al. in [19] proposed a requirement-driven dynamic services composition method for Web services. The dynamic business processes configuration method is used to select Web Services, and thus to meet customers' requirements.

Different with the above works, this paper aims to refine existing service composition plan at runtime for obtain higher effect. The underlying data of proactive data service in this paper is sensor data stream, and we try to utilize real-time analysis of sensor data to realize dynamic sensor data correlation and refine service composition.

5.2 Lag-Correlation Analysis

Many works assume that the lag time for each pair of related points in the two time series is consistent. Shifted method can be used to solve this kind of lag-correlation problem through maximizing the correlation of the two-time series by translating one time series with a constant time axis variable t. BRAID [20] used geometric progressive method and interpolation method, which can find the maximum correlation coefficient with $O(\log l)$ time complexity. Lin et al. [21] proposed a three point forecast-based probing method, which can achieve small error when the lag is large and perform well on the occasion of lag mutation. Curve registration methods can be used to eliminate difference lags. Curve registration based on feature point [22] was a simple curve alignment method, which select all the feature points (e.g. maximum value, minimum value, or zero value) and align them in vertical direction. However, it is not suit for time series whose feature points are fuzzy. Jiang et al. [23] presented a curve registration model for maximizing the correlation coefficient and used smoothing-generalized expectation maximization (S-GEM) algorithm to solve the time warping function of the model. However, the time complexity and effectiveness of the algorithm depends on the number of sampling points.

6 Conclusion

In this paper, we propose a data-driven service composition method based on our previous proactive data service model for supporting dynamic sensor correlation in IoT environment. Based on our method, we can keep modifying model-based service composition at runtime and obtain better effect, such as detect anomaly much earlier. Then we improve the Dynamic Time Warping (DTW) based algorithm to analyze the underlying sensor data and obtain the one-way lag-correlations in real-time. Lastly, we keep refine the existing service composition plan at runtime based on the sensor data correlation and mapping between service and sensor data. We apply our method in the real anomaly detection of a coal-fired power plant, and verify that our service composition method can detect anomalies much earlier with high precision and recall through a series of experiments.

References

1. Han, Y.B., Liu, C., Su, S., et al.: A decentralized and service-based approach to proactively correlating stream data. In: International Conference on Internet of Things (2016)
2. Chu, V.W., Wong, R.K., Liu, W., et al.: Traffic analysis as a service via a unified model. In: IEEE International Conference on Services Computing, pp. 195–202. IEEE (2014)
3. Zhang, J., Radia, N., Li, Z., et al.: An infrastructure supporting considerate sensor service provisioning. In: The 6th IEEE International Conference on Service Oriented Computing and Applications (SOCA), pp. 69–76. IEEE (2013)
4. Guilly, T.L., Olsen, P., Ravn, A.P., et al.: HomePort: middleware for heterogeneous home automation networks. In: IEEE International Conference on Pervasive Computing and Communications Workshops, pp. 627–633. IEEE (2013)
5. Budgaga, W., Malensek, M., Pallickara, S.L., et al.: A framework for scalable real-time anomaly detection over voluminous, geospatial data streams. In: Concurrency & Computation Practice & Experience, pp. 1–24 (2017)
6. Hibner, A., Zielinski, K. Semantic-based dynamic service composition and adaptation. In: 2007 IEEE Congress on Services, pp. 213–220. IEEE (2007)
7. Klusch, M., Gerber, A.: Semantic web service composition planning with owls-xplan. In: Proceedings of the 1st International AAAI Fall Symposium on Agents and the Semantic Web, pp. 55–62 (2005)

8. Peer, J.: A POP-based replanning agent for automatic web service composition. In: Gómez-Pérez, A., Euzenat, J. (eds.) ESWC 2005. LNCS, vol. 3532, pp. 47–61. Springer, Heidelberg (2005). https://doi.org/10.1007/11431053_4

9. Liu, X., Ma, Y., Huang, G., et al.: Data-driven composition for service-oriented situational web applications. IEEE Trans. Serv. Comput. **8**(1), 2–16 (2015)

10. Hossain, M.S., Moniruzzaman, M., Muhammad, G., et al.: Big data-driven service composition using parallel clustered particle swarm optimization in mobile environment. IEEE Trans. Serv. Comput. **9**(5), 806–817 (2016)

11. Wu, S., Lin, H., Wang, W., et al.: RLC: ranking lag correlations with flexible sliding windows in data streams. Pattern Anal. Appl. 1–11 (2016)

12. Guo, T., Sathe, S., Aberer, K.: Fast distributed correlation discovery over streaming time-series data. In: Proceedings of the 24th ACM International Conference on Information and Knowledge Management (CIKM), pp. 1161–1170 (2015)

13. Liu, X., Yang, M.C.K.: Simultaneous curve registration and clustering for functional data. Comput. Stat. Data Anal. **53**(4), 1361–1376 (2009)

14. Kate, R.J.: Using dynamic time warping distances as features for improved time series classification. Data Min. Knowl. Discov. **30**(2), 283–312 (2016)

15. Sheng, Q.Z., Qiao, X., Vasilakos, A.V., et al.: Web services composition: a decade's overview. Inf. Sci. **280**, 218–238 (2014)

16. Wu, Z., Ranabahu, A., Gomadam, K., Sheth, A., Miller, J.: Automatic composition of semantic web services using process mediation. In: International Conference on Enterprise Information Systems, pp. 453–461 (2007)

17. Canfora, G., Di Penta, M., Esposito, R., Villani, M.L.: A framework for QoS-aware binding and re-binding of composite web services. J. Syst. Softw. **81**(10), 1754–1769 (2008)

18. Kalasapur, S., Kumar, M., Shirazi, B.A.: Dynamic service composition in pervasive computing. IEEE Trans. Parallel Distrib. Syst. **18**(7), 907–918 (2007)

19. Zhang, L.J., Li, B.: Requirements driven dynamic services composition for web services and rid solutions. J. Grid Comput. **2**, 121–140 (2004)

20. Sakurai, Y., Papadimitriou, S., Faloutsos, C.: BRAID: stream mining through group lag correlations. In: ACM SIGMOD International Conference on Management of Data, pp. 599–610 (2005)

21. Lin, Z.Y., Jiang, Y., Lai, Y.X., et al.: A new algorithm on lagged correlation analysis between time series. J. Comput. Res. Dev. **12**, 2645–2655 (2012)

22. Ramsay, J.: Functional Data Analysis. Springer, New York (2006). https://doi.org/10.1007/b98888

23. Jiang, G.X., Wang, W.J.: Correlation analysis in curve registration of time series. J. Softw. **25**(9), 2002–2017 (2014)

A Dynamic Service Adaptation Algorithm for Seamless Integration of Cloud Infrastructure and Edge Devices

Liu Yang[1(✉)] and Yi Li[2]

[1] State Grid Corporation of China, Beijing, China
yang-liu@sgcc.com.cn
[2] State Key Laboratory of Advanced Power Transmission Technology,
Global Energy Interconnection Research Institute (GEIRI), Beijing, China
80726576@qq.com

Abstract. Service-oriented cloud-edge integration is a promising approach for the big IoT stream processing effectively in a distributed manner. Dynamic adaptation of cloud and edge service is of key importance to enable the seamless integration of cloud infrastructure and edge equipment. There exist several challenges, such as grasping the right moment and coping incomplete matching. Targeting at the challenges and based on our previous proactive data service model, the paper proposes a service adaptation approach, called as ALES, to enable the dynamic cloud-edge integration. The main contributions include: transforming the service adaptation problem into the improved maximal weight matching model in a dynamic bipartite graph. The $M/M/c/\infty$ model in the queuing theory is modified to optimize the Kuhn-Munkres algorithm to minimize the average response time of the request of edge service. The effectiveness of the proposed approach is demonstrated by examining real cases of Chinese State Power Grid. Experimental results verify the effectiveness and efficiency of our approach.

Keywords: Cloud-edge integration · Cloud service · Edge service · Service adapting

1 Introduction

The IoT (Internet of things), deemed as the third wave of information revolution, enables large-scale sensors to be deployed in various application fields. These sensors continuously generate stream data, which are often infinite, noisy, low-value-density, and out of order. Traditional stream data processing architectures, especially with cloud, are designed to store and process them in a centralized manner [1]. However, along with the rapid development of intelligent terminal devices, such as smartphones, tablet, and gateways, many of them have internally installed much computing power. They are regarded as edge devices when they are connected to the Internet. A new computing paradigm i.e., edge computing has emerged and greatly stimulate the process of large-scale distributed stream data from sensors [2, 3]. This paradigm stresses sensor data and its processing should be put close to the edge devices.

© Springer Nature Switzerland AG 2019
X. Liu et al. (Eds.): ICSOC 2018 Workshops, LNCS 11434, pp. 182–193, 2019.
https://doi.org/10.1007/978-3-030-17642-6_16

Today, service computing has become a mainstream integration approach for distributed system due to its standardization, flexibility, and versatility [4, 5]. Some works have already put focuses on how to integrate computing power of cloud infrastructure and edge devices with service-oriented approaches [6–9]. In these approaches, there are two kinds of services are involved, which are called as cloud services and edge services. A cloud service is deployed and run on the cloud. It is usually heavyweight, which means it consumes lots of computing resources. An edge service is deployed and run on an edge device. It is lightweight, which means it consumes much fewer computing resources. To realize the integration, some techniques are developed to compose edge services and cloud service at the build time or cooperate their instances on the runtime.

Inspecting with a real scenario in Sect. 2, we find dynamic service adaptation also means much for cloud-edge integration, which does not receive enough attentions in related works [10]. Service adaptation means to build and maintain a connection between the edge service instance and cloud service instance for event processing according to some specific event process logic. Actually, the edge devices have characteristics of extendibility and uncertainty. It can quickly scale themselves and send large-scale adaptation requests in unpredictable time. Although the cloud is powerful, it still owns limited computation resources. It means only limited cloud service instances can be supported to run concurrently. On the contrary, there may have considerable differences in magnitude between the edge service instances as well as cloud service instances. Hence, it becomes a key issue to ensure these disproportionate service instances to be adapted in the run time and each adaptation request from edge services should be handled as quickly as possible.

This paper names the above-mentioned issue as the *incomplete adaptation problem* among cloud-edge service instances. To solve it, this paper proposes an Adaptive cLoud-Edge Service instance adaptation algorithm, i.e. ALES and integrate it into our previously proposed edge-cloud integration approach [11]. The main contribution is that the improvement-based bipartite graph matching method by the optimization model of queuing theory helps to realize the ALES. The dynamic adaptation algorithm can effectually solve the dynamic and unpredictable adaptation request of large-scale edge services with limited cloud service instances and minimize the delay and response time of data processing.

2 Motivation and Problem

The motivation of this paper is the real time process of the power quality in the State Smart Grid (SSG). SSG has deployed more than 7000 Data Acquisition Terminals (DATs) on the transmission lines across the whole country. A DAT can collect the sensor stream data related to more than 2000 power indicators which can fully reflect the power quality during power transmission.

Figure 1 shows the cloud-edge integration architecture in SGG which is built based on the Seamless Integration of Cloud and Edge Service approach (SICES). DATs join into the cloud severed as the edge equipment because they are designed to execute some lightweight computation.

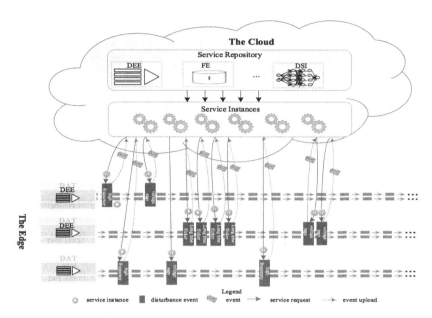

Fig. 1. The cloud-end integration architecture based on the SICES

The cloud has created a service responsivity which contains serval services: The data Disturbance Event Extraction (DEE) service, the Feature Extraction service (FE), and the Disturbance Source Identification Service (DSI). The DSI service is build based on RNN network with 24 layers and 100 units each layer and it will be updated periodically. The DSI receives and analyzes the event comes from the DEE.

However, DAT terminals are easily extensible so that large scale of DAT terminals can be added into the cloud occasionally or went down from the cloud in a unpredict time. As well as the DEE will be increased more than the DSI. During a very short counting intervals, there may be more than 7000 DAT terminals running at the edge side, so that there are more than 7000 DEE requesting for adaptation with DSI. But, it is difficult to simultaneously adapt to more than 7,000 running instances of recurrent neural network models and maintain communication with DAT terminals by factors such as technology and cost of cloud infrastructure.

Besides, due to the intrinsic characteristics of the sensor stream data, the opportunity of detecting a disturbance event has great uncertainty by the DEE service. And, the frequency, the impacted indicators and the moment of disturbance events occurrence are different and unpredictable. For example, from the moment t_1 to moment t_3, (the time interval is very short $t_3 - t_1 < 100ms$) there are several different types and different amounts of disturbance events. At t_1, there were 323 DEE instances outputted the disturbance events, there were 323 available DSI instances cloud be adapted to the DEE instances. At t_2 moment and t_3 moment, there were another 2135 and 256 DEE instances outputted the disturbance events, but there are not enough DSI instances could be adapted for them.

Above all, during cloud-edge integration, the scale of edge service instances and the opportunity of service adaptation are both dynamic changeable at the run-time, but the cloud service instances are limited. To find optimize the allocation plan to ensure that every disturbance event detected by the DEE service can be processed to meet the continually change and uncertainty of adaptation requests of edge service and reduces the overall execution cost is a key issue to seamless integrate the cloud and edge.

3   Overview of the SICES Approach

In our previous work, we have proposed an approach SICES for the seamless integration of cloud and edge based on our proactive data service model [5, 11].

The proactive data service model is defined as the Definition 1. It incorporates some configurable stream data processing capabilities and transform the original low-value density sensor data stream into a high-level event stream.

Definition 1 (Proactive Data Service Model). A proactive data service can be defined as the four tuple: $S = < uri, in\_events, out\_events, event\_handler >$。

- *uri*: the unique identifier of service;
- *in_events*: input of the service, it can be the original stream data or events stream;
- *out_events:* output of the service, different operation generates different type of event;
- *event_handler*: a combination consisting of one or more operations according to the processing logic for the received event.

The SICES [11] contains the edge side and cloud side. The proactive data service can be splitted into two parts according the operations in event hander. The proactive data service whose operations are lightweight can run on the edge equipment to pre-process the stream data. It is regarded as the edge services. As well as the service whose operations are heavyweight only runs on the cloud to receive and process the events generated by the edge side. A service can be declaratively defined as an edge service or a cloud service according to its encapsulated computing task when it is defined.

The edge service running on the edge equipment to real-time transform the low value density stream into event stream by detecting the key events (such as sampling value is too high or low) contained in the original data. When the first key events emerge, edge service instance send adaptation request to the cloud. A service schedule assigns a suitable cloud service instance to the edge service. Then, an event transmission channel is established between the edge and cloud. The events will be transmitted to the cloud service for processing. When the cloud service instance finish future processing of events, this cloud service instance is also released for the other scheduling.

In order to facilitate the scheduling process between the edge service and the cloud service instance, we propose the data structure of key nodes. It is defined as a temporary event buffer that is deployed on an edge equipment and bound to a specific edge service instance. When beginning request for a cloud service instance, the edge side caches the event stream that generated by the edge service during the adapting process.

However, as previously analyzed, there may be a mismatch between the number of edge service instances and the number of cloud service instances, which means that there are a large number of edge service instances at the same time to request limited cloud service instances for adaptation. In order to solve this problem, this paper proposes ALES based on queuing theory and dynamic bipartite graph in the Sect. 4. ALES is improved key part to be integrated into SICES. The algorithm helps to adapt the suitable cloud service instance for handling a given edge request under the condition that the average response time of all the edge service instances waiting for adaptation is the minimum.

4　The Service Adaptation Algorithm

In this section first transforms the adaptation problem into Dynamic Bipartite Graph (DBG) with a Maximum Weighted perfect Matching (MWM). At the same time, a M/M/c/∞ queuing model in the queuing theory is established for the key nodes to predict the processing time of the cloud service instances and assist the MWM of DBG to guarantee the average waiting time of event minimal.

4.1　Could-Edge Service Adaptation Model Based on the Dynamic Bipartite Graph

The algorithm of this paper uses the key nodes generated by the edge service instance as the minimum adaptation unit to for the cloud service instance. This is because a key node caches a set of events that need to be processed within a time period. Besides, one edge service instance may continuously generate different types of key nodes which require different cloud service instances for processing.

The weighted bipartite graph is an optimal solution for the scheduling and assignment problem [12]. Thus, we build a service adaptation model based on the bipartite graph.

Definition 2 (Bipartite Graph). For any graph $G = (V, E)$, if the V can be splited into two disjoint subsets, and vertexes attached to each edge belongs to different subsets, then G is a bipartite graph.

Definition 3 (Matching). A matching in G is a subset of its edges M, no two of which share an endpoint. If there is a matching M, each vertex in the graph is associated with an edge in the graph, the M is a perfect match. Give each edge $e \in E$ a weight, then G is a weight bipartite graph. If the perfect matching satisfies that the weighted sum is max, then it is a maximum weighted perfect match (WMW).

If vertex $v \in V$ is an endpoint of $e \in M$, the v is saturated. The interleave path of M refers to the path where its side alternates between $\{E-M\}$ and M. If there is an edge whose starting and ending points are unsaturated in M, then it is the augmenting path of M. According to Berge theorem, if there are no more augmenting paths, a maximum match is found.

In a period of time, there are a set of key nodes, $K = \{k_1, k_2, \ldots, k_n\}$, and a set of cloud service instances $S = \{s_1, s_2, \ldots, s_m\}$. Based on the above, the service adaptation problem between the key nodes of edge services and cloud service instances can be modeled by a weighted bipartite graph $G = (V, BE)$. In which, $V = \{K \cup S\}$ is the vertexes in G, K and S constitute the left and right vertices in G. BE is the edge set in G, which represents the assignment between key nodes that cloud service instances. The weight of the edge is expressed as ew_{ij}.

In order to reduce the execution time, we will use the waiting time T_{k_i} present the weight of edges.

$$ew_{ij} = T_{k_i} = t - k_i.t$$

In which, t is the current time, $k_i.t$ is the moment the key node emerged.

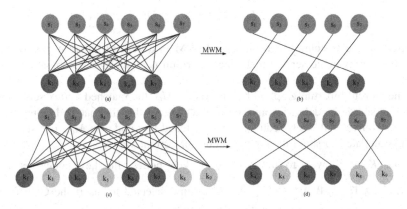

Fig. 2. The service scheduling model based on the dynamic bipartite graph

However, the key node generation is driven by the stream, there is a huge uncertain. That is to say, the left vertexes K in G is continually changed, while the cloud service instances S can be known according to the state of service scheduling. The continually changed K makes the G be dynamic, where new edges are being added and old edges are being removed.

Figure 2 shows an example of the service scheduling model. At the moment t1, there is a G, is shown as (a), we can get an MWM (b) if there is no change in G. However, some new key nodes $K' = \{k_{10}, k_{11}, k_{12}\}$ and some cloud service instances S' are inserted into G, which is shown in (c), MWM(b) should change to MWM (d). The main issue is that incoming key nodes will change the matching continually.

The queue theory always is applied in the stochastic scene. In this paper, we use the M/M/c/∞ queuing model to transform the K into a queue. The cloud service instance S served as processor for K. Assuming that ρ is the average number of key nodes in G for now. c represents the number of key nodes that can be inserted into G,

$c = m - \rho_i m$ is the maximum number of service instances in S when all service instances are free. P_0 is the probability that all the cloud service instances are free when the number of key nodes in G is i.

4.2   The Dynamic Service Adaptation Algorithm

Firstly, we improved the typical Kuhn-Munkres [13] algorithm to solve the MWM in a weighted bipartite graph. We first give preliminaries of equivalent subgraph. L is the feasible vertex label of G which is computed by the formula (1), we set the $G_L = \{(s,k)|e = (s,k) \in BE\}$, and it satisfy that $L(s) + L(k) = be.ew$, then G_L is the equivalent subgraph of G. If there is a perfect matching M^* in G_L, then M^* is the MWM of G.

$$\begin{cases} L(s) = maxew\left(s_i k_j\right) \\ L(k) = 0; \end{cases} \tag{1}$$

Based on the Matching algorithm, an MWM in a general bipartite graph can be found. Next, a dynamic service matching algorithm is given by a combination with a queue.

If the current bipartite graph G has an MWM M_G, the matched vertex sets $\mathrm{K}(M_G)$ and $S(M_G)$ should be deleted from the G, which means that the matched cloud service instance resources will be scheduled to the matched key nodes in M_G. The state of G should be updated to show the count number of current vertexes.

If the K is allowed to insert $c(c \neq 0)$ key nodes, the key nodes set $K^c = \left\{k_1^c, k_2^c, k_i^c \ldots k_c^c | T_{k_i^c} \geq W_q \& k_1^c \geq k_2^c\right\}$ should be first selected to insert the G to form a new bipartite graph. In order to obtain the maximum weighted perfect match of the bipartite graph, it is necessary to satisfy that $|S| = |K|$, which means the left and the right vertex sets should have the same number of vertexes. Therefore, when updating the bipartite graph matching model, it is need to add some virtual cloud service instances vertexes and set the edge value to 0. Otherwise the key nodes should be still wait in the queue until the condition is satisfied again. Our algorithm has realized a data structure that maintains a maximal matching, or an approximate maximum cardinality matching, in a dynamic graph. Because the time complexity of the Kuhn-Munkres algorithm [14] is $O(n^3)$, where $n = max\{|S|\}$. It can be known that when the key nodes being inserted into G, only the improved Kuhn-Munkres is called once, and the waiting time of key nodes is W_q. Thus, the time complexity of our algorithm is $O\left(W_q n^3\right)$, that is $O(n^3)$.

5   Experiment

An important constraint goal of the dynamic integration of cloud and edges in this paper is to minimize the waiting time of events. Therefore, in this section, experiments based on the actual SSG data are performed according to the following settings. All the following experiments are repeated 10 times and we adopt the average values.

5.1 Experiment Setting

Experiment Environment: The experiment is conducted based on a cloud infrastructure and edge environment. The configuration is shown in Table 1. 20 virtual machines (VMs) use 1 Gbps Ethernet fibers and switches to build the cloud infrastructure. 50 DATs are used as the edge equipment that joined into the cloud.

Dataset: The data set in this experiment is real sensor data collected from SSG. There are 354 sensors, each with 2520 indicator data values. The data sampling time is 2016-07-01 00:00:00 to 2018-01-31 23:59:59. Based on this data set, the real sensor data stream is simulated on the DAT. (Table 1)

Table 1. The configuration of the experiment environment

Role	Equipment	Hardware configuration	Software configuration
Cloud	20 VMs	2 × 8 core with 2.4 GHz CPU 128 GB Memory 1 TB RAID5	Centos7.0 Hadoop-2.6.5 JDK-1.8.5
Edge	50 DATs	32-bit embedded microprocessor LPC2214 ARM7TDMI	Embedded Red Hat JDK 10.0.1

5.2 Experiment Setup

This paper validates the effectiveness of the ALES method based on the implementation of the DEE services and the DSI services as mentioned is Sect. 2. According to the established cloud environment, the cloud can run at most 20 DSI service instances simultaneously.

The metric used in this paper is the average response time of events, which is defined as the following:

Average Response Time (Rs): Rs indicates the average response time of key nodes within a given period time. It means the time difference between the moment when the key nodes emerge and the moment when cloud service instance finishing processing it.

$$RS = \frac{\sum \left(k.T_p - k.t \right)}{l}$$

$k.T_p$ is the moment that the cloud service instance finishing processing of key node. l is the number of key nodes during the given period time.

In this paper, we will compare the average response time of disturbance events of the SICES and the SICES^{++}. SICES^{++} have integrated the ALES into SICES to optimize the problem of uncertain opportunity and the coping incomplete adaptation problems. Experiments are carried out as the followings:

(a) Verifying that the changes of average response time when increasing the number of DATs. Specifically, we initialize 20 DSI service instances on the cloud. The DATs are joined into the cloud in order 10, 20, 30, 40, and 50 respectively.

The stream speed is set to 100/s. Then, calculate the average response time of different methods under the different number of DATs;

(b) Verifying that changes of average response time under the different stream speed. Specifically, we initialize 20 DSI service instances on the cloud. 50 DATs are joined into the cloud. The stream speed is set to in order 100/s, 200/s, 300/s, 400/s, and 500/s respectively. Then, calculate the average response time of different methods under the different stream speed;

(c) Verifying that the changes of average response time when increasing the number of DSI service instances. Specifically, 30 DATs are joined into the cloud. The stream speed is set to 100/s. And the DSI service instances increasing in order 5, 10, 15, and 20 respectively. Then, calculate the average response time of different methods under the different number of DATs;

5.3   Experiment Results and Evaluation

Figure 3 gives the RS of different methods under the different DATs, the RS increases as the DATs number increases, but the SICES++ is slower than SICES. And, the RS of DACE is 28.4% lower than the RS of SICES.

Figure 4 gives the RS of different methods under the different stream speed of DATs, the RS increases as the stream speed increases, but the SICES++ is slower than SICES. And, the RS of DACE is 24.4% lower than the RS of SICES.

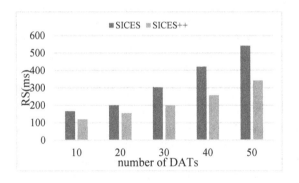

Fig. 3. The RS under different DATs numbers

Figure 5 gives the RS of different methods under the different DATs instances number, the RS decreases as the DATs instances increases, but the SICES decreases slower than SICES. And, the RS of DACE is 25.6% lower than the RS of SICES.

The experiment results show that the RS of SICES^{++} is average 26% lower than that of SICES and can be reduced by up to 36.8%. This is because when SICES schedules cloud service instances, it may cause conflicting requests for edge service instances which affect the service matching based on bipartite graphs to reduce matching efficiency. The combination of queuing theory in ALES can keep the matching of the bipartite graph in a stable state, which reduces the waiting time by reducing the bad competition during the matching process. Second, the use of queuing can predict the waiting time of key nodes, and the service adaptation scheme can be optimized and arranged in advance.

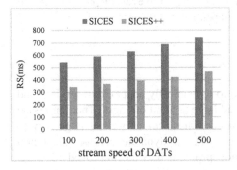

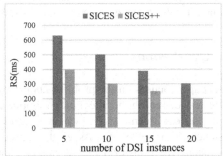

Fig. 4. The RS under different stream speed   **Fig. 5.** The RS under different DSI instances

The experiment result has demonstrated that with the dynamic adaptation algorithm enables limited cloud service instances to handle huge-scale and continually changeable adaptation requests of edge service instances.

6 Related Work

With the rise of IoT globally and edge computing, integration of edge and cloud has received much attention in research community and industry.

Varghese et al. [15] presented an Edge-as-a-Service (EaaS) platform. They aimed at realizing distributed cloud architectures and integrating the edge of the network into the computing ecosystem. Xu et al. [10] presented EAaaS, which is a scalable analytic service for enabling real-time edge analytics in IoT scenarios. Kaur et al. [13] adopted lightweight containers instead of the conventional virtual machines to reduce the overhead, response time, and overall energy consumption of fog devices. Wang et al. [8] presented a cloud-edge computing framework based on a tensor-based services model to provide high-quality proactive and personalized services for humans. However, they rely on pre-existing knowledge of the infrastructure and on statically defined data pipelines to perform efficient workload allocation across geographically distributed resources.

Some approaches related to service runtime self-adaptation using preplanning. The core operations in these approaches are planning, running and self-adaptation. Bucchiarone et al. [16] and [17] provided a self-adaptation approach using context-aware replanning. The approach could continuously monitor the abnormal situation according current context and automatically adapt the main process at runtime. The context is defined by a set of domain objects. But the adaptation goals are preconditions or effects of faulted services, and when corresponding adaptation operations fail, the final business goals can't be achieved. Alférez et al. [18] proposed a framework that used variability models to support the runtime adaptation of service compositions. The variability models recorded various variants for a business process, and feature models were created for these variants. An exception at runtime could be monitored according the changes of features in the running context, and then was solved through removing and adding some process fragments in the main process. However, the construction of variability models is complexity and closely depends on domain specialists.

7   Conclusion

This paper focuses on the problem about how to dynamically adapt cloud services and edge service during the integration of cloud and large amount of edges. The main issue is the serious mismatch of available cloud service instances as well as edge service instances. To solve this issue, the paper proposes a dynamic service adaptation approach. We transform the service adaptation problem into the improved maximal weight matching model in a dynamic bipartite graph. The M/M/c/∞ model in the queuing theory is also involved to optimize the Kuhn-Munkres algorithm to minimize the average response time of the request of edge service. The effectiveness of the proposed approach is demonstrated by examining real cases of SSG. Experimental results verify the effectiveness and efficiency of our approach.

Acknowledgment. This work was supported in part by a grant from the Technology Project of State Grid, "Research and Application of Key Technology in Big Data Analysis of Power Quality", the National Natural Science Foundation of China (Grant No. 61672042), the Program for Youth Backbone Individual, and the Beijing Municipal Party Committee Organization Department (Grant No. 2015000020124G024).

References

1. He, B., Yang, M., Guo, Z., et al.: Comet: batched stream processing for data intensive distributed computing. In: ACM Symposium on Cloud Computing, pp. 63–74. ACM (2010)
2. Ahmed, A., Ahmed, E.: A survey on mobile edge computing. In: Proceeding of the 10th IEEE International Conference on Intelligent Systems and Control, Coimbatore, India, 7–8 January 2016, pp. 1–8 (2016)
3. Lopez, P.G., Montresor, A., Epema, D., et al.: Edge-centric computing: vision and challenges. ACM SIGCOMM Comput. Commun. Rev. **45**(5), 37–42 (2015)
4. Huhns, M.N., Singh, M.P.: Service-oriented computing: key concepts and principles. IEEE Internet Comput. **9**(1), 75–81 (2005)
5. Han, Y., Liu, C., Su, S., et al.: A proactive service model facilitating stream data fusion and correlation. Int. J. Web Serv. Res. **14**(3), 1–16 (2017)
6. Cheng, B., Zhu, D., Zhao, S., et al.: Situation-aware IoT services coordination platform using event driven SOA paradigm. IEEE Trans. Netw. Serv. Manag. **13**(2), 349–361 (2016)
7. Ryden, M., Oh, K., Chandra, A., et al.: Nebula: distributed edge cloud for data intensive computing. In: IEEE International Conference on Cloud Engineering. IEEE, pp. 57–66 (2014)
8. Wang, X., Yang, L.T., Xie, X., et al.: A cloud-edge computing framework for cyber-physical-social services. IEEE Commun. Mag. **55**(11), 80–85 (2017)

9. Xiao, B., Rahmani, R., Li, Y., et al.: Edge-based interoperable service-driven information distribution for intelligent pervasive services. Pervasive Mob. Comput. **40**, 359–381 (2017)
10. Xu, X., Huang, S., Feagan, L., et al.: EAaaS: edge analytics as a service. In: IEEE International Conference on Web Services. IEEE, pp. 349–356 (2017)
11. Zhang, S., Liu, C., Han, Y., et al.: Seamless integration of cloud and edge with a service-based approach. In: IEEE International Conference on Web Services. IEEE (2018) (in press)
12. Plaxton, C.G.: Fast scheduling of weighted unit jobs with release times and deadlines. In: Aceto, L., et al. (eds.) ICALP 2008. LNCS, vol. 5125, pp. 222–233. Springer, Heidelberg (2008). https://doi.org/10.1007/978-3-540-70575-8_19
13. Azad, A., Buluc, A., Pothen, A.: A parallel tree grafting algorithm for maximum cardinality matching in bipartite graphs. In: Proceedings of Parallel and Distributed Processing Symposium, pp. 1075–1084 (2015)
14. Riesen, K., Bunke, H.: Approximate graph edit distance computation by means of bipartite graph matching. Image Vis. Comput. **27**(7), 950–959 (2009)
15. Varghese, B., Wang, N., Li, J., et al.: Edge-as-a-Service: Towards Distributed Cloud Architectures (2017)
16. Bucchiarone, A., Marconi, A., Pistore, M., et al.: Dynamic adaptation of fragment-based and context-aware business processes. In: IEEE International Conference on Web Services. IEEE, pp. 33–41 (2012)
17. Bucchiarone, A., Marconi, A., Pistore, M., et al.: Domain objects for continuous context-aware adaptation of service-based systems. IEEE International Conference on Web Services. IEEE, pp. 571–578 (2013)
18. Alférez, G.H., Pelechano, V., Mazo, R., et al.: Dynamic adaptation of service compositions with variability models. J. Syst. Softw. **91**(5), 24–47 (2014)

A Cost-Effective Time-Constrained Multi-workflow Scheduling Strategy in Fog Computing

Ruimiao Ding[1], Xuejun Li[1(✉)], Xiao Liu[2], and Jia Xu[1]

[1] School of Computer Science and Technology, Anhui University, Hefei, China
drm_ahu@qq.com, xjli@ahu.edu.cn, xujia_ahu@qq.com
[2] School of Information Technology, Deakin University, Geelong, Australia
xiao.liu@deakin.edu.au

Abstract. With the rapid development of Internet of Things and smart services, massive intelligent devices are accessing the cloud data centers, which can cause serious network congestion and high latency issues. Recently, fog computing becomes a popular computing paradigm which can provide computing resources close to the end devices and solve various problems of existing cloud-only based systems. However, due to QoS (Quality of Service) constraints such as time and cost, and also the complexity of various resource types such as end devices, fog nodes and cloud servers, task scheduling in fog computing is still an open issue. To address such a problem, this paper presents a cost-effective scheduling strategy for multi-workflow with time constraints. Firstly, we define the models for workflow execution time and resource cost in fog computing. Afterwards, a novel PSO (Particle Swarm Optimization) based multi-workflow scheduling strategy is proposed where a fitness function is used to evaluate the workflow execution cost under given deadlines. A heart rate monitoring App is employed as a motivating example and comprehensive experimental results show that our proposed strategy can significantly reduce the execution cost of multiple workflows under given deadlines compared with other strategies.

Keywords: Fog computing · Cost-Effectiveness ·
Particle Swarm Optimization · Workflow scheduling · Time constraint

1 Introduction

With the rapid development of Internet of Things (IoT) and smart services, massive intelligent devices are accessing the cloud data centers. For example, Cisco VNI report (2016–2021) predicts that the number of mobile devices per capita will reach to nearly 1.5 by 2021 and the global mobile data traffic will increase sevenfold between 2016 and 2021 [1]. Cisco Global Cloud Index (2016–2021) shows that 94% of all data center workloads will be processed by cloud computing data centers in 2021 [2]. The drastic increase in cloud data center traffic and end devices brings huge obstacles to satisfactory usage of cloud services such as heavy communication, unpredictable delays, and poor support to the mobility of end users [3, 4]. In order to alleviate these obstacles, a new computing paradigm called "fog computing" was proposed by Cisco [5]. Fog service is

© Springer Nature Switzerland AG 2019
X. Liu et al. (Eds.): ICSOC 2018 Workshops, LNCS 11434, pp. 194–207, 2019.
https://doi.org/10.1007/978-3-030-17642-6_17

similar to a lightweight cloud service and including multiple computing resources [3, 6, 7]. Fog computing can be viewed as an extension to cloud computing rather than its replacement. It aims to reduce the network congestion, reduce delays and better support the mobility of end devices [8–11].

Due to multiple types of computing resources such as end devices, fog nodes and cloud servers in the fog computing environment, how to effectively manage these resources is particularly important. Workflow system has been widely used to manage various kinds of resources and run workflow tasks effectively in a distributed computing environment [12]. Therefore, we can use workflow system to execute workflow tasks with multiple types of resources in a fog computing environment. Fog computing can provide localized computing resources so as to execute most tasks on the fog nodes instead of the cloud servers [13]. While fog nodes can achieve real-time interaction and low latency at the edge of the network, cloud servers are centralized with much more computation power and storage space [4]. Some researchers have studied the strategy of collaborative scheduling between fog and cloud computing resources, the target of these strategies is to balance the workload between fog nodes and cloud servers, as well as to optimize the energy consumption and task completion time [4, 14–17]. According to these existing studies, the way of using computing resources in the fog environment can be generally divided into three types, which are using Single layer of Cloud resources (SC), using Single layer of Fog resources (SF), and using Multi-layer Fog and Cloud resources (MFC). Although these studies have taken into account multi-layer resources in fog computing, most of their strategies are not good at processing massive parallel workflow tasks, and also did not make full use of fog nodes to reduce the time delay and resource cost.

In this paper, we aim to address the scheduling problem for multi-workflow with the goal of reducing costs under given deadlines in the fog environment. Specifically, a Cost-effective Time-constrained multi-workflow scheduling Strategy using multi-layer resources in Fog computing (denoted as CTSF) is proposed where Particle Swarm Optimization (PSO) is used to generate initial solutions for multi-layer resources [12, 18]. However, when multiple tasks are allocated to the same resource at the same time, PSO cannot solve resource conflicts among tasks. In such a situation, the Min-Min algorithm is employed further to handle the conflicts [19].

The rest of the paper is organized as follows. Section 2 demonstrates a motivating example for problem analysis. Section 3 defines all the models used in this paper. Section 4 proposes the CTSF strategy. Section 5 presents the experimental results. Finally, Sect. 6 concludes the paper and points out some future work.

2 Motivating Example

This section first describes a motivating scenario, and then compares the execution time, cost, computation time and communication time for a multi-workflow example with three different ways of using computing resources in the fog environment.

2.1   Example Scenario

The development of IoT and fog computing has great impact on healthcare systems in hospitals and smart home [20, 21]. Most healthcare systems are developed to collect and analyze the medical data of people in real time, so that medical staff such as the doctor can be promptly informed of the occurrence of some sudden emergencies [21]. Figure 1 describes the scenario of heart rate monitoring in a healthcare system which illustrates the use of both fog nodes and cloud servers in task scheduling.

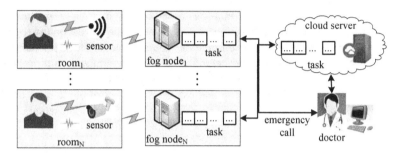

Fig. 1. A scenario of heart rate monitoring.

Figure 1 shows the healthcare system in a typical three-tier fog computing structure which includes the end device layer, the fog node layer, and the cloud sever layer. The role of the end device layer is to collect data in real time. Each room can be equipped with a variety of sensors and IoT devices to collect the real-time physical state data of the patient. For example, the fog nodes can process the video images from the sensors to get the heart rate of the patients in a non-contact fashion, then transmit the heart rate data to the cloud server for storage, and send out emergency call to the doctor if abnormal heart rate is detected. After receiving the emergency call, the doctor can inquire the patient's heart rate data from both fog nodes and cloud server, and analyzes the data for treatment. In such a fog based healthcare system, a large number of fog nodes are processing the data received from sensors for different patients so as to effectively reduce the data communication of the network and the computation workload of the cloud server. It can also timely respond to the patient's emergency situation even when the connection to the cloud sever is broken.

2.2   Three Ways of Using Fog Computing Resources

Based on the heart rate monitoring scenario described above, we now present a series of tasks to demonstrate the three ways of using fog computing resources. Using the Directed Acyclic Graph (DAG), we can visually illustrate the successive dependencies of all tasks in the workflow [22]. An example is given to show two sequential work-flows. Each workflow has three tasks, numbered 1-3 and 4-6 respectively. The workload and data size for each task are shown in Table 1. Task 1 and task 4 start simultaneously. The completion time of task 3 and task 6 determines the completion time of the two workflows. Here, we assume that fog nodes and cloud servers operate at the speeds of 1.0 GHz and 1.6 GHz respectively [23, 24], and the price of fog nodes and cloud servers are 0.12$ per hour and 0.96$ per hour respectively. The data transmission bandwidth of local area network (LAN) and wide area network (WAN) are 100 Mbps and 40 Mbps respectively [25]. The workflow deadline is specified as 15 s. The solutions corresponding to the three ways of using fog computing resources, viz. SC, SF and MFC, are shown in Fig. 2.

Table 1. Task's workload and data size.

Task	1	2	3	4	5	6
Workload (Megacycles)	3000	2800	2500	2500	3000	2000
Input (MB)	20	10	20	20	15	10
Output (MB)	15	5	15	10	10	15

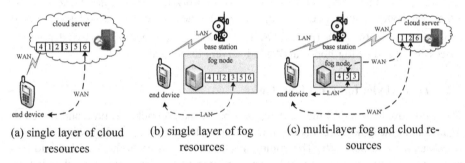

(a) single layer of cloud resources

(b) single layer of fog resources

(c) multi-layer fog and cloud resources

Fig. 2. Three ways of using fog computing resources.

Table 2. The results of three different ways of using fog computing resources.

Three ways of using resources	SC	SF	MFC
Cost($)	0.0069	$0.62 * 10^{-3}$	0.0031
Execution time(s)	25.875	18.6	13.35

As shown in Table 2, the cost of the solution generated by SC is the highest, while the cost of the solution generated by SF is the lowest but its execution time is the longest and it cannot meet the deadline. Clearly, compared with SC and SF, MFC can generate the best solution which achieves the minimum cost under the given deadline.

3 Models for Workflows in Fog Computing

3.1 Workflow and Resource Models

A workflow is represented by a DAG and it donates as $G = (V, E)$. Where $V = (v_1, v_2, \ldots, v_{N_t})$ represents the set of the ordered executable tasks, and each edge $e_{ij} = (v_i, v_j) \in E(i, j = 1, 2, \ldots N_t \text{ and } i \neq j)$ represents the constrained relationship between task v_i and v_j that the start execution time of task v_j must be later than the finish time of task v_i. Each task $v_i \in V$ has a computation workload w_i, input data and output data. The input and output data size of task v_i are denoted as In_i and Out_i. The set of all direct predecessors and successors of task v_i are denoted as $pred(v_i)$ and $succ(v_i)$. A typical workflow must have an entrance task without any predecessors and an exit task without any successors, denoted as v_{entry} and v_{exit}.

The resource model can be expressed as a collection $R = (R_1, R_2, \ldots, R_K)$ which represent fog nodes and cloud servers. Any resource in set R can communicates with each other through LAN and WAN [4] and all workflow tasks can be executed by either fog nodes or cloud servers. R_f and R_c denote the set of fog nodes and cloud servers respectively. Each resource R_k has a processing speed, r_k^f and r_k^c denote the processing speed of fog nodes and cloud servers respectively.

3.2 Time Model for Workflow Tasks

The workflow execution time contains two parts: the computation time and the communication time. The computation time of task v_i denoted as $T_i^{comp}(R_k)$, where the task v_i executed on resource R_k. The communication time can be further divided into two parts: the communication time between resources and end devices, denoted as $T_i^{comm}(R_k, IO_i)$, and the communication time between task v_i and v_j, denoted as $T_{ij}^{comm}(R_k, R_l)$, where task v_i and v_j are executed on resource R_k and R_l respectively. The data transmission direction between resources and end devices denoted as IO_i, which is a 0-1 variable. Specifically, when $IO_i = 1$, it represents the end devices will transfers the input data of the task v_i to the resource R_k. When $IO_i = 0$, it represents the resource R_k will transfers the output data of the task v_i to the end devices.

Formula (1) represents the computation time of task v_i executed on resource R_k.

$$T_i^{comp}(R_k) = \begin{cases} w_i/r_k^f, R_k \in R_f \\ w_i/r_k^c, R_k \in R_c \end{cases} \tag{1}$$

where w_i represents the workload of the task v_i, r_k^f and r_k^c denote the processing speed of fog nodes and cloud servers respectively.

The communication time between resources and end devices can be calculated by Formula (2). Formula (3) represents the communication time between task v_i and v_j.

$$T_i^{comm}(R_k, IO_i) = \begin{cases} In_i/B_L, R_k \in R_f, IO_i = 1 \\ In_i/B_W, R_k \in R_c, IO_i = 1 \\ Out_i/B_L, R_k \in R_f, IO_i = 0 \\ Out_i/B_W, R_k \in R_c, IO_i = 0 \end{cases} \tag{2}$$

$$T_{ij}^{comm}(R_k, R_l) = \begin{cases} Out_i/B_L, R_k \neq R_l, R_k, R_l \in R_f \\ Out_i/B_W, R_k \neq R_l, R_k, R_l \in R_c \\ Out_i/B_W, R_k \in R_f, R_l \in R_c \\ Out_i/B_W, R_k \in R_c, R_l \in R_f \\ 0, R_k = R_l \end{cases} \tag{3}$$

where B_L and B_W represent the bandwidth of LAN and WAN respectively. In_i and Out_i represent input and output data size of task v_i respectively. If the task v_i and v_j are allocated on the same resource, the communication time is 0.

$EST(v_i)$ and $FT(v_i)$ denote the earliest start time and the finish time of task v_i respectively. The total execution time of workflow W is donated as $T(W)$, which can be calculated by Formula (4–6), and the total execution time of multi-workflow WF_M can be calculated by Formula (7).

$$T(W) = FT(v_{exit}) + T_{exit}^{comm}(R_{exit}) \tag{4}$$

$$FT(v_i) = EST(v_i) + T_i^{comp}(R_k) \tag{5}$$

$$EST(v_i) = max_{v_j \in pred(v_i)} \left\{ T_{idle}(R_k), FT(v_j) + T_{ji}^{comm}(R_l, R_k), T_i^{comm}(R_k, IO_i) \right\} \tag{6}$$

$$T(WF_M) = max_{W \in N_w} \{T(W)\} \tag{7}$$

The execution time of the workflow is the arrival time of the output data of task v_{exit} from the resources to the end devices. The execution time of a multi-workflow is the last finish workflow execution time in all workflows. The earliest start time for a task v_i is the maximum time of $T_{idle}(R_k)$, $FT(v_j) + T_{ji}^{comm}(R_l, R_k)$ and $T_i^{comm}(R_k, IO_i)$. $T_{idle}(R_k)$ is the idle time of resource R_k, $FT(v_j) + T_{ji}^{comm}(R_l, R_k)$ is the output data of precursor task arrival time. v_{exit} is an exit task of workflow W and it executed on resource R_{exit}. $pred(v_i)$ is the set of all direct predecessors to task v_i. N_w is the number of workflows.

3.3   Cost Model for Workflow Tasks

The execution cost of multi-workflow can be calculated by Formula (8).

$$C(WF_M) = \sum_{k=1}^{K} c_{R_k}^d * t_{R_k} * x_{R_k}^d + \sum_{k=1}^{K} (p_{R_k}^r + c_{R_k}^r * t_{R_k}) * x_{R_k}^r \tag{8}$$

Formula (8) contains two parts, the first part is the execution cost of all on-demand resources and the second part is the cost of all reserved resources. This cost calculation considers the two most common ways to purchase resources in real time: on demand and reserved. Where $c_{R_k}^d$ and $c_{R_k}^r$ are the cost of on demand and reserved resource R_k respectively, t_{R_k} is execution time of the resource R_k, $x_{R_k}^d$ and $x_{R_k}^r$ represent that resource R_k is purchased as on demand or reserved resources respectively, $p_{R_k}^r$ represents the deposit required by resource R_k when it is a reserved resource. K represents the total number of resources.

4   CTSF Strategy for Multi-workflow Scheduling

4.1   Fitness Value

The fitness value is used to evaluate the quality of solutions generated by PSO based scheduling algorithm [12]. We design the fitness function to evaluate the cost under given deadlines [23, 24]. The smaller the fitness value, the lower the execution cost of the solution. The fitness value can be calculated by Formula (9).

$$fitness = (f_1 * C(WF_M)) + \left(f_2 * 10 * C(WF_M) * \frac{T(WF_M)}{deadline} \right) \qquad (9)$$

The fitness function consists of two parts: the resource execution cost under given deadlines $(f_1 = 1, f_2 = 0)$ and the resource execution cost beyond deadlines $(f_1 = 0, f_2 = 1)$. $C(WF_M)$ and $T(WF_M)$ represent the execution cost and time of the solution respectively, and *deadline* is the user specified time constraint for the workflow.

4.2   The CTSF Strategy

In the CTSF strategy, PSO is used to generate solutions and Min-Min algorithm is used to resolve the conflict on the resources. Algorithm 1 shows the process for resource conflict resolution based on the Min-Min algorithm. In Algorithm 1, when there is conflict on the resource (Line 1), we count the number of conflicting tasks and calculate the expected finish time of these tasks (Lines 2–5). The next step is to select the task with the earliest expected finish time from these tasks and allocate resources to it, and update the number of conflicting tasks (Lines 6–7). Loop Line 1 to Line 7 until there is no conflict task.

Algorithm 2 shows the CTSF strategy which mainly includes three parts: initialization, iterative evolution, and return the best task scheduling plan as the final solution. Initialization is to generate particle swarm randomly and set other parameters (Lines 1–4). Iterative evolution is divided into outer and inner loops (Lines 5–16). The outer loop controls iterations (Lines 5–16) and the inner loop controls the number of particles in the swarm (Lines 6–14). In the inner loop, we update the velocity and position of the particles [18] (Line 7). When the resource conflict problem is encountered, Algorithm 1 described above is adopted to solve the problem (Line 8). At last, we update the local optimal scheduling plan according to the fitness value (Lines 9–13). After the inner loop is finished, we select the solution with minimum fitness value as the global optimal solution (Line 15). When the iteration terminates, the algorithm return the best task scheduling plan (Line 17). Assuming the number of scheduling schemes is N, the number of iterations is D and the number of tasks is T, the computational complexity of the strategy is $O(NDT)$ [24].

Algorithm 1. Resource conflict resolution based on Min-Min algorithm

Input: particle p^k

Output: execution order of tasks in the particle p^k

1: while conflicts existed on the resource
2:     for $i = 1$ to N_{task} do /* N_{task} represents the number of conflict tasks
3:        compute the earliest start time of task i by Formula (6)
4:        compute the finish time of task i by Formula (5)
5:     end for
6:     choose the task with the earliest finish time and allocate resources to it
7:     update the number of resource conflict tasks
8: end while
9: return execution order of tasks in the particle p^k

Algorithm 2. Cost-effective PSO based time-constrained multi-workflow scheduling

Input: maximum iterations: $Iter$, population size: $Scale$, deadline: $deadline$, N_w workflows and each workflow has N_t tasks, resources: $R = (R_1, R_2, ..., R_K)$

Output: optimal solution $gbest$

1: for $k = 1$ to $Scale$ do
2:     generate the initial solution p^k and particle velocity v^k randomly
3:     set the initial solution p^k as the initial local optimal $pbest_k$
4: end for
5: for $t = 1$ to $Iter$ do
6:     for $k = 1$ to $Scale$ do
7   update particle movement velocity and solution
8:        execution solution and if a resource conflict problem is encountered, a resource conflict resolution described in Algorithm 1 is adopted to solve the problem.
9:        compute the execution time and cost of p^k and $pbest_k$ by Formula(4-8)
10:       compute the fitness value of p^k and $pbest_k$ by Formula(9)
11:       if($fitness(p^k) < fitness(pbest_k)$) then
12:          set the solution p^k as the local optimal $pbest_k$
13:       end if
14:    end for
15: choose the solution with least fitness value as the global optimal solution $gbest$
16: end for
17: return $gbest$

5   Evaluation

In this section, we evaluate the proposed multi-workflow scheduling strategy CTSF from two aspects. Firstly, we compare CTSF with other two strategies, viz. FP which only uses single layer of fog nodes and CP which only uses single layer of cloud servers. For the fairness of comparison, FP and CP both use PSO for optimization and Min-Min for conflict resolution, which is the same as in CTSF. These three strategies are compared in terms of fitness value, cost, execution time, computation time and communication time. Secondly, different resource conflict resolution algorithms in multi-layer fog and cloud resources are compared on the fitness value, cost and execution time. Besides our CTSF, other two strategies include Max-P and FCFS-P. The Max-P and FCFS-P strategy represent the use of PSO for task scheduling, and uses the Max-Min and FCFS (First Come First Served) respectively to resolve conflicts.

5.1   Experimental Settings

The simulation environment runs on a desktop computer with the following configurations: Intel core i5, dual-core 3.2 GHz CPU, 8 GB RAM, and Microsoft Windows 7 OS. The simulations are developed in Java with JDK 1.7.

The experiment contains several sequential workflows and each workflow has 8 tasks. The pricing for fog and cloud resources is show in Table 3 which is consistent to the resource pricing of Amazon's EC2 (https://aws.amazon.com/cn/ec2/pricing/). In the simulation, we consider the scenario with 3 fog nodes and 4 cloud servers in the fog environment. The CPU processing speed of fog nodes is 1.0 GHz and the cloud servers are 1.3 or 1.6 GHz. The workload of a task is generated between 30000 and 3000000 Megacycles randomly [26]. The deadlines is selected from 20% to 100% more than the average execution time of multi-workflow on the resource with 1.4 GHz CPU [27]. The input data and output data of a task is generated between 500 and 2000 MB randomly. The network bandwidth of LAN and WAN are 100 Mbps and 10 Mbps respectively [4, 6].

Table 3. The resource pricing.

Speed (GHz)	Reserved		On-demand
	Per-term ($)	Per-hour ($)	Per-hour ($)
1.0	97.5	0.07	0.12
1.3	390	0.28	0.48
1.6	780	0.56	0.96

5.2   Comparison of Scheduling Strategies with Different Resource Layers

Here, we compare the three scheduling strategies. The fitness value of three strategies is shown in Fig. 3. When the number of workflows changes from 10 to 60, the fitness value of the CTSF strategy is the lowest. With the continuously increase of the number of workflows, the gap of fitness value between CTSF and the other two scheduling strategies are growing as well. For example, when the workflow number is 10, the fitness value of CTSF is 50.6% lower than FP. When the workflow number becomes 60, the fitness value of CTSF is 81.9% lower than FP. Therefore, it shows that our CTSF strategy which uses multi-layer fog and cloud resources in the fog environment is suitable for large-scale task scheduling.

The results on the cost and execution time are shown in Figs. 4 and 5. The cost of FP in Fig. 4 is the lowest. The reason is that the price of fog nodes is lower than cloud servers. However, due to the longer execution time as shown in Fig. 5, the solution generated by FP cannot meet given deadlines. Therefore, it shows that CTSF can achieve the lowest cost while given deadline is satisfied.

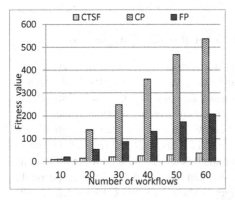

Fig. 3. Comparison of the fitness value.

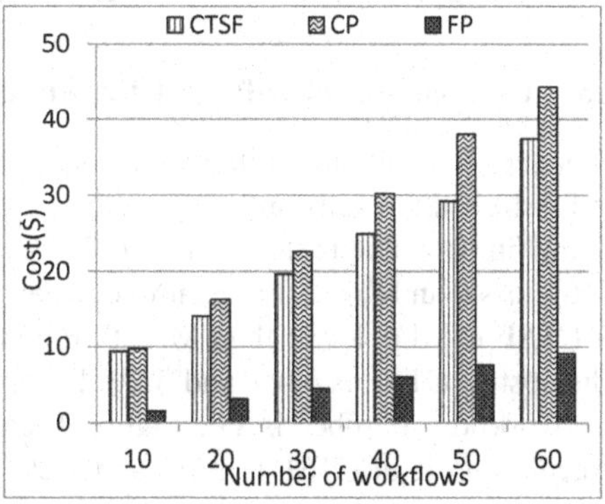

Fig. 4. Comparison of the execution cost.

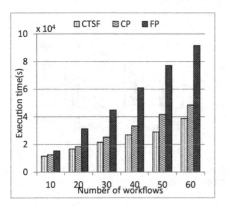

Fig. 5. Comparison of the execution time.

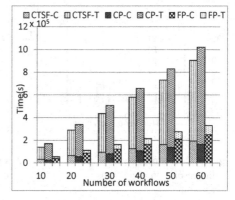

Fig. 6. Comparison of the computation time and communication time.

Figure 6 shows the results on the computation time and communication time The computation time of the CTSF, CP, and FP solution are expressed as CTSF-C, CP-C, and FP-C respectively. Similarly, the communication time (namely data transfer time) of three strategies are expressed as CTSF-T, CP-T, and FP-T respectively. Compared with CP, CTSF can reduce its task communication time. And compared with FP, CTSF can reduce its task computation time.

It can be seen that tasks with large workload but small data size are better to be executed on cloud servers as it can save a lot of communication time. In contrast, tasks with small workload but large data size are better to be executed on fog nodes as it can save computation time. We can also find out that the execution time of the workflow is not equal to the sum of computation time and communication time, because there are task waiting times due to task dependencies and task queuing.

5.3   Comparison of Different Resource Conflict Resolution Algorithms

This section compares different resource conflict resolution algorithms. Figures 7, 8 and 9 show the results on fitness value, cost and execution time respectively. The result on the fitness value is shown in Fig. 7. The fitness value of CTSF is close to Max-P, but it still less than Max-P. For example, when the workflow number is 60, the fitness value of CTSF is 8.1% lower than Max-P. Figure 8 shows the cost between three strategies. The cost of CTSF is 3.4% and 3.2% lower than Max-P and FCFS-P respectively when the workflow number is 60. Figure 9 shows the result on the execution time. The execution time of CTSF is 1.1% and 2.2% lower than Max-P and FCFS-P respectively when the workflow number is 60. Three Figures show that our CTSF strategy outperforms other two strategies on fitness value, cost and execution time.

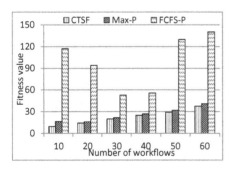
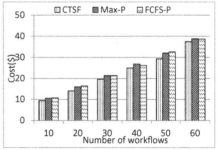

Fig. 7. The fitness value under different conflict resolution algorithms.

Fig. 8. The cost under different conflict resolution algorithms.

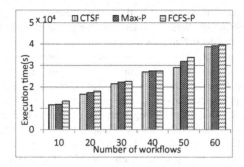

Fig. 9. The execution time under different conflict resolution algorithms.

To summarize, our CTSF strategy can achieve the best overall performance in comparison with all other strategies. CTSF is fit for multi-workflow scheduling with time constraints in the fog computing environment. The main reason is that the CTSF strategy can find the best scheduling plan with lowest cost under given deadlines through the heuristic of the PSO algorithm, meanwhile the Min-Min algorithm can effectively reduce the execution time of conflicting tasks.

6 Conclusion

Workflow scheduling in fog computing is an important yet open issue. In order to schedule a large number of parallel workflows with the goal of reducing costs under given deadlines in fog computing, this paper has proposed a novel scheduling strategy by using multi-layer fog and cloud resources. Experimental results have shown that the proposed strategy can achieve the best overall performance in cost and time compared with other strategies.

In the future, we will explore other popular multi-workflow scheduling optimization algorithms such as ant colony optimization and genetic algorithm. In the meantime, we will consider the impact of dynamic bandwidth on the scheduling plan.

Acknowledgments. This work was supported by the National Natural Science Foundation of China under No. 61672034, 61300042, and the Natural Science Foundation of Anhui Province of China under No. 1708085MF160, and the Key Natural Science Foundation of Education Bureau of Anhui Province Project No. KJ2018A0010.

References

1. Cisco visual networking index: Global mobile data traffic forecast update, 2016–2021 white paper. https://www.cisco.com/c/en/us/solutions/collateral/service-provider/visual-networking-index-vni/mobile-white-paper-c11-520862.html. Accessed 6 Jun 2018

2. Cisco global cloud index: Forecast and methodology, 2016–2021 white paper. https://www.cisco.com/c/en/us/solutions/collateral/service-provider/global-cloud-index-gci/white-paper-c11-738085.html. Accessed 6 Jun 2018

3. Li, C., Xue, Y., Wang, J., et al.: Edge-oriented computing paradigms: A survey on architecture design and system management. ACM Comput. Surv. **51**(2), 1–34 (2018)

4. Deng, R., Lu, R., Lai, C., et al.: Optimal workload allocation in fog-cloud computing toward balanced delay and power consumption. IEEE Internet Things J. **3**(6), 1171–1181 (2017)

5. Bonomi, F., Milito, R., Zhu, J., et al.: Fog computing and its role in the Internet of Things. In: 1st MCC Workshop on Mobile Cloud Computing, pp. 13–16. ACM, Helsinki (2012)

6. Mahmud, R., Kotagiri, R., Buyya, R.: Fog computing: a taxonomy, survey and future directions. In: Di Martino, B., Li, K.-C., Yang, Laurence T., Esposito, A. (eds.) Internet of Everything. IT, pp. 103–130. Springer, Singapore (2018). https://doi.org/10.1007/978-981-10-5861-5_5

7. Roman, R., Lopez, J., Mambo, M.: Mobile edge computing, fog et al.: a survey and analysis of security threats and challenges. Future Gener. Comput. Syst. **78**(2), 680–698 (2018)

8. Ni, L., Zhang, J., Jiang, C., et al.: Resource allocation strategy in fog computing based on priced timed petri nets. IEEE Internet Things J. **4**(5), 1216–1228 (2017)

9. Alonso-Monsalve, S., García-Carballeira, F., Calderón, A.: Fog computing through public-resource computing and storage. In: 2nd International Conference on Fog and Mobile Edge Computing, pp. 81–87. IEEE, Valencia (2017)

10. Bao, W., Yuan, D., Yang, Z., et al.: Follow me fog: toward seamless handover timing schemes in a fog computing environment. IEEE Commun. Mag. **55**(11), 72–78 (2017)

11. Yin, H., Zhang, X., Liu, H., et al.: Edge provisioning with flexible server placement. IEEE Trans. Parallel Distrib. Syst. **28**(4), 1031–1045 (2017)

12. Masdari, M., Valikardan, S., Shahi, Z., et al.: Towards workflow scheduling in cloud computing: a comprehensive analysis. J. Netw. Comput. Appl. **66**(5), 64–82 (2016)

13. Bittencourt, L.F., Diazmontes, J., Buyya, R., et al.: Mobility-aware application scheduling in fog computing. IEEE Cloud Comput. **4**(2), 26–35 (2017)

14. Hu, P., Ning, H., Qiu, T., et al.: Fog computing based face identification and resolution scheme in Internet of Things. IEEE Trans. Ind. Inf. **13**(4), 1910–1920 (2017)

15. Zeng, D., Gu, L., Guo, S., et al.: Joint optimization of task scheduling and image placement in fog computing supported software-defined embedded system. IEEE Trans. Comput. **65**(12), 3702–3712 (2016)

16. You, C., Huang, K., Chae, H., et al.: Energy-efficient resource allocation for mobile-edge computation offloading. IEEE Trans. Wirel. Commun. **16**(3), 1397–1411 (2016)

17. Xu, J., Palanisamy, B., Ludwig, H., et al.: Zenith: Utility-aware resource allocation for edge computing. In: IEEE International Conference on Edge Computing, pp. 47–54 (2017)

18. Pandey, S., Wu, L., Guru, S. M., et al.: A particle swarm optimization-based heuristic for scheduling workflow applications in cloud computing environments. In: 24th International Conference on Advanced Information Networking and Applications, pp. 400–407. IEEE, Biopolis (2010)

19. Kokilavani, T., George Amalarethinam, D.I.: Load balanced Min-Min algorithm for static metatask scheduling in grid computing. Int. J. Comput. Appl. **20**(2), 42–48 (2011)

20. Rahmani, A.M., Gia, T.N., Negash, B., et al.: Exploiting smart e-Health gateways at the edge of healthcare Internet-of-Things: A fog computing approach. Future Gener. Comput. Syst. **78**(2), 641–658 (2018)

21. Farahani, B., Firouzi, F., Chang, V., et al.: Towards fog-driven IoT eHealth: promises and challenges of IoT in medicine and healthcare. Future Gener. Comput. Syst. **78**(2), 659–676 (2018)

22. Ramírez-Gallego, S., Fernández, A., García, S., et al.: Big data: Tutorial and guidelines on information and process fusion for analytics algorithms with mapreduce. Inf. Fusion **42**(6), 51–61 (2018)
23. Netjinda, N., Sirinaovakul, B., Achalakul, T.: Cost optimal scheduling in Iaas for dependent workload with particle swarm optimization. J. Supercomput. **68**(3), 1579–1603 (2014)
24. Li, X., Jia, X., Zhu, E., et al.: A novel computation method for adaptive inertia weight of task scheduling algorithm. J. Comput. Res. Dev. **53**(9), 1990–1999 (2016)
25. Vaquero, L.M., Rodero-Merino, L.: Finding your way in the fog: towards a comprehensive definition of fog computing. ACM SIGCOMM Comput. Commun. Rev. **44**(5), 27–32 (2014)
26. Chen, X., Jiao, L., Li, W., et al.: Efficient multi-user computation offloading for mobile-edge cloud computing. IEEE/ACM Trans. Netw. **24**(5), 2795–2808 (2015)
27. Sarangi, S. R., Goel, S., and Singh, B.: Energy efficient scheduling in IoT networks. In: Proceedings of Symposium on Applied Computing, pp. 1–8. ACM, New York (2018)

A Brief Survey on IoT Privacy: Taxonomy, Issues and Future Trends

Kinza Sarwar[(⊠)], Sira Yongchareon, and Jian Yu

School of Engineering, Computer and Mathematical Sciences,
Auckland University of Technology, Auckland, New Zealand
{kinza.sarwar,sira.yongchareon,jian.yu}@aut.ac.nz

Abstract. Internet of Things (IoT) is a paradigm that has the capability to revolutionize on everyday life, in sectors of ranging from our homes, health, transport, industry, entertainment to interaction with government. The comfort and benefits that IoT is providing are undeniable, however, these may come with a huge risk of individual identity and data privacy. Several researches have been conducted to find a better way to eliminate privacy risks and minimize the effect on users' privacy requirements. In this context, the proposed study consists of four segments, first we analyse the privacy problems evolving with the advancement in IoT paradigm. In the second segment, we present methodology review with analysis and classification of privacy solutions. Then we provide an in-depth analysis of preserving privacy during sensors data transmission. In the last segment, we depict the future trend for end-to-end privacy in IoT.

Keywords: Internet of Things (IoT) · Privacy · Security

1 Introduction

The wide deployment of the Internet of Things (IoT) has resulted into enabling the interconnectivity of smart things worldwide, which has significantly improved every day's life [1], including pervasive health care (smart hospitals), assisted living, household activities, home security, smart supply chain, infrastructure support, smart meters for balancing bills, air quality management and so on [2]. The rapid growth in devices connectivity to internet, which are equipped with processing power and sensors are predicted to approximately reach 34 billion by year 2020 [2]. However, despite the advancement in IoT and rapid growth in IoT devices, several concerns undermine full adoption of IoT to provide convenient and flexible services, one of the main concerns is individual identity and personal data privacy in IoT environment. The data owner worries about the potential use of its sensitive or private data, and sometimes data owner does not wish to share private data without retaining level of control [2]. Affiliated with privacy concerns are also smart devices' limited memory storage, energy budget for power battery and constrained processing resources [3], which hinders the public and private key cryptography use to mitigate the privacy threats in IoT environment.

To highlight privacy concerns with IoT devices limitation, different surveys have been provided in the recent years. Authors have presented literature reviews to

© Springer Nature Switzerland AG 2019
X. Liu et al. (Eds.): ICSOC 2018 Workshops, LNCS 11434, pp. 208–219, 2019.
https://doi.org/10.1007/978-3-030-17642-6_18

highlight the privacy and security challenges in IoT and provided guidelines of existing security threats and attacks to help readers understand the challenges, concerns and issues for future directions. Literature review presented in [3] on Internet of Things security, provided classification of IoT into three layers and discussed the security concerns and attacks, and possible solutions in each layer. However, the survey [3] has only analyzed the generic security concerns with possible solution in IoT heterogeneous environment, whereas, does not explicitly analyzed privacy requirements. Other [4] systematic review covers the privacy facets and discuss the possible challenges, but the suggested solutions have been only considered for preserving content privacy during transmission, processing and storing. There has been no discussion on other different privacy requirements (for example, identity, temporal, location privacy) and how to fulfil these requirements.

Furthermore, Lopez *et al.* [5] analyzed the existing privacy threats in sensing technologies, identified the privacy problems with possible countermeasures. In addition, entailed the new privacy challenges with the evolution of technology. Although the study [5] covered the aspects of privacy in IoT, but the privacy technique trends used in achieving privacy aspects are not discussed explicitly. The advancement of IoT not only depends on addressing the privacy requirements based on security concepts with challenges, countermeasures and concerns, but with analyzing the privacy problems' solutions evolution, and how these solutions are improving with what impact on IoT technology?

Therefore, we intend to streamline the privacy trends with the impact on IoT technology using systematic literature review, that help readers to learn and understand possible privacy needs with unforeseen threats and vulnerabilities attached. The main contributions of this survey are as follow:

- We identify the privacy requirements with IoT devices limitations and evaluate the existing privacy schemes
- We classify and analyze the privacy preserving solutions adopted in IoT.
- Finally, we enumerate open research issues with future direction.

The remainder of this paper is organized as follows. Section 2 presents an overview of IoT, Privacy requirements in IoT. Section 3 provides analysis and classification of privacy-based schemes, whereas Sect. 4 discuss in-depth the privacy preservation during data transmission. Section 5 provides the open issues with future trends. Finally, concluding the study.

2   Privacy Requirements for IoT

Users are surrendering their data privacy, bit by bit; in IoT environment, without realizing/awareness of what content is being collected and used? Due to which the increasingly invisible, dense, and pervasive collection, processing, and dissemination of data during people's private lives give rise to serious privacy concerns. Therefore, to understand privacy requirement in detail, privacy has been divided into two main categories, context and content- oriented privacy as illustrated in Fig. 1.

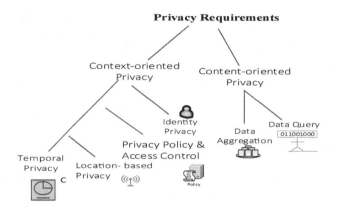

Fig. 1. Privacy requirements

2.1 Context Oriented Privacy

Context privacy focuses on protecting location and timing referring to contextual information. During the data content transmission, the focus is on protecting data using encryption techniques [5]. However, ignoring the fact that the features of the communications, including the size and number of messages being transmitted, the time and rate at which messages are being sent, the frequency spectrum used by the nodes, the source and destination of transmissions, from which attacker can manipulate the data being used [5]. Thus, hiding these features is challenging depending on the limited IoT hardware platform. Next, we analyze four context-oriented privacy problems in detail.

1. *Identity Privacy:* It is challenging to manage the identity of users in such heterogeneous IoT environments. The users' want their identity to remain anonymous during transmission. In IoT, pseudonymity can provide user anonymity, a persistent identifier to ensure that a service can be offered from initiation to completion without revealing the identity and location [6]. Whereas the periodically updated pseudonyms and certificates lead to intolerable computational cost for resource-constrained IoT nodes. In addition, it cannot resist the physically dynamic tracing attack for location identification.

2. *Privacy Policy and Access Control:* The privacy cannot be fully achieved without identifying and specifying the policies and procedures, which help to understand the requirements for the appropriate use and disclosure of protected information, user's rights, and breach notification. Policies may include the Individual's access to protected data, amendment of data, requests for restrictions on use and disclosure of data [3]. Setting up the policies and procedure in such a varying IoT devices environment is difficult while considering limited utilization of memory cost.

3. *Location- based Privacy:* In IoT, location- based privacy seems critical to be achieved, since the frequently exposed location would expose the living habitual of the IoT user. For example, a patient living in smart home suffering from dementia, would never allow intervening his/her living habits privacy to be monitored and

outsourced to doctors, cloud and centrally monitoring systems controlled at different ends. In IoT, the widely adopted technique used to hide the location is through pseudonyms [6]. However, it cannot resist tracing attack.

4. *Temporal Privacy:* The occurrence of an event is always associated with the time at which the event takes place and without this information event data is mostly meaningless. An attacker can launch DDOS attack by monitoring the traffic usage at which the events take places [5]. However temporal privacy has gained less attention in IoT environment, where more focus is on preserving content privacy.

2.2   Content-Oriented Privacy

Content Privacy focuses on protecting the privacy of data content. There are two types of adversaries which may compromise data-oriented privacy. One is an external adversary which eavesdrops the data communication between sensor nodes [5]. The second type is an internal adversary, which is also participating node but has been captured and manipulated by malicious entities to compromise private information [5]. The data collected and transmitted by the network may contain private information about individuals, businesses and valuable assets. As such, protecting these data from eavesdroppers and attackers enables content-oriented privacy. The two situations where content-oriented privacy is not sufficiently covered with the basic authentication and encryption mechanisms are during data-aggregation and when users query the network for data.

1. *Data Aggregation:* Data-aggregation is the process of combining information from different data sources as messages flow towards the base station with performing data-aggregation operators are the sum, average, maximum, and minimum [13]. Data aggregation significantly reduce the communication and energy overhead of sensor nodes and at the same time allow the base station to reduce the computational burden due to the processing of many messages. Consequently, data-aggregation is a very important process for the durability and efficiency of sensor networks [13].

2. *Data Query:* In data driven query, user queries the network or nodes for satisfying sets of conditions to ensure that data is intact and confidential. Users are afraid that their query is kept private or not? Attaining data query privacy is becoming an essential task in content-oriented privacy. Since the overhead grows exponentially with the wide spread adoption of IoT sensor devices in Internet of Things, the aim to provide perfect data query privacy is becoming more difficult [5].

3   Analysis and Classification of Privacy Based Schemes

This section provides the analysis of privacy-based schemes in IoT applications adapted to provide privacy by considering the privacy requirements, as highlighted in Sect. 2. Also classifies the privacy schemes based on the requirements. Further, timeline in Sect. 3.1 presents the scope of privacy advancement in IoT domain with the passage of time.

3.1   Timeline

From year 2005, there have been surveys highlighting the importance of privacy in IoT domain, however the full use of privacy methods has not been deployed by researchers till 2010. Figure 2, list down the methods been adopted per year for achieving privacy. In years 2010–2012 an infant stage introduction to privacy policies and legal obligation for IoT widespread adoption has been conducted. Whereas 2013 was a year for privacy with enhancements in policies considering attribute signer and identity privacy, thus opening ways for diversifying privacy in IoT. Furthermore, in year 2014, almost 3% techniques were used to preserve identity using masking and concatenation. In year 2015, advance level of elliptic curves, semantic policies and homomorphic encryption with data aggregation and trust relationship in IoT interaction has been introduced. Then the year 2016, encompasses perfect forward secrecy, user anonymity, setting privacy privileges to users and fog layer for data distribution. Wide range of privacy-preserving approaches (35%) has been proposed in year 2017–2018 for data and identity anonymization.

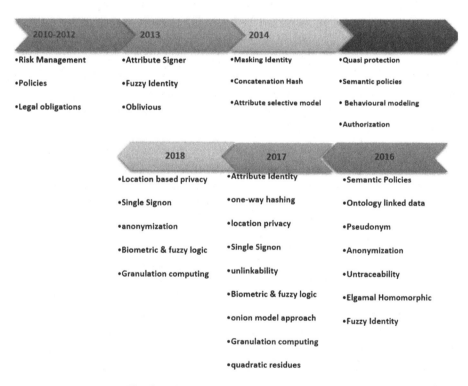

Fig. 2.   Privacy methods 2010–2016 timeline

3.2 Classification of Privacy Based Schemes

In this section, we identify the privacy preserving schemes used in IoT applications and categorized according to the attributes of privacy achieved in IoT domain, Table 1 provides the schemes preserving privacy references. The detail of each category is elaborated in following sub-sections.

Table 1. Content and context oriented privacy categories with techniques' references

Category	Reference
Temporal	[22, 30, 31]
Location- based	[6, 11, 12, 17, 25, 28]
Privacy polices & access control	[8, 18, 23, 24, 26]
Identity	[9–12, 15, 17, 18, 20, 22, 25]
Content oriented	[7, 11–15, 19–22, 25, 26, 32]

3.3 Content-Oriented Privacy

Different approaches have been used by researchers and practitioners to achieve data privacy, in [22], authentication protocol has been designed to provide RFID tags' data privacy using one-way hashing in smart city. The protocol ensures that the data of individuals are kept private while using RFID tags. However, the protocol uses basic hashing methods, which may compromise the content privacy if attacker is smart enough to launch birthday attack for hash collision. Another scheme used AES and SHA1 to design a framework for achieving content privacy in smart homes [11]. Whereas in [17] the researchers used Diffie Hellman key exchange and hashing to achieves decentralized content privacy in smart homes. However, both the schemes have their limitation of use in IoT domain, in [11] for key agreement and storage involved third party service provider, which can compromise the data integrity and privacy. Further in [17] the model gives the weak security guarantees considering basic hashing for distributed system.

Further for data-aggregation privacy requirement, authors have used different approaches [31, 32] for achieving data accuracy, flexibility and minimizing overhead. However, the performance network overhead is not optimized during the aggregation and number of collisions has been increased. In healthcare system, researchers also proposed Multi-agent architecture concept with pseudonyms method [16] for providing authority to patients to select data privacy level, only selected private information is then transmitted to medical servers [16]. Whereas patient data is transmitted to central medical server, which may be vulnerable to DDOS attack and lead to data loss in single point of failure.

3.4 Context-Oriented Privacy

For context privacy fulfillment, this subsection discusses the possible solutions being adapted in past

1. *Identity Privacy:* To achieve anonymity, as in [22] anonymous authentication protocol design used pseudo-identity and one-time-alias identity concept to enhance the quality of the residence in smart city. Another users' un-traceability scheme has been adopted using Elliptic Curve Cryptography (ECC) methods [10]. However, the scheme [22] provides anonymity using only symmetric key hashing, if keys get compromise, user identity is at stake. Further backend server can be monitoring the communication being carried out between tags leading to single point of failure. Whereas [10] is vulnerable to collusion attack leading to loss to anonymity property. In another scheme [18], anonymity model using granulation computing provided individuals privilege to set precise privacy preferences has been proposed. Authors claims it to be first anonymity model considering the autonomy of quasi identifier attributes. Whereas, the scheme does not deal with any other security property including data integrity and confidentiality. Attribute based signature scheme for user attributes privacy and anonymity has been proposed [25], however the signature attribute authority is centralised entity which can lead to data loss. Further use of ABS is computationally expensive, which makes scheme not well-suited for IoT devices.

2. *Privacy policies and Access control:* Henze *et al.* proposed a heavyweight policy [8] driven platform which offered users transparency and adaptability for configuring privacy requirements in pervasive healthcare assisting living, accordingly data is secured using AES and RSA methods. The scheme does focuses on privacy preserving of end users, whereas the use of RSA makes the scheme heavyweight. Therefore, scheme is costly, not suitable for resource constrained and low memory IoT, further regulatory requirements are kept intact even after data reaches the destination, occupying the extra memory.

Furthermore, [16] also give privileges to users to set level of privacy preferences and control the data access. Another scheme [23] which is based on Ciphertext-policy attribute based encryption defines attributes with multiple policies for encryption and then outsource data to cloud storage. The scheme has been able to mitigate collusion attack, however use of attribute-based signatures and defining policies makes it middleweight, as it incurs computational cost higher than lightweight schemes designed. Therefore, scheme is not able to support the scaling needs of IoT context [23]. Authors in [24] also defines security and privacy policy-based management using semantic ontologies. Ontology designed to provide policy rule evaluation, policy decision-based language, behavioral model and enforcement rule monitoring. However, designing ontologies for policies requires lot of energy and memory storage, which cannot be done on IoT devices.

3. *Location based Privacy:* Few efforts have been made to hide the location of nodes, preventing the trace back attacks by randomizing routing paths for source and destination [27]. Also misleading an attacker from their target by injecting bogus traffic [27]. Further, location based authentication scheme has been adopted [6] to mitigate attacks such as location privacy, man-in-the-middle and compromise. The scheme is based on lightweight hashing methods to secure location-based services in cloud-IoT paradigm. In addition, nodes un-linkability to location has also been proposed using anonymous secure framework.

Another effort considered hiding the transmission by enclosing it in innocuous messages [28]. However, most of the solutions for privacy location are designed to considered attackers and to protect either data source location or destination (or base station) location. Whereas it is of paramount importance to design a platform to secure the location privacy of source and destination simultaneously and all possible active attackers disrupting the communication rather than just considering passive attackers.

4. *Temporal Privacy:* To highlight time-driven problem [29] introduced message packet random delays in transmission to base station wireless sensor networks. However, the adopted solution is not compatible with real-time resource con-strained IoT sensor nodes, as use of random delays requires buffering at interme-diate nodes limits the one-time delivery of emergency messages. Another solution has been provided to preserve temporal privacy in real-time monitoring [30]. The solution is based on the Laplacian delays in perturbation the order of data messages and data transmission time. However still the use Laplacian delays in unclear, whether an attacker can find out original sending time [30]. Recently, a temporal privacy preservation scheme [31] has been proposed that is dependent of time-dependent priority queue, which overcomes the limitation of random delays and time-driven model approaches. However, the proposed scheme lacks to provide privacy analysis, also the discussion on applying data encryption.

Analysis of schemes based on the privacy main categories (i.e. content-oriented privacy and context-oriented privacy) is presented in Table 2, which shows the privacy features used by schemes and following under different weight (heavy, middle or light) according to the cryptographic techniques used. '+' sign shows that the techniques strongly fulfil the privacy category requirement, '-' sign shows that it does not fulfil the requirement, whereas '±' shows on average requirement is fulfilled.

From table, it can be concluded that the lightweight content-oriented privacy is provided in schemes [7, 9, 12–14, 21]. The schemes focused to achieve data privacy in IoT environment. The schemes also provided content-oriented integrity, confidentiality and authenticity. However, schemes do not provide user privacy and apply privacy policies to attain content privacy. Content privacy is also provided by [15] the method used to preserve data privacy is middleweight by using high-level protocol specifica-tion language and elliptic curve point multiplication. Whereas [19] is heavyweight scheme as it has used semantic modeling with ontologies and digital signature in smart homes, which makes scheme not well-suited for IoT resource constraint sensors/nodes.

Context-oriented privacy schemes mainly focus is to preserve the user's location and identity with embedding privacy policies. Using lightweight cryptographic meth-ods [11, 22] schemes provided user privacy, whereas [26] provides heavyweight user privacy, using multiagent architecture with data linking approach and storing data centrally at cloud.

Table 2. Privacy schemes analysis based on weights and features

Group	Integrity	Confidentiality	Authentication	Data privacy	User privacy	Privacy policies
Content-Oriented Privacy						
Lightweight [7, 9, 12–14, 21]	+	+	+	+	−	−
Middleweight [15, 20]	±	±	±	+	−	−
Heavyweight [19]	+	+	+	+	±	±
Context-Oriented Privacy						
Lightweight [11, 22]	±	±	±	±	+	±
Middleweight [25]	+	+	+	+	+	+
Heavyweight [26]	+	+	+	+	+	+

4   Open Issues and Future Trends

The identified schemes for IoT privacy development face many challenges, this section addresses series of opening research challenges and issues with convincing future trends and solutions.

4.1   Centralization

Most of the schemes [12, 16, 33] uses centralized unit (e.g. server, control centers, cloud) to store data, which leads to single point of failure and DDOS attack. An attacker may gain an access to centralized unit, deletes, inserts or updates the stored data, and may disrupt the traffic and making the centralized unit resources unavailable to the network. Therefore, mitigating this challenge is of utmost importance. Adapting data storage at distributed several units can resolve the centralization issue. Data can be stored in patches at these data stores in form of hashes, using concept of block chain. Block chain methods results in insignificant processing time, traffic and energy consumption [17]. However, the scheme mainly focuses on access use case and storing data using public keys which are fixed with cluster head. Thus, provides weak security guarantees for a distributed system. Therefore, there is a need of a distributed system with strong security and privacy model, using keys randomly generated with cluster head.

4.2   Computationally Expensive

Asymmetric crypto methods such as RSA, El Gamal, Paillier cryptosystem and homomorphic are heavyweight methods as they require larger memory and computation efficiency for mathematical operations and storage, which also results in slow communication between nodes. Use of RSA in different schemes such as [8] results in heavyweight policies driven interface, that is not suitable for IoT platform. Therefore, optimizing performance efficiency using lightweight asymmetric cryptosystems to provide same level of security as RSA, El Gamal or Paillier is required to secure and preserve privacy in IoT environment.

It is known that ECC encounters less computational and memory cost as compared to other asymmetric cryptosystems. In the recent year, ECC has been used to mitigate the computational and memory overhead issues, however mostly the schemes such as [7] stored data at central data store, which leads to single point of failure as mentioned above. Exploiting the ECC methods with distributed data stores would give a promising solution to performance overhead problem. However, in the recent year, it has been analyzed that Shor's algorithm can efficiently solve elliptic curve discrete logarithms using quantum computers. Thus, ECC security is vulnerable to quantum computing. Therefore, there is a need of lightweight quantum resistance cryptographic schemes to be fully suitable for IoT.

4.3   Preserving Temporal and Data Aggregation Privacy

During the data transmission, preserving the privacy of node packet's time instances (e.g. packet creation time, Time to Live) is of utmost importance, as an attacker can detect the time of packet creation which can lead to future communication detection and knowing the behavior of a communication, can launch attacks accordingly to gain access to unencrypted data. There are few approaches carried out to preserve temporal privacy of packet, however these approaches are not fully suitable for real-time resource constrained IoT sensor nodes. Therefore, fully preserving the temporal privacy in IoT domain is a challenge task. In addition, data aggregation in IoT has been receiving considerable attention recently, aggregating hybrid IoT devices data into one securely is a challenging task, as for saving scarce network bandwidth while providing data privacy.

5   Conclusion

In this paper, we delved into the analysis of the most important aspects of privacy in Internet of Things, which emphasis on work being done and issues that require further research. We present review with preserving privacy timeline and classification for IoT domain. We also perform analysis and classification of the privacy solutions and associated limitations in IoT paradigm. Further, summarized series of opening research challenges and issues with convincing future trends and solutions. We believe our survey may motivate researchers in developing new privacy preservation schemes with performance efficiency in the context of Internet of Things.

References

1. Yang, Y., et al.: A survey on security and privacy issues in internet-of-things. IEEE Internet Things J. **4**(5), 1250–1258 (2017)

2. Puthli, R.: The Internet of Things will be much, much bigger than mobile (2015). https://blog.itude.com/2015/03/06/the-internet-of-things-will-be-much-much-bigger-than-mobile/

3. Mendez, D.M., Papapanagiotou, I., Yang, B.: Internet of things: survey on security and privacy. arXiv preprint arXiv:1707.01879 (2017)

4. Aleisa, N., Renaud, K.: Privacy of the Internet of Things: A Systematic Literature Review (2017)

5. Lopez, J., et al.: Evolving privacy: from sensors to the internet of things. Future Gener. Comput. Syst. 75, 46–57 (2017)

6. Zhou, J., et al.: Security and privacy for cloud-based IoT: challenges. IEEE Commun. Mag. 55(1), 26–33 (2017)

7. Li, R., et al.: IoT applications on secure smart shopping system. IEEE Internet Things J. 4(6), 1945–1954 (2017)

8. Henze, M., et al.: A comprehensive approach to privacy in the cloud-based internet of things. Future Gener. Comput. Syst. 56, 701–718 (2016)

9. Srinivas, J., et al.: Provably secure biometric based authentication and key agreement protocol for wireless sensor networks. J. Ambient Intell. Humanized Comput. (2017)

10. Gope, P., Hwang, T.: A realistic lightweight anonymous authentication protocol for securing real-time application data access in wireless sensor networks. IEEE Trans. Ind. Electron. 63 (11), 7124–7132 (2016)

11. Kumar, P., et al.: Anonymous secure framework in connected smart home environments. IEEE Trans. Inf. Forensics Secur. 12(4), 968–979 (2017)

12. Amin, R., et al.: A robust and anonymous patient monitoring system using wireless medical sensor networks. Future Gener. Comput. Syst. 80, 483–495 (2018)

13. Tonyali, S., et al.: Privacy-preserving protocols for secure and reliable data aggregation in IoT-enabled smart metering systems. Future Gener. Comput. Syst. 78, 547–557 (2018)

14. Jayaraman, P.P., et al.: Privacy preserving internet of things: from privacy techniques to a blueprint architecture and efficient implementation. Future Gener. Comput. Syst. 76, 540–549 (2017)

15. Li, X., et al.: A three-factor anonymous authentication scheme for wireless sensor networks in internet of things environments. J. Netw. Comput. Appl. 103, 194–204 (2018)

16. Ivaşcu, T., Frîncu, M., Negru, V.: Considerations towards security and privacy in internet of things based eHealth applications. In: 2016 IEEE 14th International Symposium on Intelligent Systems and Informatics (SISY). IEEE (2016)

17. Dorri, A., et al.: Blockchain for IoT security and privacy: The case study of a smart home, pp. 618–623 (2017)

18. Le, J., Liao, X., Yang, B.: Full autonomy: a novel individualized anonymity model for privacy preserving. Comput. Secur. 66, 204–217 (2017)

19. Tao, M., et al.: Multi-layer cloud architectural model and ontology-based security service framework for IoT-based smart homes. Future Gener. Comput. Syst. 78, 1040–1051 (2018)

20. Challa, S., et al.: Secure signature-based authenticated key establishment scheme for future IoT applications. IEEE Access 5, 3028–3043 (2017)

21. Seo, S.-H., Won, J., Bertino, E.: pCLSC-TKEM: a pairing-free certificateless signcryption-tag key encapsulation mechanism for a privacy-preserving IoT. Trans. Data Privacy 9(2), 101–130 (2016)

22. Gope, P., et al.: Lightweight and privacy-preserving RFID authentication scheme for distributed IoT infrastructure with secure localization services for smart city environment. Future Gener. Comput. Syst. (2017)

23. Huang, Q., Yang, Y., Wang, L.: Secure data access control with ciphertext update and computation outsourcing in fog computing for internet of things. IEEE Access 5, 12941–12950 (2017)

24. Neisse, R., et al.: SecKit: a model-based security toolkit for the internet of things. Comput. Secur. **54**, 60–76 (2015)
25. Su, J., et al.: ePASS: an expressive attribute-based signature scheme with privacy and an unforgeability guarantee for the internet of things. Future Gener. Comput. Syst. **33**, 11–18 (2014)
26. Ivascu, T., Frîncu, M., Negru, V.: Considerations towards security and privacy in Internet of Things based eHealth applications, p. 275–280 (2016)
27. Yao, L., et al.: Protecting the sink location privacy in wireless sensor networks. Pers. Ubiquit. Comput. **17**(5), 883–893 (2013)
28. Shao, M., et al.: Cross-layer enhanced source location privacy in sensor networks. In: 6th Annual IEEE Communications Society Conference on Sensor, Mesh and Ad Hoc Communications and Networks, 2009 SECON 2009. IEEE (2009)
29. Kamat, P., et al.: Temporal privacy in wireless sensor networks: theory and practice. ACM Trans. Sens. Netw. (TOSN) **5**(4), 28 (2009)
30. Yang, X., et al.: A novel temporal perturbation based privacy-preserving scheme for real-time monitoring systems. Comput. Netw. **88**, 21–88 (2015)
31. Ara, A., et al.: A secure privacy-preserving data aggregation scheme based on bilinear ElGamal cryptosystem for remote health monitoring systems. IEEE Access **5**, 12601–12617 (2017)
32. Vahedi, E., et al.: A secure ECC-based privacy preserving data aggregation scheme for smart grids. Comput. Netw. **129**, 28–36 (2017)
33. Figueres, N.B., et al.: Efficient smart metering based on homomorphic encryption. Comput. Commun. **82**, 95–101 (2016)

Real-Time Estimation of Road Traffic Speeds from Cell-Based Vehicle Trajectories

Xiaoxiao Sun[1], Dongjin Yu[1(✉)], Sai Liao[1], Wanqing Li[1],
and Chengbiao Zhou[2]

[1] School of Computer Science and Technology,
Hangzhou Dianzi University, Hangzhou, China
{sunxiaoxiao,yudj}@hdu.edu.cn
[2] Hangzhou Trustway Technology Company Limited, Hangzhou, China

Abstract. This paper presents a novel approach for urban road networks to estimate traffic speeds using vehicle trajectories captured by detectors on transportation cells. By scanning and analyzing dynamic traffic streams of passing-vehicles, we calculate the real-time traffic speed of road segment separated by adjacent detectors, which are further synthesized to present the traffic speed of whole road. Compared to driving routes data with limited coverage or floating GPS data with occasional missing that are both frequently utilized for traditional road speed estimation, our approach utilizes the full coverage detector data and is proved to have more accurate and reliable results in its application for two large cities of China. An analysis and visualization system was hence developed, whose successful operation in several transportation departments indicated the efficiency of our approach. It helps to guide travelers the optimal driving routes, which greatly relieves the huge traffic stress of city road.

Keywords: Traffic trajectory · Transportation cells · Traffic speed ·
Speed estimation

1 Introduction

With the rapid development of economy and society, the numbers of vehicles in large cities increase dramatically [1]. Not only the developed countries, but also the developing countries suffer seriously from traffic congestion. As we all know, estimating dynamic road traffic speeds helps the drivers to find out the optimal routes to their destinations, and therefore relieve the huge stress of city road network [2, 3].

Currently, there are two types of data source that are most frequently employed to estimate the traffic speed: the floating-vehicle-based data captured from moving vehicles and the cell-based data captured from detectors installed along transportation cells [4, 5]. Compared to the floating-vehicle data, cell-based data have the following advantages [6–8]. (1) They cover almost all trajectories of all vehicles running on the major roads of city. Thus, they are far more representative of the traffic condition of whole city. (2) The geographical position and moving directions can be accurately captured when all vehicles pass through the detectors along transportation cells.

X. Liu et al. (Eds.): ICSOC 2018 Workshops, LNCS 11434, pp. 220–228, 2019.
https://doi.org/10.1007/978-3-030-17642-6_19

(3) Different from fixed patterns due to the driving preferences of some floating vehicles, such as taxis, the randomness of cell-based data enhances the accuracy of estimation greatly.

In this paper, by utilizing vehicle trajectories captured from the detectors installed along transportation cells, we present a novel approach to estimate road traffic speeds. By scanning and analyzing the traffic streams of passing-vehicles in real time, such as plate number, passing time, the detector passed-by etc., we calculate the real-time traffic speed of the road segment separated by adjacent detectors, which are further synthesized to present the traffic speed of whole road.

The structure of the paper is as follows: Sect. 2 is an overview of previous work in road traffic speeds estimation. In Sect. 3, we present a detailed description of our approach to estimate real-time road traffic speeds from cell-based vehicle trajectories. Section 4 demonstrates the application of our approach in two Chinese cities for their road traffic relief with a corresponding system introduced in the end. We conclude the paper and present future directions in Sect. 5.

2 Related Works

A large number of studies have been carried out on road traffic speed estimation due to its importance in road network traffic relieve. According to Wang et al., methods for traffic speed estimation can be classified to into two categories: traffic theory based methods and data-analysis based methods [9].

Traffic theory based methods requires for well-established theoretical background in transportation field. They take the effects of various factors into consideration when establishing the estimation models, like incidents, road works, traffic control measures, etc., and are usually able to better simulate the actual traffic situation. However, better simulation usually needs more complicated and intensive computation, which further led to lower method efficiency [10]. In addition, many parameters that are needed in the methods should be defined in advance, which greatly enhances the difficulty to precede the study [11].

Data analysis based methods are easier to implement since they are data–driven models who aims to mine the patterns using traffic data and conduct estimation based on those patterns [12]. Nowadays, with the development of traffic surveillance systems, more and more real-time high-frequency traffic data become available. The development of data analysis technology also accelerates the study and utilization of data-driven methods. Linear regression [13], time series [14], kalman filtering [15], nonparametric regression [16], artificial neural networks (ANNs) [17] and many other data analysis models have been utilized to predict road traffic speeds.

Generally speaking, the majority of both types of above-mentioned methods for traffic speed estimation address the problem in two steps [18]: (a) map-matching and path inference, where the optimal path (usually the shorted path) is planned and chosen on the road map (see for example [19–21]); (b) travel speed calculation and estimation, where real-time data are input and calculated to dynamic speed of every road (see for example [22, 23]). In our study, the similar two steps are adopted and detailed process is as follows: historical detector data are first utilized to generate adjacent detector pairs and to calculate the shortest path between them, then dynamic detector data are used to estimate real-time traffic speed of every road segment separated by detector pairs and the results are synthesized to present the traffic speed of whole road further.

3   Methodologies

3.1   Model Architecture

The architecture of our approach is given in Fig. 1. As we can see, various data are integrated and applied to realize the real-time estimation of road traffic speeds, including Map Data, Detectors Data and Passing-Vehicle Data. The core of the model consists of two main modules, namely, the module of *Generating Adjacent Detector-Pairs*, which generates adjacent detector pairs and calculate their shortest path based on Road Networks data (Map Data) and Detectors Data, and the module of *Calculating Traffic Speed*, which estimates the real-time traffic speed of the road segment separated by adjacent detectors based on Passing-Vehicle Data and further synthesize to present the traffic speed of whole road. Eventually, the estimated results are visualized to demonstrate the traffic situation of the whole study area.

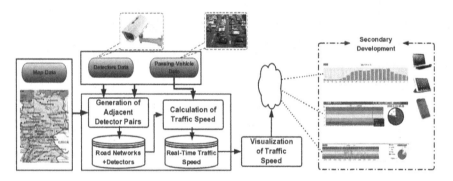

Fig. 1. The model architecture

3.2   Data Sources

For our approach, various data source are integrated and applied. The three main data sources are listed as follows: (1) *Map Data*, vector geographic data which contains the road ID (unique number), coordinate of the two endpoints and the midpoint of each road. (2) *Detectors Data*, dynamic data which contains the detector ID (unique number) and coordinate of each detector installed on the intersection or along the road. (3) *Passing-Vehicle Data*, real-time data which contains license plate number, vehicle pictures, passing detector ID and passing time, of each moving vehicle when passing detectors.

3.3   Generating Adjacent Detector Pairs

Historical detector data and passing-vehicle data were used to generate adjacent detector pairs and to calculate the shortest path between them. The detailed process is shown in Fig. 2 and described as follows:

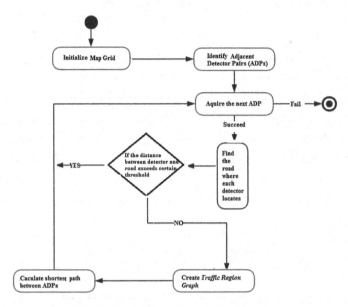

Fig. 2. Generating adjacent detector pairs

Step 1. Initializing Map Grid
The study area is divided into map grids composed of meshes with same size. A road is regarded to locate in a certain mesh if its midpoint is inside the mesh. A *"Mesh-Road List"* is thus kept to record which mesh each road locates in.

Step 2. Identifying Adjacent Detector Pairs
Two detectors passed sequentially by a certain large number of vehicles are identified as an adjacent detector pair and their info are stored into a list called *"Adjacent Detector Pair Set"*.

Step 3. Calculating Shortest Paths between Adjacent Detector Pairs
The process of calculating the shortest path between adjacent detectors is as follows (Fig. 3): (1) Find the exact mesh where the detector locates according to its coordinate. (2) Find all the roads which locate in the aforementioned mesh and acquire its neighboring 8 meshes from the *"Mesh-Road List"*. (3) Calculate distance between the detector and each road. The detector is considered to locate on one specific road if the distance between the detector and the road is the shortest. The calculation of shortest path between two adjacent detectors is therefore converted into the calculation of shortest path between two roads where the detectors locate. (4) Construct a *"Path Ladder"* (PL) that consists of multiple meshes and continuously covers these two

adjacent detectors. (5) Construct a *"Traffic Region Graph"* (TRG), in which the vertex represents the road in PL, whereas the edge represents the line connecting two adjacent vertexes, i.e., two roads with the same endpoint. The weight of edge is equal to the sum of the distance from the midpoint of each road to their connecting endpoint. (6) Find the shortest path along the map between two roads, which is as the shortest path between two adjacent detectors, using *Dijkstra*'s algorithm.

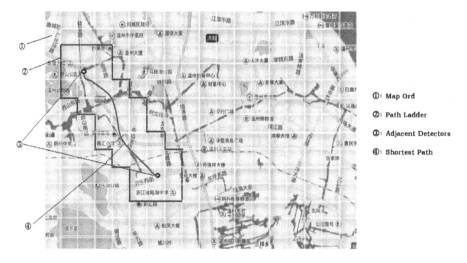

Fig. 3. The generation of adjacent detector-pairs

3.4   Estimating Real-Time Traffic Speed

Real-time detector data and passing vehicle data were used to estimate real-time traffic speed of every detector and every road further, and then to visualize the traffic situation of the whole study area. The detailed process is as follows:

Step 1. Creating "outMap"

In order to estimate traffic speed, we first create an *"outMap"* to store the latest driving information of vehicles. The inner structure of *"outMap"* is as following: *"plate number"* —> *("detector number", "passing time").*

Step 2. Calculating Passing Records Every *t* Minutes

We first read vehicle passing records collected in the nearest *T* minutes (rollback time, T > t) in ascending order according to passing time. Afterward, we create an *"inMap"* to eliminate the influence due to the overlap between two adjacent rounds of speed calculation, whose inner structure is the same as that of *"outMap"*. For each passing record, we successively search its previous passing record with the same plate number in *"inMap"* and *"outMap"* if it belongs to the overlapping portion; otherwise we only search it in *"outMap"*. We then obtain the vehicle's speed through dividing the shortest distance between two detectors sequentially passed by with the passing time interval, and save it to a list called *"Detector-Speed List"*. Meanwhile, we update the information in "*inMap*" or "*outMap*" for the next rounds of calculation. A sample of handling passing-vehicle records is shown in Fig. 4 ($t = 1$, $T = 5$).

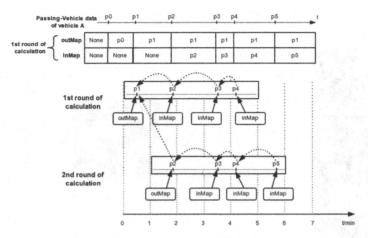

Fig. 4. The consecutive calculation of traffic speeds ($t = 1$, $T = 5$)

Step 3. Estimating Traffic Speed on Every Road

After handling all the passing-vehicle data, we employ the Grubbs' criterion ($\alpha = 0.9$) to eliminate unusual data in the "*Detector-Speed List*". We then use the average value of the remaining data as the speed of road segment separated by adjacent detectors. Finally, considering that one road may be included in more than one path separated by adjacent detectors, we calculate the real-time traffic speed v_i of road i using the weighted average of every calculated speed, as shown in Eq. 1:

$$v_i = \frac{\sum_{k \in R_i} w_{ik} \times v_k}{\sum_{k \in R_i} w_{ik}}, w_{ik} = \frac{l_i}{l_k} \tag{1}$$

where R_i is the union of all paths that include road i, v_k is the traffic speed of path k, and l_i and l_k are the lengths of road i and path k, respectively.

4 Demonstrations

We applied the presented approach in two large cities in eastern China, namely Jiaxing city and Quzhou city, each having more than 1 million residents.

In Jiaxing, we employed the traffic streams provided by 403 video detectors along transportation cells while in Quzhou, 313 video detectors were employed. In the experiment, we set the update frequency, or variable t, to 1 min, and set the rollback time, or variable T, to 5 min. Eventually, we identified 1047 adjacent detector pairs and 11,898 roads in Jiaxing. In Quzhou, 879 adjacent detector pairs and 7,801 roads were identified. Based the approach described in this paper, a system called "Real-time Road Traffic Big Data Analysis System" is developed. The system is currently steadily operated in the transportation departments in cities like Jiaxing, Quzhou and so on, as Fig. 5 shows.

Fig. 5. Real-time road traffic big data analysis system (a) Positions of detectors and car-type analysis captured by these detectors (b) Visualization of estimated real-time road traffic speeds on road maps

Monitoring of Car-type and Abnormal Vehicle Detection

All types of traffic data, including map data, dynamic detector data and real-time passing-vehicle data were integrated in our system. In this way, we're able to select the interested detector to see the real-time traffic conditions captured by the selected detector. In addition, the system also provides the function of car-type identification and abnormal vehicle detection. Figure 4(a) demonstrates the vehicles captured by detectors at 14:48:31, November 16th, 2015. It also listed abnormal vehicles, abnormal causes and their plate numbers.

Real-time Visualization of Estimated Road Speeds
Based on the integrated data and our estimation approach, road traffic speeds of all roads are visualized on the map in our system at the frequency of one minute. Green lines indicate unblocked roads; while yellow and red lines indicate busy roads and congested roads, respectively. Road names and their corresponding estimated speeds are listed in the lower right corner of the system interface for users who are interested in detailed road traffic speeds of a specific road as in Fig. 4(b).

5 Conclusions

In this paper, a real-time road traffic speed estimation approach based on the traffic stream captured by detectors along transportation cells is presented. It helps to guide travelers the optimal driving routes, which greatly relieves the huge traffic stress of city road. Compared to traditional road traffic speed estimation methods, our approach has the following advantages. (1) The data sources of our approach are all-type vehicles rather than just partial public vehicles such as taxis and buses. (2) Compared to driving routes data with limited coverage or floating GPS data which suffers from occasional missing, the data we used from detectors is more sufficient, reliable and accurate. (3) The results that our approach calculated are two-way speeds rather than one-direction speeds, which is more practical and close to reality.

The application of our approach in two large cities in eastern China indicated its efficiency and accuracy, while the successful operation of our developed system demonstrated its importance and practicality in daily life. In the future, we will try to integrate other data sources, such as loop detectors, into our approach to achieve better results.

Acknowledgments. The work is supported by National Natural Science Foundation of China (No. 61472112, No. 61702144), Key Science and Technology Project of Zhejiang Province (No. 2017C01010), and Natural Science Foundation of Zhejiang Province (No. LY12F02003).

References

1. Richards, P.I.: Shock waves on the highway. Oper. Res. **4**(1), 42–51 (1956)
2. Han, J., Li, Z., Tang, L.A.: Mining moving object, trajectory and traffic data. In: Kitagawa, H., Ishikawa, Y., Li, Q., Watanabe, C. (eds.) DASFAA 2010. LNCS, vol. 5982, pp. 485–486. Springer, Heidelberg (2010). https://doi.org/10.1007/978-3-642-12098-5_56
3. Wang, Z., Lu, M., Yuan, X., Zhang, J.: Visual traffic jam analysis based on trajectory data. IEEE Trans. Visual Comput. Graphics **19**, 2159–2168 (2013)
4. Lai, W.K., Kuo, T.H., Chen, C.H.: Vehicle speed estimation and forecasting methods based on cellular floating vehicle. Data. Appl. Sci. **6**(2), 47 (2016)
5. Liu, H., Sun, J.: Improving freeway traffic speed estimation using high-resolution loop detector data, Technical report. Center for Transportation Studies (2013)
6. Wang, Z., Ye, T., Lu, M., Yuan, X., Qu, H., Yuan, J., Wu, Q.: Visual exploration of sparse traffic trajectory data. IEEE Trans. Visual Comput. Graphics **20**, 1813–1822 (2014)

7. Bouillet, E., Ranganathan, A.: Scalable, real-time map-matching using IBM systems. In: Mobile Data Management, pp. 249–257 (2010)
8. Wang, H., Li, Z., Hurwitz, D., Shi, J.: Parametric modeling of the heteroscedastic traffic speed variance from loop detector data. J. Adv. Transp. **49**(2), 279–296 (2015)
9. Wang, J., Shi, Q.: Short-term traffic speed forecasting hybrid model based on chaos-wavelet analysis-support vector machine theory. Transp. Res. Part C **27**(2), 219–232 (2013)
10. Waller, S.T., Chiu, Y.C., Ruizjuri, N., et al.: Short Term Travel Time Prediction on Freeways in Conjunction with Detector Coverage Analysis. Austin (2007)
11. Willinger, W.: Traffic modeling for high-speed networks: theory versus practice. Inst. Math. Appl. **71**, 395 (1995)
12. Van, L.J., Hoogendoorn, S., Van, Z.H.: Robust and adaptive travel time prediction with neural networks. Technical report, Proceedings of the 6th Annual TRAIL Congress (Part 2) (2000)
13. Shan, Z., Zhao, D., Xia, Y.: Urban road traffic speed estimation for missing probe vehicle data based on multiple linear regression model. In: International IEEE Conference on Intelligent Transportation Systems, pp. 118–123. IEEE (2013)
14. Grundy, C., Steinbach, R., Edwards, P., et al.: Effect of 20 mph traffic speed zones on road injuries in London, 1986–2006: controlled interrupted time series analysis. Br. Med. J. **340** (7736), 31 (2010)
15. Wang, Y., Papageorgiou, M., Messmer, A.: Real-time freeway traffic state estimation based on extended Kalman filter: adaptive capabilities and real data testing. Transp. Res. Part A **42** (10), 1340–1358 (2008)
16. Shi, D.X., Ding, T.J., Ding, B., et al.: Traffic speed forecasting method based on nonparametric regression. Comput. Sci. **43**(2), 224–229 (2016). In Chinese
17. Jiang, X., Adeli, H.: Dynamic wavelet neural network model for traffic flow forecasting. J. Transp. Eng. **131**(10), 771–779 (2005)
18. Rahmani, M., Koutsopoulos, H.N., Jenelius, E.: Travel time estimation from sparse floating car data with consistent path inference: a fixed point approach. Transp. Res. Part C Emerg. Technol. **85**, 628–643 (2015)
19. Newson, P., Krumm, J.: Hidden Markov map matching through noise and sparseness. In: ACM SIGSPATIAL International Conference on Advances in Geographic Information Systems, pp. 336–343. ACM (2009)
20. Kim, K., Seol, S., Kong, S.H.: High-speed train navigation system based on multi-sensor data fusion and map matching algorithm. Int. J. Control Autom. Syst. **13**(3), 503–512 (2015)
21. Marchal, F., Hackney, J., Axhausen, K.W.: Efficient map matching of large global positioning system data sets: tests on speed-monitoring experiment in Zürich. Transp. Res. Rec. J. Transp. Res. Board **1935**(1), 93–100 (2005)
22. Yue, Y., Zou, H.X., Li, Q.Q.: Urban road travel speed estimation based on low sampling floating car data. In: International Conference of Chinese Transportation Professionals, pp. 1–7 (2009)
23. Shan, Z., Zhao, D., Xia, Y.: Urban road traffic speed estimation for missing probe vehicle data based on multiple linear regression models. In: International IEEE Conference on Intelligent Transportation Systems, pp. 118–123. IEEE (2013)

A Data Cleaning Service on Massive Spatio-Temporal Data in Highway Domain

Yanqing Xia[1,2(✉)], Xuefei Wang[1,2], and Weilong Ding[1,2]

[1] Data Engineering Institute,
North China University of Technology, Beijing 100144, China
xia_yan_qing@163.com
[2] Beijing Key Laboratory on Integration and Analysis of Large-Scale
Stream Data, Beijing 100144, China

Abstract. With the development of highway toll system and sensor network, massive highway toll data has been accumulated nowadays. The imperfection of raw data, such as incomplete, repetitive and abnormal data, seriously affects the efficiency of data mining modeling. Traditional cleaning methods on massive spatio-temporal data are inefficient, because the business rules are difficult to depict in various domains. On the highway toll data of Henan Province, we propose a data cleaning service through business rules. This service can efficiently clean the raw toll data with spatio-temporal attributes, including the data calibration of erroneous data and invalid data, the repair of erroneous data, and the filtering of duplicate data. Implemented through Hadoop MapReduce on toll data in highway domain, our service shows its efficiency, accuracy and scalability in extensive experiments.

Keywords: Data cleaning · Spatio-temporal data · Highway · Hadoop · Business rules

1 Introduction

In recent years, smart cities and the Internet of Things have developed steadily. Various sensors have been used in data collection of city, such as sensors of toll stations, monitoring cameras for trunk roads, and smart card readers on buses. Massive data has been accumulated rapidly and provided a data foundation for big data analysis [1]. Due to the diversity of the environment in which the sensor device, network and storage are located, the quality of the raw data is too low to analyze the data directly. There are many types of error records in massive raw data. They make the extraction of effective data difficult and inefficient. In general, 15% of the collected directly data from the sensor is incomplete or has errors [2]. Taking Henan highway toll data as an example, there are about 20% and 35% error records of the raw data in 2016 and 2017, respectively. The errors lie in these types. (1) Lack of key attributes. For example, the entry station number is "0" or the license plate number is null in one highway toll record; (2) Distortion of attribute values. For example, the entry time is 2017/4/17-10:08:45, but the exit time is 2006/1/1-02:39:31 in one toll record; (3) Redundant records. The difference between times of multiple records is only in seconds. For example, the same vehicle passed twice

© Springer Nature Switzerland AG 2019
X. Liu et al. (Eds.): ICSOC 2018 Workshops, LNCS 11434, pp. 229–240, 2019.
https://doi.org/10.1007/978-3-030-17642-6_20

on the same station in 3 s but two passing records of this vehicle are stored. These raw records are difficult to use directly for further data analysis, so data cleaning is required. Data cleaning is the process to improve the quality of the raw data, identify irrational data, and fix errors [6].

For the massive data of typical spatio-temporal attributes, the traditional data cleaning method without additional prior knowledge is time consuming and difficult to guarantee accuracy, because there are the following essential difficulties.

(1) It is difficult to depict the business rules of data cleaning services. For example, raw highway toll data has typical spatio-temporal attributes, including timestamps and toll station identities when vehicles come in and out of highway, etc. But traditional methods of data cleaning on highway toll data are immature in highway domain because the business rules are not fully considered.

(2) The efficiency and scalability of data cleaning on massive spatio-temporal data in big data environments are lower. Early methods of data cleaning were mostly used for cleaning small amounts of data. With the development of the Internet of Things, massive amounts of data were collected. Although traditional data cleaning methods can be executed in parallel, they cannot be linearly expanded and have lower efficiency.

The contributions of this paper can be summarized as follows. (1) We propose the business rules in highway domain. The data cleaning service through business rules mainly solve the data calibration of erroneous data and invalid data, the repair of erroneous data, and the filtering of duplicate data. (2) This data cleaning service is implemented by Hadoop MapReduce in big data environment, and its feasibility and scalability are proved by extensive experiments on real data.

The organization of this paper is as follows. Section 2 shows the research significance and background of related work. Section 3 elaborates the data cleaning services, including the determination of spatio-temporal data consistency, rule-based filtering and data de-duplication. Section 4 evaluates the performance and effectiveness of the cleaning service. Section 5 summarizes the conclusion.

2   Background

2.1   Motivation

The work of this paper is originated from the highway big data analysis system of Henan Province. The system can conduct routine business analysis of public travel and traffic management through big data technology, and provide the current and historical traffic conditions on the highway network for the traveler. So the traffic management can guide traffic on the highway to alleviate traffic congestion. Currently, the system has been operated by the Henan Provincial Department of Transportation and was available in October 2017. Highway toll data consists of static data and dynamic data. Static data includes information of highway toll stations and road segments, etc. Dynamic data includes information of vehicles passing through toll stations. The toll data has four characteristics including complexity, real-time, massive lines, and dynamic. Complicated conditions of highway traffic make the collected data varied. The toll data is received in real time and updated in seconds. The dynamical increase of highway data forms massive historical raw data. The massive highway toll data not only has spatial attributes, but also has temporal attributes [3]. There are 1.5 billion highway toll records from 2016 to 2017. The data involves 660 million vehicles, 37 highways and 279 toll stations. The toll data includes 12 attributes as shown in Table 1. These data is typical spatio-temporal data, which includes three attributes, six entity attributes, two time attributes, and four spatial attributes.

Table 1. The attributes of toll data in highway domain

Attribute	Notation	Type
CARDNETWORK	Identity of staff	Entity
CARDID	Identity of MTC card	
VEHICLECLASS	Class of vehicle	
VEHICLETYPE	Type of vehicle	
VEHICLELICENSE	License plate number	
ETCCPUID	Identity of ETC card	
ENTRYTIME	Timestamp of entry station	Time
EXITTIME	Timestamp of exit station	
ENTRYSTATION	Identity of entry station	Space
ENTRYLANE	Identity of entry barrier gate	
EXITSTATION	Identity of exit station	
EXITLANE	Identity of exit barrier gate	

Through above various attributes, the traffic volume of the highway can be analyzed from different perspectives. But low quality data is a hindrance for further analysis of data and user experience [4]. On the one hand, the timestamps between the data are inconsistent. The raw data is stored by month but some data is not stored in a reasonable temporal range. It is a certain challenge to define the correctness of the temporal range for the dynamic and flexible structure of the highway. For example, in one record of April 2017, there is an entry time of "2017/4/4 14:07:52" and an exit time of "2006/1/1 00:19:18", we can determine the exit time by the entry time, but it is difficult to determine whether the overall time is logical. Then, the highway network is connected, but there is no circular route on the highway. In general, vehicles entering from a toll station will not go out from the same toll station. On the other hand, the given data is illegal. It is more common to have attribute values missing in the raw data. This lack of completeness is difficult to explain the validity of the data. For example, a vehicle passed through the exit and entrance station, but there is no information of license plate number in one record. Finally, there will be two redundant records but have different timestamps. For example, there is a vehicle A's entrance time at the S1 toll station and the entrance time is "2017/4/4 10:07:15". There is another vehicle A's entrance time at the S1 toll station and the entrance time is "2017/4/4 10:07:18". Such records cause storage redundancy and even errors of subsequent statistics of traffic.

In addition, most of the existing parallel processing methods need to process GB-level data, and a large amount of I/O causes a delay in data cleaning. In the case of increasing data volume, the existing methods cannot be linearly scaled. Therefore, we use the big data platform to study the scalable method for data cleaning of massive spatio-temporal attributes data.

2.2 Related Work

Data cleaning is mainly used for cleaning raw data, such as identifying unreasonable data and repairing erroneous data. It plays an important role in cyberspace such as RFID, sensors, and ETL processes [14]. Usually data cleaning involves multiple steps such as defining the type of error, identifying the erroneous data, and repairing the erroneous data [5]. We will introduce the relevant work from the following two aspects:

(1) For identifying erroneous data. The errors of the raw data can be classified into the following types, including inconsistency, repeatability, incompleteness, and invalidity. Correspondingly the process of identifying the erroneous data requires determining whether the data violates the rule constraints [7]. To date, many related techniques have been applied to verify whether data violates the rule constraints, such as similarity join, clustering, and classification [5]. Traditionally, rule constraints can lead us to fix erroneous data attributes, but may not explain which attributes are correct or incorrect. In recent years, rule-based data cleaning has been proposed, and when there are sufficient conditional constraints, the erroneous data can be accurately identified [8]. At present, sensors have been widely used in smart cities, and more and more data that has spatio-temporal attributes is generated, especially in real-time application scenarios [9]. However, the spatio-temporal data cannot be fully used in the traditional methods. The service proposed in this paper will clean the raw data from two aspects: whether the temporal attribute of the data is consistent and whether the data violates the spatio-temporal associated rules.

(2) For repairing erroneous data. Once the erroneous data is identified, it can be fixed by business rules and corrected the erroneous attributes. In the area of repairing data, the researchers have proposed a number of suggestive methods. Some researchers use a fixed rule containing evidence patterns, negative patterns and real values to automatically repair erroneous data [15]. And some researchers try to use CCFDs to determine a method for repairing erroneous data that is inconsistent with content-related data [13]. In practical applications, the method of repairing erroneous data is different in different fields [6]. For example, in the field of smart grids, researchers have proposed the eChIDNA system to process data streams between software and data transmission to achieve the repair of erroneous data [14]. It can be seen that the data repair is mostly carried out by the business rules of the field. In the highway traffic field, the business rules of the data cleaning service are still relatively lacking.

In summary, recent researches still lack effective methods to identify data inconsistencies and repair invalid data on massive spatio-temporal data. Some researchers have given data cleaning methods in the field of urban public transport [16].

Although our researches are not in the same field, they have provided us with many ideas that are worthy to reference. In this paper, for the actual needs of the highway field, the data cleaning service is carried out through Hadoop MapReduce, which is the parallel processing of massive historical spatio-temporal data.

3   Data Cleaning Service on Massive Spatio-Temporal Data

3.1   Overview

In this paper we take highway toll data as an example to illustrate the data cleaning service on spatio-temporal data. The methodology of data cleaning service in this paper is shown in Fig. 1. We get the data for one month each time, so the following services clean raw data at month granularity. The input here is massive highway toll data collected by sensors and other devices, and import the data into the distributed file system HDFS. After calibrating data on spatio-temporal association and filtering data based on business rules, the valid data is output to the non-relational database HBase or HDFS.

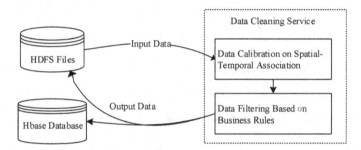

Fig. 1. The methodology

It can be seen that there are two main steps in cleaning services from Fig. 1: (1) Data calibration on spatio-temporal association. Spatio-temporal data will be judged and corrected in terms of whether the temporal attribute is out of business ranges, whether the spatial attributes are valid, and whether the spatio-temporal attributes are consistent. (2) Data filtering based on business rules. The valid data obtained after the previous step will be judged whether the license plate number is legal, deleted null value and removed the redundant data. The two steps are performed by a MapReduce job, and the flow diagram is shown in Fig. 2.

On the left is the Map task. Spatio-temporal data will be judged in terms of whether the license plate number is legal, whether the temporal attribute is out of business ranges, whether the spatial attributes are valid, whether the spatio-temporal attributes are consistent and deleted null value. On the right is the Reduce task. We remove the redundant data.

The specific implementation of the Map task and Reduce task is described in the following sections.

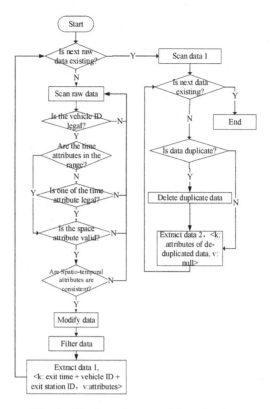

Fig. 2. The flow diagram of data cleaning

3.2 Data Calibration Through Spatio-Temporal Association

The inconsistency of raw data is unavoidable, especially on values of temporal attribute. The legality judgment of temporal attributes in can be divided into two categories: whether the entry time and exit time of the raw data are legal and whether one of the entry time and exit time is legal. Then we judge whether the illegal temporal attribute can be repaired according to the rules of spatio-temporal association. The legality judgment of temporal attributes is that the entry station cannot be same as the exit station in one toll record. This data cleaning method will be introduced by taking the actual highway toll data of April 2017 as an example.

Pattern 1: The temporal attributes are illegal. Raw toll records as example are shown in Fig. 3. It can be seen that the time when the vehicle entered the toll station 60113 was "2006/1/1 02:52:37", and the time of the vehicle passed the exit toll station 1015 was "2006/1/1 02:52:37". It is found that neither time belongs to April 2017, so we can delete this record in this case.

Pattern 2: The spatial attributes are invalid. The entry and exit toll station in one toll record are at the same station. Normally, since the highway network does not have a ring shape, a vehicle cannot leave from the station A and enter the highway on the station A. If the exit toll station number is same as the entry toll station number in one record, this record is invalid and it will be rejected.

```
20060101025237_1015        column=A:CARDID, timestamp=1531224514611, value="101163322"
20060101025237_1015        column=A:CARDNETWORK, timestamp=1531224514611, value="2016120998"
20060101025237_1015        column=A:ENTRYLANE, timestamp=1531224514611, value=0
20060101025237_1015        column=A:ENTRYSTATION, timestamp=1531224514611, value=60113
20060101025237_1015        column=A:ENTRYTIME, timestamp=1531224514611, value="2006/1/1 02:52:37"
20060101025237_1015        column=A:ETCCPUID, timestamp=1531224514611, value=""
20060101025237_1015        column=A:EXITLANE, timestamp=1531224514611, value="105"
20060101025237_1015        column=A:EXITSTATION, timestamp=1531224514611, value=1015
20060101025237_1015        column=A:EXITTIME, timestamp=1531224514611, value="2006/1/1 02:52:37"
20060101025237_1015        column=A:VEHICLECLASS, timestamp=1531224514611, value=1
20060101025237_1015        column=A:VEHICLELICENSE, timestamp=1531224514611, value="\xE8\x93\x90\xE8\xB1\x
20060101025237_1015        column=A:VEHICLETYPE, timestamp=1531224514611, value=1
```

Fig. 3. A record of toll data whose entry and exit time are illegal

Pattern 3: The spatio-temporal attributes are inconsistent. Figure 4 shows the toll record which the entry time or exit time is illegal. It can be seen that the time when the vehicle entered the toll station 60103 was "2017/4/17 06:50:32", and the time when the vehicle passed the exit toll station 1015 was "2006/1/1 02:57:14". It can be judged that the entry time belongs to April 2017, which is legal time, but the exit time is in January 2006. So we change the time "2006/1/1 02:57:14" to "2017/4/18 02:57:14" by the order of entry and exit. The road network structure of highway is connected, and toll stations are space-dependent. We can calculate the mileage between the entry station and exit station. If the minimum speed of the vehicle is 80 km/h and special traffic conditions such as traffic accidents are not considered, it can be concluded that the maximum travel time between the two stations is 3 h. According to a certain temporal range, we calculated the interval between the entry time and the repaired exit time. It can be concluded that the repaired exit time of the data is out of the legal temporal range, so this record is eliminated. On the other hand, if the repaired time is in a reasonable temporal range, the repaired record is retained.

```
20060101025714_1015        column=A:CARDID, timestamp=1531224521995, value="4556979"
20060101025714_1015        column=A:CARDNETWORK, timestamp=1531224521995, value="2016120998"
20060101025714_1015        column=A:ENTRYLANE, timestamp=1531224521995, value=1
20060101025714_1015        column=A:ENTRYSTATION, timestamp=1531224521995, value=60103
20060101025714_1015        column=A:ENTRYTIME, timestamp=1531224521995, value="2017/4/17 06:50:32"
20060101025714_1015        column=A:ETCCPUID, timestamp=1531224521995, value=""
20060101025714_1015        column=A:EXITLANE, timestamp=1531224521995, value="105"
20060101025714_1015        column=A:EXITSTATION, timestamp=1531224521995, value=1015
20060101025714_1015        column=A:EXITTIME, timestamp=1531224521995, value="2006/1/1 02:57:14"
20060101025714_1015        column=A:VEHICLECLASS, timestamp=1531224521995, value=1
20060101025714_1015        column=A:VEHICLELICENSE, timestamp=1531224521995, value="\xE8\x93\x90\xE8\xB
20060101025714_1015        column=A:VEHICLETYPE, timestamp=1531224521995, value=1
```

Fig. 4. A record of toll data whose entry or exit time is illegal

In order to ensure the spatial rationality and temporal consistency of raw data, we judge the legality of spatial and temporal attributes of raw data reasonably, delete raw data that both spatial and temporal attributes are unreasonable, and repair the time-repairable raw data.

3.3   Data Filtering Based on Business Rules

According to the attributes given in Table 1 of Sect. 2.1, in addition to the verification of the temporal and spatial attributes of the toll data, we need to check attributes such as the license plate number, the identity of ETC card and the identity of MTC card, and judge the legality of attributes by the business rules. According to the different business rules, it is mainly divided into the following three patterns:

Pattern 4: The license plate number is illegal. The license plate number is the most critical information of a vehicle and is the record identifier of all its passage or illegal behavior. In one toll record, the license plate number is "黄豫ND8030<黄豫 ND8030>". The front field is manually recorded, and the back field is stored by the camera. In this paper we filter the license plate numbers with a regular expression to check the legal license plate number. The segmentation of regular expression is shown in Table 2. It consists of four fields: the license plate color of the vehicle, the province to which it belongs, the license plate number of the vehicle, and the vehicle type.

Table 2. Business rules of vehicles' license plate numbers.

Attribute	Regular expression
License plate color	([蓝白黄黑])?{1}
Province	[京津冀沪渝豫云辽黑湘皖鲁新苏浙赣鄂桂甘晋蒙陕吉闽贵粤青藏川宁琼使领]
License plate number	{1}[A-Z]{1}[A-Z0-9]{4}
Vehicle type	[A-Z0-9挂学试警港澳]{1}

Pattern 5: The data that some critical attributes are null is invalid. In addition to the above attributes, some attributes are null in the raw data, which are not repairable but critical. For example, if the entry and exit toll station number are "0" in one raw record, the toll station numbers cannot be judged according to the business rules. This type of data is considered as invalid data. When neither ETC ID nor MTC ID exists in one record, the record cannot be determined the vehicle type. This type of data is considered as invalid data, too. These invalid data will be directly culled.

Pattern 6: There are redundancy duplicate data. In an unstable sensor network environment, it is likely that multiple passes of the same vehicle at the same toll station are identified and stored.

Definition: Duplicate record. For the same vehicle, if there are multiple toll records at the same toll station S (exit/entry), we extract the time t_i (exit/entry), $\Delta t = |t_i - t_{i+1}|$. If $\Delta t < 1$ min, the records are duplicate.

Identified duplicate records may exist in valid raw data and need to be de-duplicated. According to the definition of duplicate record, if a record is duplicate, the record of t_{i+1} needs to be removed. Otherwise, the record is not a duplicate record but may be a record of an illegal vehicle such as a fake plate vehicle.

In the data cleaning process, it is necessary to determine whether there is duplicate data. If you want to judge and cull the duplicate data in a MapReduce job, you must ensure that any key in the middle of the job is sorted in the Shuffle task. So you can de-duplicate the sorted data of the same key value in the Reduce task. Therefore, the reduce task is to be performed after the map task is completed.

Finally, the entire cleaned valid data is stored in the HBase database or HDFS file to prepare data for subsequent data analysis.

4 Experiment

4.1 Environment

We use the Linux operating system (CentOS 6.7, JDK 1.7) in experiments. We use big data platform of Cloudera Manager (CDH5.10.0) to deploy the cluster, install components such as Zookeeper, HBase, HDFS, and implement the monitoring and management of cluster. The cluster has three nodes, one master node and two slave nodes, each node runs 21G of memory, and the host memory is 1.8T.

In the CDH environment, the MapReduce framework is used for data cleaning. Here, we need to set the parameter "mapred.reduce.slowstart.completed.maps=1" of the MapReduce job. This parameter can be set to perform Shuffle task when the Map task is completed.

The experimental data is the toll data of the highways in Henan Province. We cleaned one month of data each time. We used the actual data for each month from 2016 to 2017. There were on average 35,000,000 pieces of records each month, each record contained 12 attributes to describe the behavior of the vehicle on the highway.

4.2 Evaluation

The raw data of April 2017 was used for experimental evaluation and analysis.

Experiment 1: We cleaned the data of April 2017. There were a total of 45,983,889 raw toll records in April. The raw toll data was imported from the oracle database into the distributed file system HDFS. After the data was cleaned by our service, the valid data was stored in the HBase corresponding table.

The cleaned data had a total of 35,929,491 valid records. Among them, there were 506,706 pieces of temporal erroneous records and 5,721,457 pieces records of incorrect license plate number. In the preliminary statistics, 78% of the data were valid data. It indicated the feasibility of the proposed method in this paper.

In addition, we evaluated the performance with different amounts of raw data.

Experiment 2: The raw data was segmented, and then the amount of data for each process was increased by multiples. We took different data volumes to analyze the total temporal consumption and the size of average data on the cleaned data. The result is shown in the Fig. 5.

It can be seen that the performance of spatio-temporal data-based cleaning and rule-based filtering has good scalability with increasing data size, and the execution time does not increase linearly with the increase of data volume. With a 6x increase in scale, execution time is always in the minute level through parallel computing by MapReduce. Moreover, as the amount of data increases, the processing time per unit data amount decreases, so the method has good scalability.

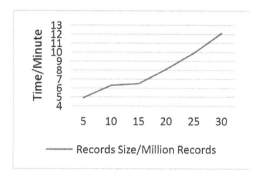

Fig. 5. Data cleaning execution

For accurate verification, we added manually generated dirty data to the cleaned raw data. Then we cleaned it again and evaluated its verification.

Experiment 3: We extracted the data of one month that has been cleaned, modified half of the data and created abnormal data. We modified the data in three aspects: (1) The temporal and spatial properties of the vehicle were modified randomly; (2) The correctly license plate numbers were changed to an unreasonable license plate number or a blank value; (3) We copied and modified part of the data and added the duplicated data to the cleaned data. Then Data cleaning processing was performed on the three types of artificial dirty records, and after the processing was completed, the cleaned data was scanned to distinguish whether all the artificial dirty data were eliminated.

In the experiment, the modification ratio of the data was set to 5%, 10%, 15%, 20%, 25%, and 30%. The three dirty data are respectively cleaned according to the repaired ratio. We calculated the proportion of cleaned data in total effective data. The result is shown in the Fig. 6.

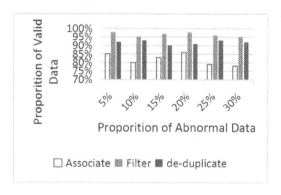

Fig. 6. Proportion of artificial anomalies after cleaning

From the experimental results, it can be seen that in the artificial dirty data, the most fluctuation of the three dirty data is the accuracy of the spatio-temporal associated attribute value, but the ratio of correct data is still above 78%; for the dirty data of artificial license plate number, the accuracy of the cleaned data maintains above 95%; for artificial duplicate data, the accuracy of the cleaned data keeps above 90%. In the case of three different artificial dirty data, the accuracy of the data cleaning service is relatively stable after the introduction of different amounts of artificial dirty data, and it even achieves 98% correctness. In general, we believe that the accuracy should be decrease because more abnormal data will be considered as invalid data. In fact, in the filtering method of this article, the proportion of the cleaned data in the correct data is independent of the size of the exception data: any data is scanned once and judged once. In addition, in this experiment, some artificial dirty data cannot be distinguished whether it is a violation, because most of the modifications do not violate the rules we define.

According to the above experiments, the data cleaning service proposed in this paper can effectively verify the validity of data with spatio-temporal attributes and has good scalability for cleaning data of different scales.

5 Summary

In this paper, taking highway domain as example, a data cleaning service on massive spatio-temporal data is proposed. This service can guarantee the validity of spatial and temporal attributes of data, the spatio-temporal consistency, and the de-duplication of data. Execution time of the data cleaning service is in seconds and the service has higher accuracy and scalability. In the future, we will consider more illegal patterns according to the business feedbacks and custom requirements to provide effective support for further data analysis.

References

1. Anagnostopoulos, I., Zeadally, S., Exposito, E.: Handling big data: research challenges and future directions. J. Supercomput. **72**(4), 1494–1516 (2016)
2. Zhong, M., Lingras, P., Sharma, S.: Estimation of missing traffic counts using factor, genetic, neural, and regression techniques. Transp. Res. Part C Emerg. Technol. **12**(2), 139–166 (2004)
3. Lee, W.H., Tseng, S.S., Shieh, J.L., et al.: Discovering traffic bottlenecks in an urban network by spatiotemporal data mining on location-based services. IEEE Trans. Intell. Transp. Syst. **12**(4), 1047–1056 (2011)
4. Carey, M.J., Jacobs, S., Tsotras, V.J.: Breaking BAD: a data serving vision for big active data. In: Proceedings of the 10th ACM International Conference on Distributed and Event-Based Systems, pp. 181–186. ACM, Irvine (2016)
5. Ganti, V., Sarma, A.D.: Data cleaning: a practical perspective. Morgan & Claypool Publishers, Williston (2013)

6. Tang, N.: Big data cleaning. In: Chen, L., Jia, Y., Sellis, T., Liu, G. (eds.) APWeb 2014. LNCS, vol. 8709, pp. 13–24. Springer, Cham (2014). https://doi.org/10.1007/978-3-319-11116-2_2

7. Fan, W., Geerts, F., Tang, N., Yu, W.: Inferring data currency and consistency for conflict resolution. In: Proceedings of the 29th International Conference on Data Engineering (ICDE 2013), pp. 470–481. IEEE (2013)

8. Wang, J., Tang, N.: Towards dependable data repairing with fixing rules. In: Proceedings of the 2014 ACM SIGMOD International Conference on Management of Data, pp. 457–468. ACM, Snowbird (2014)

9. Sun, D., Zhang, G., Zheng, W., Li, K.: Key Technologies for Big Data Stream Computing. Big Data: Algorithms, Analytics, and Applications. CRC Press, Taylor & Francis Group, USA (2014)

10. Beskales, G., Ilyas, I.F., Golab, L.: Sampling the repairs of functional dependency violations under hard constraints. Proc. VLDB Endow. **3**, 197–207 (2010)

11. Chu, X., Ilyas, I.F., Papotti, P.: Holistic data cleaning: putting violations into context. In: Proceedings of 2013 IEEE 29th International Conference on Data Engineering (ICDE 2013), pp. 458–469 (2013)

12. Fan, W., Li, J., Ma, S., Tang, N., Yu, W.: Towards certain fixes with editing rules and master data. VLDB J. **21**, 213–238 (2012)

13. Du, Y., Shen, D., Nie, T., Kou, Y., Yu, G.: Determining repairing sequence of inconsistencies in content-related data. In: Bouguettaya, A., et al. (eds.) WISE 2017. LNCS, vol. 10569, pp. 524–539. Springer, Cham (2017). https://doi.org/10.1007/978-3-319-68783-4_36

14. Wang, J., Tang, N.: Dependable data repairing with fixing rules. Data Inf. Qual. **8**(3–4), 1–34 (2017)

15. Vincenzo, G., Magnus, A., Marina, P.: eChIDNA: continuous data validation in advanced metering infrastructures. IEEE PES Innovative Smart Grid Technologies, Europe

16. Ding, W., Cao, Y.: A data cleaning method on massive spatio-temporal data. In: Wang, G., Han, Y., Martínez Pérez, G. (eds.) APSCC 2016. LNCS, vol. 10065, pp. 173–182. Springer, Cham (2016). https://doi.org/10.1007/978-3-319-49178-3_13

Tracking a Person's Behaviour in a Smart House

Gavin Chand, Mustafa Ali, Bashar Barmada$^{(\boxtimes)}$,
Veronica Liesaputra, and Guillermo Ramirez-Prado

Computer Science Department,
Unitec Institute of Technology, Auckland, New Zealand
{bbarmada, vliesaputra, gprado}@unitec.ac.nz

Abstract. This paper proposes to use machine learning techniques with ultrasonic sensors to predict the behavior and status of a person when they live solely inside their house. The proposed system is tested on a single room. A grid of ultrasonic sensors is placed in the ceiling of a room to monitor the position and the status of a person (standing, sitting, lying down). The sensors readings are wirelessly communicated through a microcontroller to a cloud. An intelligent system will read the sensors values from the cloud and analyses them using machine learning algorithms to predict the person behavior and status and decide whether it is a normal situation or abnormal. If an abnormal situation is concluded, then an alert with be risen on a dashboard, where a care giver can take an immediate action. The proposed system managed to give results with accuracy exceeding 90%. Results out of this project will help people with supported needed, for example elderly people, to live their life as independent as possible, without too much interference from the caregivers. This will also free the care givers and allows them to monitors more units at the same time.

Keywords: Smart home · People with supported needs · Behavior tracking · Ultrasonic sensors · Machine learning

1 Introduction

Everyone has the right to live safely and independently in the environment around them. Especially people with supported needs require to feel this independency inside their home, and that they are not continuously monitored by care givers. The advance of Internet of Thing and machine learning is pushing toward smarter homes. Houses can be safer and more comfortable, hazards and risks can be detected and reported, and occupants and caregivers can utilize their time more efficiently.

The aim of the project proposed here is to enable people with supported needs to live their lives well and independently, with least amount of intervention from the caregivers, by creating a smart home using non-intrusive sensors. The proposed system will satisfy the following criteria: Being aware of people's behavior, and track and trace them in the house. Notify caregivers when the occupant needs help or do some actions that might hurt them. Identify factors that caused some hazardous actions to occur. The assumed scenario is that there is only one permanent occupant for a single house, plus a caregiver who can intervene occasionally.

© Springer Nature Switzerland AG 2019
X. Liu et al. (Eds.): ICSOC 2018 Workshops, LNCS 11434, pp. 241–252, 2019.
https://doi.org/10.1007/978-3-030-17642-6_21

Different types of sensors (e.g. water flow, electricity flow, ultrasonic, pressure) can be used and connected to a number of Microcontrollers to help with the prediction [11]. At this stage of the project we only focus on ultrasonic sensors. All data collected from the microcontrollers will be sent wirelessly to a gateway in the house, which will send the data through a cloud to a main server for processing. The server will use data mining techniques to analyze the data to track and trace the occupant, and distinguish between normal and abnormal behaviors. This process will lead to identify situations that need attention, and predict factors that contribute to hazardous issues. The analyzed data will be visualized onto an online dashboard, enabling caregivers to monitor the current situation and to receive alerts from the system, no matter where they are, for any case that needs attention.

The main challenge of the proposed system is to preserve the privacy of the house occupants. For that no video or audio monitoring is permitted. In general, Occupants should not feel that they are monitored, for that all sensors should be seamlessly integrated and blended to normal household items. Research showed that if house occupants knew that they were monitored, their behavior would change. This is called Hawthorne effect [1, 2]. Another challenge is that the system should be able to distinguish among different people in the house, by distinguishing among their behaviors. The main behavior belongs to the occupant of the house, and any other behavior deviating from this main behavior will belong to someone else, could be the caregiver. Machine learning techniques will be used to make about the behavior.

In this paper we create a grid of ultrasonic sensors in the ceiling of a room. Each sensor covers a spot in the room to indicate the height of the occupant. All sensors collectively should track the movement of the occupant, and through the connected micro controller, the data is sent to a central unit for processing and decision making. The ultrasonic sensor that we propose to use for indoor environment is HRLV-MaxSonar-EZ0 that can detect objects between 30 cm to 5 m.

In the below sections we provide a review of previous research about smart homes for people that need support. Then we concentrate on using ultrasonic sensors to track people in the smart environment, and the decision making process using machine learning techniques. Section 3 describes the system architecture proposed here and the discussion about the results. Finally, the conclusion is in Sect. 4.

2 Smart Homes for People of Supported Needs

Many projects were investigating the usage of IoT and different types of sensors to create smart homes to suit certain requirements. [3] tries to setup a security alarm system for elderly that involves cameras to sense the motion if there is any abnormality, where all data are stored locally for future analysis. The project in [4] is trying to create a smart home for elderly people to live an independent life, which involves camera for facial recognition and PIR (Passive Infrared) sensors for motion detection. In [5], in addition of monitoring the subject's movement using cameras and infrared sensors, they also introduce different sensors, such as pressure sensor mats, stove temperature sensors, switches on doors, and bed sensor, to predict the normal and abnormal activities of the subject under observation. [6] proposes a smart location tracking using an array of pressure sensors under the floor tiles. The size of the tile is 60×60 cm and each is equipped with 4 pressure sensors on the corners. In [7] a wearable smart sensors are used to detect the fall of a person and distinguish it from the normal activities. Some of the sensors used in their system are accelerometer and chardiotachometer to estimate the impact of the fall.

2.1 Ultrasonic Sensors in Smart Homes

Ultrasonic sensors detect how far objects are from the current point by sending ultrasonic waves toward the objects and measure the time of the returned wave to estimate the distance. Ultrasonic sensors are used in varieties of applications including motion detection, robotics, navigation systems and people detection.

In smart homes, ultrasonic sensors are used either as part of their intelligent monitoring system, or as a standalone monitoring system. Ultrasonic sensors can be mounted on ceiling and/or wall [8]. [9] claims to give an accurate 3D tracking of human activities in a living area using mathematical models to predict the position. Their proposed system uses more than 300 ultrasonic sensors in $3.5 \times 3.5 \times 2.7$ m room, which makes it very expensive and it impractical to monitor people without noticing. In [4] ultrasonic sensors are used to predict how full the trash bin is, as part of the house intelligent system. In [10], a 6×6 ultrasonic grid is installed on the ceiling of approximately 4×4 room to monitor the movement of a child as a child-mother distance and child-stranger distance. Kalman filter is used to track the direction of the movement of the child taking into consideration the last two readings from the sensors.

The sensitivity of the ultrasonic sensors is affected by many factors such as Temperature and high noise [6]. For the work presented here, the room temperature is assumed to be moderate and there is no high noise situation.

2.2 Mining Sensors Data

The history of all the events captured by the sensors at a particular time at a specific location can be used to discover activities, abnormal behavior and to predict the next actions that the resident intent to do [11]. In the following section, we will describe some research that has been done in this area.

Given a raw sensor events tagged with a date and time, [12] applies a priory algorithm [13] to get the most frequently occurring sequences of events that happened in a house. It then identifies the temporal relations between two events as defined in [14]: before, contains, overlaps, meets, starts, started-by, finishes, finished-by and equal relations. The probability of an event A occurs given that we have observed the occurrence of event B is calculated by the total number of times A has any temporal relations with B divided by the total number of times event B occurred. [12] uses the probability theory to calculate the likelihood of event A occurring based on every event that has occurred on the day until that point in time. It also calculates the mean and standard deviations of event A occurred throughout the resident's history. An event is considered abnormal if the likelihood of that event is close to 0 and its frequency is greater than mean + 2 standard deviations.

They then evaluated their algorithm on a real and synthetic dataset. In the synthetic data, all of the expected anomalies are detected and no false positives are reported. In the real data, no anomalies are reported because it does not contain anomalous event. Unfortunately, we do not really know how well their algorithm performed since they do not explain what anomalous event they have introduced to the synthetic dataset or how did they generate the events in the real and synthetic datasets. Furthermore, from the snippets of their raw sensor events, it seems that they have placed the sensors to some objects in the room.

Many researchers have developed Hidden Markov Model (HMM) to detect anomalous behavior observed in a day using different set of features such as the tempo and timing of the events [15], and the analysis of the resident's walking trajectories [16]. Given those features and a sequence of events observed so far, the model has to first predict what are all the possible next events. If the next observed event is not in the list of possible events, the event will be marked as abnormal. Because state duration is not explicitly modeled, [17] found that those models fail to detect abnormal behavior caused by a person performing an activity longer or shorter than usual.

Although [15] and [16] models can accurately predict anomalous behavior caused by a resident performing an activity in the order that is different than what was previously observed, they cannot distinguish which activity sequence is abnormal when the order of activities is identical but the duration of one or more activities vary. Hence, [17] have developed a HMM where the state duration is included as a state variable and they called it ESD-HMM.

They then evaluated their ESD-HMM model on a single person performing the following activities in a kitchen in any order they want: preparing cereal, making toast, preparing dinner, cooking dinner, and cooking a bacon and eggs breakfast. The discrete observations are stove, bench, sink, fridge and door. Undefined is used for all other observations. Those activities are chosen because it highlights the fact that a resident might visited the same areas in the room to perform two different types of activities. For instance, to prepare cereal and toast, the sequence is [door, fridge, bench, sink, bench, fridge, door]. We can only distinguish them by looking at the time spent at kitchen's bench—it takes longer to prepare a toast than a cereal. Their evaluation found that ESD-HMM can predict a person's activity with 100% accuracy while HMM can only obtain 81.43% accuracy. [17] also evaluated how both models can detect anomalous behavior given 24 normal sequence of observations but the activity's duration is either shorter or longer than the normal ones. They found that ESD-HMM can reliably distinguish normal and abnormal sequence, better than the HMM model.

[18] creates a Relational Markov Networks model to accurately predict the location of a person based on: (a) temporal information such as time of the day and duration; (b) geographic evidence such as the types of business and whether they are near a commonly visited place like restaurant or store; (c) sequential information on which activities usually followed by a certain activity and how often those activities occurred while the user is at the same place; and (d) context information such as the number of different homes and workplaces the user has.

They have tested their model and basic HMM on 2 datasets: (1) location traces of a single person over period of four months and (2) location traces of five people over period of a week. They found that their Relational Markov Networks achieved 7% error rate on the first dataset and 18% error rate on the second dataset. Their model accuracy is improved when they trained their model based on the information from more subjects. The model created using basic HMM performed worse by 10% than the Relational Markov Networks on both datasets. Although this model was designed to identify a person's outdoor location, the authors suggested that it can also be used to estimate the person's indoor location and activities, and should perform better than the generative HMM.

From all the above, we can see that the essential features for accurately predicting an abnormal behavior are the sensor values, temporal information such as time, duration, tempo, trajectories, and the location where the event takes place. Through those features, we can not only track a person's location but also identify their activities and determining whether that activity is abnormal.

3 Proposed System Architecture

The system architecture is proposed as a mesh of ultrasonic sensors on the smart house ceiling. Sensors are wired to small microcontroller boards enabled with WiFi. The proposed system uses Arduino ESP32 microcontrollers for this purpose. Such devices send the data from the sensor grid to a database on a server over the network. A machine learning system is used to look for events or patterns on the data to describe different behaviors of the occupant in the house. There is a web interface frontend installed on the server publicly available, for a caregiver to access and monitor. Figure 1 show the general architecture of the proposed system.

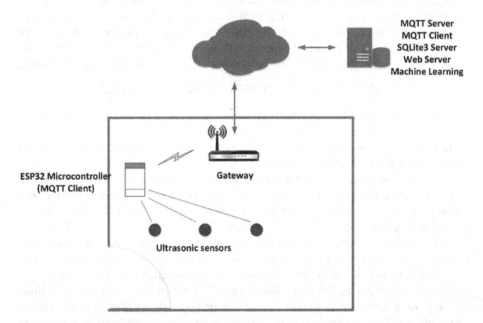

Fig. 1. General architecture of the proposed system. The readings from the ultrasonic sensors are directed through the microcontrollers to the server for processing.

Data from sensors can give static and dynamic information from the environment. The first one is when a sensor is activated due to the event on the presence of a person, and their location can be computed; the later refers to patterns, a series of these events measured through time, which define behavior patterns, such as walking, running, or sitting. Behavior patterns will later be classified as normal, abnormal, no activity, sitting, standing, laying, etc.

Mosquitto, an open-source local MQTT server (usually called an MQTT broker), is installed and setup on the server, and used to route the sensors' readings from the Arduino ESP32 microcontrollers (MQTT Clients) to a database. Later, Weka is used for the machine learning training to decide on the best model to make decision about the behaviors. A web-based dashboard is also created on the server to show the activities of the house occupant, and can be accessed by the caregiver to monitor these activities.

MB1003 EZ0 ultrasonic sensors are placed on the ceiling with 60 cm apart from each other on a grid, as they were tested to have a 30 cm radius reach. [19] provides a detailed study for optimum distribution of ultrasonic sensors in smart homes, their locations, their angles and the distances among them. Readings come from the sensor 10-bit ADC convertor. Analog voltage bits (0 to 1023) can be read directly and give a proportional distance from the sensor to an object in mm. Each bit corresponds to 5 mm.

In this prototype, as shown in Fig. 2, we only used 9 sensors to cover the area of interest, which is the grey area shown in Fig. 2, where most of the activities of the occupant happen. The 9 sensors are connected to the microcontroller, which is then connected to the LAN using its WiFi adapter. The microcontroller sets up a session with the broker using MQTT protocol and publishes the signals periodically to the broker. Signals are concatenated and published on an MQTT topic.

The analog inputs on the microcontroller are used with sampling rate of 1 sample/s. An MQTT client, coded with Python, is also running on the same server where the broker sits. It sets up a session with the broker, subscribes to the topic where sensor signals are published, and stores them on a SQLite3 database on the server itself. Topic payload is a string containing the sensor values concatenated in the following format:

$$1299:976:1296:1328:976:1166:384:912:1313$$

These values represent an estimation of the distance from a sensor to an object, which are functions to the analog it values.

Once the Client receives a new message on the topic, a timestamp is generated and included with the data sample.

For data mining and decision making, the experimentation came in three different parts: (1) Track location, (2) Predicting Activity and (3) Predicting Behavior. For tracking location, no machine learning is required, one may know the position of a person directly from the values of the sensors.

For Activity Prediction, activities are measured on trajectories on 3 sensors and synthetic data is generated based on those values. In this research, we try to study how accurate the prediction will be for the activity and the abnormal behavior. The inputs of the intelligent system are the observations that are detected at a certain point in time, they are not a sequence of events. The evaluation has shown that it is possible to accurately predict a resident's activity and detect an anomaly behavior based only on the sensor value, duration on each sensor and the range time of day.

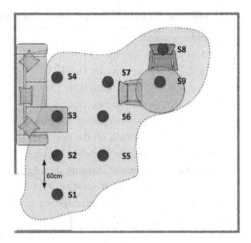

Fig. 2. Sensors layout. 9 ultrasonic sensors are used to cover the grey area in the room, where most of the occupant activities happen.

Two different data sets are used with different sets. For the first set, the behaviours are "abnormal", "normal" and "no activity". For the second set, the activities are "no activity", "sitting", "standing", "laying", "walking" and "running" for the second one. Each training data set has 20 attributes (Time, S1, ..., S9, Duration Sensor 1, ..., Duration Sensor 9 and Behavior). First set has 1953 instances and second one has 1486.

Actual sensor readings were used to define occupant states and Table 1 shows the combination of these 9 sensors to determine on the activities. From the change of state of sensors over time activities are defined. "Duration Sensor" attribute is used to capture, in second, how long a sensor state remains unchanged. This is used to show for how long each sensor holds a value during an activity. Behaviour is the class attribute in both data sets, it classifies the readings into activities. The time attribute of sensor readings is not the exact time, but a time range, which ranges from seconds to minutes to hours depending on rules for each sensor reading a different time is displayed.

Different classifiers were run through Weka, a data mining open source tool, focusing on accuracy, recall, precision and ROC area.

Normal activity and No activity have more instances compared to abnormal activity when the number of instances splits into activities. This is because a room is more likely to have no activity, or a person is more likely to be carrying out normal activity compared to abnormal activity.

Figure 3 represents how each type of instance for the class attribute (Activities) are divided. Most instances are categorized as No activity, Standing and Sitting. Laying, Walking and Running have less compared to the others. The reason for this distribution is because a person is more likely to sit and stand in a room and there is a high chance of no activity happening in the room. A person is less likely laying, walking or running in the room.

Table 1. The observations used in the proposed smart system

Sensors	Threshold	Activity
S1, S2, S5, S7	850 < x < 940	No activity
S3, S4	730 < x < 760	No activity on couch
S9	630 < x < 650	No activity on table
S6, S8	720 < x < 740	No activity on chair
S1	815 < x < 835	Abnormal, laying on ground
S8, S9	600 < x < 625	Abnormal, on the desk
S8, S9	100 < x < 110	Abnormal, standing on chair
S9	30 < x < 55	Abnormal, standing on table
S1	265 < x < 280	Abnormal if duration > 15 min, standing
S3, S4	665 < x < 685	Abnormal if duration > 4 h, laying on couch
S1	265 < x < 280	Abnormal
S5 (2 s later)	265 < x < 280	
S1	265 < x < 280	Abnormal, running
S5 (1 s later)	265 < x < 280	
S1, S8	430 < x < 440	Normal, sitting in chair
S6, S8	430 < x < 440	Normal, sitting on chair
S1	265 < x < 280	Normal, duration < 15 min
S1	230 < x < 280	Normal, walking
S5 (2 s later)	230 < x < 280	
S3, S4	665 < x < 685	Normal, laying on couch
S3, S4	515 < x < 540	Normal, sitting on couch
S1	265 < x < 280	Normal, between 6 am to 11 pm
S5 (2 s later)	265 < x < 280	
S1	600 < x < 625	Normal, duration < 15 min, sitting on floor

The values produced by some sensors can be used to clearly distinguish the resident's activities and behaviours, which allow data classification and create an accurate model. For instance, as shown in Fig. 4, the abnormal activities for S9 can be easily detected if the sensors produced a low value as it signifies that the resident is standing on the table. The majority of the sensor values are high because most of the time there is no one under that sensor (i.e. no activity), which also contributes to the false negatives. Figure 5 shows that the laying down activity is the easiest to detect as its produced the longest observed duration. The different colours differentiate each different type of instance in the class attribute. From the data we can see the colours are not overlapping with each other that much and there are only a few colours that cross into other territories.

Weka is used to create a model and train it using the datasets. Validation and test dataset are used to evaluate the performance of our trained model. The results are combined to check the integrity of the entire dataset and whether the classifier/s are providing accurate results. Cross validation is used to evaluate the predictive models.

No.	Label	Count	Weight

Name: Behaviour   Type: Nominal
Missing: 0 (0%)   Distinct: 6   Unique: 0 (0%)

No.	Label	Count	Weight
1	No Activity	262	262.0
2	Standing	304	304.0
3	Laying	180	180.0
4	Sitting	427	427.0
5	Walking	193	193.0
6	Running	120	120.0

Fig. 3. The classification of class attribute activities

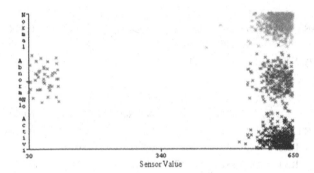

Fig. 4. Scatter plot of instances classified as normal, abnormal and no activities based on the sensor value observed in S9

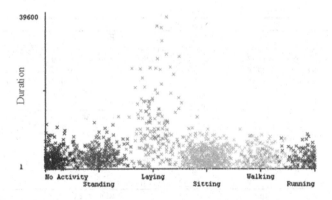

Fig. 5. Scatter plot of instances classified as no activity, standing, laying, sitting, walking and running based on the duration value observed in S1

The top 3 classifiers chosen to be compared for the first and second dataset are PART, Lazy IBK and Lazy KStar. The IBK model shows the best percentages of correctly classified instances for the first dataset at classifying behaviours, as shown in Table 2. ROC area is found out to have a very high average. Training, Validation and Test results for Data Set A are also shown in the table. Meanwhile, Lazy KStar is the best classifier for the second dataset, as shown in Table 3

Table 2. The top 3 classifiers ART, Lazy IBK and Lazy KStar for data set A

Training Data Set A

	CCI %	rms error	ROC Area		
			No Activity	Abnormal	Normal
PART	86.2471	0.2599	0.987	0.942	0.927
Lazy IBK	87.1795	0.2877	0.972	0.899	0.88
Lazy KSTAR	86.014	0.293	0.989	0.894	0.941

Validation Data Set A

	CCI %	rms error	ROC Area		
			No Activity	Abnormal	Normal
PART	83.7349	0.2699	0.983	0.918	0.914
Lazy IBK	87.0482	0.2865	0.961	0.883	0.882
Lazy KSTAR	84.3373	0.3073	0.988	0.869	0.939

Test Data Set A

	CCI %	rms error	ROC Area		
			No Activity	Abnormal	Normal
PART	84.4311	0.2773	0.982	0.927	0.914
Lazy IBK	86.2275	0.3011	0.978	0.912	0.877
Lazy KSTAR	84.4311	0.3047	0.983	0.887	0.939

Table 3. The top 3 classifiers ART, Lazy IBK and Lazy KStar for data set B.

Training Data Set B								
	CCI %	rms error	ROC Area					
			No Activity	Standing	Laying	Sitting	Walking	Running
PART	83.828	0.1907	0.945	0.992	0.999	0.999	0.842	0.927
Lazy IBK	81.9857	0.2438	0.96	0.834	1	0.926	0.628	0.803
Lazy KSTAR	89.9693	0.1746	0.987	0.991	1	0.997	0.959	0.931

Validation Data Set B								
	CCI %	rms error	ROC Area					
			No Activity	Standing	Laying	Sitting	Walking	Running
PART	85.8268	0.1969	0.967	1	1	1	0.928	0.783
Lazy IBK	79.9213	0.2543	0.985	0.861	1	0.926	0.701	0.673
Lazy KSTAR	89.7638	0.1769	0.991	0.998	1	0.999	0.944	0.813

Test Data Set B								
	CCI %	rms error	ROC Area					
			No Activity	Standing	Laying	Sitting	Walking	Running
PART	87.451	0.1718	0.965	1	1	1	0.954	0.852
Lazy IBK	79.2157	0.2626	0.98	0.862	1	0.911	0.664	0.668
Lazy KSTAR	89.8039	0.179	0.989	0.999	1	0.998	0.953	0.978

4 Conclusion

In this paper we proposed a smart house for residents of supported needs to allow them live as independent as possible by their own, with minimum interference from care-givers. Several IoT sensors are proposed to monitor the activities and the behaviour of the resident, including ultrasonic, pressure, water flow and electricity flow. To preserve the privacy of the resident and to make sure that their behaviour stays as normal as possible, all these sensors should be hidden and blended with the surrounding envi-ronment. In addition, no cameras or any recording mechanisms are used. The readings from different sensors are collected through microcontrollers and wirelessly commu-nicated to a server over a cloud, where processing using data mining algorithms is used to determine on the behaviour of the occupant. To monitor these activities and beha-viours, a web-based dashboard is created, when caregivers can access. If an abnormal behaviour is detected, then an alert will notify the caregiver to take action.

To prove the proposed concept, the paper showed a prototype of the system using ultrasonic sensors installed on the ceiling of a room. 9 sensors are installed in a room to cover the areas that most of the activities take place. Readings from the sensors are published through Arduino ESP32 microcontroller via MQTT protocol to a MQTT broker, and then stored in a SQLite3 database. For the data mining part, three different parts are considered: (1) Track the location, which does not need any datamining, since it can be determined directly from the sensors, (2) Predicting Activity and (3) Predicting Behaviour. The time attribute is also considered to predict the activities and behaviours.

Different activities are considered: "no activity", "sitting", "standing", "laying", "walking" and "running", and different behaviours are considered: "abnormal", "normal" and "no activity". Datamining algorithms are applied using Weka to deter-mine the activities and behaviours. For behaviours classification, the top 3 classifiers that give more than 84% accuracy are PART, Lazy IBK and Lazy KStar. For activities classification, again same top 3 classifiers give accuracy more than 80%.

The next step in this project, is to include other types of sensors, such as pressure sensors, water flow sensors, electricity sensors, and other sensors, to increase the accuracy of the prediction process for the activities and behaviours of the house occupant. Also, by studying the activities of the occupant we should be able to dis-tinguish between the current house occupant and another person, such as the caregiver.

References

1. Steinmetz, J., Xu, Q., Fishbach, A., Zhang, Y.: Being observed magnifies action. J. Pers. Soc. Psychol. **111**(6), 852–865 (2016)
2. Adair, J.G.: The hawthorne effect: a reconsideration of the methodological artifact. J. Appl. Psychol. **69**(2), 334–345 (1984)
3. Ansari, A.N., Sedky, M., Sharma, S.: An internet of things approach for motion detection using raspberry Pi. In: Proceedings of 2015 International Conference on Intelligent Computing and Internet of Things, Harbin, China (2015)

4. Lee, C., Park, S., Jung, Y., Lee, Y., Mathews, M.: Internet of things: technology to enable the elderly. In: The Second IEEE International Conference on Robotic Computing (IRC), Laguna Hills, CA, US, pp. 358–362 (2018)
5. Demiris, G., et al.: Smart Home Sensors for the Elderly: A Model for Participatory Formative Evaluation, Alan Institute for Artificial Intelligence (2006)
6. Lee, T.S., Kwon, Y.M., Kim, H.G.: Smart location tracking system using FSR (Force Sensing Resistor). In: ICAT 2004 International Conference on Automotive Technology, Istanbul – Turkey (2004)
7. Wang, J., Zhang, Z., Li, B., Lee, S., Sherratt, R.S.: An enhanced fall detection system for elderly person monitoring using consumer home networks. IEEE Trans. Consum. Electron. **60**(1), 23–29 (2014)
8. Nadee, C., Chamnongthai, K.: Ultrasonic array sensors for monitoring of human fall detection. In: 12th International Conference on Electrical Engineering/Electronics, Computer, Telecommunications and Information Technology (ECTI-CON). Hua Hin, Thailand (2015)
9. Nishida, Y., Aizawa, H., Hori, T., Hoffman, N.H., Kanade, T., Kakikura, M.: 3D ultra-sonic tagging system for observing human activity. In: Proceedings 2003 IEEE/RSJ International Conference on Intelligent Robots and Systems. Las Vegas, NV, USA (2003)
10. Cheng, R., Heinzelman, W., Sturge-Apple, M., Ignjatovic, Z.: A motion-tracking ultrasonic sensor array for behavioral monitoring. IEEE Sens. J. **12**(3), 707–712 (2012)
11. Gottfried, B., Guesgen, H.W., Hübner, S.: Spatiotemporal reasoning for smart homes. In: Augusto, J.C., Nugent, C.D., (eds.) Designing Smart Homes, pp. 16–34. Springer, Heidelberg (2006). https://doi.org/10.1007/11788485_2
12. Vikramaditya, J., Diane, C.: Anomaly detection using temporal data mining in a smart home environment. Methods Inf. Med. **47**, 70–75 (2008). https://doi.org/10.3414/ME9103
13. Agrawal, R., Srikant, R.: Mining sequential patterns. In: Yu, P.S., Chen, A.L.P. Proceedings of the Eleventh International Conference on Data Engineering, Taipei, Taiwan, pp. 3–14. IEEE Computer Society, 6–10 March 1995
14. Allen, J.F., Ferguson, G.: Actions and events in interval temporal logic. J. Logic Comput. **4** (5), 531–579 (1994)
15. Brand, M., Kettnaker, V.: Discovery and segmentation of activities in video. IEEE Trans. Pattern Anal. Mach. Intell. **22**(8), 844–851 (2000)
16. Nguyen, N.T., Bui, H.H., Venkatesh, S., West, G.: Recognising and monitoring high-level behaviours in complex spatial environments. In: IEEE Computer Society Conf. Computer Vision and Pattern Recognition, Wisconsin, USA (2003)
17. Lühr, S., Venkatesh, S., West, G., Bui, H.H.: Explicit state duration HMM for abnormality detection in sequences of human activity. In: Zhang, C., Guesgen, H.W., Yeap, W.-K. (eds.) PRICAI 2004. LNCS (LNAI), vol. 3157, pp. 983–984. Springer, Heidelberg (2004). https://doi.org/10.1007/978-3-540-28633-2_125
18. Liao, L., Fox, D., Kautz, H.: Location-based activity recognition using relational Markov networks. In: Proceedings of the International Joint Conference on Artificial Intelligence, pp. 773–778. Professional Book Center, Edinburgh, Scotland (2005)
19. Pham, V.T., Qiu, Q., Wai, A.A.P., Biswas, J.: Application of ultrasonic sensors in a smart environment. Pervasive Mob. Comput. **3**(2), 180–207 (2007)

An Efficient In-Memory R-Tree Construction Scheme for Spatio-Temporal Data Stream

Ting Zhang, Lianghuai Yang$^{(\boxtimes)}$, Donghai Shen, and Yulei Fan

School of Computer Science and Technology,
Zhejiang University of Technology, Hangzhou 310014, China
yanglh@zjut.edu.cn

Abstract. In this paper, we proposed an efficient R-tree construction method by bulk loading over spatial-temporal data stream. The core idea is to partition spatial-temporal data stream into time windows and construct an R-tree for each time window. In each time window, we parallelized space partitioning and data stream reception during R-tree construction; and then we adopted sorting-based bulk loading scheme to optimize R-tree construction, which avoided unnecessary synchronization overhead and accelerated the R-tree construction. In addition, to reduce the sorting cost of R-tree bulk loading, sampling-based space partitioning scheme was introduced. Theoretical analysis and experiments demonstrated the effectiveness of our proposed method.

Keywords: R-tree · Data stream · In-memory index · Big data

1 Introduction

With the rapid development of location-based services (LBS), location aware services, such as traffic monitoring, child safety, and friend search, play an increasingly important role in daily life. The spatio-temporal data arrive continuously with high arrival rate and massive data size with multiple attributes, and we call them spatio-temporal data streams. LBS applications require new query processing techniques to deal with both spatial and temporal domains in real-time. Indexes are the infrastructure to expedite query process.

For spatial indexing, many scholars have proposed various bulk construction methods, especially R-tree, but these methods are still not adequate when processing big streaming data. They usually consider only static data or apply bulk updating to existing spatial indexes. However, for spatio-temporal stream data, they may be disordered or unlimited, and should be handled in real-time for massive spatio-temporal data stream. As such, this paper proposes an efficient in-memory R-tree construction scheme. Our main contributions are as follows:

1. A novel bulk loading algorithm called DSortLoad is proposed based on the idea of double-sorting data within time window. It constructs R-tree index by firstly building an R-tree skeleton and assigning keys to the tree later;

© Springer Nature Switzerland AG 2019
X. Liu et al. (Eds.): ICSOC 2018 Workshops, LNCS 11434, pp. 253–265, 2019.
https://doi.org/10.1007/978-3-030-17642-6_22

2. A bulk loading algorithm named SSortLoad is proposed, which sorts sampled time window data. It uses sorted sampling data to derive the spatio-temporal data partitioning scheme, so it is much faster in construction than DSortLoad.

2 Related Work

Some commonly used spatial indexes are R-tree [1], grid index [2], k-d tree index [3], quadtree index [4], and variants of R-tree such as R^+-tree [5] and R*-tree [6]. Among them, R-tree is the most widely used one. The Packed R-tree [8] is the first R-tree with bulk loading scheme, and much progress has been made since then [7]. It sorts the spatial objects based on a certain dimension coordinate. Objects are filled into R-tree leaf nodes in turn. So the spatial utilization of packed R-tree is almost 100%. Kamel and Ibrahim [9] proposed an R-tree bulk constructing scheme based on space filling curve Hilbert. It uses the space filling curve to assign Hilbert values to the space objects, and sorts the spatial objects by Hilbert values and fills the R-tree leaf nodes with the spatial objects in order. Leutenegger et al. [10] proposed a STR algorithm called Sort-Tile-Recursive algorithm which is closer to the Packed R-tree, but it takes a step forward. When partitioning, various dimensions are considered comprehensively, and each time roughly partitioned by one dimension, thus it can get a good result in the global scope. García et al. [11] proposed the TGS algorithm, which is characterized by top-down and greedy split which is suitable for irregular datasets. However, the R-tree construction speed of TGS is slower than others, because of its top-down and greedy split characteristics. In addition, the VAMSplit R-tree [11], which was proposed by White and Jain, is similar to TGS. It used a top-down greedy dataset split scheme as well, however, in each step, the construction algorithm determines the split dimensions and split positions through the maximum variance, and then splits dataset according to the selected dimensions and positions.

   However, with massive spatio-temporal data, the traditional stand-alone systems can no longer afford management and computation. Tan et al. [12] proposed CloST, a distributed spatio-temporal data analysis and storage system based on Hadoop, which include three layers storage called bucket, region and block. Cary et al. [13] proposed R-tree constructing scheme over MapReduce framework, which consists of three steps: grouping data objects by partition functions, constructing a single small R-tree for each group of data, and merging all small R-trees into a large R-tree. Zhong et al. [14] proposed a distributed spatio-temporal index, which includes disk-based MDR^+-tree index and key-based B-tree index for high throughput access and near real-time data retrieval. [15] studied spatio-temporal query patterns under Hadoop, which included a geospatial data organization method, a two-layer distributed index framework, and a query processing architecture that combines distributed index with MapReduce; they also implemented a distributed storage prototype system exHDFS [16] for storing large scale temporal data. Eladwy et al. [17] proposed a distributed spatio-temporal system for processing and storing satellite data called SHAHED. This system partitions the temporal attribute into year, month and day, then partitions the spatial attribute by a novel multi-resolution quadtree method, and finally encodes the partitioned grids by the Z-curve. Li et al. [18] uses Hilbert curve to encode data objects, and implements the R-tree bulk construction method over MapReduce. Similarly, Liu [19] uses Hilbert curve and MapReduce to study the parallel construction method of spatial index, and generates the spatial partition function by random sampling.

Nishimura et al. [20] proposed the concept of an IndexLayer on HBase called MD-HBase. MD-HBase exploits linearization to encode the spatial data, and then uses the k-d tree or quadtree to partition the regions into conceptual subspace, finally extracts the longest common prefix as the key of the regions and stores the data in HBase. Wang et al. [21] proposed the SICC index, which is R-tree variant for indexing less overhead boundary segments while ensuring query efficiency. Ma et al. [22] proposed a three-layer index called UQE-Index based on the spatio-temporal characteristics of massive Internet data. It uses B^+ tree to index time intervals, and uses k-d tree to dynamically partition data in time intervals and index them with the R-tree. Cai et al. [23] proposed a distributed storage system DITIR that supports efficient trajectory data insertion and real-time time range query. DITIR extracts first few layers of R-tree, which is constructed in the previous time window, to achieve efficient indexing of high-speed data streams. However, this method is based on the assumption that the key distribution of input data tuples will not change too much over a period.

3   Problem Statement

Spatial data stream is continuous, real-time and has unlimited scale, and each stream tuple has location information. To support efficient retrieval related to location, a suitable spatial index needs to be devised. Here, spatial data stream is partitioned into continuous time windows. For each time window, all data is indexed by constructing an inner R-tree. In this process, the time-window-oriented bulk R-tree construction method needs to improve throughput and reduce latency by considering characteristics of spatial stream data, so as to quickly complete R-tree index construction and provide near real-time querying.

W_1, W_2, ..., W_k in Fig. 1 represent time windows for receiving spatial stream tuples. $T_{dealy\text{-}time}$ denotes the time required to build R-tree index for all stream tuples in a time window, that is, the construction delay. In order to provide near real-time query, $T_{dealy\text{-}time}$ is desired to be as short as possible. $T_{wait\text{-}time}$ denotes the time interval from the completion of R-tree construction of previous time window to the start of next time window. R-tree index construction method needs to ensure that $T_{wait\text{-}time}$ is greater than or equal to zero.

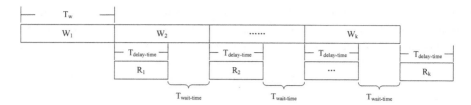

Fig. 1. Receiving spatial stream tuples and construct R-tree index

4   Novel and Improved R-Tree Index Construction Scheme

We denote the ith time window W_i at t_i: $W_i = \{<t_{ik}, lon_{ik}, lat_{ik}> \mid k = 1,2,\ldots, |W_i|\}$, where t_{ik} is the time stamp of a stream tuple, lon_{ik} and lat_{ik} are longitude and latitude of a spatial object respectively, $|W_i|$ refers to the number of tuples in W_i. In this paper, a two-level index structure is assumed for stream data; the top-level is a B^+ tree with window timestamp as the key, and its leaf node points to an inner R-tree of time window W_i. This section focuses on the construction of the inner R-tree (Fig. 2).

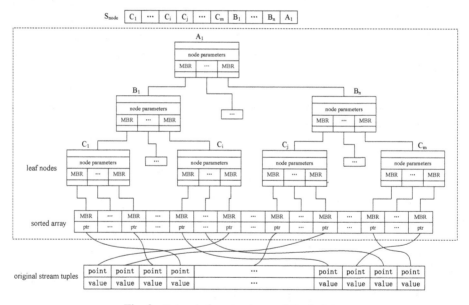

Fig. 2. R-tree index structure and its skeleton

4.1   DSortLoad Algorithm

The first solution proposed is a bulk loading R-tree construction algorithm based on double sortings of time window data (DSortLoad). In DSortLoad, we firstly select the horizontal dimension (longitude) as the sorting criterion to perform a full sorting of spatial data in time window. The specific process is to use the multiple data fragment sorting and a merge sorting in time window, to complete full sorting of spatial data in the entire time window. The next step is to calculate the structure of R-tree index and then apply for storage resources needed to build R-tree skeleton. Because we can know the number of all stream tuples when the current time window ends, so we can start the calculation after it immediately. Since DSortLoad is based on the STR method for R-tree bulk loading, we will also perform horizontal group after sorting stream tuples, and complete group vertical sorting with latitude as sorting criterion in each group. When group vertical sorting of spatial stream tuples, the calculation of R-tree structure and resources allocation of R-tree construction are completed, we can parallel fill in leaf node layer of R-tree and update MBR information of all nodes with stream tuples, from bottom to top and left to right. The concrete construction process is shown in Fig. 3. This method is divided into five stages: P1 (horizontal sort), P2 (calculate structure), P3 (construct skeleton), P4 (group vertical sort), and P5 (bulk loading).

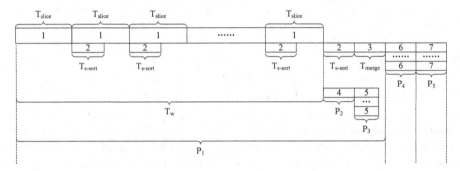

Fig. 3. Description of DSortLoad

Horizontal Sort

The P1 stage divides time window into equal-length time slices. T_{slice} represents the duration of each slice. After each slice is cached, quick sort method is used to complete sorting based on horizontal dimension of stream tuples. In Fig. 3, $T_{s\text{-}sort}$ indicates sorting time of each slice. T_{slice} is generally larger than $T_{s\text{-}sort}$. At the end of the entire time window, a number of sorted slices are formed, then merge sorting can be performed. T_{merge} indicates the time of merge sorting.

Calculate Structure

When the time window is finished, R-tree structure parameters can be calculated. This process can be executed in parallel with horizontal sorting of the last data slice within the time window and the merge sorting of all slices. The parameters that need to be calculated at this stage include: the height of the R-tree, the number of internal nodes, the number of leaf nodes, and the number of child nodes of each node. In addition, we need to divide stream tuple arrays horizontally and perform vertical sorting operation on stream tuples in each group, so we need to calculate grouping length according to the number of stream tuples and the capacity of each node. According to the calculation results, we can know the total number of nodes in the tree, and then we can apply for an array of nodes with required length in memory.

Construct Skeleton

This process constructs R-tree skeleton structure in parallel from left to right and from bottom to top. Through calculating R-tree structure parameters, we can determine the size of R-tree, the position of each node in R-tree, and the relationship between upper and lower levels, which can helps us construct the skeleton of R-tree. In addition, it should be noted that the spatial range of each R-tree node is described by the MBR. Although we do not know the MBR of each R-tree node, it does not affect the R-tree skeleton construction, the calculation of MBR can be put into the bulk loading stage of R-tree construction. We need to initialize node parameters and link nodes, but leaf nodes are not filled with stream tuples in this stage.

Group Vertical Sort

When merge sorting on spatial stream tuples in the time window is completed, we also need to group data horizontally and sort stream tuples in each group according to vertical dimension, called group vertical sort. The group vertical sort stage of stream tuples needs to be divided into two processes in practice: horizontal group and group vertical sort. Through the horizontal sort stage, we obtain a sorted array with length r. Each inner R-tree node has b child nodes, and each leaf node have b stream tuples. All tuples should be divided into $\sqrt{r/b}$ groups on average, so each group contains $b * \sqrt{r/b}$ stream tuples. Since all tuples are already in order, we only need to mark the location of each $b * \sqrt{r/b}$ tuple to complete the horizontal group process of stream tuples. For tuples in each group, we sort it by quick sort according to its vertical dimension coordinate value (latitude value). The process of each group is independent of each other. Therefore, even if we concurrently sort each group of the entire stream tuple array, we can guarantee the correctness of the final result. In addition, in group vertical sort, different groups need to be sorted in different order. Tuples that belong to different groups but have adjacent subscripts can also close to each other in spatial position. Therefore, in the process of R-tree bulk loading, we only need to take b stream tuples to fill in R-tree leaf nodes in turn.

Bulk Loading

The bulk loading process logically operates nodes from left to right and bottom to top, as well as obtains stream tuples to complete the construction of the entire R-tree. We divide the R-tree construction into two processes: leaf nodes filling process and MBR updating process. Through double sortings, different groups are sorted in ascending or descending order according to their positions, so that different stream tuple groups have been stored in the array in sequence, then the leaf nodes filling process only needs to assemble every b stream tuples into a leaf node. Since the range of stream tuples corresponding to each leaf node has been determined, and loading process of each leaf node is independent of each other, so they can also be processed in parallel. After filling data into leaf nodes, we need to update MBR information of leaf nodes. This process logically updates each node from bottom to top and left to right.

4.2 SSortLoad Algorithm

The second algorithm is bulk loading R-tree construction algorithm based on sorting sampling data of time window (SSortLoad), as shown in Fig. 4. In general, data distribution can be approximated by sampling data. Therefore, we can use sampling data to formulate grouping rules in advance, so that stream tuples can be divided into different groups according to established grouping rules in data receiving process.

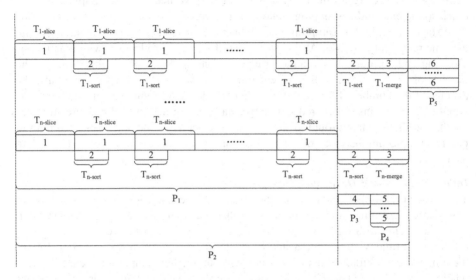

Fig. 4. Description of SSortLoad

Data Sampling

We plan to use sampling data to formulate grouping strategy, but the grouping strategy needs to be calculated before we use the SSortLoad algorithm to construct R-tree. In this paper, the process of system startup is divided into three stages: cold start of sampling data, sorting sampling data, and continuous sampling with dynamic adjustment of grouping strategy. Throughout the system, we use a reservoir sampling algorithm to sample continuously arriving spatial data stream. The whole process is shown in Fig. 5.

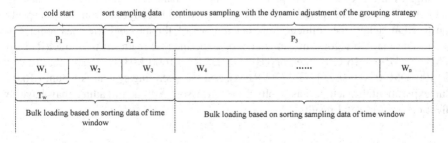

Fig. 5. Overall running processes of system

The first stage is cold start of sampling data, and the time range is $[0, t_{full}]$, where t_{full} means that enough samples data have been collected. In this stage, we first use DSortLoad algorithm to process data in time window. When the system starts running, we first apply for a sample array of length k, which is used to accept longitude values of sampled data. And then, we only need to store first k stream tuples in the array according to the order they arrived. The second stage is sorting sampling data, and the time range is $(t_{full}, t_{build}]$, where t_{build} indicates when grouping strategy initialization is completed. Before we formulate grouping strategy, we need to sort sampling data by quick sort to ensure that grouping strategy can be completed simply and efficiently. The third stage is continuous sampling with dynamic adjustment of grouping strategy, and the time range is (t_{build}, ∞). At this stage, two things need to be deal with: continuous sampling and formulating dynamic grouping strategy. We will roughly estimate the number of stream tuples in the current time window. In the estimation, we take the average of the number of tuples in first c time windows as predictive value in next time window. It maintains an ordered sampling data queue in memory. When stream tuples handler needs to obtain grouping strategy, it only needs to obtain groups according to predicted tuple numbers of current window and node capacity from sorted sampling data.

Data Reception and Horizontal Group
The time window that starts earlier than t_{build} will be loaded in R-tree according to DSortLoad algorithm, and the time window that starts later than t_{build} will be loaded in R-tree according to SSortLoad algorithm. Then we will describe the SSortLoad algorithm for the time window with a start time later than t_{build}. as shown in Fig. 4. Before the time window starts, we obtains groups with the predicted tuple numbers of current window and the node capacity from sorted sampling data, and apply arrays to accept data of each group. During the arrival of stream tuples, they are divided into different group. After the end of the time window, this stage will also end, and we will get all horizontal groups of stream tuples.

Group Vertical Sort/Calculate Structure/Construct Skeleton/Bulk Loading
These stage are the same as these corresponding stages of DSortLoad.

5   ExperimentEvaluation

This section compares and analyzes DSortLoad and SSortLoad. The experiment investigates three data stream parameters: data stream rate, time window and the number of slices. The performance is compared and analyzed from four aspects: construction delay, the influence of the number of threads and the maximum data stream rate that the algorithm can bear. The experimental platform uses Intel(R) Core (TM) i7-4790, 16 GB memory(Hynix DDR3 1600 MHz), Seagatehard disk (ST1000DM003-1ER62, 1 TB, 7200RPM), and the operating system is Ubuntu 16.04. Our experimental machine has 4 physical cores, so the hyperthreading may have an effect on experimental results.

5.1   The Number of Threads vs. Performance of Two Algorithm

The experiment uses 100 million tuples and then we observe the change of algorithm's performance by changing the number of threads as shown in Fig. 6. The left side is DSortLoad's while the right side is SSortLoad's, and the same as below. As shown in Fig. 6, the time of delay, bulk loading or group vertical sort of DSortLoad and SSortLoad decrease rapidly with the increase of the number of threads at first, but when the number of threads reaches a certain level, since the CPU is already fully loaded, it remains basically unchanged. For DSortLoad, the time of quick sort and merge maintains a steady state. For SSortLoad, sometimes there will be a certain fluctuation for the time of delay, bulk loading or group vertical sort, this is because of constant thread switching when the number of threads is more than 4, which will cause a certain time overhead.

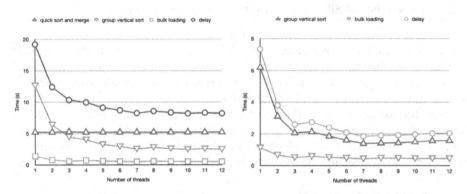

Fig. 6. Fixing window's time and stream tuples in DSortLoad and SSortLoad

When we set time window to 120 s, the number of slices to 10 and data volume to 100, 50 and 10 million, the change of R-tree construction delay of DSortLoad and SSortLoad as the number of threads increases gradually is shown in Fig. 7. No matter how big the data amount is, construction delay of DSortLoad and SSortLoad will decrease rapidly and then remain basically unchanged as the number of threads increases. When the number of threads reaches a certain number, it will be affected by bottlenecks of other resources such as CPU, making it difficult to reduce the construction delay.

From Figs. 6 and 7, although in both cases, delay time of DSortLoad and SSortLoad are reduced, but SSortLoad is always better than DSortLoad no matter how big the number of threads is.

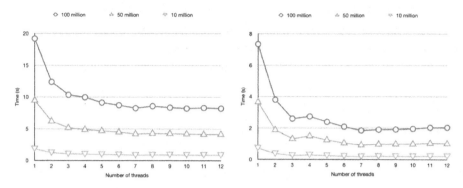

Fig. 7. Fixing window's time and varying stream tuples in DSortLoad and SSortLoad

5.2 The Number of Slices vs. Performance of Two Algorithm

When the time window is set to 120 s, the amount of data is 100 million, and the number of threads is 6. We observe the change of performance of DSortLoad and SSortLoad by changing the number of slices as shown in Fig. 8. For DSortLoad and SSortLoad, the time of delay, quick sort and merge decreases rapidly with increasing the number of slices, but when the number of slices reaches a certain level, they start to increase because data in each slice is reduced, so the time of quick sort in the slice is reduced obviously but the time of merge sort of all slices will increase more. But the time of group vertical sort of DSortLoad and the time of bulk loading of DSortLoad and SSortLoad are keeping stable because they are independent of the number of slices.

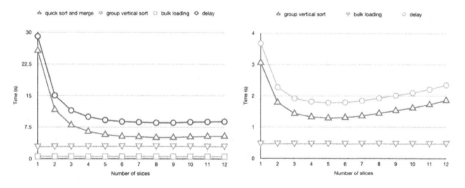

Fig. 8. Fixing window's time and stream tuples in DSortLoad and SSortLoad

When we set time window to 120 s, the number of threads to 6 and data volume to 100, 50 and 10 million, the change of R-tree construction delay of DSortLoad and SSortLoad as the number of slices increases gradually is shown in Fig. 9. No matter how big the data amount is, construction delay of DSortLoad and SSortLoad will decrease rapidly and then increase with the increase of the number of slices, and will reach the best when the number of slices is around 8 and 5 for DSortLoad and SSortLoad respectively.

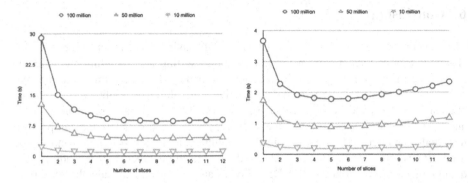

Fig. 9. Fixing window's time and varying stream tuples in DSortLoad and SSortLoad

From Figs. 8 and 9, although in both cases, delay time of DSortLoad and SSort-Load are reduced, but SSortLoad is always better than DSortLoad no matter how big the number of slices is.

5.3 Data Stream Rate vs. Performance of Two Algorithm

Different data stream rate is expressed as fixed time window and varied stream data tuples, so we only change stream data amount for comparing performance of DSort-Load and SSortLoad. When the number of slices is 10 and the number of threads is 1, the change of performance of DSortLoad and SSortLoad as the number of stream data tuples increases gradually is shown in Fig. 10. No matter how big the number of stream data tuples is, performance of SSortLoad is better than DSortLoad, that is, SSortLoad can withstand larger data stream rate than DSortLoad.

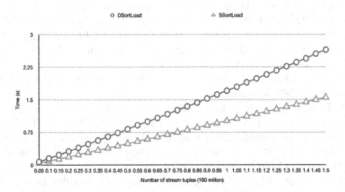

Fig. 10. Varing data stream rate in DSortLoad and SSortLoad

6 Conclusion

This paper is aimed at the application of completely saving data stream, combined with characteristics of data stream, using bulk loading, sorting and sampling technologies for near real-time construction of R-tree index in memory based on time windows. We proposed DSortLoad and SSortLoad respectively for different application scenarios, both of them have their own advantages. SSortLoad not only has less memory usage and hear larger data stream rate, but also has less construction delay and can provide near real-time queries. However, it needs to sample data in advance, so it can only be used after system startup for a while, and the execution efficiency depends on the quality of grouping strategy; But DSortLoad can be run directly and the execution efficiency is stable. So DSortLoad can be used in the initial stage of system, and SSortLoad can be used when sufficient data is sampled. In the future, we will further study DSortLoad and SSortLoad construction schemes for distributed scenarios, and R-tree constructed by two algorithms will be quantitatively compared.

References

1. Guttman, A.: R-trees: a dynamic index structure for spatial searching. In: ACM Sigmod International Conference on Management of Data, pp. 47–57 (1984)
2. Liu, D., Li, Q., Cheng, J.: Indexing on main memory spatial object. Remote Sens. Environ. **11**(4), 302–308 (1996)
3. Bentley, J.L.: Multidimensional binary search trees used for associative searching. Commun. ACM **18**(9), 509–517 (1975)
4. Finkel, R.A., Bentley, J.L.: Quad trees a data structure for retrieval on composite keys. Acta Informatica **4**(1), 1–9 (1974)
5. Sellis, T.K., Roussopoulos, N., Faloutsos, C.: The R + -Tree: a dynamic index for multi-dimensional objects. In: Proceedings of the 13th International Conference on Very Large Data Bases, pp. 507–518. Morgan Kaufmann Publishers Inc (1987)
6. Beckmann, N., Kriegel, H.P., Schneider, R., et al.: The R*-tree: an efficient and robust access method for points and rectangles. ACM Sigmod Rec. **19**(2), 322–331 (1990)
7. Roussopoulos, N., Leifker, D.: Direct spatial search on pictorial databases using packed R-trees. ACM Sigmod Rec. **14**(4), 17–31 (1985)
8. Zhang, M., Lu, F., Shen, P., et al.: The evolvement and progress of R-Tree family. Chin. J. Comput. **28**(3), 289–300 (2005)
9. Kamel, I., Faloutsos, C.: On packing R-trees. In: Proceedings of the Second International Conference on Information and Knowledge Management, pp. 490–499 (1993)
10. Leutenegger, S.T., Edgington, J., Lopez, M.A.: STR: a simple and efficient algorithm for R-tree packing. In: Proceedings of the 13th International Conference on Data Engineering, pp. 497–506. IEEE Computer Society (1997)
11. García, R.Y.J., López, M.A., Leutenegger, S.T.: A greedy algorithm for bulk loading R-trees. In: Proceedings of the 6th ACM International Symposium on Advances in Geographic Information Systems, pp. 163–164 (1998)
12. Tan, H., Luo, W., Ni, L.M.: CloST: a Hadoop-based storage system for big spatio-temporal data analytics. In: Proceedings of the 21st ACM International Conference on Information and Knowledge Management, pp. 2139–2143 (2012)

13. Cary, A., Sun, Z., Hristidis, V., Rishe, N.: Experiences on processing spatial data with MapReduce. In: Winslett, M. (ed.) SSDBM 2009. LNCS, vol. 5566, pp. 302–319. Springer, Heidelberg (2009). https://doi.org/10.1007/978-3-642-02279-1_24

14. Zhong, Y., Fang, J., Zhao, X.: VegaIndexer: a distributed composite index scheme for big spatio-temporal sensor data on cloud. In: Geoscience and Remote Sensing Symposium, 2013 IEEE International, pp. 1713–1716 (2013)

15. Zhong, Y., Zhu, X., Fang, J.: Elastic and effective spatio-temporal query processing scheme on Hadoop. In: Proceedings of the 1st ACM SIGSPATIAL International Workshop on Analytics for Big Geospatial Data, pp. 33–42 (2012)

16. Zhong, Y., Fang, J., Zhao, X.: A distributed storage scheme for big spatio-temporal data. Chin. High Technol. Lett. **23**(12), 1219–1229 (2013)

17. Eldawy, A., Mokbel, M.F., Alharthi, S., et al.: SHAHED: a MapReduce-based system for querying and visualizing spatio-temporal satellite data. In: 2015 IEEE 31st International Conference on Data Engineering, pp. 1585–1596 (2015)

18. Li, X., Zheng, W.: Parallel spatial index algorithm based on Hilbert partition. In: 2013 International Conference on Computational and Information Sciences, pp. 876–879 (2013)

19. Liu, Y.: Research on Key Techniques of High Performance Spatial Query Processing for Large Scale Spatial Data. National University of Defense Technology (2013)

20. Nishimura, S., Das, S., Agrawal, D., et al.: MD-HBase: a scalable multi-dimensional data infrastructure for location aware services. In: Proceedings of the 2011 IEEE 12th International Conference on Mobile Data Management, vol. 01, pp. 7–16. IEEE Computer Society (2011)

21. Wang, S., Maier, D., Ooi, B.C.: Fast and adaptive indexing of multi-dimensional observational data. Proc. VLDB Endowment **9**(14), 1683–1694 (2016)

22. Ma, Y., Rao, J., Hu, W., et al.: An efficient index for massive IOT data in cloud environment. In: Proceedings of the 21st ACM International Conference on Information and Knowledge Management, pp. 2129–2133 (2012)

23. Cai, R., Lu, Z., Wang, L., et al.: DITIR: distributed index for high throughput trajectory insertion and real-time temporal range query. Proc. VLDB Endowment **10**(12), 1865–1868 (2017)

ASOCA: Adaptive Service-Oriented and Cloud Applications and ISyCC: IoT Systems for Context-Aware Computing

Introduction to the 3rd Edition of the International Workshop on Adaptive Service-Oriented and Cloud Applications ASOCA 2018

The ASOCA 2018 workshop was held in conjunction with the 16th International Conference on Service Oriented Computing (ICSOC 2018) on November 12, 2018 in Hangzhou, China.

The workshop address the adaptation and reconfiguration issues of the Service-oriented and cloud applications and architectures. ASOCA session gathered about twenty attendees. The discussions following the presentations. We received 16 submissions, out of which 2 papers were accepted. For this edition, the ASOCA program was merged with the program of the third workshop on IoT systems provisioning and management for context-aware smart cities (ISYCC'18). The presentations of the two workshops were held during the same session.

We would like to thank the authors for their submissions, the program committee for their reviewing work, and the organizers of the ICSOC 2018 conference for their support which made this workshop possible.

Organization

Workshop Organizers

Ismael Bouassida Rodriguez   ReDCAD, University of Sfax, Tunisia
Khalil Drira   LAAS-CNRS and Univ. de Toulouse, France
Shizhan Chen   Tianjin University, Tianjin, China

Dynamic Task Allocation for Data-Intensive Workflows in Cloud Environment

Xiping Liu[(⊠)], Liyang Zheng, Chen Junyu, and Lei Shang

Jiangsu Key Laboratory of Big Data Security and Intelligent Processing,
School of Computer Science, Nanjing University of Posts
and Telecommunications, Nanjing, China
liuxp@njupt.edu.cn

Abstract. Cloud environment provides high performance computing services to process massive data for data-intensive workflows. Due to the different functional requirements, tasks in a workflow might be allocated to multiple cloud servers. The massive data among these tasks have to be transferred and this greatly increases the execution cost. To decrease the transferred data size during the workflow execution, this paper proposes a dynamic task allocation method based on the data dependencies. The workflow with data dependencies and typical control logic, i.e., sequential, parallel, and exclusive choice, is described based on process algebra. The data size relevant to a data dependency can be obtained only after the task is executed. Each task is allocated to a certain server according to relevant data size and maximal data paths. A case study is presented to illustrate the feasibility and effect of the proposed method and the related work is discussed based on the case study.

Keywords: Dynamic task allocation · Data-intensive workflows · Cloud environment · Data dependency · Maximal data path

1 Introduction

Cloud environment provides on-demand network access to massive computing resources [1]. In cloud environment, service providers can deploy their services to cloud servers in an elastic way instead of maintaining their own servers in a much higher price. With increasingly abundant services emerged in cloud environment, many data-intensive workflows have been executed on cloud servers [2, 3].

To make a data-intensive workflow efficiently executed in cloud environment, it is important to reasonably arrange tasks in the workflow to suitable servers [4]. Many researchers have been putting effort on this issue [3, 5]. Moghadam et al. [6] proposed a multi-objective optimization model and three-level implementation structure to decrease the workflow completion time consisting of data communication cost, waiting time, and task processing time. Kumar et al. [7] presented two load balanced workflow scheduling algorithms to minimize the makespan and maximize average cloud utilization. Rodriguez et al. [8] presented a particle swarm optimization algorithm to minimize the overall execution cost under the deadline constraints. Choi et al. [9] proposed a data-locality aware workflow scheduling method with considerations of data transfer time and task parallelism to improve the execution time.

© Springer Nature Switzerland AG 2019
X. Liu et al. (Eds.): ICSOC 2018 Workshops, LNCS 11434, pp. 269–280, 2019.
https://doi.org/10.1007/978-3-030-17642-6_23

These studies mainly focus on the completion time optimization of workflows while the monetary cost is few considered. However, how much to pay for the services are also a very important criterion for the workflow execution [3, 10]. For a data-intensive workflow, tasks usually need to process large volumes of data and most of cost is paid for data transmission [3, 11].

Some effort is put into the data transmission cost reduction [12, 13], while they requires estimation on data to be transferred before the execution. However, it is usually hard to evaluate the transferred data size in advance in many application scenarios. Moreover, tasks of workflows might be in some exclusive choice branches and would not be executed, which also brings challenges for the allocation. To decrease the transferred data size during the execution of a data-intensive workflow in cloud environment, this paper propose a method to dynamically allocate a task to a cloud server according to the real execution situation of this workflow.

The rest of this paper is organized as follows: Sect. 2 presents a motivating example and relevant analysis. Section 3 describes the data-intensive workflow allocation problem in cloud environment. Section 4 proposes a dynamic task allocation method based on the problem description. Section 5 illustrates the proposed method through a case study based on the motivating example and discusses the related work. Finally, Sect. 6 concludes the paper.

2   A Motivating Example and Analysis

Figure 1 presents a workflow example with eleven tasks, where each task has some functional requirements representing what to do and the edges among tasks represent the control flow. For example, task 5 is executed after task 4 and both of these two tasks are in an exclusive choice branch (this branch might not be executed according to the result of task 1. The data dependencies among tasks could be presented through ordered pairs, such as <1, 2>, <2, 6>. The real data size to be transferred from task 1 to task 2 is usually hard to estimate before the execution of task 1, although the size is very important for the allocation of tasks in a data-intensive workflow.

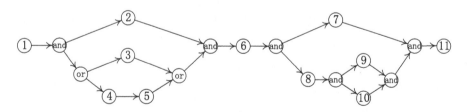

Fig. 1. A workflow example

To deploy a data-intensive workflow in cloud environment, the candidate cloud servers for each task should be first found. If a service satisfying functional require-ments of a task locates on a server, this server could be a candidate server.

Not all candidate servers of a task have the opportunity to execute the task. Taking above workflow as an example, if the branch with task 3 is not chosen, no candidate servers for task 3 need to be selected. Moreover, if server A is a candidate server of both task 7 and task 9 and task 7 is already allocated to server A, then A cannot be allocated to task 9 as they should be executed in a parallel way.

Given multiple available servers, a task should select one with highest possibility to decrease more transferred data. Taking above workflow as an example, suppose that task 6 has three candidate servers A, B, and C, where A and B are not selected by any task yet while B is also the candidate server of task 7, C is selected by task 2 and task 2 need to transfer 1 GB data to task 6. At the time to allocate for task 6, C will definitely decrease 1 GB, B might decrease some data (task 7 might not be allocated to B and even so the decreased size is unknown), A seems no benefit. In this case, allocating task 6 to C might be more reasonable.

The real situation is much more complicated than above example. The allocation for a task must consider both the relevant control flow and data dependencies with known size or unknown size. The detailed problem description and allocation method are presented as following sections. To make the method description more concise, process algebra is adopted to define a workflow, although there are multiple workflow representation methods [14–16].

3 Problem Description

The data-intensive workflow to be allocated in cloud environment is described as follows.

Definition 1 (W). A workflow is defined as a triple $W = <T, D, E>$

- $T = \{t_i \mid t_i$ represents the ith task in a workflow, $i = 1, 2, ..., n\}$ provides the task set;
- $D = \{d_{i,j} \mid d_{i,j}$ represents the data dependency from t_i to t_j and the value is 0 or 1, $i, j = 1, 2, ..., n\}$ provides the data dependency set;
- $E = t_i \mid (E \cdot E) \mid (E + E) \mid (E \parallel E)$, E represents an expression consisting of finite operators and tasks from T, where $\cdot$ represents sequential, $+$ represents exclusive choice, and $\parallel$ represents parallel. E provides the control logic of the workflow.

An expression can be simplified by deleting unnecessary parentheses "(" and ")", with the given precedence order $\cdot > \parallel > +$. For example, the workflow in Fig. 1 can be represented as $t_1 \cdot (t_2 \parallel (t_3 + t_4 \cdot t_5)) \cdot t_6 \cdot (t_7 \parallel t_8 \cdot (t_9 \parallel t_{10})) \cdot t_{11}$.

A cloud server involved in the allocation of a data-intensive workflow is represented as s_p, where $p = 1, 2, ..., m$. Each task in a workflow might have multiple candidate cloud servers.

Definition 2 (CS_i). The candidate servers for the ith task are defined as a set $CS_i = \{s_p \mid s_p$ can provide a service satisfying the functional requirement of $t_i, p \in 1, 2, ..., m\}$.

Generally speaking, it is possible to decrease the transferred data among tasks only if s_p is a server that can provide multiple services to process multiple tasks of a workflow. The servers with ability to handle more tasks in the workflow would be preferred to be the candidate servers.

Definition 3 (TS_p). The tasks that s_p can handle are defined as a set $TS_p = \{t_i \mid t_i$ could be executed on s_p, $i = 1, 2, \ldots, n\}$.

Obviously, CS_i and TS_p provide similar information in different ways and both of them are used in the allocation algorithms. Each task t_i could be allocated to a server in CS_i and tasks in the same TS_p have the opportunity to decrease the transferred data if they have data dependencies. However, some tasks in the same TS_p should not be allocated to the same server, if they are in different parallel branches. Each task in a parallel branch might have some conflict tasks.

Definition 4 (CT_i). The tasks conflicting with the ith task are defined as a set $CT_i = \{t_j \mid t_j$ and t_i have conflict on the selection of servers, $j \in 1, 2, \ldots, n\}$.

Taking Fig. 1 as an example, $CT_7 = \{t_8, t_9, t_{10}\}$, $CT_9 = \{t_7, t_{10}\}$, etc. Different servers must be selected for conflict tasks to keep them parallel.

Given a workflow with exclusive choice branch, not all tasks would be executed. For example, the real execution result of Fig. 1 might be $t_1 \cdot (t_2 \| t_3) \cdot t_6 \cdot (t_7 \| t_8 \cdot (t_9 \| t_{10}))$ $\cdot t_{11}$ or $t_1 \cdot (t_2 \| t_4 \cdot t_5) \cdot t_6 \cdot (t_7 \| t_8 \cdot (t_9 \| t_{10})) \cdot t_{11}$. If a task is in exclusive choice branch and this branch is not chosen, it is unnecessary to allocate this task.

Definition 5 (ET). The executed tasks in a workflow model are defined as a set $ET = \{t_i \mid t_i$ is executed, $i \in 1, 2, \ldots, n\}$.

The result to allocate tasks in a data-intensive workflow in cloud environment can be defined as follows.

Definition 6 (R). The result consisting of n tuples is defined as $R = \{<t_i, as_i> \mid t_i$ is allocated to as_i, $as_i \in CS_i$, $\forall as_i \forall as_{i'} \cdot (t_{i'} \in CT_i \rightarrow as_i \neq as_{i'})$, $t_i \in ET\}$.

Given W and CS_i ($i = 1, 2, \ldots, n$), many feasible solutions could be found and R with less transferred data would be better. For two tasks t_i and t_j with $d_{i,j} = 1$, the data size to be transferred from t_i, denote as $ds_{i,j}$, could be obtained only after t_i is executed. The total transferred data during the execution can be computed based on Eq. (1).

$$sumD(R) = \sum_{(d_{i,j}=1) \wedge (as_i \neq as_j)} ds_{i,j} \qquad (1)$$

4   Dynamic Task Allocation Oriented to Data Size Optimization

To decrease the transferred data, it is a straightforward way to allocate tasks with bigger transferred data size to the same server. However, the data size corresponding to each data dependency is unknown and it's hard to get a global optimal solution before the execution.

In our dynamic task allocation method, a task is allocated only after all its precedent tasks are executed. The allocation for a task is based on relevant data dependencies with known or unknown data size, the conflict tasks and the candidate servers. The concrete method is proposed as follows.

4.1   Preparations Before the Execution

For a task t_i to be allocated, the server is selected from CS_i according to the transferred data which could be possibly decreased. The data relevant to t_i could be the one transferred to t_i (which size is known) or the one transferred from t_i (which size is unknown as t_i is not executed yet). To decrease transferred data size as much as possible, the maximal data path is defined and used for the server selection.

Definition 7 (MDP_i). The maximal data paths starting from t_i are defined as a set $MDP_i = \{P_{i,u} \mid P_{i,u}$ is a subset of T and the tasks in $P_{i,u}$ could form a path $v_0 v_1 ... v_k ...$ making $d_{v_{k-1} v_k} = 1$, where $v_0 = i$, $v_k \neq i$, and $v_k \in 1, 2, ..., n, \forall P_{i,u} \forall P_{i,u'}(P_{i,u} \not\subset P_{i,u'})\}$.

Taking Fig. 1 as an example, $MDP_6 = \{P_{61}, P_{62}, P_{63}\}$, where $P_{61} = \{t_6, t_7, t_{11}\}$, $P_{62} = \{t_6, t_8, t_9, t_{11}\}$ $P_{63} = \{t_6, t_8, t_{10}, t_{11}\}$. For the allocation of t_6 based on unknown transferred data, the server with max intersection with P_{6u} would be preferred to decrease more transferred data.

Table 1 lists the relevant notations, where CT_i and MDP_i could be obtained according to W through following algorithms.

Table 1. Notation list

Notations	Descriptions	Notations	Descriptions
t_i	ith task	CS_i	Candidate servers for t_i
s_p	pth server	TS_p	Tasks that s_p can deal with
$d_{i,j}$	Data dependency from t_i to t_j	CT_i	Tasks conflicting with t_i
$ds_{i,j}$	Data size transferred from t_i to t_j	MDP_i	Maximal data paths starting from t_i

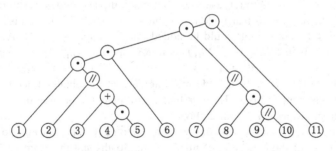

Fig. 2. A full binary tree example for a workflow

Based on the workflow model, a full binary tree could be easily built to represent the control flow among tasks by putting tasks on leaf nodes and operators on interior nodes. Figure 2 presents the binary tree built according to the workflow in Fig. 1. CT_i for each task in a parallel branch could be obtained through the binary tree traversal, as Algorithm 1 shows.

Algorithm 1. Obtaining conflict task sets

```
Input: W, the full binary tree built from E of W
Output: CTᵢ, i=1, 2, ..., n
 1  Trav(nd)
 2    switch (nd.data){
 3      case '//': h←h+1, fₕ←ls, LSₕ←∅, Trav(nd.left)
 4                 fₕ←rs, RSₕ←∅, Trav(nd.right)
 5                 for each tᵢ in LSₕ
 6                   add each task in RSₕ into CTᵢ
 7                 for each tᵢ in RSₕ
 8                   add each task in LSₕ into CTᵢ
 9                 h←h-1, break
10      case '+': Trav(nd.left), Trav(nd.right), break
11      case '·': Trav(nd.left), Trav(nd.right), break
12      default: if h>0
13                 for j from 1 to h
14                   if fₕ=ls
15                     Add nd.data into LSₕ
16                   else if fₕ=rs
17                       Add nd.data into RSₕ
18                 break
19  for each tᵢ
20    CTᵢ←∅
21  h←0, Trav(root)
```

In Algorithm 1, h means the height of a node '‖' as a parallel branch might be embedded in another one. Taking $E = t_7 \| t_8 \cdot (t_9 \| t_{10})$ as an example, the first '‖' ($h = 1$) has left child t_7 and right child '·', where '·' has left child t_8 and right child '‖' ($h = 2$). The flag f_h is used to represent which branch the leaf nodes of subtrees belong to. Based on h and f_h, each leaf node in a subtree with root '‖', i.e. a task in parallel branches with different height, could be added into corresponding sets. According to this algorithm, t_7 is in LS_1, t_8 is in RS_1, t_9 is in RS_1 and LS_2, t_{10} is in RS_1 and RS_2, and CT_i could be easily obtained, such as $CT_7 = \{t_8, t_9, t_{10}\}$, $CT_9 = \{t_7, t_{10}\}$.

MDP_i for each task might include multiple sets and is obtained according to the data dependencies among tasks. The warshall algorithm could be modified to search for maximal data paths, as Algorithm 2 shows.

In Algorithm 2, $PS_{i,j}$ represents the set of nodes on a data path from t_i to t_j. $MDPE_i$ represents the set of the end tasks of maximal data paths starting from t_i. A maximal data path starting from a task t_i does not include any t_k in an exclusive choice branch as these tasks might not be executed and the relevant data dependencies might be useless for decreasing transferred data size. For this case, the path from t_i to t_j through an optional task t_k is not taken into account, except that t_i and t_k are in the same exclusive choice branch. If t_i can reach t_j through t_k, a data path ending at t_k is shorter than a data path ending at t_j and would not be a maximal data path starting from t_i, so t_k would be deleted. Moreover, the data path from t_i to t_j should be added into $PS_{i,j}$. As long as $PS_{i,j}$ is renewed, it should be simplified by deleting sets contained by another set.

Algorithm 2. Obtaining maximal data path sets

```
Input: W
Output: MDPᵢ, i=1, 2,...,n
 1  for each dᵢ,ⱼ
 2     if dᵢ,ⱼ=0
 3        PSᵢ,ⱼ←∅
 4     else add {tᵢ, tⱼ} into PSᵢ,ⱼ, add tⱼ into MDPEᵢ
 5  for k from 1 to n
 6     for each tᵢ with dᵢ,ₖ=1
 7        if tₖ is in an exclusive choice branch
 8           then if tᵢ is not in the same exclusive choice branch
 9              then break
10        for each tⱼ with dₖ,ⱼ=1
11           if dᵢ,ⱼ=0
12              dᵢ,ⱼ←1, add tⱼ into MDPEᵢ
13           delete tₖ from MDPEᵢ
14           add PSᵢ,ₖ∪PSₖ,ⱼ into PSᵢ,ⱼ
15           for each set x in PSᵢ,ⱼ
16              if x is a subset of another set in PSᵢ,ⱼ
17                 delete x from PSᵢ,ⱼ
18  for each tᵢ
19     u←1
20     for each tⱼ in MDPEᵢ
21        for each set x in PSᵢ,ⱼ
22           Pᵢ,ᵤ←x, u←u+1
```

4.2 Dynamic Task Allocation During the Execution

Given a data-intensive workflow W, CT_i and MDP_i for each t_i can be obtained through above algorithms. Then t_i can be allocated based on CS_i, TS_p, CT_i, MDP_i and $ds_{j,i}$ (the known size of data transferred from t_j to t_i), where CT_i is only useful for t_i in a certain parallel branch. The concrete algorithm is shown as follows.

Generally, t_1 and t_n are the first and the last task of a workflow with n tasks (a dummy start or end task could be added to get such a workflow). So the first task to be allocated to t_1 at line 20, and the allocation is terminated after t_n is allocated. The process $A(i)$ (line 1 to line 19) is used to allocate t_i. After the execution of a task is finished, $getCandT()$ would detect the executed task and return the tasks which could be allocated next. If there is more than one task in CdT, the tasks would be dynamically allocated one by one in the order decided through line 26 to line 36.

To decide which task in CdT should be allocated first, three principles are applied to get a smaller candidate task set. After that, if there is still more than one task (this case does not happen often), the task to be allocated would be randomly selected from $CT3$.

Algorithm 3. Dynamic task allocation

```
Input: W, CSi, TSp, CTi, MDPi, i=1, 2, …, n
Output: R, sumD(R)
 1  A(i)
 2    if CTi≠∅
 3      for each tj in CTi∩ET
 4        if asj∈CSi
 5          delete asj from CSi
 6    for each sp in CSi
 7      sumSp←0
 8    for each tj in ET
 9      if dj,i=1∧asj∈CSi
10        sumSp←sumSp+dsj,i     //sp=asj
11    if max(sumSp)=0
12      maxI←0, maxIs←-1
13      for each set Pi,u in MDPi
14        for each sp in CSi
15          if |Pi,u∩TSp|>maxI
16            maxI←|Pi,u ∩Sp|, maxIs←p
17      asi←SmaxIs
18    else asi←sp
19    add ti into ET
20  A(1)
21  CdT←∅
22  while tn is not in ET
23    while CdT=∅
24      CdT←getCandT()
25    while CdT≠∅
26      if |CdT|>1
27        CdT1←{ti in CdT with least |CSi|}
28        if |CdT1|>1
29          CdT2←{ti in CT1 with max sumDT(i)}    //by Eq.(2)
30          if |CdT2|>1
31            CdT3←{ti in CT2 with max |Pi,u|}
32            while CdT3≠∅
33              delete ti from CdT3 and CdT, A(i)
34          else delete the only task ti in CdT2 from CdT, A(i)
35        else delete the only task ti in CdT1 from CdT, A(i)
36      else delete the only task ti from CdT, A(i)
37  compute sumD(R) by Eq. (1)
```

The first principle is that the task with the least $|CS_i|$ is preferred. Generally, the multiple tasks in CdT are the first tasks of multiple parallel branches and require different servers. If t_i with less $|CS_i|$ is allocated later, it is possible that all the candidate servers of t_i are already allocated to other parallel tasks and another new server must be recruited to process t_i, while more servers usually means more possible transferred data.

The second principle to choose a task is that the one with max $sumDT(i)$ is preferred. $sumDT(i)$ represents the total known data size to be transferred from some executed tasks which might be decreased by allocating relevant tasks to the same server. It can be computed by following Eq. (2).

$$sumDT(i) = \sum_{d_{j,i}=1 \wedge (as_j \in CS_i)} ds_{j,i} \qquad (2)$$

The third principle is that the one with max $|P_{i,u}|$ is preferred. The more tasks a maximal data path has, the higher the possibility to decrease unknown data size to be transferred is.

To decide which server a task t_i should be allocated to, it is necessary to compute the transferred data which could be possibly decreased. Before that, if CT_i is not empty and a server s_p in CS_i is already allocated to a task t_j in CT_i ($as_j = s_p$), the server s_p must be first deleted from CS_i to keep t_i and t_j parallel. For each server s_p in reduced CS_i, the total transferred data size to be decreased if t_i is allocated to s_p, i.e. $sumS_p$, is computed based on $ds_{j,i}$ with $as_j = s_p$ and $d_{j,i} = 1$. The server s_p with max $sumS_p$ is first preferred as it can decrease a certain amount of data. If no transferred data could be decreased as no task with data dependency to t_i is executed on a server in CS_i, the server s_p with max intersection to a maximal data path starting from t_i is preferred as it might decrease more transferred data by involving more data dependencies.

5   A Case Study and Discussion

Based on the control flow of eleven tasks given in Fig. 1 and the Definition 1, a data-intensive workflow is randomly generated and represented as $W = <T, D, E>$, where $T = \{t_i \mid i = 1, 2, \ldots, 11\}$, $E = t_1 \cdot (t_2 \parallel (t_3 + t_4 \cdot t_5)) \cdot t_6 \cdot (t_7 \parallel t_8 \cdot (t_9 \parallel t_{10})) \cdot t_{11}$, and the subset of D satisfying $d_{i,j} = 1$ is $\{d_{1,2}, d_{1,3}, d_{1,4}, d_{2,6}, d_{2,7}, d_{3,6}, d_{4,5}, d_{4,6}, d_{4,8}, d_{4,11}, d_{5,6}, d_{6,7}, d_{6,8}, d_{6,9}, d_{6,11}, d_{7,11}, d_{8,9}, d_{8,10}, d_{9,11}, d_{10,11}\}$. The relevant CS_i for each task is presented in Table 2 and TS_p can be easily obtained from CS_i.

Table 2. CS_i for tasks in W

CS_1	$\{s_1, s_2, s_3\}$	CS_2	$\{s_3, s_4\}$	CS_3	$\{s_2, s_3\}$	CS_4	$\{s_1, s_2\}$
CS_5	$\{s_2, s_4\}$	CS_6	$\{s_1, s_3\}$	CS_7	$\{s_2, s_4\}$	CS_8	$\{s_1, s_3\}$
CS_9	$\{s_1, s_3\}$	CS_{10}	$\{s_3\}$	CS_{11}	$\{s_1, s_3, s_4\}$		

Before the execution, CT_i for each task in a parallel branch and MDP_i for each task could be obtained according to Algorithms 1 and 2. Tables 3 and 4 present the details.

Table 3. CT_i for a task in a parallel branch

CT_2	$\{t_3, t_4, t_5\}$	CT_3	$\{t_2\}$	CT_4	$\{t_2\}$	CT_5	$\{t_5\}$
CT_7	$\{t_8, t_9, t_{10}\}$	CT_8	$\{t_7\}$	CT_9	$\{t_7, t_{10}\}$	CT_{10}	$\{t_7, t_9\}$

Table 4. MDP_i for tasks in W

MDP_1	$\{t_1, t_2, t_6, t_7, t_{11}\}, \{t_1, t_2, t_6, t_8, t_9, t_{11}\}, \{t_1, t_2, t_6, t_8, t_{10}, t_{11}\}$	MDP_2	$\{t_2, t_6, t_7, t_{11}\}, \{t_2, t_6, t_8, t_9, t_{11}\}, \{t_2, t_6, t_8, t_{10}, t_{11}\}$
MDP_3	$\{t_3, t_6, t_7, t_{11}\}, \{t_3, t_6, t_8, t_9, t_{11}\}, \{t_3, t_6, t_8, t_{10}, t_{11}\}$	MDP_4	$\{t_4, t_5, t_6, t_7, t_{11}\}, \{t_4, t_5, t_6, t_8, t_9, t_{11}\}, \{t_4, t_5, t_6, t_8, t_{10}, t_{11}\}$
MDP_5	$\{t_5, t_6, t_7, t_{11}\}, \{t_5, t_6, t_8, t_9, t_{11}\}, \{t_5, t_6, t_8, t_{10}, t_{11}\}$	MDP_6	$\{t_6, t_7, t_{11}\}, \{t_6, t_8, t_9, t_{11}\}, \{t_6, t_8, t_{10}, t_{11}\}$
MDP_7	$\{t_7, t_{11}\}$	MDP_8	$\{t_8, t_9, t_{11}\}, \{t_8, t_{10}, t_{11}\}$
MDP_9	$\{t_9, t_{11}\}$	MDP_{10}	$\{t_{10}, t_{11}\}$

According to Algorithm 3, a final allocation result R can be obtained based on W, CS_i given before the execution and the real execution details, i.e. $ET = T\text{-}\{t_3\}$ and data size of each data dependency shown in Table 4.

Table 5. Transferred data size of each data dependency

$ds_{1,2}$	$ds_{1,3}$	$ds_{1,4}$	$ds_{2,6}$	$ds_{3,6}$	$ds_{4,5}$	$ds_{4,6}$	$ds_{4,8}$	$ds_{4,11}$	$ds_{5,6}$	$ds_{6,7}$	$ds_{6,8}$	$ds_{6,9}$	$ds_{6,11}$	$ds_{7,11}$	$ds_{8,9}$	$ds_{8,10}$	$ds_{9,11}$	$ds_{10,11}$
7	–	5	4	–	6	12	7	9	8	3	9	11	6	14	11	13	8	9

At the beginning, t_1 is first allocated. As there is no data transferred from other tasks for t_1, the server to allocate to it is the one which TS_p has biggest intersection with three sets in MDP_1. In this case, s_3 selected as TS_1 has six common elements with P_{13}. After t_1 is executed, CdT gets two candidate tasks to be allocated, i.e. t_2 and t_4 (the exclusive choice branch $t_4 \cdot t_5$ but not t_3 is chosen). As $|CS_4| = |CS_2|$ and $sumDT(2) = 7 > sumDT(4) = 0$ ($s_3 \notin CS_4$ and it is impossible to make t_4 and t_1 on the same server), t_2 is preferred to be allocated first (to s_3) and then t_4 is allocated to s_1 with the biggest intersection to sets in MDP_4. Then, t_5 is allocated to s_2 based on MDP_5. To allocate t_6, $sumS_1$ and $sumS_3$ are computed respectively by Eq. (2) based on $ds_{4,6}$ and $ds_{2,6}$ and $<t_6, s_1>$ is obtained. For t_7 and t_8, t_8 is allocated first according to the principles and $<t_8, s_1>$, $<t_7, s_4>$ are obtained. For t_9 and t_{10}, t_{10} is allocated to the only candidate server s_3 first and t_9 is allocated to s_1 based on $sumS_1$ and $sumS_3$. Finally, t_{11} is allocated to s_1 as $sumS_1 = 23$, $sumS_3 = 9$, and $sumS_4 = 14$. The total transferred data for this allocation scheme $sumD(R) = 62$ can be computed by Eq. (1).

Given this case, few studies provide effective allocation methods to decrease the transferred data in the execution of a workflow. Some methods are proposed to minimize the completion time [6–9, 18] while little optimization on the data transmission is mentioned. Some methods [12, 13, 19] are proposed to optimize the data relevant cost while they usually need the estimated data size before the execution. Moreover, most of allocation methods [6–9, 13, 18, 19] do not consider exclusive choice branches which are necessary to represent the typical control logic in some data-intensive workflows.

It is hard to apply other current method on the discussed problem in this paper. As a comparison, an allocation result is given based on a basic rule, i.e. the server in CS_i with more $|TS_p|$ is preferred for each t_i. With the exact same input and execution situation, $R' = \{< t_1, \ s_3 >, < t_2, \ s_3 >, < t_4, \ s_1 >, < t_5, \ s_4 >, < t_6, \ s_3 >, < t_7, s_4 >, < t_8, s_3 >, < t_9, s_1 >, < t_{10}, s_3 >, < t_{11}, s_3 >\}$ is obtained, and the total transferred data for this scheme is $sumD(R) = 94$. Comparing to the original total data size of the workflow, i.e. 152-the sum of items in Table 5, R' can decrease some transferred data while it still gets much bigger data than R obtained by our method.

6   Conclusions and Future Work

For some data-intensive workflows run in cloud environment, users have strong intention to decrease the transferred data size and the data size is dynamically decided during the execution of workflows but not before the execution. A dynamic allocation method is proposed to handle this situation, where the typical three control flow (including sequential, parallel and exclusive choice) and the unknown size for each data dependency among tasks are two main challenges. Before the execution, conflict tasks for each task in a parallel branch are obtained based on revised tree traversal operations. Moreover, maximal data paths starting from each task, including the one in an exclusive choice branch, are also obtained based on the improved warshall algorithm. During the execution, tasks are dynamically allocated one by one in the order decided by the control flow definition and some basic principles. The cloud server for each task is carefully selected to get a best decision for possible max decreased data. The case study illustrates the feasibility and effect of our method.

As it is hard to exactly estimated the task execution time on different cloud server in some data-intensive application scenarios, conflict tasks are roughly inferred based on parallel logic in our method. In the future, conflict tasks could be further refined based on the task execution time and provide more options for tasks in parallel branches.

References

1. Rimal, B.P., Choi, E.: A service-oriented taxonomical spectrum, cloudy challenges and opportunities of cloud computing. Int. J. Commun Syst **25**(6), 796–819 (2012)
2. Diaz-Montes, J., Diaz-Granados, M., Zou, M., Tao, S., Parashar, M.: Supporting data-intensive workflows in software-defined federated multi-clouds. IEEE Trans. Cloud Comput. **6**(1), 250–263 (2018)
3. Alkhanaka, E.N., Leea, S.P., Rezaeia, R., Parizi, R.M.: Cost optimization approaches for scientific workflow scheduling in cloud and grid computing: a review, classifications, and open issues. J. Syst. Softw. **113**(3), 1–26 (2016)
4. Lenhard, J., Ferme, V., Harrer, S., Geiger, M., Pautasso, C.: Lessons learned from evaluating workflow management systems. In: Braubach, L., et al. (eds.) ICSOC 2017. LNCS, vol. 10797, pp. 215–227. Springer, Cham (2018). https://doi.org/10.1007/978-3-319-91764-1_17
5. Masdari, M., ValiKardan, S., Shahi, Z., Azar, S.I.: Towards workflow scheduling in cloud computing: a comprehensive analysis. J. Netw. Comput. Appl. **66**, 64–82 (2016)

6. Moghadam, M.H., Babamir, S.M., Mirabi, M.: A multi-objective optimization model for data-intensive workflow scheduling in data grids. In: IEEE 41st Conference on Local Computer Networks Workshops, pp. 25–33 (2016)

7. Kumar, M.S., Gupta, I., Jana, P.K.: Forward load aware scheduling for data-intensive workflow applications in cloud system. In: International Conference on Information Technology, pp. 93–97 (2016)

8. Rodriguez, M.A., Buyya, R.: Deadline based resource provisioning and scheduling algorithm for scientific workflows on clouds. IEEE Trans. Cloud Comput. 2(2), 222–235 (2014)

9. Choi, J., Adufu, T., Kim, Y.: Data-locality aware scientific workflow scheduling methods in HPC cloud environments. Int. J. Parallel Prog. 45(5), 1128–1141 (2017)

10. Smanchat, S., Viriyapant, K.: Taxonomies of workflow scheduling problem and techniques in the cloud. Future Gener. Comput. Syst. 52, 1–12 (2015)

11. Gupta, M., Jain, A.: A survey on cost aware task allocation algorithm for cloud environment. In. 4th IEEE International Conference on Signal Processing, Computing and Control, pp. 642–646 (2017)

12. Yuan, D., Yang, Y., Liu, X., Zhang, G., Chen, J.: A data dependency based strategy for intermediate data storage in scientific cloud workflow systems. Concurr. Comput. Pract. Exp. 24(9), 956–976 (2012)

13. Bilgaiyan, S., Sagnika, S., Das M.: Workflow scheduling in cloud computing environment using cat swarm optimization. In: IEEE International Advance Computing Conference (IACC), pp. 680–685 (2014)

14. Xie, Y., Chen, S., Ni, Q., Hanqing, W.: Integration of resource allocation and task assignment for optimizing the cost and maximum throughput of business processes. J. Intell. Manuf. (2017). https://doi.org/10.1007/s10845-017-1329-z

15. Guerfel, R., Sbaï, Z., Ayed, R.B.: Model checking of cost-effective elasticity strategies in cloud computing. In: Braubach, L., et al. (eds.) ICSOC 2017. LNCS, vol. 10797, pp. 80–92. Springer, Cham (2018). https://doi.org/10.1007/978-3-319-91764-1_7

16. Baeten, J.C.M., Middelburg, C.A.: Process Algebra with Timing. Springer, New York (2002). https://doi.org/10.1007/978-3-662-04995-2

17. Bousselmi, K., Brahmi, Z., Gammoudi, M.M.: QoS-aware scheduling of workflows in cloud computing environments. In: IEEE 30th International Conference on Advanced Information Networking and Applications, pp. 737–745 (2016)

18. Mishra, S.K., Puthal, D., Sahoo1, B., Jena, S.K., Obaidat, M.S.: An adaptive task allocation technique for green cloud computing. J. Supercomput. 74(1), 370–385 (2018)

19. Bessai, K., Youcef, S., Oulamara, A., Godart, C., Nurcan, S.: Bi-criteria workflow tasks allocation and scheduling in cloud computing environments. In: IEEE Fifth International Conference on Cloud Computing, pp. 638–645 (2012)

A Data Dependency and Access Threshold Based Replication Strategy for Multi-cloud Workflow Applications

Fei Xie$^{(\boxtimes)}$, Jun Yan$^{(\boxtimes)}$, and Jun Shen$^{(\boxtimes)}$

University of Wollongong, Wollongong, NSW 2500, Australia
fx439@uowmail.edu.au, {jyan,jshen}@uow.edu.au

Abstract. Data replication is one of the significant sub-areas of data management in cloud based workflows. Data-intensive workflow applications can gain great benefits from cloud environments and usually need data management strategies to manage large amounts of data. At the same time, multi-cloud environments become more and more popular. We propose a cost-effective and threshold-based data replication strategy with the consideration of both data dependency and data access times for data-intensive workflows in the multi-cloud environment. Finally, the simulation results show that our approach can greatly reduce total cost of data-intensive workflow applications by considering both of data dependency and data access times in multi-cloud environments.

Keywords: Multi-cloud · Data management · Data replication · Data dependency · Data access times

1 Introduction

In recent years, the increasing amount of data becomes major challenges for all organizations, such as data congestion problems [5, 8, 16], lower data management cost effectiveness [4] and lower data management efficiency [17]. The emergence of cloud computing technologies constructs a novel paradigm for developing and deploying distributed applications.

Cloud storage is not only the adoption of physical hardware but also a highly integrated system which includes network devices, data storage devices, servers, official applications, common access interfaces, network access and client-side programs. Multi-cloud uses two or more cloud computing services in order to allow users to share the workload across multiple cloud service providers. Multi-cloud is commonly used by several famous applications, such as OpenStack and Microsoft Azure [20]. It allows heterogeneous cloud environments to satisfy the user requirements, and can help users minimize the data loss risks and downtime in order to achieve better cloud computing power and quality of service. It can also help users avoid single vendor lock-in risks to a large extent [20]. Multi-cloud is always used to support global or cross-regional collaborative work because the cloud services in multi-cloud always rely on hardware in multiple locations. By using the multi-cloud environment, it is more agile and scalable than only using a single cloud to perform the tasks and share the data [14].

© Springer Nature Switzerland AG 2019
X. Liu et al. (Eds.): ICSOC 2018 Workshops, LNCS 11434, pp. 281–293, 2019.
https://doi.org/10.1007/978-3-030-17642-6_24

A data-intensive workflow such as a scientific workflow may consist of hundreds of complex tasks and huge amount of data. Data management in such a scenario is still a difficult research challenge as moving large amount of data can be cost-ineffective [19]. Data-intensive workflow applications may benefit greatly from multi-cloud because a multi-cloud environment satisfies their cross-regional computation and massive data storage requirements better by leveraging computation and storage capacities of many data centers [15].

The past research works have addressed this challenging problem in two directions by using data placement and replication strategies. Parameters such as data dependency and data access times have been used separately from the data perspective to develop different strategies in order to achieve a better data management performance [2, 12]. Without the consideration of data dependency, highly-dependent data may be stored in locations distant from one another. This may increase the data access cost and the response time. At the same time, without the consideration of data access times, frequently-accessed data may be stored in a remote location. It may also have a significant influence on the total cost, the response time, and the access delay.

In this paper, we propose a data dependency and access threshold based data replication strategy with the consideration of both data dependency and data access times for data-intensive workflows in the multi-cloud environment. In our approach, the data dependency and data access times of datasets are balanced to dynamically control the creation of data replicas. The simulation shows that our approach is more cost-effective than approaches that consider the data dependency or data access times only. The remainder of the paper is organized as follows. Section 2 reviews the major related work and presents the motivation of our work. Then Sect. 3 describes our data replication approach in details. Section 4 discusses the simulation results. Finally, Sect. 5 concludes this paper.

2 Related Work

Cloud computing is known as an emerging and fast growing area of service delivery in information technology aspects. This novel approach is marked as one of the top five emerging technologies that will have a significant improvement on quality of science as well as the society within the next 20 years [1]. In general, cloud technology aims to shift several IT dimensions to remote facilities such as central data storage rather than local processing on capable distant servers instead of stationary or portable devices, integrated data rather than distributed data, and the replacement of dispersion applications by centralized ones [10].

In this paper, we particularly focus on data management challenges in multi-cloud environments by using data replication strategy. Data replication is the strategy of creating multiple data copies and storing the copies in multiple sites [11, 18]. Data replication can help users save cost [7] and response time [13] when tasks are being processed, and improve the data availability [3, 9, 17] and reliability [6].

Several approaches have been proposed for data replication in cloud environments. In [2], authors propose a Latest Access Largest Weight (LALW) strategy in order to select a popular file and calculate a suitable number of copies and grid sites for data replication in data grids by considering access frequency to exhibit the importance for access history in different time intervals. In [12], authors propose a Fair-Share Replication (FSR) strategy that takes both access load and storage load into account to determine the replicas creation. An average access frequency is used to compare with the access frequency of targeted datasets to find the popular file and rank the file. In [3], authors propose a dynamic, cost-aware data replication strategy by identifying the minimum number of replicas in order to satisfy the desired availability, get the maximum value and keep the total weight less than or equal to the peak budget at the same time.

Based on the findings from past research, either data dependency or data access times can significantly influence the data management solution. The attribute of data dependency considers the relationship between two datasets from the perspective of tasks. The attribute of data access times considers the number of access times of a dataset accessed by tasks. We argue that both data dependency and data access times should be considered jointly in order to improve the data management performance.

3 Approaches

By taking both data dependency and data access times into consideration, our approach aims to create replicas for datasets that are both highly dependent and frequently accessed. This also balances the number of the replicas created and the total cost saved. A summary of the notations used in our approach and their definitions is given in Table 1.

Table 1. Notations.

Symbol	Meaning
G	A workflow application
T	The set of tasks in the workflow application G
E	The set of edges in the workflow application G
D	The set of datasets in the workflow application G
$|T(d_i)|$	The number of tasks in T which use the dataset d_i
$Dep(d_i, d_j)$	The data dependency between the dataset d_i and d_j
DCD_w	Within-DataCenter Data Dependency
DCD_b	Between-DataCenter Data Dependency
HDD	High-Dependent Dataset
AT_{total}	The sum of all data access times of all datasets
AT_{avg}	The average access times of all datasets
$\varnothing$	Threshold value for data access times candidate pool
N_D	The total number of datasets
HAD	Hot-Access Dataset
DC	The set of data centers in the multi-cloud environment
CSP	The set of cloud service providers in the multi-cloud environment
$TCost$	Total cost

(*continued*)

Table 1. (*continued*)

Symbol	Meaning
$TCost_{max}$	The total cost when there are no replication happened
$TCost_{current}$	The current total cost value when Ø stay at a specific value
$NR_{current}$	The current number of replicas when Ø stay at a specific value
μ	The cost reduction per replica
$Cost_s$	Data storage cost
$time_s$	The storage duration
$Cost_t$	Data transmission cost
DC^*	The set of data centers with all initial datasets and replicas
γ	The data storage rate of the cloud service provider csp

3.1 Prerequisite

Before the start of our data replication strategy, we assume that initial dataset and task placement has been completed by using a data and task placement strategy. Datasets and tasks have been allocated into geographically-dispersed data centers in DC from different cloud service providers in CSP.

3.2 Workflow Application Model

A workflow application $G = (T, E)$ is modelled as a Directed Acyclic Graph (DAG), where T is the set of vertices as tasks and E is a set of edges as the control dependencies between the tasks. In the workflow application G, the child task can only start after its parent tasks have finished and the associated control dependencies have been transferred to the child task.

3.3 Data Dependency Model

The data dependency represents the data relationship between each two datasets in D. The data dependency between datasets d_i and d_j is defined as the ratio of the number of tasks that use both d_i and d_j to the total number of workflow tasks T [19]. Therefore, the data dependency can be calculated as follows in Eq. 1.

$$Dep(d_i, d_j) = \frac{|(T(d_i) \cap T(d_j))|}{|T|} \tag{1}$$

In multi-cloud environments, we define Within-DataCenter Data Dependency (DCD_w) and Between-DataCenter Data Dependency (DCD_b). DCD_w is the data dependency between the dataset d_i and all other datasets within the same location of d_i. DCD_b is the data dependency between the dataset d_i and all other datasets within the different locations of d_i. DCD_w and DCD_b are both represented as a 2-tuple (dc, d).

A $DCD(dc, d)$ function is used to calculate DCD_w and DCD_b for each dataset d in each data center dc. For each dataset d_i in D, we calculate their DCD_w and DCD_b based on its location dc in DC as follows in Eqs. 2 and 3.

$$DCD_w(dc, d_i) = \sum_{j=1}^{n} Dep(d_i, d_j), i \neq j, \left(d_i \text{ and } d_j \text{ store in the same location}\right) \quad (2)$$

$$DCD_b(dc, d_i) = \sum_{j=1}^{n} Dep(d_i, d_j), i \neq j, \left(d_i \text{ and } d_j \text{ store in different locations}\right) \quad (3)$$

For a dataset d placed in the data center dc, if its $DCD_b (dc, d) > DCD_w(dc, d)$, we partition the dataset d into a new set of datasets called High-Dependent Dataset HDD. A $DepCompare()$ function is used to compare DCD_w and DCD_b for each dataset d in D in order to partition the datasets into High-Dependent Dataset HDD.

3.4   Data Access Times Model

Data access times is the number of times of a dataset accessed by all tasks in a single execution of the workflow. We count data access times AT for each dataset d in D during workflow execution period by the function $AT(d)$. Then we calculate the sum of all data access times of all datasets AT_{total} as follows in Eq. 4 and set the threshold $\varnothing$. A $ATCalculation()$ function is used to calculate the value of AT_{total} and AT_{avg}.

$$AT_{total} = \sum_{i=1}^{n} AT(d_i), d_i \in D \quad (4)$$

Then we calculate the average data access times of all datasets ET_{avg} with the total number of datasets N_D as follows in Eq. 5.

$$AT_{avg} = \frac{AT_{total}}{N_D} \quad (5)$$

If $AT(d) > \varnothing * AT_{avg}$ then, we partition the dataset d into a new set of datasets called Hot-Access Dataset HAD. The threshold value $\varnothing$ can be dynamically changed from 0 to N_D in order to optimize the total cost and the number of replicas. The $ATCompare()$ function is designed to compare the value between $AT(d)$ and $\varnothing * AT_{avg}$ in order to determine if a dataset d in D should be categorized into HAD.

3.5   Eligible Replicated Dataset Candidate Pool

We compare HDD and HAD in order to identify the eligible dataset candidates for replication, which are the overlapping elements in both HDD and HAD. These eligible dataset candidates are both highly dependent and highly accessed. Replicas of these datasets should be created and placed into appropriate data centers using our replica placement strategy.

3.6 Multi-cloud Environment Model

Multi-cloud is the use of two or more cloud computing services in order to allow users to share the workload across multiple cloud service providers. A multi-cloud environment is represented as a 2-tuple $MC = (DC, CSP)$, where

- DC: $\{dc_1, dc_2, dc_3, \ldots, dc_p\}$ is the set of data centers in the multi-cloud environment.
- CSP: $\{csp_1, csp_2, csp_3, \ldots, csp_u\}$ is the set of cloud service providers in the multi-cloud environment.
- Each dc has only one csp, while one csp may have multiple dc.

3.7 Cost Model for Multi-cloud

The total cost $TCost$ is defined as the sum of the data storage cost $Cost_s$ and the data transmission cost $Cost_t$, as follows in Eq. 6.

$$TCost = \sum Cost_s + \sum Cost_t \qquad (6)$$

The data storage cost $Cost_s$ is dependent on the data storage rate of the cloud service provider γ, the size of the dataset $Size(d)$, and the storage duration $time_s$. As each cloud service provider has its own data storage pricing model, it is necessary and indispensable to consider the data storage cost rates γ of different dc in DC. Data storage cost $Cost_s$ for the dataset d can be presented as follows in Eq. 7.

$$Cost_s = \sum\nolimits_{dc=1}^{p} \gamma * Size(d) * time_s \qquad (7)$$

The data transfer cost $Cost_t$ is dependent on the transfer cost ratio α, the size of the dataset $Size(d)$, and the data access times of the dataset $AT(d)$. Therefore, data transfer cost $Cost_t$ for the dataset d can be presented as follows in Eq. 8.

$$Cost_t = \alpha * Size(d) * AT(d) \qquad (8)$$

3.8 Recommend Value of $\varnothing'$

A recommend value of $\varnothing'$ will return when the result of following Eq. 8 (μ) is optimal, where $TCost_{max}$ denotes the total cost when there are no replication happened, and $TCost_{current}$ and $NR_{current}$ denotes the current total cost value and the current number of replicas respectively when $\varnothing$ stay at a specific value. We insert an evaluation parameter μ to evaluate cost reduction per replica in Eq. 9. Therefore when μ stays at a maximum value at a specific value of $\emptyset$, it means the cost reduction per replica is optimal and this value of $\emptyset$ can be returned as the recommend value $\emptyset'$.

$$\mu = \frac{TCost_{max} - TCost_{current}}{NR_{current}} \tag{9}$$

3.9 Algorithms

Our data replication algorithms include two sub-algorithms as follows.

```
Algorithm 1. Data replication loop
Input: DC, D, CSP, Ø
Output: DC*: set of data centers with all initial da-
tasets and replicas
Ø': A recommended value of Ø
1.   begin
2.           Insert workflow G
3.           Dynamically change threshold parameter Ø from
0 to N_D by step 0.01
4.                   start Algorithm 2
5.                   List all eligible datasets
6.                   Place all eligible datasets
to related task locations
7.                   Account the number of repli-
cas NR_current
8.                   Calculate TCost_current based on
the placed location for all replicas
9.                   Account the TCost_max when
there are no replication happened
10.                  Calculate each value of evalu-
ation parameter μ at different value of Ø
11.                  end Algorithm 2 after Ø reach N_D
12.          Find the best value of μ
13.                  return Ø' and DC*
14.  end
```

```
Algorithm 2. Eligible replicated dataset creation
Input: DC, D, CSP, Ø
Output: eligible replicated datasets
1.  begin
2.  for (each dataset d, d ∈ D) do
3.          Locate the location of all datasets
4.          Calculate all data dependencies for each da-
taset
5.              for (each data center dc, dc ∈ DC) do
6.                  Calculate DCDw and DCDb by function
DCD(dc, d)
7.                      Compare DCDw and DCDb for
each dataset d in D by function DepCompare()
8.                          While (DCDb(d) > DCDw(d)) do
9.                          Generate HDD candidate pool
10.                         end while
11.         Continue
12.         Calculate all data access times for each d
13.             ATCalculation()
14.                 ATCompare()
15.                     While (AT(d) > Ø * ATavg) do
16.                     Generate HAD candidate pool
17.                     end while
18.         if  d ∈ {HAD ∩ HDD}
19.             then d is a eligible replicated da-
taset
20.             end if
21.         end for
22.             return all datasets and eligible repli-
cated datasets
23.     end for
24.     end
```

4   Simulations

4.1   Simulation Settings

Our simulations are conducted on CloudSim. We performed three scientific workflows, 25 nodes Montage workflow, 30 nodes CyberShake workflow and 30 nodes LIGO Inspiral workflow in order to simulate the effectiveness of our strategy. The data items of Montage workflow includes d_1 to d_{18} which are accessed by tasks {1, 45, 45, 45, 45, 45, 107, 107, 1, 1, 1, 1, 1, 1, 1, 1, 1, 1} times respectively and has the data size from d_1

to d_{18} {0.29, 4000, 4000, 4000, 4000, 4000, 0.26, 270, 7.2, 2.3, 2.8, 21, 12, 7.2, 165430, 165430, 6600, 320} respectively. The data items of CyberShake workflow includes d_1 to d_5 which are accessed by tasks {90, 572, 574, 200, 1} times respectively and has the data size from d_1 to d_5 {220, 5500, 0.3, 2000, 2100} respectively. The data items of LIGO Inspiral workflow includes d_1 to d_8 which are accessed by tasks {42, 84, 42, 14, 79, 14, 35, 42} times respectively and has the data size from d_1 to d_8 {800, 150, 8600, 230, 300, 320, 940, 1200} respectively. The pricing model of four adopted cloud service providers (Amazon, Microsoft, AT&T and Google) is shown in Table 2. Besides, we set the storage duration $time_s$ as 1 for the cost calculation convenience in order to make the consistence of each data storage time in every different *CSP*.

Table 2. The pricing model of adopted multi-cloud service providers

Cloud service provider	Storage service	Storage price (per data unit)
Amazon	Amazon S3	0.025
Microsoft	Microsoft Azure	0.034
AT&T	AT&T Cloud Storage	0.040
Google	Google Cloud Storage	0.026
Data transfer cost	0.070 per data unit	

After eligible datasets are determined, we create replicas for them and distribute the replicas to all task locations which require these replicas as input datasets and have enough available storage space. The reason of this placement operation is that replicas are frequently required by tasks which require these replicas as input datasets. Therefore, replicas may store as near as task locations for reducing the data movement cost.

4.2   Simulation Results

In the first simulation, we tested four scenarios on all three scientific workflow applications. As shown in Fig. 1, it is obvious that our strategy can significantly decrease the total cost compared with other three approaches in all three data-intensive workflows. Our strategy has a 94.12%, 99.10%, and 69.91% decrease respectively in Montage, CyberShake and LIGO Inspiral workflow to compare with the no replication scenario of those three workflows. Besides, our strategy has a 40.11% and 92.49% reduction respectively in Montage and CyberShake workflow to compare with the data dependency adoption only scenario of those two workflows. Apart from that, our strategy has a 31.41%, 92.80% and 67.32% decrease respectively in Montage, CyberShake and LIGO Inspiral workflow to compare with the data access times adoption only scenario of those three workflows.

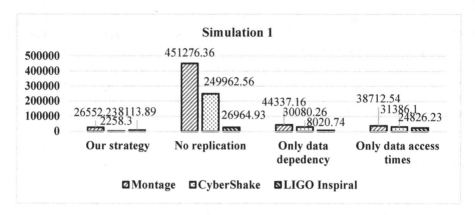

Fig. 1. The result of simulation 1

In the second simulation, we change the threshold $\varnothing$ to dynamically adjust *HAD* in order to view the impact on the number of replica created and the total cost saving.

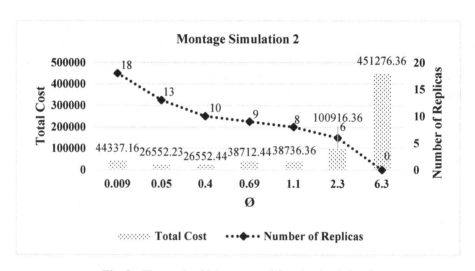

Fig. 2. The result of Montage workflow in simulation 2

As shown in Fig. 2, there is an obvious fluctuation on the total cost and the number of replicas when the value of $\varnothing$ dynamically increase from 0 to N_D in the Montage workflow. It is recommended that the cost reduction per replica remains at a maximum level when $\varnothing$ stays at 2.3 in the Montage workflow. Similarly, we can find the results of CyberShake and LIGO Inspiral workflow in our simulation 2 as follows in Figs. 3 and 4 as follows. It is recommend that the total cost and the number of replicas exist in an acceptable level when $\varnothing$ stays in the range from 0.79 to 1.79 in the CyberShake workflow, and when $\varnothing$ stays at 0.95 in the LIGO Inspiral workflow.

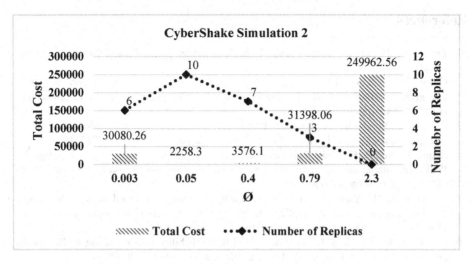

Fig. 3. The result of CyberShake workflow in simulation 2

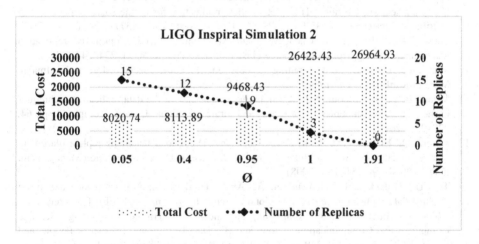

Fig. 4. The result of LIGO Inspiral workflow in simulation 2

5   Conclusions

To conclude, data replication is commonly used to decrease access latency, improve data availability, and reduce data transfer cost by creating data replicas to geographically-distributed data centers. In this paper, we propose a data dependency and access threshold based data replication strategy with the consideration of both data dependency and data access times jointly for data-intensive workflows in the multi-cloud environment. The simulation results shows that our data replication strategy can greatly reduce the total cost of data-intensive workflow execution and suggest a recommended value of ∅ in order to find the optimal performance by using our strategy.

References

1. Buyya, R., Broberg, J., Gościński, A.: Cloud Computing: Principles and Paradigms. Wiley, Hoboken
2. Chang, R-S., Chang, H-P., Wang, Y-T.: A dynamic weighted data replication strategy in data grids. In: IEEE/ACS International Conference on Computer Systems and Applications, AICCSA 2008, pp. 414–421 (2008)
3. Gill, N.K., Singh, S.: A dynamic, cost-aware, optimized data replication strategy for heterogeneous cloud data centers. Future Gener. Comput. Syst. **65**, 10–32 (2016)
4. Janpet, J., Wen, Y-F.: Reliable and available data replication planning for cloud storage. In: IEEE 27th International Conference on Advanced Information Networking and Applications (AINA), pp. 678–685 (2013)
5. Khalajzadeh, H., Yuan, D., Grundy, J., Yang, Y.: Improving cloud-based online social network data placement and replication. In: IEEE 9th International Conference on Cloud Computing (CLOUD), pp. 678–685 (2016)
6. Li, W., Yang, Y., Yuan, D.: Ensuring cloud data reliability with minimum replication by proactive replica checking. IEEE Trans. Comput. **65**(5), 1494–1506 (2016)
7. Lin, J.-W., Chen, C.-H., Chang, J.M.: QoS-aware data replication for data-intensive applications in cloud computing systems. IEEE Trans. Cloud Comput. **1**(1), 101–115 (2013)
8. Liu, G., Shen, H., Chandler, H.: Selective data replication for online social networks with distributed datacenters. IEEE Trans. Parallel Distrib. Syst. **27**(8), 2377–2393 (2016)
9. Long, S.-Q., Zhao, Y.-L., Chen, W.: MORM: a multi-objective optimized replication management strategy for cloud storage cluster. J. Syst. Archit. **60**(2), 234–244 (2014)
10. Marinescu, D.C.: Cloud Computing: Theory and Practice. Elsevier/Morgan Kaufmann, Morgan Kaufmann is an imprint of Elsevier, Boston (2013)
11. Milani, B.A., Navimipour, N.J.: A comprehensive review of the data replication techniques in the cloud environments: Major trends and future directions. J. Netw. Comput. Appl. **64**, 229–238 (2016)
12. Rasool, Q., Li, J., Oreku, G.S., Zhang, S., Yang, D.: A load balancing replica placement strategy in data grid. In: Third International Conference on Digital Information Management, ICDIM 2008, pp. 751–756 (2008)
13. Tos, U., Mokadem, R., Hameurlain, A., Ayav, T., Bora, S.: A performance and profit oriented data replication strategy for cloud systems. In: International IEEE Conferences on Ubiquitous Intelligence & Computing, Advanced and Trusted Computing, Scalable Computing and Communications, Cloud and Big Data Computing, Internet of People, and Smart World Congress (UIC/ATC/ScalCom/CBDCom/IoP/SmartWorld), pp. 780–787 (2016)
14. Wang, C., Lu, Z., Wu, Z., Wu, J., Huang, S.: Optimizing multi-cloud CDN deployment and scheduling strategies using big data analysis. In: IEEE International Conference on Services Computing (SCC), pp. 273–280 (2017)
15. Wang, T., Yao, S., Xu, Z., Jia, S.: DCCP: an effective data placement strategy for data-intensive computations in distributed cloud computing systems. J. Supercomput. **72**(7), 2537–2564 (2016)
16. Wu, X.: Data sets replicas placements strategy from cost-effective view in the cloud. Sci. Program. **2016**, 13 (2016)

17. Ye, Z., Li, S., Zhou, J.: A two-layer geo-cloud based dynamic replica creation strategy. Appl. Math. Inf. Sci. **8**(1), 431–439 (2014)
18. Yuan, D., Cui, L., Liu, X.: Cloud data management for scientific workflows: Research issues, methodologies, and state-of-the-art. In: 10th International Conference on Semantics, Knowledge and Grids (SKG), pp. 21–28 (2014)
19. Yuan, D., Yang, Y., Liu, X., Chen, J.: A data placement strategy in scientific cloud workflows. Future Gener. Comput. Syst. **26**(8), 1200–1214 (2010)
20. Zhang, Q., Li, S., Li, Z., Xing, Y., Yang, Z., Dai, Y.: CHARM: a cost-efficient multi-cloud data hosting scheme with high availability. IEEE Trans. Cloud Comput. **3**(3), 372–386 (2015)

Support Context-Adaptation in the Constrained Application Protocol (CoAP)

Yuji Dong[1,2], Kaiyu Wan[2(✉)], Yong Yue[2], and Xin Huang[2]

[1] University of Liverpool, Liverpool L69 3BX, UK
yuji.dong@outlook.com
[2] Xi'an Jiaotong Liverpool University, Suzhou 215123, China
{kaiyu.wan,yong.yue}@xjtlu.edu.cn

Abstract. The number of interconnected smart devices has already rapidly increased, and the Internet of Things (IoT) has presented tremendous potential in various domains such as smart cities, healthcare and industrial automation. To integrate the IoT applications to Web to utilise the advantages of Internet infrastructures, the Constrained Application Protocol (CoAP) is proposed as one of the standardised protocols for IoT applications. However, the REST architecture style, which is the foundation of Web, was not designed for IoT applications and thus cannot satisfy all the requirements of IoT applications. To efficiently monitor the IoT resources asynchronously, the IETF (Internet Engineering Task Force) extended the CoAP with Resource Observe mechanism. However, the Resource Observe mechanism benefits sensors rather than actuators. For the actuator resources, the CoAP cannot support the context-adaptation, and therefore it cannot always correctly estimate system states and handle complex physical behaviours. In this paper, we extend the CoAP with a context-adaptation mechanism to enrich the system states estimation and other operations in the protocol level for physical behaviour modelling and implementation. The extended mechanism is implemented in the Californium (CF) framework.

Keywords: Context-adaptation · CoAP · Internet of Things

1 Introduction

IoT is envisioned to integrate the physical world into computer-based systems. Recent years, with the advanced technology development such as sensors, networking and data processing, IoT has illustrated great potential in various fields [9]. When connecting IoT devices into the Internet, the IoT devices and services are expected to interoperate at the application layer. Inspired by the success of the World Wide Web, Guinard [10] proposed the concept of Web of Things, which advocates using the REST (Representational State Transfer) architectural style to design IoT applications and using the ubiquity of HTTP to interact with devices. HTTP over TCP has problems in constrained environments,

© Springer Nature Switzerland AG 2019
X. Liu et al. (Eds.): ICSOC 2018 Workshops, LNCS 11434, pp. 294–305, 2019.
https://doi.org/10.1007/978-3-030-17642-6_25

though, in particular with the small frame sizes and the lossy links of low-power wireless communication, because it requires more resources to keep the connection. Instead of adding the compression techniques to solve the problems, the IETF designed a new Web protocol from scratch: the Constrained Application Protocol (CoAP) [16]. CoAP follows the style of REST but is tailored to the requirements of low-cost devices and IoT application scenarios. It uses a compact binary format and runs over UDP or DTLS when security mechanisms are enabled, which also enables multicast communication. On the top, the request/response sub-layer enables RESTful interaction through the well-known methods GET, PUT, POST, and DELETE as well as response codes that are defined under the HTTP specification. CoAP resources are addressable by URIs, and Internet Media Types are used to represent resource states. RESTful caching and proxying enable network scalability.

However, the application layer protocol is responsible for the application level support, where the RESTful API is not sufficient for all functional requirements of the IoT systems. Thus recently the resource observes [11] mechanism is designed to fit the sensors' requirements as the publish-subscribe model.

Even though the resource observe mechanism can already naturally cooperate with the functionalities of the sensors, the CoAP has no primary support for the actuators from the context-adaptation perspective. However, the Context-Adaptation support on the unreliable network (like Internet-based network) is critical to implement the physical behaviours in the IoT systems. In this paper, we will give some general models for the physical behaviour modelling and related implementations from the Context-Adaptation perspective.

The rest of the paper is organised as follows. Section 2 explains the related work and background. Then the Sect. 3 is the main body to support the Context-Adaptation in CoAP. This section is divided into three parts including the motivation, Context-Adaptation Messaging Model and Adapt Option. The Sect. 4 explains the implementation based on the Californium (CF) framework and the Sect. 5 gives the conclusion and future works.

2   Related Work

The context adaptation has played an important role in continuously changing physical environment, especially in the complex IoT systems. In [2], a design for adaptation approach is proposed to support the development, deployment and execution of systems in dynamic environments by exploiting service refinement and re-configuration techniques. In [15], the MAPE-K feedback loop is used to support a synchronisation and adaptation mechanism for the real-world process as a process-based framework. It uses a different perspective from combining processes' virtual world and real world effects to build self-adaptive IoT systems. The work can achieve a high level of autonomy and resilience against failures for physical world process. In [4], the authors provide the methodology of using a model-based service-oriented architecture with service composition to support self-adaptation. The work is solid and also provides fault tolerance mechanism.

In [3], the service adaptation is achieved using service composition for automatic reconfiguration based on the rich interface specifications. Following this idea, they used the Discrete-Time Markov Chains in a language to describe the impact of adaptation tactics and the assumption about the environment.

Different from other solutions, the support from protocol level is more general than other approaches, especially when the CoAP becomes one of the IoT standard protocols. There is much work based on the CoAP from different perspectives such as the Security [14], cooperation with the Cloud Computing [19], and the applications [13]. However, the CoAP has no general Context-Adaptation support, which limits its capabilities in many complex IoT scenarios. The closest idea is in [18], where the author designed the IoT application building blocks called RESTlets for direct binding of sensors and actuators based on CoAP. However, different from creating the extra individual building block in [18], we intend to extend the CoAP itself with the related behaviour models to support from protocol level; therefore the user can have the benefit from the infrastructural protocol without requiring any specific techniques.

3   Context-Adaptation in CoAP

3.1   Motivation

Scalability, extensibility and interoperability among heterogeneous things and their environments, are key requirements and challenges in the IoT systems. Since these requirements are similar to the Web, which is one of the most successful distributed systems, the Web of Things (WoT) concept is proposed to integrate the smart things into the Web (the application layer) rather than the Internet (the network layer). To achieve the integration, some common patterns used for the Web such as the REST model are applied in the IoT applications [8]. HTTP (Hypertext Transfer Protocol) [7] is the classical implementation of REST architectural style. However, the devices and networks in the IoT environments may be extremely constrained; thus the typical approaches around the HTTP protocol can be too heavy to support the IoT systems. The IETF Constrained RESTful Environments (CoRE) working group, therefore, designed the CoAP following the REST architectural style with tailored features for IoT applications and Machine-to-Machine (M2M) scenarios with resource-constrained devices [1].

However, the REST architectural style was mainly designed for the World Wide Web, which has many different requirements compared to the IoT applications. REST architectural style is network-centric [8], which means the basic operations like GET, POST, PUT and DELETE are defined in the protocol level as the unified interface. While this design principle supports the Web's scalability and interoperability, it also constrains the request-response model and operations for the different web resources. However, the request-response model with four basic operations is not sufficient for the IoT applications' requirements.

A typical example is an environment monitoring case when a client is interested in having a current representing of a resource (sensor) over a while, for example, when we use a temperature sensor to detect the abnormal temperature in the industrial environments. Compared to the active roll polling requesting to get the information, we prefer to let the sensor notify the system when the temperature value is out of the normal range. The IETF community, therefore, extends the CoAP with the *Observing Resources* mechanism based on the *Observe Design Pattern* with which the targeted resource can be used to observe the detailed environments and make the notification if the observations satisfy specific pre-defined policies.

Although the extended *Observing Resources* mechanism provides the basic messaging model for most sensors, the actuators' requirements from using the CoAP are not satisfied. In our previous work [6], the issues of using the REST architecture style in the IoT systems are discussed, and the solution is proposed as the Feedback-based Adaptive Service-Oriented Paradigm (FASOP).

CoAP is an application layer protocol based on the REST model; therefore it also inherits the issues from the REST architectural style. In the IoT systems, CoAP's messaging model cannot always guarantee the correct system states estimation; therefore it hardly supports complex physical behaviours.

For example, in the scenario to turn on/off a light, a standard CoAP solution will provide a RESTful interface which accepts PUT/POST operation to trigger the controller of the light. If the client receives the response with code "200 OK", the operation to the light is expected to succeed. However, the light itself cannot obtain the information of whether the light is operated successfully because the operation of the light has a physical effect. Therefore the response code of "200 OK" cannot guarantee the successful operation, which may lead to wrong system states estimation. In the large complex IoT systems, the wrong state's estimation may cause big issues, and it is difficult to diagnose them. For more complex scenarios such as controlling a robot via CoAP, the disadvantage from the lack of related behaviour models in CoAP becomes more obvious. If we intend to remotely control a robot driving in speed a via CoAP, the normal method is to give a PUT/POST operation message to the robot with the complete command. However, the response from the robot's actuator cannot indicate whether the command is executed correctly because the robot's actuator can only know if the command is executed without knowing the effect from the command.

To solve this kind of problems, extra services could be used to detect the context change. For the former example, we can use extra light and speed sensors to detect the effect from the CoAP command so that the interface can give the client a correct response. Figure 1 expresses how the FASOP is used in the basic request-response model for the issues of using the REST model in the IoT systems.

Not only for correct states estimation, but IoT systems also need the context-adaptation model to support many complex behaviours. If the context-adaptation model can have real-time support, it can even model complex physical behaviours to support the robots' behaviours based on the calculus models.

Compared to the general paradigm proposed in [6], the context-adaptation support in CoAP is more comfortable to be reused. The context-adaptation support in the protocol has many advantages compared to other solutions because the protocol is one of the necessary infrastructures for the IoT applications and it can provide the general support without specific middlewares.

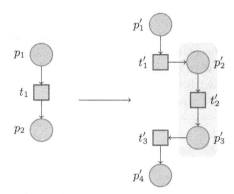

Fig. 1. To apply the feedback-based adaptive service-oriented paradigm in the basic request-response model to support context-adaptation

3.2   Context-Adaptation Messaging Model

The main purpose of the Context-Adaptation support is to support the complex physical behaviours modelling and development over the unreliable networks. Because scalability is one of the key concerns in the IoT applications, based on the conclusion in [5], the decentralised control solution is preferable. The Context-Adaptation Messaging Model is a lightweight model extended from the original messaging models in CoAP to keep them compatible; therefore the feedback control loops would not extremely affect the scalability of CoAP.

As a decentralised approach, the management of the decentralised feedback loops is a complicated problem as the contexts and targets can always change. To enable the basic request-response model to support context-adaptive behaviours, the requested targets need to obtain all the required context information. Based on the existing messaging models and mechanisms in CoAP, we propose the following two patterns to locate and retrieve the context information.

1. The requested message self-contains all the addresses of the required context information, and the requested node will issue another request to the addresses of the contexts information. The final response will include the requested behaviours and all the changes in the related contexts information during the period.
2. The *Resource Observe* mechanism can make the pre-register between different IoT nodes. If the requested node already registers itself to several other nodes and the requested message does not contain other addresses, the requested node will send back the requested behaviours and the changes of the pre-registered contexts information during the period.

Apart from the direct request-response process, the CoAP also provides the proxy mechanism to let the proxy forward some messages. Since the proxy allows more flexible and efficient ways to handle the messages [17], we also support the Context-Adaptation Messaging Model with the proxies involved.

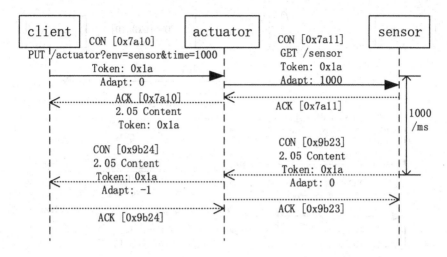

Fig. 2. Basic context-adaptation messaging model without proxy

Messaging Model Without Proxy. The Fig. 2 illustrates the basic Context-Adaptation Messaging Model extended from the direct request-response model. To provide reliable control, the context-adaptive requests are required to transfer with a reliable transmission, which means the message has to be marked as Conformable (CON). When the *actuator* receives the requested context adaptive message, it will issue another request to the specified *sensor*. Since the message is still marked as the context-adaptive request, the requested sensor will monitor the environments during the given period and respond to the requested *actuator* with the context changing information. Then the actuator can combine the data and send back to the original client.

In the Fig. 3, the context adaptive request does not specify another node's address and the requested *actuator* has already *Resource Observe* another sensor, so the *actuator* wait for the given period and eventually respond with the possible changed context information. This form of the Context-Adaptation Messaging Model can hide the details about the required *sensor* if the IoT applications do not want the client to know the *sensor*. However, it requires the pre-register with *Resource Observe*, which may affect the scalability if the IoT applications contain too many this kind of dependencies.

Messaging Model with Proxy. The proxy can play an important role in the real IoT applications because the powerful devices can be used to handle large amounts of computation and network pressure as the proxies. The Fig. 4 illustrates an example of requesting a context-adaptive message from a *proxy*. Different from the other forwarding messages, if the *Proxy* detects a context-adaptive message, it will split the message into two messages and issue two different requests to the *actuator* and the *sensor* respectively. The proxy is

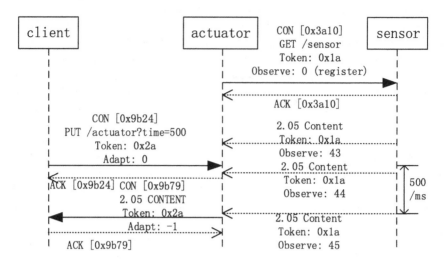

Fig. 3. Context-adaptation messaging model in observing resources without proxy

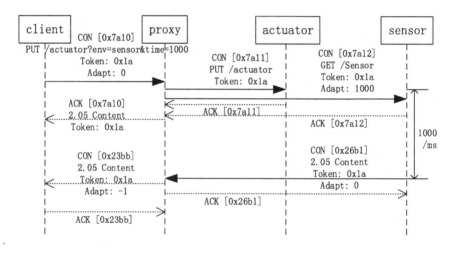

Fig. 4. Basic context-adaptation messaging model with proxy

responsible for managing the Context-Adaptation Messaging Model and carries all the pressures of handling all the incoming requests from different nodes. In this case, it is just a normal original CoAP message for the requested *actuator*.

In Fig. 5, the messages sequences are similar to the case in Fig. 3. The difference is that the *proxy* takes the responsibility of managing the Context-Adaptation Messaging Model, so the context-adaptive message for the requested actuator is a normal original request. The advantage of using a proxy to support the Context-Adaptation Messaging Model with Resource Observe mechanism is that the proxies can manage complex dependencies as a centralised node to reduce the pressures for other resource-constrained nodes.

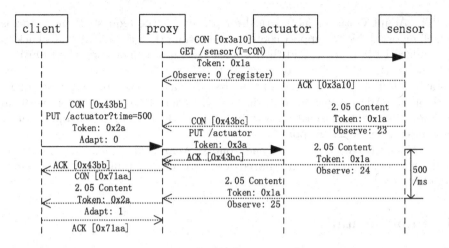

Fig. 5. Context-adaptation messaging model in observing resources with proxy

3.3   The Adapt Option

Similar as the Observe Option for Resource Observe mechanism, the Adapt Option's format is defined in the Table 1 where C stands for Critical, U stands for Unsafe, N stands for No-Cache-Key and R stands for Repeatable. If it is included in a PUT request or a response message, the requested node knows it is a context-adaptive message.

When the Adapt Option is included in a PUT request with the value 0, it extends the PUT method so it will parse the requested URI to detect if there is any required node's address. Then the requested node will check if itself is observing any valid resource. The requested node handles the context-adaptive message following the Context-Adaptation Messaging Model described in Sect. 3.2. When the Adapt Option is included in a PUT request with an option value which is not 0 or −1, it extends the PUT method, so it not only retrieves a current representation of the target resource but also records the representation of the target resource during the given period based on the option value.

The option value −1 is the exceptional value which is used to confirm the end of a context adaptive request. If the response contains an Adapt Option with the option value −1, the receiving node knows that the response is from a context-adaptive request and it can do the further analysis and decision based on the response.

Table 1. The adapt option

No.	C	U	N	R	Name	Format	Length	Default
128		x	-		Adapt	uint	0-3 B	(none)

The Adapt Option is not critical for processing the request. If the server is unwilling or unable to support context-adaptation, then the request falls back to a standard PUT request, and the response does not include the Adapt Option.

The Adapt Option is not part of the Cache-Key: a cacheable response obtained with an Adapt Option in the request can be used to satisfy a request without an Adapt Option, and vice versa. When a stored response with an Adapt Option is used to satisfy a standard GET/PUT request, the option must be removed before the response is returned.

To track the entire process of one Context-Adaptation Messaging, the *Token* is used to confirm if the transferred messages are contained in one context-adaptive request.

4   Implementation

We have implemented some Context-Adaptation Messaging Models based on the open-source framework - "Californium (CF)", which is a great Java implementation of CoAP for IoT cloud services [12].

The Californium (CF) framework is implemented in a 3-staged architecture including network stage, protocol stage and business logic stage. Since the architecture has three decoupled stages, the Context-Adaptation Messaging Model could be easily extended in the protocol stage, and we do not need to re-write all the necessary transport protocols.

In the implementation, we add three new classes - *AdaptingEndpoint*, *AdaptRelation* and *CoapAdaptRelation*. Similar as the Observe Mechanism in Californium (CF) framework, the resource can support the Context-Adaptation by creating an *AdaptRelation* to define the context-adaptation relationships between the actuators and sensors. The users can manage the *AdaptRelation*'s life-cycles to support their business logic.

To satisfy the functional requirements in the Context-Adaptation Message Model, we also modify some existing classes in the Californium (CF) framework to cooperate with the *AdaptRelation*. For example, we set up a reversed number - "128" in the CoAP Option Number Registry to define the "Adapt" option. The classes like *OptionSet*, *Request*, *CoapClient* and *CoapResource* are all modified with some new attributes and methods to make the CoAP resources support our Context-Adaptation Messaging Models.

Figure 6 is a state machine which specifies the implementation from the perspective of a resource supporting context-adaptation. It starts from the state that the resource receives a request containing the adapt option.

If the request has a valid URL with parameter *env*, or the requested resource already has *ObserveRelation*, the resource will create a new *AdaptRelation* and initialise it with the related parameters. After the new *AdaptRelation* is initialised, the resource will create a new request to send to another resource based on the parameter *env* from the incoming request's URL. If the *AdaptRelation*

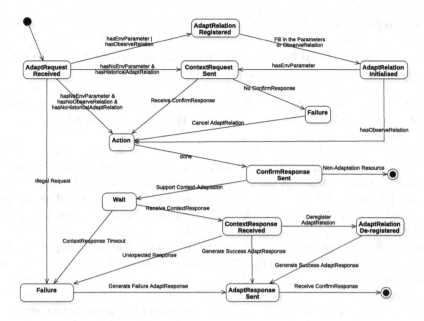

Fig. 6. The state machine to support context-adaptation in CoAP

is created based on *ObserveRelation*, the resource can directly do the action based on the incoming request without sending a request to another resource. The resource can also have historical *AdaptRelation*, and if it does, the existing *AdaptRelation* can be used without creating a new one.

If the incoming request cannot satisfy the context-adaptation conditions, it will be degraded to a request following the original request-response model. In this case, after the resource's action is done, the resource will respond to the requesting resource and end the context-adaptation model.

If the context-adaptation conditions are satisfied, the resource will enter to *Wait* state after it finishes its action. The waiting time is depending on the parameter in the *AdaptRelation*. In the successful mode, the resource can receive the *ContextResponse* which detects the context changing from another resource. Then the resource can decide whether to de-registered the *AdaptRelation* or not. If the *AdaptRelation* is kept, the next context-adaptive request coming to this resource does not need to create a new *AdaptRelation*.

The errors can be in different stages and all traceable. Therefore the resource supporting context-adaptation can provide richer information to estimate the system states. No matter whether the resource's action succeeds, the resource can generate the related *AdaptResponse* and send it back to the requesting client.

The current implementation is still a simple prototype and does not support *Proxy*. To fully support context-adaptation in CoAP could be extremely difficult and we consider many problems as the future work. For example, the permissions from the requests and requested resources may be different; thus the current implementation may cause some security issues.

5 Conclusion

This paper has described how context-adaptation can be applied to the CoAP to improve system states estimation and functionally enrich the physical modelling abilities in the IoT systems from the protocol level. Compared to other context-adaptation solutions, the Context Adaptation in CoAP is a more general infrastructure level support, especially when the CoAP has already been one of the standards for IoT systems.

However, to provide precise Context Adaptation in CoAP is difficult. In this paper, we give the four types of Messaging Models to support general context adaptation. The implementation is based on the Californium (CF) framework, and we did not implement the messaging models with a proxy. The current context-adaptation support for CoAP still face some issues such as security problems, which are considered as the future work.

In the future, we consider adding the QoS and Security support in the Context-Adaptation support in CoAP to achieve real-time property. If the CoAP has real-time context-adaptation, it can be used in more complex IoT systems with complex physical behaviours. As part of future work, we also intend to apply the current extended CoAP in some real-world applications to test it.

References

1. Bormann, C., Castellani, A.P., Shelby, Z.: Coap: an application protocol for billions of tiny internet nodes. IEEE Internet Comput. **16**(2), 62–67 (2012)
2. Bucchiarone, A., De Sanctis, M., Marconi, A., Pistore, M., Traverso, P.: Design for adaptation of distributed service-based systems. In: Barros, A., Grigori, D., Narendra, N.C., Dam, H.K. (eds.) ICSOC 2015. LNCS, vol. 9435, pp. 383–393. Springer, Heidelberg (2015). https://doi.org/10.1007/978-3-662-48616-0_27
3. Camara, J., Canal, C., Salaün, G.: Behavioural self-adaptation of services in ubiquitous computing environments. SEAMS **9**, 28–37 (2009)
4. Cubo, J., Canal, C., Pimentel, E.: Model-based dependable composition of self-adaptive systems. Informatica **35**, 51–62 (2011)
5. de Lemos, R., et al.: Software engineering for self-adaptive systems: a second research roadmap. In: de Lemos, R., Giese, H., Müller, H.A., Shaw, M. (eds.) Software Engineering for Self-Adaptive Systems II. LNCS, vol. 7475, pp. 1–32. Springer, Heidelberg (2013). https://doi.org/10.1007/978-3-642-35813-5_1
6. Dong, Y., Wan, K., Yue, Y.: A feedback-based adaptive service-oriented paradigm for the internet of things. In: Braubach, L., et al. (eds.) ICSOC 2017. LNCS, vol. 10797, pp. 137–148. Springer, Cham (2018). https://doi.org/10.1007/978-3-319-91764-1_11
7. Fielding, R., et al.: Hypertext transfer protocol-http/1.1. Tech. rep. (1999)
8. Fielding, R.T.: Architectural styles and the design of network-based software architectures. Ph.D. thesis, University of California, Irvine (2000)
9. Gubbi, J., Buyya, R., Marusic, S., Palaniswami, M.: Internet of things (IOT): a vision, architectural elements, and future directions. Future Gener. Comput. Syst **29**(7), 1645–1660 (2013)
10. Guinard, D., Trifa, V., Wilde, E.: A resource oriented architecture for the web of things. In: Internet of Things (IOT) 2010, pp. 1–8. IEEE (2010)

11. Hartke, K.: Observing resources in the constrained application protocol (CoAP) (2015)
12. Kovatsch, M., Lanter, M., Shelby, Z.: Californium: scalable cloud services for the internet of things with CoAP. In: 2014 International Conference on the Internet of Things (IOT), pp. 1–6. IEEE (2014)
13. Kuladinithi, K., Bergmann, O., Pötsch, T., Becker, M., Görg, C.: Implementation of CoAP and its application in transport logistics. In: Proceedings IP+ SN, Chicago, IL, USA (2011)
14. Raza, S., Shafagh, H., Hewage, K., Hummen, R., Voigt, T.: Lithe: lightweight secure coap for the internet of things. IEEE Sens. J. 13(10), 3711–3720 (2013)
15. Seiger, R., Huber, S., Heisig, P., Assmann, U.: Enabling self-adaptive workflows for cyber-physical systems. In: Schmidt, R., Guédria, W., Bider, I., Guerreiro, S. (eds.) BPMDS/EMMSAD -2016. LNBIP, vol. 248, pp. 3–17. Springer, Cham (2016). https://doi.org/10.1007/978-3-319-39429-9_1
16. Shelby, Z., Hartke, K., Bormann, C.: The constrained application protocol (CoAP) (2014)
17. Tanganelli, G., Vallati, C., Mingozzi, E., Kovatsch, M.: Efficient proxying of CoAP observe with quality of service support. In: 2016 IEEE 3rd World Forum on Internet of Things (WF-IoT), pp. 401–406. IEEE (2016)
18. Teklemariam, G.K., Van Den Abeele, F., Moerman, I., Demeester, P., Hoebeke, J.: Bindings and restlets: a novel set of coap-based application enablers to build IOT applications. Sensors 16(8), 1217 (2016)
19. Zhou, J., et al.: Cloudthings: a common architecture for integrating the internet of things with cloud computing. In: 2013 IEEE 17th International Conference on Computer Supported Cooperative Work in Design (CSCWD), pp. 651–657. IEEE (2013)

ADMS: AI and Data Mining for Services

ADMS: First Workshop on AI and Data Mining for Services

Anup K. Kalia[1], Jin Xiao[1], Fanjing Meng[1], Larisa Shwartz[1], and Ying Li[2]

[1]IBM T.J. Watson, Yorktown Heights, NY, USA
[2]Peking University, Beijing, China

Introduction

The ADMS 2018 workshop was held in conjunction with the 16th International Conference on Service Oriented Computing (ICSOC 2018) held on November 12–15, 2018 in Hangzhou, China. The workshop focused on topics from service management that has been increasingly challenging for IT enterprises due to variety of customers producing data at a large volume and velocity. At any given point, these enterprises need to know a myriad of information regarding the status, risk or compliance, business objectives, and operational health of the services involved. Further, business goal alignment and customer experience need to be prioritized and, accordingly, managed in an agile and optimized manner. To do so, enterprises are constantly seeking novel technologies and solutions in cognitive platforms, advanced analytics and learning, and interactive frameworks. With the proliferation of cloud computing, microservice architectures and IoT data fabrics, the enterprises face new challenges in operating their business with increased efficiency, reduced cost, faster time-to-market, and enhanced customer experience. For example, enterprises such as Amazon and Google can create, deploy and market new features or capabilities multiple times within the same day.

The problem of rapid change in enterprises demands the exploration of new directions and possible innovations. To be successful in this endeavor, we require forums of both academic and industry researchers, and practitioners. Thus, the first edition of the workshop became successful with 10 submissions. From the submissions, we selected four full papers and one short paper. We would like to extend our gratitude to authors for their submissions, the program committee for their reviews, and the organizers of ICSOC 2018 to make the first edition of the ADMS workshop successful.

Fast Nearest-Neighbor Classification Using RNN in Domains with Large Number of Classes

Gautam Singh[1], Gargi Dasgupta[2], and Yu Deng[3(✉)]

[1] IBM Research-India, New Delhi 110070, DL, India
{gautamsi,gaargidasgupta}@in.ibm.com
[2] IBM Research-India, Bangalore 560045, KA, India
[3] IBM T.J. Watson Research Center, Yorktown Heights, New York 10598, NY, USA
dengy@us.ibm.com

Abstract. In scenarios involving text classification where the number of classes is large (in multiples of 10000 s) and training samples for each class are few and often verbose, nearest neighbor methods are effective but very slow in computing a similarity score with training samples of every class. On the other hand, machine learning models are fast at runtime but training them adequately is not feasible using few available training samples per class. In this paper, we propose a hybrid approach that cascades (1) a fast but less-accurate recurrent neural network (RNN) model and (2) a slow but more-accurate nearest-neighbor model using bag of syntactic features.

Using the cascaded approach, our experiments, performed on data set from IT support services where customer complaint text needs to be classified to return top-N possible error codes, show that the query-time of the slow system is reduced to $1/6^{th}$ while its accuracy is being improved. Our approach outperforms an LSH-based baseline for query-time reduction. We also derive a lower bound on the accuracy of the cascaded model in terms of the accuracies of the individual models. In any two-stage approach, choosing the right number of candidates to pass on to the second stage is crucial. We prove a result that aids in choosing this cutoff number for the cascaded system.

Keywords: RNN · Multi-stage retrieval · Nearest neighbor

1 Introduction

In the spectrum of text classification tasks, number of class labels could be two (binary), more than two (multi-class) or a very large number (more than 10000). In industry, text classification tasks with large number of classes arise naturally. In the domain of IT customer support, a user complaint text is classified to return top-N most likely error codes (from potentially 10000 s of options) that product could be having. Another example is from the domain of health insurance where

© Springer Nature Switzerland AG 2019
X. Liu et al. (Eds.): ICSOC 2018 Workshops, LNCS 11434, pp. 309–321, 2019.
https://doi.org/10.1007/978-3-030-17642-6_26

patients inquire whether their insurance covers a certain diagnosis or treatment. Such patient queries need to be classified into top-N appropriate medical codes to look up against a database and serve an automated response to the patient.

In the given setting, enough training samples are not available to adequately train an effective ML-based model [13]. For dealing with this challenge, Dumais et al. [6] propose a hierarchical classification where a hierarchy among class labels is known before-hand. For example, an item is classified into top-level categories ("computer" or "sports") and then further classified into sub-categories ("computer/hardware", "computer/software" etc.). In another approach [13], the hierarchy among classes is not known. Instead, from the "flat" class labels, a hierarchy is constructed through repeated clustering of the classes.

In this paper, we adopt a different approach. As the number of class labels grows, the task of text classification starts to increasingly resemble the task of document retrieval (or search). Our approach makes use of this observation. Retrieval methods using sophisticated features are effective but very slow at prediction time. ML models on the other hand are fast but imprecise in the given setting. A common approach in retrieval domain uses two-stages (1) *filtering stage*, a fast, imprecise and inexpensive stage that generates t candidate documents and (2) *ranking stage*, a sophisticated retrieval module that uses complex features (phrase-level or syntactic-level) to re-rank the candidate documents. The two stage retrieval approach mitigates the trade-off between speed and accuracy. By analogy, in this paper, we use a statistical ML based model as the first stage (i.e. candidate generation). This stage is fast but has low accuracy. Next, we use expensive syntactic NLP features and similarity scoring on the candidate classes in the second-stage to generate final top-N predicted classes. This stage is slow but more accurate.

A number of ML-based models exist for text classification such as regression models [11], Bayesian models [8] and emerging deep neural networks [4,7,9, 17,18]. On the other hand, many approaches use syntactic NLP-based features for text classification based on similarity of nearest neighbor [12,15]. Another approach uses *word2vec* to incorporate word similarity into nearest-neighbor-based text classification task [16]. For candidate generation, hashing has been a well-known technique. Hashing techniques can either be *data-agnostic* (such as locality sensitive hashing [1,3]) or *data-dependent* such as learning to hash [14]. Candidate generation is also classified as *conjunctive* if the candidates returned contain all the terms in query and *disjunctive* if the candidates contain at least one term from the query [2,5].

The main contributions of this paper are as follows:

1. We propose a hybrid model for text classification that cascades a fast but less-accurate recurrent neural network model and a slow but more-accurate retrieval model which uses bag of syntactic features. We experimentally show that the query time of the slow-retrieval model is reduced to $1/6^{th}$ after cascading while improving upon its accuracy (Sect. 4).

2. We prove a meaningful lower bound on the accuracy of cascaded model in terms of the accuracies of the individual models. The result is generic and can be applied on any cascaded retrieval model (Sect. 4.1).
3. Choosing the number of candidate classes t to pass on to the second stage in any cascaded model is crucial to the performance. If t is too small, the accuracy of the second stage suffers. If t is too large, the speed of the model suffers. To choose this, past works typically perform grid search or test on t values at regular intervals within a desirable range. In this paper, we prove that in order to choose the best t, we need to test the accuracy of the cascaded model only on few special values of t rather than all possible values within a desirable range. The result is generic and can be applied to any cascaded retrieval modelx (Sect. 4.2).
4. We show that our cascaded model outperforms a baseline for speeding-up the slow retrieval model using locality sensitive hashing (LSH) (Sect. 5).

2   Nearest-Neighbor Model Using Bag of Syntactic Features

In this section, we describe the aforementioned slow nearest-neighbor based model. In this technique, we first perform dependency parsing on the text. A dependency parser, $depparse(s)$ takes a sentence s as input and returns a tree (V, E)

$$V, E = depparse(s) \tag{1}$$

where V is a set of all nodes or words in sentence s and E is a set of all edges or 3-tuples in the tree.

$$E = \{(w_1, w_2, r) | \exists \text{ directed edge } r \text{ from } w_1 \rightarrow w_2\} \tag{2}$$

Any directed edge $(w_1, w_2, r) \in E$ represents some grammatical relation r between the connected words w_1 and w_2. These relations might have labels such as *nsubj, dobj, advmod,... etc.* and these represent some grammatical function fulfilled by the connected word pair.

Next, we take word-pairs using each edge in the dependency tree and concatenate their word vectors [10] to get a bag of *syntactic* feature vectors. This is shown in Algorithm 1. In the algorithm, notice that weights are assigned to the words during concatenation. These weights are based on heuristics and higher weight is given to nouns, adjectives and verbs than other parts of speech.

Computing Similarity of Text with a Class in Training Set. Given a text query q, we next compute its similarity with a particular class b in training set. Let the set of texts in the training set corresponding to class b be called $X(b)$. Let the $Z(b)$ denote the set of bags of syntactic features corresponding to each text in $X(b)$. Let $z(q)$ denote bag of syntactic features for the query text.

$$sim(q, b) = \max_{vecset \in Z(b)} \sum_{u \in z(q)} \max_{v \in vecset} cosine(\mathbf{u}, \mathbf{v}) \tag{3}$$

Algorithm 1. Generate Bag of Syntactic Features

1: **procedure** GENERATEBAGOFSYNTACTICFEATURES(s)
2:     $(V, E) \leftarrow$ dependency parse tree of sentence s
3:     $vectorset \leftarrow$ empty set
4:     **for** $(w_1, w_2, rel) \in E$ **do**
5:         $\mathbf{v}_1 \leftarrow word2vec(w_1)$
6:         $\mathbf{v}_2 \leftarrow word2vec(w_2)$
7:         $\omega_1 \leftarrow wordweight(w_1)$
8:         $\omega_2 \leftarrow wordweight(w_2)$
9:         $\mathbf{v} \leftarrow (\omega_1 \mathbf{v}_1, \omega_2 \mathbf{v}_2)$
10:         $vectorset.add(\mathbf{v})$
        return $vectorset$

In the above similarity metric, we compute the cosine of feature vectors of the query text and texts corresponding to class b in the training set. The similarity of the best matching text is taken as the similarity score for class b. Next, the N highest scoring classes for the given query are returned.

3   Recurrent Models for Text Classification

For text classification using recurrent models, text is converted into a sequence of word-vectors and given as input to the model. In recurrent models, the words in text may be processed from left to right. In each iteration, previous hidden state and a word are processed to return a new hidden state. In this paper, we experiment with two kinds of recurrent models (1) GRU [4] and (2) LSTM [7]. We describe below the details only for the GRU model.

GRU model is parametric and defined by 6 matrices $\mathbf{U}^z$, $\mathbf{U}^r$, $\mathbf{U}^h$, $\mathbf{W}^z$, $\mathbf{W}^r$, $\mathbf{W}^h$ and output matrix $\mathbf{O}$. The recurrence equations are given below.

Initialization Initialize the hidden state as a zero vector.

$$\mathbf{h}_0 = \mathbf{0}$$

Iteration For j^{th} iteration, $j \in [1, m]$, compute the following

$$\mathbf{z}_j = \sigma(\mathbf{U}^z \mathbf{v}_j + \mathbf{W}^z \mathbf{h}_{j-1})$$

$$\mathbf{r}_j = \sigma(\mathbf{U}^r \mathbf{v}_j + \mathbf{W}^r \mathbf{h}_{j-1})$$

$$\mathbf{h'}_j = tanh(\mathbf{U}^h \mathbf{v}_j + \mathbf{W}^h(\mathbf{h}_{j-1} \circ \mathbf{r}_j))$$

$$\mathbf{h}_j = (1 - \mathbf{z}_j) \circ \mathbf{h'}_j + \mathbf{z}_j \circ \mathbf{h}_{j-1}$$

where m is the number of words in text and σ refers to the sigmoid function.

Termination and Computing Output Probability Distribution. The latest hidden state $\mathbf{h}_m$ is subjected to a softmax layer to generate an output probability distribution $\mathbf{y} = softmax(\mathbf{Oh}_m)$. We return the classes corresponding to top-N probability values in $\mathbf{y}$.

4   Cascaded Model for Fast and Accurate Retrieval

Retrieval model using bag of syntactic features is an example of nearest-neighbor classification. For a given query q, this demands that the similarity score be computed with every sample in the training set. On the contrary, if we filter a few candidate classes using the first stage of cascading, the slowness of the retrieval model is overcome. We denote the recurrent machine learning model as M_1 and the slow nearest-neighbor classifier as M_2.

Notations. The correct class to which query q belongs is denoted by b_q. We denote the set of candidate classes returned by the first stage by T and number of such candidates by $t = |T|$. We use $M_1(q, t)$ denote the set of t classes returned by the first stage. We denote the number of classes to be returned by the second stage as N. Therefore $t > N$. $M_2^T(q, N)$ denotes the set of N classes returned by the second stage after inspecting the set of classes T returned by the first stage. We use $M_2(q, N)$ to denote the set of N classes returned by the second stage if it were to inspect all classes in the training set without any cascading. We define an empirical accuracy metric over a validation set S_{valid} containing user-queries as follows.

$$accuracy = \frac{|\{q \mid q \in S_{test}, b_q \in M(q, N)\}|}{|S_{test}|} \approx P(b_q \in M(q, N)) \quad (4)$$

The numerator is the number of queries with correct classes in the top-N suggestions returned by text classifier M. The denominator is the total number of queries.

Before describing the proofs, we define two empirical quantities $\rho(t)$ and $\alpha(t)$ associated to the cascaded model which are easy to estimate as follows using a validation set.

$$\rho(t) = \frac{|\{q \mid q \in S_{valid}, b_q \in M_1(q, t), b_q \in M_2(q, N)\}|}{|\{q \mid q \in S_{valid}, b_q \in M_2(q, N)\}|} \quad (5)$$
$$\approx P(b_q \in M_1(q, t) \mid b_q \in M_2(q, N))$$

$$\alpha(t) = \frac{|\{q \mid q \in S_{valid}, b_q \in M_1(q, t)\}|}{|\{q \mid q \in S_{valid}\}|} \approx P(b_q \in M_1(q, t)) \quad (6)$$

It is easy to compute $\rho(t)$ as follows. $\alpha(t)$ is analogously computed.

1. Run both M_1 and M_2 on the validation set and store the match scores for each class.

2. For each t, find the number of classes which are present both in top-t for M_1 and top-N for M_2. Also find the number of classes which are present in top-N for M_2.
3. Find the ratio of the above two numbers for each t.

In this paper, we assume that empirical estimates of probability values using the validation set are good approximations of their actual values.

4.1   Lower Bound on Accuracy of Cascaded Model

The idea is to show that the accuracy of the cascaded model is lower bounded by accuracy of the slow-model times $\rho(t)$. This is given in following theorem.

Theorem 1. *For a cascaded model consisting of stages M_1 and M_2,*

$$P(b_q \in M_1(q,t), b_q \in M_2^T(q,N)) \geq \rho(t)P(b_q \in M_2(q,N)) \tag{7}$$

In order to prove the above, we go through the following lemma.

Lemma 1. *Let q by any query such that $b_q \in M_1(q,t)$, then*

$$b_q \in M_2(q,N) \implies b_q \in M_2^T(q,N) \tag{8}$$

Proof (of Lemma 1). Since $b_q \in M_1(q,t)$, hence the first stage removes only some incorrect classes and not the correct class b_q. Now since the correct class is in top-N for M_2 without any cascading, hence, after cascading using M_1, the candidate classes that M_2 inspects contain fewer incorrect classes. Thus, introduction of cascading either improves or maintains the rank of the correct class returned in top-N. This gives us the above lemma.   □

Proof (of Theorem 1). Using Lemma 1,

$$b_q \in M_1(q,t) \cap M_2(q,N) \implies b_q \in M_1(q,t) \cap M_2^T(q,N) \tag{9}$$

This implies that,

$$
\begin{aligned}
P(b_q \in M_1(q,t) \cap M_2^T(q,N)) &\geq P(b_q \in M_1(q,t) \cap M_2(q,N)) \\
&= P(b_q \in M_1(q,t), b_q \in M_2(q,N)) \\
&= P(b_q \in M_1(q,t) \mid b_q \in M_2(q,N))P(b_q \in M_2(q,N)) \\
&= \rho(t)P(b_q \in M_2(q,N))
\end{aligned}
\tag{10}
$$

□

4.2   Picking Best t

Given a cascaded model, choosing the number of candidates t to pass on to the second stage is crucial. If t is too small, then accuracy suffers as it becomes more likely that the correct class has not passed the first stage. If t is too large, then the query time suffers. The first stage also acts as an elimination round and large t dilutes this elimination process by crowding out the correct class.

Text classification models used in each stage are typically complex. Studying their combined behavior in a cascaded setting may not be straightforward. Thus, choosing t is a challenge. Typically, the only reliable way to do this is to run the cascaded model on all possible values of t and pick a t which produces the highest accuracy on a validation set within a desirable range of t. This process might be time-consuming as the slow model (as a part of cascaded model) needs to be re-run for every t being checked. In the following theorem, we show that not all values of t need to be checked. Given that $\alpha(t)$ has same value for two distinct values of t, the theorem shows that choosing the smaller value of t offers at least as much accuracy as choosing the larger one. This implies that we need to check only those values of t where $\alpha(t)$ changes value.

Theorem 2. *Let q be any query. For t_1, t_2 such that $t_2 > t_1$, if $\alpha(t_1) = \alpha(t_2)$ then*

$$P(b_q \in M_1(q, t_1) \cap M_2^{T_1}(q, N)) \geq P(b_q \in M_1(q, t_2) \cap M_2^{T_2}(q, N)) \qquad (11)$$

In other words, for a given value of $\alpha(t) = \alpha_0$, the accuracy is maximized when

$$t = arg \min_{\alpha(t)=\alpha_0} \alpha(t) \qquad (12)$$

For proof of above theorem, we go through the following lemma.

Lemma 2. $\forall t_1, t_2$ *such that $t_2 > t_1$,*

$$b_q \in M_1(q, t_1) \implies b_q \in M_1(q, t_2) \qquad (13)$$

Proof (of Lemma 2). If the correct class is returned in top-t_1 by the first stage for a given query, then for $t_2 > t_1$, the correct class is also a part of top-t_2 classes returned by the first stage. $\qquad \square$

Proof (of Theorem 2). We start from the condition given in the theorem i.e., $\alpha(t_1) = \alpha(t_2)$ and using Eq. 6, we get

$$P(b_q \in M_1(q, t_1)) = P(b_q \in M_1(q, t_2)) \qquad (14)$$

Using above Eq. 14 and Lemma 2, we get the equality of the set of queries for whom the correct class have passed through the first stage.

$$\{q \mid b_q \in M_1(q, t_1)\} \equiv \{q \mid b_q \in M_1(q, t_2)\} \qquad (15)$$

Now consider the set of queries which are correctly classified in top-N by the cascaded model using $t = t_2$,

$$\{q \mid b_q \in M_1(q, t_2) \cap M_2^{T_2}(q, N)\} \qquad (16)$$

Now, when t_2 is reduced to t_1, we know on one hand that the number of classes passing to the second stage is smaller i.e., t_1. On the other hand, we know from set equivalence in Eq. 15 that the exact same queries contain their correct classes in the candidate classes being passed on. These two observations imply that only incorrect classes have been removed in the first stage while going from t_2 to t_1. This reduction in number of classes being passed on can either improve or keep same the rank of the correct class returned in the top-N by the second stage in the cascaded setting. Therefore,

$$b_q \in M_1(q, t_2) \cap M_2^{T_2}(q, N) \implies b_q \in M_1(q, t_1) \cap M_2^{T_1}(q, N) \qquad (17)$$

This implies that

$$P(b_q \in M_1(q, t_1) \cap M_2^{T_1}(q, N)) \geq P(b_q \in M_1(q, t_2) \cap M_2^{T_2}(q, N)) \qquad (18)$$

$\square$

4.3   Baseline for Query Time Improvement

This section describes the LSH-based baseline for candidate generation. In the training set, for every syntactic feature vector $\mathbf{v}$, the ith bit of the hash code is given as

$$h_i(\mathbf{v}) = sgn(\mathbf{w}_i^T \mathbf{v}) \qquad (19)$$

where $\mathbf{w}_i$ are randomly picked. We create a hash-table Φ_{class} whose indices are hash-codes of syntactic features in the training set and values are the sets of corresponding class labels. We create a similar hash-table Φ_{text} whose values are texts corresponding to the hash-codes instead of class labels. For candidate generation, we use two implementations of the conjunctive approach (1) *Class-based* where returned candidate classes contain to all hash-codes computed from the query text. (2) *Text-based* where returned candidate classes have at least one text that contains all hash codes computed from the query text.

5   Experiments and Inferences

In this section, we describe the experiments which demonstrate performances of our proposed techniques and verify the bounds.

Data Set. Two kinds of documents from the domain of IT support are used to generate data set for our experiments (1) product reference documents and (2) past problem requests. From 300 MB of product reference documents, we extracted a total of 55 K distinct error codes and a total of 15 K distinct error code text descriptions. We combined the error codes corresponding to each of 15 K distinct error code descriptions to reduce data sparsity per class and to get 15 K error-code classes. From the past problem requests, we extracted 40 K problems with known error-code classes. Out of these, 90% are used for training while remaining is set aside for validation and testing. Notice that the mean

Table 1. Examples of user-queries and error-code class descriptions returned by our models with highlighted correct response

User query	Top-10 error description suggestions
Getting media err detected on device	System lic detected a program exception, a problem occurred during the ipl of a partition, partition firmware detected a data storage error, tape unit command timeout, interface error, **tape unit detected a read or write error on tape medium,** tape unit is not responding, an open port was detected on port 0, contact was lost with the device indicated, destroy ipl task
hmc appears to be down	**licensed internal code failure on the hardware management console hmc,** system lic detected a program exception, service processor was reset due to kernel panic, the communication link between the service processor and the hardware management console hmc failed, platform lic detected an error, power supply failure, processor 1 pgood fault pluggable, system power interface firmware spif terminated the system because it detected a power fault, detected ac loss, a problem occurred during the ipl of a partition, platform lic failure
Failed power supply	A fatal error occurred on power supply 1, power supply failure, the power supply fan on un e1 failed, **detected ac loss,** a fatal error occurred on power supply 2, power supply non power fault ps1, the power supply fan on un e2 failed the power supply should be replaced as soon as possible, a non fatal error occurred on power supply 1, the power supply fan on un e2 experienced a short stoppage

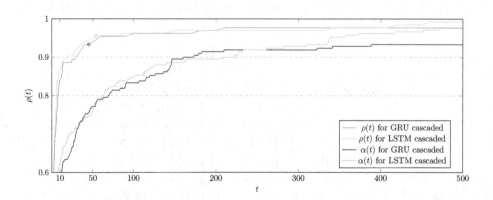

Fig. 1. Plot showing dependence of $\rho(t)$ and $\alpha(t)$ on t for the cascaded model on the described data set.

Table 2. Computing relevant t values for cascaded models

M_1	$\frac{P(b_q \in M_1(q,N))}{P(b_q \in M_2(q,N))}$	t crossing	t values when ρ changes value
GRU	0.933	45	45, 55, 91, 179, 210
LSTM	0.955	54	54, 82, 141, 337, 452

Table 3. Heat map showing word weights assigned by GRU model to user queries

My	tape	drive	has	been	giving
error	once	every	week		

Need	to	have	adapter	replaced

Flashing	power	button	and	warning	light

Table 4. Accuracies and CPU times of cascaded model comprising of syntactic-bigram vector model followed by M_1 for varying t for suggestion of top-10 error-code classes

M_1	t	Accuracy	Time taken (in s)		
			Mean	Min	Max
LSTM	54	63.33%	9.09	0.73	49.98
	82	64.76%	12.23	1.12	63.60
	141	**65.23%**	14.51	1.23	75.00
	337	64.29%	23.35	2.09	114.4
	452	62.86%	23.46	2.35	108.2
GRU	45	60.95%	9.85	1.22	50.23
	179	63.33%	18.93	2.25	89.97
	210	**64.29%**	20.10	2.31	93.18
	400	63.81%	25.89	2.51	117.1
	500	63.33%	29.15	2.66	131.6

Table 5. Accuracies and CPU times of various models for suggestion of top-10 error-code classes

Model	Accuracy	Time taken (in s)		
		Mean	Min	Max
LSTM	61.43%	0.013	0.004	0.112
GRU	60.00%	0.014	0.005	0.062
sn-Vectors	64.29%	84.60	12.54	294.92
sn-Bigrams	63.33%	41.42	8.97	133.51
BOW	43.33%	12.80	7.32	28.19

Table 6. Baseline accuracies (in top-10) and CPU times of LSH-based implementations (for reducing query time of bag of syntactic features technique) for varying number of permutations P.

LSH version	P	Accuracy	Time taken (in s)		
			Mean	Min	Max
Cluster based	5	62.38%	35.1	0.001	142.2
	10	60.47%	10.3	0.001	27.12
	15	57.14%	5.82	0.001	19.39
	20	56.66%	5.79	0.001	19.75
Text based	1	64.28%	46.1	0.001	194.2
	3	61.90%	13.5	0.001	41.23
	5	55.23%	1.31	0.001	11.30

number of texts corresponding to each error code class is approximately 2–3, which is too few for adequate training of statistical ML-based models (Tables 1 and 3).

In Fig. 1, we show the plots of $\rho(t)$ and $\alpha(t)$ for cascaded models having M_1 as the GRU model and the LSTM model. Notice that to guarantee the usefulness of the cascaded model, the accuracy of the cascaded model should be at least as much as the less accurate model. The smallest value of t that achieves this can be found by using the lower bound in Theorem 1. Thus,

$$\rho(t)P(b_q \in M_2(q, N)) \geq P(b_q \in M_1(q, N)) \tag{20}$$

or,

$$\rho(t) \geq \frac{P(b_q \in M_1(q, N))}{P(b_q \in M_2(q, N))} \tag{21}$$

Thus, as shown in Table 2, for GRU model, $\rho(t) \geq 0.933$ or $t \geq 45$. Similarly, for LSTM model, $\rho(t) \geq 0.955$ or $t \geq 54$. These thresholds on t are shown in Fig. 1 on the $\rho(t)$ plots.

In Table 4, we show the accuracies and CPU times of the cascaded model for varying t for M_1 as the GRU and the LSTM model. Notice that according to Theorem 2, we only need to check the accuracies for t where $\alpha(t)$ (shown in Fig. 1) changes value. Therefore Table 4 shows accuracies for some of those t values.

On comparing the accuracy of CPU times of the cascaded model (in Table 4) and the bag of syntactic features model (depicted in Table 5 as sn-Vectors), we see that cascading reduces query time to $1/6^{th}$ using LSTM and $1/4^{th}$ using GRU model. Cascading using LSTM model also improves the accuracy.

Table 5 shows accuracy and CPU times of other uncascaded models such as (1) fast, machine learning based LSTM and GRU models, (2) bag of syntactic bigrams which uses exact string match for finding similarities between syntactic-bigrams after lemmatizing the words and (3) the bag of words model.

In Table 6, we show the results of the two versions of the LSH based baseline. The accuracy and CPU time are shown for varying number of permutations (number of bits in the hash code). Increasing the number of bits leads to fewer nearest-neighbor candidates which decreases the accuracy and improves query time. Comparing results in Tables 4 and 6, we infer that our proposed cascaded model outperforms the described baseline. Notice that when LSH generates the candidate classes, even though the accuracy gets close to LSTM's, it does so at a larger price paid in terms of latency. This is because LSH candidates are less precise and therefore we need a lot more of them to result in a comparable accuracy. Since the number of candidates is greater, it makes the nearest-neighbor slower than when LSTM was used to generate candidate classes.

6   Conclusion and Future Work

We proposed a cascaded model using fast RNN-based text classifiers and slow nearest-neighbor based model relying on sophisticated NLP features.

We successfully resolved challenges posed by large number of classes, very few training samples per class and slowness of nearest-neighbor approach. We derived a generic lower bound on the accuracy of a 2-stage cascaded model in terms of accuracies of individual stages. We proved a result that eases the effort involved in finding the appropriate number of candidates to pass on to the second stage. We outperformed an LSH-based baseline for query time reduction.

Some problems that need further work naturally emerge. One is investigating insights when 2-stage cascading is extended to multi-stage. Another is exploring other machine learning models operate in a cascaded setting.

References

1. Andoni, A., Indyk, P.: Near-optimal hashing algorithms for approximate nearest neighbor in high dimensions. In: 2006 47th Annual IEEE Symposium on Foundations of Computer Science, FOCS 2006, pp. 459–468. IEEE (2006)
2. Asadi, N., Lin, J.: Effectiveness/efficiency tradeoffs for candidate generation in multi-stage retrieval architectures. In: Proceedings of the 36th International ACM SIGIR Conference on Research and Development in Information Retrieval, pp. 997–1000. ACM (2013)
3. Broder, A.Z., Charikar, M., Frieze, A.M., Mitzenmacher, M.: Min-wise independent permutations. J. Comput. Syst. Sci. **60**(3), 630–659 (2000)
4. Cho, K., et al.: Learning phrase representations using rnn encoder-decoder for statistical machine translation. arXiv preprint arXiv:1406.1078 (2014)
5. Clarke, C.L., Culpepper, J.S., Moffat, A.: Assessing efficiency-effectiveness trade-offs in multi-stage retrieval systems without using relevance judgments. Inf. Retrieval J. **19**(4), 351–377 (2016)
6. Dumais, S., Chen, H.: Hierarchical classification of web content. In: Proceedings of the 23rd Annual International ACM SIGIR Conference on Research and Development in Information Retrieval, pp. 256–263. ACM (2000)
7. Hochreiter, S., Schmidhuber, J.: Long short-term memory. Neural Comput. **9**(8), 1735–1780 (1997)
8. McCallum, A., Nigam, K., et al.: A comparison of event models for Naive Bayes text classification. In: AAAI-98 Workshop on Learning for Text Categorization, Madison, WI, vol. 752, pp. 41–48 (1998)
9. Mikolov, T., Karafiát, M., Burget, L., Cernocky, J., Khudanpur, S.: Recurrent neural network based language model. In: Interspeech, vol. 2, p. 3 (2010)
10. Mikolov, T., Sutskever, I., Chen, K., Corrado, G.S., Dean, J.: Distributed representations of words and phrases and their compositionality. In: Advances in Neural Information Processing Systems, pp. 3111–3119 (2013)
11. Schütze, H., Hull, D.A., Pedersen, J.O.: A comparison of classifiers and document representations for the routing problem. In: Proceedings of the 18th Annual International ACM SIGIR Conference on Research and Development in Information Retrieval, pp. 229–237. ACM (1995)
12. Sidorov, G., Velasquez, F., Stamatatos, E., Gelbukh, A., Chanona-Hernández, L.: Syntactic dependency-based n-grams as classification features. In: Batyrshin, I., Mendoza, M.G. (eds.) MICAI 2012. LNCS (LNAI), vol. 7630, pp. 1–11. Springer, Heidelberg (2013). https://doi.org/10.1007/978-3-642-37798-3_1

13. Tsoumakas, G., Katakis, I., Vlahavas, I.: Effective and efficient multilabel classification in domains with large number of labels. In: Proceedings of ECML/PKDD 2008 Workshop on Mining Multidimensional Data (MMD 2008), pp. 30–44 (2008)

14. Wang, J., Zhang, T., Sebe, N., Shen, H.T., et al.: A survey on learning to hash. IEEE Trans. Pattern Anal. Mach. Intell. **40**, 769–790 (2017)

15. Wang, S., Manning, C.D.: Baselines and bigrams: simple, good sentiment and topic classification. In: Proceedings of the 50th Annual Meeting of the Association for Computational Linguistics: Short Papers-Volume 2, pp. 90–94. Association for Computational Linguistics (2012)

16. Ye, X., Shen, H., Ma, X., Bunescu, R., Liu, C.: From word embeddings to document similarities for improved information retrieval in software engineering. In: Proceedings of the 38th International Conference on Software Engineering, pp. 404–415. ACM (2016)

17. Zhang, X., Zhao, J., LeCun, Y.: Character-level convolutional networks for text classification. In: Advances in Neural Information Processing Systems, pp. 649–657 (2015)

18. Zhou, P., Qi, Z., Zheng, S., Xu, J., Bao, H., Xu, B.: Text classification improved by integrating bidirectional LSTM with two-dimensional max pooling. arXiv preprint arXiv:1611.06639 (2016)

TaxiC: A Taxi Route Recommendation Method Based on Urban Traffic Charge Heat Map

Yijing Cheng[1,2], Qifeng Zhou[1,2(✉)], and Yongxuan Lai[3]

[1] Shenzhen Research Institute of Xiamen University, Shenzhen, China
[2] Automation Department, Xiamen University, Xiamen, China
chengyj97@163.com, zhouqf@xmu.edu.cn
[3] School of Software, Xiamen University, Xiamen, China
laiyx@xmu.edu.cn

Abstract. A successful taxi route recommendation system is helpful to achieve a win-win situation for both increasing drivers' income and improving passengers' satisfaction. The critical problem in this system is how to find the optimal routes under the highly time-varying and complex traffic environment. By investigating the main factors and comparing various route recommendation methods, in this paper, we handle the taxi route recommendation issue from a new perspective. The relationships between the cruising taxis and passengers are regarded as attraction or repulsion between electric charges. Then based on urban traffic charge heat map, we propose a simple yet effective taxi route recommendation method named TaxiC. TaxiC considers four key factors: the number of passengers, travel distance, traffic conditions, vacant competition, and then recommends driving direction in real time for drivers to help them find the next passengers more efficiently and reduce the cruising time. The experimental results on a real-world data set extracted from 5398 taxis in Xiamen city demonstrate the effectiveness of the proposed method.

Keywords: Taxi route recommendation · Traffic charge · GPS trajectories

1 Introduction

Taxi is one of the most common means of public transportation in urban cities. Due to the flexibility of the pick-up position and driving route, taking taxi is a relatively more convenient and faster way of going out compared with other public transport such as bus and metro. Passengers hope to get to the cab as soon as possible, while taxi drivers wish to reduce the cruising time to increase their income. However, in practice, it is not easy for a driver to schedule and select the best route to find the next passenger, since the optimal path is dynamic with the change of traffic conditions, distance, location, and the number of passengers

© Springer Nature Switzerland AG 2019
X. Liu et al. (Eds.): ICSOC 2018 Workshops, LNCS 11434, pp. 322–334, 2019.
https://doi.org/10.1007/978-3-030-17642-6_27

and vacant cabs in different time. And only relying on the drivers' experience is often inefficient and may result in reduced performance, especially for the raw recruits.

With the development of networking and data processing technologies, real-time GPS trajectories can be collected, which makes it possible to combine a broad set of GPS trajectories with data mining technology [9,11–13] to support taxi operations and route planning, such as passengers' mobility behavior prediction [5,10], profitability map deriving [2,7], spatial-temporal clustering [14], and Coulomb's-Law-based recommendation system [6]. Although these methods do work to some extent they still have some limitations: (1) Passengers' mobility behavior is hard to predict and differs a lot under different circumstances; (2) Most of the study mainly focuses on road segments [3,4] with more passengers and hotspots recommendation, while neglecting the competition among vacant taxis, which may produce an invalid recommendation and result in extra cruising [8].

To overcome these limitations, in this paper, we propose a simple yet effective taxi route recommendation method named TaxiC. TaxiC mainly consists of two steps, first computing the traffic charge by considering four key factors: the number of passengers, travel distance, traffic conditions, vacant competition, and then recommending a driving directions after a region analysis and further considering the value of PVR (the ratio between the number of passengers and the number of vacant taxis). We use taxi trajectory information and passenger information extracted from 5398 taxis over the period of July 2014 of Xiamen city to verify TaxiC on the average revenue of taxi drivers. The experimental results demonstrate the superiority of the proposed method as compared to the state-of-the-art approaches.

2   Related Work

Recently, with the help of taxi service platforms (e.g. Didi Taxi), taxis can pick up passengers much more easily than ever before. However, it's impossible for a taxi to pick up all of its passengers via taxi service platforms, taxi drivers still need to cruise sometimes. Therefore, an effective recommendation system is indispensable. There are many kinds of recommendation systems which are based on passengers' mobility behavior and real-world GPS trajectories and the main difference lies in the weight put on the two factors [1].

When we consider real-world GPS trajectories to be of more importance, we can derive some kind of map for taxi drivers to refer to. A simple yet practical method in which a Spatial-Temporal Profitability (STP) map is derived from historical trajectories for the purpose of recommending profitable locations to taxi drivers is presented by Powell et al. [7]. However, this method just help make drivers' experience more precise and clearer, so it may be ineffective since taxi drivers still play a very important role. Dong et al. [2] propose to calculate the score of each road segment based on real-world GPS trajectories. Then the profitable cruising route is derived based on the scores.

When passengers' mobility behavior is thought highly of, we need to start from the passengers' side. Li et al. [5] propose an improved ARIMA based prediction method to forecast the spatial-temporal variation of passengers in hotspots, and with this method, taxi drivers can reduce their cruise time and distance on the process of finding their next passengers. An adaptive routing method based on the daily logs of taxis is proposed by Yamamoto et al. [10]. In this method, taxis will be assigned the most efficient path where many passengers are waiting as they cruise, and the assignment changes dynamically corresponding to the changes of taxis' positions. This can not only increase profitability but also reduce competition.

3   Problem Formulation

3.1   Notations

Since traffic situation is highly time-varying and very sensitive to locations, to generate the traffic charges, we should first do the spatial and temporal transformation to the original traffic information to produce $region(i, j)$.

- Spatial processing: This process is dividing the map into grids with comparable areas. In this study, we split the map by $0.005°$ of longitude and $0.005°$ of latitude [6], and each grid is regarded as a region.
- Temporal processing: To overcome the time-varying, it is necessary to analyze the traffic condition with a proper time granularity. In this study, we regard half an hour as a period [6].

After above preprocessing, all the basic information to generate traffic charges can be extracted from GPS trajectories and passenger information. The important notations are listed as follows Table 1:

Table 1. Important notations

Notation	Description
$P_t^{(d)}(i, j)$	The number of passengers
$V_t^{(d)}(i, j)$	The number of vacant taxis
$A_t^{(d)}(i, j)$	The number of taxis
$S_t^{(d)}(i, j, k)$	Speed of taxis of a specific set
$M_t^{(d)}(i, j, k)$	Revenue of orders of a specific set

Note: all of the terms is calculated in $region(i, j)$ at time slot t, day d.

3.2 Traffic Charge Definition

According to the property of attraction or repulsion between electric charges, the definition of traffic charge in longitude i and latitude j at time slot t of the day d is stated as follows:

$$C_t^{(d)}(i,j) = \frac{P_t^{(d)}(i,j)}{avg\{P_t^{(d)}(i,j)\}} \times (1 - \frac{V_t^{(d)}(i,j)}{A_t^{(d)}(i,j)})$$

$$\times (1 + \frac{avg\{S_t^{(d)}(i,j,k)\}}{\max_{k \in \Omega}\{S_t^{(d)}(i,j,k)\}}) \times (1 + \frac{avg\{M_t^{(d)}(i,j,k)\}}{\max_{k \in \Omega}\{M_t^{(d)}(i,j,k)\}}), \qquad (1)$$

where $i = 1, 2, ..., n_{lon}, j = 1, 2, ..., n_{lat}$, and Ω stands for a set of taxi IDs in current region.

The traffic charge contains information from four dimensions: $\frac{P_t(i,j)}{avg\{P_t(i,j)\}}$ reflects that passengers affects the traffic charge positively, while the negative sign before $\frac{V_t(i,j)}{A_t(i,j)}$ indicates that vacant taxis is no good to the traffic charge. And $\frac{avg\{S_t(i,j,k)\}}{\max\{S_t(i,j,k)\}}$ means that better the traffic condition is, more revenue taxi drivers can earn. Besides, a region with higher pay per order($\frac{avg\{M_t(i,j,k)\}}{\max\{M_t(i,j,k)\}}$) is more favored. In summary, a region with higher traffic charge is supposed to have more underlying passengers, less competition, better traffic condition, and higher revenue per order.

Since the traffic condition is changing all the time, TaxiC combines the historical information and real-time update to calculate the final traffic charges:

$$C_F = \omega \times C_H + (1 - \omega) \times C_R, \qquad (2)$$

where C_H represents the historical traffic charge and C_R stands for the real-time traffic charge, ω is the weight tradeoff between C_H and C_R.

4 Recommendation Model

4.1 System Framework

Figure 1 shows the framework of TaxiC, which is mainly composed of three parts: historical trajectories calculation, real-time trajectories update, and real-time online driving direction recommendation. All of the trajectories contain both spatial and temporal information. The historical traffic charges are calculated on the historical trajectories, real-time trajectories are included in calculating the real-time traffic charges, and then the final traffic charges are the tradeoff between historical and real-time traffic charges.

At each time slot, given a final real-time charge heat map generated by the final traffic charges of all regions, and considering the PVR of the current region (where the taxi is located at) compared with the adjacent regions, our recommendation system will give one optimal driving direction for the taxi driver to find the next passenger.

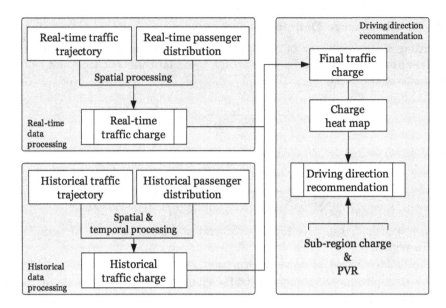

Fig. 1. System framework

4.2   Driving Direction Recommendation

Driving is a human behavior with a strong subjective property and is closely related to the real-time situation. Therefore, our recommendation system gives one optimal driving direction instead of specific driving routes when an intersection occurs. By saying driving 'direction', we refer to the general direction the driver should be heading for, not turning left or right specifically. Thus drivers can cruise more freely and take advantage of their driving experience towards the optimal routes.

To further consider the behavior of other vacant taxi drivers and the situation of current and adjacent sub-regions, we define PVR, the ratio between the number of passengers and the number of vacant taxis, to predict the behavior of vacant taxi drivers around the potential passengers. A heat map of time slot t in all regions is given to show the high charge regions, which are theoretically the most likely places vacant taxi drivers would go. In summary, our recommendation strategy for each vacant taxi driver in $region(i,j)$ is:

1. If the traffic charge in $region(i,j)$ is greater than a threshold θ (the average charge of sub-regions), the driver should continue to cruise in the current sub-regions to get passengers.
2. If not, then consider the PVR in $region(i,j)$. If the PVR is greater than a threshold δ (the average PVR of all regions), the driver continues to cruise; otherwise, the driver should change the driving direction towards regions with higher traffic charges.

To decide the specific direction, we need to find $region(i_s, j_s)$ outside the current sub-region, whose traffic charge is above θ, and the distance between $region(i_s, j_s)$ and $region(i, j)$ is the shortest at the same time:

$$\underset{(i_s, j_s) \notin \Gamma_s}{arg\,min}\{dist(R_{ij}, R_{i_s j_s}) \mid C_t^{(d)}(i_s, j_s) \geq \theta\}, \qquad (3)$$

where Γ_s is the set of longitude and latitude of the sub-regions, R_{ij} and $R_{i_s j_s}$ represent $region(i, j)$ and $region(i_s, j_s)$ respectively.

Then the specific direction is calculated as follows:

$$\overrightarrow{dir} = \overrightarrow{R_{ij} R_{i_s j_s}} \qquad (4)$$

For example, as shown in Fig. 2, if the traffic charges in sub-region is less than θ and in region A, B, C, and D are all greater than θ, then the system will recommend a driving direction to region A because the distance between region A and the current region is the shortest.

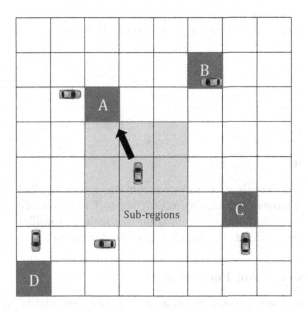

Fig. 2. An example of changing driving direction

As shown in Algorithm 1, the whole process continues until the driver picks up a passenger. After dropping off the passenger, the system updates the current time t_c, the longitude lon_c and the latitude lat_c, and start the process all over again.

ALGORITHM 1. Online Driving direction recommendation

Input:
d, C_H, C_R,t_c, lon_c, lat_c,$PVR_t^{(d)}$,ω,θ, δ,$isVacant$
Output:
dir: the recommended driving direction
$isVacant = 1$
while $isVacant == 1$ **do**
$\quad (i,j) \leftarrow getRegionSlot(lon_c, lat_c)$
$\quad C_{t_c}^{(d)}(i,j) \leftarrow formula(1)\&(2)$
$\quad$ **if** $a\ passenger\ is\ picked\ up$ **then**
$\quad\quad | \quad isVacant \leftarrow 0$; **break**
$\quad$ **end**
$\quad$ **if** $C_{t_c}^{(d)}(i,j) \geq \theta$ **then**
$\quad\quad |$ continue
$\quad$ **else**
$\quad\quad$ **if** $PVR_t^{(d)}(i,j) \geq \delta$ **then**
$\quad\quad\quad |$ continue
$\quad\quad$ **else**
$\quad\quad\quad | \quad \overrightarrow{dir} \leftarrow getNewDirection(C_{t_c}^{(d)}(i_s,j_s))$
$\quad\quad\quad | \quad$ /*to get the direction with higher traffic charges*/
$\quad\quad$ **end**
$\quad$ **end**
end

---

5   Experiments

5.1   Data Set

The data set used to evaluate our system contains a total of 5398 taxi trajectory information and passenger information of Xiamen (China) over the period of July 2014. After data preprocessing, approximately over 220 million GPS position records and over 7 million customer information are included.

5.2   Recommendation Performance

To evaluate proposed recommendation system, we first divide Xiamen Island into 34×27 regions, i.e., each small region spans $0.005°$ of longitude and $0.005°$ of latitude. The longitude of the whole area ranges from $118.05°$E to $118.217°$E and latitude $24.433°$N to $24.567°$N. The whole data set is split up into two parts: one including data for the first 21 days is considered as historical data, and the rest is the testing data. The time slot is set to be 0.5 h and the weight between the historical and real-time traffic charge $\omega = 0.8$.

Figure 3 shows the traffic charge heat maps of 2:00~2:30 am and 9:00~9:30 am in July 1st (Tuesday). We can see that the charges of 9:00~9:30 am are significantly higher than that of 2:00~2:30 am. We also note that there is one region with much higher traffic charge in 2:00~2:30 am. According to the satellite map, Xiamen Railway Station is within that region.

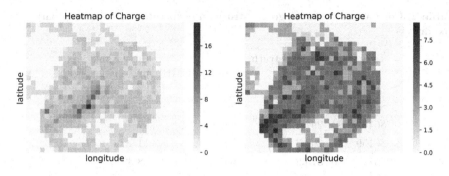

Fig. 3. Traffic charge of 2:00~2:30(left) and 9:00~9:30(right) on July 1st

Then we randomly choose **50** taxi drivers (5 for each day in the testing set) to simulate their driving routes over the period from 7:00 am to 12:00 am using TaxiC. Here we let sub-regions be 5×5 grids centered on the region the taxi is in. As we have mentioned above, the specific driving routes are determined under probability, which means that every time the results of the simulation would be different. Therefore, for each taxi driver, we average the results from 10 simulations as the final result. The experimental results show that the average revenue over this period increased by 10.26%, which is better compared with 8% increase using urban traffic coulombs law [6]. Table 2 shows part of the experimental results.

Figure 4 shows the ground-truth (in left) and experimental (in right) pick-up and drop-off locations of one taxi driver (7:00am to 12:00am). Comparing the details in the two sub-figure, we can find that the distance between one drop-off point and the next pick-up point is shortened. That is to say, the cruising time between dropping off one passenger and picking up the next one is shortened, which means the driver spends less time finding passengers thus leading to the increase of total income.

Table 3 shows the comparisons of TaxiC with other state-of-the-art route recommendation methods. Given a heat map, the randomized model will randomly offer a driving direction. We can see that this model can earn drivers an average revenue of 768.6(RMB), which is 6.58% less than that of the ground truth, in this respect, we know how important the drivers' experience is. The second method is the modified HITS model [15], which only takes profits into consideration, i.e., taxi drivers will be guided to the regions with highest profits and other factors like competition are not concerned about. Besides, STP model in [7] generate an STP map, which is similar to heat map, but what we care about is the traffic charges and STP focuses on profitability scores. Therefore, the driving direction recommended by STP points to the region with the highest score. Among all of the five methods, TaxiC model earns the highest average revenue. Specifically, when adopting TaxiC, the average revenue is 12.76%, higher than that of the ground truth, while the average revenue generated by STP and HITS is only 9.93% and 2.54% higher respectively.

Table 2. Comparisons between ground-truth and experimental revenue of part of the taxi drivers

Taxi ID	Ground-truth revenue (RMB)	TaxiC revenue(RMB)	Increasing percentage (%)
86182**04	269.5	290.1	7.64
86182**84	297.3	320.9	7.94
86159**87	262.3	291.8	11.25
86159**76	315.2	343.8	8.32
86147**21	247.3	264.9	6.64
86147**15	249.3	301.8	17.39
86147**57	279.6	333.1	16.06
86134**15	252.6	287.5	13.82
86134**52	275.1	299.60	8.91
86134**82	328.9	349.8	6.35
86134**82	250.3	288.98	15.45
86135**89	240.0	279.78	16.58
86134**44	294.4	314.4	6.79
86134**41	253.8	297.58	17.25
86134**43	276.8	300.92	8.71
...	...	...	...
Average	261.56	288.40	10.26

Fig. 4. Comparison of pick-up and drop-off locations.(The red circle and the blue triangle stand for the pick-up and drop-off points respectively, and the numbers represent the order of the passengers.) (Color figure online)

Table 3. Comparisons with other methods

Method	Average revenue (RMB)	Increasing percentage (%)
Random	768.6	−6.58
HITS	843.6	2.54
STP	904.4	9.93
Ground truth	822.7	0
TaxiC	927.68	12.76

5.3 Parameter Tuning

The Weight ω. We simulate the driving routes under different ω. Part of the results are listed in Table 4. We can find that the recommendation performance is best when $\omega = 0.5$, followed by $\omega = 0.8$. When the historical traffic charges are barely taken into consideration, the increase in revenue is not significant. While when ω is less than 0.5, the revenue of more taxi drivers shows a noticeable decline.

Table 4. Results under different ω

Taxi ID	$\omega = 0.8$ (%)	$\omega = 0.5$ (%)	$\omega = 0.2$ (%)	$\omega = 0.0$ (%)
86182**04	7.64	11.87	3.35	3.56
86182**84	7.94	1.22	−5.44	1.18
86159**87	11.25	10.05	4.90	0.82
86159**76	8.32	6.99	−1.61	−3.38
86147**21	6.64	17.20	11.52	8.09
86147**15	17.39	15.00	10.98	1.29
86147**57	16.06	7.33	4.89	5.41
86134**15	13.82	16.07	5.82	5.62
86134**52	8.91	21.37	1.45	2.07
86134**82	6.35	2.46	−1.19	−6.99
86134**82	15.45	11.59	−4.39	5.51
86135**89	16.58	14.73	1.62	−2.54
86134**44	6.79	10.39	−3.33	−4.58
86134**41	17.25	9.26	4.05	5.20
86134**43	8.71	10.3	1.48	0.61
...	...	...	...	...
Average	10.26	11.25	3.35	2.76

Note: 'Average' represents the average values of all 50 samples.

Parameters θ and δ. First let θ_0 be the average charge of the sub-regions and δ_0 be the average PVR of all regions. We change θ under $\delta = \delta_0$, and change δ under $\theta = \theta_0$. Experimental results are shown in Table 5 and Fig. 5. We can see that the performance is better when $\theta = 1.0\theta_0, 1.2\theta_0$ or $\delta = 1.0\delta_0, 1.2\theta_0$. According to Algorithm 1, if θ and δ get larger, taxi drivers would change driving directions more frequently, and too frequent changes in direction may result in unsatisfactory outcomes. On the other hand, if θ and δ are too small, taxi drivers would be more likely to stick to the previous directions rather than changing directions, which lead to little increase in revenue, and that is the reason why results are much less satisfactory when $\theta = 0.5\theta_0$ or $\delta = 0.5\delta_0$.

Table 5. Results under different θ and δ

$\delta = \delta_0$	Increasing percentage(%)	$\theta = \theta_0$	Increasing percentage(%)
$\theta = 1.5\theta_0$	6.93	$\delta = 1.5\delta_0$	7.19
$\theta = 1.2\theta_0$	9.83	$\delta = 1.2\delta_0$	11.29
$\theta = \theta_0$	10.26	$\delta = \delta_0$	10.26
$\theta = 0.8\theta_0$	4.35	$\delta = 0.8\delta_0$	5.48
$\theta = 0.5\theta_0$	2.70	$\delta = 0.5\delta_0$	1.44

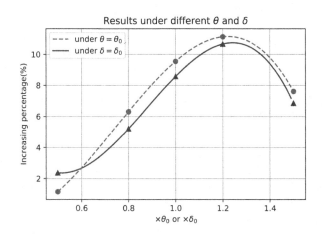

Fig. 5. Results under different θ and δ

6 Conclusion

In this paper, we propose a traffic-charge-based online driving direction recommendation system for taxi drivers named TaxiC. The proposed system takes both real-time and historical traffic situations into consideration, and the recommendation strategy also considers the behaviors of other taxi drivers. Moreover, to have a more intuitive understanding of the traffic charges, we provide a traffic charge heat map of all regions for taxi drivers. The experimental results show TaxiC can help taxi drivers selecting one optimal route and reduce the cruise time.

In our future work, improvements will be made on the accuracy of regional division. That is to say, we will apply the concept of traffic charges to the road-segment level. What's more, we need to focus on passengers more. For example, the waiting time of passengers before being picked up should be taken into consideration. Once both taxi drivers and passengers are considered, the recommendation system will be more practical and effective.

Acknowledgment. This work is supported by the Natural Science Foundation of Fujian Province (China) under Grant No. 2017J01118, by Shenzhen Science and Technology Planning Program under Grant No. JCYJ20170307141019252, and by the National Natural Science Foundation of China under Grant No. 61503313.

References

1. Chow, C., Mokbel, M.F.: Trajectory privacy in location-based services and data publication. SIGKDD Explor. **13**(1), 19–29 (2011)
2. Dong, H., Zhang, X., Dong, Y., Chen, C., Rao, F.: Recommend a profitable cruising route for taxi drivers. In: 2014 IEEE 17th International Conference on Intelligent Transportation Systems (ITSC), pp. 2003–2008. IEEE (2014)
3. Hwang, R.H., Hsueh, Y.L., Chen, Y.T.: An effective taxi recommender system based on a spatio-temporal factor analysis model. Inf. Sci. **314**, 28–40 (2015)
4. Li, B., et al.: Hunting or waiting? discovering passenger-finding strategies from a large-scale real-world taxi dataset, pp. 63–68 (2011)
5. Li, X., et al.: Prediction of urban human mobility using large-scale taxi traces and its applications. Front. Comput. Sci. **6**(1), 111–121 (2012)
6. Lyu, Z., Lai, Y., Li, K.-C., Yang, F., Liao, M., Gao, X.: Taxi route recommendation based on urban traffic coulomb's law. In: Bouguettaya, A., et al. (eds.) WISE 2017. LNCS, vol. 10569, pp. 376–390. Springer, Cham (2017). https://doi.org/10.1007/978-3-319-68783-4_26
7. Powell, J.W., Huang, Y., Bastani, F., Ji, M.: Towards reducing taxicab cruising time using spatio-temporal profitability maps, pp. 242–260 (2011)
8. Qian, S., Zhu, Y., Li, M.: Smart recommendation by mining large-scale GPS traces, pp. 3267–3272 (2012)
9. Seidl, D.E., Jankowski, P., Tsou, M.: Privacy and spatial pattern preservation in masked GPS trajectory data. Int. J. Geogr. Inf. Sci. **30**(4), 785–800 (2016)
10. Yamamoto, K.: Adaptive routing of multiple taxis by mutual exchange of pathways. Int. J. Knowl. Eng. Soft Data Paradigms **2**(1), 57–69 (2010)

11. Ying, J.J., Lu, E.H.C., Kuo, W.N., Tseng, V.S.: Urban point-of-interest recommendation by mining user check-in behaviors, pp. 63–70 (2012)
12. Yuan, J., Zheng, Y., Zhang, L., Xie, X., Sun, G.: Where to find my next passenger. In: Proceedings of the 13th International Conference on Ubiquitous Computing, pp. 109–118. ACM (2011)
13. Yuan, N.J., Zheng, Y., Zhang, L., Xie, X.: T-finder: a recommender system for finding passengers and vacant taxis. IEEE Trans. Knowl. Data Eng. **25**(10), 2390–2403 (2013)
14. Zhang, M., Liu, J., Liu, Y., Hu, Z., Yi, L.: Recommending pick-up points for taxi-drivers based on spatio-temporal clustering. In: 2012 Second International Conference on Cloud and Green Computing (CGC), pp. 67–72. IEEE (2012)
15. Zheng, Y., Zhang, L., Xie, X., Ma, W.: Mining interesting locations and travel sequences from GPS trajectories. In: International World Wide Web Conferences, pp. 791–800 (2009)

Event Log Reconstruction
Using Autoencoders

Hoang Thi Cam Nguyen[1] and Marco Comuzzi[2(✉)]

[1] Trusting Social, Ho Chi Minh City, Vietnam
hoang.cam.nguyen@trustingsocial.com
[2] Ulsan National Institute of Science and Technology, Ulsan, Republic of Korea
mcomuzzi@unist.ac.kr

Abstract. Poor quality of process event logs prevents high quality business process analysis and improvement. Process event logs quality decreases because of missing attribute values or after incorrect or irrelevant attribute values are identified and removed. Reconstructing a correct value for these missing attributes is likely to increase the quality of event log-based process analyses. Traditional statistical reconstruction methods work poorly with event logs, because of the complex interrelations among attributes, events and cases. Machine learning approaches appear more suitable in this context, since they can learn complex models of event logs through training. This paper proposes a method for reconstructing missing attribute values in event logs based on the use of autoencoders. Autoencoders are a class of feed-forward neural networks that reconstruct their own input after having learnt a model of its latent distribution. They suit problems of unsupervised learning, such as the one considered in this paper. When reconstructing missing attribute values in an event log, in fact, one cannot assume that a training set with true labels is available for model training. The proposed method is evaluated on two real event logs against baseline methods commonly used in the literature for imputing missing values in large datasets.

Keywords: Event log · Business process · Data quality · Neural network

1 Introduction

Historical information about execution of business processes can be recorded in so-called *event logs* using data produced by enterprise information systems. A record in an event log is an individual event that occurred in a particular process instance, or *case*, and includes attributes such as a case identifier, timestamp of occurrence, activity name, i.e., what was executed, and resource identifier, i.e., who was in charge of execution/supervision. Event logs enable a plethora of process analyses, such as process discovery, conformance analysis, performance analysis or organisational information mining [21].

This work received fundings from NRF Korea Project Number 2017076589.

X. Liu et al. (Eds.): ICSOC 2018 Workshops, LNCS 11434, pp. 335–350, 2019.
https://doi.org/10.1007/978-3-030-17642-6_28

The quality of data-enabled analysis strongly depends on the quality of the underlying data used for it [2]. This holds also for event log-enabled business process analysis. For instance, in the monitoring of process KPIs, low quality information about resource identifiers, i.e., inaccurate or incomplete resource attribute values in event logs, prevents calculating an entire class of indicators related with individual resources' efficiency in executing the tasks to which they are assigned.

A certain level of errors in event logs, unfortunately, is often unavoidable, particularly where manual logging is involved. Mans et al. [11], for instance, report that errors in event logs of health care processes mainly occur due to manual logging and that, among them, missing or incorrect case id and resource information occur at higher frequency than missing or abnormal timestamps. Therefore, more research is needed to address the challenge of improving the quality of event logs, which in turn will enable higher quality analyses of business processes.

Quality of data, in general, can be enhanced by (i) improving the way in which data are captured while they are being generated and (ii) improving the quality of data after they have been acquired [2]. In this paper we focus on (ii), that is, improving the quality of existing event logs. There are two stages to improve the quality of data that have been acquired, namely data *cleaning* and *imputation*. The former refers to identifying and removing abnormal values in a dataset, whereas the latter is the process of replacing, or reconstructing, missing values with reliable substituted values. In this paper, we focus on reconstructing missing attribute values in event logs. These values may be missing because they have never been acquired or because of the result of removing abnormal values. The objective, in this case, is to *impute* a substituted value that most truthfully reflects the execution of the business process that has generated the event to which the missing attribute belongs.

Traditional data imputation methods, such as mean or median value substitution, are not very effective with event logs, since one cannot assume that attribute values follow a known specific distribution. Instead of using traditional methods, this paper proposes to adopt machine learning techniques to learn a model of data from which missing values can be then imputed. The core idea underlying the proposed method is to treat imputation as a special case of machine learning-enabled process predictive monitoring. While predictive monitoring aims at predicting the next value of an attribute in a case [20], e.g., the next activity to be executed, by looking at what happened in an event log in the past, when imputing missing values we can look at the entire event log to impute a value for missing attributes. From a methodological standpoint, predictive monitoring is a supervised learning problem, since previous history in an event log can be used to extract a set of correctly labelled observations to train a model. In reconstructing missing attribute values, however, correct observations are, by definition, not available for training a learning model. Therefore, event log reconstruction becomes a case of unsupervised learning.

The method proposed in this paper uses *autoencoders*, i.e., a class of deep feed-forward neural networks that aim at reconstructing their own input after having learnt a hidden (or *latent*) distribution of the input data [8]. The autoencoders developed in this paper to impute missing attribute values in an event log are able to handle both numerical, e.g., timestamps, and categorical attributes, e.g., activity names and resource identifiers. They have been tested on real event logs randomly perturbed with missing values.

The paper is organised as follows. Section 2 discusses related work on event log quality, while autoencoders are introduced in Sect. 3. The method to impute missing attributes values is described in Sect. 4 and its evaluation is presented in Sect. 5. Conclusions are eventually drawn in Sect. 6.

2   Related Work

Various methods have been proposed to handle missing data in large datasets, such as deletion of observations with missing values or reconstructing data using statistical and artificial intelligence techniques. Promising results have been shown particularly in imputation of medical domain datasets [4, 17]. It should be noted, however, that an event log has unique characteristics which make it different from other types of datasets, such as the ones traditionally used in health care or social science research. While an individual record in other datasets, e.g., medical datasets, can be considered as a complete observation of a phenomenon, an event in an event log is only part of a case. Cases represent the actual observations to train a model, either for predictive monitoring or missing values reconstruction. This multi-layered structure of event logs, combined with temporal relations among events determined by timestamps, require learning models, such as neural networks, able to learn higher dimensional models of data.

Data quality issues in event logs have been classified by Bose et al. [5] and, in the specific context of process mining in the health care, by Mans et al. [11]. Bose et al., in particular, have identified missing, incorrect, imprecise, and irrelevant data as type of sources of event log quality degradation. The focus of this paper is on missing data, which, however, may also derive from removing incorrect or imprecise data.

The work of Suriadi et al. [19] classifies a set of event log imperfection patterns that may guide the event log quality improvement phase. Patterns help understanding the sources of imperfection in an event log and, therefore, can guide the improvement of logging activities during process execution. In this paper, we focus on a closely related, but different issue, that is, reconstructing missing values in an event log that has already been acquired.

The quality of event logs is strictly related with detecting noise in event logs, i.e., infrequent behaviour, and with repairing event logs. Noise is typically removed in a pre-processing phase, using frequency-based approaches [7, 15]. As such, it can be seen in our context as a data *cleaning* activity. Several ad-hoc methods have been proposed for identifying and repairing event logs by reconstructing missing events. Rogge-Solti et al. [14] propose a method based on

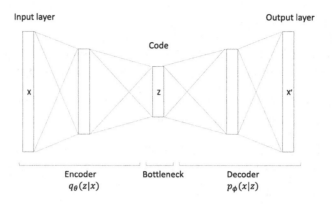

Fig. 1. The *butterfly* architecture of an autoencoder with five layers.

stochastic Petri nets and Bayesian networks. A similar approach can then be used to improve process documentation [13]. Bayomie et al. [3] have proposed a method to reconstruct the value of case identifiers in an unlabeled event log. These approaches take a different perspective from the one considered in this paper, since they assume that a process model is available. Missing events or attribute values can be then reconstructed by combining process knowledge with knowledge discovery techniques. In this paper, the only information available for reconstructing missing values in an event log is the event log itself and we do not assume any knowledge about the process that has generated an event log. Nolle et al. [12] have proposed to use autoencoders for denoising event logs, showing remarkable performance, albeit on artificially generated logs. Even in this case, however, noise in event logs is defined at the event level, e.g., missing or duplicated events, rather than at the event attribute level as we consider in this paper.

3   Autoencoders

Autoencoders are a class of neural networks used for unsupervised learning and as generative models [8]. Given a dataset $X = \{x^i\} \in \mathbb{R}^n$, an autoencoder tries to learn a vector X' having a distribution similar to X. This is done in two separate processes (see Fig. 1 for a standard representation of an autoencoder). First, a vector Z, i.e., a *code*, is formed (or *encoded*) from X to learn a hidden, or *latent* model $q_\theta(z|x)$ of the data, where θ are the weights and biases of the encoder; second, a decoder $p_\phi(x|z)$ reconstructs a vector X' having similar distribution to X from the code Z (ϕ are the weights and biases of the decoder neural network). Several hidden layers can be stacked in between input and output layers in both processes, allowing a model to create a higher dimensional representation of the data. The autoencoder of Fig. 1, for instance, uses one hidden layer for both encoding and decoding, leading to a 5-layered deep neural network, and adopts a so-called *butterfly* architecture, in which the size of the input is greater than the number of neurons in the hidden layer, which is greater than the code dimension.

The number of hidden units in the bottleneck layer, i.e., the dimension of the code, can be lower or higher than n. If the size of the code is lower than n, then an autoencoder is forced to learn a *compressed* representation of X, by identifying a limited number of interesting features characterising the latent distribution of X. If the size of the code is higher than n, then an autoencoder can still be used to learn interesting structures in data, particularly if specific constraints on hidden units are enforced, e.g., sparcity of hidden units when processing pixels of an image.

Autoencoders initially have been used for dimensionality reduction and feature learning. The basic idea of autoencoders (with code size lower than n) is similar to the one of Principal Components Analysis (PCA) [1], that is, to project high dimensional data onto a manifold, which can represent data with a lower dimensional code. Unlike PCA, autoencoders are not restricted to linear transformations and they are able to reconstruct their output from latent variables. Autoencoders have been successfully applied in many real-world problems, such as paraphrase detection [18] or anomaly detection [16]. Nowadays, they also find several applications as generative models, since the learnt code Z can be used to generate new datasets from the same latent distribution of input X.

Similar to other feed-forward neural networks, the neurons in the hidden layers of an autoencoder compute the weighted sums of the input neurons and biases, which are then passed through a non-linear transformation guided by some activation function, such as sigmoid function. The learning process in an autoencoder aims at optimising a loss function $L(X, X')$, where L is a suitable likelihood function. L can be formulated based on the ultimate objective of the training process. When the data resemble a vector of probabilities, i.e., values comprised between 0 and 1, as in the method proposed in the paper, the loss function in Eq. 1 is used to optimize. This loss function considers the average cross-entropy of N observations x_i in X.

$$L(X, X') = \frac{1}{N} \sum_{i=1}^{N} x_i \log x_i' + (1 - x_i) \log(1 - x_i') \tag{1}$$

Variational autoencoders (VAE) [10] are a variant of autoencoders (AE), which add additional constraints on the encoded representation to be learnt. A VAE, in fact, is an autoencoder with added constraints on the encoded representation Z. In particular, the features in a code Z learnt by a VAE are forced to roughly follow a given probabilistic distribution $p(z)$, e.g., a unit gaussian distribution. This helps when VAE are used as a generative model, since new output data roughly similar to the input data can be generated by drawing values from such a distribution and passing them into the decoder part of the neural network.

The loss function to be optimised in a VAE for one datapoint $x_i \in X$ is shown in Eq. 2. The first term is the reconstruction term, or expected negative log-likelihood of x_i, taken in respect of the encoder's distribution over the code. If the decoder's output does not reconstruct the data well, then this term will be high. The second term is the Kullback-Leibler (KL) divergence (expanded in Eq. 3).

The KL divergence measures how closely the latent code z matches the chosen probability distribution $p(z)$. A common choice is to choose the unit gaussian distribution $N(0, 1)$ as $p(z)$. For more details about the internal functioning of VAE, we refer to [8].

$$l_i(\theta, \phi) = -E_{z \sim q_\theta(z|x_i)} \left[\log p_\phi(x_i|z) + KL(q_\theta(z|x_i) \| p(z)) \right] \qquad (2)$$

$$KL(q_\theta(z|x_i) \| p(z)) = E_q[\log q_\theta(z|x)] - E_q[\log p(x|z)] + \log p(x) \qquad (3)$$

4   Method

This section presents in detail the proposed method for reconstructing missing attribute values in event logs. The steps of the proposed method are shown in Fig. 2. A low quality event log, i.e., with missing values, is taken as input. In a pre-processing phase, event logs are transformed into a format that can be fed into autoencoders. As discussed later in this section, for an autoencoder, each case in an event log represents an observation x belonging to the input X. Hence, each case in an event log is transformed into a matrix of events and features that can be fed into an autoencoder. As far as model training is concerned, in this paper we experiment with traditional autoencoders (AE) and variational autoencoders (VAE), which require the same type of input. The model learnt from input data is then used to reconstruct missing values in an event log. The output of this step is a set of ouput matrices, one for each case in an event log. In a post-processing phase, for each case the values in the output matrix are then translated back into the traditional format of event logs by applying the inverse of the transformation adopted in the pre-processing phase.

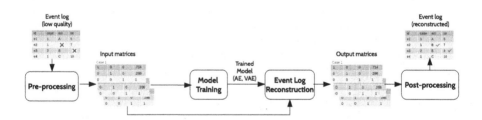

Fig. 2. Event log reconstruction method.

Before discussing the steps of the proposed method in more detail, let us introduce some required notation of event logs. Let $\mathcal{E}$ be the event universe, i.e. the set of all possible event identifiers. Events are characterised by attributes, e.g., they belong to a particular case, have a timestamp, correspond to an activity, and are executed by a particular person. Let $AN = \{a_1, \ldots, a_n\}$ be a set of all possible attributes names and $\mathcal{D}_{a_i}$ the domain of attribute a_i, i.e., the set of all possible values for the attribute a_i. Attributes can be numerical or categorical. Numerical

Event log			
id	case	act	tst
e1	1	A	5
e2	1	B	7
e3	2	B	3
e4	1	C	10

Normalisation of attributes "act" (discrete) and "tst" (continuous)

id	case	C_A	C_B	C_c	C_{tst}
e1	1	1	0	0	0
e2	1	0	1	0	0.4
e3	2	0	1	0	0
e4	1	0	0	1	1

Input of autoencoder

Case 1				
e1	1	0	0	0
e2	0	1	0	0.4
e4	0	0	1	1

Case 2				
	0	0	0	0
	0	0	0	0
e3	0	1	0	0

Fig. 3. Event log pre-processing: example.

attributes, e.g., timestamps, assume value within a certain numerical interval, that is, $\mathcal{D}_{a_i} = [v_{i,min}, v_{i,max}] \subseteq \mathbb{R}$. Categorical attributes assume values within a given set, such as a set of activity identifiers (strings) for the activity label attribute, i.e., $\mathcal{D}_{a_i} = \{v_{i,1}, \ldots, v_{i,K}\}$. For any event $e \in \mathcal{E}$ and attribute name $a \in AN$, $\#_a(e) \in \mathcal{D}_a$ is the value of attribute named a for event e.

Let $\mathcal{D}_{id}$ be the set of event identifiers, $\mathcal{D}_{case}$ the set of case identifiers, $\mathcal{D}_{id}$ the set of activity labels, $\mathcal{D}_{tst}$ the set of possible timestamps, and $\mathcal{D}_{res}$ the set of possible resource identifiers. For each event $e \in \mathcal{E}$, we define a set of standard attributes:

- $\#_{id}(e) \in \mathcal{D}_{id}$ is the event identifier of e;
- $\#_{case}(e) \in \mathcal{D}_{case}$ is the case identifier of e;
- $\#_{tst}(e) \in \mathcal{D}_{tst}$ is the timestamp of e;
- $\#_{act}(e) \in \mathcal{D}_{act}$ is the activity name of e;
- $\#_{res}(e) \in \mathcal{D}_{res}$ is the resource involved in e;

In the pre-processing phase, an event log is transformed into a suitable format to be fed into an autoencoder. Autoencoders require as input observations coded as a matrix of numerical values. Values should also be normalised. If, in fact, attribute values vary across different ranges, then attributes characterised by larger ranges would be more important than other attributes characterised by smaller ranges during the learning phases. A common choice is to normalise attribute values between 0 and 1. To meet this requirement, an event log is pre-processed as described in the following to transform each case into a matrix C of values $c_{i,j}$ comprised between 0 and 1 of fixed size (see Fig. 3 for an example).

Categorical attributes (see encoding of the activity attribute in Fig. 3) are encoded using a one-of-K scheme. That is, for an attribute a_i a column in the autoencoder input matrix is created for each value $v_{i,k} \in \mathcal{D}_{a_i}$. A row is then created for each event e in an event log, with values:

$$c_{i,k}(e) = \begin{cases} 1 & \text{if } \#_{a_i}(e) = v_{i,k} \\ 0 & \text{otherwise} \end{cases}$$

for $k = 1, \ldots, K$.

Numerical attributes $\#_{a_i}(e)$ (see encoding of timestamps in Fig. 3) are encoded by normalising their value between a minimum value L_{min} and a maximum value L_{max} assumed by attribute a_i within the case to which event e belongs. That is, for a numerical attribute a_i, a column is created such that, for each event e in an event log:

$$c_i(e) = \frac{\#_{a_i}(e) - L_{min}}{L_{max} - L_{min}}, \tag{4}$$

with $L_{max} = \#_{a_i}(e_{max})$, $L_{min} = \#_{a_i}(e_{min})$ and

$$e_{max} = \{e \in \mathcal{E} : \#_a(e) \leq \#_a(e') \wedge \#_{case}(e) = \#_{case}(e') \Rightarrow e' = e, \forall e' \in \mathcal{E}\} \tag{5}$$

$$e_{min} = \{e \in \mathcal{E} : \#_a(e) \geq \#_a(e') \wedge \#_{case}(e) = \#_{case}(e') \Rightarrow e' = e, \forall e' \in \mathcal{E}\} \tag{6}$$

Alternatively, numerical attributes values can be normalised using the minimum and maximum values $l_{i,min}$ and $l_{i,max}$ in $\mathcal{D}_{a_i}$. This choice, however, is highly sensitive to abnormally high values in the domain $\mathcal{D}_{a_i}$. For both categorical and numerical attributes, missing values are encoded to the value 0.

Obtained rows are then grouped by case id and ordered by timestamp value. As a result, an individual case is represented by a $p \times q$ matrix, where p is the number of activities in the case and q is the number of columns resulting from the normalisation described above. Since an autoencoder requires a fixed-size matrix as input for all observations, zero-padding is applied to all cases for which $p < p_{max}$, where p_{max} is the highest number of activities in a case in an event log (see zero-padding of the first two rows for case 2 in Fig. 3, in which it is assumed that case 1 is the one with highest number of activities in the event log). In the experiments that we conducted, the results do not depend on the position of the zero-padding rows in an input matrix.

The objective of the model training step is to train a model that can learn the *latent* distribution of data in an event log. Once a model has been trained, each case in an event log is reconstructed into an output matrix of elements $c'_{i,j}$ of size $p \times q$. As a result of the event log reconstruction step, in an output matrix missing attributes values (denoted by 0 in the input matrix) are mapped to valid values for numerical attributes and to probabilities for the categorical attributes. In other words, the task of reconstructing a missing value of a numerical attribute is a regression task, while reconstructing values of categorical attributes is a classification task.

To define the loss function to be optimsed, during model training we introduce a masking matrix to distinguish missing values and zero-padding values from non-zero values in an input matrix. The loss function, in fact, must be designed in such a way that 0 values in an input matrix should not be learnt, since they correspond to either artificially added zero-padding values or initially missing values. Elements $m_{i,j}$ of the masking matrix $M \in \mathbb{R}^{p \times q}$ are defined as:

$$m_{i,j} = \begin{cases} 0 & \text{if } c_{i,j} = 0 \text{ (missing or 0-padding)} \\ 1 & \text{otherwise} \end{cases} \tag{7}$$

As introduced in Sect. 3, we consider a cross entropy-based loss function for AE, shown in Eq. 8, which uses the masking matrix of Eq. 7 and in which cross-entropy is averaged across all values in an input matrix. For VAE, we consider the loss function defined in Sect. 3 and $p(z) = N(0, 1)$.

$$L(x, x') = \frac{1}{p \times q} \sum_{i=1}^{p} \sum_{i=1}^{q} c_{i,j} \cdot m_{i,j} \log c'_{i,j} + (1 - c'_{i,j}) \cdot m_{i,j} \cdot \log(1 - c'_{i,j}) \quad (8)$$

The last step is to post-process the output matrices to reconstruct an event log in its traditional format. In this post-processing step missing values of numerical attributes are transformed into valid values in an event log by inverting Eq. 4, whereas an output value a_i of a categorical attribute is reconstructed by softmax activation, that is, the attribute value $a_{i,k}$ with highest probability value $c'_{i,k}$ in an output matrix is chosen as reconstructed value.

5   Evaluation

This section first describes the datasets used in the evaluation of the proposed method. Then we discuss the evaluation criteria and finally present the results of the experiments.

We have evaluated the proposed method using real-life process event logs publicly available[1]. While deep learning normally requires sufficient amounts of high dimensional data for more efficient and stable performance [6], i.e., large-sized datasets, the performance of the proposed method has been explored under extreme situations as well. We therefore have chosen one *small* dataset, from the Business Process Intelligence (BPI) 2013 Challenge, and one *large* dataset, from the BPI 2012 Challenge:

- **BPI 2013 Challenge.** This log comprises 1,487 cases and 6,660 events with 7 different activities obtained from an incident and problem management process at Volvo IT Belgium. The highest number of activities in a case is 35.
- **BPI 2012 Challenge.** This log consists of 13,087 cases and 262,200 events capturing a process of loan and overdraft application in a Dutch financial institute. There are 36 different activities observed in the process and the highest number of activities in a case is 175.

Event logs downloaded in the standard XES format have been converted into csv files for pre-processing. Case id, timestamp of completed activities and activity name are attributes common to both datasets. Hence, our experiments focus on these three attributes.

The downloaded event logs are clean and complete, so there is a need to introduce missing values to evaluate the proposed method. We restrict the proposed model to imputing the values of timestamp of completed activities,

---

[1] at: https://data.4tu.nl/repository/collection:event_logs_real.

Table 1. Example of missing attribute value setting (BPI Challenge 2012 event log)

Case ID	Activity	Complete timestamp
Case 1	A_SUBMITTED-COMPLETE	01/10/2011 07:38:45
Case 1	A_PARTLYSUBMITTED-COMPLETE	01/10/2011 07:38:45
Case 1	A_PREACCEPTED-COMPLETE	NaT
Case 1	NaN	NaT
Case 1	NaN	01/10/2011 18:36:46

as an example of numerical attribute, and activity name, as an example of categorical attribute. The remaining attribute, i.e., case id, is maintained accurate and complete.

Since we are interested in investigating the impact of informative missingness on the performance of our algorithm, we consider 30%, 35%, 40% and 50% as ratios of attribute values missingness in event logs. To decide which values to set as missing, we randomly sample two integers x_1 and x_2 from a discrete uniform distribution, with x_1 signifying the event in which a value is set as missing, i.e., the *row* in an event log, and x_2 the attribute to be set as missing, i.e., the *column* in an event log. Then, we set the observation at the location identified by x_1 and x_2 as missing. Table 1 shows an example of setting missing values using a fragment of the BPI Challenge 2012 dataset. In this case, x_1 is drawn from a uniform distribution in the range $[1, 5]$, that is, 5 events belong to the log, and x_2 from a uniform distribution in range $[1, 2]$, i.e., only 2 attributes can be missing (activity or timestamp). In Table 1, 4 missing values have been set, for $(x_1, x_2) \in \{(3, 2), (4, 1), (4, 2), (5, 1)\}$. Note that numerical missing attributes are set to NaN, whereas categorical missing attributes are set to NaT. As a result of this procedure, the propensity for an attribute value to be missing is completely random.

The pre-processed data are split into training, validation and testing set with the ratios of 60%, 20% and 20% without shuffling, since the pre-processed data are ordered based on timestamp values and this order must be preserved. For testing, we choose the model showing the best performance on the validation set among the ones obtained at each epoch during training. The actual number of missing values introduced in the experiments is shown in Table 2. For demonstration purpose, we consider AE and VAE with five layers, as shown in Fig. 1. We adopt a *butterfly* architecture in both cases, with input size (resulting after pre-processing), number of neurons in hidden layers and code dimension equal to 280, 100, 50 for the small event log BPI 2013 and 6475, 300, 100 for the large event log BPI 2012. Based on guidance from the literature [8,10], internal neurons use *TanH* and *ReLU* activation functions in AE and VAE, respectively. Neurons in the last layer before output use sigmoid as activation function to squash the output between 0 and 1. Additional internal layers may be stacked in the encoding and decoding layers to increase the performance of the learning process while deteriorating the time performance.

Table 2. Number of missing values in each dataset

Data	Missingness ratio	Variable	Train	Validate	Test	Total
BPI 2013	30%	Time	1,371	327	317	2,015
		Activity	1,352	321	308	1,981
	35%	Time	1,577	374	399	2,350
		Activity	1,523	408	381	2,312
	40%	Time	1,799	432	425	2,656
		Activity	1,797	423	452	2,672
	50%	Time	2,226	545	535	3,306
		Activity	2,146	654	554	3,354
BPI 2012	30%	Time	47,329	16,546	14,501	78,376
		Activity	47,624	16,971	14,349	78,944
	35%	Time	55,546	19,584	16,930	92,060
		Activity	55,183	19,457	16,840	91,480
	40%	Time	63,500	22,125	19,154	104,779
		Activity	63,485	22,333	19,163	104,981
	50%	Time	79,253	27,901	23,902	131,056
		Activity	79,431	27,777	23,936	131,144

The input data has been loaded into the model using a mini batch-size of 16, and the weights have been initialised by Xavier uniform initialiser to assist in faster convergence, avoiding local minima and exploding/vanishing gradient descent. We have trained the model with 100 epochs using the learning rate of 0.005 with an exponential decay factor of 0.9. The parameters are optimised using the Adam algorithm [9] with $\beta_1 = 0.9$ and $\beta_2 = 0.999$. We train the model until the termination condition of early stopping is met, or the maximum number of epochs is reached. We monitor the training procedure by manually terminating the training when the loss on the validation dataset has not improved after 10 iterations.

After model training, we let the model do the event log reconstruction (see Fig. 2) on the test set. The performance of the regression task (for numerical attributes) is evaluated using the Mean Absolute Error (MAE) and the Root Mean Square Error (RMSE), while for the classification task (for categorical attributes), we consider the accuracy score.

The method has been implemented in Pytorch[2]. A companion Web site, including source code and experiments is publicly available[3]. Experiments run on an Intel i7 Linux machine equipped with 16GB memory and a GeForce GTX 1080 GPU. One epoch training takes approximately 3 s for the large event log BPI 2012 and 0.2 s for the smaller event log BPI 2013.

---

[2] https://github.com/pytorch.

[3] https://github.com/hoangnguyen3892/event-log-reconstruction.

Table 3. Model performance for timestamp value reconstruction, measured by Mean Absolute Error (MAE) and Root Mean Squared Error (RMSE) in days.

Event log	Missingness	Metric	VAE	AE	BL_1	BL_2	BL_3	BL_4
BPI 2013	30%	MAE	7.23	6.70	8.68	14.35	8.97	12.90
		RMSE	13.50	13.32	16.47	19.40	16.43	18.42
	35%	MAE	7.80	7.34	15.35	19.88	15.45	18.67
		RMSE	14.38	14.21	113.84	113.94	113.83	113.85
	40%	MAE	8.52	7.70	10.14	16.79	10.93	15.34
		RMSE	15.95	13.99	18.21	23.53	18.42	22.03
	50%	MAE	8.65	8.32	19.10	26.05	19.68	26.27
		RMSE	14.92	14.73	139.66	140.02	139.62	140.14
BPI 2012	30%	MAE	0.98	0.77	1.12	1.46	1.09	1.13
		RMSE	2.12	1.92	3.80	3.86	3.70	3.68
	35%	MAE	1.07	0.81	1.15	1.49	1.11	1.13
		RMSE	2.23	1.95	3.78	3.85	3.66	3.64
	40%	MAE	1.08	0.89	1.18	1.54	1.13	1.19
		RMSE	2.23	2.10	3.89	3.97	3.79	3.78
	50%	MAE	1.17	1.06	1.43	1.85	1.39	1.43
		RMSE	2.40	2.46	4.29	4.42	4.19	4.18

The performance of the proposed method is evaluated against baseline imputation methods commonly used in the literature. For imputing the values of categorical attributes, i.e., activity name in our experiments, a traditional approach is to consider the most frequent observation [17]. In our experiments, the baseline BL for missing activity values is the most frequent activity name in an event log. For imputing values of numerical attributes, the median or mean value are often considered [17]. In our experiments, we consider 4 possible baselines for imputing missing timestamps values, i.e., reconstructing timestamp values using the median (BL_1) and mean (BL_2) duration of all activities in an event log, and using the median (BL_3) and mean (BL_4) duration of the activity to which a missing timestamp belongs. Note that, if both activity name and timestamp are missing for an event, then the activity name is imputed first using the proposed method, and this imputed value is used to calculate the baseline values of the missing timestamp.

Tables 3 and 4 show the results of timestamp and activity name reconstruction, respectively.

Timestamp Value Reconstruction. Results in Table 3 show that, in relative terms, both VAE and AE perform better than the baselines BL_{1-4}. The mean and maximum case duration is 8.62 days and 137.22 days, respectively, for the BPI 2012 event log and 178.88 days and 2254.88 days, respectively, for the BPI 2013 event log. The performance of the proposed method on the BPI 2012 event log is rather stable, with MAE and RMSE not exceeding 11.6% (0.13%) and 27.8% (0.07%) of mean (maximum) case duration, respectively. The performance in respect of the BPI 2013 event log is substantially less stable. The high variability of results for the BPI 2013 event log is due to the distribution of activity durations. Activities in this event log tend to have very short or very long duration, which makes it difficult to learn the time characteristics in the logs. This is also supported by the noticeable gap between mean (BL_1, BL_3) and median (BL_2, BL_4) imputation for this event log. Mean values are in fact affected by extreme values or outliers in the dataset, and therefore achieves worse results.

Activity Name Reconstruction. Results in Table 4 show a remarkable efficiency of the proposed method to reconstruct missing activity names. We can also observe that the performance of reconstructing missing activity names is more stable compared to missing timestamp reconstruction, even under high levels of information missingness. The model is able to impute missing values efficiently with higher accuracy than baselines from the very first iterations. This may be due to the fact that a sequence of activities in an event log tend to follow a particular pattern determined by the process control flow. This pattern can be learned by our model during the training process, which helps improving the accuracy of activity imputation.

Table 4. Model performance for missing activity label reconstruction, measured by accuracy.

Data	Missingness	VAE	AE	BL
BPI 2013	30%	73.05%	78.57%	44.16%
	35%	74.80%	75.33%	46.46%
	40%	73.70%	78.76%	44.47%
	50%	71.48%	76.33%	47.11%
BPI 2012	30%	69.05%	79.19%	10.77%
	35%	64.88%	78.69%	10.32%
	40%	64.33%	75.92%	10.28%
	50%	60.78%	74.90%	10.17%

Effect of Missingness Ratio. As the number of missing attribute values increases, the performance of the proposed reconstruction models deteriorates. However, the missingness ratio does not appear to have a large effect on the activity name imputation performance (see Table 4). As remarked before, this may be due to the patterns of sequence of activities. Once these control flow structures have been learned by a model, they easily can be used to reliably impute missing values. It seems, therefore, that the performance of the model should be evaluated in the future in respect of the complexity of a process model control flow.

Note that the results do not vary extensively in the baseline methods using the mean and median values. This is because we only consider completely random missing values, which do not have a significant impact impact on average values calculate from the dataset.

Comparison Between Two Proposed Learning Models. Overall, AEs seem to perform better than VAEs in most scenarios. In addition, VAEs converge slower than AEs under the same settings. This should not surprise, since VAE are by definition better suited to *generative* use cases, i.e., when the objective is to generate new datasets X' with a similar distribution to the input X, whereas AEs suit better the use case of exact reconstruction of the input dataset X, through the steps of encoding and decoding. The problem considered in this paper is more similar to the latter one, since we aim at reconstructing exactly a set of missing values in an event log.

6   Conclusions

This paper has presented a method to reconstruct missing attribute values in event logs. This increases the event logs quality by reducing the number of missing values, which in turn enables higher quality business process analysis. The method proposed uses autoencoders, a special class of feed-forward deep neural networks that aim at reconstructing their own input. Even though the performance of reconstructing timestamp values is unstable, especially in the case of the small-sized dataset, we have showed that autoencoders give better results than baseline imputation methods when applied to two real-life event logs.

The proposed method has been evaluated for imputing the values of missing timestamps and activity labels. However, it can be generalised to other variables that typically belong to an event log. For instance, cost can be considered as a numerical variable, whereas resource identifier is a categorical variable that can be handled similarly to activity names. Given its central role in uniquely identifying cases, imputing the value of missing *case id* values is more challenging and deserves the development of ad-hoc methods.

The work presented has several limitations. First, the bias introduced by the distribution of the values of timestamps leads to poor imputation of timestamps when compared to activity names. Also, the proposed method only considers two variables for training and it can be improved by considering other existing information in event logs or by extracting more features. Addressing these limitation is a direction for future work. Moreover, future research should also look beyond improving event log quality after they have been acquired, by considering how a process logging infrastructure can be intsrumented with data quality controls. Another interesting avenue for future research concerns investigating the impact of control flow complexity on the efficiency of reconstructing the values of activity labels. Finally, we also aim at evaluating the actual impact of event log quality improvement on the results of process mining analysis.

References

1. Abdi, H., Williams, L.J.: Principal component analysis. Wiley Interdisc. Rev. Comput. Stat. **2**(4), 433–459 (2010)
2. Batini, C., Cappiello, C., Francalanci, C., Maurino, A.: Methodologies for data quality assessment and improvement. ACM Comput. Surv. **41**(3), 16 (2009)
3. Bayomie, D., Helal, I.M.A., Awad, A., Ezat, E., ElBastawissi, A.: Deducing case IDs for unlabeled event logs. In: Reichert, M., Reijers, H.A. (eds.) BPM 2015. LNBIP, vol. 256, pp. 242–254. Springer, Cham (2016). https://doi.org/10.1007/978-3-319-42887-1_20
4. Beaulieu-Jones, B.K., Moore, J.H.: Missing data imputation in the electronic health record using deeply learned autoencoders. In: Pacific Symposium on Biocomputing, pp. 207–218. World Scientific (2017)
5. Bose, R.J.C., Mans, R.S., van der Aalst, W.M.: Wanna improve process mining results? In: 2013 IEEE Symposium on Computational Intelligence and Data Mining (CIDM), pp. 127–134. IEEE (2013)
6. Chen, X.W., Lin, X.: Big data deep learning: challenges and perspectives. IEEE Access **2**, 514–525 (2014)
7. Cheng, H.-J., Kumar, A.: Process mining on noisy logs-can log sanitization help to improve performance? Decis. Support Syst. **79**, 138–149 (2015)
8. Doersch, C.: Tutorial on variational autoencoders. Arxiv preprint (2016)
9. Kingma, D.P., Adam, J.Ba.: A method for stochastic optimization. CoRR, abs/1412.6980 (2014)
10. Kingma, D.P., Welling, M.: Auto-encoding variational Bayes. ArXiv e-prints, December 2013
11. Mans, R.S., van der Aalst, W.M.P., Vanwersch, R.J.B., Moleman, A.J.: Process mining in healthcare: data challenges when answering frequently posed questions. In: Lenz, R., Miksch, S., Peleg, M., Reichert, M., Riaño, D., ten Teije, A. (eds.) KR4HC/ProHealth -2012. LNCS (LNAI), vol. 7738, pp. 140–153. Springer, Heidelberg (2013). https://doi.org/10.1007/978-3-642-36438-9_10
12. Nolle, T., Seeliger, A., Mühlhäuser, M.: Unsupervised anomaly detection in noisy business process event logs using denoising autoencoders. In: Calders, T., Ceci, M., Malerba, D. (eds.) DS 2016. LNCS (LNAI), vol. 9956, pp. 442–456. Springer, Cham (2016). https://doi.org/10.1007/978-3-319-46307-0_28
13. Rogge-Solti, A., Mans, R.S., van der Aalst, W.M.P., Weske, M.: Improving documentation by repairing event logs. In: Grabis, J., Kirikova, M., Zdravkovic, J., Stirna, J. (eds.) PoEM 2013. LNBIP, vol. 165, pp. 129–144. Springer, Heidelberg (2013). https://doi.org/10.1007/978-3-642-41641-5_10
14. Rogge-Solti, A., Mans, R.S., van der Aalst, W.M.P., Weske, M.: Repairing event logs using timed process models. In: Demey, Y.T., Panetto, H. (eds.) OTM 2013. LNCS, vol. 8186, pp. 705–708. Springer, Heidelberg (2013). https://doi.org/10.1007/978-3-642-41033-8_89
15. Rogge-Solti, A., Senderovich, A., Weidlich, M., Mendling, J., Gal, A.: In log and model we trust? In: EMISA, pp. 91–94 (2016)
16. Sakurada, M., Yairi, T.: Anomaly detection using autoencoders with nonlinear dimensionality reduction. In: Proceedings of 2nd Workshop on Machine Learning for Sensory Data Analysis, MLSDA 2014, pp. 4–11 (2014)
17. Shah, A.D., Bartlett, J.W., Carpenter, J., Nicholas, O., Hemingway, H.: Comparison of random forest and parametric imputation models for imputing missing data using mice: a caliber study. Am. J. Epidemiol. **179**(6), 764–774 (2014)

18. Socher, R., Huang, E.H., Pennin, J., Manning, C.D., Ng, A.Y.: Dynamic pooling and unfolding recursive autoencoders for paraphrase detection. In: Shawe-Taylor, J., et al. (ed.) Advances in Neural Information Processing Systems, vol. 24, pp. 801–809 (2011)
19. Suriadi, S., Andrews, R., ter Hofstede, A.H., Wynn, M.T.: Event log imperfection patterns for process mining: towards a systematic approach to cleaning event logs. Inf. Syst. **64**, 132–150 (2017)
20. Tax, N., Verenich, I., La Rosa, M., Dumas, M.: Predictive business process monitoring with LSTM neural networks. In: Dubois, E., Pohl, K. (eds.) CAiSE 2017. LNCS, vol. 10253, pp. 477–492. Springer, Cham (2017). https://doi.org/10.1007/978-3-319-59536-8_30
21. van Eck, M.L., Lu, X., Leemans, S.J.J., van der Aalst, W.M.P.: PM^2: a process mining project methodology. In: Zdravkovic, J., Kirikova, M., Johannesson, P. (eds.) CAiSE 2015. LNCS, vol. 9097, pp. 297–313. Springer, Cham (2015). https://doi.org/10.1007/978-3-319-19069-3_19

MLE: A General Multi-Layer Ensemble Framework for Group Recommendation

Xiaopeng Li[1], Jia Xu[1], Bin Xia[1(✉)], and Jian Xu[2]

[1] Jiangsu Key Laboratory of Big Data Security and Intelligent Processing, Nanjing University of Posts and Telecommunications, Nanjing, People's Republic of China
bxia@njupt.edu.cn
[2] School of Computer Science and Engineering, Nanjing University of Science and Technology, Nanjing, China
dolphin.xu@njust.edu.cn

Abstract. As the number of users and locations has increased dramatically in location-based social networks, it becomes a big challenge to recommend point-of-interests (POIs) meeting users' preference. In traditional recommendation tasks, personalized recommendations performs well, however, these methods also have many disadvantages such as the long-tailed problem and the strong assumption. Further, in general scenarios, a group of users (e.g., colleagues, friends, and family members) often visit a specific location to enjoy time together (e.g., meal and shopping). Thus, it is more meaningful to recommend locations to the group than to individuals. However, the existing group recommendation approaches also have some limitations that hardly capture the preferences of a group of users effectively. To make full use of the users' preferences and improve the effectiveness of group recommendation, in this paper, we propose a multi-layer ensemble framework which has a two-step fusion process. For the first step, we employ several personalized recommendation methods to generate the recommendations for individuals, and the recommendation list is obtained using the proposed fusion approach based on the supervised learning. For the second step, we utilize several ranking aggregation algorithms to fuse the recommendations list of individuals in the group and propose an unsupervised learning based ranking algorithm (URank) to further fuse the results of ranking aggregations to obtain the final group recommendation list. The experiments are conducted on a real-world dataset, and the results demonstrate the effectiveness of our proposed general framework.

Keywords: Group recommendation · Ranking aggregation ·
Unsupervised learning · General ensemble model

1 Introduction

In the era of information explosion, recommender systems (RSs) are widely used to address the problem of information overload, where the users can efficiently

© Springer Nature Switzerland AG 2019
X. Liu et al. (Eds.): ICSOC 2018 Workshops, LNCS 11434, pp. 351–366, 2019.
https://doi.org/10.1007/978-3-030-17642-6_29

obtain the valuable information. Recently, the development of smartphones and the location positioning service boosts the emergence of the location-based social networks (LBSNs), such as Foursquare and Gowalla. Using Foursquare APP, users can post check-in records while visiting the locations, and share the experience with friends. These check-in data provide the opportunities to analyze users' preferences and recommend point-of-interests (POIs) for each individual. With the variety of personalized recommendation services, our daily lives become more convenient; hence the location-based recommender system has become one of the hot research topics such as [21,22].

For the personalized recommendations, the major works are divided into many domains, such as: content-based, collaborative filtering, model-based, association rule-based, and hybrid recommendation. The most representative and effective approach is the matrix factorization which is a collaborative filtering based algorithm, such as Biased Matrix Factorization (BMF), Probabilistic Matrix Factorization (PMF), and Neural Collaborative Filtering (NCF), BMF is effective to address the bias of rating from different users, however, it cannot overcome the problem of long-tailed data where the unpopular objects may be hardly recommended. In addition, PMF combines the traditional matrix factorization with the theory of probability and statistics, and predicts users' preferences based on Gaussian distribution. However, the assumption is strong that the data cannot strictly obey the standard normal distribution. Furthermore, NCF, which is a neural network based algorithm, is proposed to solve the problem of the generalized matrix factorization, however, the over-fitting problem affects the performance of recommendation. These state-of-the-art matrix factorization approaches address some significant problems in the personalized recommendation tasks. Meanwhile, each approach has its own disadvantage that decreases the performance of recommendations.

In practical scenarios, the personalized recommendations have some limitations, such as cold-start. If users can be clustered properly, the group recommendations can effectively overcome the problem of missing data and provide fair and appropriate suggestions for group activities. Therefore, ranking aggregation is applied to fuse the personalized recommendation lists to generate group recommendations. Ranking aggregation is mainly categorized into the score-based and order-based aggregation. In the score-based aggregation, each item in a specific recommendation list is given a particular score based on its rank. Fagin's Algorithm (Fagin), which is a classical score-based algorithm, scans the sorted lists in parallel to generate the final aggregation list. However, the effectiveness of the algorithm decreases as the group size increases. Different from the score-based aggregation, the order-based method adopts the order of each item to generate the ranking aggregation list instead of using the score. MedRank has been admitted that is extremely efficient. The rule of MedRank algorithm picks the group's preference that has the best median rank. However, the output of the algorithm is not satisfactory, because the order is used instead of the score for aggregation. Inspired by PageRank, MC_4 algorithm applies the Markov chain to aggregate rankings.

In this paper, we propose a multi-layer ensemble framework which has a two-step fusion process for the group location recommendation. In the personalized recommendation (i.e., the first step), we employ BMF, PMF, and NCF to generate the recommendations, and fuse the recommendations of these models to obtain the personalized recommendation list for each user. In this step, we calculate the weights of each algorithm by the gradient descent method, and re-predict the missing values in the interaction matrix based on these weights. In the group recommendation (i.e., the second step), we propose an unsupervised learning based ranking algorithm (URank), which can be used in the ranking aggregation for the group recommendation and models fusion. Then, we use four ranking aggregation approaches (i.e., Fagin, MedRank, MC_4, and URank) to merge the personalized recommendation lists in the group, respectively. Then, we further fuse the results of these four approaches to obtain the unique recommendation list for the group using URank. In the TopN recommendation problem, experimental results based on the real-world dataset show that our proposed multi-layer ensemble framework has better performance in group recommendation than traditional algorithms.

The main contribution of this paper is summarized below:

1. We propose an unsupervised learning based ranking algorithm (URank). It can be applied not only to the group recommendation task, but also to fuse models.
2. In this paper, we propose a multi-layer ensemble framework which has a two-step fusion process (the personalized recommendation and the group recommendation). In different recommendation processes, we fuse the results of sub-algorithms to remedy disadvantages of them.
3. The experimental results show the effectiveness of our proposed models which outperform other state-of-the-art methods in topN recommendation.

2   Related Work

2.1   Personalized Recommendation

RSs, which play a crucial role to overcome the information overload, have been widely applied in many domains (e.g., news, e-commerce, and social networks). With the development of RSs, a large number of experiments and theories have shown that the matrix factorization (MF) outperforms other algorithms and has become the baseline method to extract the latent feature of users and items. Koren et al. proposed the PMF method, which adopts a probabilistic linear model with Gaussian observation noise to predict the result [8]. It can handle large datasets and deal with users who have few interaction information. Salakhutdinov presented a fully Bayesian treatment of Probabilistic Matrix Factorization (BPMF) by placing hyperpriors over the hyper-parameters to perform approximate inference [18]. Rendle et al. proposed a Bayesian Personalized Ranking (BPR) criterion [17], which is the maximum posterior estimator from a Bayesian analysis and measures the difference between the rankings of user-purchased items and the rest items. With the development of deep neural networks, the algorithm based on neural network has been used in RSs. He et al. proposes a general framework to give the model non-linearities [7]. In other field, Xu et al. designed incentive mechanisms to minimize social costs [23, 24].

2.2 Group Recommendation

In the recommendation system, we often encounter such problems: recommend items to a group of users. The method used in most studies is ranking aggregation [4]. Although ranking aggregation is recently being used in a broad range, the origin of it was in the eighteenth century. The two methods popularized at that time was Borda's method and Condorcet method. In many methods based on Borda, Argentini et al. proposed the method which is perhaps the most representative one [1]. It works based on the objects' positions in input rankings directly. Condorcet vote is another popular traditional method, which works based on the pairwise comparisons of items. Dwork et al. used the Locally Kemeny optimal ranking as the fused ranking [3], it is implemented by finding a Hamiltonian path. Moreover, some other methods apply stochastic optimization algorithms such as the cross-entropy Monte Carlo algorithm for searching the optimal ranking [13]. In 2010, Qin et al. proposed a probabilistic model (CPS) [15], which was defined with a coset-permutation distance, and models the generation of a permutation as a stagewise process. In 2015, Ding et al. proposed an instant-runoff ranking fusion method (IRRF) using the result of traditional batch mode ranking fusion methods and a top-2 comparison based instant-runoff ranking fusion method (T2-IRRF), which is an improved IRRF by introducing more local comparison information into the selection of the best item in each round.

2.3 Fusing Recommendation Models

Fusing recommendation models have been well studied to improve the prediction performance; a method combines the predictions of different algorithms, or the same algorithm with different parameters to obtain a final prediction. These algorithms have been successfully used, for instance, in the Netflix Prize contest consisting of the majority of the top performing solutions [14]. The most basic strategy is to acquire the final prediction based on the mean over all the prediction results or the majority votes, such as: Burnham and Anderson [2]. Meanwhile, most of the related works in the literature point out that ensemble learning has been used in recommender system as a way of combining the prediction of multiple algorithms to create a stronger rank, such as linear regression, restricted boltzmann machines (RBM), and gradient boosted decision trees (GBDT), Jahrer et al. propose a fusion model to apply the adaptive learning rate [11], with a modest performance increase. However, the methods mentioned above all have their optimization direction, so the performance improvement of the model is one-sided.

3   Multi-layer Ensemble Framework

3.1   Preliminaries

In this paper, we assume that there exist a set of users $U = \{u_1, u_2, ...\}$ and a set of locations $V = \{v_1, v_2, ...\}$, $\#u$ and $\#v$ denotes the number of users and locations respectively. Therefore, the user-location interaction matrix based on the check-in records is defined as below:

$$y_{ij} = \begin{cases} r_{ij}, & u_i \ visited \ v_j \\ 0, & otherwise \end{cases} \tag{1}$$

where r_{ij} represents the times the user u_i has been to the location v_j. In this paper, the major recommendation algorithms are based on the technique of matrix factorization. Therefore, we employ p_i and q_j to represent the predefined latent features of users and locations, respectively and the preferences of users $\hat{Y}$ (i.e., user-location interaction matrix) are predicted using the latent features.

3.2   Model Framework

Figure 1 illustrates the multi-layer ensemble framework for the group recommendation. The framework is divided into two parts: the personalized recommendation and the group recommendation. For the personalized recommendation part, we consider the interaction matrix of users and locations as the input,

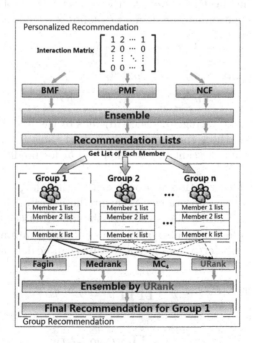

Fig. 1. Model framework

and three model-based recommendation algorithms (i.e., Biased Matrix Factorization, Probabilistic Matrix Factorization, and Neural Collaborative Filtering) are used to generate recommendations for individuals. Then, we propose an ensemble model that fuses the results of the model-based algorithms to obtain a recommendation list for each user. For the second part, we fuse the recommendation list of individuals in the group using four ranking aggregation approaches (i.e., Fagin, MedRank, MC_4, and URank) to obtain the group recommendation lists. Then we employ URank, which is our proposed unsupervised learning based ranking algorithm, to further fuse the results of four ranking aggregations for providing the final recommendation list for each group. Due to the multi-layer ensemble of personalized and group recommendation approaches, the effects of disadvantage of each approach will be decreased and users' preferences can be captured effectively.

3.3   Personalized Recommendation

For the personalized recommendation part, Biased Matrix Factorization (BMF), Probabilistic Matrix Factorization (PMF), and Neural Collaborative Filtering (NCF) are applied to generate the recommendation list for individuals.

BMF is a traditional matrix factorization approach considering the rating bias of each user [8]. In other words, due to the characteristics of individuals, the distribution and preference of rating (or check-in) will be totally different. For a user, 3 (the range of rating is 0–5) may be a general rate, but for another user, 3 may be a high rate. Therefore, the consideration of rating (or check-in) bias will decrease the effect according to the characteristics of individuals. The biased matrix factorization can be defined as follows:

$$b_{ij} = \mu + b_i + b_j, \tag{2}$$

$$\hat{y}_{1ij} = \mu + b_i + b_j + p_i^T q_j, \tag{3}$$

$$min \sum (y_{ij} - \hat{y}_{1ij})^2 + \lambda \|\Theta\|, \tag{4}$$

where b_{ij} represents the rating (or check-in) bias of the user u_i in the location v_j. Then we minimize the error between the actual value y_{ij} and the predicted value $\hat{y}_{1ij}$ using gradient descent to obtain b_i and b_j for predicting the unbiased rating (or check-in).

PMF is a matrix factorization approach considering the perspective of probability [12]. PMF has two assumptions: (1) the prediction error (between the actual value and the predicted value) obeys the Gaussian distribution, and (2) the latent features of users and locations also obey Gaussian distributions. Therefore, the distribution of prediction error and latent features can be defined as follows:

$$p\left(Y|P, Q, \sigma^2\right) = \prod_{i=1}^{\#u} \prod_{i=1}^{\#v} \left[N(y_{ij}|p_i^T q_j, \sigma^2)\right], \tag{5}$$

$$p(P|\sigma_P^2) = \prod_{i=1}^{\#u} N(p_i|0, \sigma_P^2 I), \tag{6}$$

$$p(Q|\sigma_Q^2) = \prod_{j=1}^{\#v} N(q_j|0, \sigma_Q^2 I). \tag{7}$$

Then, the latent features of users and locations will be obtained by minimizing the loss function as below:

$$minE = \frac{1}{2} \sum_{i=1}^{\#u} \sum_{j=1}^{\#v} I_{ij}(y_{ij} - \hat{y}_{2ij}) + \frac{\lambda_P}{2} \|P\|^2 + \frac{\lambda_Q}{2} \|Q\|^2, \tag{8}$$

$$\hat{y}_{2ij} = p_i^T q_j, \tag{9}$$

where I_{ij} denotes whether the user u_i has been to the location v_j, and λ_P and λ_Q are regularization parameters.

From the perspective of neural networks, NCF introduces non-linearity to learn the interaction information, rather than a handcraft that has been done by the traditional matrix factorization model [7]. The prediction function of NCF model is defined as follows:

$$\hat{y}_{3ij} = a_{out} \left(h^T \left(p_i \odot q_j \right) \right) \tag{10}$$

where a_{out} and h denotes the activation function and edge weights of the output layers, respectively. Intuitively, if we allow h to be learned from data without the uniform constraint, it will result in a variant of MF that allows varying importance of latent dimensions. If we use a non-linear function for a_{out}, it will generalize MF to a nonlinear setting which might be more expressive than the linear MF model. In this paper, we implement a generalized version of MF under NCF that considers the sigmoid function $\sigma(x) = 1/(e^{-x})$ as a_{out} and learns h from data with the log of loss.

BMF, PMF, and NCF have good performance in general scenarios, however, these approaches also have their disadvantages. For example, BMF doesn't work well if the dataset has the long-tailed problem; PMF works based on the strong assumptions; NCF, as a neural network based approach, will overfit the dataset. Therefore, we propose an approach to fuse the results of three basic models $(\hat{Y}_1, \hat{Y}_2, \hat{Y}_3)$ to decrease the effects of these disadvantages. In this paper, we fuse the recommendations lists based on RMSE between the ground truth and the predicted value. The loss function (i.e., RMSE) is defined as below:

$$RMSE = \sqrt{\frac{1}{\#u\#v}} \cdot \sqrt{\sum_{i=1}^{\#u} \sum_{j=1}^{\#v} \left(y_{ij} - \sum_{k=1}^{3} d_k \hat{y}_{kij} \right)^2} \tag{11}$$

where $d_k (k = 1, 2, 3)$ denotes the weight of each basic algorithm. Equation 11 is a continuously derivable function, so the parameter d_i can be deduced using the gradient descent method, and the obtained weights $d_k (k = 1, 2, 3)$ determine the impact of each basic model on the final recommendation list. The gradient direction of d_k is defined as below:

$$\nabla d_k = \frac{\partial RMSE}{\partial d_k} = \frac{1}{2}\sqrt{\frac{1}{\#u\#v}\left[\sum_{i=1}^{\#u}\sum_{j=1}^{\#v}\left(y_{ij}-\sum_{k=1}^{3}d_k\hat{y}_{kij}\right)^2\right]^{-\frac{1}{2}}}$$

$$\cdot\sum_{i=1}^{\#u}\sum_{j=1}^{\#v}2\left(y_{ij}-\sum_{k=1}^{3}d_k\hat{y}_{kij}\right)(-\hat{y}_{kij}),\tag{12}$$

and the update formula of d_k is:

$$d_k = d_k - \gamma\nabla d_k\tag{13}$$

where γ denotes the learning rate of the method. When Eq. 11 coverages, the final recommendation list for individuals will be obtained based on the ensemble model considering the learned weights $d_k(k = 1, 2, 3)$.

3.4   Group Recommendation

The group recommendation part aims to aggregate recommendation lists of group members into a unique recommendation list for the group. In this part, we employ four ranking aggregation approaches (i.e., MedRank, Fagin, MC_4, and URank) to fuse the recommendation lists. These approaches will be briefly introduced in the following sections.

MedRank is an order-based rank aggregation algorithm [6]. The main idea of MedRank is: the item, which appeared in more than half of the number of ranking lists, will be remained in the final aggregated ranking. For example, given three rankings $R_1 : [A, B, C, D]$, $R_2 : [B, A, D, C]$, $R_3 : [B, C, A, D]$. To count the elements in the first position of each ranking list, we find that the number of B is 2, which is more than half of the number of rankings ($2 > 1.5$). Therefore, B is considered as the first position in the aggregated ranking list. Then, B is removed from the three ranking lists and the elements in the first position will be counted and selected. In this way, we will obtain the aggregated ranking $[B, A, C, D]$.

Different from MedRank, Fagin is a score-based rank aggregation algorithm and is well-suited for the group recommendations [5]. For example, there are three rankings: $R_1 : [A : 1.0, B : 0.8, C : 0.5, D : 0.3, E : 0.1]$, $R_2 : [B : 0.8, C : 0.7, A : 0.3, D : 0.2, E : 0.1]$, $R_3 : [D : 0.8, C : 0.6, A : 0.2, E : 0.1, B : 0]$. If a top-2 recommendation is demanded, then we take the top-2 elements from these rankings into a new list until all values of k elements in the new list are taken in the original three lists, and $C : [0.5, 0.7, 0.6], B : [0.8, 0.8, 0], A : [1.0, 0.3, 0.2], D : [0.3, 0.2, 0.8]$ are the generated. Therefore, the aggregated list is $[C : 0.6, B : 0.53, A : 0.5, D : 0.43]$.

Because the ranking aggregation is similar to traditional page rank, Dwork et al. creatively applies the Markov chain (MC) to aggregate rankings, and proposes MC series algorithm [4]. These algorithms calculate their transition probability matrix by different rules, then get a new sort according to the smooth distribution of the transition matrix. The rule followed by the MC_4 algorithm is as follows: choose the candidate a, then pick another candidate b uniformly from the union of all candidates ranked by vectors. If most voters ranked b higher than a, go to b. Otherwise, stay in a.

URank, which is our proposed unsupervised ranking aggregation method, considers normalized Discounted Cumulative Gain (nDCG) as the ranking metric, specifically as follows: r_{t_j} represents the actual rating of the item t_j (ranked in position j, i,e., $\sigma(t_j) = j$). DCG and nDCG at Top-n are defined as:

$$DCG = r_{t_1} + \sum_{j=2}^{n} \frac{2^{r_{t_j}}}{\log_2(j)} \tag{14}$$

$$nDCG = \frac{DCG}{IDCG} \tag{15}$$

where $IDCG$ is the maximum possible gain value that is obtained with the optimal re-order of the n items in $t_1, ..., t_n$.

If nDCG is considered as the metric to fuse the multiple ranking lists, there exist two significant problem: **a.** nDCG is often applied to evaluate the ordering performance with labels. However, the current scenario is an unsupervised problem, we cannot utilize nDCG according to the traditional point of view. **b.** Because the ranking list is ordered by a series of discrete values, it is non-trivial to learn weights using the gradient descent. To overcome the problem **a**, we propose a strategy instead of the traditional way: (1) initialize the weights of different models; (2) get the integrated order by the weighted results and calculate nDCG between integrated order and the order of each basic model; (3) calculate the accumulation of nDCG. The formula is defined as below:

$$E(w) = \sum_{k=1}^{3} \frac{1}{IDCG_k} \sum_{j=1}^{\#v} \frac{2^{s_{kj}} - 1}{\log_2(1 + \pi(j))}, \tag{16}$$

where $IDCG_k$ denotes the normalization parameter and k denotes the index of the models. $\pi(j)$ is a symbolic function and denotes the ranking position of the location v_j:

$$\pi(j) = 1 + \sum_{m=1, m \neq j}^{\#v} I[f_w(j) \succ f_w(m)], \tag{17}$$

where $\succ$ denotes the order relationship of the rank, and $f_w(j)$ is a linear function that represents the sort score of the location v_i. I is a 0–1 recognition function:

$$I = \begin{cases} 1, & f_w(j) \succ f_w(m) \\ 0, & other \end{cases} \tag{18}$$

Therefore, Eq. 16 can be rewritten as:

$$E(w) = \sum_{k=1}^{3} \frac{1}{IDCG_k} \sum_{j=1}^{\#v} \frac{2^{s_{kj}} - 1}{\log_2\left(2 + \sum_{m=1, m \neq j}^{\#v} I[f_w(j) \succ f_w(m)]\right)} \tag{19}$$

Note that, Eq. 19 is not a continuous function, so we cannot calculate the optimal w by partial derivatives, this is the problem **b** mentioned above. To overcome the problem **b**, a natural way for the approximation is to approximate the indicator function I using a logistic function [16]. Therefore, $\pi(j)$ can be replaced using $\hat{\pi}(j)$:

$$\hat{\pi}(j) = 1 + \sum_{m=1;m\neq j}^{\#v} \frac{exp(-\alpha(f_w(j) - f_w(m)))}{1 + exp(-\alpha(f_w(j) - f_w(m)))} \tag{20}$$

Table 1 shows the comparison between $\hat{\pi}(j)$ and $\pi(j)$. When $\alpha > 0$ is a scaling constant(e.g., 50, 100, 150), $\hat{\pi}(j)$ is a continuous and differentiable function. Thus, Eq. 19 can be rewritten as:

Table 1. Examples of position approximation

object	s_i	$\pi(i)$	$\hat{\pi}(x)(\alpha = 100)$
object$_1$	4.20074	2	2.00118
object$_2$	3.12378	4	4.00000
object$_3$	4.40918	1	1.00000
object$_4$	1.55258	5	5.00000
object$_5$	4.13330	3	2.99882

$$E(w) = \sum_{k=1}^{3} \frac{1}{IDCG_k} \sum_{j=1}^{\#v} \frac{2^{s_{kj}} - 1}{\log_2\left(2 + \sum_{m=1;m\neq j}^{\#v} \frac{exp(-\alpha(f_w(j)-f_w(m)))}{1+exp(-\alpha(f_w(j)-f_w(m)))}\right)} \tag{21}$$

It can be proved that Eq. 21 is a convex function. To solve Eq. 21, we use the gradient ascent based on the chain derivation rule:

$$\nabla w_k = \frac{\partial E(w)}{\partial w} = \sum_{k=1}^{3} \frac{1}{IDCG_k} \sum_{j=1}^{\#v} \frac{\frac{2^{s_{kj}}-1}{\log_2(1+\hat{\pi}(j))}}{\partial \hat{\pi}(j)} \frac{\hat{\pi}(j)}{\partial w \beta_k} \tag{22}$$

The updated w_k is defined as below:

$$w_k = w_k + \eta \nabla w_k \tag{23}$$

Therefore, in this paper, we use the aforementioned approaches (i.e., MedRank, Fagin, MC_4, and URank) to fuse the recommendation lists of group members to generate a recommendation list for the group respectively. Then URank is applied to fuse the results from each ranking aggregation approach to obtain the unique ranks for the group.

4 Experimental Evaluation

4.1 Experimental Setup

Check-In Dataset. We evaluated the performance of our method on LBSN datasets. Foursquare is a famous LBSN that allows people to post check-in records in Twitter when they visit a specific venue based on the location information. We collected user's check-in data by calling Twitter and Foursquare's API interface. The dataset contains 419,509 tweets published by 49,823 users among 18,899 locations from August 2012 to July 2013 in Manhattan [19].

Baseline. To evaluate the effectiveness of our proposed model, in the personalized recommendation part, we consider the traditional recommendation algorithms (i.e., BMF, PMF, and NCF) as the baseline method, respectively. In the group recommendation part, we use three ranking aggregation algorithms (i.e., Fagin, MedRank, and MC_4) and the proposed algorithm (i.e., URank) to generate the final group recommendation results based on the personalized recommendations using BMF, PMF, and NCF, respectively. Therefore, the combination of a personalized recommendation algorithm and a ranking aggregation algorithm is considered as a baseline model. Based on different combinations of personalized recommendation algorithms and ranking aggregations, we conducted 20 models on the real-world dataset.

Evaluation Metrics. To assess our proposed framework, we use well-known criteria for TopN recommendation, such as Recall, Precision, and F1-score. The criteria are defined as below:

$$Recall = \frac{\sum_{u \in U} |R(u) \cap T(u)|}{\sum_{u \in U} |T(u)|}$$

$$Precision = \frac{\sum_{u \in U} |R(u) \cap T(u)|}{\sum_{u \in U} |R(u)|}$$

$$F1 - score = \frac{2 \times precision \times recall}{precision + recall}$$

where U is the set of all users, $R(u)$ is the recommendation list based on the preference of user u in the training dataset, and $T(u)$ is the set of user u's behaviors in the test dataset.

4.2 Results and Discussion

In this section, we aim to evaluate the effectiveness of the multi-layer fusion framework for the group location recommendation and answer the following questions:

- Which is the best combination for the recommendation framework?
- What is the performance of proposed framework on different types of groups?

Effectiveness. In this section, we compare the 20 combinations of personalized and group recommendation approaches, and the experimental results are shown in the Table 2. We analyze the experimental results from two aspects: personalized recommendations and group recommendations. For personalized recommendation, we compare the three traditional recommendation algorithms (i.e., BMF, PMF, NCF) with the fusion algorithm we proposed. As observed in Table 2, our proposed fusion model outperforms other traditional personalized recommendation approaches in RMSE. It means that the model we proposed has more strong ability to fit data than the other three models. In addition, the performance of our framework at TopN (N=20, 40, 60) location recommendations for the group also outperforms other models. We also compare the ensemble model with each ranking aggregation (i.e., Fagin, MedRank, and MC_4). From the Table 2, we can see that the proposed framework has better performance in the group recommendation than each ranking aggregation algorithm. The experimental results show that the multi-layer ensemble framework effectively decrease the effect of disadvantages in each approach.

Table 2. Performance comparison

Method	Person	$Fuse_2$	N=20			N=40			N=60		
	RMSE	nDCG	Pre	Rec	F1	Pre	Rec	F1	Pre	Rec	F1
BMF-Fagin	0.897	null	0.086	0.088	0.087	0.079	0.135	0.097	0.072	0.182	0.103
BMF-MedRank	0.897	null	0.087	0.091	0.089	0.072	0.131	0.093	0.071	0.180	0.102
BMF-MC_4	0.897	null	0.082	0.096	0.091	0.078	0.133	0.098	0.073	0.181	0.104
BMF-$URank$	0.897	null	0.089	0.087	0.088	0.082	0.140	0.103	0.074	0.181	0.105
BMF-$fuse_2$	0.897	0.891	0.090	0.087	0.088	0.080	0.137	0.101	0.076	0.179	0.107
PMF-Fagin	0.879	null	0.102	0.081	0.090	0.091	0.130	0.107	0.082	0.181	0.113
PMF-MedRank	0.879	null	0.098	0.083	0.090	0.093	0.128	0.108	0.083	0.187	0.115
PMF-MC_4	0.879	null	0.091	0.079	0.085	0.083	0.121	0.098	0.077	0.166	0.105
PMF-$URank$	0.879	null	0.099	0.086	0.092	0.096	0.131	0.111	0.085	0.179	0.115
PMF-$fuse_2$	0.879	0.887	0.103	0.085	0.093	0.101	0.131	0.114	0.084	0.183	0.115
NCF-Fagin	0.872	null	0.108	0.075	0.089	0.092	0.123	0.105	0.083	0.166	0.111
NCF-MedRank	0.872	null	0.103	0.073	0.085	0.093	0.127	0.107	0.085	0.172	0.114
NCF-MC_4	0.872	null	0.096	0.071	0.082	0.082	0.109	0.094	0.075	0.154	0.101
NCF-$URank$	0.872	null	0.107	0.073	0.087	0.090	0.121	0.103	0.082	0.174	0.111
NCF-$fuse_2$	0.872	0.902	0.111	0.074	0.089	0.104	0.129	0.115	0.086	0.170	0.114
$fuse_1$-Fagin	0.853	null	0.120	0.082	0.097	0.104	0.142	0.120	0.093	0.192	0.126
$fuse_1$-MedRank	0.853	null	0.118	0.080	0.096	0.105	0.143	0.121	0.096	0.195	0.128
$fuse_1$-MC_4	0.853	null	0.110	0.075	0.089	0.088	0.120	0.102	0.083	0.169	0.111
$fuse_1$-$URank$	0.853	null	0.122	0.081	0.097	0.103	0.142	0.119	0.089	0.187	0.121
$fuse_1$-$fuse_2$	0.853	0.893	**0.125**	**0.085**	**0.101**	**0.103**	**0.147**	**0.121**	**0.103**	**0.208**	**0.138**

Different Combination. To evaluate the combination of personalized recommendation approaches and ranking aggregations for the group recommendation, we divide the experiments into two categories: re-merge with unused approach and re-merge with used approach. In the first category, we select three of the ranking aggregation algorithms (i.e., Fagin, MedRank, MC_4, URank) as sub-algorithms, and the remaining one is used as the method of fusing models to

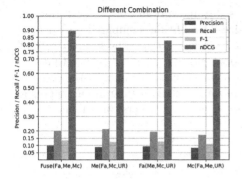

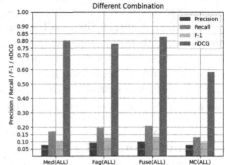

Fig. 2. Triple combination.   **Fig. 3.** Quadruple combination.

generate the final result. As observed in Fig. 2, we can find that the performance of the group recommendation is worse than other combinations significantly when the MC_4 algorithm is applied to re-merge the results of models.

In addition, if URank is used to re-merge the recommendation lists aggregated by Fagin, MedRank, and MC_4, the recommendations have better performance. In the second category, we use all four ranking aggregation algorithms as sub-algorithms, and apply an algorithm from them as the method to re-merge the recommendation lists of models (See Fig. 3). As observed in Fig. 3, if we re-merge the recommendation lists of four ranking aggregations using URank, the performance is better than that of other combinations. Note that, compared the experimental results in Figs. 2 and 3, the overall performance will be decreased if we re-merge the recommendation lists with used approaches.

Group Method. To evaluate the performance of proposed framework on different types of groups, we use two ways to group users and conduct the experiments respectively. (I) Random grouping: divide all users into groups randomly; (II) Similar grouping: group similar users based on the interaction matrix.

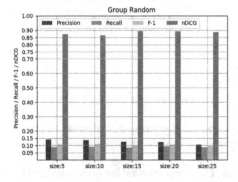

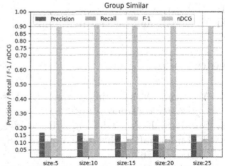

Fig. 4. Group random   **Fig. 5.** Group similarity

As observed in Figs. 4 and 5, our proposed framework has better performance in the similar group at the small group size. In addition, compared with Precision, Recall, F1-score of similar groups and random groups, the performance of similar groups is better than that of random groups. This is because that the personalized recommendation lists in the similar group have many intersections. Therefore, when performing TopN group recommendation, the ranking aggregation algorithm tends to select the same object meet members' preference.

5 Conclusion and Future

In this paper, we propose the general multi-layer ensemble framework for the group recommendation. We evaluate the framework on a real-world dataset and the experimental results show the effectiveness of our approach. In addition, we further evaluate the performance of the proposed framework in two aspects: (1) different combinations of algorithms and (2) the effect of the grouping method. For the first question, in the group recommendation part, the experimental results show that if URank is used to further fuse the results of four ranking aggregation methods, the two-step fusion will improve the performance of recommendations. For the second question, the performance of ensemble framework also works better in the similar groups than the random groups.

In the future, we want to continue our research and explore the relationship between group recommendation and personal recommendation; we also hope to validate our findings through experiments with other datasets. Since the results of personalized recommendations have a significant impact on the results of group recommendations, we will try different personalized recommendation algorithms and ranking aggregation algorithms to further improve our performance. Meanwhile, according to life experience, the decision of the group is affected by each member is different in some cases, so weighting the results of the members in the group is also necessary for research. We also hope introduce methods in other fields(event mining) to perfect our framework [9,10,20].

Acknowledgments. The work was supported in part by the National Natural Science Foundation of China (Grant No. 61472193, No. 61872193, No. 61802205 and No. 61872186), the Natural Science Research Project of Jiangsu Province under Grant 18KJB520037, and the research funds of NJUPT under Grant NY218116.

References

1. Argentini, A.: Ranking aggregation based on belief function theory. Ph.D. thesis, University of Trento (2012)
2. Burnham, K.P., Anderson, D.R.: Model selection and multimodel inference: a practical information-theoretic approach. Springer, New York (2003). https://doi.org/10.1007/b97636
3. Dwork, C., Kumar, R., Naor, M., Sivakumar, D.: Rank aggregation revisited (2001)

4. Dwork, C., Kumar, R., Naor, M., Sivakumar, D.: Rank aggregation methods for the web. In: Proceedings of the 10th International Conference on World Wide Web, pp. 613–622. ACM (2001)

5. Fagin, R., Kumar, R., Sivakumar, D.: Efficient similarity search and classification via rank aggregation. In: Proceedings of the 2003 ACM SIGMOD International Conference on Management of Data, pp. 301–312. ACM (2003)

6. Fagin, R., Lotem, A., Naor, M.: Optimal aggregation algorithms for middleware. J. Comput. Syst. Sci. **66**(4), 614–656 (2003)

7. He, X., Liao, L., Zhang, H., Nie, L., Hu, X., Chua, T.S.: Neural collaborative filtering. In: Proceedings of the 26th International Conference on World Wide Web, pp. 173–182. International World Wide Web Conferences Steering Committee (2017)

8. Koren, Y., Bell, R., Volinsky, C.: Matrix factorization techniques for recommender systems. Computer **42**(8), 30–37 (2009)

9. Liu, Z., Li, T., Wang, J.: A survey on event mining for ict network infrastructure management. ZTE Commun. **14**(2), 47–55 (2016)

10. Liu, Z., Li, T., Zhou, Q.: Application driven big data mining. In: ZTE Technology, pp. 49–52 (2016)

11. McKenzie, T.G., et al.: Novel models and ensemble techniques to discriminate favorite items from unrated ones for personalized music recommendation. In: Proceedings of the 2011 International Conference on KDD Cup 2011, vol. 18, pp. 101–135. JMLR.org (2011)

12. Mnih, A., Salakhutdinov, R.R.: Probabilistic matrix factorization. In: Advances in Neural Information Processing Systems, pp. 1257–1264 (2008)

13. Pihur, V., Datta, S., Datta, S.: Rankaggreg, an R package for weighted rank aggregation. BMC Bioinform. **10**(1), 62 (2009)

14. Piotte, M., Chabbert, M.: The pragmatic theory solution to the Netflix grand prize. Netflix Prize Documentation (2009)

15. Qin, T., Geng, X., Liu, T.Y.: A new probabilistic model for rank aggregation. In: Advances in Neural Information Processing Systems, pp. 1948–1956 (2010)

16. Qin, T., Liu, T.Y., Li, H.: A general approximation framework for direct optimization of information retrieval measures. Inf. Retrieval **13**(4), 375–397 (2010)

17. Rendle, S., Freudenthaler, C., Gantner, Z., Schmidt-Thieme, L.: BPR: Bayesian personalized ranking from implicit feedback. In: Proceedings of the Twenty-fifth Conference on Uncertainty in Artificial Intelligence, pp. 452–461. AUAI Press (2009)

18. Salakhutdinov, R., Mnih, A.: Bayesian probabilistic matrix factorization using markov chain Monte Carlo. In: Proceedings of the 25th International Conference on Machine Learning, pp. 880–887. ACM (2008)

19. Xia, B., Li, T., Li, Q., Zhang, H.: Noise-tolerance matrix completion for location recommendation. Data Mining Knowl. Discov. **32**(1), 1–24 (2018)

20. Xia, B., Li, T., Zhou, Q.F., Li, Q., Zhang, H.: An effective classification-based framework for predicting cloud capacity demand in cloud services. IEEE Trans. Serv. Comput. (2018)

21. Xia, B., Li, Y., Li, Q., Li, T.: Attention-based recurrent neural network for location recommendation. In: 2017 12th International Conference on Intelligent Systems and Knowledge Engineering (ISKE), pp. 1–6. IEEE (2017)

22. Xia, B., Ni, Z., Li, T., Li, Q., Zhou, Q.: Vrer: context-based venue recommendation using embedded space ranking svm in location-based social network. Expert Syst. Appl. **83**, 18–29 (2017)

23. Xu, J., Li, H., Li, Y., Yang, D., Li, T.: Incentivizing the biased requesters: truthful task assignment mechanisms in crowdsourcing. In: 14th Annual IEEE International Conference on Sensing, Communication, and Networking (SECON), pp. 1–9. IEEE (2017)

24. Xu, J., Rao, Z., Xu, L., Yang, D., Li, T.: Mobile crowd sensing via online communities: incentive mechanisms for multiple cooperative tasks. In: IEEE 14th International Conference on Mobile Ad Hoc and Sensor Systems (MASS), pp. 171–179. IEEE (2017)

Does Your Accurate Process Predictive Monitoring Model Give Reliable Predictions?

Marco Comuzzi[1]([⊠]), Alfonso E. Marquez-Chamorro[2], and Manuel Resinas[2]

[1] Ulsan National Institute of Science and Technology, Ulsan, Republic of Korea
mcomuzzi@unist.ac.kr
[2] Universidad de Sevilla, Sevilla, Spain
{amarquez6,resinas}@us.es

Abstract. The evaluation of business process predictive monitoring models usually focuses on accuracy of predictions. While accuracy aggregates performance across a set of process cases, in many practical scenarios decision makers are interested in the reliability of an individual prediction, that is, an indication of how likely is a given prediction to be eventually correct. This paper proposes a first definition of business process prediction reliability and shows, through the experimental evaluation, that metrics that include features defining the variability of a process case often give a better prediction reliability indication than metrics that include the probability estimation computed by the machine learning model used to make predictions alone.

Keywords: Business process · Predictive monitoring · Reliability

1 Introduction

The ubiquitous support of information systems and the emerging availability of Internet-of-Things (IoT) technology enable the collection of large amount of data during process execution for process analysis, design and enhancement. Data collected during process execution, usually in the form of *event logs*, are the input of process predictive monitoring, which aims at predicting specific aspects of interests regarding cases currently executing, e.g., which activities are going to be executed next, when a case will terminate, or the value of specific process performance indicators.

Research on business process predictive monitoring recently has focused intensely on the adaptation of existing machine learning techniques to solve new predictive monitoring problems with higher accuracy [4]. From a practical standpoint, however, when making decisions within the scope of an individual process

This work has partially received fundings from the European Union's Horizon 2020 research and innovation programme under the Marie Sklodowska-Curie grant agreement No 645751 (RISE_BPM), grants TIN2015-70560-R (MINECO/FEDER, UE) and P12-TIC-1867 (Andalusian R&D&I program), and NRF Korea Project Number 2017076589.

X. Liu et al. (Eds.): ICSOC 2018 Workshops, LNCS 11434, pp. 367–373, 2019.
https://doi.org/10.1007/978-3-030-17642-6_30

case, decision makers such as process owners or users are not only concerned with the accuracy of a prediction model, but also, and often most importantly, with having a means to gauge the *reliability* of an individual prediction. For instance, when deciding whether to renegotiate an agreement with a client to extend the service completion due date or assign more resources to this client to meet the agreed due date, a service provider may rely on a due date predictive model of their internal processes which is 80% accurate on average. However, because these decisions are taken on a per-case basis, a service provider clearly requires a measure to understand to what extent they can rely on, or *trust*, a specific prediction made for each particular client.

In this paper, we focus on predicting business process *outcomes* at the level of individual process instances. Process outcomes, for instance, can be the satisfaction of violation of specific SLA properties, such as process instance execution time being below a certain threshold negotiated by a service provider with customers, or the fulfillment or violation of specific constraints, e.g., regarding order of activities, during process execution.

Accuracy of a predictive model of process outcomes is calculated by aggregating prediction results across a test set of previous cases. As such, it does not give an indication of how much decision makers can *trust* an individual prediction based on new data or, in other words, about the likelihood that a new individual prediction is eventually correct. Machine learning models often define specific metrics for the reliability of predictions, such as the classification probability in decision trees. Other model-independent reliability measures can be defined, which can be based on sensitivity of a prediction or on *transduction*. With sensitivity analysis, a prediction is considered more reliable if the variability of predictions made for similar input data is limited. With transduction reliability is assessed by comparing predictions using models trained with and without a particular new example [1]. However, these measures are based only on the training data and do not take into account features the system generating data used to learn a model.

We argue that, besides the data collected and the chosen learning model, the reliability of an individual prediction may depend on a variety of other factors characterising the *variability* of the *system* generating the data, that is, in our case, the business process. A prediction, for instance, is likely to be more reliable when a process case is almost complete or, more generally, when the choices available to complete a case are limited. Variability may also be associated with the time elapsed to execute a specific case, e.g., the longer a case has been executing, the closer it may be to its termination and, therefore, the fewer the possible choices available for its completion. Part of this knowledge about variability of process cases while making predictions may be already embedded by a predictive model in the learning phase, particularly in the case of complex non linear models, such as neural networks. It is practically impossible, however, to disentangle this knowledge from the internal functioning of a training algorithm in order to obtain a measure of reliability for an individual prediction [1].

The aim of this paper is to put forward the issue of the reliability of individual prediction in business process outcomes predictive monitoring. In order to do so, in Sect. 2 we provide an initial definition of a measure of process prediction reliability that combines prediction probabilities available for the chosen machine learning model with features of a process case, such as its expected completion time or expected number of activities to be executed before case completion. Then, in Sect. 3, we evaluate the proposed metric using a real world business process event log and state of the art predictive monitoring techniques. The results show that metrics that include terms capturing process variability provide a better indication of the reliability of an individual prediction, than any intrinsic reliability metric available for the chosen learning model alone. Conclusions are briefly drawn in Sect. 4. We argue that the issue identified by this paper will spark a new area of research in the field of process predictive monitoring focusing on the definition of prediction reliability metrics well suited for the scenario of business process execution.

2 Model

As a general case of business process outcomes prediction, we consider the scenario of predicting the value of process performance indicators (PPIs) for process cases that are currently executing. Let $\mathcal{P}$, $\mathcal{I}$, and $\mathcal{T}$ represent the universe of processes, PPIs, and the time domain, respectively. Hence, a process $P \in \mathcal{P}$ is associated with M process performance indicators $PPI_m \in \mathcal{I}$. Each indicator $PPI_m \in \mathcal{I}$ assumes value within a domain D_m, which can be numerical or categorical and possibly infinite.

Let $\mathcal{C}_P$ be the universe of cases of a process P. We define the *value* v and *predicted value* $\hat{v}$ of a PPI for a case as follows:

- $v : \mathcal{C}_P \times \mathcal{I} \times \mathcal{T} \to D_m \cup \{\bot\}$, written $v_j^t(PPI_m)$, mapping a case $j \in \mathcal{C}_P$ and an indicator PPI_m onto a value in the domain D_m at a given time instant t. Note that the undefined value $\bot$ is used when the value of PPI_m cannot be calculated at time t. For instance, the execution time of a case can only be calculated after a case has completed;
- $\hat{v} : \mathcal{C}_P \times \mathcal{I} \times \mathcal{T} \to D_m \cup \{\bot\}$, written $\hat{v}_j^t(PPI_m)$, mapping a case $j \in \mathcal{C}_P$ and an indicator PPI_m onto a value a *predicted* value in the domain D_m at a given time instant t. A predicted value is obtained using some prediction model trained with data generated during process execution. The undefined value $\bot$ is used when a predicted value cannot be calculated based on available data.

Note that, for a given case j and indicator PPI_m, at any given time t, only one of $v_j^t(PPI_m)$ and $\hat{v}_j^t(PPI_m)$ is available. If for a case j the value $v_j^t(PPI_m)$ cannot be calculated and it is not yet possible to generate a predicted value $\hat{v}_j^t(PPI_m)$, then both value and predicted value are undefined.

The objective of this paper is to define a metric to measure the reliability of predicted PPI values $\hat{v}_j^t(PPI_m)$. In order to be a reliability metric, the proposed metric (i) must assume only values between 0 and 1, with 1 signifying that there is a 100% likelihood that the predicted value of a PPI is eventually correct, (ii) it must assume the value 1, i.e., 100% reliability, when the actual value of a PPI $v_j^t(PPI_m)$ becomes available, and (iii) it should increase as the likelihood of a predicted value to be correct increases. Properties (i) and (ii) are guaranteed by design in the proposed definition given below. Property (iii) drives the design of the proposed reliability metric and its achievement is demonstrated by the experimental evaluation.

The problem of defining a reliability metric for SLA prediction is the problem of defining a function $r : \mathcal{C}_P \times \mathcal{I} \times \mathcal{T} \to [0, 1]$, written as $r_j^t(PPI_m)$, to indicate the reliability of an individual predicted value of an indicator PPI_m for the j-th case of process P at time t.

In this paper, we propose the following definition of $r_j^t(PPI_m)$:

$$r_j^t(PPI_m) = w_1 \cdot adv_j^t(PPI_m) + w_2 \cdot time_j^t(PPI_m) + w_3 \cdot pred_j^t(PPI_m).$$

That is, with $\sum_w = 1$, the proposed reliability metric is comprised of the weighted sum of the following 3 terms: (i) $adv_j^t(PPI_m)$ considering the advancement in execution of the j-th instance at time t; (ii) $time_j^t(PPI_m)$ considering the time elapsed since the j-th instance has started; and (iii) $pred_j^t(PPI_m)$ refers to a value of probability estimate of the prediction as defined by the prediction technique in use, e.g., prediction probability in decision tree-based classification. Note that this value may not be available when the prediction technique in use does not provide any kind of prediction reliability.

Regarding the first term $adv_j^t(PPI_m)$, let l_j be the number of activities executed thus far in the j-th case. We assume that an estimate of the remaining number of activities to be executed in the j-th case $\hat{l}_j$ is available. This estimate can be obtained is several ways, e.g., naively by considering the average number of remaining activities in all previous cases that matched the execution thus far of the current case, using a predictive monitoring technique [4], by matching the current execution trace with the most similar previous case, or by considering the average number of activities on all possible paths to complete a process execution, possibly weighted by the probabilities of taking specific paths, if available.

Then, $adv_t^j = f(l_j, \hat{l}_j)$, where f is a monotonic increasing *activation function* with values between 0 and 1 and $\lim_{\hat{l}_j \to 0} f(l_j, \hat{l}_j) = 1$, e.g., $f(l_j, \hat{l}_j) = \frac{l_j}{l_j + \hat{j}_l}$.

The second term $time_j^t(PPI_m)$ also relies on an estimate of the remaining time to complete the execution of a process case. This can also be calculated in several ways, e.g., using predictive monitoring or by averaging the remaining execution time of previous similar cases available in an event log.

Let t_j^{ex} be the time elapsed from the start of case j and $\hat{t}_j$ the estimate of the remaining time required to complete case j, then $time_t^j = f(t_j, \hat{t}_j)$, where f is a monotonic increasing *activation function* with values between 0 and 1, e.g., $f(t_j, \hat{t}_j) = \frac{t_j}{t_j + \hat{t}_l}$.

3   Evaluation

This section presents a simple experimentation to assess the validity of the proposed reliability metric definition. In particular, our aim is to show that higher prediction reliability is achieved when the weights of the *adv* and *time* terms in the reliability metric definition are not zero, to show that including information about case variability improves reliability of predictions.

A real-life event log from the IT Department of a regional public administration was used in the experimentation. This dataset represents an incident management log. In this scenario, a service level agreement (SLA) is established considering certain key performance indicators (KPIs). This SLA determines the penalties derived from the under-fulfillment of a threshold for each of the KPIs. Thus, predictive monitoring is necessary to anticipate the possibility of violating the SLA and, therefore, incurring into penalties. We consider one specific KPI (named K20), which indicates abnormal idle time during the resolution of an incident. An incident management case, in fact, may remain idle due to a variety of reasons, such as unavailability of personnel or scheduling errors. Idle time is clearly unproductive and should be avoided. The KPI K20 states that idle time should not exceed a certain threshold in any given case.

This event log consists of 174.989 process cases, each of them with 15 attributes. Beside standard attributes of events in event logs, such as activity name, timestamp, and resource, each event contains additional information about, for instance, the type of incident, its priority or the service center to which it was assigned[1]).

For our experimentation, we have divided this dataset in three parts: 60% as training set, 20% for validation and 20% as test set. We have trained the model with the training set and estimated the different parameters related to the reliability using the validation set. As encoding we have considered a sliding window of 2 events, since empirical evaluation has showed this is a good window size. Each feature vector is composed by the different attributes of the 2 events of the event window, while the last position corresponds to the class, which indicates a value of the KPI to be predicted. Each attribute can be nominal or a real number. More detailed information of the encoding is provided in [3].

The reliability of predicted values of indicator K20 is $rel_j^t(K20) = w_1 \cdot adv_j^t(K20) + w_2 \cdot time_j^t(K20) + w_3 \cdot pred_j^t(K20)$. To compute the term $adv_j^t(K20)$, we use the activation function described above using the average number of activities in all previous cases as an estimate of the remaining number of activities. A similar method has been adopted for $time_j^t(K20)$, i.e., we have considered the elapsed time from the beginning of the case for each activity. Then, the average total execution time of the cases is calculated, and this is used as an estimate of the remaining execution time for each validation case. A decision tree algorithm has been used as model. Then, the third term $pred(K20)$ is the predicted class probability for each case of the validation set.

---

[1] Description of the attributes can be found at https://goo.gl/ye68ei.

We have computed the values of reliability $rel_j^t(K20)$ for each case j in the event log and each possible combination of the weights w_1, w_2, w_3, sampling weights values at intervals of 0.1. To assess the validity of the reliability metric, we have divided the predictions according to their calculated reliability value in intervals of size 0.1. For instance, the reliability interval $(0.3, 0.4]$ contains all predictions for which $0.3 < rel_j^t(K20) \leq 0.4$. Then, we have defined a sensitivity-based estimation of prediction errors for all the intervals as follows. For each interval, we first obtain the number of correct (P) and incorrect (NP) predictions to determine the sensitivity $(Sens)$ of the prediction, with $Sens = P/(P+NP)$. Then, we determine the deviation of this value $Sens$ from the center of the interval. If the proposed reliability metric is valid, for instance, this means to assume that the interval $(0.3, 0.4]$ should contain approximately 35% of correct predictions, 45% for the next interval and so on. Finally, we have obtained the average error (avg_err) for all deviations and all possible values of weights. An extract of the results showing the combinations of weights values with lowest average error is shown in Table 1.

Table 1. Experimental results.

w_{adv}	w_{time}	w_{pred}	avg_err	P_corr	p_value
0.0	0.0	1.0	0.2164	0.6162	0.1926
0.1	0.0	0.9	0.2167	0.1126	0.8318
0.2	0.0	0.8	0.1784	0.6332	0.1771
0.3	0.0	0.7	**0.1532**	0.8342	0.0389
0.2	0.1	0.7	**0.1544**	0.9269	0.0078
0.3	0.2	0.5	0.1633	0.4258	0.3997
0.5	0.0	0.5	0.1533	0.6184	0.1906

We can appreciate how the average error decreases when considering the terms adv and $time$ in the reliability definition. For instance, for $w_{pred} = 1$ the average error is 0.2164, while the best results are achieved for $w_{adv} = 0.3$ and $w_{pred} = 0.7$ $(avg\_err = 0.1532)$ or $w_{adv} = 0.2$, $w_{time} = 0.1$ and $w_{pred} = 0.7$ $(avg\_err = 0.1544)$. An improvement of 5% points is achieved in these cases by including the variability terms adv and $time$.

The fifth column of Table 1 shows the Pearson correlation coefficient between the sensitivity measure and the center of intervals. These two values should be correlated for an accurate estimation of the reliability [2]. The significance level $(\alpha \leqslant 0.05)$ of the correlation is reported in the sixth column. As we can see, the positive correlation has statistical significance for the best combinations of weights cited above.

To summarise, even if very limited, our experimentation shows that a reliability metric that includes terms capturing process variability is more likely to estimate correctly the probability that a prediction will be eventually correct than considering only a reliability parameter typical of the chosen machine learning model, i.e, predicted class probability of decision trees in our case.

4   Conclusions

The objective of this paper has been to signal the need to define metrics of reliability of individual process predictive monitoring predictions and outline some preliminary ideas on how to face it. The empirical results, in particular, highlight that prediction reliability is higher when terms capturing case variability are included.

Future work should look at refining the initial definition provided in this paper and at assessing the impact of a high quality reliability metric on real world process predictive monitoring use cases.

References

1. Bosnić, Z., Kononenko, I.: An overview of advances in reliability estimation of individual predictions in machine learning. Intell. Data Anal. **13**(2), 385–401 (2009)
2. Bosnić, Z., Kononenko, I.: Estimation of individual prediction reliability using the local sensitivity analysis. Appl. Intell. **29**(3), 187–203 (2008)
3. Márquez-Chamorro, A., Resinas, M., Ruiz-Cortés, A., Toro, M.: Run-time prediction of business process indicators using evolutionary decision rules. Expert Syst. Appl. **87**(Supplement C), 1–14 (2017)
4. Marquez-Chamorro, A.E., Resinas, M., Ruiz-Cortes, A.: Predictive monitoring of business processes: a survey. IEEE Trans. Serv. Comput. **11**, 962–977 (2017)

PhD Symposium

PhD Symposium Preface

Service-oriented computing (SOC) has rapidly evolved with technologies such as Web services, Cloud services, and the Internet of Things. While this has provided industry and practitioners with the opportunities to develop a new generation of products and services, it has also raised many fundamental research challenges and open questions. The International Conference on Service Oriented Computing (ICSOC) is the premier international forum for academics, industry researchers, developers, and practitioners to report and share groundbreaking work in service-oriented computing.

The International PhD Symposium on Service Computing was held in conjunction with the 16th International Conference on Service Oriented Computing (ICSOC 2018) on November 12–15, 2018 in Hangzhou, China. This is the 14th edition of the series held in conjunction with the ICSOC conferences in Malaga (2017), Banff (2016), Goa (2015), Paris (2014), Berlin (2013), Shanghai (2012), Paphos (2011), San Francisco (2010), Stockholm (2009), Sydney (2008), Vienna (2007), Chicago (2006), and Amsterdam (2005).

The ICSOC PhD Symposium is an international forum for PhD students working in all the areas related to the service computing. Its goals are:

- To bring together PhD students and established researchers in the field of service oriented computing,
- To enable PhD students to interact with other PhD students and to stimulate the exchange of ideas among participants,
- To provide PhD students an opportunity to present, share and discuss their research in a constructive and critical atmosphere, and
- To provide PhD students with critical and constructive feedback from experts on their already completed and, more importantly, planned research work.

To achieve these goals, the symposium operates in a workshop format, giving PhD students an opportunity to showcase their research and providing them with ample feedback from both senior researchers and fellow PhD students. Each submission was reviewed by three members of the program committee and after a thorough review process, 5 papers out of 9 were accepted to constitute the program of the PhD symposium. The authors of 4 papers made oral presentations in the symposium. Several distinguished professors attended the symposium and discussed topics related to the successful completion of PhDs and subsequent employment opportunities with the authors.

We acknowledge the support of the contributors to this PhD symposium and express our gratitude to the program committee members for the time and effort they have put into reviewing papers.

January 2018

Djamal Benslimane
Aditya Ghose
Zhongjie Wang

Organization

Program Committee

Christoph Treude	University of Adelaide, Australia
Xianzhi Wang	Singapore Management Univeristy, Singapore
Stephan Reiff-Marganiec	University of Leicester, UK
Shizhan Chen	Tianjin University, China
Zakaria Maamar	Zayed University, Dubai, United Arab Emirates
Richard Chbeir	University of Pau & Pays Adour, Bayonne, France
Franck Morva	Paul Sabatier University, Toulouse, France
Mourad Oussalah	University of Oulu, Finland

Service Negotiation in a Dynamic IoT Environment

Fan Li[(✉)]

Trinity College Dublin, College Green, Dublin, Ireland
fali@scss.tcd.ie

Abstract. In the Internet of Things (IoT), billions of physical devices connecting over the Internet provide a near real-time state of the world in a service-oriented way. The demand-driven service-provision paradigm may need a negotiation process to tailor the service properties before creating the service level agreement (SLA). Existing negotiation techniques are focused on the cloud computing, however, SLA negotiation is rarely discussed in the IoT environment. Thus, we extended a commonly-used web service negotiation framework based on characteristics of the IoT, integrated with a game theory-based negotiation strategy, and evaluated its performance under a simulation platform. Based on the result, we identified the research questions and outlined future directions.

Keywords: Decentralized SLA negotiation ·
SLA negotiation framework · IoT

1 Introduction

The Internet of Things (IoT) envisages a large number of physical objects, connecting over the Internet at an unparalleled rate to provide. The functionalities provided by these devices can be offered as a service [11,20,22]. Similar to cloud computing, IoT services can be consumed in a demand-driven way [10], as IoT applications have a flexible service quality demand and pricing mechanism [7].

To resolve the possible preference conflicts between service providers and consumers, a negotiation process is conducted for both parties expressing their own demands and preferences [6]. When a consensus is reached, the on-demand cost-effective service is tailored in the form of a Service Level Agreements (SLA), which is a contract between a service consumer and a provider in the context of a particular service provisioning [12,19]. Currently, SLA management has not been fully considered in the IoT middlewares [15,16]. Compared with the cloud computing, challenges of SLA negotiation in the IoT emerge from the following aspects:

Supervised by: Siobhán Clarke, Siobhan.Clarke@scss.tcd.ie

Supported by Science Foundation Ireland (SFI) under the project SURF - grant 13/IA/1885.

- **Large-scale distributed environment**: In the IoT, a huge number of IoT devices geographically distributed in different locations are likely to engage in service provisioning [17]. The emergence of fog computing implies that multiple services offering the same or similar functionalities may exist and be deployed in different cloud platforms or fog nodes(e.g. gateways, base stations, routers, etc.).
- **Deep heterogeneity**: The smart objects in the IoT have various device features, resource capabilities and service properties [26], which makes negotiation information heterogeneous.
- **Highly dynamic**: In the IoT, considering the unstable wireless network [9] and the mobility of autonomous service providers (ASP)[1] [17], the availability of negotiating participants is unpredictable.

Many existing negotiation approaches assume a centralized mediator platform that does not consider the strong spatial dimension of the IoT services, and the communication problems between mobile negotiation entities are neglected [5,8,13,13,14,21,24,24,25,29,30]. This is not a practical assumption with the scale of localized sensors deployed in different IoT platforms and potential number of ASPs available in the IoT. In order to identify the necessary research questions of relating to the design of an automatic SLA negotiation framework for the IoT middleware, we conducted a preliminary experiment by extending the negotiation model of a standard web service SLA specification. We proposed a purely decentralized negotiation framework where distributed gateways behave as brokers that automatically negotiate with multiple service providers on behalf of consumers.

The remainder of this paper is organized as follows. Section 2 describes our preliminary design based on a current SLA negotiation specification. Section 3 outlines the experimental setup, and evaluates our extended negotiation framework. Section 4 identifies research questions and provides a short discussion about future research directions.

2   Preliminary Design

Although research on SLA negotiation in the IoT environment is very limited, it is possible to extend or modify current existing negotiation frameworks so that they can be applied to SLA negotiation of IoT services. Considering the Web Services Agreement (WS-Agreement) [3] is a commonly used SLA standard, WS-Agreement Negotiation language forms the basis of our negotiation model in the preliminary experiment. Details of the WS-Agreement negotiation protocol and data format can be found in [3,23].

The extension involves three parts: extending the WS-Agreement with a set of IoT domain-specific vocabularies, extending the WS-Agreement Negotiation

---

[1] We define ASP as providers who can autonomously decide when to offer the services (e.g. a traffic condition information service provided by a smart vehicle traveling data recorder on a taxi can be online or offline at any time according to the configuration set by the driver.).

protocol with four additional phases according to the IoT characteristics, and integrating it with the mixed negotiation strategy which demonstrates a good balance of success rate and utility when negotiating with incomplete information [28]. Due to the page limit, this paper focuses on the extension of the WS-Agreement negotiation protocol. The extended SLA specification and description of negotiation strategy are omitted.

The negotiation model in WS-Agreement Negotiation includes three phases: negotiation initialization, multi-round bilateral negotiation, and SLA creation. This model assumes that consumers have the prior knowledge about the available services and the negotiation information of corresponding providers, which is infeasible in the IoT. Also, this protocol does not consider the communication problems arising from an unstable network, mobility, and availability of negotiating parties.

To address these problems, we assume a set of gateways are deployed in the environment, which works in a distributed manner to provide functionalities including service discovery, SLA negotiation, and QoS monitoring. These gateways can be mobile (e.g., a smartphone) or static (e.g., a Raspberry Pi internally installed on a bus station) connected by WiFi. Since static gateways are likely to provide a more stable and reliable negotiating services than mobile gateways, we assume the static gateways are responsible for negotiating services and forwarding messages while the mobile gateways are only responsible for forwarding messages. The Service providers who are offering SLA-supported services outline their contact information and functionalities of services in a partially completed SLA (i.e., SLA templates), and list all the negotiable service properties with default values in the template. The templates (SLAT) are formalized by the extended SLA specification, and published to gateways so that their offering can be understood and discovered when requests are received. Based on these assumptions, we extended the WS-Agreement Negotiation protocol with four additional phases:

- **Connection overlay maintenance**: This overlay controls how to forward messages during the negotiation process. When a new gateway joined the network, it identifies surrounding gateways by broadcasting *ping* messages, which contains the gateway information such as location, identifier, and mobility. If the gateway receives a reply from another gateway, it stores the gateway information in a local route table as a neighbour. If the new joined gateway is mobile, it resends the message when moving more than a pre-defined distance. Each gateway periodically checks the connections with its neighbouring mobile gateways to remove the invalid links.
- **Distributed SLAT registration and updating**: Services providers publish services by sending template registration messages to surrounding gateways. Mobile gateways forward the messages to their neighbouring gateways until they are received by a static gateway, which stores them in its local repository. To avoid storing invalid SLATs, static gateways periodically check the availability of SLATs and remove the ones that are out of date.

- **Negotiation customization and request forwarding**: Negotiation requests are forwarded in the connection overlay until a candidate service that can potentially satisfy the request is found, or the message reaches the maximum hop limit. The match-making process is implemented by content-based filtering. If more than one SLAT is matched in a gateway's repository, the gateway ranks the services according to the utility function specified in [28]. The gateway submits a negotiation customization message to the provider who offers the highest utility as a handshake to test provider's availability and customize the negotiation context such as specifying negotiation protocol and SLA schema. After a successful handshake, the multi-round negotiation process modeled by WS-Agreement Negotiation is performed.
- **Consumer locating**: Considering the mobility of consumers and the requests forwarding mechanism, a consumer may not be able to receive the response from the negotiating gateway. A *locating* message, consisting of the consumer identifier and negotiation response, is designed to locate a consumer if the negotiating gateway fails to receive an acknowledgment (ACK) from the consumer within a specified time. The gateway which receives the *locating* message sends a *ping* message to the consumer, if an *ACK* is received, the gateway parses the negotiation response from the message and sends it back to the user. Otherwise, the message is forwarded to neighbouring gateways until the maximum hop limit is reached.

3   Experiment Setup and Evaluation

The negotiation protocol we propose includes six phases: connection overlay maintenance, SLAT distribution, negotiation customization and request forwarding, bilateral negotiation, SLA creation, and consumer locating. To assess its feasibility, we integrated the mixed concession-tradeoff QoS negotiation strategy [27] into the bilateral negotiation phase to evaluate offers and generate counteroffers and implemented it using *Simonstrator* [18] (a peer to peer simulator for distributed mobile applications) to simulate a smart city scenario. In the simulation, static gateways were evenly distributed in the environment while mobile gateways, service providers, and consumers were randomly distributed. These mobile entities followed a social movement pattern provided by *Simonstrator* with five pre-defined speeds: walk speed (0.42 m/s to 0.5 m/s), bike speed (3.6 m/s to 4.2 m/s), car speed (16.7 m/s to 27.8 m/s), mixed speed (0.01 m/s to 27.8 m/s), and static speed (0.01 m/s) as a comparison. We created 136 IoT service prototypes based on examples proposed in IoT literature [2,4,26], and completed the dataset with 300 web service prototypes generated from an existing OWLS-SLR dataset [1]. Based on the prototypes, we generated 436 SLATs by randomly assigning QoS values according to the predefined variation range. We regarded the requested QoS values as reserved values of a consumer, and computed the preferred values by increasing the reserved values by a random number varying between 5 to 20. The negotiation timeout was set to 10 min. The maximum negotiation round was set to 20. The static gateways validated

SLATs every 30 min against the expiry date specified in the SLATs, and checked the connections with neighbouring mobile gateways every 10 min. All the entities were connected by WiFi, and TCP send-and-reply mode was applied to interactions. The *Churn* model provided by *Simonstrator* was used to simulate the availability of hosts.

The evaluation metrics were success rate, response time and percentage of received responses. We assumed performance was affected by five factors: the number of gateways, the number of service providers, the number of SLATs, and the ratio of static providers. Figure 1 shows the simulation results under the influence of different factors. For each test case, only one variable changed while others were unchanged. The result shows that negotiation failures were mainly caused by three reasons: timeout, absence of matched services, and no agreement is reached before the deadline. Except for the last failure which was affected by the negotiation strategy and the preferences of negotiating parties, the other failures were closely related to the IoT characteristics. In this experiment we only considered QoS negotiation, however, the functional properties such as location and sampling parameters may be negotiable in the IoT. The negotiation strategy should not only measure QoS attributes but also assesses the functional service properties.

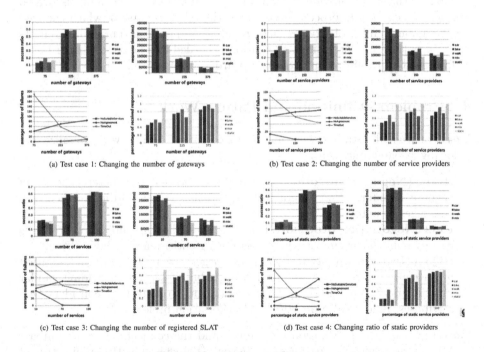

(a) Test case 1: Changing the number of gateways

(b) Test case 2: Changing the number of service providers

(c) Test case 3: Changing the number of registered SLAT

(d) Test case 4: Changing ratio of static providers

Fig. 1. Negotiation performance

The failure "timeout" indicated that network connection was lost during the negotiation process, or a negotiating party could not be connected at that moment. This was proved by the simulation result of test case 1 and 4. Figure 1(a) shows that the average response time drops from approximately 6.5 min to 0.5 min as the number of gateways increased from 75 to 375. Although the speed of movement had a negative impact on the success rate, in that the entities moving at the higher speed caused more failures, deploying more gateways diminished this impact since it generated a more dense connection overlay which increased the chance for mobile entities to be connected with the system. However, if the speed of movement dropped to nearly zero, the improvement in success rate was not as obvious as the others because the chance of being connected with other gateways in different locations was eliminated. This conclusion is illustrated in Fig. 1(d) in that the highest success rate is achieved when half of the providers are static. However, mobility also made communication more challenging and caused more timeout failures. The negative impact on the success rate was obvious when all the providers were mobile. The absence of matched services indicates that even the services that match the requested criteria exist in the environment, random distribution of SLATs creates obstacles to retrieve all the available negotiation information when messages have hop limits. This was proved by the simulation result of test case 2 and 3. Figure 1(b) shows that increasing the number of providers from 50 to 250 reduced such failures. It can be inferred that more providers means more candidate services can be discovered during the negotiation process. This was verified by test case 3, which changed the maximum number of services each provider could publish. This failure reflects that a negotiation information aggregation is needed in a large-scale distributed environment to facilitate the request forwarding mechanism.

4   Problem Definition and Future Work

Based on the literature review and the experiment result, we generalize the following research questions:

- **RQ1 (Negotiation object):** How to address the heterogeneity of negotiation information generated by different parties according to their own languages or ontologies?
- **RQ2 (Negotiation protocol):** How to address the communication problems in a dynamic environment where negotiating entities are mobile?
- **RQ3 (Negotiation strategy):** How to get the most optimized solution in an environment that has multiple distributed services providing similar functionality? What is the proper negotiation strategy that considers QoS attributes, functional properties, and negotiation preference?

Since the template distribution mechanism and the connection overlay impact greatly on the negotiation performance in the IoT. Inspired by the architecture of the cellular network, designing a hierarchical architecture that might effectively address the mobility and scalability issues is our future work.

References

1. OWLS-SLR - Datasets. http://lpis.csd.auth.gr/systems/OWLS-SLR/datasets. html
2. Al-Fuqaha, A., Guizani, M., Mohammadi, M., Aledhari, M., Ayyash, M.: Internet of Things: a survey on enabling technologies, protocols, and applications. IEEE Commun. Surv. Tutor. **17**(4), 2347–2376 (2015)
3. Andrieux, A., et al.: Web services agreement specification (ws-agreement). In: Open Grid Forum, vol. 128, p. 216 (2007)
4. Cabrera, C., Palade, A., Clarke, S.: An evaluation of service discovery protocols in the Internet of Things. In: Proceedings of the Symposium on Applied Computing, pp. 469–476. ACM (2017)
5. Di Nitto, E., Di Penta, M., Gambi, A., Ripa, G., Villani, M.L.: Negotiation of service level agreements: an architecture and a search-based approach. In: Krämer, B.J., Lin, K.-J., Narasimhan, P. (eds.) ICSOC 2007. LNCS, vol. 4749, pp. 295–306. Springer, Heidelberg (2007). https://doi.org/10.1007/978-3-540-74974-5_24
6. Elfatatry, A., Layzell, P.: Negotiating in service-oriented environments. Commun. ACM **47**(8), 103–108 (2004)
7. Grubitzsch, P., Braun, I., Fichtl, H., Springer, T., Hara, T., Schill, A.: ML-SLA: multi-level service level agreements for highly flexible IoT services. In: 2017 IEEE International Congress on Internet of Things (ICIOT), pp. 113–120. IEEE (2017)
8. Hasselmeyer, P., Mersch, H., Koller, B., Quyen, H., Schubert, L., Wieder, P.: Implementing an SLA negotiation framework. In: Proceedings of the eChallenges Conference (e-2007), vol. 4, pp. 154–161 (2007)
9. Kalasapur, S., Kumar, M., Shirazi, B.A.: Dynamic service composition in pervasive computing. IEEE Trans. Parallel Distrib. Syst. **18**(7), 907–918 (2007)
10. Kantarci, B., Mouftah, H.T.: Sensing services in cloud-centric Internet of Things: a survey, taxonomy and challenges. In: 2015 IEEE International Conference on Communication Workshop (ICCW), pp. 1865–1870. IEEE (2015)
11. Karnouskos, S., Savio, D., Spiess, P., Guinard, D., Trifa, V., Baecker, O.: Real-world service interaction with enterprise systems in dynamic manufacturing environments. In: Benyoucef, L., Grabot, B. (eds.) Artificial Intelligence Techniques for Networked Manufacturing Enterprises Management. Springer Series in Advanced Manufacturing, pp. 423–457. Springer, London (2010). https://doi.org/10.1007/978-1-84996-119-6_14
12. Ludwig, H., Keller, A., Dan, A., King, R.P., Franck, R.: Web service level agreement (WSLA) language specification. In: IBM Corporation, pp. 815–824 (2003)
13. Mišura, K., Žagar, M.: Negotiation in Internet of Things. Automatika časopis za automatiku, mjerenje, elektroniku, računarstvo i komunikacije **57**(2), 304–318 (2017)
14. Mu, N., Rui, L., Guo, S., Qiu, X.: Generalized Lagrange based resource negotiation mechanism in MANETs. In: 2014 10th International Conference on Network and Service Management (CNSM), pp. 218–223. IEEE (2014)
15. Mubeen, S., Asadollah, S.A., Papadopoulos, A.V., Ashjaei, M., Pei-Breivold, H., Behnam, M.: Management of service level agreements for cloud services in IoT: a systematic mapping study. IEEE Access **6**, 30184–30207 (2018)
16. Palade, A., Cabrera, C., Li, F., White, G., Razzaque, M., Clarke, S.: Middleware for Internet of Things: an evaluation in a small-scale IoT environment. J. Reliable Intell. Environ. **4**(1), 3–23 (2018)

17. Razzaque, M.A., Milojevic-Jevric, M., Palade, A., Clarke, S.: Middleware for Internet of Things: a survey. IEEE Internet Things J. **3**(1), 70–95 (2016)
18. Richerzhagen, B., Stingl, D., Rückert, J., Steinmetz, R.: Simonstrator: simulation and prototyping platform for distributed mobile applications. In: Proceedings of 8th International Conference on Simulation Tools and Techniques (SIMUTOOLS), pp. 99–108. ACM, August 2015
19. Saravanan, K., Rajaram, M.: An exploratory study of cloud service level agreements-state of the art review. KSII Trans. Internet Inf. Syst. **9**(3), 843–871 (2015)
20. Shelby, Z., Hartke, K., Bormann, C.: The Constrained Application Protocol (CoAP) (2014)
21. Swiatek, P., Rucinski, A.: IoT as a service system for ehealth. In: 2013 IEEE 15th International Conference on e-Health Networking, Applications & Services (Healthcom), pp. 81–84. IEEE (2013)
22. Thoma, M., Meyer, S., Sperner, K., Meissner, S., Braun, T.: On IoT-services: survey, classification and enterprise integration. In: 2012 IEEE International Conference on Green Computing and Communications (GreenCom), pp. 257–260. IEEE (2012)
23. Waeldrich, O., et al.: WS-Agreement Negotiation Version 1.0, p. 64 (2011)
24. Yan, J., Zhang, J., Lin, J., Chhetri, M.B., Goh, S.K., Kowalczyk, R.: Towards autonomous service level agreement negotiation for adaptive service composition. In: 10th International Conference on Computer Supported Cooperative Work in Design, 2006. CSCWD 2006, pp. 1–6. IEEE (2006)
25. Yaqub, E., et al.: A generic platform for conducting SLA negotiations. In: Wieder, P., Butler, J., Theilmann, W., Yahyapour, R. (eds.) Service Level Agreements for Cloud Computing, pp. 187–206. Springer, New York (2011). https://doi.org/10.1007/978-1-4614-1614-2_12
26. Zanella, A., Bui, N., Castellani, A., Vangelista, L., Zorzi, M.: Internet of Things for smart cities. IEEE Internet Things J. **1**(1), 22–32 (2014)
27. Zheng, X.: QoS Representation, Negotiation and Assurance in Cloud Services. Queen's University, Canada (2014)
28. Zheng, X., Martin, P., Brohman, K., Da Xu, L.: Cloud service negotiation in Internet of Things environment: a mixed approach. IEEE Trans. Ind. Inf. **10**(2), 1506–1515 (2014)
29. Zulkernine, F., Martin, P., Craddock, C., Wilson, K.: A policy-based middleware for web services SLA negotiation. In: IEEE International Conference on Web Services 2009. ICWS 2009, pp. 1043–1050. IEEE (2009)
30. Zulkernine, F.H., Martin, P.: An adaptive and intelligent SLA negotiation system for web services. IEEE Trans. Serv. Comput. **4**(1), 31–43 (2011)

Towards Energy and Time Efficient Resource Allocation in IoT-Fog-Cloud Environment

Huaiying Sun[1,2(✉)], Huiqun Yu[1(✉)], and Guisheng Fan[1(✉)]

[1] Department of Computer Science and Engineering,
East China University of Science and Technology, Shanghai, China
ecustshy@foxmail.com, {yhq,gsfan}@ecust.edu.cn
[2] Shanghai Key Laboratory of Computer Software Evaluating and Testing,
Shanghai, China

Abstract. As the number of IoT devices with limited resources and the corresponding observed data grow exponentially, the method of offloading all tasks to a remote data center becomes expensive, even inefficient. How to optimize the energy consumption of application requests from IoT devices satisfying the deadline constraint is also a challenge. Fog computing is closer to users, featuring the lower service delay but less resource than the remote cloud. Fog does not mean to replace cloud. They are complementary to each other, and cooperation between them is worth studying. The main points of this paper are: (1) Proposing a general IoT-fog-cloud computing architecture that fully exploits the advantages of fog and cloud. (2) Formulating the energy efficient computation offloading and dynamic resource scheduling (eoDS) problem, then proposing an eoDS algorithm to solve the problem, reducing the energy consumption and completion time of application requests (3) Compared with cloud nodes, the mobility of fog nodes is higher. For this, we propose the fog functional areas reconstruction method to adaptively deal with the changing environment, improving the resource utilization of fog.

Keywords: IoT-fog-cloud · Resource scheduling ·
Energy consumption · Completion time

1 Introduction

In the early stage of the highly discrete Internet of things (IoT) technology, it is impossible to rely solely on the use of the centralized cloud structure, which drives the computing towards decentralized resources [1]. For example,

Advisor—Huiqun Yu, Guisheng Fan.
This work is partially supported by the NSF of China under grants No. 61772200, 61602175 and 61702334, Shanghai Pujiang Talent Program under grants No. 17PJ1401900. Shanghai Municipal Natural Science Foundation under Grants No. 17ZR1406900 and 17ZR1429700. Educational Research Fund of ECUST under Grant No. ZH1726108. The Collaborative Innovation Foundation of Shanghai Institute of Technology under Grants No. XTCX2016-20.

© Springer Nature Switzerland AG 2019
X. Liu et al. (Eds.): ICSOC 2018 Workshops, LNCS 11434, pp. 387–393, 2019.
https://doi.org/10.1007/978-3-030-17642-6_32

unmanned vehicles can not only depend on the cloud for real-time video processing or short time data storage, because this will cause unacceptable decision making delay [2]. Fog computing is realized by scattered computing and storing resources on the edge of the network, which is close to the data source [3]. It is the extension of cloud, promoting the operation of limited computation, storage and network resources. However, with the exponential growth of IoT devices, the corresponding observed data grow exponentially, the method of offloading all tasks to a remote data center becomes expensive, even inefficient [4]. Thus, how to optimize the energy consumption of IoT devices satisfying the time constraint required by application requests is still a challenge at present [5]. Fog does not mean to replace cloud, but to compensate for the lack of cloud, the interaction and cooperation between fog and cloud is worth studying [1].

Therefore, the main points of my PhD project including: (1) Proposing a general framework for IoT-fog-cloud computing, which can make full advantages of fog (close to the user, lower delay) and cloud (far away from the user, more resource). (2) Formulating the energy efficient computation offloading and dynamic resource scheduling (eoDS) problem as the energy efficiency cost minimization problem. To solve this problem, we propose the eoDS algorithm, which includes 2 parts: computing offloading selection and transmission power allocation. It aims at reducing the energy consumption and completion time of application requests considering the computing ability of devices and the dynamic network environments. (3) Compared with cloud nodes, the mobility of fog nodes is higher. For this problem, we propose the functional areas reconstruction method, which consists of two parts: the selection of central nodes and the division of functional areas, to adaptively deal with the changing environment, improving the resource utilization of fog.

2   Related Work

Chang et al. [1] proposed an approach to solve the energy consumption optimization problem meeting the delay requirement in fog computing system. Yousefpour et al. [2] proposed a method which firstly judges whether the estimated waiting time of a task on the local IoT device will exceed the preset threshold α, if not, a fog node is selected randomly. If α is actually exceeded, the task will be forwarded to an adjacent fog node before reaching the largest forwarding number N_{fwd}. If N_{fwd} is exceeded, then it will be forwarded to the cloud. Yang et al. [6] proposed an optimal offloading algorithm based on the Markov Decision Process, which is used for mobile devices in a discontinuous connection of the micro-cloud /fog system, considering the user's local load and the availability of the micro-cloud. Jalali et al. [7] proposed a generic fog data flow processing and analysis model and architecture, which is very common in the cloud but has not been fully studied in the fog structure by analyzing the common attributes of various typical applications like the video mining and event monitoring etc. Verma et al. [8] proposed a method for fog-cloud environment, which combines data backup and load balancing based on the availability of data to assign user requests to fog or cloud. This method is effective but expensive. Wang et al. [9] proposed a CachinMobile method to continuously improve the energy efficiency of fog nodes by caching the request data on the terminal user's mobile phone to the fog node. Wen et al. [10] proposed a fog business framework based on parallel genetic algorithm. The framework focuses on the optimization of the selection and placement of fog resources and IoT devices. Pham et al. [11] proposed a task scheduling algorithm in fog-cloud environment for balancing performance and overhead. However, it does not consider the problem of energy consumption.

3 The Architecture and Resource Allocation Method

Figure 1 shows a general architecture of IoT-fog-cloud, containing 3 layers. The first is the Local layer, which contains the IoT devices. Then is the Fog layer, which includes fog severs and controllers that can be located at different geographic locations. They could be some not fully utilized severs (although these servers maybe specially allocated for local use, they can be used to provide services to IoT nodes when they are idle or not fully utilized, as long as the fog and the IoT providers can reach an agreement) or some computable gateway servers, routers, switches, etc [11]. The third layer is the Cloud layer comprising the cloud severs. Although cloud is usually located far away from the IoT devices, its sufficient storage and processing capabilities provide an essential support for the implementation of IoT applications [1,8]. The computable nodes in each layer of the architecture are partitioned into multiple domains, and each domain only realizes a certain IoT application, such as the green circle area of corresponding layers in Fig. 1. The nodes of an area in Local layer (for example, the devices in a factory)can communicate with the fog/cloud nodes which implement the same IoT application, for example, offloading the tasks to fog/cloud nodes.

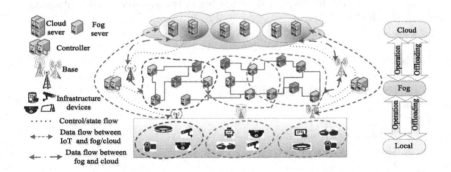

Fig. 1. System architecture (Color figure online)

Fog and cloud can be connected to base stations through LTE link or wired backhaul [10]. IoT nodes then can send application requests, QoS requirements and application parameters (such as data size) to the controller through LTE connection. Cloud, fog, and IoT nodes will send their processing rates, task arrival rates etc to the controller. Controller then will allocate resources to the application request. If the controller assigns the task of a request to the fog/cloud node, the IoT node will send the task data through LTE link to the base station. The base station will transfer the data to cloud or fog through the wired backhaul, and cloud/fog will return the processing results to the corresponding IoT node in the same way. Controller virtualized IoT, fog and cloud nodes into a resource pool. It provides flexibility in allocating resources for application requests, assigning tasks to the local IoT device, the fog node, or the cloud node appropriately. There is an access control mechanism in it ensuring the controller can always assign application requests to the authenticated computable nodes. The energy efficiency cost (EEC) for a task m of request n on the fog described similar to [12] is shown by Eq. (1). $CT^f_{n,m}, E^{f,trs}_{n,m}$ denote the time and energy

---

Algorithm 1. The energy efficient computation offloading and dynamic resource scheduling (eoDS) method

---

Input: M: a sequence of tasks of an application request from device n; The size and the clock circles required to finish each task; A set of predecessor tasks with task $m \in M$, $\{pare(m)\}$; The available computable resource;

Output: : optimal resource allocation policy;

1 **for** $m = 1$ *to* M **do**
2   /* whether to fog */
3   decide whether to offload task m to the fog layer by Computation offloading selection algorithm;
4   **if** $(a_{n,m} == 1)$ **then**
5   offload m to fog, flag=1;
6   /* Transmission power allocation */
7   assign the optimal Transmission power to the current task for data transmission by Newton iteration based transmission power allocation method;
8   **end**
9   /* not to fog, further considering the cloud*/
10   **else**
11   decide whether to offload task m to the cloud layer by Computation offloading selection algorithm;
12   **end**
13   **if** $(a_{n,m} == 1 \ and \ flag == 0)$ **then**
14   offload m to cloud, flag=1;
15   the same as the step 7;
16   **else**
17   task m will be assigned to the current IoT device;
18   **end**
19   **end**
20   flag=0;
21 **end**

required by task execution on the fog. $K_{n,m}^f$ denotes the energy efficiency cost of task m on fog (the case of local/cloud is similar). $\lambda_{n,m}$ is the weight. For the request n with a task set M, the corresponding energy and time cost to be minimized is described by (2). $\alpha_{n,m}, \beta_{n,m}, \delta_{n,m} \in \{0,1\}$, the sum of them is 1, indicating that a task only can be assigned to one executing place.

$$K_{n,m}^f = \lambda_{n,m}^t CT_{n,m}^f + \lambda_{n,m}^e E_{n,m}^{f,trs}(S), (\lambda_{n,m}^t + \lambda_{n,m}^e = 1) \tag{1}$$

$$min \sum_{m=1}^{M} K_{n,m} = \sum_{m=1}^{M} \alpha_{n,m} K_{n,m}^l + \beta_{n,m} K_{n,m}^f + \delta_{n,m} K_{n,m}^c \tag{2}$$

Then, we propose the eoDS algorithm, which includes 2 parts: computing offloading selection and transmission power allocation, aiming at reducing the energy consumption and completion time of application request from IoT device. Fog layer can handle most of the tasks to reduce the overall service delay and the energy consumption of application request [2,3]. Thus, the eoDS used in controller first considers whether a task is more suitable to be executed on the local or on the fog according to the overheads on them (line 2–8 in Algorithm 1). If the case that on fog is better, it then adopts the transmission power allocation method to assign the optimal transmission power to the current task, else it will further consider whether the cloud can be a better choice (line 9–19 in Algorithm 1). If the case that on the cloud is better, the task will be assigned to the cloud and it also will adopt the transmission power allocation method to assign the optimal transmission power to the current task. Otherwise it will stay at the local node.

4   Preliminary Experiment and Results

To evaluate the effectiveness of the proposed method, we extend iFogSim [3] to simulate the IoT-fog-cloud environment in Sect. 3. IFogSim is an extension to the CloudSim framework [5], which has been widely used to simulate different computing modes. We take the methods in [1,2] (we refer them to Md1 and Md2 respectively) as the baselines. The experiment parameters are also set according to [1,2]. Md1 in [1] is an approach which is to solve the energy consumption optimization problem meeting the delay requirement, while it does not consider the dependencies between tasks in the application request and the cooperation between fog and cloud. The common thing in Md2 and eoDS is that they both take fog and cloud into consideration, while the core of Md2 is different from eoDS as mentioned in Sect. 2.

We compare the average energy efficiency cost (EEC) values under 3 different modes, namely, the no fog (NF) mode, all fog (AF) mode, fog and cloud (FaC) mode. Figure 2(a) shows the EEC value of the application request in 3 different modes. From the graph, we can see that the EEC values of NF mode and AF mode are very similar, while the EEC value in FaC mode is obviously better than the other two modes. This is because the FaC mode contains both advantages

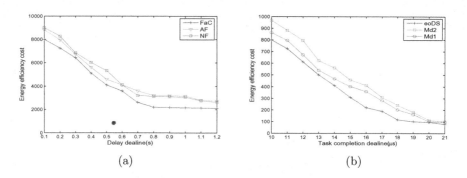

Fig. 2. Simulation results

of AF and NF compared with AF and NF, and the use of resources is more flexible. Figure 2(b) shows the EEC values corresponding to tasks with different completion time constraints in the application request. The corresponding EEC with relatively loose deadline is smaller, eoDS is more obviously better than Md1 and Md2. This is because, under the same condition, for eoDS, tasks of application request will be assigned to the local /fog/cloud node according to the general overhead on the local /fog/cloud node, meanwhile the assignment of the task data transmission power is optimized for the fog/cloud execution. The graph shows that when the deadline constraints are magnified to a certain extent, the energy efficiency costs of them tend to be similar. This maybe because the looser constraints of the task requirements and the relative adequacy of the required resources, the more similar tasks assigning results of them.

5   Conclusion and Future Work

Our initial evaluation has shown the potential of the proposed method. We will further evaluate the performance of the method. While in the previous, we assume that the specific domains in fog/cloud for executing different types of applications are known in prior. Compared with cloud nodes, the mobility of fog nodes is higher. For this problem, we further propose a fog functional area reorganization method, which consists of two parts: the selection of central nodes and the division of functional areas, to improve the resource utilization of fog. In essence, the division process can group the logical similar fog devices regarding various resource related standards. Thus, we plan to adopt the spectral clustering to do the division. Each selected central node will perform a spectral clustering considering the available computation and memory resources of the available fog devices. For example, if a central node aims to create a computing optimization function domain, the corresponding spectral clustering [13] will identify all similar fog devices with sufficient processing resources. Each central node (for example, the red nodes in fog layer shown in Fig. 1) creates its own functional domain, so a fog node (like the yellow nodes in Fig. 1) can belong to multiple functional domains only if it has sufficient resource.

References

1. Chang, Z., Zhou, Z., Ristaniemi, T., et al.: Energy efficient optimization for computation offloading in fog computing system. In: GLOBECOM 2017-2017 IEEE Global Communications Conference, pp. 1–6. IEEE (2018)
2. Yousefpour, A., Ishigaki, G., Jue, J.P.: Fog computing: towards minimizing delay in the Internet of Things. In: IEEE International Conference on Edge Computing, pp. 17–24. IEEE (2017)
3. Huang, B., Bouguettaya, A., Dong, H., Chen, L.: Service mining for Internet of Things. In: Sheng, Q.Z., Stroulia, E., Tata, S., Bhiri, S. (eds.) ICSOC 2016. LNCS, vol. 9936, pp. 566–574. Springer, Cham (2016). https://doi.org/10.1007/978-3-319-46295-0_36
4. You, C., Huang, K., Chae, H., et al.: Energy-efficient resource allocation for mobile-edge computation offloading. IEEE Trans. Wireless Commun. 16(3), 1397–1411 (2017)
5. Mahmoud, M.M.E., Rodrigues, J.J.P.C., Saleem, K., et al.: Towards energy-aware fog-enabled cloud of things for healthcare. Comput. Electr. Eng. 67, 58–69 (2018)
6. Yang, Z., Niyato, D., Wang, P.: Offloading in mobile cloudlet systems with intermittent connectivity. IEEE Trans. Mob. Comput. 14(12), 2516–2529 (2015)
7. Jalali, F., Vishwanath, A., Hoog, J.D., et al.: Interconnecting fog computing and microgrids for greening IoT. In: Innovative Smart Grid Technologies - Asia, pp. 693–698. IEEE (2016)
8. Verma, S., Yadav, A.K., Motwani, D., et al.: An efficient data replication and load balancing technique for fog computing environment. In: International Conference on Computing for Sustainable Global Development. IEEE (2016)
9. Wang, S., Huang, X., Liu, Y., et al.: CachinMobile: an energy-efficient users caching scheme for fog computing. In: International Conference on Communications in China, CIC, pp. 1–6. IEEE (2016)
10. Wen, Z., Yang, R., Garraghan, P., et al.: Fog orchestration for Internet of Things services. IEEE Internet Comput. 21(2), 16–24 (2017)
11. Pham, X.-Q., Huh, E.-N.: Towards task scheduling in a cloud-fog computing system. In: Asia-Pacific Network Operations and Management Symposium, pp. 1–7 (2016)
12. Chen, X., Jiao, L., Li, W., et al.: Efficient multi-user computation offloading for mobile-edge cloud computing. IEEE/ACM Trans. Networking 24(5), 2795–2808 (2016)
13. Ulrike, V.L.: A tutorial on spectral clustering. Statist. Comput. 17(4), 395–416 (2007)

AppNet: A Large-Scale Multi-layer Heterogeneous Complex App Network for Intelligent Program Search

Jianmao Xiao[1], Shizhan Chen[1(✉)], Zhiyong Feng[1], and Jian Yang[2]

[1] College of Intelligence and Computing, Tianjin University, Tianjin, China
{zt_xjm,shizhan,zyfeng}@tju.edu.cn
[2] Computing Department, Macquarie University, Sydney, NSW, Australia
jian.yang@mq.edu.au

Abstract. The resources of mobile application in the app stores contains a vast amount of code and knowledge, which is of great significance to intelligent program search technology, but how to organize and utilize these multi-source heterogeneous data efficiently and integrate semantic information is still a key problem. In this paper, WordNet based AppNet, a multi-layer heterogeneous complex app network model was proposed, it completely describes the hierarchical structure between app-related tags, attributes, and code and in which aims to explore its application in the intelligent program search. Firstly, we expound the construction mechanism of AppNet and describe how does it realize mapping with WordNet, and then two simple real application scenarios were conducted based on AppNet in which to verify its validity and feasibility. We believe that the proposed AppNet model will provide researchers with more efficient ideas in the field of intelligent software development and search.

Keywords: Program search · App network · Ontology · Semantics

1 Introduction

Nowadays, mobile apps occupy a large share of our everyday life. Consumers spend much of their time in apps [1], which means the search function in app store becomes essential.

The traditional app search technology mainly regards the program as general text information and uses a common search engine technology to build a keyword-based program search engine, but the efficiency of this search does not meet the needs of users. So [2] leverage user reviews to find out important features of apps and bridge vocabulary gap between app developers and users to improve accuracy for mobile app retrieval, and provides an independent unbiased search for mobile apps with semantic search capabilities. However, the semantic information involved is limited.

Owing to the problem that the search results are incomplete and imprecise based on the above app search mechanism, so the intelligent program search

© Springer Nature Switzerland AG 2019
X. Liu et al. (Eds.): ICSOC 2018 Workshops, LNCS 11434, pp. 394–399, 2019.
https://doi.org/10.1007/978-3-030-17642-6_33

technology is proposed to solve the problem. One of the main directions of intelligent program search technology is to achieve accurate search based on semantic information. Hill et al. proposed "natural language source code localization" can be applied to a large number of data. They make semantic guesses about the name of the variable in the source code and build a database that contains the use of the massive source code variable and the morpheme expansion set [3]. Stolee et al. proposed that the problem of program search is summed up as a constraint solving problem, which provides a <input-output> method of data pair and constraint solving to search the code based on semantics. But due to the complexity of the analysis process, the method is still only in the theoretical stage [4]. Actually, although the program search technology has been studied by many researchers in recent years, there is still a certain gap in achieving truly intelligent program search till now [5].

It can be noticed from the above description that the use of the semantic information of the program is of great significance to the search for intelligent programs. So in this work, we proposed an multi-layer complex app network model AppNet based on WordNet [6] ontology to explore the intelligent search for app and program at semantic level.

The structure of this article is as follows: We first give a description of the AppNet model structure in detail and discuss the construction process and value at each layer of the model (Sects. 2 and 3), then two simple applications were conducted by exploit AppNet (Sect. 4), finally we give a perspective of possible research work in the future based on this proposed model (Sect. 5).

2   The Proposed AppNet Model

We have designed the multi-layer heterogeneous complex app network model called AppNet as shown in Fig. 1. The model is divided into three layers, we call it Tag layer, App layer, and the Code layer. AppNet can be further formalized as a five-tuple APN, $APN = <Tg, As, Co, TR, CR>$, where Tg represents the tag layer, As represents the app layer, Co represents the code layer, and TR represents the relationships between the tags, CR represents the relationships between the codes.

The three layers of AppNet are independent and also interrelated for each other. As described from top to bottom, the contents of the tag layer are extracted from app's information in app store, which contains two levels of content, the first level is the app's own category tag in the app store, the other level of the content is extracted from the description of the app and user reviews information by using the topic model technology. Since the vocabulary of the reviews in tag layer is basically nouns, verbs and so on. Therefore, we can use the obtained tag data, and based on the WordNet related hierarchy, semantics and inference technology to complete the mapping of app tag data to the WordNet ontology, and realize the construction of tag layer of app, Its essence can be regarded as a tag semantic network.

The app layer in the middle consists primarily information that the app displays in the app store. It includes the app classification, review information, rating and other attributes which can be considered a multi-attribute entity network. At the bottom, the code layer reflects the internal attributes of the app. It is mainly for the app's source program, including the related files, components, libraries, packages, classes and functional code modules that make up the app. Its essence is a relationships network between code. AppNet's tag layer and app layer, app layer and code layer, and the three layers are connected by the app to form three-layer heterogeneous complex app network. It completely depicts the attributes of the app from the semantic and the code level. Its starting point is to structure the related datasets.which is available to the app. The essence is to build an ontology for mobile apps. At present, we had built a AppNet demo website that can be accessed through http://www.fangzhifeng.top/appnet.

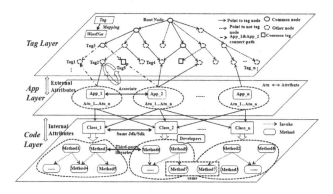

Fig. 1. The model architecture of AppNet

3   Construct AppNet

AppNet is a project that fully describe the app from multiple dimensions. We have crawled a real data set from the current popular app store (Apple App store&Google Play). Till now, it contains 20000 apps, 12063 App_Tags, 1,8245,8892 methods, and 26 self-attributes, among which app and apk are in one-to-one correspondence.

3.1   Data Collection

AppNet contains three layers. The tag layer data was obtained by extract the description and review information related to the app. The app layer data was directly obtained by the app description page, and mainly includes the name, classification, version, developers and user reviews, and other related information of the app, based on these multi-dimensional data, we can make use of machine learning related technologies to predict the app version or app recommendation on the app layer. And for the code layer the data is mainly from the apk decompiling. The following Subsects. 3.3 and 3.4 will introduce the tag layer and code layer in detail.

3.2   Data Processing

For the tag layer, the main idea is to use NLP technology to process the crawling description information and the review text data, and the processing flow as shown in Fig. 2. Here, we use the nltk package to perform word segmentation, remove stop words, stem extraction, and other operations on these text data, and then use the LDA topic model to select feature words as the final tag data for the app.

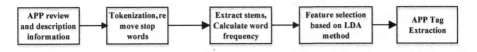

Fig. 2. Tag collection process

As for the code layer, we mainly focus on the method data after the apk decompile, through our actual decompilation, the number of methods after each apk decompilation is about in range $(10^3 - 10^4)$. When there is an call or other dependencies relationships between the methods, then the edges are constructed. So the invocation relationship between all the methods under each app constitutes the method network. For each app, do the same thing, and then the code for multiple apps can be associated through the app layer and the tag layer.

3.3   Tag Layer

According to the tag data obtained in Sect. 3.2, we can know that the data vocabulary is basically nouns, verbs, adjectives, etc., so that all the corresponding tag nodes can be found in the WordNet. Tag network construction mechanism as shown in Fig. 3, through the tag data and WordNet node matching, the corresponding tag network can be obtained and this is equivalent to establishing a logical tag network on the WordNet.

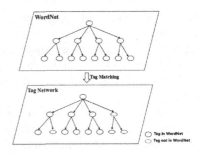

Fig. 3. Tag network construction mechanism

Based on the tag network, we can mining the association between apps. The key to implementing an association is to find a path that connects two apps. As shown in Fig. 1, App_1->Tag1->Tag3->Tag5->App_2 is a path from App_1 to App_2, then an association between A_pp1 and App_2 is achieved.

The essence of the tag layer is a semantic tag network. Therefore, we can implement various applications through the tag network for the app (Sect. 4 gives an simple application: App query expansion). In future, the AppNet would be do more work in the code layer, and would provide a feasible way for the real intelligent program search.

3.4   Code Layer

Currently the source code data of AppNet is mainly obtained by decompile apk, we divide the code into code written by the developer, the code that calls the JDK or SDK, and the third-party library code, which actually exists the call and the dependency relationships. Here we focus on the method-level data, since each apk has a large number of method, the dependencies relationships between

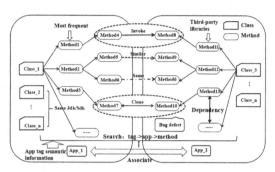

Fig. 4. Methods network

methods and classes are complex. Their invocation, dependency and other relationships constitute a method network.

As shown in Fig. 4. Each app has its own corresponding method network, and the same app or different apps has method relationships such as similar (Method5 and Method9), same (Method6), called (Method4 and Method8) or clone (Method7 and Method10) and so on. The essence of the code layer can be seen as an ontology of app-related codes, based on the above method network data and relationships, a lot of things can be done in future.

4   AppNet Applications

App query expansion in app stores. In our work, we implement semantic-based query extension based on tag semantic network, since the tag network is based on the WordNet ontology, so we can perform app retrieval and recommendation based on keyword-related synonyms set and antonym set, etc., and our results (see in website in Sect. 2) show that it had been greatly improved in the recall rate of the app.

Another application is to construct the code knowledge base. The process of construct the knowledge base as shown in Fig. 5. Owing to the combination of tag semantic labels information in the AppNet, the knowledge base also contains semantic information indirectly. Therefore, based on this knowledge base, there are also a lot of things could be done based on AppNet in future, such as implementing semantic-based code generation, app development requirements discovery, etc. These will be my follow-up major research work.

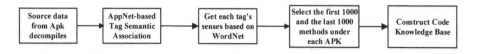

Fig. 5. The app code knowledge base construction process

5 Discussion and Future Work

Our future work has two goals:

Completing AppNet. We will continue to add more Internet data resources, such as Github, Stack overflow and other open source communities datas to expand our model.

Exploiting AppNet. We hope that AppNet will become an important resource in the field of intelligent program development. Therefore, we envision the following possible applications.

(1) Program generated automatically based on the code network. When the AppNet contains enough data and code knowledge, we will try to use the complex networks and deep learning related technologies to achieve program auto-completion and generation.
(2) Intelligence development for software. AppNet integrates the full attribute information of the app, and with the help of NLP and ontology related technologies, we believe that the AppNet would provide a feasible way to realize intelligent development for software.

Acknowledgements. This work is supported by the National Natural Science Foundation of China grant No.61572350 and the National Key R&D Program of China grant No.2017YFB1401201.

References

1. Datta, A., Dutta, K., Kajanan, S., Pervin, N.: Mobilewalla: a mobile application search engine. In: Zhang, J.Y., Wilkiewicz, J., Nahapetian, A. (eds.) MobiCASE 2011. LNICST, vol. 95, pp. 172–187. Springer, Heidelberg (2012). https://doi.org/10.1007/978-3-642-32320-1_12
2. Duan, H., Zhai, C., Cheng, J., Gattani, A.: Supporting keyword search in product database: a probabilistic approach. Proc. VLDB Endow. **6**(14), 1786–1797 (2013)
3. Hill, E., Pollock, L., Vijay-Shanker, K.: Improving source code search with natural language phrasal representations of method signatures. In IEEE/ACM International Conference on Automated Software Engineering, pp. 524–527. IEEE (2011). https://doi.org/10.10007/1234567890
4. Stolee, K.T., Elbaum, S., Dwyer, M.B.: Code search with input/output queries: generalizing, ranking, and assessment. J. Syst. Softw. **116**(C), 35–48 (2016)
5. Liu, B.B., Dong, W., Wang, J.: A survey of intelligent search and construction methods of program. Ruan Jian Xue Bao/J. Softw. 2017 (in Chinese). http://www.jos.org.cn/1000-9825/0000.htm
6. Fellbaum, C.: WordNet: An Electronic Lexical Database. Bradford Books, Cambridge (1998)

A Goal-Driven Context-Aware Architecture for Distributing Cognitive Service Group

Siyuan Lu[(⊠)]

School of Software and Microelectronics, Peking University, Beijing, China
larrylu0426@icloud.com

Abstract. Cognitive service is an emerging service paradigm in service-oriented computing. It can comprehend data in the same way as the human. Cognitive services require sufficient information to understand service scenarios. Actually, to achieve a goal sometimes requires multiple services with order dependencies and prerequisites to work collaboratively. When an exception event occurs during the service group working, the conventional approach is to restart or stop the service based on the exception type. If the environment information is changed much fast and retrieved unpractically, the exception event can cause the delayed response of the service group. If the goal of the service group is time-aware and service result is preferred, the regular policy is hard to match the requirement. In this paper, we address the problem of delayed response caused by exception events raised from the distributing cognitive service group. A novel architecture is proposed to ensure the overall consistency and real-time reaction of distributing cognitive service group.

Keywords: Service-oriented computing · Cognitive service · Context awareness

1 Introduction

Cognitive services require sufficient information to understand service scenarios. To obtain sufficient information, cognitive services often require multiple data sources. Furthermore, multiple resource (e.g., computing, storage, and cache) nodes are often required to achieve the desired result. Because each data source has different device characteristics and physical locations, only part of the data from the service environment can be obtained, and the service environment cannot be fully represented. Therefore, it is necessary to integrate the data from all channels to represent the service environment. Actually, to achieve a goal sometimes requires multiple services with order dependencies and prerequisites to work collaboratively. The functions and features of each service are different to a large extent and all have the independent operational capability. These individuals need work together for an ultimate goal while communication and consistency of each other. We gather these services as a cluster and name it "distributing cognitive service group".

When an exception event occurs during the service group working, the regular approach is to restart or stop the service based on the exception type. Restarting the service need to abandon the current service progress and then retrieve the previous data

© Springer Nature Switzerland AG 2019
X. Liu et al. (Eds.): ICSOC 2018 Workshops, LNCS 11434, pp. 400–406, 2019.
https://doi.org/10.1007/978-3-030-17642-6_34

to execute again. Even, it needs to choose another available resource node due to the current invalid one. In any case, all manners need a broad temporal and resource cost. If the environment information is changed much fast and retrieved unpractically, the broken-down service accumulates large amount of context data required to handle in time. Other related services need to wait for the invalid service to be valid. Further, the exception event can cause the delayed response of the service group. If the goal of the service group is time-aware and service result is preferred, the regular policy is hard to match the requirement. This is a severe challenge about service high availability and instantaneity.

In this paper, we propose a novel service architecture for multiple cognitive services to promote the adaptability to the environment and robustness of service group. We introduce the concept of context-aware to achieve the perception, understanding, and decision of the exception and deviation across the service collaboration and service working then assess the impact of both on the achievement of goals. Depending on the degree of impact, the influenced service decides to ignore or handle the exception, further, to continue or restart even stop the service. The significance of context is to provide an overall consistent basis for the service group and a prerequisite for the execution of the service. When the exception and deviation rise, the relationship between the goal and the current service working progress state is considered according to the overall status of the service group at that time, and the high availability of the service is guaranteed under the condition of ensuring the overall consistency and real-time response. The distributing cognitive service group based on this architecture can acquire the expected result with the unexpected exception.

To achieve it, this paper will first give the overview of cognitive service and research on combing service computing and contextual computing. Second, give a high-level design of the proposed architecture and some related concept explanations in short. Next, we enumerate some challenge points and give some insight from us about how to solve them. The paper closes with a conclusion.

2   Related Work

Cognitive service is an emerging service paradigm in service-oriented computing. It's able to comprehend data in the same as the human. For instance, the human face recognition service not only can find where the human faces are but also can know who they are, even mind the human character information (e.g., affect, sex) from the face shape, skin color, expression and so on. The cognition process doesn't need the human intermediary. In a word, cognitive service makes service more intelligent. So far, there are few relevant studies in this field. There is no clear clarification of cognitive service across the academia and industry. Microsoft is working on this field even has published several cognitive services with the API such as Emotion, LUIS, Speaker Recognition [1].

From the perspective of cognitive service, Context is a powerful, and longstanding concept to depict the interaction environment which is usually complexing and variety [10]. Interaction with service is by explicit the information given by users, and the context is implicit, e.g., the environment information surrounding the service and user. Context is useful to interpret explicit interaction [2, 4], giving the input information more rich implications. According to Hong et al. "to provide adequate service for the users, applications and services should be aware of their contexts and automatically adapt to their changing contexts-known as context-awareness" [5].

To combine the service with context, one popular approach existed in many studies is to make context as a middleware embedded into the existed service system to provide the context cognition capacity for automatically adapt to extremely dynamic computing environments. From the context side, the combination involves the definition of context lifecycle divided into four necessary stages [9]: context acquisition, context modeling, context reasoning and context disposition. From the service side, the combination involves the condition to trigger services and the relationship/dependency between them. Gu et al. [3] presented a service-oriented context-aware middleware (SOCAM) architecture for the building and rapid prototyping of context-aware mobile services. The core of this work is to define an ontology-based approach to model various contexts for supporting semantic representation, context reasoning and context knowledge sharing and provide an original insight about context-aware service system architecture. However, this proposal only considered the service automation rather than service efficiency and availability. Other related works about the context-aware service-oriented middleware such as Hydra [6], SCIMS [7] and CAMEO [8] have given an enormous contribution on the context side for providing more comprehensive context representation to promote more effective service response capacity. Nevertheless, considering the capacity of context, service can exploit the change context information to perceive the exceptions raised from the service environment and make a right decision to reduce the negative impact. Further, on the other hand, context is meaningful to promote the service robustness and high availability.

3 Proposal

In this section, we mainly introduce the high-level design of proposed architecture which involves two main topics as bellow (related discussion detail is in the subsection):

- Which concepts are essential to define a cognitive service and how the functional cognitive services work together to achieve the specific goal.
- How to use known information to define the service environment context and use context for ensuring the goal achievement punctually during the service working period.

3.1   Overview on Distributing Cognitive Service Group

According to the functional requirement, cognitive service need use known data to satisfy user's expected result, for instance, customers can use Meeting Record service to extract the speech content of attendees from the audio data and video data which can be acquired from meeting room monitor device and phone. The attendee information can be an optional data to help the service to comprehend the speech content deeper.

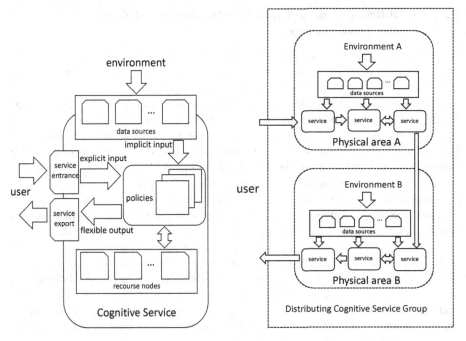

Fig. 1. Cognitive service structure.   **Fig. 2.** DCSG topology

Based on this kind of service workflow, we define some essential concepts for cognitive service to match the service functional requirement as below and Fig. 1 illustrates the cognitive service structure we defined, further, based on this structure, we consider the data source location to divide the service area and form the distributing cognitive service group (DCSG) illustrated in Fig. 2.

Explicit Input: User need to provide the satisfactory input data, which is the main part of data used to comprehend the in-depth information for obtaining expected result.

Data Source and Implicit Input: Cognitive service can access and acquire the necessary and additional service context data from data source then fusion and form the implicit input to assist the reasoning process for enhancing the depth for service result.

Resource Node: Cognitive service need to be deployed on several resource nodes for using the computing and storage capability. Resource nodes popularly can be physical or virtual machines (e.g., server) and also can be containers (e.g., Docker). These nodes are usually managed by a cluster manager service.

Policy: Policy is the processing operation to obtain the expected result from the input data.

Flexible Output: Due to the quality variety of input information, cognitive service can conclude different result depth. So, the service output is very flexible.

3.2   A Goal-Driven Context-Aware Architecture for Distributing Cognitive Service Group

To achieve the goal, the service group needs to perceive the overall working progress. We use service context to recognize the exception and make a corresponding decision to handle it. The overall architecture is illustrated in Fig. 3.

The most important consideration about service context is the service environment definition and corresponding service context representation. Context modeling is a regular method to build a context space for representing the interaction environment. The range of service environment is limited to involve two fields: **service outside environment** and **service inside environment**. Service outside environment represents the service input data including explicit input, and implicit input, service inside environment describes the service runtime status and dependent resource status.

Two core service components which are **controller service** and **daemon service** provide the capacities of capturing the exception and deviation and making decisions to solve them. Daemon services deploy on the host platform to acquire the service inside environment context for perceiving and control the functional service. Controller service responds to all daemon service and has a global perception of the whole service group. If a service inside exception raises, the daemon service deployed on host platform locating the broken-down service will firstly respond and try to solve it following some predefined rules and reports the impact to controller service for judging the impact globally.

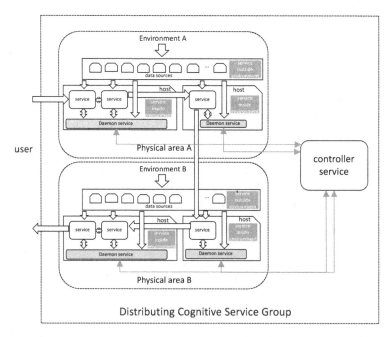

Fig. 3. A goal-driven context-aware architecture for distributing cognitive service group

Considering the encapsulation of third-party service, we decouple the dependency between perception capability and functional service inside. In this way, the existed service system can be easy to transfer to this novel architecture.

4 Challenge

The service architecture defined in our proposal may bring some challenges to our research. The most pressing challenge is when the controller service is down, the functional services will disconnect with the controller service. It means that functional services will lose the ability to perceive each other and controller service will lose the memory of service progress during its downtime. We need to present a progress retrieving approach to decrease this impact. Further, we are ready to evaluate the architecture performance by comparing with different state-of-the-art ones. So, the evaluation work is considered as the future work to be thought and finished.

5 Conclusion

In this paper, we address the problem of delayed response caused by exception event raised from the distributing cognitive service group. A novel architecture is proposed to ensure the overall consistency and real-time response of distributing cognitive service group. In the future, to evaluate the effect of it, we will develop a simple smart home system based on this architecture. Moreover, to solve a series of problems about controller service doesn't work, we will present a progress retrieving approach.

References

1. Microsoft Cognitive Service. https://azure.microsoft.com/en-us/services/cognitive-services/. Accessed 4 June 2018
2. Chan, A.T., Chuang, S.-N.: MobiPADS: a reflective middleware for context-aware mobile computing. IEEE Trans. Softw. Eng. **29**(12), 1072–1085 (2003)
3. Gu, T., Pung, H.K., Zhang, D.Q.: A service-oriented middleware for building context-aware services. J. Netw. Comput. Appl. **28**(1), 1–18 (2005)
4. Santos, L.O., Poortinga, R., Vink, P.: A service-oriented middleware for context-aware applications. In: Proceedings of 5th International Workshop on Middleware for Pervasive and Ad-Hoc Computing (2007)
5. Jong-yi, H., Eui-ho, S., Sung-Jin, K.: Context-aware systems: a literature review and classification. Expert Syst. **36**(4), 8509–8522 (2009)
6. Eisenhauer, M., Rosengren, P., Antolin, P.: HYDRA: a development platform for integrating wireless devices and sensors into ambient intelligence systems. The Internet of Things, pp. 367–373. Springer, New York (2010). https://doi.org/10.1007/978-1-4419-1674-7_36

7. Kabir, M.A., Han, J., Yu, J., Colman, A.: SCIMS: a social context information management system for socially-aware applications. In: Ralyté, J., Franch, X., Brinkkemper, S., Wrycza, S. (eds.) CAiSE 2012. LNCS, vol. 7328, pp. 301–317. Springer, Heidelberg (2012). https://doi.org/10.1007/978-3-642-31095-9_20

8. Khan, A.J., Jayarajah, K., Han, D., Misra, A., Balan, R., Seshan, S.: CAMEO: a middleware for mobile advertisement delivery. In: Proceeding of the 11th Annual International Conference on Mobile Systems, Applications, and Services, pp. 125–138. ACM (2013)

9. Charith, P., Arkady, Z., Christen, P., Dimitrios, G.: Context aware computing for the internet of things: a survey. IEEE Commun. Surv. Tutor. 16(1), 414–454 (2014)

10. Cabrera, O., Franch, X., Marco, J.: Ontology-based context modeling in service-oriented computing: a systematic mapping. Data Knowl. 110, 24–53 (2017)

Crossover Service Phenomenon Analysis Based on Event Evolutionary Graph

Mingyi Liu$^{(\boxtimes)}$, Zhongjie Wang, and Zhiying Tu

School of Computer Science and Technology, Harbin Institute of Technology,
Harbin, China
{liumy,rainy,tzy_hit}@hit.edu.cn

Abstract. Nowadays, crossover and convergence between services has become a new phenomenon in service market, especially in China. This work aims at analyzing the inner and external formation mechanism of crossover service, which have great significance to the sustainable development of this new ecosystem. Previously, a traditional concept based knowledge graph extracted from crossover service News was constructed for crossover service event analysis. The crossover modes and the statistics of appearances were found in that experiment. Due to the limitation of motivation analysis of the inference method based on static concept structure, the Event Evolutionary Graph (EEG) is introduced to improve the event analysis, and moreover to achieve the event prediction in this undergoing experiment. Generic EEG can represent the event evolution rules and patterns, but due to the characteristics of crossover services, this experiment will adapt event modeling method and its training method. This work in progress methodology would explain the inner and external formation reason of crossover service, and furthermore achieve the assisted decision-making for potential crossover organizations based on event prediction.

Keywords: Crossover service · Event evolutionary graph ·
Service event prediction

1 Introduction

With the development of modern service industries, the crossover and convergence between services is becoming more and more obvious [4]. Crossover service refers to the services that originally belong to different domains, whereafter interoperate with each other to create a brand new service. It brings dramatic changes of the user experience, which cannot be provided by any single service. New retail, a upgrade version of the traditional e-commence, is a typical crossover service. It involves logistics, warehousing, marketing, finance, wholesale procurement, manufacturing, insurance, e-commerce, and etc. These services are converged to give users a new shopping experience and method.

Supervised by Zhongjie Wang, Zhiying Tu.

© Springer Nature Switzerland AG 2019
X. Liu et al. (Eds.): ICSOC 2018 Workshops, LNCS 11434, pp. 407–412, 2019.
https://doi.org/10.1007/978-3-030-17642-6_35

The essential of crossover is to collaborate, which is also the traditional research issue of service orchestration and choreography. In the past decade, most of the relevant researches, no matter process-based, interaction-based, or QoS constraints oriented, focus on the functional completeness, performance, or user satisfaction of the converged solutions [6]. In other words, these researches have explained the phenomena of service convergence from the aspects of business interoperability, quality configurability, or context-awareness. However, few studies have analyzed the living environment of crossover services that includes physical context, marketing and social environment, not to mention the explorations of general rules and mechanism of crossover phenomena by comprehensively analyzing the service business features and domain related features with this environment.

Knowledge graph, which evolved from semantic network [5], was ideally designed for the elementary inference from concept to concept. It is one of the best choices for analyzing the crossover service phenomena from the semantic level. Since big data drives the scale of the knowledge graph rising rapidly, the high-dimensional entities with sparse relations badly weaken the efficiency and accuracy of the inference. Recently, the representation learning proposes an embedding way to transfer the graph into a low-dimensional space, where entities and relations represented as vectors make the relational calculus efficiently. However, we more likely consider the knowledge graph as a static structure for entity-relation representation, which is less sensitive to the dynamic events. Thus, this paper introduces the event evolutionary graph to better represent the dynamic emergence of crossover service events, further more to achieve event prediction.

2 Completed Work

Our previous work proposed an entity-event network called Service Collaboration Network (SCN) to well clarify the historical cooperation facts between services by retrieving the valuable information from the Internet News.

The SCN is an undirected graph $G = (V, E)$, where V is a set of nodes in the graph used to represent all service entities and E is a set of edges in the graph used to represent all collaboration events. Each node in the graph is also labeled with the domain category. For any two nodes $u, v \in V$, and the edge $e \in E$ connecting these two nodes, it means that the service entity u and v have a collaboration event e.

Figure 1 demonstrates an example of SCN, in which each node represents a specific service entity with domain exclusive color, and each edge represents a service collaboration event. The label of each edge is the textual description about the collaboration fact of the two entities on the endpoints of this edge.

Based on the SCN, an empirical analysis experiment on the law of crossover service was conducted. It revealed that the crossover ability of the enterprises from different domains can be ranged into various levels, because many reasons: inherent shortages of primary industry (such as countryman is less motivated), policy orientation (such as China Manufacturing 2020), and moreover

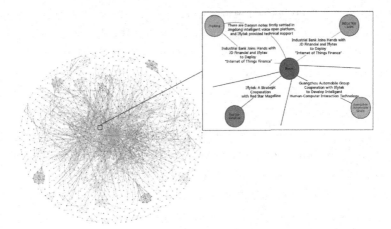

Fig. 1. Service Collaboration Network

the appetency of market capital and new techniques varies in different enterprises, domains, and even regions. We also proved that some crossover patterns are exactly existing, such as (1) new techniques always drive crossover services emergence; (2) the enterprises with abundant financial resources not only invest in the crossover, but business crossover is becoming their favorite; (3) Sometimes, the crossover is the surviving way for newly-established firms.

These findings are interesting for us to understand the crossover service phenomena. However, the above explorations mainly focus on the studies of service entities in crossover service cooperation events rather than service cooperation events themselves. Actually, there are various complex relations between service collaboration events, such as temporal relationship and logical causality. Service Collaboration Network treats service collaboration events as edges, so the relationship between events is not so obvious and hard for analysis. Therefore, Service Collaboration Network is hard to explain the exact reasons of the emergence of a specific crossover service. And also, it is difficult to predict the development trend of this crossover service.

3 Proposal

3.1 Concept of Event Evolutionary Graph

There are two important concepts in Event Evolutionary Graph [4]: events and events relationship. Events are represented by abstract, generalized, semantically complete predicate phrases that contain event triggers and other necessary components to maintain the semantic completeness of the event. Events relations include temporal relationship and causality. The temporal relation focuses on the partial order relationship between the two events in time, for example, "pay" after "eat" in the restaurant. The causal relationship between events is a subset

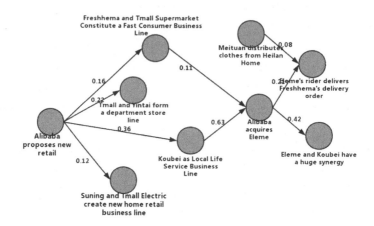

Fig. 2. Event Evolutionary Graph

of the temporal relationship, emphasizing the cause and effect, e.g. nuclear leak causes marine pollution.

Event Evolutionary Graph is a directed graph that describes the evolution of events and causation between events. Nodes in the graph represent abstract, generalized events, and directed edges represent the relationship between events. The edge is also marked with the transition probability information between events. Figure 2 gives an example to illustrate Event Evolutionary Network.

3.2   Construct Event Evolutionary Graph

Data Collection and Data Clean. We acquire two kinds of datum, one is the official announcement of the service entity, and another is the IT technology News from different websites. This data acquisition is a 24/7 and real time process, in which only the time information and body text information are retained. In addition, we will construct a online filter to determine whether the captured News is relevant.

Crossover Service Event Chains Extraction. A service event chain is partially ordered set of service events that share a common service entity which called protagonist entity. In the generic EEG, an event is represented by a pair of the verb lemma and the grammatical dependency relation between the verb and entity, which can be easily extracted by NLP toolkit. However, due to the complexity of crossover service events, the generic event extraction algorithm needs to be modified to accommodate crossover service events. For example, in the generic event, no matter Yahoo! is acquired by either Alibaba or Verizon, these two company acquisition events will be considered as the same event. Actually these are two exactly distinguishing facts, not only the participants but also the market influences are totally different. After the crossover service events are extracted, there are many works on inferring temporal relations [2,7].

Construct EEG Based on the Extracted Event Chains. Putting all crossover service event chains together into EEG. Different expressions of the same type of event will be encountered during the construction of the EEG. These events should be merged into one. EEG can be formally denoted as $G = (V, E)$, where $V = \{v_1, v_2, ..., v_n\}$ is the node set and E is the edge set. Each node $v \in V$ represent a crossover service event, and each $e \in E$ is a directed edge with a weight. The weight ω of a directed edge $v_i \rightarrow v_j$ can be computed by:

$$\omega(v_i|v_j) = \frac{count(v_i, v_j)}{\sum_k count(v_i, v_k)} \tag{1}$$

where $count(v_i, v_j)$ means the frequency of bigram (v_i, v_j) appears in crossover service event chains. Weights will be an important part of the input to the event prediction model.

3.3   Predict Crossover Service Event Based on EEG

The EEG can reflect the rules and patterns of event evolution, which is very suitable for event prediction. The EEG stored in the graph structure has the same difficulties with the traditional knowledge graph. Thus, neural node embeddings, a powerful representation for graph-structure data, will be used to express semantic information between nodes using low-dimensional dense vectors while maintaining graph structure information.

As mentioned above, the event information could be transferred into a sequential data, so Recurrent Neural Network (RNN) is selected for the further processing. Because it has been proved that RNN is the most effective neural networks in dealing with the front-to-back correlation between sequential inputs. In addition, attention mechanism will be involved in the event prediction as well, to avoid various misleadings, caused by different context events, in correct event subsequent identification. In conclusion, the further experiment will use an end-to-end RNN with attention mechanism to solve the problem of crossover service event prediction.

4   Challenges

There are two major challenges when applying the Event Evolutionary Graph to represent the crossover service events.

- How to describe crossover service event? How to make the description of a crossover service event in generalizable model? Generic EEG is pure event description abstract without any consideration of time and concrete entities [1]. Normally, only a small number of entities are considered in the event [3]. In contrast, crossover service events are much more complex than these generic events which are sensitive to the time and the participating entities. The number of participating entities within the crossover service events is large, and the relations among them are complex. In addition, retaining the complete semantics of the event from massive non-structure text is a huge challenge as well.

– How to incrementally train the graph? Service events are time-sensitive, so when we make predictions or recommendations, the latest service events will greatly affect the results. Thus, to update/retrain the graph in time or even in real time is another challenge.

References

1. Chambers, N., Jurafsky, D.: Unsupervised learning of narrative event chains. In: Proceedings of ACL-08: HLT, pp. 789–797 (2008)
2. Frermann, L., Titov, I., Pinkal, M.: A hierarchical bayesian model for unsupervised induction of script knowledge. In: Proceedings of the 14th Conference of the European Chapter of the Association for Computational Linguistics, pp. 49–57 (2014)
3. Granroth-Wilding, M., Clark, S.C.: What happens next? event prediction using a compositional neural network model. In: Thirtieth AAAI Conference on Artificial Intelligence (2016)
4. Li, Z., Ding, X., Liu, T.: Constructing narrative event evolutionary graph for script event prediction. In: Proceedings of the 27th International Joint Conference on Artificial Intelligence, pp. 4201–4207. AAAI Press (2018)
5. Liu, Z., Sun, M.S., Lin, Y., Xie, R.: Knowledge representation learning: a review. J. Comput. Res. Dev. **53**(2), 247–261 (2016)
6. Sheng, Q.Z., Qiao, X., Vasilakos, A.V., Szabo, C., Bourne, S., Xu, X.: Web services composition: a decade's overview. Inform. Sci. **280**, 218–238 (2014)
7. UzZaman, N., Llorens, H., Derczynski, L., Allen, J., Verhagen, M., Pustejovsky, J.: Semeval-2013 task 1: Tempeval-3: evaluating time expressions, events, and temporal relations. In: Second Joint Conference on Lexical and Computational Semantics (* SEM), Volume 2: Proceedings of the Seventh International Workshop on Semantic Evaluation (SemEval 2013), vol. 2, pp. 1–9 (2013)

Demonstrations

16th International Conference on Service Oriented Computing (ICSOC) - Demo Track

Antonio Bucchiarone[1], Wei Emma Zhang[2], and Ying Zou[3]

[1]Fondazione Bruno Kessler, Trento, Italy
bucchiarone@fbk.eu
[2]Macquarie University, Australia
w.zhang@mq.edu.au
[3]Queen's University, Canada
ying.zou@queensu.ca

Abstract. The goal of the ICSOC Demo track is to provide opportunities for participants from academia and industry to present their latest development in Service Oriented Computing. Interactive systems, design-support tools, platforms and novel applications have been presented. A *Best Demo Award*, has been given to a demo that the entire ICSOC Conference attendance voted to be the best in quality, execution, and impact among all the accepted demos in the conference.

Motivation and Objectives

The demonstration track focuses on tools or research prototypes that showcase the innovations in Service-Oriented Applications. Areas of interest for demonstrations include all topics for ICSOC 2018. Specific topics of interest include, but not limited to, the following:

- Modeling Business Services and Service Value Networks
- Flexible Service Composition and Mashups
- Adaptive Service-based Systems
- Business Process Interaction and Choreographies
- Business Intelligence and Analytics for Services
- Services on the Cloud (XAAS)
- Service Integration and Orchestration
- Service Engineering Tools and Methodology
- Service Design Methods and Tools
- Service Change Management Systems
- Service Operations and Management
- Service Applications and Implementations
- Service-oriented Architecture Showcases
- Quality of Service Design and Management
- Service Security, Privacy, and Trust
- Service Vocabularies and Ontology

- Cloud Computing Services and Engineering
- Grid and Scientific Computing Services
- Pervasive and Mobile Services
- Embedded and Real-time Services
- Testbeds for Service Technologies and Concepts
- Social Networks and Services
- Internet of Things Services
- Data-aware Services including Artifact-Centric Systems
- Services for Big Data
- Human-mediated Services
- RESTful Web Services
- Open API
- Service Adaptation and Customization
- Service Governance
- Formal Methods for Web Services
- Validation and Verification of Services
- Elastic Service Computing
- RFID, sensor data and services related to the Internet of Things
- Services related linked open data

Accepted Papers

Thirty-one demo papers have been submitted, while Fourteen have been accepted (45% of acceptance rate) and presented during the demo session. This year at ICSOC we have also organized a short session where tool demo authors can pitch their demos to the attendees of the conference. The presentation for each demo was limited to *** one minute *** with one slide. In the following, details on the demos presented are given:

- **Improved Architectures/Deployments with Elmo.** Arjan Lamers, Marko van Eekelen, Sung-Shik Jongmans
- **CEA: A Service for Cognitive Event Automation.** Larisa Shwartz, Jinho Hwang, Hagen Volzer, Michael Nidd, Murilo Goncalves Aguiar, Marcos Vinicius Landivar , Paraiso Letusa Valero
- **BluePlan: A Service for Automated Migration Plan Construction using AI.** Malik Jackson, John Rofrano, Jinho Hwang, Maja Vukovic
- **ELeCTRA: induced usage limitations calculation in RESTful APIs.** Antonio Gamez-Diaz, Pablo Fernandez, Ana Ivanchikj, Cesare Pautasso, Antonio Ruiz-Cortes
- **Offering Artificial Intelligence Development Situation Analysis Service for Users.** Xiujuan Xu, Yu Liu
- **TReAT: A Tool for Analyzing Relations between Tasks in a Process.** Pengbo Xiu, Jian Yang, Weiliang Zhao

- **iCOP: IoT-enabled Policing Processes.** Francesco Schiliro, Amin Beheshti, Samira Ghodratnama, Farhad Amouzgar, Boualem Benatallah, Jian Yang, Quan Z. Sheng, Fabio Casati, Hamid Reza Motahari-Nezhad
- **iSheets: A Spreadsheet-based Machine Learning Development Platform for Data-driven Process Analytics.** Farhad Amouzgar, Amin Beheshti, Samira Ghodratnama, Boualem Benatallah, Jian Yang, Quan Z. Sheng
- **SORCER: A Decentralised Continuous Integration Platform for Service-Oriented Software Systems.** Jameel Almalki, Haifeng Shen
- **On Anomaly Detection and Root Cause Analysis of Microservice Systems.** Zijie Guan, Jinjin Lin, Pengfei Chen
- **RESTalk Miner: Mining RESTful Conversations, Pattern Discovery and Matching.** Ana Ivanchikj, Ilija Gjorgjiev, Cesare Pautasso
- **slay Engine for Large-Scale SLA Management.** Shashank Rajamoni, Robert Engel, Bryant Chen, Heiko Ludwig, Alexander Keller
- **Paving the Way for Autonomous Cars in the City of Tomorrow: A Prototype for Mobile Devices Support at the Edges of 5G Network.** Fatma Raissi, Clovis Anicet Ouedraogo, Sami Yangui, Frederic Camps, Nejib Bel-Hadj Alouane. **Best Demo Award**
- **Juno: An Intelligent Chat Service for IT Service Automation.** Jin Xiao, Anup Kalia, Maja Vukovic

Demo Track Chairs

Dr. Antonio Bucchiarone is senior researcher in the DAS (Distributed Adaptive Systems) research unit of Fondazione Bruno Kessler, Trento, Italy. His area of focus are self-adaptive (collective) systems, applied formal methods, run-time service composition and adaptation. He has been actively involved in various research projects in the field of Collective and Adaptive (Service-based) Systems including the following FP7 projects: ALLOW Ensembles, ALLOW, S-Cube, Sensoria. He was general chair of the IEEE International Conference on Self-Adaptive and Self-Organizing Systems (SASO 2018), in Trento, Italy. Moreover, he has taken part in the organization and in the program committees of conferences and workshops, among which SASO 2016, SA-TTA at ACM SAC from 2013 to 2017, the FoCAS Workshop on Fundamentals of Collective Adaptive Systems (2014 and 2015), and the eCAS Workshop on Engineering Collective Adaptive Systems in 2016. He has been also the chair of the Doctoral Symposium at SASO 2015 and ICSOC 2018 and co-chair of the Engineering Collective Adaptive Systems (eCAS) workshop at the Self-Adaptive Self-Organizing (SASO) conference in 2017.

Wei Emma Zhang is currently a senior postdoctoral research fellow in Department of Computing at Macquarie University. Her research interests include Internet of Things, text mining, data mining and knowledge base. She received PhD degree in computer science from the University of Adelaide in 2017. She has authored or coauthored more than 40 papers so far. She has been actively involved in various IoT projects, including projects funded by Australian Research Council and industry projects. She has also served on various conference committees and international journals in different roles such as track chair, proceeding chair, PC member and reviewer. She is the member of the IEEE and ACM.

Dr. Ying (Jenny) Zou was named Canada Research Chair in Software Evolution in recognition of her research on the methods and tools for supporting the development and evolution of service-oriented applications. Dr. Ying Zou is a Professor in the Department of Electrical and Computer Engineering and cross-appointed to the School of Computing at Queen's University in Canada. She is a visiting scientist of IBM Centers for Advanced Studies (CAS), IBM Canada. She was awarded with 2014 IBM CAS Research Faculty Fellow of the Year. Dr. Zou also won twice IBM Faculty Awards in 2007 and 2008. She has published over 145 research papers in the high quality international conferences and journals, such as the International Conference on Software Engineering (ICSE), ACM Joint Meeting on European Software Engineering Conference and Symposium on the Foundations of Software Engineering (ESEC/FSE), and the International Conference on Service-Oriented Computing (ICSOC), IEEE Transactions on Software Engineering (TSE), IEEE Transactions on Services Computing (TSC) and the International Journal of Empirical Software Engineering (EMSE).

Dr. Zou has leveraged her research collaborations with academic and industrial partners, attracted new research funding and recruited and trained a high number of highly qualified personnel. Dr. Zou has demonstrated her leadership through the organization of international conferences/workshops. For example, she recently served in the program committee for the International Conference on Software Engineering (ICSE) 2019, Awards co-chair in the International Working Conference on Mining Software Repositories (MSR) 2019, and the tool demonstration track co-chair in the International Conference on Service-Oriented Computing (ICSOC) 2018. She is a regular program committee member for many leading international conferences, such as ICSOC, MSR and the International Conference on Software Maintenance and Evolution (ICSME). She is an associated editor for the IEEE Transactions on Services Computing from 2019. She is a senior IEEE member and a Member-at-Large in the IEEE Computer Society Technical Council on Software Engineering (TCSE).

Acknowledgment. The workshop chairs would like to thank ICSOC 2018 organizers for providing the full support and ensuring the success of the tool demo track. We thank the authors of the submitted papers, to have chosen the demo track as place where to propose their work. We would also like to thank also the reviewers, for their careful work in evaluating the papers.

Improved Architectures/Deployments with Elmo

Arjan Lamers[1,2], Marko van Eekelen[2,3], and Sung-Shik Jongmans[2,4(✉)]

[1] First8 B.V., Nijmegen, The Netherlands
[2] Department of Computer Science,
Open University of the Netherlands, Heerlen, The Netherlands
ssj@ou.nl
[3] Institute for Computing and Information Sciences, Radboud University Nijmegen, Nijmegen, The Netherlands
[4] Department of Computing, Imperial College London, London, UK

Abstract. Manually reasoning about candidate refactorings to alleviate bottlenecks in service-oriented systems is hard, even when using high-level architecture/deployment models. Nevertheless, it is common practice in industry. Elmo is a decision support tool that helps service-oriented architects and deployment engineers to analyze and refactor architectural and deployment bottlenecks in service-oriented systems.

Keywords: Services · Refactoring · Architecture · Deployment

1 Highlights

Elmo is a decision support tool that helps service-oriented architects and deployment engineers to analyze and refactor architectural and deployment bottlenecks in service-oriented systems. We first summarize the highlights:

- *Elmo uses a light-weight, high-level, **whiteboard-style notation** to model architectures/deployments (Fig. 1).* This is important, as business executives often base their decisions on such "whiteboard models": the ability to explain consequences of architecture/deployment refactorings in a simple notation that is naturally understandable to executives is vital in industry.
- *Elmo **automatically analyzes potential bottlenecks** in architecture and deployment models.* The analysis performed by Elmo is based on the formal semantics of Elmo's whiteboard-style notation [8,15]. The user can subsequently manipulate the models (by selecting refactorings from a list) to improve the models and eliminate the bottleneck. In addition to this:
- *Elmo **automatically infers refactorings** of architectures/deployments, guaranteed to achieve a given goal.* Using graph exploration algorithms, Elmo is capable of exploring the space of possible refactorings (up to a given depth), and if multiple chains of refactorings achieve the same goal, Elmo automatically compares the other pros and cons of these chains. However:

X. Liu et al. (Eds.): ICSOC 2018 Workshops, LNCS 11434, pp. 419–424, 2019.
https://doi.org/10.1007/978-3-030-17642-6_36

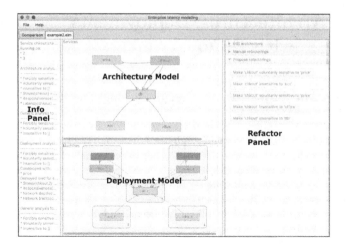

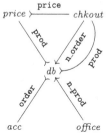

Fig. 1. Elmo (blurred: simplified e-commerce system)

Fig. 2. Architecture model of a simplified e-commerce system (cf. Fig. 1)

- *Elmo **does not carry out** refactorings.* Elmo is geared toward providing decision support: its sole purpose is to help architects and deployment engineers (1) to find the best solution for a refactoring problem, and (2) perhaps more importantly, to convince executives that this solution should indeed be implemented. Actual implementation of refactorings is beyond Elmo's scope.
- *Elmo **works purely qualitatively** instead of quantitatively.* Once performance issues start to manifest, Elmo avoids a need for brittle and expensive additional performance measurements (profiling, monitoring, simulations, etc.), relying exclusively on dependency analyses between services.
- *Elmo is being developed and **evaluated with industry** partner First8.* This already led to promising initial results. First8 is a software company that specializes in custom business-critical systems; refactoring service-oriented systems to improve performance is an important activity of First8.

2   Motivation

In current industrial practice, architects and deployment engineers need to *manually* reason about candidate refactorings to alleviate bottlenecks in service-oriented systems. Even when using high-level architecture/deployment models, this has three major issues. *First*, reasoning about refactorings is an intellectually demanding activity, and often requires architects to make simplifying assumptions and/or apply additional abstractions. This leads to imprecise refactoring proposals, which may be more costly, more risky, and less effective than necessary. *Second*, as refactoring proposals are based on experience and best-practices, architects can easily overlook less-intuitive refactorings that may very well be most-effective for a given system. *Third*, predicting how different refactorings will interact with each other is hard (e.g., an improvement in the architecture may be canceled out by an improvement in the deployment, due to resource sharing). In a large-scale project, First8 architects indeed struggled with these issues, which strongly motivated Elmo's development.

3   The Tool

Elmo is shown in Fig. 1, in the context of a simplified e-commerce system (see the demo for details [9]). Using the graphical interface, Elmo allows an architect to construct architecture/deployment models. As shown in Fig. 1, these models are lightweight, and they look similar to architectural whiteboard diagrams.

Formally [8,15], the models are graphs; Fig. 2 shows an example (i.e., an architecture model of the same simplified e-commerce system as in Fig. 1). Vertices represent services (architecture) or service instances (deployment), while edges represent service calls. We distinguish between *pushes* (denoted as $s_1 \longrightarrow s_2$, meaning that s_1 initiates an information flow from s_1 to s_2) and *pulls* (denoted as $s_1 \longrightarrow\!\!\!\prec s_2$, meaning that s_1 initiates an information flows from s_2 to s_1), as these impact performance differently. Calls are furthermore annotated with the type of information involved. One or more instances of services can be *deployed* on one or more *machines*.

Each time information is pushed to or pulled from a service s, work needs to be done and *stress* is imposed on s. The stress set of s ($Stress(s)$) is defined as the set of services that may impose stress directly or indirectly by being stressed themselves. Service instances sharing the same machine also share their stress. A related notion is *responsiveness* ($Resp(s)$), which indicates how quickly a service s is able to deliver its work. It consists both of the stress set of the service, as well as the stress of the services from which it needs to pull information. Based on stress and responsiveness, three qualitative sensitivity levels can be defined: service a is *insensitive* to service b if b never impacts a (formally: $b \notin Resp(a)$); a is *willingly sensitive* to b if b impacts a *only* on a's initiative (formally: $b \in Resp(a) \wedge b \notin Stress(a)$); a is *unwillingly sensitive* to b if b impacts a *also* on b's initiative (formally: $b \in Stress(a)$). For instance, if service s_1 pushes information to service s_2, the performance of s_2 is sensitive to s_1, *unwillingly* (i.e., s_2 has no control). In contrast, if s_1 pulls information from s_2, the performance of s_1 is sensitive to s_2, *willingly* (i.e., s_1 chooses to depend on s_2).

These models can be used to explore sensitivity characteristics of the system: an architect can select service (-instances) and Elmo evaluates and highlights its sensitivities. Possible refactorings are immediately shown with resulting effects; these refactorings are formally guaranteed to preserve the existing behavior [8]. An architect can then apply the suggested refactorings to the architecture/deployment model, to try out ideas and compare results of different strategies. Also, using memory-optimized graph exploration algorithms, Elmo can automatically suggest a chain of refactorings towards a given goal (e.g., "make service s_4 insensitive to service s_1").

Elmo is open-source [10] and implemented in JavaFX. The refactorings currently supported are: splitting and merging services, changing pushes to pulls and vice versa, changing deployments of services, and adding caches and/or queues.

4   Working with Elmo

The typical Elmo workflow looks as follows. First, architects and deployment engineers sit together to manually construct a high-level architecture/deployment model of the system (initially on a whiteboard; subsequently in Elmo).[1]

A typical goal is improving performance of a service, or preparing for increased load on an endpoint provided by a service. Given such a goal, a natural starting point (the service-under-investigation) is often clear.

Depending on the aims of the architects and deployment engineers, they can subsequently select Elmo's "sensitivities perspective" (to improve a service's performance) or its "impact perspective" (to find potential scalability issues). In the former case, Elmo computes and shows to which services the service-under-investigation is sensitive; in the latter case, Elmo computes and shows which services will be impacted by an increased load on the service-under-investigation.

Based on Elmo's analyses, the architects and deployment engineers can subsequently pick services that, undesirably, are sensitive to the service-under-investigation (or vice versa), formulate a refactoring goal to alleviate these sensitivities, and let Elmo explore the search space. Finally, Elmo reports candidate refactorings, along with a number of metrics to compare them against each other. The architects and deployment engineers can evaluate these options, and apply the one of their choice to the model.

5   First Industrial Case Study

JoinData is a digital highway for farm-generated data, used nation-wide in the Netherlands. It allows for data exchange in the agricultural sector. For example, milking-robots on the farm, suppliers of animal feed, or laboratories that provide reports on soil can exchange information with accountancy firms, governmental organisations, or farm management systems. *EDI-Circle* is the messaging component of the JoinData platform and acts as a hub that receives, adapts and routes messages between parties. Due to expected growth, the scalability and performance of EDI-Circle need to improve. We compared (1) the manual analysis and proposed course of action by the lead architect of the EDI-Circle project with (2) Elmo's automated analysis.

The service-under-investigation was determined to be the *download* service s, the primary service provided by EDI-Circle. Elmo's analysis confirmed that s had

---

[1] Note that although this is currently a manual activity, we are planning to investigate integration of Elmo with existing tools to (semi-)automatically generate models of existing service-oriented systems (e.g., [11]).

many sensitivities. The proposed solution by the architect was "to change the whole system, since everything is connected", by trying to improve the through-put of *all* services involved, starting with the database. Elmo's analysis, however, showed that some services to which s was sensitive, logically should not affect s's performance. Elmo therefore proposed a much more localized chain of refac-torings, *excluding the database*, specifically aimed to alleviate these unnecessary sensitivities. This solution was not proposed by the architect; to find it, Elmo explored a space of 1,143,227 possible scenarios. This is first evidence that Elmo can offer significant benefits.

6 Related Work and Novelty

- *Qualitative vs. quantitative.* Contrasting a large body of work on quantitative modeling (e.g., [2,4,12,14,21]), the models that First8 architects today use (and thus supported by Elmo) are *intentionally* qualitative. Although quan-titative models can be more accurate, such models require load functions, detailed descriptions, or actual implementations; these are often demanding to obtain. Also, calculating the performance of the architecture/deployment might not be instantaneous, but may require a lengthy simulation. Finally, small changes in deployments or algorithms, can have a big impact on per-formance, rendering painfully obtained performance measurements obsolete. To our knowledge, no other tools exist that take a similar approach to ours to aid in reasoning about refactorings of service-oriented systems, their archi-tectures, and their deployments. This places Elmo in a unique position.
- *Design refactorings vs. implementation refactorings.* There are also other architecture tools that aid in refactoring an existing architecture. They help in visualizing the architecture, detecting code smells like dependency cycles or validating architecture rules (e.g. [3,5,16,19,20]). These tools work at the implementation/code level and do not take actual deployment into account, nor can they evaluate performance sensitivities like Elmo does.
- *Monitoring.* Application Performance Monitoring (e.g. [1,6,7,17]) tools pro-vide a quick insight in actual interaction between services and aid in detecting real problems. They can only do this when software is actually deployed, not during design. Whereas these tools can identify performance bottlenecks, they have only very limited support for finding solutions. Elmo, in contrast, can automatically compute series of refactorings to achieve a given goal.
- *Modeling techniques.* UML Component Diagrams enable architects to docu-ment dependencies between components/services. A key difference with our approach is that component diagrams do not distinguish between push and pull operations [13] (i.e., component diagrams model *dependencies* between components, but they do not model the *directions of information flows* that push and pull operations additionally convey); in our model, this is vital infor-mation to reason about sensitivities between services. To provide such infor-mation in UML, complementary behavioral diagrams (e.g., *UML Sequence Diagrams*) can be used, but then the level of detail becomes too low for our

purpose, while at the same time a maintenance burden emerges. Also, mixing different types of diagrams is cumbersome.

It may be interesting to investigate whether a new *UML Profile* can be used to *extend* component diagrams with Elmo-like features (although we note that the UML specification suggests to use profiles for component diagrams only to capture information about whether the interface of one component "is suitable for consumption by the depending component" [18]).

References

1. AppDynamics LLC: AppDynamics. https://www.appdynamics.com
2. Bertoli, M., Casale, G., Serazzi, G.: JMT: performance engineering tools for system modeling. SIGMETRICS Perform. Eval. Rev. **36**(4), 10–15 (2009)
3. Bischofberger, W., Kühl, J., Löffler, S.: Sotograph – a pragmatic approach to source code architecture conformance checking. In: Oquendo, F., Warboys, B.C., Morrison, R. (eds.) EWSA 2004. LNCS, vol. 3047, pp. 1–9. Springer, Heidelberg (2004). https://doi.org/10.1007/978-3-540-24769-2_1
4. Brebner, P.: Real-world performance modelling of enterprise service oriented architectures: delivering business value with complexity and constraints (abstracts only). SIGMETRICS Perform. Eval. Rev. **39**(3), 12 (2011)
5. Caracciolo, A., Lungu, M.F., Nierstrasz, O.: A unified approach to architecture conformance checking. In: WICSA, pp. 41–50. IEEE Computer Society (2015)
6. Datadog: Datadog. https://www.datadoghq.com
7. DynaTrace LLC: DynaTrace. https://www.dynatrace.com
8. van Eekelen, M., Jongmans, S.S., Lamers, A.: Non-quantitative modeling of service-oriented architectures, refactorings, and performance. Tech. Rep. TR-OU-INF-2017-02, Open University of The Netherlands (2017)
9. Elmo Team: Elmo video. https://youtu.be/Oi9kxqh_GBs
10. Elmo Team: Elmo website. http://www.open.ou.nl/ssj/elmo
11. Granchelli, G., Cardarelli, M., Francesco, P.D., Malavolta, I., Iovino, L., Salle, A.D.: Microart: a software architecture recovery tool for maintaining microservice-based systems. In: ICSA Workshops, pp. 298–302. IEEE (2017)
12. Juan Ferrer, A., et al.: OPTIMIS: a holistic approach to cloud service provisioning. Future Gener. Comp. Syst. **28**(1), 66–77 (2012)
13. Kobryn, C.: Modeling components and frameworks with UML. Commun. ACM **43**(10), 31–38 (2000)
14. Kounev, S.: Performance modeling and evaluation of distributed component-based systems using queueing petri nets. IEEE Trans. Softw. Eng. **32**(7), 486–502 (2006)
15. Lamers, A., van Eekelen, M.: A lightweight method for analysing performance dependencies between services. In: Celesti, A., Leitner, P. (eds.) ESOCC Workshops 2015. CCIS, vol. 567, pp. 93–110. Springer, Cham (2016). https://doi.org/10.1007/978-3-319-33313-7_7
16. Lattix LDM2: Lattix Architect 10. http://lattix.com
17. New Relic: New Relic Inc. https://newrelic.com
18. Object Management Group: Unified Modeling Language 2.5.1 (2017). https://www.omg.org/spec/UML/2.5.1/
19. SonarSource: SonarQube. https://www.sonarqube.org
20. Structure101: Structure101 Studio. https://structure101.com
21. Zhu, L., Liu, Y., Bui, N.B., Gorton, I.: Revel8or: model driven capacity planning tool suite. In: ICSE, pp. 797–800. IEEE Computer Society (2007)

CEA: A Service for Cognitive Event Automation

Larisa Shwartz[1], Jinho Hwang[1(✉)], Hagen Völzer[2], Michael Nidd[2],
Murilo Goncalves Aguiar[3], Marcos Vinicius Landivar Paraiso[3],
and Letusa Valero[3]

[1] IBM T.J. Watson Research Center, New York, USA
{lshwart,jinho}@us.ibm.com
[2] IBM Zurich Research Lab, Zurich, Switzerland
{hvo,mni}@zurich.ibm.com
[3] IBM Global Technology Services, São Paulo, Brazil
{murilog,mparaiso,letusa}@br.ibm.com

Abstract. The IT service management is transforming or evolving with artificial intelligence. A data-driven and knowledge-based approach potentiates the IT service management optimization and automation with the goal of delivering better business outcomes. In this demo, we show our framework, cognitive event automation (CEA), that applies artificial intelligence to the automated resolution of incident tickets, and the methodology and technologies for creating knowledge by analyzing tickets, eliminating those that do not require action as well as auto-resolving those that do. The case study shows CEA can help the IT service management system to deliver better business outcomes.

Keywords: Cognitive systems · Data analytics · Event management

1 Design and Operation

As the number of industries experiencing digital disruption growing, using information technology to enable business advantage becomes a critical success factor for enterprises. We demonstrate here a framework that focuses on IT service management optimization and automation with the goal of transforming IT Service management lifecycle to deliver better business outcomes through a data-driven and knowledge-based approach.

We focus our discussion on applying artificial intelligence (AI) to the automated resolution of incident tickets, and the methodology and technologies for creating knowledge by analyzing tickets, eliminating those that do not require action as well as auto-resolving those that do. The framework relies on novel domain specific techniques in data mining and machine learning to generate insights from operational context, among them generation of predictive rules, deep neural ranking and hierarchical multi-armed bandit algorithms.

© Springer Nature Switzerland AG 2019
X. Liu et al. (Eds.): ICSOC 2018 Workshops, LNCS 11434, pp. 425–429, 2019.
https://doi.org/10.1007/978-3-030-17642-6_37

Our framework, cognitive event automation (CEA), consists of analytical micro-services that target knowledge and model building through off-line learning, as well as micro-services utilized at run-time. CEA allows to fully automate event handling flow for isolated anomalies as well as for complex syndromes (i.e. correlated events) manifested by business workload performance degradation. Through taking advantage of AI that incorporates on-line learning and feedback loop analysis of historical data, CEA continuously improves recommendations for automated resolution of complex syndromes.

CEA first detects a syndrome by identifying a group of symptoms which have a common root cause. It then enriches the syndrome information with probable root causes and their diagnostics. Subsequently the diagnostics are run on the systems which exhibited anomalous behavior. The data collected is used for the root cause disambiguation. Finally, the derived root cause is submitted to a Resolution Planning Engine (RPE). It returns an optimized plan of actions for the remediation of the identified root cause. RPE is an artificial intelligence (AI) planner that uses cost-optimal planning with applications in plan recognition, diagnosis and explanation generation.

Coordinated execution of the plan performed by appropriate automation engines on each segment of the hybrid environment. All details captured during resolution and healing of a complex symptom are stored in IBM's Data Lake and used for further analysis and continual improvement across all customers. New capabilities improve the quality of services provided to customers, drive enhanced yield for automated event and incident resolution, and offer an increased operational visibility for clients and service providers alike.

2   System Overview

Analytical systems need higher flexibility to accommodate dynamic addition of the business functionalities, and larger scalability for processing power of growing data size. The data or processing models in nature can change frequently, thus data processing components should always be ready for the replacement when models or routines are changed or upgraded. That is, the components may run as stateless and this allows them to be replaced anytime the new versions are ready. In addition, the data processing components need to be available all the time or the results returned could be misleading or malformed.

The microservice is a new computing paradigm with new architectural style that overcomes the limitations of monolithic architectural style. The microservice architecture consists of a collection of loosely coupled services, each of which implements a business functionality. The microservice architecture enables scalability, flexibility, and also continuous devops (development/deployment) of large, complex applications. Especially, it enables an organization to evolve its technology stack [2,3,5]. CEA uses the IBM microservices framework (Amagam8 or Istio in Kubernetes) to support the data processing components.

The microservice framework itself can cope with failure scenarios when with multiple services, but the virtual machine failure is not well supported.

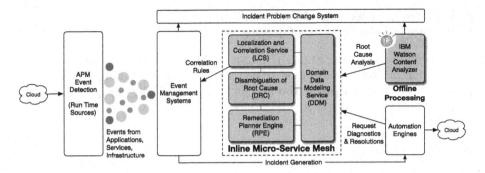

Fig. 1. Architecture of Cognitive Event Automation

CEA adopts the docker swarm cluster to provide the virtual machine availability. Figure 1 illustrates the architecture of CEA. In large, the CEA framework consists of two components: offline processing and inline processing. The details are in the following sections.

2.1 Offline Processing

The services for off-line processing used for building knowledge corpus and modeling. Domain Data Modeling service include:

- Pattern recognition with frequency analysis of the clusters
- Build a knowledge corpus of root causes and associated dependencies for these complex incidents [4, 7]
- Recommender system for automation for troubleshooting of a single symptom or a complex event

Correlation and Localization Service (CLS) is an off-line service as well. CLS identifies clusters of events attributable to a complex incident as well as clusters of correlated events. Often, multiple alerts have the same root cause, but distinct tickets are generated for them, which translates into unnecessary tickets with unnecessary overhead, uncoordinated ticket response, response without full information. By identifying this clusters and providing correlation rules, CLS aliviate and some cases eliminate these issues. [1] It also quantifies the opportunity and computes a KPI to measure progress.

2.2 Inline Processing

Inline processing is provided by services with capabilities for reasoning over gathered runtime data and knowledge corpus built off-line. Disambiguation of Root Causes (DRC) is build as a recommender system that

- Enriches event data using knowledge corpus
- Determining possible root causes

– Identifies steps necessary for full diagnosis
– Provides optimal sequence of diagnostics steps

Remediation Planning Engine (RPE) is an AI planing that provides sequence of steps for problem remediation. RPE is capable of generating a number of possible cost-optimum plans, the system recommends the top plan (shortest path) [6].

3   Case Study

One of leading financial organizations in Latin America has a number of locations and IT environments that varies greatly. The company has both external service provider as well as internal support for their IT environments. While they would like to keep supporting some of their IT internally, they recognize that it becomes time and resource consuming, and often challenging from skills perspective. IBM is an external service provider for the company, and they selected IBM to enable automation for insuring consistent quality of provided support, and also embarking on continuous-learning solution. The first of a kind solution Cognitive Event Automation (CEA) is able to correlate multiple symptoms into one composite incident and orchestrate an automated troubleshooting and resolution through use of Watson and AI infused automated reasoning. The company experienced a drop of incident tickets of 15%, and was able to take advantage of self-configurable automations to achieve the level of automated resolution of well above 60% of their incidents from monitoring, and to reduce number of complex incidents that become major incidents in half. It allowed the company to keep their workforce focused on their immediate business, knowing that their IT is well supported through machine to machine cognitive process.

4   Conclusion

In this demo, we have showed the cognitive event automation framework that is a data-driven and knowledge-based IT service management system. CEA applies artificial intelligence to the automated resolution of incident tickets, and the methodology and technologies for creating knowledge by analyzing tickets, eliminating those that do not require action as well as auto-resolving those that do. The case study shows CEA can help the IT service management optimization and automation with the goal of delivering better business outcomes.

References

1. Botezatu, M.M., Bogojeska, J., Giurgiu, I., Voelzer, H., Wiesmann, D.: Multi-view incident ticket clustering for optimal ticket dispatching. In: Proceedings of the 21st ACM SIGKDD International Conference on Knowledge Discovery and Data Mining, pp. 1711–1720. ACM (2015)
2. Dragoni, N., Lanese, I., Larsen, S.T., Mazzara, M., Mustafin, R., Safina, L.: Microservices: how to make your application scale. CoRR abs/1702.07149 (2017). http://arxiv.org/abs/1702.07149
3. Francesco, P.D., Malavolta, I., Lago, P.: Research on architecting microservices: trends, focus, and potential for industrial adoption. In: 2017 IEEE International Conference on Software Architecture (ICSA), pp. 21–30, April 2017
4. Perng, C., Thoenen, D., Grabarnik, G., Ma, S., Hellerstein, J.: Data-driven validation, completion and construction of event relationship networks. In: Proceedings of the ninth ACM SIGKDD, pp. 729–734. ACM (2003)
5. Sill, A.: The design and architecture of microservices. IEEE Cloud Comput. **3**(5), 76–80 (2016)
6. Sohrabi, S., Riabov, A.V., Udrea, O., Hassanzadeh, O.: Finding diverse high-quality plans for hypothesis generation. In: ECAI Frontiers in Artificial Intelligence and Applications, vol. 285, pp. 1581–1582. IOS Press, The Netherlands (2016)
7. Wang, Q., Zhou, W., Zeng, C., Li, T., Shwartz, L., Grabarnik, G.Y.: Constructing the knowledge base for cognitive it service management. In: 2017 IEEE International Conference on Services Computing (SCC). IEEE (2017)

BluePlan: A Service for Automated Migration Plan Construction Using AI

Malik Jackson[1], John Rofrano[2], Jinho Hwang[2(✉)], and Maja Vukovic[2]

[1] University of Maryland Baltimore County, Baltimore, MD, USA
mjacks3@umbc.edu
[2] IBM T.J. Watson Research Center, New York, USA
{rofrano,jinho,maja}@us.ibm.com

Abstract. Migration of legacy applications to Cloud has been growing steadily over the past years, driven by the promise of greater flexibility, scalability, and lower management costs. However, the complexity of the migration tasks and activities makes transformation of the current service and application architectures a long and difficult process that involves months of migration planning and execution. In this paper, we present a service application *BluePlan* and its implementation, which employs an artificial intelligence (AI) planner that optimizes the end-to-end migration planning with constraints, and creates migration plans for execution. The AI planner service serves to expedite and simplify the migration planning process by defining the clients' constraints and resources in a simplified format that abstracts the user's need to hard-code domains and problems. This capability is exposed as a service and evaluated for migration plans for over 500 hundred clients with varying independent memory, cpu and time constraints in the span of a few minutes, thereby enabling migration project manager and migration architects to reason about potential migration plans, and replan as needed.

Keywords: AI planning · Cloud computing · Cloud migration

1 Introduction

Cloud Migration projects are typically long running engagements that comprise multiple sub-processes including: analysis and understanding of the client's operating environment, a design phase where servers are grouped into migration waves, the setup of the target environment and pre-configuration, migration execution, post-execution processing, and finally testing of the target environment [4,5,10].

Once the migration opportunity is uncovered, the design phase is critical in enabling an efficient plan of action for migration, which takes into account number of business and technical dependencies such as application release dates, change windows, resource availability of the infrastructure (e.g. provisioned landing pads), etc. While individual servers get migrated, it is really the business

© Springer Nature Switzerland AG 2019
X. Liu et al. (Eds.): ICSOC 2018 Workshops, LNCS 11434, pp. 430–434, 2019.
https://doi.org/10.1007/978-3-030-17642-6_38

applications that are being moved so understanding what IT assets comprise a business application and migrating them together is essential for success. To date, this uses algorithms to discover server affinity [1,11,12], and the rest of the planning is project management driven [3,8]. As a result, the project manager needs to handle any dependencies and/or constraints that arise as the migration is scheduled for execution. This is not often straightforward, especially when considering the scale of the client's environment, reaching over 10 K endpoints, and multiple interdependencies [6,7,9].

In this demo, we show the use of our AI planning service to schedule and manage the design phase of migration processes, thereby enabling a project manager to reason about multiple what-if scenarios and look into alternative cost or time driven choices.

2 System Overview

AI or automated planning is the realization of strategies or action sequences with domain definition and problem scenarios [2]. Unlike classical control and classification problems, the solutions are complex and must be discovered and optimized in multidimensional space.

PDDL (Planning Domain Definition Language) provides a syntax for representing planning problems. Traditional AI planning problems are represented and solved using two inputs: a domain file and a problem file. A domain file is composed of the name of the domain; a list of predicates, and each predicate's variables (recall that a predicate represents a single property of a state) a list of actions to change the state of the world; for each action, its parameters, preconditions, and effects may be stated. A problem file lists the domain, objects that can be used in place of variables, a description of the initial state (using the predicates listed in the domain file), and goal criteria (again, using predicates). The same domain file will be useful for many different problem scenarios.

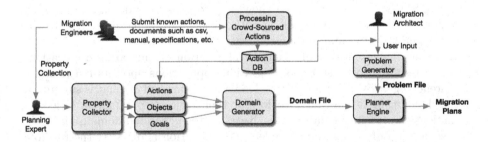

Fig. 1. Architecture of the AI planner service for cloud migration

Figure 1 illustrates the architecture of the service utilizing AI planning for cloud migration. The end product of the service are the migration plans, providing instruction on moving servers to the cloud in an efficient manner with respect their resource costs and dependencies.

The core of the service revolves around the planner engine, for which we have used a derivative of the well-known, Fast-Forward planner called the Metric-FF planner. We utilized this planner primarily because of its continued support, public license usage rights and its compatibility with PDDLv2.1+; 2.1 and later versions support a number of packages that extend the functionality of the language. Among these, we are particularly interested in fluents, which allow for numeric variables, (earlier versions of PDDL typically only utilize binary variable values) and functions which are built in with templates for operating on them, typing, which assigns a rigid type to each object, and adl, which permits disjunctions and equality statements in more contexts.

The system is also comprised of the domain and problem files, defined earlier. In the context of migration, most of the defined actions and predicates deal with server/application statuses and shutdown/startups, while the problem file instantiates them.

Subject Matter Experts (SMEs) of migration planning may appreciate the computational complexity of planning engines, but not necessarily the complexity of its syntax and logical rules when trying to model a scenario. Therefore, we thought to generate these files ourselves given sufficient knowledge, currently in the form of spreadsheets, from the user. The syntax of the spreadsheet data is specified on the application. While the data must be formatted descriptively to parse/translate it into PDDL and is not yet finalized, we intend to design an intuitive format that should be relatively easy to encode.

In the domain file, necessary information can be broken down into actions, object types, predicates, functions, and goals within the context of changes required to reach the desired state with actions. Our system's interface allows users to upload files containing object/predicate/function and goal information where it is then processed by the Property Collector module and used to craft a domain file. Since general action steps within migration might differ from one SME to another, we thought to build a database to collect them and allow public entities to change and enrich the list themselves.

While SMEs generally have the knowledge to model the domain, users such as migration architects (MAs), along with clients they want to migrate to the cloud, should have the information to create problems within a specific domain. A MA's knowledge base should include information on migrating applications including resource costs, status of migration applications upon its initial state, and intended goals which they may upload and use instead of what is submitted in the domain. MAs may need to format their object's parameters based on the actions created in the database or based on the generated domain file itself. This separation of domain and problem file generation allow MAs the freedom to morph their data for any domain model and SMEs to create domains for any number of problem cases. We will now take a more in depth look at a use case of our service from our development.

3 Case Study

To demonstrate the usage of our service, we developed a use case for the migration of 500 servers to a set of theoretical cloud hosts. We assume the servers are running on their original hosts with arbitrary applications running that, along with the system itself, must be shut down before the actual migration step can take place. Since there are usually more servers needing to move than is physically possible in a single migration session, we define multiple groups of servers to be moved which we call "waves".

In our domain knowledge file, our primary resources of intrigue include quantities of CPU, memory, and effort hours allocate-able during each "wave" of migration, as well as the cost associated with each individual server. We define effort hours as the average amount of time needed to complete an individual migration, given standard subject matter skill level and connection speeds. Our primary predicates are intuitively related to waves and the state of the servers, such as migration_status, server_status and shutdown server apps.

In the action database for our service, we loaded in actions for shutting down and starting up the server and its applications. In addition to parameters affected, the system must know pre-conditions and post-conditions of the action: before migration for instance, the system and its action must be shut down.

In our problem file we list all objects to be instantiated as well as values for predicates and functions that utilize those particular objects. Values for the cpu cost, memory cost, and effort hours cost in this use case were randomized, being whole integers between 2 and 32, 10 and 50, and 1 and 5 respectively. We also initialize values for our wave with capacities of 10, 128, and 96 for memory, cpu, and effort.

Our goal statement in this model and problem is simply to migrate all clients in a wave. In doing this, the planner will need to shut down all server applications before shutting down and migrating all servers. While the actions exist to require it, we do not mandate the system turn on the system or its applications. Since turning them back on only elongates the path to the goal state, we should not expect to see any system or services started in our plan.

Sending the required information through the service, we eventually arrive at the generation of our migration plans. The system shuts down all applications and servers before migrating them based on available resources. The plan generates in the matter of a few minutes after parsing 500 object initialized objects spanning over three thousand lines of PDDL initializations. As expected, it does not waste actions by turning any applications or servers back on to reach the desired goal.

4 Conclusion

We have shown the use of our AI planning service to schedule and manage the design phase of migration processes. The system design allows migration subject matter experts to have flexible definitions of migration and create plans with migration preferences. Our use case study with the migration of 500 servers shows the effectiveness of the AI planner. Furthermore, the study testifies the validity of our system in providing an abstraction for creating planning problems that prevent needing any knowledge of PDDL to solve.

References

1. Branch, J.W., Murthy, K., Shwartz, L., Olsson, E., Larsen, R.A.: Bizmap: a framework for mapping business applications to it infrastructure. In: 2015 IFIP/IEEE International Symposium on Integrated Network Management (IM), pp. 1377–1383 (2015)
2. Herry, H., Anderson, P., Wickler, G.: Automated planning for configuration changes. In: Proceedings of the 25th International Conference on Large Installation System Administration, pp. 5–5. LISA 2011, USENIX Association, Berkeley (2011). http://dl.acm.org/citation.cfm?id=2208488.2208493
3. Hwang, J.: Computing resource transformation, consolidation and decomposition in hybrid clouds. In: 2015 11th International Conference on Network and Service Management (CNSM), pp. 144–152, November 2015
4. Hwang, J.: Toward beneficial transformation of enterprise workloads to hybrid clouds. IEEE Trans. Netw. Serv. Manag. **13**(2), 295–307 (2016)
5. Hwang, J., Huang, Y.W., Vukovic, M., Jermyn, J.: Cloud transformation analytics services: a case study of cloud fitness validation for server migration. In: 2015 IEEE International Conference on Services Computing, pp. 387–394, June 2015
6. Hwang, J., Vukovic, M., Anerousis, N.: FitScale: scalability of legacy applications through migration to cloud. In: Sheng, Q.Z., Stroulia, E., Tata, S., Bhiri, S. (eds.) ICSOC 2016. LNCS, vol. 9936, pp. 123–139. Springer, Cham (2016). https://doi.org/10.1007/978-3-319-46295-0_8
7. Jermyn, J., Hwang, J., Bai, K., Vukovic, M., Anerousis, N., Stolfo, S.: Improving readiness for enterprise migration to the cloud. In: Proceedings of the Middleware Industry Track, pp. 5:1–5:7. Industry papers. ACM, New York (2014). https://doi.org/10.1145/2676727.2676732
8. Kim, I.K., Zeng, S., Young, C., Hwang, J., Humphrey, M.: A supervised learning model for identifying inactive VMS in private cloud data centers. In: Proceedings of the Industrial Track of the 17th International Middleware Conference, pp. 2:1–2:7. Middleware Industry 2016. ACM, New York (2016). https://doi.org/10.1145/3007646.3007654
9. Nidd, M., Bai, K., Hwang, J., Vukovic, M., Tacci, M.: Automated business application discovery. In: 2015 IFIP/IEEE International Symposium on Integrated Network Management (IM), pp. 794–797, May 2015
10. Vukovic, M., Hwang, J.: Cloud migration using automated planning. In: NOMS 2016–2016 IEEE/IFIP Network Operations and Management Symposium, pp. 96–103, April 2016
11. Wu, D., Hwang, J., Vukovic, M., Anerousis, N.: BlueSight: automated discovery service for cloud migration of enterprises. In: Drira, K., Wang, H., Yu, Q., Wang, Y., Yan, Y., Charoy, F., Mendling, J., Mohamed, M., Wang, Z., Bhiri, S. (eds.) ICSOC 2016. LNCS, vol. 10380, pp. 211–215. Springer, Cham (2017). https://doi.org/10.1007/978-3-319-68136-8_27
12. Zhang, B., Hwang, J., Ma, L., Wood, T.: Towards security-aware virtual server migration optimization to the cloud. In: 2015 IEEE International Conference on Autonomic Computing, pp. 71–80, July 2015

ELeCTRA: Induced Usage Limitations Calculation in RESTful APIs

Antonio Gamez-Diaz[1]([⊠]), Pablo Fernandez[1], Cesare Pautasso[2],
Ana Ivanchikj[2], and Antonio Ruiz-Cortes[1]

[1] Universidad de Sevilla, Seville, Spain
{agamez2,pablofm,aruiz}@us.es
[2] Software Institute, Faculty of Informatics, USI Lugano, Lugano, Switzerland
{cesare.pautasso,ana.ivanchikj}@usi.ch

Abstract. As software architecture design is evolving to microservice paradigms, RESTful APIs become the building blocks of applications. In such a scenario, a growing market of APIs is proliferating and developers face the challenges to take advantage of this reality. For example, third-party APIs typically define different usage limitations depending on the purchased Service Level Agreement (SLA) and, consequently, performing a manual analysis of external APIs and their impact in a microservice architecture is a complex and tedious task. In this demonstration paper, we present ELeCTRA, a tool to automate the analysis of induced usage limitations in an API, derived from its usage of external APIs. This tool takes the structural, conversational and SLA specifications of the API, generates a visual dependency graph and translates the problem into a *constraint satisfaction optimization problem* (CSOP) to obtain the optimal usage limitations.

1 Motivation

In recent years, there has been a clear trend towards the micro-service architectural style where each component (i.e. micro-service) can evolve, scale and get deployed independently. This style increases the flexibility of the system and has been applied in demanding web applications such as eBay, Amazon or Netflix.

From an engineering perspective, a key element of these architectures, with respect to the modeling and implementation of microservices, is the use of the RESTful paradigm. From a business perspective, this microservice architecture tendency represents a recent shift in software engineering towards API-driven building and consumption, fostering a breeding landscape for RESTful API market in which composite service providers face new issues, such as, how to set their usage limitations accordingly to 3rd party providers' usage limitations [6].

This work has been partially supported by the European Commission (FEDER), the Spanish and the Andalusian R&D&I programs (grants TIN2015-70560-R (BELI), P12–TIC–1867 (COPAS) and TIN2014-53986-REDT (RCIS)) the FPU scholarship program, granted by the Spanish Ministry of Education, Culture and Sports (FPU15/02980).

X. Liu et al. (Eds.): ICSOC 2018 Workshops, LNCS 11434, pp. 435–438, 2019.
https://doi.org/10.1007/978-3-030-17642-6_39

Automatic discovery of usage limitations requires the serialization of developers' knowledge regarding the SLA usage limitations based on the API structure and the implemented RESTful conversation [8]. This automatic discovery becomes crucial when there are frequent changes in the usage limitations of the external services or when the microservice architecture itself experiences changes. In this automatic discovery of usage limitations scenario, a key concept is the *boundary service* that corresponds to an API that has the closest interaction with the end-user by means of actions in the GUI. Specifically, each action in the GUI triggers what we coin as *root operations* (composed by a given path and an HTTP method) that are typically related to the user story. Commonly, as a facade, all the boundary services are deployed behind an API Gateway [7] that enhances the security of the infrastructure.

Given the frequent and multiple ways in which the third party APIs' usage limitations evolve and are likely to keep evolving, when building an application, we need to adapt our customer's expectations regarding the performance of the tool (i.e., how many operations can be generated over time and how long it will take to produce an operation). Therefore, to rapidly react to these changes, there is a need of automating the process to obtain the usage limitations that a provider can offer to its end-users based on certain optimal criteria in a microservice architecture, such as minimizing the requests made to the third-party providers. Specifically, the problem addressed is finding the usage limitations of a root operation induced by the rest of the services (internal and external) composing the microservice architecture. Despite the fact that knowing the usage limitations in the internal services can be useful, calculating the usage limitations in the root operations (i.e., the operations closer to the end users) is more valuable since they help the service provider to set its own usage limitations to end users and to understand the induced service level agreement he can offer to its users.

In this demonstration paper, we propose a tool that, given: (i) the external usage limitations (as derived from the purchased SLA) as well as the boundary service structure and root operation conversation; it translates the problem into a *constraint satisfaction optimization problem* (CSOP) to obtain the induced usage limitations for the specified root operation.

2   Using ELeCTRA to Calculate the Usage Limitations

In order to illustrate the problem, let us consider the following example: we have developed a report generation application for the internal evaluation of the researchers in our university. For this purpose, we needed to collect, per researcher, the quality indicators of his/her publications. After considering different bibliometric providers, we opted for the Scopus API [4] as it provides the set of publications as well as the CitesScore^{TM} index, an impact factor index calculated by Elsevier. Specifically, our application depends upon four Scopus APIs. Per researcher, the following invocations are needed: (i) retrieving the simple list of publications; (ii) collecting the details regarding each publication; (iii) gathering the details concerning each publication's venue (journal or conference).

Each of these Scopus APIs present different usage limitations [6], so, depending on the input and the usage limitations of each API operation, the induced usage limitations for our end-users will vary. The question to be addressed is: *what is the maximum amount of researchers per week for which this report can be generated without over-passing the Scopus API usage limitations?*

We use ELeCTRA[1] to answer the question. First, we have to model the structural viewpoint of each Scopus RESTful service using the Open API Specification (OAS) [3], as well as the usage limitations by using the SLA4OAI Specification [5]. Each of these models should be publicly available through an URL. Finally, using the embedded editor in ELeCTRA, the x-conversation model is introduced to define the dependencies between the internal and external services, as well as the parameters needed to calculate automatically the usage limitations. This example is preloaded at ELeCTRA and can be accessed by selecting the *simple example*. ELeCTRA is composed of two different microservices (ELeCTRA-DOT and ELeCTRA-CSOP) and a user interface (ELeCTRA-UI) accessible through a web browser. This UI includes a textual editor so that a user can directly modify the *x-conversation* document and visualize the *OAS* and *SLA4OAI* models. When the user saves the model, two actions are carried out. On the one hand, an invocation to ELeCTRA-DOT, the graphical representation microservice, is performed. The *x-conversation* model is parsed and according to a set of rules, it is converted to a graph using the *dot* [1] notation. A png image is returned back to the UI. On the other hand, a request to ELeCTRA-CSOP, the CSOP model generator and solver microservice, is developed in order to calculate the usage limitations for the boundary operation.

ELeCTRA-DOT first represents all the RESTful requests (i.e., each pair of method and path) as the nodes of the graph by using the structural information present in the OAS model. Then, an edge between two operations is included if they are related in the *x-conversation* model. Next, this edge is labeled with the information about the number of invocations based on the x-conversation mode. Finally, for each operation of each service, the usage limitations information is retrieved by means of the SLA4OAI extension. ELeCTRA-CSOP, on the other hand, is the main microservice in this tool, since it is responsible for transforming the *x-conversation* model to a constraint satisfaction optimization problem in order to obtain the usage limitations for an operation. By using a set of rule constructs, the *x-conversation* is transformed into a set of parameters (e.g., the values of the usage limitations, the number of invocations from an operation to the next one), variables (e.g., the quota of the boundary operation to be maximized) and constraints (e.g., the sum of the requests made to a certain operation should not overpass the quota value for this operation). Specifically, this microservice uses the MiniZinc's [2] syntax, a language designed for specifying constrained optimization and decision problems over integers and real numbers. Once the problem has been successfully translated and validated, ELeCTRA-CSOP invokes the solver through the MiniZinc interface and gets the response back. Then, ELeCTRA-UI

---

[1] https://electra.governify.io.

receives the information and sends the updated usage plans to ELeCTRA-DOT to complete the remaining usage limitations. Finally, all this information is presented to the end user.

3   Instructions for the Organizers

This software tool is bundled into a v10.6.0 Node.js application, running in a Windows 10 system which should have installed (and added to the user PATH environment variable) Minizinc v2.1.7 and Graphviz v2.38.0.

Nevertheless, for the sake of simplicity and portability, authors have packed the entire app into a Docker Image[2]. Therefore, any x86_64 machine with Docker[3] will be able to run the application by typing: `docker run -p 8080:80 isagroup/governify-electra`.

Furthermore, to avoid any installation issue, the online web application is deployed at: https://electra.governify.io.

The demonstration video is available at: http://youtu.be/axbkDax1N9g.

References

1. Graphviz. https://graphviz.gitlab.io/_pages/doc/info/lang.html
2. Minizinc. http://www.minizinc.org/downloads/doc-latest/minizinc-tute.pdf
3. Open API Specification. https://www.openapis.org
4. Scopus API. https://dev.elsevier.com/api_docs.html
5. SLA4OAI Specification. https://github.com/isa-group/SLA4OAI-Specification
6. Gamez-Diaz, A., Fernandez, P., Ruiz-Cortes, A.: An analysis of RESTful APIs offerings in the industry. In: Maximilien, M., Vallecillo, A., Wang, J., Oriol, M. (eds.) ICSOC 2017. LNCS, vol. 10601, pp. 589–604. Springer, Cham (2017). https://doi.org/10.1007/978-3-319-69035-3_43
7. Gámez-Díaz, A., Fernández-Montes, P., Ruiz-Cortés, A.: Towards SLA-driven API gateways. In: JCIS (2015)
8. Ivanchikj, A., Pautasso, C., Schreier, S.: Visual modeling of RESTful conversations with RESTalk. J. Softw. Syst. Model. **17**(3), 1031–1051 (2018). https://doi.org/10.1007/s10270-016-0532-2

---

[2] https://hub.docker.com/r/isagroup/governify-electra.
[3] https://docs.docker.com/install/.

Offering Artificial Intelligence Development Situation Analysis Service for Users

Xiujuan Xu[1,2], Tingting Jiang[1,2], Shimin Shan[1,2], Jun Ni[1,2], Kai Wang[1,2], Zhenlong Xu[3], and Yu Liu[1,2(✉)]

[1] School of Software, Dalian University of Technology, Dalian 116620, China
{xjxu,yuliu}@dlut.edu.cn
[2] Key Laboratory for Ubiquitous Network and Service Software of Liaoning Province, Dalian 116620, China
[3] School of Management, Dalian University of Technology, Dalian 116620, China

Abstract. With the development of artificial intelligence (AI) industry, the research field is more and more closely related to AI industry. It is increasingly important to analyze the development trend of AI, predict and grasp the research direction, and provide industrial transformation in time. There are many kinds of AI classification, and the scale of literature data is also very large. In this paper we propose a visual analysis system based on micro-service architecture, which is an efficient, robust and easily extended and easy-to-use visual platform for AI development situation analysis. Our paper describes the usage of the system in detail.

1 Introduction

This paper provides users with AI development situation analysis and visualization services. Web-based remote visualization system: the remote visualization system provides high-performance visualization capabilities to end users who may not have sufficient local software and hardware resources by separating the visualization server from the end-user platform. In particular, remote systems address the visualization of large data sets that can't be stored locally or transmitted to the local platform. Meanwhile, the micro-service architecture improves the expansibility of system functions with visual charts. Users can get the analysis of all aspects of the data provided by users, as well as the chart service and so on [1]. Main operations include: user data upload; select chart type, and set the chart's vertical and horizontal axes. A typical use case is as follows:

Tina is a scholar in the field of AI. She wants to know the research institutions and countries that have published more research results at the forefront of the industry in AI so as to focus on those top research. Therefore, she opened the corresponding service page of the system website, uploaded the current data information to the corresponding data template, and selected the data fields needed to be analyzed: published literature results, references, research institutions, countries and chart types.

© Springer Nature Switzerland AG 2019
X. Liu et al. (Eds.): ICSOC 2018 Workshops, LNCS 11434, pp. 439–442, 2019.
https://doi.org/10.1007/978-3-030-17642-6_40

Our system receives a request from Tina and will complete the following tasks for its selection. (1) The data uploaded by Tina will be abstracted into a data model. (2) The system provides the correct service interface for the selected chart types. (3) The field data selected by the service will be analyzed accordingly. (4) The system displays the data analysis results to Tina in visual charts.

Our main work includes the following aspects. According to the data provided by the user, the system will complete the establishment of data model. According to user's chart service and the need to display the data of field selection, the system will automatically generate the visual charts required by the user. Meanwhile, the system supports the interaction between the interface and the user to remind and supplement the missing input information and realize personalized configuration charts automatic generation of visual chart to meet the needs of users. At the same time, our system could support the interaction with the user interface to remind complement of lack of input information, and can realize the personalized configuration chart. Finally, after the user's modification and improvement, the output chart information will meet the user's needs basically [2].

The demonstration introduced in this paper is accessible via the link http://dcy.beyondcloud.cn/starter.html.

2   System Structure

Our system provides personalized visualization services for website users' data analysis needs. Figure 1 fully illustrates the composition of the system, including each service module, and the flow of data between modules.

As showed in Fig. 1, user query refers to the information selected by a user, including field information, chart type information, and so on. User data DB refers to the data source where a user needs to upload data locally.

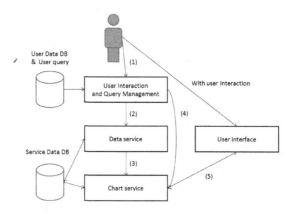

Fig. 1. System structure

The system is provided to all registered users, through the use of mobile tools such as computers or mobile phones. It can achieve the use of all functions.

User Interaction and Query Management (UIQM): This module mainly realizes the interaction between users and the system. A user could upload the data required for analysis and input the demand field request information and chart request into the system. The user passes in the information from the data stream 1 to the module, and the analytical information uploaded by the user is passed into the data service by the data stream 2, and the data service is modeled internally [3].

Data service: First, the data service receives a user's data file and saves it into the user database. Second, our system builds a data model for the data, and passes the model information into the chart service through the data flow 3. Finally, the model will be used to create charts for the next level of service.

Chart service: The user through the data flow 4-chart type to configure the field information request, also receives the data flow of 3 data information, the final internal operations to automatically generate visual chart. This model can produce a graphic interface, provided to the user interaction interface. The main work of this interface is the user to make custom changes to your chart service operations. And it eventually gets data analysis results in the form of a chart to show to the user [4] (detailed information on data flow 5).

3 Use Case

We break down Tina's operation and describe in detail her operation process: analysis published many research achievements, research institutions and countries at the forefront of the industry. UIQM analyzes Tina's uploaded data as well as input requests to continue the data flow. UIQM analyses Tina's chart selection 'histogram', and input field request: axis parameter: 'affilname' institution name, country, number of references, number of papers.

The query indicates that this request of the use case obtains a data analysis result, including the establishment of the chart and the selection of the chart display field in the operational process. All processes are shown below: (1) Create the data model: The data service automatically creates the data model according to the data input by a user. Tina input the paper information data table, including the fields of scholar, publication, number of references, institution, country, etc., to create the paper information model. (2) Create chart: 2 create charts: fields for selection: affilname institution name, country, number of references, number of papers generate the selected chart Histogram.

The chart results obtained by Tina show the following analysis results:

(1) The countries with the most published research results are the United States, China and the UK, respectively published papers: 37,351, 19,196, 8,049.
(2) The institutions with the most research achievements are: Carnegie University, published papers: 2682, cited number: 33,531; Stanford University, published papers: 2,115, citations: 31,239; Microsoft Research, published papers: 1,280, citations: 34,816.

(3) As well as the information of other cutting-edge institutions, the number of published papers and number of references are shown in the figure as a line with different colors.

Service models are connected through interfaces and combined together to complete users' requests. The data service establishes a data model and passes the model into the chart service to generate the corresponding data analysis results, which satisfies Tina's analysis demand for cutting-edge institutions.

4   Conclusions

In this work, we created an AI development analysis system by the way of a data visualization platform. Based on the results of the demand analysis, the micro service granularity is divided according to different requirements to meet the user's data analysis requirements. A fundamental challenge for any process-aware information system is to ensure compliance of modeled and executed business processes with imposed compliance rules stemming from guidelines, standards and laws.

For future work: (1) We will strengthen the security protection of the system to ensure that the data in the system is not infringed, and the data security and confidentiality of the user are ensured. We need integrate and improve users' data management according to their needs further. (2) In response to the actual demand for explosive growth of data in the field of AI, the system's microservice support content will not be able to meet the needs of users. The timely update and expansion of services will be the direction in the future. (3) To facilitate the use of many non professionals, we will improve the user interaction and use simplification.

Acknowledgment. This work was supported in part by the Natural Science Foundation of China grant 61502069, 61672128, 61702076; the Fundamental Research Funds for the Central Universities (DUT18JC39, DUT17JC45).

References

1. Rademacher, F., Sachweh, S., Zündorf, A.: Analysis of service-oriented modeling approaches for viewpoint-specific model-driven development of microservice architecture. CoRR abs/1804.09946 (2018)
2. Kibria, M.G., Nguyen, K., Villardi, G.P., Zhao, O., Ishizu, K., Kojima, F.: Big data analytics, machine learning and artificial intelligence in next-generation wireless networks. IEEE Access, **99**:1 (2018). abs/1711.10089
3. Butka, P., Smatana, M., Novotná, V.: Interactive visualization of query results set from information retrieval using concept lattices. In: Borzemski, L., Świątek, J., Wilimowska, Z. (eds.) ISAT 2017. AISC, vol. 655, pp. 128–137. Springer, Cham (2018). https://doi.org/10.1007/978-3-319-67220-5_12
4. Kłoda, R., Piwiński, J., Szewczyk, R., Ostaszewska-Liżewska, A., Duchna, K.: Visualization river water level using internet technologies. In: Szewczyk, R., Havlik, D. (eds.) Recent Trends in Control and Sensor Systems in Emergency Management. AISC, vol. 675, pp. 14–22. Springer, Cham (2018). https://doi.org/10.1007/978-3-319-70452-4_2

TReAT: A Tool for Analyzing Relations Between Tasks in a Process

Pengbo Xiu$^{(\boxtimes)}$, Jian Yang$^{(\boxtimes)}$, and Weiliang Zhao$^{(\boxtimes)}$

Department of Computing, Macquarie University, Sydney, Australia
pengbo.xiu@outlook.com, {jian.yang,weiliang.zhao}@mq.edu.au

Abstract. It is challenging to analyze the control flow relations of tasks in a complex business process. To solve this problem, quite a few process abstraction and reduction techniques have been proposed. However, existing approaches are lacking of the support for network structures in control flows. In this demonstration, we present a graphical Web application, **TReAT** (**T**asks **Re**lation **A**nalyzing **T**ool). With TReAT, users can model their business processes and analyze relations between tasks in a process. Most common control flow structures including the network structure are supported by TReAT.

Keywords: BPM · Petri net · Web application · jsPlumb

1 Introduction

Process models are normally employed as central tools by business process management teams for capturing, understanding, analyzing, and improving work in organizations. Detailed analysis of business requirements often requests process modelers to extract specific relations between tasks in process models. One scenario is change management of service-based business processes introduced in our precious work [1]. From the perspective of a service provider, the consistency between service interfaces and its internal business process may be violated after changes occurring. The consistency requires that the flow relations of input and output messages performed by service interfaces are same with relations of the corresponding messages in the internal business process. It is easy to figure out that in Fig. 1A, the process and its provided service are consistent with each other, because the operations of the service and their related tasks of the process have the same sequential control flow relation. But for a much more complex process as Fig. 1B, it is difficult to find out the relations between the highlighted tasks without a comprehensive analysis.

In [1], we proposed a Petri-net-based process model with a set of control flow patterns. Then we developed an algebra-based method. A "postmark" is "pressed" on each token in each marking of a Petri net. The relations between highlighted tasks could be figured out by analyzing the postmark of the final marking of the Petri net. More details about the method are described in [1].

© Springer Nature Switzerland AG 2019
X. Liu et al. (Eds.): ICSOC 2018 Workshops, LNCS 11434, pp. 443–446, 2019.
https://doi.org/10.1007/978-3-030-17642-6_41

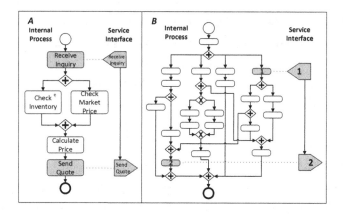

Fig. 1. The consistency between a provided service and the internal process

In this paper, we propose a Web application, TReAT[1], with functionalities to enable the modeling of a business process by Petri net and the analysis of the control flow relations between tasks. Existing model reduction or abstraction approaches [2, 3] can only handle the symmetrical structures that could be nested arbitrarily but could not overlap. Different with these work, our tool can support the non-symmetrical structures like a control dependency between two tasks from two parallel branches. In other words, by using this tool, complicated network structures in a process can be analyzed. A screen-shot of TReAT is shown in Fig. 2.

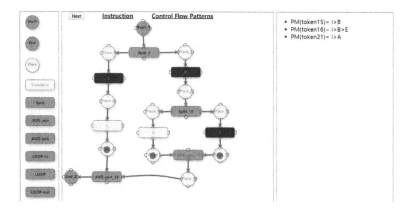

Fig. 2. A screen-shot of TReAT.

---

[1] The Web application at: https://git.io/fAlAA.
  A demo video is available at: https://youtu.be/MvYnjkXEhT8.

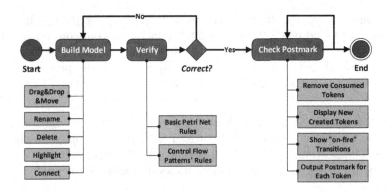

Fig. 3. The operation process of TReAT and its function modules

2   Overview of TReAT

TReAT is a Web application developed with HTML, CSS, JavaScript, jQuery, and jsPlumb. TReAT employs jsPlumb as the data visualization library that provides a means for developers to visually connect elements on their web pages by using SVG or Canvas [4]. The application can be executed with most browsers. It is not necessary to download and install other applications and plug-ins.

Figure 3 shows the operation process of TReAT with three packages (*Build Model*, *Verify*, and *Check Postmark*). The function modules of each package are shown as well. Details of these packages are described as follows.

Build Model. Users build their process models on the Web page.

- *Drag&Drop&Move* module enables users to drag a node from the left column, then drop it into the center column, and adjust the position of the node.
- *Rename* module enables a user to edit the node name by double clicking it.
- *Delete* module enables a user to delete a node by hovering the mouse on it and clicking the "×".
- *Highlight* module enables a user to highlight a transition by hovering the mouse on it and clicking the "★".
- *Connect* module supports to connect two nodes. A user can click one of four endpoints of one node and holds the arrow to point to an endpoint of another node. A connection can be removed by clicking it.

Verify. After building up a process model, users can click the "Verify" button to check the compliance with modeling rules. The modeling rules include the basic Petri Net rules and the control flow patterns rules.

- The *Basic Petri Net Rules* require that a net must consist of places, transitions, and arcs. Arcs can run from a place to a transition or vice versa, but never between places or between transitions.

- The *Control Flow Patterns' Rules* are as follows: 1. the process must have only one start/end place, 2. start/end place must have only one output/input arc, 3. each white node (non-starting/ending places and the task transitions) must have only one input arc and one output arc. 4. the process structure must follow the patterns on "Control Flow Patterns" page of TReAT.

Check Postmark. If no error being detected, the "Verify" button will be replaced by the "Next" button and a token with ID will appear in the starting place. The postmark of the token is shown in the right column. When the "Next" button being clicked, four function modules will be executed.

- *Remove Consumed Tokens* module detects and removes tokens in the input places of "on-fire" transitions.
- *Display New Created Tokens* module locates the output places of "firing" transitions and displays tokens in these transitions.
- *Show "on-fire" Transitions* module finds the "on-fire" transitions in the new marking and changes their borders into red.
- *Output Postmark for Each Token* module runs postmark algorithm and provides the output in the right column. The meanings of the algebraic expressions can be interpreted according to the instruction page of TReAT.

3   Conclusion and Future Work

TReAT has been developed in this work. This tool can help users to model their business process and analyze relations between tasks. Different with existing work, this tool can handle the network structures in business processes. For future extension on this application, a function module for automatically translating popular process modeling languages (e.g. BPMN, BPEL, and UML) into the Petri-net-based languages will be developed. This module will enable users to import their process modeled in BPMN directly to the application without translating and drawing the Petri-net-based model manually.

References

1. Xiu, P., Zhao, W., Yang, J.: Correctness verification for service-based business processes. In: IEEE International Conference on Web Services, pp. 752–759 (2017)
2. Esparza, J., Hoffmann, P.: Reduction rules for colored workflow nets. In: Stevens, P., Wąsowski, A. (eds.) FASE 2016. LNCS, vol. 9633, pp. 342–358. Springer, Heidelberg (2016). https://doi.org/10.1007/978-3-662-49665-7_20
3. Fdhila, W., Indiono, C., Rinderle-Ma, S., Reichert, M.: Dealing with change in process choreographies: design and implementation of propagation algorithms. Inf. Syst. **49**, 1–24 (2015)
4. jsPlumb Github Page. https://github.com/jsplumb/jsplumb. Accessed 29 Aug 2018

iCOP: IoT-Enabled Policing Processes

Francesco Schiliro[1,2], Amin Beheshti[1(✉)], Samira Ghodratnama[1],
Farhad Amouzgar[1], Boualem Benatallah[3], Jian Yang[1], Quan Z. Sheng[1],
Fabio Casati[4], and Hamid Reza Motahari-Nezhad[5]

[1] Macquarie University, Sydney, Australia
{amin.beheshti,jian.yang,michael.sheng}@mq.edu.au,
{francesco.schiliro,samira.ghodratnama,farhad.amouzgar}@hdr.mq.edu.au
[2] Australia Federal Police, Canberra, Australia
[3] University of New South Wales, Sydney, Australia
boualem@cse.unsw.edu.au
[4] University of Trento, Trento, Italy
fabio.casati@unitn.it
[5] EY AI Lab, San Jose, USA
hamid.motahari@ey.com

Abstract. Analyzing data-driven and knowledge intensive business processes is a key endeavor for today's enterprises. Recently, the Internet of Things (IoT) has been widely adopted for the implementation and integration of data-driven business processes within and across enterprises. For example, in law enforcement agencies, various IoT devices such as CCTVs, police cars and drones are augmented with Internet-enabled computing devices to sense the real world. This in turn, has the potential to change the nature of data-driven and knowledge intensive processes, such as criminal investigation, in policing. In this paper, we present a framework and a set of techniques to assist knowledge workers (e.g., a criminal investigator) in knowledge intensive processes (e.g., criminal investigation) to benefit from IoT-enabled processes, collect large amounts of evidences and dig for the facts in an easy way. We focus on a motivating scenario in policing, where a criminal investigator will be augmented by smart devices to collect data and to identify devices around the investigation location and communicate with them to understand and analyze evidences. We present iCOP, IoT-enabled COP assistant system, to enable IoT in policing and to accelerate the investigation process.

Keywords: Process data science · Data Analytics ·
Internet of things · Knowledge Lake · Law enforcement · Policing

1 Introduction

The introduction of Information and Communications Technology (ICT) has been a success factor for conducting police investigations. Advances in technology have improved the ways police collects, uses, and disseminates data and information. This include the advent of always-connected mobile devices, backed by

© Springer Nature Switzerland AG 2019
X. Liu et al. (Eds.): ICSOC 2018 Workshops, LNCS 11434, pp. 447–452, 2019.
https://doi.org/10.1007/978-3-030-17642-6_42

access to large amounts of open, social and police-specific private data. Among all these advances and technologies, the Internet of things (IoT) [2,11], i.e., the network of physical objects augmented with Internet-enabled computing devices to enable those objects sense the real world, can be a valuable asset for law enforcement agencies and has the potential to change the processes in this domain such as detection, prevention and investigation of crimes [6]. For example, considering cases such as Boston Bombing, one challenging task for the police officers and investigators would be to properly identify and interact with other officers on duty as well as Internet-enabled devices such as CCTV and drones, to enable fast and accurate information collection and analysis.

In this paper, we present a framework and a set of techniques to assist knowledge workers (e.g., a criminal investigator) in knowledge intensive processes (e.g., criminal investigation) to benefit from IoT-enabled processes, collect large amounts of evidences and dig for the facts in an easy way. We focus on a motivating scenario in policing, where a criminal investigator is augmented by smart devices (e.g., cell phone and watch) to collect data (e.g., recording voice, taking photos/videos and using location-based services), to identify the Things (e.g., CCTVs, police cars, officers on duty and drones) around the investigation location and communicate with them to understand and analyze evidences. This will accelerate the investigation process for cases such as Boston bombing (USA) where fast and accurate information collection and analysis would be vital. We implement a research prototype and present an IoT-enabled COP assistant system (iCOP), to: (i) facilitate the evidence collection: through an evidence-based GUI framework for policing. The goal is to provide a coherent and rigorous approach to improve the effectiveness and efficiency of a police officer in the field when responding to, detecting and preventing crime, and (ii) develop and explore how an evidence-based interface on a smart mobile device can be deployed in policing to provide an IoT-enabled approach, to interrogate a 'policing knowledge hub': an IoT infrastructure that can collaborate with internet-enabled devices to collect the data, extract events and facts, and link different part of the story using a real-time dashboard.

The iCOP framework will take a structured provision of knowledge approach, delivering a range of functions. This will include a workflow technology that controls how the frontline police officer gets information and job tasks. We leverage our previous work, i.e. Knowledge Lake [5], to transform the raw IoT data into a contextualized data and knowledge represented as a set of data summaries. The summaries, include a set of facts, information, and insights extracted from the raw data (ingested from open, social and IoT data sources) using data curation techniques [4] such as extraction, linking, annotation, and classification. The rest of the paper is organized as follows. In Sect. 2, we present an overview of the iCOP, while in Sect. 3 we describe our demonstration scenario.

2   System Overview

We present iCOP, IoT-enabled COP assistant system, to enable IoT in policing and to enable fast and accurate evidence collection and analysis. Figure 1 illustrates the iCOP Architecture. The main components include: IoT-Enabled Data Collection, Data Transformation and Data Analytics.

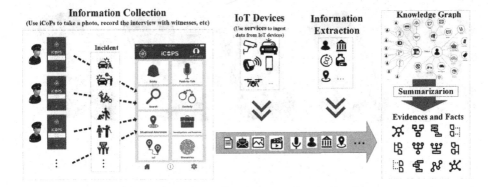

Fig. 1. The iCOP architecture.

IoT-Enabled Data Collection. The research questions at this level is how IoT can assist with responding, detecting crime as well as preventing crime [6]. The goal here is to contribute to research and thinking towards making the police officers more effective and efficient at the frontline, while augmenting their knowledge and decision management processes through information and communication technology. The proposed framework enables: (i) Manual Data Collection: at this level, the frontline police can take a photo of the scene, record video and audio, as well as writing notes and statements in an easy way; and (ii) IoT-Enabled Data collection: at this level, we develop ingestion services to extract the raw data from IoT devices such as CCTVs, location sensors in police cars and smart watches and police drones. We have used our previous work, Data Lake services [4], to organize this information in the data lake, i.e., centralized repository containing raw data stored in various data islands.

Data Transformation. At this level and inspired by Google Knowledge Graph [14] - a system that Google launched in 2012 that understands facts about people, places and things and how these entities are all connected - we focus on constructing a 'policing knowledge hub': an IoT infrastructure that can collaborate with Internet-enabled devices to collect data, understand the events and facts and assist law enforcement agencies in analyzing and understanding the situation and choose the best next step in their processes. We leverage our previous work, Knowledge Lake services [3,5,10], to automatically extract features (from keyword to named entities), enrich the extracted features and link them to external knowledge bases, such as Wikidata (wikidata.org/) and more. In particular, we use the Knowledge Lake [5] to automatically transform the raw data in the Data Lake into contextualized data and knowledge, i.e., facts, information, and insights extracted from the raw data using data curation techniques such as extraction, linking, summarization, annotation, enrichment, and classification.

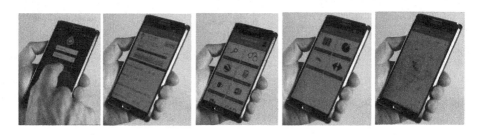

Fig. 2. iCOP screenshots.

Data Summaries and Analytics. At this level, we provide a set of services to summarize the constructed knowledge graph, and to extract complex data structures such as timeseries, hierarchies, patterns and subgraphs and link them to entities such as business artifacts, actors, and activities. We will use the concept of Folder and Path (presented in our previous work [7–9]) to summarize the knowledge graph and to model, organize, index and query such complex data structures and to consider them as first-class entities in the Knowledge Graph. We present a real-time dashboard that enables the knowledge workers interact with the data in an easy way. The dashboard will enable monitoring the entities (e.g., IoT devices, people, and locations) and dig for the facts (e.g., suspects and evidences) in an easy way.

3 Demonstration Scenario

The demonstration scenario consists of three parts: *(Step 1) Information Collection:* first, we would like that the attendee appreciates the difficulties that an investigator can encounter when dealing with data collection phase. The iCOP mobile application, will enable the investigators to identify the relevant datasets (e.g. private, open and social data sources) and link them to the current investigation case. *(Step 2) IoT-Enabled Data Collection:* by activating the location-based services in the iCOP system, it is possible to automatically identify the Internet-enabled devices around the location area. For example, the investigator can identify and interact with IoT devices such as CCTVs, police cars and drowns. *(Step 3) Data Transformation and Evidence Discovery:* we present data summaries and analytics services as well as the real-time dashboard to enable the attendees interact with the data in an easy way. In this step, we leverage our previous work, i.e. Knowledge Lake [5], to transform the raw IoT data into a contextualized data and knowledge represented as a set of (tagged [12]) data summaries. Figure 2 illustrates some screenshots of the iCOP system.

4   Conclusion and Related Work

The existing body of policing research shows significant strides in the adoption of technology in some areas in the police department [1]. A significant number of investigators have focused on the role of mobile devices in helping the police respond to current policing challenges and improve their effectiveness [13]. Today, law enforcement agencies use data analysis, crime prevention, surveillance, communication, and data sharing technologies to improve their operations and performance. In this context, IoT services has the potential to improve knowledge exchange, communication practices, and analysis of information within the police force. To achieve this goal, in this paper, we presented iCOP, IoT-enabled COP assistant system, to enabling IoT in policing. The iCOP provides techniques to assist investigators benefit from IoT to identify the best next steps. The current version of iCOP has been implemented as a research prototype. As future work, we are turning iCOP into a fully functional system.

References

1. Allen, D., Wilson, T., Norman, A., Knight, C.: Information on the move: the use of mobile information systems by UK police forces. Inf. Res. **13**(4), 13–14 (2008)
2. Bandyopadhyay, D., Sen, J.: Internet of things: applications and challenges in technology and standardization. Wireless Pers. Commun. **58**(1), 49–69 (2011)
3. Beheshti, A., Benatallah, B., Motahari-Nezhad, H.R.: Processatlas: a scalable and extensible platform for business process analytics. Softw. Pract. Exper. **48**(4), 842–866 (2018)
4. Beheshti, A., Benatallah, B., Nouri, R., Chhieng, V.M., Xiong, H., Zhao, X.: Coredb: a data lake service. In: Proceedings of the 2017 ACM on Conference on Information and Knowledge Management, CIKM, pp. 2451–2454 (2017)
5. Beheshti, A., Benatallah, B., Nouri, R., Tabebordbar, A.: Corekg: a knowledge lake service. PVLDB **11**(12), 1942–1945 (2018)
6. Beheshti, A., et al.: iProcess: enabling IoT platforms in data-driven knowledge-intensive processes. In: Weske, M., Montali, M., Weber, I., vom Brocke, J. (eds.) BPM 2018. LNBIP, vol. 329, pp. 108–126. Springer, Cham (2018). https://doi.org/10.1007/978-3-319-98651-7_7
7. Beheshti, S.M.: Organizing, querying, and analyzing ad-hoc processes' data. Ph.D. thesis, University of New South Wales, Sydney, Australia (2012)
8. Beheshti, S., Benatallah, B., Motahari-Nezhad, H.R.: Galaxy: a platform for explorative analysis of open data sources. In: Proceedings of the 19th International Conference on Extending Database Technology, EDBT, pp. 640–643 (2016)
9. Beheshti, S., et al.: Process Analytics - Concepts and Techniques for Querying and Analyzing Process Data. Springer, Cham (2016). https://doi.org/10.1007/978-3-319-25037-3
10. Beheshti, S.M.R., Venugopal, S., Ryu, S.H., Benatallah, B., Wang, W.: Big data and cross-document coreference resolution: Current state and future opportunities. arXiv preprint arXiv:1311.3987 (2013)
11. Dustdar, S., Nastic, S., Scekic, O.: Smart Cities - The Internet of Things People and Systems. Springer, Cham (2017). https://doi.org/10.1007/978-3-319-60030-7

12. Maamar, Z., Sakr, S., Barnawi, A., Beheshti, S.-M.-R.: A framework of enriching business processes life-cycle with tagging information. In: Sharaf, M.A., Cheema, M.A., Qi, J. (eds.) ADC 2015. LNCS, vol. 9093, pp. 309–313. Springer, Cham (2015). https://doi.org/10.1007/978-3-319-19548-3_25
13. Schiliro, F., et al.: The role of mobile devices in enhancing the policing system to improve efficiency and effectiveness. In: Au, M.H., Choo, K.K.R. (eds.) Mobile Security and Privacy. Elsevier, Amsterdam (2016)
14. Singhal, A.: Introducing the knowledge graph. Google Blog (2012)

iSheets: A Spreadsheet-Based Machine Learning Development Platform for Data-Driven Process Analytics

Farhad Amouzgar[1], Amin Beheshti[1(✉)], Samira Ghodratnama[1],
Boualem Benatallah[2], Jian Yang[1], and Quan Z. Sheng[1]

[1] Macquarie University, Sydney, Australia
{amin.beheshti,jian.yang,michael.sheng}@mq.edu.au,
{farhad.amouzgar,samira.ghodratnama}@hdr.mq.edu.au
[2] University of New South Wales, Sydney, Australia
boualem@cse.unsw.edu.au

Abstract. In the era of big data, the quality of services any organization provides largely depends on the quality of their data-driven processes. In this context, the goal of process data science, is to enable innovative forms of information processing that enable enhanced insight and decision making. For example, consider the data-driven and knowledge-intensive processes in Australian government's office of the e-Safety commissioner, where the goal is to empowering all citizens to have safer, more positive experiences online. An example process, is to analyze the large amount of data generated every second on social networks to understand patterns of suicidal thoughts, online bullying and criminal/exterimist behaviour. Current processes leverage machine learning systems, e.g., to perform automatic mental-health-disorders detection from social networks. This approach is challenging for knowledge workers (end-user analysts) who have little knowledge of computer science to use machine learning solutions in their data-driven processes. In this paper, we present a novel platform, namely iSheets, that makes it easy for knowledge workers of all skill levels to use machine learning technology, the way people use spreadsheet. We present and develop a Machine Learning (ML) as a service framework and a spreadsheet-based ML development platform to enable knowledge workers in data-driven processes engage with ML tasks and uncover hidden insights through learning in an easy way.

Keywords: Process data science · Data analytics · Machine learning

1 Introduction

Process data science is an interdisciplinary field that uses scientific methods and techniques to extract knowledge and insights from process related data [5, 7]. The goal of process data science, is to enable innovative forms of information processing that enable enhanced insight and decision making. Accordingly, in the era of

© Springer Nature Switzerland AG 2019
X. Liu et al. (Eds.): ICSOC 2018 Workshops, LNCS 11434, pp. 453–457, 2019.
https://doi.org/10.1007/978-3-030-17642-6_43

big data, the quality of the services any organization provides largely depends on the quality of their data-driven processes [2–4,9]. For example, consider the data-driven and knowledge-intensive processes in Australian government's office of the e-Safety commissioner (esafety.gov.au/), where the goal is to empowering all citizens to have safer, more positive experiences online. An example process, is to analyze the large amount of data generated on social networks to understand patterns of suicidal thoughts, online bullying and criminal/exterimist behaviour. Current processes leverage machine learning systems, e.g., to perform automatic mental-health-disorders detection from social networks.

Machine Learning (ML) combines techniques from statistics and artificial intelligence to create algorithms that can learn from empirical data and generalize to solve problems in various domains. One of the main challenges in Machine Learning is to enable users to subscribe and use ML application software in the cloud. This task is challenging as building ML services or AI-based application is different from building traditional software-as-a-service (SaaS) services. For example, for training models, each training problem is different and analysts need a toolbox to explore different algorithms and pick the best ones that apply to building a particular model. In this context, it is important to make these models available as a service so that others can easily replicate the training as well as the test environments. This will enable knowledge workers of all skill levels (e.g., an end-user with limited computer science background to data scientists) to access and reuse ML services in their processes.

In this paper, we present a novel platform, namely iSheets, that makes it easy for knowledge workers of all skill levels to use machine learning technology, the way people use spreadsheet. We present and develop a Machine Learning (ML) as a service framework and a spreadsheet-based ML development platform to enable knowledge workers engage with ML tasks and produce reliable, repeatable decisions and results as well as uncovering hidden insights through learning (from relationships and trends in the data) in an easy way.

Platforms such as Google (cloud.google.com), Microsoft (microsoft.com/en-us/ai/), and Amazon (aws.amazon.com/machine-learning/) Cloud's AI as well as TensorFlow (tensorflow.org/) provide modern machine learning services, with pre-trained models and a service to generate tailored models. While we support the same functionality, the added value of our approach is a novel platform that makes it easy for knowledge workers in knowledge-intensive processes of all skill levels to use machine learning technology, the way people use spreadsheet. The rest of the paper is organized as follows. In Sect. 2, we present an overview of the platform, while in Sect. 3 we describe our demonstration scenario.

2   System Overview

We present a platform, namely iSheets, to make it easy for knowledge workers of all skill levels to use machine learning technology, the way people use spreadsheet. The main components include: Machine Learning as a Service and Spreadsheet-based ML data transformation.

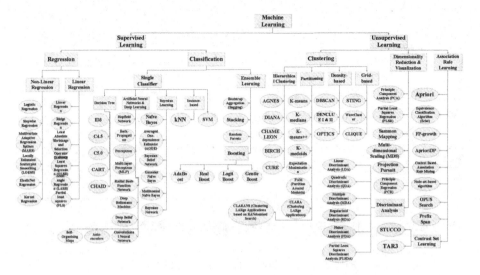

Fig. 1. The taxonomy of the Machine Learning algorithms used as a service to enable the knowledge workers interact with the summaries in an easy way [4].

Machine Learning as a Service. The objective of Machine Learning techniques is to figure out how to automatically perform tasks by generalizing from examples. In this part, we have identified many useful machine learning algorithms and wrapped them as services to enable us to summarize the process related data, and to extract complex data structures such as timeseries, hierarchies, patterns and subgraphs and link them to entities such as business artifacts, actors, and activities. Figure 1, illustrates the taxonomy of these services. The taxonomy includes the mainstream learning algorithms such as Linear Regression, Logistic Regression, SVM, Decision Trees, k-means and tagging [10]. These ML services use machine learning algorithms to predict, classify, and cluster, raw data to extract hidden insights for varieties of client applications. The server application saves the learned model and generates the output for new datasets. We support a set of algorithms organized in categories such as Supervised Learning, Unsupervised Learning and Reinforcement Learning. Each one of these classes requires a specific type of JSON structure for communication which is also provided by the framework.

Spreadsheet-Based ML Data Transformation. A spreadsheet is an interactive computer application for organization, analysis and storage of data in tabular form. In existing applications (e.g., Microsoft and Google Spreadsheets), the data stored in spreadsheet cells is usually text, a numeric value, or a formula. In this paper, we introduce new types of hyper cells in spreadsheet to enable analysts summarize the data in terms of its features (to group set of related entities) and interrelations (to group set of related patterns). We use an open source Web-based spreadsheet project (handsontable.com/) and extended it to link to ML services and enable storing data summaries in the hyper cells.

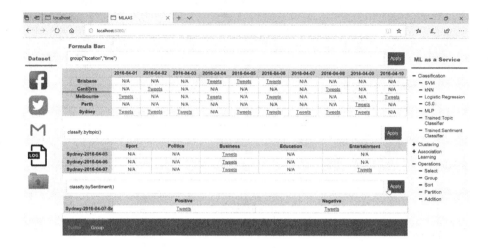

Fig. 2. Screenshot of the iSheets platform.

As illustrated in Fig. 2, the end user analyst can: (i) load the process related data into the spreadsheet; (ii) select all or range of cells; (iii) drag and drop the ML algorithm; and (iv) apply follow on analysis to the data.

3   Demonstration Scenario

The demonstration scenario focuses on assisting knowledge workers in the e-Safety department, to analyze the big data generated on Social Networks to save lives including proactive detection to understand patterns of suicidal thoughts, online bullying and criminal/exterimist behaviour. The demonstration scenario consists of three parts: *Step 1: Preprocessing.* In this step, we present to the attendee that the iSheets platform supports different types of datasets, e.g., from process logs to social network data. We illustrate that the system is able to automatically extract various features from the dataset (for this we use our previous work [8]) and also deal with large amount of data. For example, we load a Twitter dataset consists of 15 million Tweets. *Step 2: ML as a Service.* In this step, we present the iSheets platform and focus on two examples: classifying the tweets in twitter based on their topics and sentiments [11]. We present that the iSheets platform provides modern machine learning services with pre-trained models. *Step 3: Spreadsheet-based ML Data Transformation.* In this step, we enable the attendee to play with the spreadsheet-based interface, to load a dataset, apply ML services to the selected cells (simply by dragging and dropping the ML service) and to extract knowledge and insights from the data summaries in hyper cells based on the specific goal they have in mind. For example, to understand the social issues (related to a specific topic and in locations of interest) discussed on Twitter, the attendee may filter the tweets based on the location (e.g., tweets twitted from Sydney), group the tweets based on their topics (e.g., politics, health and social security) and classify them based on their sentiment [11].

4   Conclusion and Related Work

In recent years, machine learning and service oriented computing have driven advances in many different fields [3,6,11]. The availability of large datasets for tackling problems in these fields, invention of more sophisticated machine learning models, and the development of cloud ML/AI platforms (e.g., Google, Microsoft and Amazon Cloud's AI), enable the easy use of large amounts of computational resources for training ML models [1]. While we support similar line of work, the added value of our approach is a novel platform that makes it easy for knowledge workers in knowledge-intensive processes to use machine learning technology, the way people use spreadsheet.

References

1. Abadi, M., Barham, P., Chen, et al.: Tensorflow: a system for large-scale machine learning. In: OSDI, vol. 16, pp. 265–283 (2016)
2. Beheshti, A., Benatallah, B., Nouri, R., Chhieng, V.M., Xiong, H., Zhao, X.: CoreDB: a data lake service. In: Proceedings of the 2017 ACM on Conference on Information and Knowledge Management, CIKM 2017, Singapore, pp. 2451–2454, 06–10 November 2017
3. Beheshti, A., Benatallah, B., Nouri, R., Tabebordbar, A.: CoreKG: a knowledge lake service. PVLDB 11(12), 1942–1945 (2018)
4. Beheshti, A., et al.: iProcess: enabling IoT platforms in data-driven knowledge-intensive processes. In: Weske, M., Montali, M., Weber, I., vom Brocke, J. (eds.) BPM 2018. LNBIP, vol. 329, pp. 108–126. Springer, Cham (2018). https://doi.org/10.1007/978-3-319-98651-7_7
5. Beheshti, S.M.: Organizing, querying, and analyzing ad-hoc processes' data. Ph.D. thesis, University of New South Wales, Sydney, Australia (2012)
6. Beheshti, S., Benatallah, B., Motahari-Nezhad, H.R.: Galaxy: a platform for explorative analysis of open data sources. In: Proceedings of the 19th International Conference on Extending Database Technology EDBT, pp. 640–643 (2016)
7. Beheshti, S., et al.: Process Analytics - Concepts and Techniques for Querying and Analyzing Process Data. Springer, Switzerland (2016). https://doi.org/10.1007/978-3-319-25037-3
8. Beheshti, S., Tabebordbar, A., Benatallah, B., Nouri, R.: On automating basic data curation tasks. In: Proceedings of the 26th International Conference on World Wide Web Companion, Perth, Australia, pp. 165–169, 3–7 April 2017
9. Beheshti, S.M.R., Venugopal, S., Ryu, S.H., Benatallah, B., Wang, W.: Big data and cross-document coreference resolution: Current state and future opportunities. arXiv preprint arXiv:1311.3987 (2013)
10. Maamar, Z., Sakr, S., Barnawi, A., Beheshti, S.-M.-R.: A framework of enriching business processes life-cycle with tagging information. In: Sharaf, M.A., Cheema, M.A., Qi, J. (eds.) ADC 2015. LNCS, vol. 9093, pp. 309–313. Springer, Cham (2015). https://doi.org/10.1007/978-3-319-19548-3_25
11. Pang, B., Lee, L., et al.: Opinion mining and sentiment analysis. Found. Trends® Inf. Retrieval 2(1–2), 1–135 (2008)

SORCER: A Decentralised Continuous Integration Platform for Service-Oriented Software Systems

Jameel Almalki and Haifeng Shen[✉]

College of Science and Engineering, Flinders University, Adelaide, Australia
{alma0141,haifeng.shen}@flinders.edu.au

Abstract. Continuous integration (CI) is a key practice where developers integrate frequently via a shared repository to enable automated build, test, and release of software systems. While enabling CI in a centralised development environment has been a common practice, no much work has been done to effectively support CI of decentralised service-oriented systems where centralised repositories are unavailable. This paper presents SORCER, a decentralised interface-based continuous integration platform that makes it easy for developers to perform integrated build and test of service-oriented systems whose service constituents are owned and managed by different organisations to only expose their interfaces without access to their source codes.

Keywords: Continuous integration · Service-Oriented Architecture · Service compatibility · Versioning

1 Introduction

Enabling continuous integration (CI) in a centralised software development environment has been a common practice through a dedicated CI server monitoring code changes in a central repository and executing integration tests whenever changes are detected. However, with the rise of distributed software development, particularly using Service-Oriented Architecture (SOA) [3,6], it becomes increasingly important to continuously maintain the evolution of each constituent service to ensure that when integrated into the common project, they still operate in a stable and reliable manner. However, as individual services may be owned and managed by different stakeholders, they typically do not expose their underlying implementation details and are only accessible via APIs [2,8] and as such it is difficult if not impossible to perform centralised storage, testing, deployment or execution of code assets across organisational boundaries, as happens with the traditional CI approach.

To address this issue, we proposed SORC (Service-Oriented Revision Control) [7], a decentralised interface-based continuous integration model that is particularly optimised for developing SOA-based systems. It relies on decentralised

© Springer Nature Switzerland AG 2019
X. Liu et al. (Eds.): ICSOC 2018 Workshops, LNCS 11434, pp. 458–464, 2019.
https://doi.org/10.1007/978-3-030-17642-6_44

communication between service providers and consumers to enable discovery and consumption of service versions. It uses a versioning scheme to facilitate compatibility across different versions of multiple services [1]. To demonstrate the viability and the effectiveness of this model, this paper presents SORCER, a reference implementation of the SORC model for WSDL/SOAP web services that makes it easy for developers to perform integrated build and test of service-oriented systems whose service constituents are owned and managed by different organisations to only expose their interfaces without access to their source codes. It is worth clarifying that SORCER provides a platform for developers to manage software changes and perform CI rather than doing integrated build and test for developers. It is also worth mentioning WSDarwin [4], which is closely related to SORCER as it also handles the evolution of service interfaces. However, WSDarwin is a toolkit for automatically detecting changes in a service interface so that consumers can adapt to the changes, whereas SORCER is a continuous integration platform that facilitates timely communication between providers and consumers so that consumers are always well informed of the changes in the interface and also given the flexible options of adapting to a new incompatible version or staying with an old compatible version of the interface.

2 SORC: A Decentralised Interface-Based CI Model

The current CI model adopts a centralised approach where developers are required to regularly share their code changes via a central repository managed by a version control tool such as *Github* so that newly added updates can be built, tested, and run by an automated CI server such as *Jenkins*, which needs to access all code with the latest committed updates by developers in order to build and test a new release. As illustrated by Fig. 1(a), there are three separate cycles in the current CI model: (a) each developer performs the edit/build/test cycle on a local replica of the shared code base checked out from the central repository, (b) each developer needs to first update their local replica with the latest code changes made by other developers from the repository before stepping into the edit/build/test cycle and finally commit their code changes back to the repository after they are tested successful, and (c) the CI server continuously fetches all the code changes from the repository as they are committed by developers, undertakes automated integration through build/test/run, and sends the integration feedback to the relevant developers.

In contrast, as illustrated in Fig. 1(b), there is no central repository or a dedicated server where all software artefacts of a project can be stored, tested, deployed and run. Instead, there are multiple involved organisations, each of which independently develops and manages software services that are only accessible via APIs, consequently requiring a decentralised approach to CI. The SORC model has the following key distinctive features compared to the current CI model: (a) there is only one cycle, whereas there are three separate cycles in the current model, (b) each developer individually maintains multiple versions of their own service (both code and interface), whereas the central repository keeps all the versions of the entire project (code only) in the current model, (c) developers communicate directly by exchanging service descriptors and by provisioning/consuming services, while developers communicate indirectly via the central repository by exchanging code changes in the current model, and (d) CI is undertaken by each developer and requires the consumed services to be available from other developers, whereas CI is delegated to a standalone server, which does not require support from developers other than just sending them feedback in the current model.

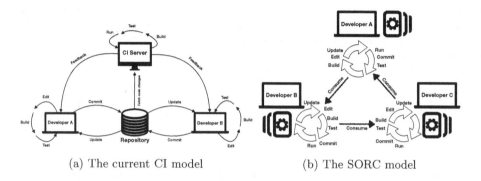

(a) The current CI model   (b) The SORC model

Fig. 1. The current and proposed continuous integration models

In the SORC model, service provisioning/consumption takes the following steps: (1) the consumer locates the service by checking out the provider's discovery file, (2) the consumer obtains the service description that explains what the service does and how it is to be invoked, (3) the consumer generates a local proxy class of the remote service, which contains necessary details for invoking the service and is a representation of the service interface at that point in time [5], and (4) the consumer uses the class as if the remote service is present locally. Over time, the interface is susceptible to changes as the service gains new features or functionality and therefore the SORC model is focused on managing interface changes that occur during the service lifecycle, allowing developers to version their services and, at the same time, maintain multiple releases that are accessible to peer developers. It controls and manages services through standard interfaces, making it possible to compare different versions, consume older versions, or review the list of changes made to a service interface.

3   SORCER: A Concept Demonstrator

SORCER provides the three utilities of *commit*, *checkout*, and *update* to support continuous integration: *commit* used by a service provider to register and publish new versions so that they can be discovered and consumed by other developers, *checkout* used by a developer to discover available services provisioned by other developers and further bind to selected services with the help of locally generated proxy classes, and *update* used by a service consumer to migrate the local proxy from the current version to a new version of the consumed service.

We present a hypothetical yet realistic use case scenario, a tourist information application that offers two types of information, including weather forecast details for a specific geographic location and the currency exchange rates in that specific location, as shown in Fig. 2. There are three developers involved in this scenario. DeveloperA is responsible for the main application that consumes the weather forecast and currency exchange rate services maintained by the remote DeveloperB and DeveloperC, respectively. All developers run the SOR-CER framework within their IDEs during the development process. As shown in Fig. 3, DeveloperA creates an application that consumes the weather forecast and currency exchange services maintained by the remote DeveloperB and DeveloperC. The integration is initiated when the developers create their respective projects and publish them on web servers. Next, using the SORCER plugin, all developers are required to configure their projects.

Fig. 2. A tourist information application

A key innovation in SORCER is that versioning of service interfaces and consumption of any version are built into the continuous process. For example, when DeveloperB commits a compatible change by adding a new method `getLatLong` to the service, this new version is assigned with the name `WeatherService_1_1`. DeveloperA runs the *update* command to automatically generate the proxy class for the new version. However, when DeveloperB commits an incompatible change to the service, where the original method `getWeatherData` is renamed to `getWeatherDetails`, this new version will be assigned with the name

WeatherService_2_0. After DeveloperA runs the *update* command, they will be prompted to decide on whether to upgrade to the new incompatible version.

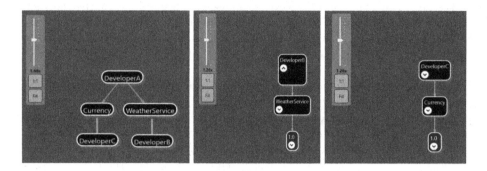

Fig. 3. Developing a tourist information application with SORCER

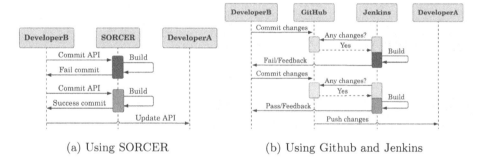

(a) Using SORCER   (b) Using Github and Jenkins

Fig. 4. Continuous integration workflows of the tourist information application

The case scenario is intended to demonstrate the viability of the SORC model and the SORCER platform for supporting continuous integration of a SOA-based system as well as to showcase their potential advantages over the existing technology stack, e.g., *GitHub + Jenkins*. Figure 4 shows the CI workflows using the two technology stacks. As depicted by Fig. 4(a), having configured the weather forecast system as a team project, DeveloperB is now ready to commit the first version of the service - WeatherService_1_0 to be invoked by DeveloperA. DeveloperA is now ready to checkout the latest changes of the associated service, after which a corresponding proxy is generated on the local machine. Finally, after generating the local proxy, the weather forecast service appears in DeveloperA's project space with a list of provisioned methods. Figure 4(b) illustrates a different workflow using *GitHub + Jenkins*. First, DeveloperB creates WeatherService and pushes it to a shared folder on GitHub. Next, DeveloperA clones the WeatherService project into his local repository, and is now able to develop a `WeatherService`-based client application and push it to GitHub. DeveloperB is also able to make further changes (both compatible and incompatible) to the existing service on GitHub. Upon detection of an updated version of the `WeatherService`, the Jenkins server builds and compiles the project to check whether the application still runs with the new version of the service.

An online video of using SORCER for continuous integration of the tourist information application can be found at https://youtu.be/uM8HEBDNjf4.

Implementation of the prototype has primarily adopted .NET technology stack including the Web Service framework based on Windows Communication Foundation and DISCO-based service discovery. It is worth noting that using the .NET stack does not contradict the technology agnostic nature of SOA, and the described approach can be easily adjusted to other SOA technologies.

To demonstrate continuous integration of the tourist information application using SORCER, we need two personal computers connected by a local area network, which are respectively used by DeveloperA (the tourist information application) and DeveloperB (the WeatherService Web service). Each computer should have the following software installed:

- Internet Information Services (IIS) 10.0
- Windows Communication Foundation (WCF) 4.5
- Visual Studio 2015
- SORCER plugin for Visual Studio 2015

4   Conclusion and Future Work

This paper has focused on the issue of enabling continuous integration in the context of developing interface-based service-oriented software systems that span across multiple organisations. The presented prototype - SORCER - implements a decentralised architecture for project integration, making it a promising solution for addressing the challenges associated with the distributed nature of service-oriented software systems. We are conscious about limitations of this work. Future research will involve going beyond WSDL/SOAP-based web services and expanding the scope of interface-based continuous integration to the REST architecture and micro-services, as well as supporting other service description languages, such as Web Application Description Language (WADL) and Swagger. We are working towards making SORCER publicly available so that we can collect real-world projects to conduct more rigorous evaluations.

References

1. Almalki, J., Shen, H.: A lightweight solution to version incompatibility in service-oriented revision control systems. In: Proceedings of the 24th Australasian Software Engineering Conference (ASWEC), pp. 59–63 (2015)
2. Dautov, R., Paraskakis, I., Stannett, M.: Utilising stream reasoning techniques to underpin an autonomous framework for cloud application platforms. J. Cloud Comput. **3**, 13 (2014)

3. Erl, T.: Service-oriented architecture: concepts, technology, and design. Pearson Education India (2005)
4. Fokaefs, M., Stroulia, E.: WSDarwin: studying the evolution of web service systems. In: Bouguettaya, A., Sheng, Q., Daniel, F. (eds.) Advanced Web Services, pp. 199–223. Springer, New york (2014). https://doi.org/10.1007/978-1-4614-7535-4_9
5. Frank, D., Lam, L., Fong, L., Fang, R., Khangaonkar, M.: Using an interface proxy to host versioned web services. In: Proceedings IEEE International Conference on Services Computing, pp. 325–332 (2008)
6. Papazoglou, M.P.: Service-oriented computing: concepts, characteristics and directions. In: Proceedings of the Fourth International Conference on Web Information Systems Engineering (WISE), pp. 3–12 (2003)
7. Sarib, A.S.B., Shen, H.: SORC: service-oriented distributed revision control for collaborative web programming. In: Proceedings of the IEEE 18th International Conference on Computer Supported Cooperative Work in Design (CSCWD), pp. 638–643 (2014)
8. Wei, Y., Blake, M.B.: Service-oriented computing and cloud computing: challenges and opportunities. IEEE Internet Comput. 14(6), 72–75 (2010)

On Anomaly Detection and Root Cause Analysis of Microservice Systems

Zijie Guan, Jinjin Lin, and Pengfei Chen$^{(\boxtimes)}$

School of Data and Computer Science, Sun Yat-sen University, Guangzhou, China
{guanzj5,linjj23}@mail2.sysu.edu.cn, chenpf7@mail.sysu.edu.cn

Abstract. In this demonstration, we design and implement a prototype of proof for causal graph building, anomaly detection and root cause analysis of microservice systems. The system comprises two core functionalities: (i) monitoring of systems and services; (ii) Application anomaly detection and root cause analysis. In the first part, the key metrics for the health of a system and an application, are collected by backend and plotted with dynamic charts in the frontend, which can help operators spot the overall system status. In the second part, the system can automatically build a causal graph of the microservice applications, indicating the dependencies between different modules, without instrumenting any source code. When an anomaly of a service instance is detected, it will be highlighted in the graph. A root cause inference function is also applied to analyze the root cause and returns a ranked list of root cause candidates to operators.

Keywords: Microservice · Root cause analysis · Monitoring system · Kubernetes

1 Introduction

The current software architecture is shifting from monolithic to microservice architecture rapidly. In microservice architecture, an application is decoupled to different modules according to their business functions. However, these decoupled modules usually contain complex interactions. Therefore, an abnormal module may cause other relevant modules to be abnormal, which makes operators difficult to diagnose anomalies. In order to maintain the application performance as expected, we need a monitoring system to know the overall health status of the applications, to detect abnormal service instance efficiently and even to do a root cause inference to help operators diagnose anomalies.

In this demo paper, we design and implement a prototype of proof for microservices in Kubernetes environment [2], which is mainly based on the technology of Microscope [1] in backend for causal graph building, anomaly detection and root cause analysis. Microscope is a new method proposed by us in [1], which can identify and locate the abnormal services with a ranked list of possible root causes in microservice environments, without instrumenting the source code.

© Springer Nature Switzerland AG 2019
X. Liu et al. (Eds.): ICSOC 2018 Workshops, LNCS 11434, pp. 465–469, 2019.
https://doi.org/10.1007/978-3-030-17642-6_45

2   System Design

The system is mainly designed for enterprise operators and DevOps developers in Kubernetes environment and includes two core functionalities in all: (i) monitoring of systems and applications; (ii) application anomaly detection and root cause analysis.

In order to help operators to know the overall system status, we design the system and application monitoring function. The key metrics for the health of a system or an application, such as service latency, throughputand system resources (e.g., CPU, memory, network utilization), are collected and plotted with dynamic charts in the frontend in real time.

In practice, its important for operators to diagnose anomalies of application as soon as possible for reducing enterprise loss. However, instrumenting the application code to provide the relevant data takes a lot of effort and it's a waste of resources. Therefore, we design the application anomaly detection and root cause analysis function, which depend on the novel technology of Microscope [1] in backend.

3   Function and Implementation

3.1   System Overview

The architecture of Microscope is presented in Fig. 1. The system works on Kubernetes platform where applications are deployed with one or more nodes. As for data collection, we apply sysdig [3] with filebeat [4] to gather and transport the network connection data storing in elasticsearch [5] with prometheus [6] to collect and storage the metrics data. Based on the data, Microscope system provides the functionalities of anomaly detection, casual graph building and root cause analysis, finally giving the result by the web front end.

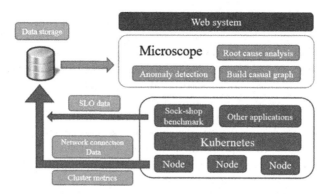

Fig. 1. The architecture diagram of Microscope system.

3.2 System and Application Monitoring

Microscope system[1] temporarily applies default metrics dashboard through Grafana [7], and customized dashboards can be set up in the future version. Microscope system displays system resources usage status in pie charts with the detailed figures. Recourse utilization over time is shown by linecharts which give detailed information of pods and containers in the system. As for applications running on the platform, the performance is an important monitoring index which is closely related to the application users experience. The system shows the network traffic status and latency of each service as the performance measurements on each application.

3.3 Application Anomaly Detection and Root Cause Analysis

Causal Graph Building. By applying the method of causal graph building with Microscope [1] in backend, the system can automatically generate the whole causal graph of all service instances on Kubernetes. Then the causal graph can be shown in frontend with a filter, where arrows indicate the direction of dependency between service instances. The users can select different applications at different instances level, such as services level or pod level in Kubernetes. The service latency of each service instances is displayed on the node and update in real time.

Anomaly Detection. We use the three-sigma method to detect the abnormal services or pods base on the SLO (Service Level Object) data. Unexpected anomalies (e.g. hardware problems, network errors, code bugs) may occur in the system which may impact the users of the applications. The first metrics to monitor is latency, which presents historical users access waiting time. Any services or pods latency continuously exceed the normal range of three-sigma is defined as abnormal and the node of this service or pod will turn red to remind the user as its shown in Fig. 2. With the pod name and IP displayed on the graph, the user of our system can make corresponding response quickly.

Root Cause Analysis. When the root cause analysis function is called, the cause inference engine starts from the root node (front-end in the Sock-shop benchmark) and traverses the causality graph along the edges. After the traversal, the engine gets a set of root cause candidates. Then the engine calculates a ranking score for each root cause candidates and finally the system gives an ordered list of root cause with ranking score where higher score indicates higher likelihood of real root cause.

---

[1] Please via https://pan.baidu.com/s/1Nd9ysS22FaYHN5GDPRzbdQ to watch the video of Microscope system.

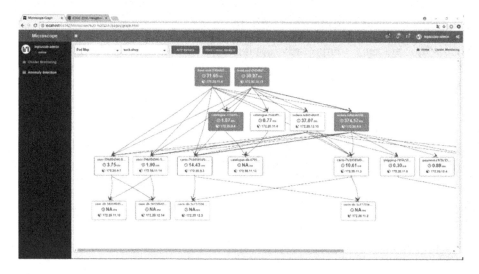

Fig. 2. An example of abnormalscenario.

4   Conclusion and Future Work

In this paper, we demonstrate a prototype system for microservice cluster with system and application monitoring functionality as well as application anomaly detection and root cause analysis basing on the Microscope [1]. We deployed a microservices benchmark, namely Sock-shop [8] to validate the system and the results show Microscope was in working order.

As part of future work, we plan to integrate Microscope system with alarm setting and alarm reduction functionalities. In order to handle the alarms immediately in the enterprises, different types or scope of alarms can be assigned to related staff by the alarm setting function. Furthermore, alarm reduction function based on root cause analysis can aggregate related alarms and help operators to diagnose the root cause of anomalies, which is expected by our users.

Acknowledgments. The work described in this paper was supported by the National Key R&D Program of China (2018YFB1004804), the National Natural Science Foundation of China (61802448) and the Guangdong Province Universities and Colleges Pearl River Scholar Funded Scheme 2016.

References

1. Jinjin, L., Pengfei, C., Zibin, Z.: Microscope: pinpoint the abnormal services with causal graphs in micro-service environments. In: Proceedings of the 16th International Conference on Service Oriented Computing (ICSOC 2018) (2018, to appear)
2. Kubernetes. https://kubernetes.io/
3. Sysdig. https://sysdig.com/opensource/
4. Filebeat. https://www.elastic.co/products/beats/filebeat

5. Elasticsearch. https://www.elastic.co/products/elasticsearch
6. Prometheus. https://prometheus.io/
7. Grafana. https://grafana.com
8. Sock-shop. https://microservices-demo.github.io/

RESTalk Miner: Mining RESTful Conversations, Pattern Discovery and Matching

Ana Ivanchikj, Ilija Gjorgjiev, and Cesare Pautasso[✉]

Software Institute, Faculty of Informatics, USI, Lugano, Switzerland
{ana.ivanchikj,ilija.gjorgjiev,cesare.pautasso}@usi.ch

Abstract. REST has become the architectural style of choice for APIs, where clients need to instantiate a potentially lengthy sequence of requests to the server in order to achieve their goal, effectively leading to a RESTful conversation between clients and servers. Mining the logs of such RESTful conversations can facilitate knowledge sharing among API designers regarding design best practices as well as API usage and optimization. In this demo paper, we present the RESTalk Miner, which takes logs from RESTful services as an input and uses RESTalk, a domain specific language, to visualize them. It provides interactive coloring to facilitate graph reading, as well as statistics to compare the relative frequency of conversations performed by different clients. Furthermore, it supports searching for predefined patterns as well as pattern discovery.

Keywords: REST APIs · RESTful conversations · Mining ·
Pattern search · Visualization

1 Introduction

As the number of RESTful services is growing, with over 15'000 publicly available REST APIs [5] in the ProgrammableWeb repository[1] as of 2018, mining their logs can bring to interesting insights regarding how different clients actually use REST APIs. This can help developers detect unexpected usage patterns of their APIs by comparing different clients' conversations, or to pinpoint interactions which are worth optimizing as they are being used by most of the clients. For instance, if there is a sequence of several requests which are frequently followed, the API designer might decide to provide in the first request a direct link of the last request, thus avoiding the clients having to make the intermediary requests. Bugs might also become evident, such as unauthorized access to some resources or frequent error messages after a certain sequence of requests. Mining techniques have been successfully applied in the area of business processes for almost two decades, resulting in process discovery, conformance checking, prediction of delays, process redesign recommendation etc. [2]. Similar to business

---

[1] http://www.programmableweb.com.

© Springer Nature Switzerland AG 2019
X. Liu et al. (Eds.): ICSOC 2018 Workshops, LNCS 11434, pp. 470–475, 2019.
https://doi.org/10.1007/978-3-030-17642-6_46

processes, the use of REST APIs also requires a particular sequence of interactions [3]. In this case they are HTTP request-response interactions between clients and servers with the goal of retrieving or modifying the state of one or more resources managed by a service provider [14]. We call the set of all possible client-server interactions, aimed at achieving a certain goal, a RESTful conversation [4,7,8]. As process mining builds on data mining and process model-driven approaches, mining of RESTful services also requires a model-driven approach to RESTful conversations. To that end, in [9] we have proposed RESTalk, a domain specific language for modeling and visualization of RESTful conversations and we use a simplified version of the same in the RESTalk Miner. Although different mining tools with graph visualization already exist [1,15,16], their visualization is not REST domain specific nor do they offer pattern searching or pattern discovery functionalities. Patterns [10] represent a systematic form of knowledge sharing as they establish a common vocabulary to describe recurring RESTful conversations [11] which is becoming increasingly important in the API-driven development [6]. Patterns can be used to pinpoint and discuss API design best practices or the absence of the same.

2   RESTalk Miner

The input to RESTalk Miner[2] is a log file from a given server containing log entries of interactions with different clients, complying to the following format:

$$\overbrace{DD/MM/YYYY}^{\text{Date}} \ \overbrace{HH:MM:SS}^{\text{Time}} \ \overbrace{3.171.112.202}^{\text{Client IP Address}} \ \overbrace{POST}^{\text{Method}} \ \overbrace{/job}^{\text{URI}} \ \overbrace{202}^{\text{Status Code}}$$

Additionally there is an optional input, i.e., a file which contains the URI templates derived from an Open API specification of the API. For instance, to abstract the following URI /content/ serial/ title /issn/03029743 this URI template can be used /content/ serial/ title /issn/:id. Such abstraction ensures that identical method calls to the same type of resource are visualized as one request. The main default output of the RESTalk Miner is a simplified RESTalk graph showing all the conversations different clients have initiated with the server. Alternatively, the user can select to visualize only the conversations of clients of interest. Most of the nodes in the graph take the form of a juxtaposed request-response containing information about the HTTP method, URI, response status code and the number of log entries in which this request/response pair has appeared. If different log entries indicate that the server has used different responses to the same request, the request and the responses are represented as separate nodes with an exclusive gateway node in-between to emphasize the existence of alternative responses. An exclusive gateway node is also used to show alternative paths that clients have taken during their interactions with the server. A node with a round form is used to mark the start and the end of a conversation of a particular client, while edges depict the sequence flow between nodes.

---

[2] https://github.com/USI-INF-Software/RESTfulConversationMining.

Based on user's preference, the graph can be flattened by abstracting from the URI information and showing only the methods that have been called and the response status codes. For the RESTalk visualization, dagre-d3 library [12,13] has been used to render the internal data structure into an SVG DOM tree which is displayed by the Web browser.

RESTalk Graph and Comparative Statistics Visualization. Once the above mentioned graph has been generated, the user can activate or deactivate different interactive visualizations: **node frequency coloring** which colors nodes from red to yellow depending on the number of log entries that contain the particular request/response pair; **edge frequency thickness** which adjusts the thickness of the edges based on how many clients follow the same path; **edge delay coloring** which colors the edges from red to yellow depending on the time difference between the nodes that the edge connects; **edge probability** which shows a probability of an alternative path being taken after an exclusive gateway; **status coloring** which colors responses based on their status codes; **conversation path coloring** which colors in a unique color all the requests made by the same client and in a mix of colors the nodes which are shared between clients in case multiple clients are selected (Fig. 1). The tool also provides the user with pie chart visualization of statistical data regarding the analyzed clients of the RESTful service. The **number of nodes** pie chart shows how many request/response nodes belong to each individual client as a percentage of the total number of nodes, i.e., how lengthy each conversation is; the **uniqueness of nodes** pie chart shows how many nodes are unique to just one client, how many are shared between two, three clients etc. Clicking on a certain slice of the pie colors in the same color in the graph the nodes it refers to; the **shared nodes** pie chart shows the number of nodes shared between specific clients; while the **dynamic sharing** pie chart uses the same computation as the shared nodes pie charts, but only for the clients selected by the user.

Pattern Discovery, Matching and Visualization. RESTalk Miner supports two types of pattern searches. Searching for unknown patterns, i.e., pattern discovery, and searching for known patterns, i.e., pattern matching. The pattern discovery can help identify new API design approaches and best practices, while the pattern matching can allow to search for patterns of interest. When **searching for unknown patterns** the user specifies the number of request/response nodes the pattern should contain and the minimal number of clients that must have used that pattern. If patterns that match these criteria are identified, they appear in a dropdown list and the user can decide to visualize them and/or save them. Saved patterns can be used later as **known patterns** to be searched for in other conversations. The user can also upload patterns she knows based on her experience or best practices and search for them in the given conversation. Such patterns need to be described in JSON with a log object describing the conversation pattern to be matched (Fig. 2). Each log entry has the same structure as the logs described above, with the difference that any of the elements (Method, Status Code, URI, etc.) can be substituted by a * symbol, meaning

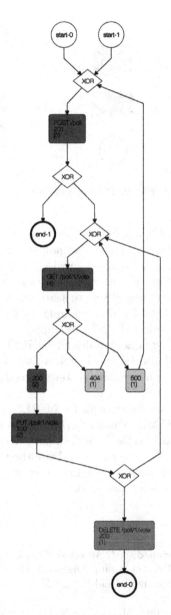

Fig. 1. Overlapping vs. unique parts of conversations

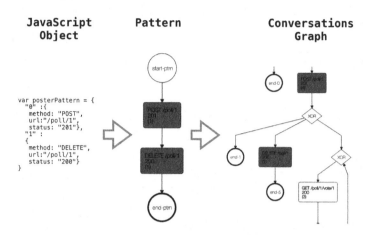

Fig. 2. Pattern matching

that any value of that element will be considered a match when searching for the pattern. URI values can also be used as placeholders, i.e., ensuring that the same URI is used in different requests without precisely specifying the URI value. An optional separator element in the pattern description allows for log entries not to be direct successors. For instance, if we are searching for a pattern with two log entries (POST /example/1, DELETE /example/1), if we use this separator element in the pattern description (POST /example/1 ... DELETE /example/1), an occurrence of POST /example/1 followed by PUT /example/1 followed by DELETE /example/1 will also be considered a match. Such description of the pattern we are searching for allows for greater expressiveness to match targeted patterns.

A screencast of the main functionalities of RESTalk Miner is available at https://youtu.be/N94clNa5Mlg. Future work includes providing full support of the RESTalk constructs, such as the hyperlink flow, which will require additional input collected in the logs. We also plan to release the tool as a Web Application with user registration functionality so that the user can save the mined RESTful conversations and the discovered patterns.

References

1. Disco. https://fluxicon.com/disco/. Accessed 20 Aug 2018
2. van der Aalst, W.M.P.: Process Mining: Discovery, Conformance and Enhancement of Business Processes. Springer, Heidelberg (2011). https://doi.org/10.1007/978-3-642-19345-3
3. van der Aalst, W.M.P., Song, M.: Mining social networks: uncovering interaction patterns in business processes. In: Desel, J., Pernici, B., Weske, M. (eds.) BPM 2004. LNCS, vol. 3080, pp. 244–260. Springer, Heidelberg (2004). https://doi.org/10.1007/978-3-540-25970-1_16
4. Benatallah, B., Casati, F., et al.: Web service conversation modeling: a cornerstone for E-business automation. IEEE Internet Comput. **8**(1), 46–54 (2004)

5. Fielding, R.T.: Architectural styles and the design of network-based software architectures. Ph.D. thesis, University of California, Irvine (2000)
6. Goteti, H.: API driven development, bridging the gap between providers and consumers. Technical report, CA Technologies (2015). http://rewrite.ca.com/us/articles/application-economy/apis-bridging-the-gap-between-providers-and-consumers.html
7. Haupt, F., Leymann, F., Pautasso, C.: A conversation based approach for modeling REST APIs. In: Proceedings of the 12th WICSA 2015, Montreal, May 2015
8. Hohpe, G.: Let's have a conversation. IEEE Internet Comput. **11**(3), 78–81 (2007)
9. Ivanchikj, A., Pautasso, C., Schreier, S.: Visual modeling of RESTful conversations with RESTalk. Softw. Syst. Model. **17**(3), 1031–1051 (2018)
10. Meszaros, G., Doble, J.: A pattern language for pattern writing. Pattern Lang. Program Des. **3**, 529–574 (1998)
11. Pautasso, C., Ivanchikj, A., Schreier, S.: A pattern language for RESTful conversations. In: Proceedings of EuroPLoP, p. 4. ACM (2016)
12. Pettitt, C.: Directed graph layout for Javascript (2012–2014). https://github.com/dagrejs/dagre
13. Pettitt, C.: A D3-based renderer for Dagre (2013). https://github.com/dagrejs/dagre-d3
14. Richardson, L., Amundsen, M., Ruby, S.: RESTful Web APIs. O'Reilly, Sebastopol (2013)
15. Stroinski, A., et al.: RESTful web service mining: simple algorithm supporting resource-oriented systems. In: Proceedings of ICWE, pp. 694–695. IEEE (2014)
16. Verbeek, H., Buijs, J., Van Dongen, B., van der Aalst, W.M.: Prom 6: the process mining toolkit. Proc. BPM Demonstration Track **615**, 34–39 (2010)

Cross-Client SLA Management
with the ysla Language and Engine

Shashank Rajamoni[1]([⊠]), Robert Engel[1], Bryant Chen[1], Heiko Ludwig[1],
and Alexander Keller[2]

[1] Almaden Research Center, IBM Research, San Jose, CA, USA
shashank.rajamoni@ibm.com
[2] IBM Global Technology Services, Chicago, IL, USA

Abstract. Due to lack of standardization and automation, large-scale
Service Level Agreement (SLA) management remains challenging for IT
service providers. For instance, flexible re-use of SLA definitions across
different client engagements is often poorly supported by current SLA
management frameworks. In this demonstration we present the *ysla
Engine*, a new SLA management framework implementing the YAML-
based *ysla* language for modeling SLAs. ysla provides novel semantic constructs for adaptable SLA templates that formally separate metrics definitions from associated customer-specific classification/categorization
taxonomies for monitored subjects. In our demonstration we model the
common, but intricate industry use case of SLAs for incident management and demonstrate how ysla-based SLA templates and SLAs can
foster cross-client SLA re-usability.

Keywords: SLA · Performance monitoring · Cloud computing ·
Re-usability

1 Introduction

In the Cloud services market, Service Level Agreements (SLAs) specify requirements and expectations with respect to services to be delivered. In particular,
enterprise customers frequently demand detailed SLAs. Due to lack of standardization and automation in SLA management technology [6, pp. 39–40], SLAs are
commonly negotiated on a per-deal basis and specified in natural language as an
addendum to service contracts. SLAs across different providers and clients often
share some commonalities, such as the general semantics of commonly used performance metrics and Service Level Objectives (SLOs). However, aside from differences in agreed service levels, they often differ in various details with regards
to metrics definitions. In particular, different *classification/categorization taxonomies* (e.g., different notions of severity of incidents to be resolved in different
timeframes, different categories of micro-services with corresponding maximal
response times, etc.) can raise challenges with regard to re-usability of metrics definitions in SLA templates across business engagements. In many existing approaches to SLA management (e.g., [2–4,7]) this can result in a need to

© Springer Nature Switzerland AG 2019
X. Liu et al. (Eds.): ICSOC 2018 Workshops, LNCS 11434, pp. 476–480, 2019.
https://doi.org/10.1007/978-3-030-17642-6_47

customize SLA templates for new engagements instead of being able to re-use them in an unmodified form. For instance, prepared metrics definitions in SLA templates cannot be easily adapted for different classes of incidents without repetitive specification of SLA constructs (e.g., specifying different SLOs for all individual incident classes as a possible work-around).

In this demonstration paper we present the *ysla* Engine, a new SLA management framework that implements the *ysla* language [1] for modeling SLAs. The framework supports configurable reusable building blocks called *Templates* and *Scopes* that allow the separation of metrics definitions from definitions of *classification/categorization taxonomies* with which they are to be used. We show how streamlined UI-supported SLA modeling with the ysla language and Engine can foster the re-use of metrics definitions in Templates across client engagements in unmodified form. The resulting improvements in conciseness and re-usability of SLAs can in turn enable standardization and automation within individual service providers, and/or the Cloud service provider industry as a whole.

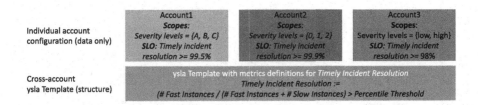

Fig. 1. Using Templates and Scopes for separating structural elements based on classification/categorization constructs from the parameterization of SLAs ysla

2   The ysla Engine

The ysla Engine is an SLA monitoring service based on the recently developed YAML-based *ysla* language for modeling SLAs [1]. The ysla language draws on several existing concepts for SLA modeling from current literature, such as *metrics*, *SLOs*, *Event-Condition-Actions* (ECAs), and *Monitors* (see, for instance, [5]). In addition, ysla introduces novel constructs for reusable SLA building blocks (*Templates*) and classification/categorization of observation data (*Scopes*). ysla *Scopes* allow for (i) the classification of metrics observation data based on values of contextual attributes, and (ii) assigning specific values to ysla variables for such groups. In other words, they allow for the definition of classes of input data together with corresponding associated parameters for expression evaluation. In combination with metrics definitions with placeholder variables, this enables the concise reuse of SLA templates for clients with different classification/categorization taxonomies for otherwise equivalent monitored subjects (e.g., for different notions of incident severity categories as illustrated in Fig. 1).

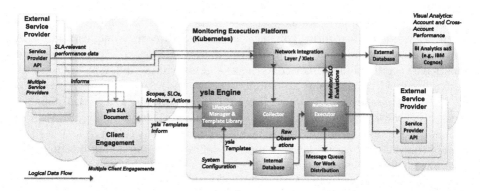

Fig. 2. Implementation and possible deployment of the ysla Engine

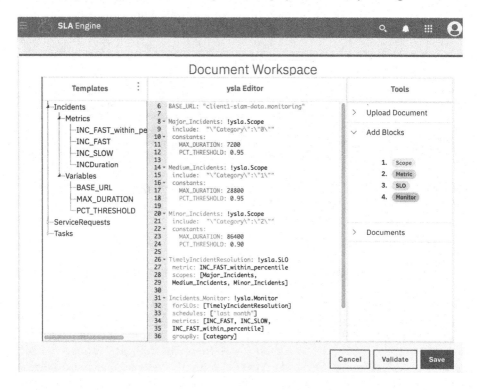

Fig. 3. ysla Editor UI with templates sidebar

From an architectural point of view, the ysla Engine is implemented in three different micro-services, namely *Collector*, *Executor*, and *Lifecycle Manager*, as shown in Fig. 2. The Lifecycle Manager service provides the overall UI to the system and manages the overall system configuration. Once an ysla document is uploaded and activated, the Collector service will begin collecting observations

Table 1. Maximal incident resolution times specified in an SLA

Incident classification	Maximum resolution time
Major incident	99% resolved within 2 h
Medium incident	95% resolved within 8 h
Minor incident	90% resolved within 24 h

from light-weight monitoring adapters for external APIs, so-called Xlets, as defined in the metrics definitions in the ysla document. Analogously, the Executor service of the ysla Engine will begin evaluating monitored metrics and SLOs according to the schedules specified in the ysla document and persist the results in an external database. Dashboards in IBM Cognos Analytics are used to visualize the resulting time series data for further analysis by the account manager.

3 Demonstration

In our demonstration, we model the use-case of SLAs for incident management. An SLA between a Cloud service provider and a client may require that certain percentiles of incidents of various severity categories need to be resolved within correspondingly defined time durations (e.g., Table 1). Other clients' SLAs may have very similar SLOs in place, however, they may define other parameters for the required percentiles, the maximal durations, as well as make use of different classification systems for severity categories. In our demonstration of the ysla Engine, we walk through the process of modeling and deploying a client-specific SLA for incident management using the ysla Editor UI as shown in Fig. 3. In particular, we show how ysla's novel language features, specifically Templates and Scopes, enable the concise modeling of different classification taxonomies across different clients without repetitive specification of metrics or SLOs from the predefined templates. Furthermore, we demonstrate how the deployment and subsequent execution of such SLAs in the ysla Engine allows for the straightforward generation of time series data for the defined SLO-relevant metrics, which is further loaded into IBM Cognos Analytics dashboards for in-depth visual analytics. A video demonstrating the above scenario can be found here: https://ibm.ent.box.com/v/ysla-engine-demo.

References

1. Engel, R., Rajamoni, S., Chen, B., Ludwig, H., Keller, A.: ysla: reusable and configurable SLAs for large-scale SLA management. In: 4th IEEE International Conference on Collaboration and Internet Computing, CIC, pp. 317–325 (2018)
2. Kouki, Y., de Oliveira, F., Dupont, S., Ledoux, T.: A language support for cloud elasticity management. In: 14th IEEE/ACM International Symposium on Cluster, Cloud and Grid Computing (CCGrid), pp. 206–215, May 2014

3. Lamanna, D.D., Skene, J., Emmerich, W.: SLAng: a language for defining service level agreements. In: 9th IEEE Workshop on Future Trends of Distributed Computing Systems, FTDCS 2003, p. 100. IEEE (2003)
4. Ludwig, H., Keller, A., Dan, A., King, R., Franck, R.: A service level agreement language for dynamic electronic services. E-Commer. Res. **3**(1–2), 43–59 (2003)
5. Mohamed, M., Anya, O., Tata, S., Mandagere, N., Baracaldo, N., Ludwig, H.: rSLA: an approach for managing service level agreements in cloud environments. Int. J. Coop. Inf. Syst. **26**(02), 1742003 (2017)
6. Stamou, A.: Systematic SLA data management. Ph.D. thesis, Univ. of Geneva (2014)
7. Tebbani, B., Aib, I.: GXLA a language for the specification of service level agreements. In: Gaïti, D., et al. (eds.) AN 2006. LNCS, vol. 4195, pp. 201–214. Springer, Heidelberg (2006). https://doi.org/10.1007/11880905_17

Paving the Way for Autonomous Cars in the City of Tomorrow: A Prototype for Mobile Devices Support at the Edges of 5G Network

Fatma Raissi[1,2] (ID), Clovis Anicet Ouedraogo[2] (ID), Sami Yangui[2,3](✉) (ID), Frederic Camps[2], and Nejib Bel Hadj-Alouane[1]

[1] National Engineering School of Tunis, OASIS,
University of Tunis ElManar, Tunis, Tunisia
`hadj-alouane@laas.fr`
[2] LAAS-CNRS, Université de Toulouse, Toulouse, France
[3] INSA Toulouse, Université de Toulouse, Toulouse, France
`{raissi,ouedraogo,yangui,camps}@laas.fr`

Abstract. The road to fully and secure autonomous cars is still long and exceedingly complicated. For instance, like smart city and virtual reality, self-driving cars need the infrastructure and data networks to catch up before it become common, safe and widely used. 5G telco network is considered as the required key concept that could enable autonomous cars operation. It would enable edge analytics and intelligence capabilities that are still missing in the current autonomous cars. This paper proposes one more slice of the next-generation self-driving automobile. It introduces a prototype that implements an autonomous car traveling into smart city. The car relies on emerging computing models such as Multi-access Edge Computing to perform part of the computation at the edges of 5G, in the surroundings of the car. The ultimate goal is to reduce latency and allow the car to make rapid decisions during the trip.

Keywords: 3GPP IMS · 5G · Autonomous car · IoT · IoMT · MEC

1 Motivating Use Case and Scope of the Demonstration

As autonomous vehicles achieve initial and critical self-driving steps, some supporters claim that fully driverless cars are around the corner. However, the recent experiments, and unfortunately accidents, prove that technology and cities are not quite ready for autonomous cars yet. For instance, the preliminary investigation report published in May 2018 by the National Transportation Safety Board (NTSB) - following the Uber's deadly accident that occurred in Tempe, Maricopa County, Arizona - claims that car saw the pedestrian 6 s before the crash but did not brake [1]. At the beginning, the car wrongly assumed that the crossing pedestrian was a "passive object" and took the decision not to brake.

© Springer Nature Switzerland AG 2019
X. Liu et al. (Eds.): ICSOC 2018 Workshops, LNCS 11434, pp. 481–485, 2019.
https://doi.org/10.1007/978-3-030-17642-6_48

Then, it decided it needed to brake 1.3 s before striking the pedestrian. This accident highlighted two major issues with the current autonomous cars, i.e. nascent machine-learning systems and excessive reaction delays in critical situations. This work proposes to address the second limitation by enabling edge calculation and analytics in the car surroundings. The ultimate goal is to reduce the latency delays and then, contributing in reducing the car reaction time.

On one hand, autonomous car applications are latency-sensitive. Decisions need to be taken and sent to actuators very fast to ensure road users' safety (e.g. braking to stop the car following identifying a red traffic light from the camera streaming flow). On the other hand, these applications are location-aware. Precise location information are critical for systems like navigation and driving lanes change. Notably, the fifth-generation (5G for short) wireless telco network is a potential solution that could address the previously mentioned requirements [2]. 5G relies on key concepts such as Network Function Virtualization[1] (NFV), Software-defined Network[2] (SDN), Multi-access Edge Computing[3] (MEC) and Next-generation Protocols[4] (NGP). Specifically, 5G specifications recommend slicing the network into several logic and functional entities that could be virtualized to enable agile and cost-effective operating. The control plane is handled by SDN that supports dynamic reshape of the traffic while MEC provides computing capabilities at the edge of the 5G network. MEC environment is characterized by ultra-low latency and high bandwidth, as well as, real-time access. MEC resources are accessible through NGP and/or Radio Area Network (RAN).

This work aims at contributing to enabling the use of autonomous car within 5G setting. More specifically, it fully focuses on enabling the interactions between the car and the edges of the 5G network on the road. This is quite challenging for three major reasons: (i) the heterogeneity of the edge devices in terms of computing capabilities, supported runtimes and communication protocols, (ii) the unpredictable location and availability of these edge devices (connected/disconnected), as well as, their workload prior to the car travel and (iii) the mobility of the car that adds complexity when optimizing the latency and delays between the car and the core network through fixed and/or mobile edge nodes. The proposed solution relies on the 3GPP IP Multimedia Subsystem[5] (IMS) technology to tackle the two first challenges and MEC to tackle the third one. It proposes an architecture and a proof-of-concept that use a telco Presence Server (PR) to discover the available edge nodes during the car trip in a smart city and then, place the car software components over well-selected edge nodes to reduce the latency and consequently, improve the car reaction face to sudden changes during its movement. The reader should note that the placement is dynamically calculated and subject to change, on the fly, during the car trip to ensure optimal latency all the time.

---

[1] https://www.etsi.org/technologies-clusters/technologies/nfv.

[2] https://trac.tools.ietf.org/html/rfc7426.

[3] https://www.etsi.org/technologies-clusters/technologies/multi-access-edge-computing.

[4] https://www.etsi.org/technologies-clusters/technologies/next-generation-protocols.

[5] http://www.3gpp.org/more/109-ims.

2   Prototype Architecture and Demonstration Overview

This section discusses the developed prototype and describes the execution scenario of the demo. The whole system is depicted in Fig. 1. It consists of three domains. The *Autonomous Car* domain involves the required hardware and software that implements the self-driving car. The *5G Network* domain is the telco service provider that enables the car to outsource part of its calculation, invokes remote services and so on. Finally, the *Smart City* domain represents the context where the whole prototype is running. Basically, autonomous cars travel in smart cities that are equipped with 5G network for the proper functioning of these cars. The rest of this section details the prototype functioning, as well as, the different technologies and devices that were used to implement each domain.

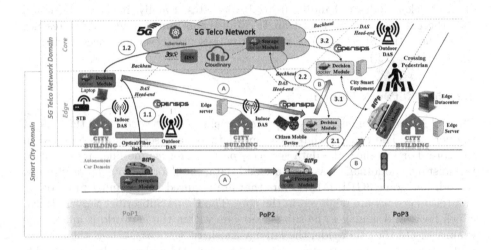

Fig. 1. Overview of the developed prototype.

2.1   Autonomous Car Domain

The SunFounder Smart Video Car Kit for Raspberry Pi is used as autonomous car. It is equipped with high-definition camera and PRoxSonar-EZ1 ultra-sound sensor. As for the software, a service-based application for the car navigation was developed. It implements two functionalities (i.e. control of the automated vehicle and obstacle avoidance) that were selected from the comprehensive list of autonomous car applications listed in [3]. The motivation behind considering these two functionalities is the obvious sensitivity with regard to latency. The developed application consists of three modules, i.e. *Perception* module, *Decision* module and *Storage* module. The *Perception* module relies on the car's sensor and camera to collect the navigation video stream, as well as, the sensor's data. These data are first cleaned (e.g. performing a noise reduction on the video stream, optimizing the brightness and the resolution on the video stream, aggregating the sensor data metrics) before being combined to build a model of the surrounding world and identify all the objects nearby like pedestrians and traffic lights. These information are then forwarded to the *Decision* module (action 1.1) that implements the so-called "driving policies" and determines how the vehicle should respond following a given situation (e.g. speed up, brake, steer left or right). Finally, the navigation data are forwarded to the *Storage* module (action 1.2) that takes care of saving it in datacenters for prospective batch processing (e.g. offline machine-learning systems). Each one of these modules was implemented with one or several HTTP REST python services. The modules are wrapped with their required libraries (e.g. OpenCV lib for the video stream processing) in Docker containers that enable, in addition to the modules hosting and execution, easy and fast migration procedure. The end-to-end orchestration of the Docker nodes is handled using Kubernetes. Finally, it should be noted that the car includes on board an IP Multimedia Subsystem (IMS) presence server client (i.e. SIPp[6] tool) to request the presence server instances during its trip (see Sect. 2.2.).

2.2   5G Network Domain

The *5G Network* domain includes prototype entities at the core and the edge of the network. The compute-intensive and data storage services are deployed in the core. For instance, the data services, part of *Storage* module, are executed in a distant Cloudinary instance, a cloud datacenter for video content storage. In addition, some 3GPP IMS servers that are required for the inner functioning of a telco network are deployed in the core. The Home Subscriber Server (HSS), which hosts and manages the subscribed cars within the network, is among the examples. On the other side, the latency-sensitive services, such as the services that make up the *Decision* module, are placed on edge nodes, as close as possible to the car. In addition, an adapted distribution of the open source IMS Presence Server OpenSips4 is deployed at the edge. In accordance with telco network specifications, a dedicated OpenSips instance is associated to each Point of Presence (PoP) and covers a specific geographic zone. The edge nodes, located in a given geographic zone, subscribe to their related OpenSips instance and notifies it of any changes that might happen during runtime (e.g. disconnection, movement).

2.3   Smart City Domain

Lego bricks (e.g. pedestrians, roads) are used to model the smart city where the car will be traveling. The city is broken up into several geographic zones assimilated as logic PoP of the 5G network. Each PoP has its own access point, Distributed Antenna Systems (DAS) and a dedicated OpenSips. For each PoP, several edge devices are assigned. The edge nodes are represented using heterogeneous devices such laptops, smartphones and Raspberry Pi devices. It should be

---

[6] http://sipp.sourceforge.net/.

noted that edge nodes could be mobile and switch from one PoP to another during runtime. When crossing a given PoP (action A, respectively B), the autonomous car discovers the list of available edge nodes in that zone and proceed to placing the *Decision* module services over the best edge node so that the communication delays with the car are minimized (actions 2.1 and 2.2, respectively 3.1 and 3.2). This operation is repeated for each visited PoP during the car trip.

References

1. Preliminary report highway HWY18MH010. https://bit.ly/2s6Nnbe. Accessed 2 Sept 2018
2. Di Taranto, R., Muppirisetty, L.S., Raulefs, R., Slock, D., Svensson, T., Wymeersch, H.: Locationaware communications for 5G networks. IEEE Signal Process. Mag. **31**(6), 102–112 (2014)
3. Pagnon, W.: Overview of techniques and applications for autonomous vehicles. Lovotics **2**(5) (2014)

Juno: An Intelligent Chat Service for IT Service Automation

Jin Xiao$^{(\boxtimes)}$, Anup K. Kalia, and Maja Vukovic

IBM T.J. Watson, Yorktown Heights, NY, USA
{jinoaix,anup.kalia,maja}@us.ibm.com

Abstract. Juno is a chat-based service that interacts with user through natural language, in order to understand, assist and execute the user's service request with a IT Service Management (ISM) system.

1 The Need for Juno

IT service request processing and execution makes up a significant portion of any large enterprise's IT operations. Traditionally, IT service request processing is quite labor-intensive involving many personnel of varied IT expertise. A helpdesk support person is needed to understand and determine the type of IT service required, generates a IT service ticket and dispatching it to appropriate systems operation team. Before the systems operation team can operate on the ticket, the required action or change is scrutinized by various security expert, client manager and sometimes the client's operations team, to ensure that the actions to be performed adhere to the security policies and infrastructure consistencies. Once approved, the systems operation team will pickup the tickets and attempt to perform the requested actions. Sometimes, the ticket may not contain sufficient information to fulfill all of the parameters of a change (e.g., didn't mention which drive a Disk should be mounted on) or contain incidental errors (e.g., ask to patch a DB2 database "dbinst1" that does not reside on the specified machine x, although DB2 database "dbinst0" does reside on x). The ticket then have to be discussed with the requester for further clarity and correction. This process overall is labor-intensive, error-prone and slow. Over the past few years, significant strides have been made in making IT service management process simpler and more automated [1–4]. Automation platforms supports large variety of change automata ranging from OS support, to databases, hardware configurations, etc. Typically these automata take inputs on the parameters and options to suite the specific target environment and the particular change request. IT service management (ISM) systems are created to help streamlining and expediting the request creation, dispatching and approval process. IBM Control Desk (ICD) is such a representative system IBM Global Technology Service uses for IT service request management. Moreover, helpdesk support is replaced by a self-service catalog user interface. A service catalog contains a listing of pre-approved services a service requester can use to facilitate a service request action. Each catalog service takes on a web-based form that contains the required parameters

© Springer Nature Switzerland AG 2019
X. Liu et al. (Eds.): ICSOC 2018 Workshops, LNCS 11434, pp. 486–490, 2019.
https://doi.org/10.1007/978-3-030-17642-6_49

and configuration options for automata execution. Furthermore, these catalogs are designed as end-system-centric, whereby a requester should first specify the end system to be acted on. Over time with the use of these self-service catalogs, some challenges have emerged: (1) requester may not necessarily know what the change action they are looking for is called or where it's located in the catalog. For instance, "grant user access to mailbox" could be located in User Account Management, Mailbox Management, or Security Services. This sometimes causes frustrating browsing experience; (2) requester may not know the name/value of a parameter that is valid for the change action. Frequently, the requester needs to look up fully qualified domain names for servers, the exact database name on a server, etc.; (3) Sometimes, an action's parameter list and configuration items can be sizable, and it is difficult for a requester to look up all of the configuration values and entity names. For instance, to add a MQ channel, the parameter includes: server name, MQ application name, Queue manager name, channel name, queue type, etc. The net effect being even with a self-service user interface, requesters (especially new users) tend to have a lot of questions and need to do many lookups. Juno is designed and created to be an intelligent self-service chatbot to address these challenges. Its aim is to be a virtual helpdesk support agent for a user that can directly engage Juno in a conversational format that does not require the user to browse the service catalog and to assist the user in parameter fulfillment through recommendation, auto-fill and validations. Our experience suggest that Juno serves as a much smoother and guided user experience to the service requesters.

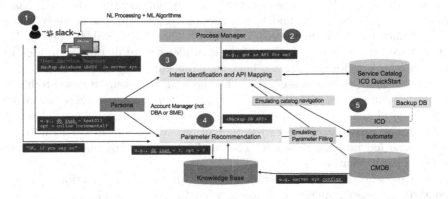

Fig. 1. The Juno architecture

2 The Juno Architecture

Juno is a collection of micro-services that communicates through APIs. The chat front-end of Juno (i.e., the chatbot) is built for a specific chat application, and is independent of the back-end reasoning and execution engines of Juno. The entire Juno service can operate across multiple chat applications, and service multiple users at the same time. As depicted in Fig. 1, Juno consists of process manager, intent identifier, parameter recommender, execution engine, knowledge base, and persona.

Process manager handles the authentication and authorization process, as well as session management. It is the interface to the chatbot. When a user initiates a conversation with Juno via chat, the process manager first authenticates the user. The authentication process involves establishing and linking a user's chat identity to his/her back-end ISM identity. Secondly, based on the user's ISM identity, the user's role and access rights to the target infrastructure and the authorized set of actions are also established. These access rights will be used throughout the session to ensure the user's interaction with Juno and the backend ISM are compliant with security policies. The process manager also keeps track of ongoing requests the user may have initiated during the session and is able to therefore bridge the chatbot's dialogue state to Juno's internal processing state.

The intent identifier employs natural-language processing, feature extraction and classification techniques to map a requester's requested action to a service catalog entry if there exists one. The service catalog entries are a priori onboarded to Juno as a meta catalog. The meta catalog entry for a service entry consists of: API descriptions of the automata associated with the service entry, the action utterances, the parameter key-values, parameter utterances, and types of the parameters. This design facilitates a dynamic approach to onboarding new service catalog entries to Juno. The Intent identifier creates a weighed feature map of the API parameters and actions. When a request is received, for example, "backup database db001 on server xyz". The intent identifier does NL-based preprocessing, tokenization and lemmatization to generate list of likely action and parameter related phrases (e.g., "backup", "database", "db001", etc.). The phrases are further searched with Intent identifier's word dictionary to identify normalized tokens for them (e.g., "back up", "backup" maps to "backup"; "db", "database" maps to "database", etc.). The normalized tokens are used to fit the weighed feature maps of APIs for classification. Furthermore, likely parameter value word phrases such as "db001" are also searched in Juno's knowledge base to determine if they exist, and what type of parameter they are. This information is also fed into the classifier. The resulting top ranked matches are then returned to the chatbot.

The parameter recommender is involved for further interaction with the requester via process manager. Based on what the requester selects, the parameter recommender takes the features generated by the intent identifier and loads the service API corresponding to the selected service entry. Different from the meta catalog entry, the service API associated with the entry contains further technical details on the parameter key-values, types of parameters, associated concepts in the knowledge base, value constraints (e.g., Integer) and defaults, as well as mapping information to generate backend data payload to the backend ISMs (this demo uses ICD as the ISM that takes in a structured XML payload). The parameter recommender first fits the word tokens into parameters required, it does verification with the knowledge base to ensure the word tokens are entities exists in the target infrastructure, the requester have access rights to it, have the right concept (e.g., "db001" is indeed a database), and the right system dependencies (e.g. "xyz" is indeed a server and "db001" is hosted on "xyz"). The outcome of this step produces a valid partially complete API payload. Then the recommender does auto-fulfillment on parameters where it can conclusively determine the value for. In the instance of "backup database db001 on server xyz", the API also requires a database application name. Since the recommender is able to determine the existence and validity of "db001" and "xyz", also "db001" is hosted on "xyz", it performs a lookup in the knowledge base for the name of the database application that hosts "db001" on server "xyz", and fulfills that parameter. In the case, where there's an inconsistency on the requester's provided values. For example, "xyz" is not a valid server, or "xyz" does not host any database called "db001", then the user is provided recommendations for the valid candidate server that hosts "db001", and the valid databases that is hosted on "xyz". The parameter recommender interacts with the user via process manager to systematically recommend parameters (as we'll see in the demo), until all parameters of the API is fulfilled.

The execution engine serves as the interface to the backend ISM system. It takes a completed service API and translates into the native payload the backend ISM expects. For this demo, XML payloads are generated to create and process requests in ICD. The execution engine can also pull request status from the ISM, and pull configuration items from Configuration Management Database (CMDB). The CMDB is the ISM's representation of the target infrastructure.

The persona service is persistent across sessions. It records a requester's identity, access rights (cached from ISM), request history, ongoing request status, as well as any linguistic utterance associations specific to the user (e.g., server "xyz" is referred to by the requester as "ICD test server").

The knowledge base is a service that is heavily used by the intent identifier and parameter recommender service to: search for existence of an entity, understand the concept type of the entity, and how the entity is situated in the target infrastructure. The CMDB of a ISM is injested to automatically generate/update the knowledge base.

3   What Is in the Demo

In this quick demo of Juno we have a Slack chatbot built that communicates with the Juno service. The dialogue management for the Slack chatbot is minimal, mostly passing process manager's response directly to the user.

First, users issue browsing command to retrieve the list of target systems they have access to. Notice that the user "Anup" and user "Jin" have access to different systems. Then, Juno guides user through a series of commands, many of which requires Juno to auto-fill parameters, correct user errors, and/or recommend parameter values. Because ISM system interaction takes time, we only show the ISM path once during this demo.

4   How to View This Demo

The demo file is titled "Juno_DEMO_ICSOC_2018.mp4". It is a MP4 video format, no sound, any MP4 viewer should be able to play this video. Thank you.

References

1. Alès, Z., Duplessis, G.D., Şerban, O., Pauchet, A.: A methodology to design human-like embodied conversational agents. In: International Workshop on Human-Agent Interaction Design and Models, Valencia, pp. 1–16 (2012)
2. Ayachitula, N., et al.: IT service management automation - a hybrid methodology to integrate and orchestrate collaborative human centric and automation centric work-flows. In: Proceedings of the 4th International Conference on Services Computing, Salt Lake City, pp. 574–581. IEEE (2007)
3. Kalia, A.K., Telang, P.R., Xiao, J., Vukovic, M.: Quark: a methodology to transform people-driven processes to chatbot services. In: Maximilien, M., Vallecillo, A., Wang, J., Oriol, M. (eds.) ICSOC 2017. LNCS, vol. 10601, pp. 53–61. Springer, Cham (2017). https://doi.org/10.1007/978-3-319-69035-3_4
4. Kalia, A.K., Xiao, J., Bulut, M.F., Vukovic, M., Anerousis, N.: Cataloger: catalog recommendation service for IT change requests. In: Maximilien, M., Vallecillo, A., Wang, J., Oriol, M. (eds.) ICSOC 2017. LNCS, vol. 10601, pp. 545–560. Springer, Cham (2017). https://doi.org/10.1007/978-3-319-69035-3_40

Author Index

Printed in the United States
by Bookmasters

Printed in the United States
By Bookmasters